Sixth Edition

Mastering Excel® 2007

A Problem-Solving Approach

Sixth Edition

Mastering Excel® 2007

A Problem-Solving Approach

JAMES GIPS

BOSTON COLLEGE

Learning Solutions

New York Boston San Francisco
London Toronto Sydney Tokyo Singapore Madrid
Mexico City Munich Paris Cape Town Hong Kong Montreal

Cover Art: Portrait of Erasmus of Rotterdam, by Hans Holbein the Younger, 1523, courtesy of the Louvre, Paris/Superstock.

Pearson Learning Solutions, 501 Boylston Street, Suite 900, Boston, MA 02116
A Pearson Education Company
www.pearsoned.com

Printed in the United States of America

1 2 3 4 5 6 7 8 9 10 V036 15 14 13 12 11 10

000200010270581340

LR/JR

ISBN 10: 0-558-81797-1
ISBN 13: 978-0-558-81797-8

CONTENTS

Chapter 1 Introduction 1

What is Excel? • A little history • What is Microsoft Office? • Why learn to use Excel?

Chapter 2 Creating simple worksheets 7

The basic idea • So what? • Getting started with Excel • Changing which cell is active • The size of the worksheet • Entering information into cells • Correcting typing errors • Undo and Redo • Simple formulas • Evaluating formulas • You try evaluating a formula • Using cell addresses in formulas • Saving the workbook • The name of the workbook • Printing the worksheet • Closing the workbook and starting a new one • Exiting from Excel

Chapter 3 Changing the appearance of cells 31

Column width • Selecting cells • Formatting cells • Alignment • Help! • Formatting numbers • Borders • Colors • Example • 3-D shading • The Format Painter button • Displaying the formulas • Finding a look for your worksheets • Minimizing the Ribbon

Chapter 4 Simple functions and the Fill operation 53

Built-in functions save you typing • The variety of functions • Arguments and ranges • Pointing • A common error: circular reference • Overuse of the SUM function • The AutoSum button • The Insert Function tool • Nested functions • The Fill operation • Using the Fill Handle • Filling by double-clicking • Goal Seek • Auto Fill • Using Auto Fill to fit a straight line • Summary

Chapter 5 Operations on cells 75

Moving cells • Erasing a range of cells • Deleting rows and columns • Inserting rows and columns • Sorting • Attaching a comment to a cell • Copy and Paste • Paste Options • Using the keyboard instead of the mouse • Copying and Pasting from the web • Getting updated external data from the web • Linking to files and web pages

Chapter 6 Relative vs. absolute addressing 99

An example where the Fill operation seems to fail • Absolute addressing • Peter Minuit • Splitting the window • Naming cells • Mixed addressing • Panes

Chapter 7 Common operations 123

Validating inputs • Cell protection • Conditional Formatting • Text boxes • Adding shapes, clip art, pictures, WordArt, and SmartArt

Chapter 8 Workbooks with multiple worksheets 137

Moving between worksheets • Using multiple worksheets • Working with multiple sheets at the same time • Calculations across worksheets • Viewing multiple sheets and workbooks • Linking workbooks

Chapter 9 The problem-solving process 149

1. Problem definition • 2. Design • 3. Implementation • 4. Testing • 5. Documentation

Chapter 10 Charts and trendlines 155

Fundamentals of charting • When to use different types of charts • Creating charts • Charting noncontiguous ranges • Multiple sets of data in the same chart • Scatter charts • Using and printing charts • Trendlines • 3-D charts

Chapter 11 Logical functions 179

The IF function • Another example • Nested IF functions • You try • Logical functions AND, OR, NOT • Another example • Testing IF functions

Chapter 12 Functions related to IF **207**

The COUNTIF function • The SUMIF function • Using IF functions in extra columns • The VLOOKUP function • Using VLOOKUP for exact matches • The IFERROR function • Combining VLOOKUP and Data Validation • Looking up text • Two-dimensional lookups with INDEX and MATCH • Catching and preventing errors in INDEX and MATCH • Form Controls

Chapter 13 Dates and times **239**

Serial numbers • An error in Excel • A second date system • Entering dates into the worksheet • Using dates directly in formulas • The TODAY function • The DATE function • Date formats • Date functions for converting from serial numbers • Example: How many days until July 1? • Hours, minutes, and seconds • The NOW function • Time formats • Entering a time into a cell or formula • Example: Testing the engines • Time functions for converting from serial numbers

Chapter 14 Financial functions **255**

Calculating loan payments with the PMT function • Using the Insert Function tool • Calculating future values using the FV function • The basic idea of these financial functions • The NPER function • The RATE function • The PV function • Making investment decisions using IRR • Net present value • Investments with arbitrary dates for cash flows • Winning the lottery • Other financial functions

Chapter 15 Random numbers and simulation **283**

The RAND function • Flipping coins • Queuing problems • Santa Claus's afternoon • Generating random integers using RANDBETWEEN • Rolling a pair of dice 100,000 times

Chapter 16 Data management with tables **311**

What is a table? • Sorting tables • Finding records with Filters • Adding the Total Row to a table • Pivot tables

Chapter 17 Analyzing data using the Analysis ToolPak **329**

Getting access to the Analysis ToolPak • What is in the Analysis ToolPak? • The Descriptive Statistics tool • Using the Histogram tool • Using the Correlation tool • Using a t-Test tool • Using the Regression tool

Chapter 18 Solver 347

Solver • Using Solver to maximize profits • Using Solver for a linear programming problem • Using Solver on a transportation problem

Index 363

CHAPTER 1

INTRODUCTION

OBJECTIVES

In this chapter you will learn:

- The major uses of Excel
- The origin of spreadsheet programs

WHAT IS EXCEL?

Excel is a best-selling computer program published by Microsoft Corporation of Redmond, Washington. The program has been put to a wide variety of uses.

The most important and most common use of the program is as a **spreadsheet**. In a spreadsheet program, the main memory of the computer is divided into rows and columns. The computer is used to perform mainly numeric computations. An example of the use of Excel as a spreadsheet is shown in Figure 1-1. Here, one enters in the Net Sales and different Operating Expenses for each of the quarters. The computer calculates the Year To Date totals in column F, the Total Operating Expenses figures in row 16 and the Operating Income figures in row 18.

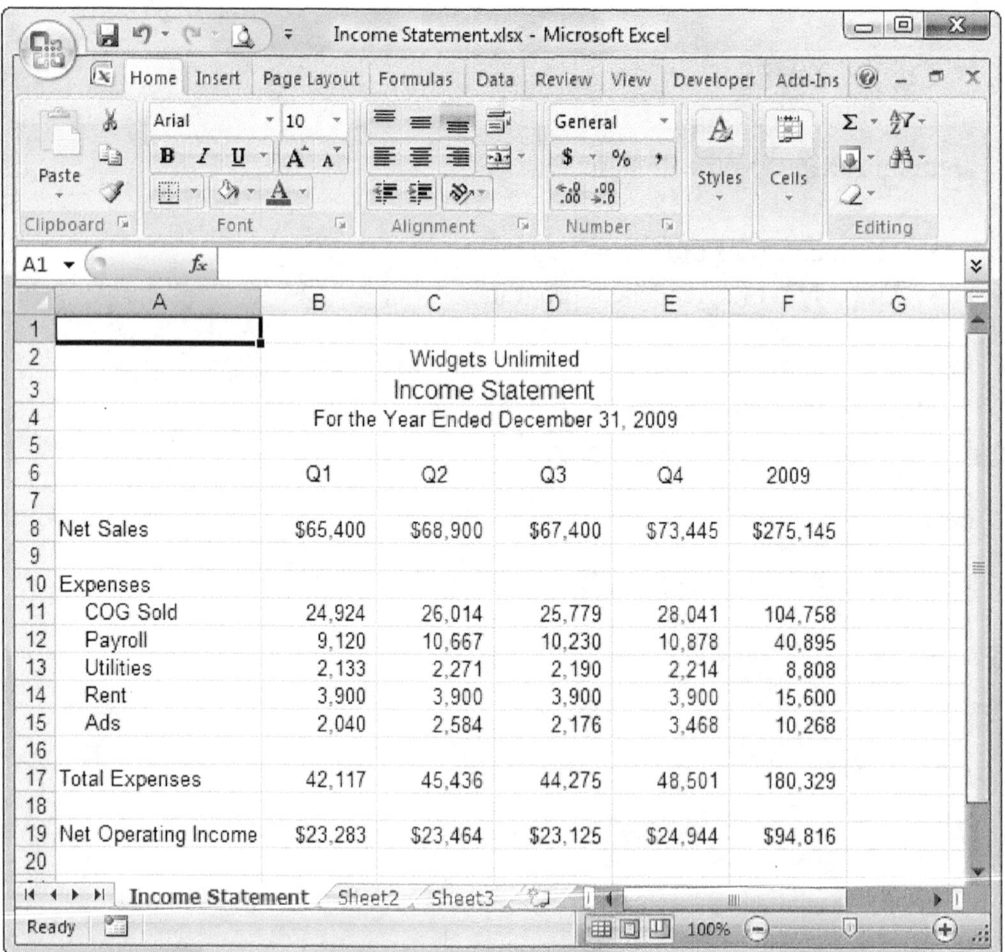

	A	B	C	D	E	F	G
1							
2			Widgets Unlimited				
3			Income Statement				
4			For the Year Ended December 31, 2009				
5							
6		Q1	Q2	Q3	Q4	2009	
7							
8	Net Sales	$65,400	$68,900	$67,400	$73,445	$275,145	
9							
10	Expenses						
11	COG Sold	24,924	26,014	25,779	28,041	104,758	
12	Payroll	9,120	10,667	10,230	10,878	40,895	
13	Utilities	2,133	2,271	2,190	2,214	8,808	
14	Rent	3,900	3,900	3,900	3,900	15,600	
15	Ads	2,040	2,584	2,176	3,468	10,268	
16							
17	Total Expenses	42,117	45,436	44,275	48,501	180,329	
18							
19	Net Operating Income	$23,283	$23,464	$23,125	$24,944	$94,816	
20							

Figure 1-1. A typical Excel spreadsheet.

Another important use of Excel is for creating **business graphics**. In business graphics the computer draws bar charts, line charts, pie charts, and other types of charts used in business. Excel draws these charts based on numbers in the spreadsheet. For example, the chart in Figure 1-2 was drawn by Excel from the numbers shown in Figure 1-1.

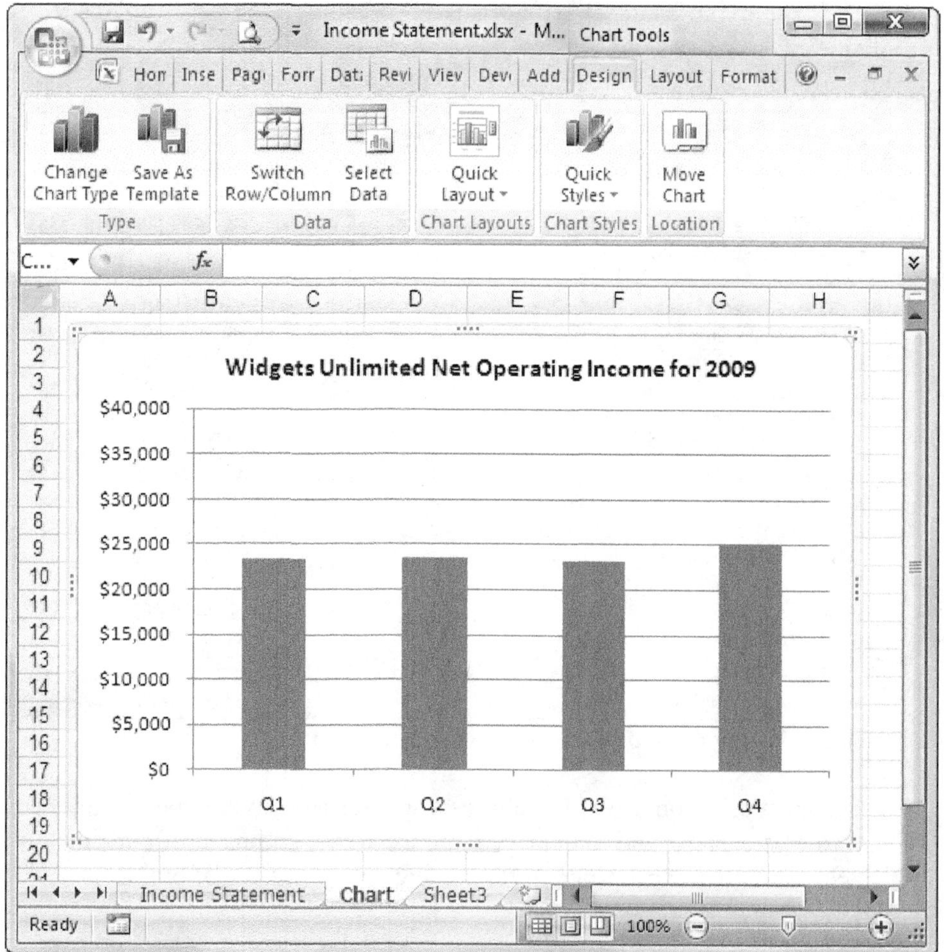

Figure 1-2. A chart drawn from the values in the worksheet in Figure 1-1.

A third use of Excel is for **data management**. In data management the computer is used to deal with large amounts of information. An example is the worksheet in Figure 1-3, which shows the homes for sale in a town.

In the real estate worksheet, each row corresponds to a different home for sale. Excel could be instructed to find all the homes with more than 3 bedrooms that have oil heat. Or, the program could be instructed to rearrange the rows so they are in order by the price.

CURRENT LISTINGS

ADDRESS	BDRMS	BATHS	LOT	AGE	PRICE	HEAT
12 Elm Street	5	3	0.4	48	$490,000	Gas
46 Hearthstone Road	5	2	1.2	3	$645,000	Oil
690 Rice Avenue	3	1	0.6	25	$179,950	Oil
90 Bay Road	2	1	0.25	33	$148,400	Oil
455 Nathan Street	2	1	0.3	16	$91,400	Elec
18 Garden Street	2	1	0.4	12	$112,000	Elec
203 Somerset Avenue	4	2	0.3	98	$359,600	Gas
34 Farley Place	7	4	2.3	52	$860,000	Oil
26 Lantern Lane	3	1	0.3	9	$504,300	Solar
11 Panama Street	3	1	0.5	38	$227,890	Gas
155 Auburn Blvd.	5	2	1.0	5	$568,000	Oil
132 Jamaica Way	4	2	0.3	67	$429,500	Gas
315 Fremont Avenue	3	1	0.4	8	$932,800	Nuclear
1322 Bellevue Road	6	3	0.3	56	$533,500	Elec
5 Pond Street	4	3	1.5	2	$475,400	Oil
349 Hill Road	2	1	1.2	34	$175,500	Oil

Figure 1-3. Part of a real estate database in Excel.

The most common use of Excel is as a spreadsheet. While we certainly cover how to use Excel to create charts and to manage data, we will spend most of our time on the many uses of Excel as a spreadsheet program for solving a wide variety of problems.

A LITTLE HISTORY

In the bad old days of computers, before the advent of personal computers and spreadsheet programs, people who wanted to use the computer to solve some numerical or financial problem usually had to write a special-purpose computer program in a language like BASIC or Fortran. It is much easier to create a spreadsheet in Excel to solve a problem than it is to write a computer program. A problem that requires 1 hour to solve using a spreadsheet program like Excel might require 10 hours or more to solve by writing a program.

The idea of a spreadsheet program was invented by Dan Bricklin when he was an MBA student at the Harvard Business School.

> Sitting there in the spring of 1978, I came up with the idea of the electronic spreadsheet. With all those other classmates to contend with the professor, there's lots of time for daydreaming, especially if you sit in the front row and the professor looks out above you. I invariably made simple addition mistakes in my homework. I wanted to do what the professor did on his blackboard: he would erase one number and Louis in the back of the room would give him all the calculations that he had done all night to recalculate everything. I wanted to keep the calculations and just erase one number on my paper and have everything recalculated. (Dan Bricklin, "VisiCalc and Software Arts: Genesis to Exodus," *The Computer Museum Report*, Summer 1986, p. 8.)

Dan Bricklin and a friend, Bob Frankston, wrote the first spreadsheet program, for the Apple II, and called it VisiCalc ("Visible Calculator"). VisiCalc was published by a small company, Personal Software, in 1979. VisiCalc became wildly popular, the best-selling computer software of its day. Personal Software changed its name to VisiCorp and brought out related software, including VisiPlot and VisiTrend, which were written by Mitch Kapor.

Mitch Kapor became a product manager for the company, but then left to form a company called Lotus Development. Lotus brought out the program 1-2-3 for the IBM PC in 1983. The developers of VisiCalc thought that the Apple III, the ill-fated successor to the very popular Apple II, was the computer of the future and targeted their advanced version of VisiCalc for the Apple III. Bricklin and Frankston also became involved in a messy lawsuit with VisiCorp. Lotus concentrated on the IBM Personal Computer from the beginning. Lotus 1-2-3 became the best-selling applications program of its time. Later, Lotus bought out the rights to VisiCalc, which is published no more.

The arch rival of Lotus Development in the personal computer software market was Microsoft Corporation. Microsoft was best known for developing MS-DOS, the original Disk Operating System of the IBM Personal Computer and compatibles. Lotus 1-2-3 was the most popular spreadsheet program for DOS machines. Microsoft introduced a spreadsheet program called Multiplan to compete with Lotus 1-2-3. Multiplan evolved into Excel. When Microsoft switched over from DOS to Windows, Lotus was slow to update 1-2-3. Microsoft took advantage of the situation to make Excel the most popular spreadsheet program for the Windows market. With the introduction of new versions of Windows, the dominance of Excel accelerated. Lotus Development was bought out by IBM in 1995. Microsoft Excel since has captured the vast majority of the spreadsheet market.

Excel is the third spreadsheet program to dominate the market. VisiCalc dominated the Apple II market. Lotus 1-2-3 dominated the MS-DOS market. Excel dominates the Windows and Macintosh markets.

All spreadsheet programs are reasonably similar. All are elaborations on Dan Bricklin's original idea. Once you learn Excel it is straightforward to learn to use any spreadsheet program.

WHAT IS MICROSOFT OFFICE?

Microsoft Office is a **suite** of programs brought out by Microsoft and sold together as one package. The Microsoft Office package includes Excel, Word (a word-processing program), PowerPoint (a presentation program), Outlook (an email and calendar program), and perhaps OneNote (a digital notebook program), Access (a database program), and other programs, depending on which edition of Office you purchase. The exact combinations in the packages vary over time. The idea is that the programs work together so that it is easy to create a spreadsheet in Excel, use it in a report created in Word and in a presentation created in PowerPoint.

WHY LEARN TO USE EXCEL?

Excel is widely used for many problems. Many of its most devoted users work with financial and accounting problems, including budgets, cash flow projections, sales reports, balance sheets, and expense accounts.

Some of these applications tabulate past results. For example, we were budgeted to spend so much in each of these different categories. So far this year we have spent this much in each of these areas. How much is left in our budget?

Other applications look to the future. We hope to sell so many copies of this proposed product at a certain price. Our expenses for the product are expected to be so much. How much money will we earn? What if certain expenses are 25% more than expected, how will this affect our profits? What if we sell only so many copies? What if we lower our price and increase our advertising budget? This is known as using Excel to perform "**What if**" analysis. "What if" analysis is an area where spreadsheet programs excel. Indeed, if you look back at the quote from Dan Bricklin, the inventor of spreadsheet programs, "What if" analysis is the specific type of application for which spreadsheet programs were developed.

As the years have gone by, computers have become more and more powerful in their hardware so they support more and more powerful software. With each new version of Excel new features are added. Excel has become a powerful tool for statistical analysis, for operations research, for management science, and for engineering and scientific calculations. Excel is used for non-numerical problems as well. It is used for alphabetizing lists, for drawing charts, and for looking at databases. Excel is used in marketing research, in sales analysis, and in human resource management.

A good working knowledge of Excel is a requirement for many professional positions. Many a student has obtained a good summer internship just on the basis of expertise with Excel.

Learning Excel is an important skill you will be able to use for the rest of your life. I hope you soon will see why.

CHAPTER 2

CREATING SIMPLE WORKSHEETS

OBJECTIVES

In this chapter you will learn how to:

- Enter information into an Excel worksheet
- Move to different cells of the worksheet
- Correct errors
- Create and evaluate formulas
- Create simple worksheets
- Save your work on the disk
- Print your work

THE BASIC IDEA

A simple Excel **worksheet** is shown in Figure 2-1. This worksheet was set up to give price quotes for potential customers. There are three products: widgets, grommits, and connectors. Widgets cost $1.19 each. Grommits cost $2.49 each. Connectors cost $0.69 each. A 6% sales tax is added to each order.

In Excel, the complete document or file you are working on is called a **workbook**. Each workbook contains various worksheets. Think of the workbook as being the electronic equivalent of a three-ring binder and the worksheets as being electronic sheets of paper.

Each worksheet is divided into **columns** and **rows**. The columns have letter names (A, B, C, ...). The rows have numbers for names (1, 2, 3, ...). The intersection of each row and column is called a **cell**. Each cell has a name. Cell E7 is in column E and row 7. That is, the name of each cell is the letter name of its column followed by the number name of its row.

Each cell can be **blank** or it can contain **text**, a **number**, or a **formula**. Text can be a word or phrase. Cells F4 and B7 in the worksheet in Figure 2-1 contain text. Cells D6 and E7 contain numbers.

The key to electronic spreadsheets is the formulas. Cells in column F in the worksheet in Figure 2-1 contain formulas.

The formula in cell F6 is

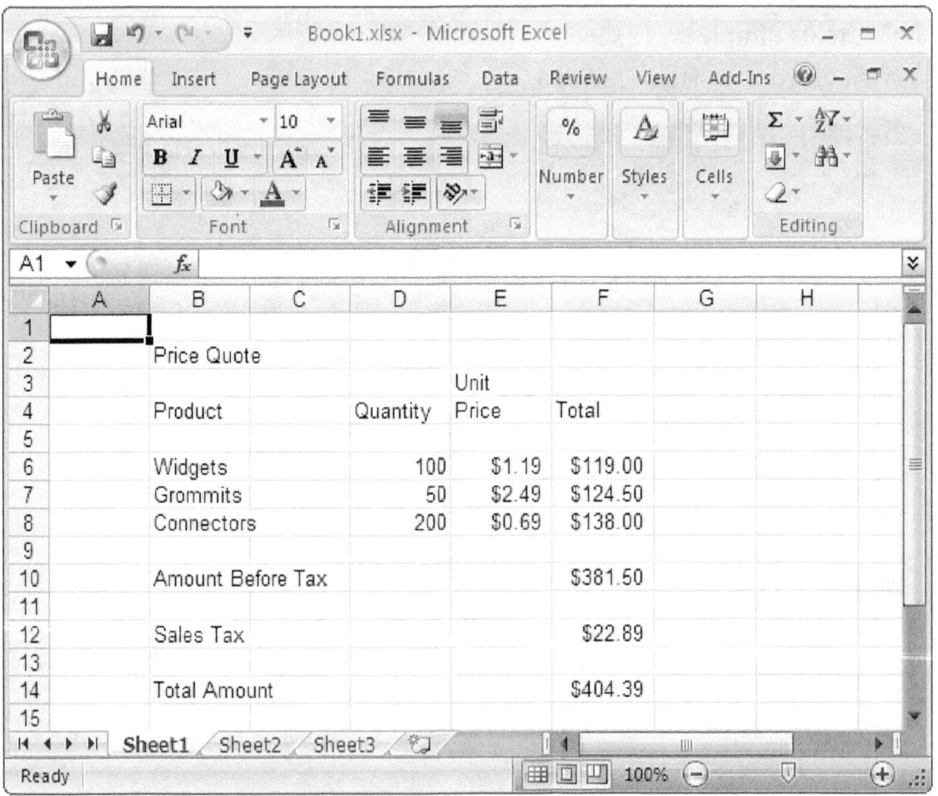

Figure 2-1. A simple worksheet for giving price quotes.

=D6*E6

The initial equal sign indicates that this is a formula. In Excel, the asterisk means multiplication. This formula tells Excel that the number displayed in cell F6 is the number in cell D6 multiplied by the number in cell E6. The formula has been typed into the cell, but the computer normally displays the result of evaluating the formula in the cell. That is, the computer displays 119.00, the result of the multiplication, in the cell.

The formulas in the worksheet are shown in Figure 2-2. Here the actual formulas are displayed in the cells, rather than the values that result from calculating the formulas. The formula in cell F7 is

=D7*E7

so the value in cell F7 is the result of multiplying the number in D7 times the number in E7. Similarly, the formula in cell F8 is

=D8*E8

Cell F10 contains the total for the order before sales tax. This value is calculated by the

	A	B	C	D	E	F
1						
2		Price Quote				
3					Unit	
4		Product		Quantity	Price	Total
5						
6		Widgets		100	1.19	=D6*E6
7		Grommits		50	2.49	=D7*E7
8		Connectors		200	0.69	=D8*E8
9						
10		Amount Before Tax				=F6+F7+F8
11						
12		Sales Tax				=F10*6%
13						
14		Total Amount				=F10+F12
15						

Figure 2-2. The Price Quote worksheet with the underlying formulas displayed rather than the values that result from evaluating the formulas.

computer by adding the values in F6, F7, and F8. The formula is

=F6+F7+F8

The Sales Tax is 6% of the Amount Before Tax. The formula for the sales tax in cell F12 is

=F10*6%

Finally, the Total Amount is the sum of the Amount Before Tax and the Sales Tax. This formula, in cell F14, is

=F10+F12

SO WHAT?

Here we have spent a lot of money for a computer and the Excel software. Plus we have to take the time to learn to use the computer and Excel. Wouldn't it just be easier and faster to do this by hand? You could do the same "worksheet" with paper and pencil. For $10 you could buy a calculator to do the arithmetic. Why bother with a computer?

In using a computer the benefit usually is not in the first time you perform some action. The benefit is in the repetition, especially in the ability to make changes. The major benefit of using a word-processing program is in the ability to make changes or revisions without retyping the entire manuscript. Similarly, the payoff of an Excel worksheet is in the third or the tenth or the hundredth time you use the worksheet.

What happens with our price quote worksheet? The potential customer says, "Oh, no. I don't want 50 grommits. I want 150 grommits." If you are using paper and pencil, you must erase the numbers in F7, F10, F12, and F14 and then recalculate the new amounts. The next person you speak with has new quantities to order. You would have to do the calculations all over again for that person's order. If you give out hundreds of price quotes each day, you would have to redo the calculations hundreds of times.

Watch what happens on the computer. We change the number in cell D7 from 50 to 150. The formulas in cells F7, F10, F12, and F14 are recalculated automatically by the computer and the results of these calculations appear automatically in the cells. (See Figure 2-3.) Similarly, we change the price for widgets from $1.19 to $0.98 by changing the number in cell E6 from $1.19 to $0.98. As soon as we make the change, the formulas in cells F6, F10, F12, and F14 are recalculated automatically by Excel.

The key to Excel is in the automatic recalculation of the formulas. Text, numbers, and formulas are entered into the worksheet. Whenever any number is changed, the relevant formulas are recalculated by the computer automatically. The speed of the computer allows the recalculation to be done almost instantaneously.

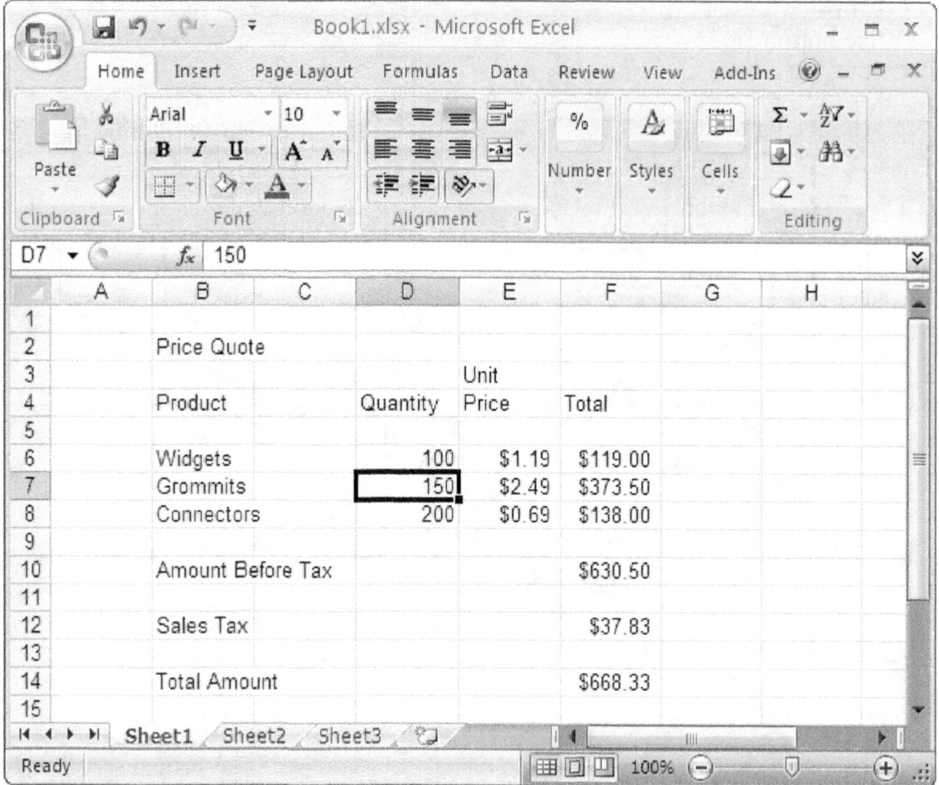

Figure 2-3. When we change the number in D7 from 50 to 150, the formulas in F7, F10, F12, and F14 automatically are recalculated.

An Excel worksheet has been described as an electronic piece of paper with a built-in pencil, eraser, and calculator. You enter the labels, numbers, and formulas into the worksheet. The computer performs all of the calculations automatically. Change one cell and the computer automatically recalculates the formulas.

As we proceed you will learn how to create larger and more complicated worksheets, involving thousands of calculations. Excel also provides us with a straightforward way of organizing and solving complicated problems.

Now we will take a look at the process of actually using Excel on the computer.

GETTING STARTED WITH EXCEL

We start up Excel just as we would any other program, by double-clicking on the Excel icon on the desktop or by finding Excel under Programs in the Windows Start menu. The initial screen displayed depends somewhat on what was specified by recent users. As one example, the interface is available in different color schemes.

A new blank workbook is shown in Figure 2-4. The various elements of the Excel window are indicated in the figure.

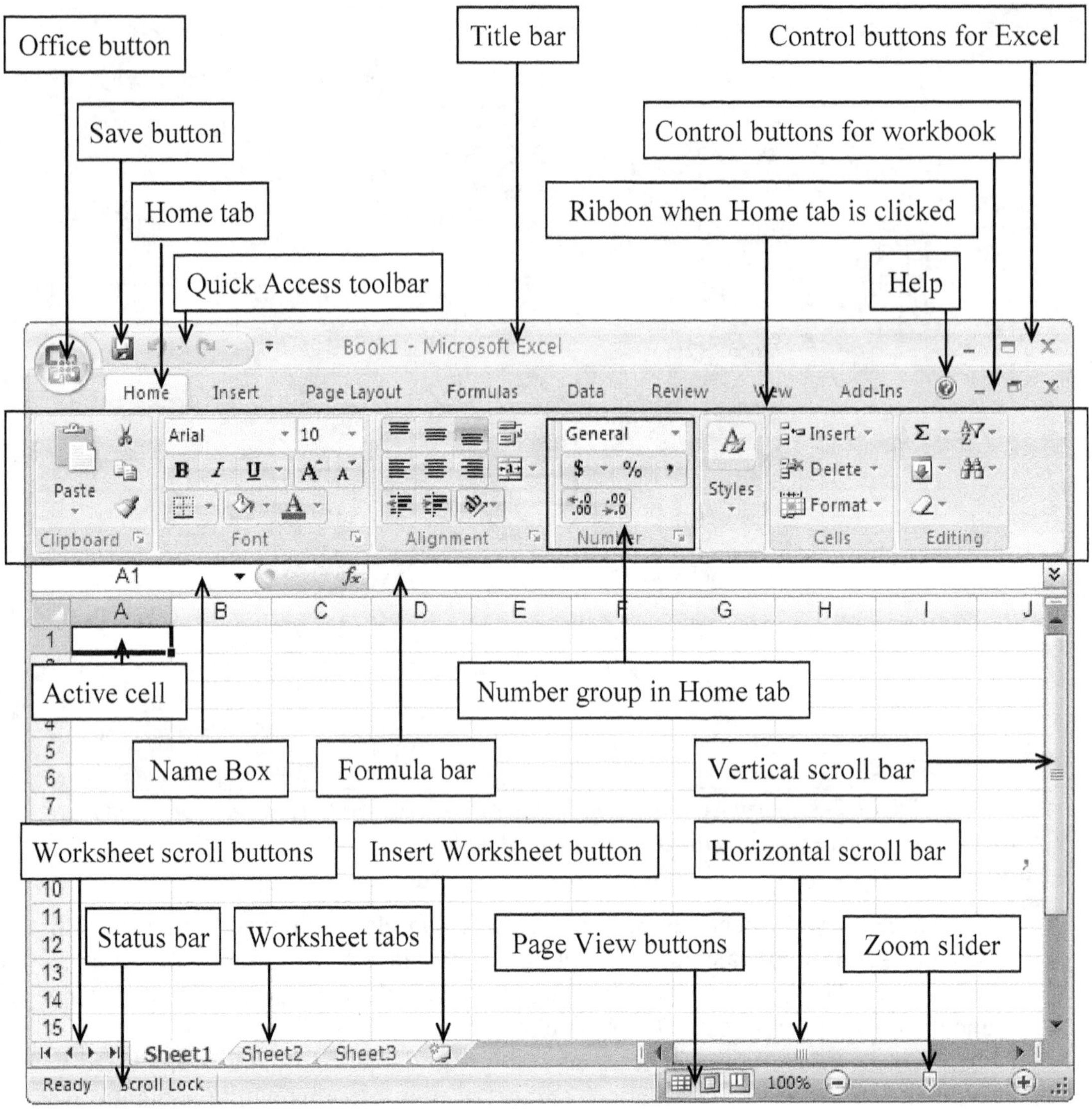

Figure 2-4. Elements of Excel window.

In the center of the top of the screen we see the **Title bar**. The Title bar tells us we are working in Excel and gives us the name of the active workbook. The current workbook we are working on is called "Book1". When we save the workbook on the disk we will give it a more descriptive name.

Clicking on the **Office button** causes a menu to drop down, as shown in Figure 2-5. On the left of the Office button menu are common operations like creating a new workbook and saving the current workbook. On the right of the menu are recent workbooks we have worked on that can be loaded back into Excel. (My list of recent workbooks is disturbingly boring.) At the bottom of the menu are the **Excel Options** button, which we will discuss later, and an **Exit Excel** button. A much more common way of exiting Excel is to click on the X button at the very top right of the entire Excel window.

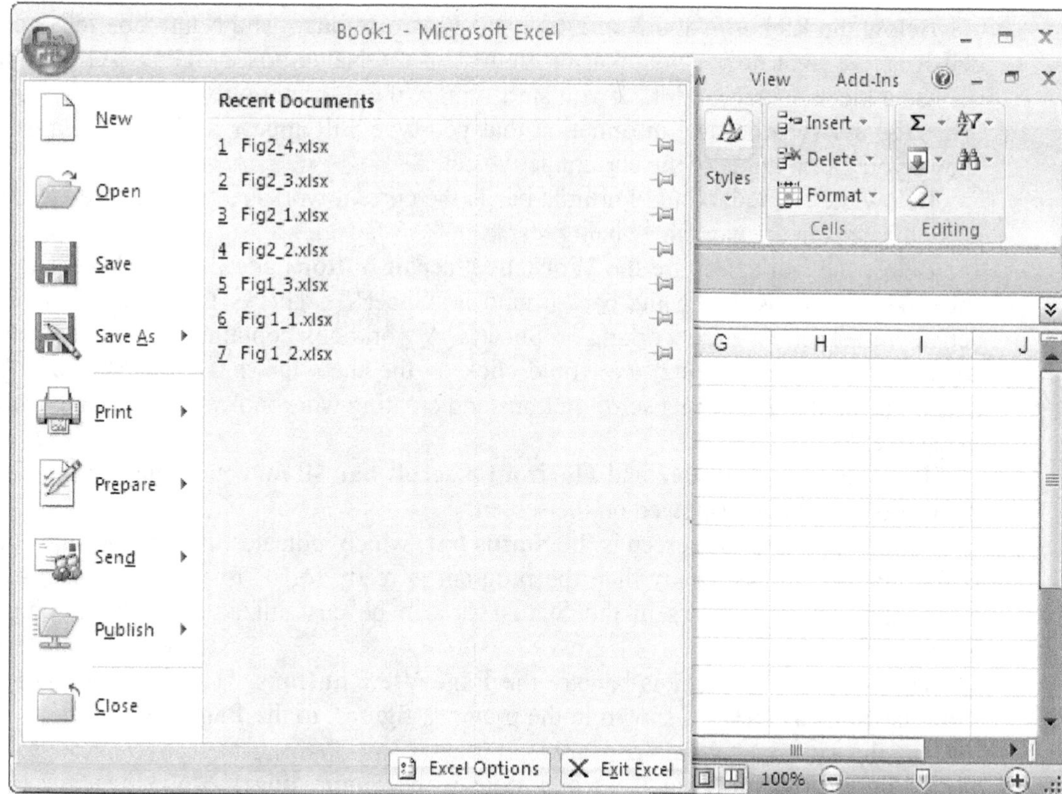

Figure 2-5. The Office menu.

To the right of the Office button is the Quick Access toolbar. Initially this toolbar contains a **Save button**, an **Undo button**, and a **Redo button**.

The Excel window in Figure 2-4 shows the Ribbon as it is displayed when the **Home tab** is clicked. This allows various commands to be issued to Excel by clicking on the different buttons in the Ribbon. Clicking any of the other tabs (**Insert**, **Page Layout**, etc.) causes different buttons to be displayed. For example, the buttons displayed in the Ribbon after clicking the Insert tab are shown in Figure 2-6. Also, if the mouse is pointing at the Ribbon you can use the scroll wheel on the mouse to scroll through the various tabs.

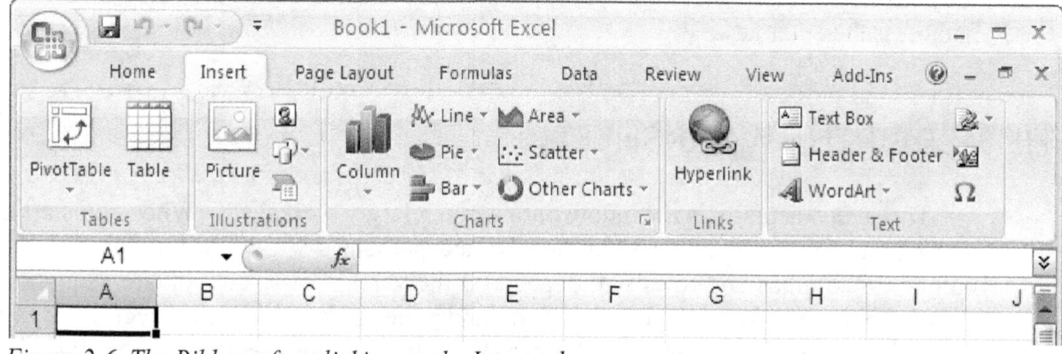

Figure 2-6. The Ribbon after clicking on the Insert tab.

Below the Ribbon is the **Name box** and **Formula bar**. The Name box tells you which cell is active right now. Note that in Figure 2-4 the Name box contains "A1" and that cell A1 has a black box around it. If you start typing, the information will go into cell A1. Cell A1 is the **active cell**. The information that you type will appear in the Formula bar, which shows you the contents of the current active cell.

Below the Name box and Formula bar is the current worksheet itself. We start out with all of the cells in the worksheet being blank.

Below the worksheet are the **Worksheet scroll buttons** and the **Worksheet tabs**. The sheet tab in bold with a white background is "Sheet1". This is the name of the currently active worksheet. We are working on Sheet1. A workbook contains multiple worksheets. If we want to work on Sheet2, we would click on the sheet tab that says "Sheet2". We will discuss using the Worksheet scroll buttons and creating workbooks with multiple worksheets in Chapter 8.

The **Vertical scroll bar** and **Horizontal scroll bar** allow you to change the portion of the worksheet that is displayed on the screen.

At the bottom of the screen is the **Status bar**, which indicates the current status of Excel. If the Status bar says Ready then the program is ready for us to issue commands or enter information. What appears in the Status bar can be customized by right-clicking on the Status bar.

To the right of the status bar are the **Page View buttons**. These allow you to switch from the **Normal view**, as shown in the previous figures, to the **Page Layout view**, which is the way the worksheet would appear when printed.

To the right of the View Control buttons is the **Zoom slider**. Move the slider to the left to see more cells in smaller size. Move the slider to the right to see fewer but larger cells.

CHANGING WHICH CELL IS ACTIVE

When we start up Excel, cell A1 is the active cell. Cell A1 is the cell in the top left of the worksheet. If we want to enter information into cell A1, we simply type the information and then press the Enter key.

If we want to enter information into another cell, we need to change it to the active cell. There are three basic ways to do this. First, we can use the mouse to point to the new cell and then click the (left) button. Second, we can use the **arrow keys** on the keyboard to move the active cell in any direction. Third we can type the address of the cell into the Name Box and press the enter key.

THE SIZE OF THE WORKSHEET

The screen actually is a window onto a much larger worksheet. When you start up Excel you might see 12 columns (A through L) and perhaps 25 rows (1 through 25). The exact number of columns and rows will depend on the version of Excel you are using, the size of your monitor, the size of your window, and other factors. Each Excel 2007 worksheet contains 16,384 columns and 1,048,576 rows! The columns are named A through Z and then

AA, AB, AC, through ZZ and then AAA, AAB, all the way to XFD. The rows are named 1 through 1,048,576. Some quick calculations show that in order to display all of the cells in the worksheet at the same size they usually appear on my screen would require a screen a quarter of a mile wide and 4 miles high!

ENTERING INFORMATION INTO CELLS

Suppose we want to enter the Price Quote worksheet in Figure 2-1 into the computer. We start with a blank worksheet, make cell B2 the active cell, and type the text Price Quote. Notice that the text appears both in the cell and in the formula bar at the top of the screen (Figure 2-7). Notice also that buttons with an X and a check mark appear to the left of the formula bar when you begin typing.

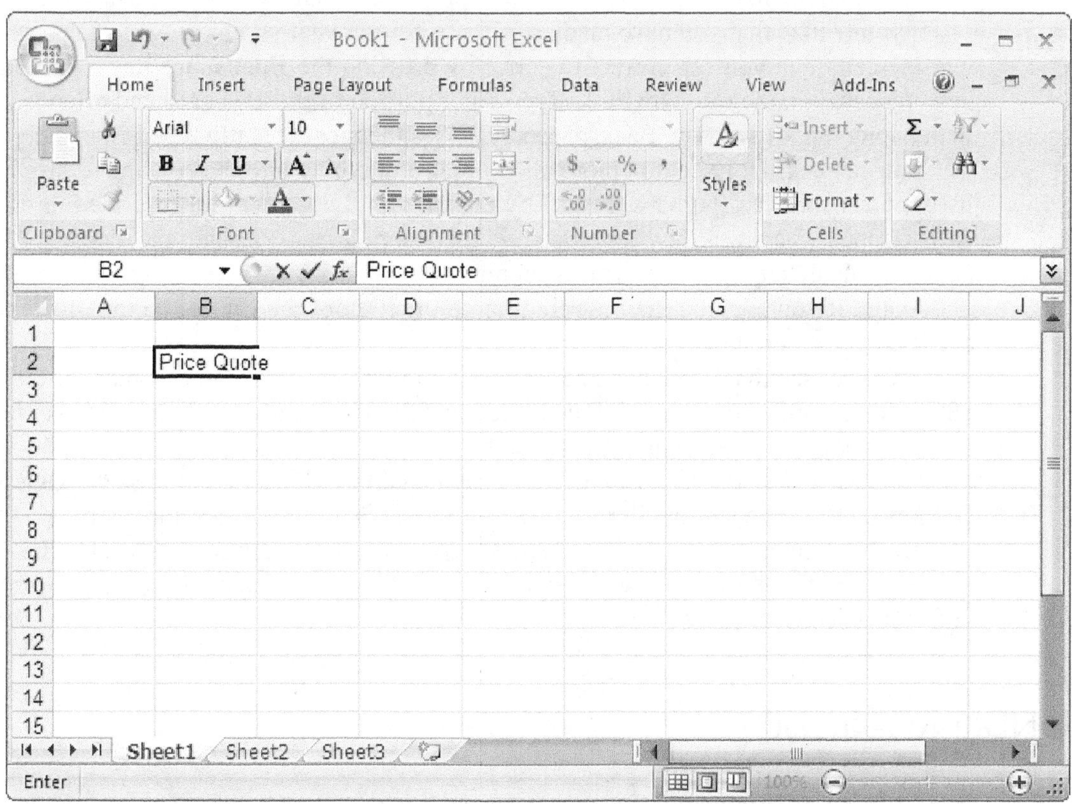

Figure 2-7. Entering text into a cell.

Once we have typed in Price Quote we either press the Enter key on the keyboard or click on the **Enter button** (the check mark). The text is "entered" into the cell.

We move the active cell down to cell B4 using the down arrow or by clicking on B4. Type the word Product, and so on.

How does Excel know which cells contain formulas and which contain text or numbers? The program looks at the first keystroke, at the first character that we type into a cell. If the first character in a cell is an equal sign (=) then the cell contains a formula. If the first entry in the cell is just about any other character then the cell does not contain a formula. If the cell contains a formula, Excel displays the result of evaluating that formula in the cell.

This is an important point, a common source of error. Begin each formula with an equal sign. If you begin a cell entry with a letter or a space, rather than an equal sign, the cell actually will contain text rather than a formula to be evaluated. If you type C7*D7 into a cell the computer will take this to be the text C7*D7 rather than a formula because it begins with a C, a letter. The computer will not evaluate the formula. Rather it simply will display C7*D7 in the cell as text.

CORRECTING TYPING ERRORS

The best way to correct a typing error depends on when the error is discovered.

If you realize that you have made a mistake before what you have typed has been entered into the cell, then you can correct the error by pressing the **Backspace key**. The Backspace key is located on the top right of the typewriter portion of the keyboard and often is indicated with a long left arrow. The Backspace key erases the most recently typed character.

You can instruct Excel to ignore all your current typing into the cell and return the cell to its previous contents (perhaps, blank) by clicking on the **Cancel button**, the button with an X that appears between the Name box and the Formula bar. Pressing the **Esc key** ("Escape" key) is equivalent to pressing the Cancel button.

Again, if you click on the Enter button, to the right of the Cancel button, the text will be accepted and entered into the cell.

If you realize that you have made a mistake in text or a formula or a number that already has been entered into a cell, simply make the cell active and correct the entry either in the Formula bar or in the entry in the cell itself.

To erase an existing entry in a cell, make the cell active and then press the **Delete key** or **Del key** on the keyboard or click on Delete in the Cells group of the Home tab.

It is a common mistake to try to erase a cell by typing a space in the cell. It looks as if the cell is erased but really the cell contains text, namely a space. This can have subtle but unfortunate consequences.

UNDO AND REDO

Have you ever done or said something and wished immediately that you could undo it or take it back? Excel provides that opportunity.

The button in the Quick Access toolbar with an arrow that curves counterclockwise is the Undo button. Clicking on this button will cause the most recent action taken to be undone. You can click on the Undo button several times to undo several of the most recent actions. Clicking on the tiny triangle to the right of the arrow shows a menu that allows you to undo multiple entries and actions at once.

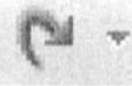

If you undo an action and are sorry, you can press the Redo button and Excel will redo the action.

SIMPLE FORMULAS

The key part of Excel is the formulas. As discussed previously, formulas begin with an equal sign.

Examples of formulas include

= 3+4*5

= C4 / 5 + 7

= (D3+G5) * (H7 - (5+D6) / 8)

Formulas can contain numbers, cell addresses (like C4 or H7), arithmetic operators, and parentheses.

The arithmetic operators include

+	addition
-	negation or subtraction
*	multiplication
/	division
%	percent (placed after a value, as in 25%)
^	exponentiation

The minus sign can be used in two ways, as the negation of a single value (-3) and as the subtraction of one number from another (6-4).

The percent operator causes the number to the left of the percent sign to be divided by 100.

The exponentiation operator raises a number to a power. For example, 2^3 means 2^3, which is 8. As another example, 64^0.5 means $64^{0.5}$. This calculates the square root of 64, which is 8.

EVALUATING FORMULAS

What would be the result of evaluating the formula =3+4*5? Is it 35? Is it 23?

The correct answer depends on whether the computer performs the addition first or the multiplication first, on the **order of precedence** of the arithmetic operators. Generally, multiplication is done before addition. Thus, the value of the formula =3+4*5 would be 23. If we want the addition to be performed first, we would type =(3+4)*5. The parentheses tell the computer to perform the operation inside, in this case the addition, first. The value of =(3+4)*5 would be 35.

What would be the value of the formula =6-5-1? Is it 0? Is it 2?

The correct answer depends on which subtraction the computer performs first. That is, it depends on whether =6-5-1 is the same as =(6-5)-1 or whether it is the same as =6-(5-1). Excel performs the left subtraction before the right subtraction so to the computer =6-5-1 is the same as =(6-5)-1, which evaluates to 0.

Here are the general rules that Excel follows when evaluating simple formulas:

1. Evaluate anything in parentheses first.

2. Evaluate the arithmetic operators in the following order:
   (a) negation (as in -7)
   (b) percent
   (c) exponentiation
   (d) multiplication or division
   (e) addition or subtraction

3. In case of tie, evaluate the operators from left to right.

YOU TRY EVALUATING A FORMULA

What would be the result of evaluating the formula

=23+((5+9)*3)/7-5

This problem uses each of the three general rules above. Try it before reading further. Write down your answer.

The computer first would add 5+9 to get 14. Then it would multiply the 14 times 3, which is 42. It would divide the 42 by 7 to get 6. Then it would add 23 and 6 to obtain 29. Finally it would take the 29 and subtract 5 to obtain the final answer of 24.

USING CELL ADDRESSES IN FORMULAS

Consider again the Price Quote worksheet in Figure 2-1. Suppose that in cell F6 instead of the formula =D6*E6 we put =100*1.19. (See Figure 2-8.) Would this formula work? It might first appear that this new formula works fine. After all, the result of evaluating this new formula would be the same as evaluating the original formula, namely 119. But, what would happen if we then changed the number in cell D6 from 100 to 300? The result of evaluating the original formula would change accordingly. But the result of evaluating the new formula =100*1.19 would not change at all, since the new formula does not refer to the numbers in the cells. It is very important that you use cell addresses in your formulas rather than the numbers that (now) are in the cells.

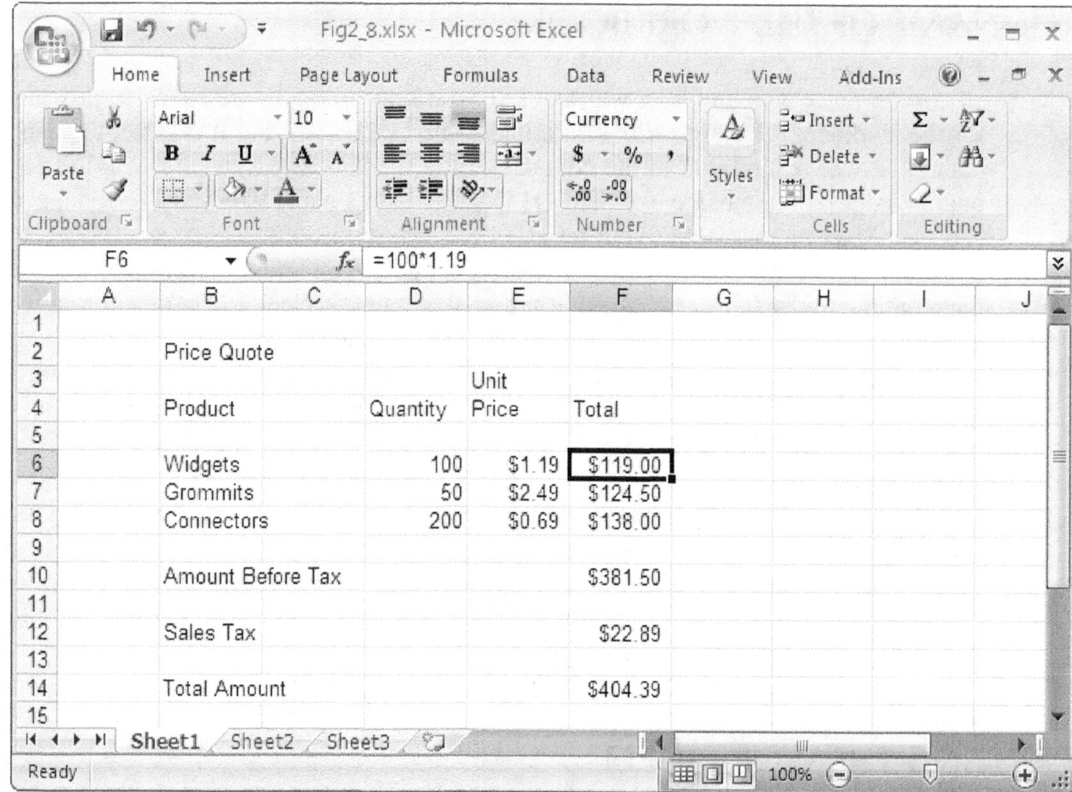

Figure 2-8. A common mistake is to put the current values in formulas instead of the cell addresses. It looks as if this formula works, but if the value in D6 is changed, the value in F6 will not change accordingly.

SAVING THE WORKBOOK

When you enter information into a worksheet on the screen, the information is saved in the primary memory of the computer. The primary memory is temporary, working memory. If you lose electric power or if Excel quits on you unexpectedly or if you turn off the computer then the information that is in primary memory will be erased. In order for the computer to remember a workbook from one session to the next, the workbook must be saved on disk. It is your responsibility to save the workbook on disk. It is advisable to save your work on the disk early and often.

The easiest way to instruct Excel to save your current workbook is to click on the **Save button** in the Quick Access toolbar. You also can select Save in the Office menu.

The first time you save a workbook you will be asked to fill in a file name and to select the disk and directory in which the workbook should be saved. File names are discussed in the next section.

The basic unit in Excel is the workbook. A workbook contains multiple worksheets. Thus far we have been working only with the first sheet, "Sheet1", of the workbook. When you click on the Save button or select Save in the Office menu, Excel always saves the entire workbook on the disk, even though you may have used only a single sheet.

THE NAME OF THE WORKBOOK

In the process of saving a workbook for the first time you are asked to provide a name for the workbook. Excel provides an initial name like Book1, but it is better to change it to a name that will remind you of the contents of the workbook. If you are working on the first quarter sales report, a name like SalesQ1 is better than a name like Mary or John, even if you can't get Mary or John out of your mind.

File names can be up to 255 characters in length. You are not allowed to include certain punctuation marks (/ ? : * " < > !) in the file names. Excel 2007 files normally have an extension, a last name, of .xlsx, which indicates to the computer that it is an Excel 2007 workbook. Previous versions of Excel used files with a .xls extension. If you want to save the Excel workbook so someone with an older version of Excel can read it, it's best to use Save As... in the Office menu and save the workbook as an "Excel 97-2003 Workbook", which is a .xls file.

The name of the current workbook appears in the Title bar at the top of the window. (See Figure 2-8.)

The easiest way to change the name of the workbook is to select Save As... in the Office menu, enter in the new name, and then save the workbook on the disk using that name. The new name will be retained for the current workbook.

PRINTING THE WORKSHEET

To print the current worksheet select Print in the Office menu.

If you would like to see the worksheet as it would be printed, you can click on the Page Layout button to the right of the Status bar in the middle of the very bottom of the Excel window.

CLOSING THE WORKBOOK AND STARTING A NEW ONE

Suppose you just have completed one of the computer exercises that follow. You have constructed a worksheet, tested it, and saved it. Now you would like to start over on a new exercise. To do this you can select Close in the Office menu. This closes the workbook you are working on. ("Close" means the workbook is erased from the primary memory of the computer and from the screen.) If you have not yet saved the workbook before closing it, the computer will ask you if you wish to save your work on the disk before it vanishes.

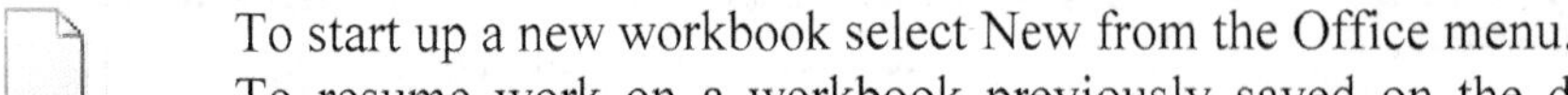

To start up a new workbook select New from the Office menu.

To resume work on a workbook previously saved on the disk, select Open from the Office menu. Alternatively, if you have worked on the document recently on this computer it might appear on the right of the Office menu, where you can select it directly.

EXITING FROM EXCEL

To exit from Excel, click on the Exit Excel button at the bottom right of the Office menu. You will be asked if you would like to save any unsaved workbooks that you have been working on. Alternatively, you can click the **Close button** at the very top right of the Excel window, to the right of the Title bar.

PAPER AND PENCIL EXERCISES

2-1. Consider the following worksheet:

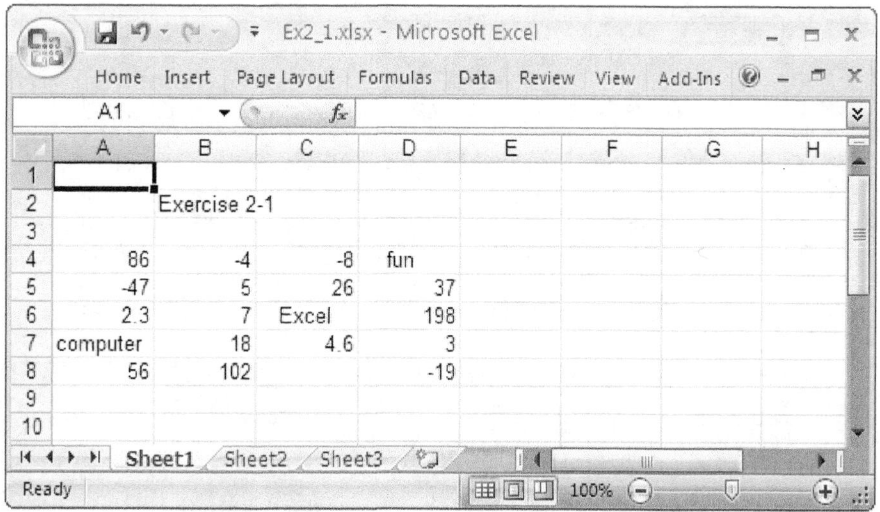

	A	B	C	D	E	F	G	H
1								
2		Exercise 2-1						
3								
4	86	-4	-8	fun				
5	-47	5	26	37				
6	2.3	7	Excel	198				
7	computer	18	4.6	3				
8	56	102		-19				
9								
10								

What would be the result of evaluating each of the following formulas? Write out your answers on paper. Do not use the computer.

(a) =B7+1

(b) =B6+2*D7

(c) =C4*(D7+B4)-6*C5+A8

(d) =C4*25%-3-B4

(e) =256/C4/2/B4

(f) =B5^2+B4^3

(g) =-B6-B4*-B3*2/C4+B5^D7-1

2-2. Salespeople earn a base salary of \$10,000 per year plus a commission of 4% of sales. The following worksheet has been created for our four salespeople. Columns E and G and row 11 contain formulas.

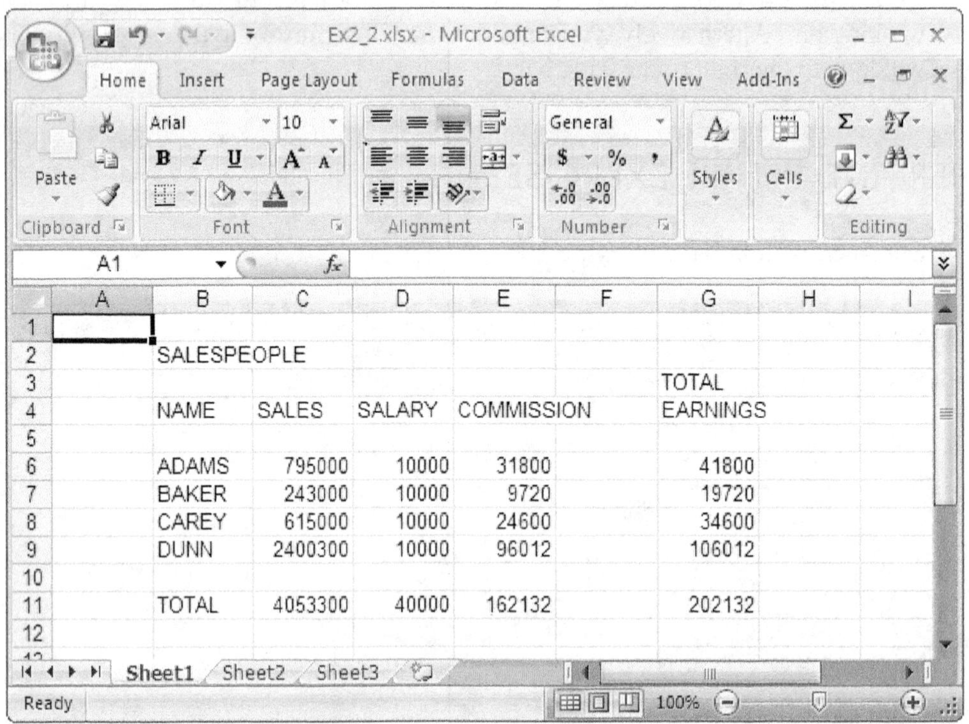

	A	B	C	D	E	F	G
1							
2		SALESPEOPLE					
3							TOTAL
4		NAME	SALES	SALARY	COMMISSION		EARNINGS
5							
6		ADAMS	795000	10000	31800		41800
7		BAKER	243000	10000	9720		19720
8		CAREY	615000	10000	24600		34600
9		DUNN	2400300	10000	96012		106012
10							
11		TOTAL	4053300	40000	162132		202132
12							

(a) Cell E6 gives Adams' Commission. What is the formula in E6?

(b) Cell E7 gives Baker's Commission. What is the formula in E7?

(c) Cell G7 gives Baker's Total Earnings. What is the formula in G7?

(d) Cell E11 gives the Total Commission. What is the formula in E11?

(e) Cell G11 gives the Grand Total of the Earnings. What is the formula in G11?

(f) Give an alternative formula for G11.

COMPUTER EXERCISES

2-3. Start up Excel. You should see a blank Excel worksheet.

(a) Use the arrow keys to move the active cell right and left and down and up.
Use the mouse to move the active cell.
Move the active cell to F12.
Move the active cell to K23.

(b) Use the arrows, scroll bars, and mouse, or the Name bar to return to A1.

(c) Enter your name in cell D4.
Type Exercise 2-3 in cell D5.
(You should type your name and the exercise number at the top of each worksheet you do for homework.)

(d) Type the number 140 in cell B2.
Type the number 233 in cell B3.
Type the formula =B2+B3 in cell B5.
(The number 373 should appear now in B5.)

(e) Change the number in cell B2 to 56.
(The total in B5 should change automatically to 289.)

(f) Change the number in cell B3 to 375.6.
(The total in B5 should change again.)

(g) Save the workbook on your disk and exit from Excel.

2-4. Put your name in cell J3. Put Exercise 2-4 in cell J4.

(a) Enter the worksheet at the top of the next page exactly as shown. When you enter the formulas into cells G10, G14, G17, and G20, the results of evaluating the formulas should show in the cells.

(b) Change the number in G7 to 14125.
(The numbers in G10, G14, G17, and G20 should change automatically.)

(c) Change the number in D15 to 106.
(The numbers in G17 and G20 should change.)

(d) Save and then close the workbook.

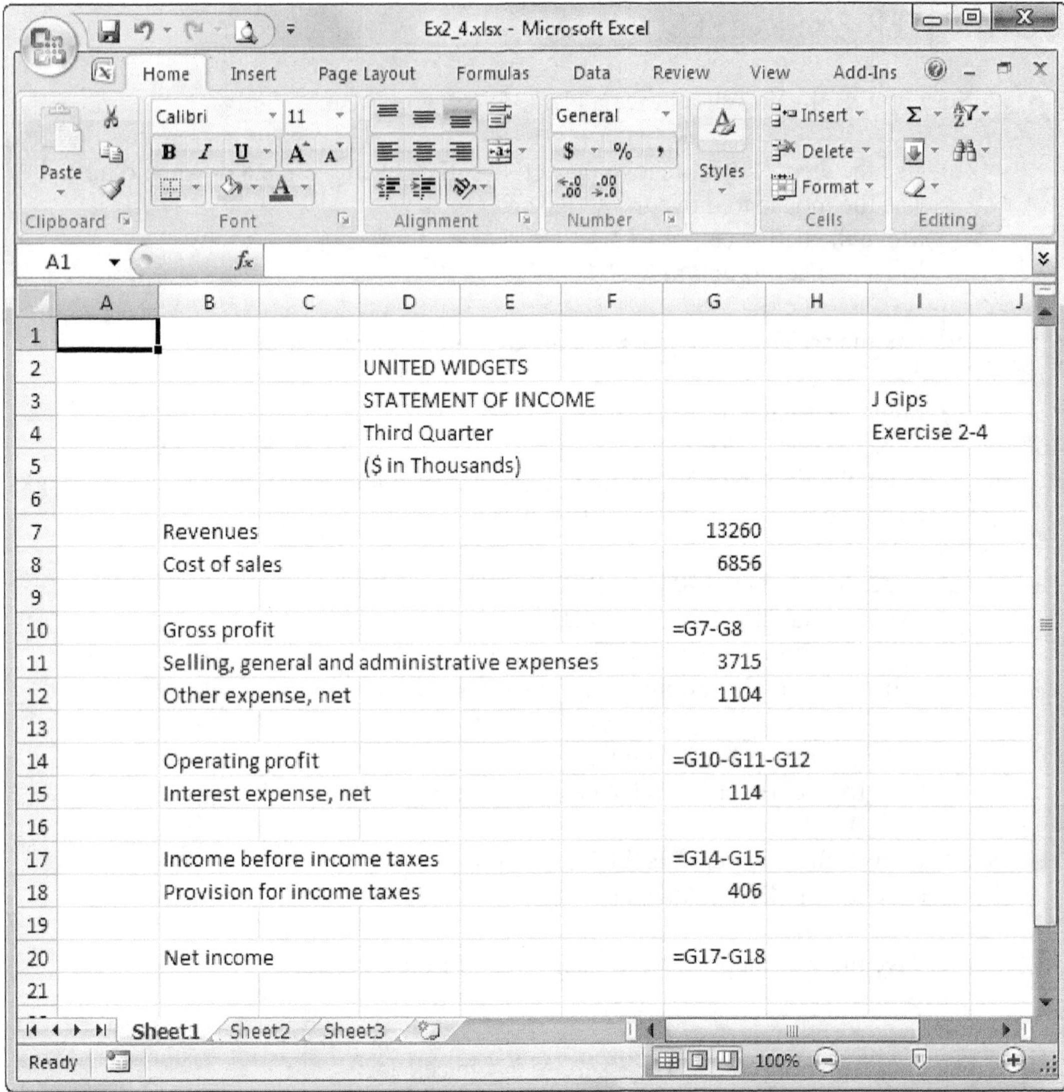

2-5. Enter the worksheet of Exercise 2-2 into the computer. Remember that columns E and G and row 11 contain formulas. Change Carey's Sales to 615,000. Do all the other numbers change appropriately?

2-6. Create a well-labeled worksheet that allows you to enter two numbers: the number of feet (for example, 6) and inches (for example, 2) in a person's height. The worksheet then should calculate the person's height in centimeters. Try your worksheet on the following heights: 5 feet 3 inches, 6 feet 2 inches, and 7 feet 4.5 inches. One inch equals 2.54 centimeters.

2-7. Create a worksheet to convert a temperature from Fahrenheit to Celsius. The formula is $C = 5/9\ (F - 32)$. Try your worksheet on temperatures of 0 degrees Fahrenheit, 32 degrees Fahrenheit, and 85 degrees Fahrenheit.

2-8. Create a well-labeled worksheet that allows you to enter a person's weight in kilograms and height in centimeters and calculates the person's weight in pounds and height in inches.

2-9. The cash drawer at the local market has room for $20 bills, $10 bills, $5 bills, $1 bills, quarters, dimes, nickels, and pennies. Create a worksheet that allows a person to enter in how many of each type of bills and coins are in the cash drawer and calculates the total value of the money in the drawer. So for example if the drawer contains two $5 bills and three quarters, there would be $10.75 in the drawer.

2-10. At Lou's Discount Furniture Store, Lou, the owner, marks furniture at twice his wholesale cost plus $80. If you bargain with him, he'll drop the price as much as 15%. Create a worksheet that allows you to enter the wholesale cost and calculates the list price and the best discount price. Try your worksheet with a sofa that wholesales for $550 and then for a table that wholesales for $200.

2-11. When a star runs out of nuclear fuel, it may collapse into a black hole if its radius becomes small enough, below the event horizon so no light escapes. The event horizon depends on the mass of the star and is given by the formula

$$R = 2\ G\ M\ /\ c^2$$

where G is Newton's constant, M is the mass of the star, c is the speed of light, and R is the radius of the event horizon.

(a) Create a worksheet that allows you to enter the mass of a star in kilograms and determines the radius of its event horizon in kilometers. What would be the maximum radius of a black hole for a star with the same mass as our Sun? (The mass of the Sun is 1.9891×10^{30} kg.)

(b) A black hole does emit some radiation. The "temperature" of a black hole depends only on its mass and is given by the formula

$$T = \hbar\ c^3\ /\ (\ 8\ \pi\ k\ G\ M\ )$$

where $\hbar$ is Planck's constant and k is Boltzmann's constant. Add to your worksheet a calculation of the apparent temperature of the black hole. What would be the apparent temperature of a black hole with the mass of the Sun?

2-12. Create a currency conversion worksheet. At the top of the worksheet put in the current conversions from dollars to euros and from dollars to yen in separate well-labeled cells. You should obtain these values off the web or from today's newspaper. Below that, your worksheet should have three parts. The first part should allow you to enter in a price in dollars and obtain the equivalent values in euros and yen. The second part should allow you to convert from euros to dollars and yen. The third part should allow you to convert from yen to dollars and euros. Try your worksheet on $29.98, €507, and ¥5,640,000.

2-13. People in cold climates often are concerned about the wind chill factor. People say, "Well it's 20 degrees out but because of the wind it feels like -5 degrees." The National Weather Service recently revised its formula for calculating the wind chill factor based on a year-long study involving volunteers with sensors on their faces doing 90-minute stints on a treadmill in a controlled climate chamber. The new official formula for calculating the wind chill factor from the National Weather Service is

$$W = 35.74 + 0.6215\, T - 35.75\, (V^{0.16}) + 0.4275\, T\, (V^{0.16})$$

where W is the wind chill adjusted temperature, T is the air temperature in Fahrenheit, and V is the wind velocity in miles per hour. Create a worksheet for calculating the wind chill factor given a temperature and wind velocity. Try your worksheet for a 30 degree day with a 10 mile per hour wind and for a -5 degree day with a 40 mile per hour wind.

2-14. The atomic weight of carbon is 12.011. The atomic weight of hydrogen is 1.0079. The atomic weight of oxygen is 15.9994. Create a worksheet that allows you to enter the number of carbon atoms, hydrogen atoms, and oxygen atoms in a molecule and calculates (i) the total number of atoms in the molecule and (ii) the molecular weight of the molecule. Try your worksheet on ethane C_2H_6 and on sucrose $C_{12}H_{22}O_{11}$.

2-15. You recently were given a beautiful framed, personally signed photograph of your favorite athlete. You'd like to know what it will be worth in the future. The formula for calculating the future value of an investment that increases at a constant rate is $F = P\,(1 + R)^N$ where P is the present value, R is the annual rate of increase, and N is the number of years. Create a worksheet that has as input the present value of your autographed photo, the annual rate of increase, and the number of years you will keep it and as output the future value.

(a) Try your worksheet with values of $500, 5%, and 10 years.

(b) Try your worksheet with values of $1,000, 7%, and 20 years.

(c) If the signed photograph is worth $1,000 today, at what annual rate must it increase to be worth $20,000 in 20 years? You should do this by trial and error to find the rate to the tenth of a percent that results in a value just over $20,000.

2-16. Create a worksheet for joggers that allows you to enter two numbers: a distance in miles and the number of minutes required to run the distance. The worksheet then should calculate two quantities: the average number of minutes per mile and the average miles per hour for the run. Try the worksheet on the following runs: 1 mile in 4 minutes, 3.5 miles in 42 minutes, and 26.21875 miles in 129.7 minutes.

2-17. The Widget Division factory purchases 25,000 couplers per year for use in its widget manufacturing process. The Director of Purchasing has determined that it costs $20.00 (in personnel and computer time) for the company to process an order to purchase couplers. It costs the company $4.00 per year to carry a coupler in inventory (including space allocation, breakage, theft, and insurance). As the new Analyst, you are asked to determine how many couplers should be ordered at one time. If you order 100 couplers at a time, orders will be arriving almost daily so you will have low carrying costs but you will have to pay for 250 purchases per year. If you order 100,000 couplers at a time, you will have low purchase costs but very high inventory carrying costs.

The Economic Order Quantity (EOQ) is the amount that should be ordered at one time to minimize carrying and ordering costs. The EOQ is calculated by $\sqrt{2DO/C}$ where D is the annual demand, O is the cost for processing an order, and C is the annual carrying cost for a unit in inventory.

(a) Create a worksheet for determining the Economic Order Quantity. You should have an appropriate heading at the top. You should have separate well-labeled cells for the annual demand, order cost, and annual unit carrying cost. Your worksheet should work for any quantities entered. (Note that the square root of a quantity can be calculated by raising the quantity to the 0.5 power.) How many couplers should be purchased at a time? Try your worksheet on the numbers in the first paragraph.

(b) Suppose demand for widgets increases dramatically and now we need to purchase 100,000 couplers per year. How many should be purchased at a time? Change the value in the cell that contains the annual demand.

2-18. Our company sells products globally. The company is organized into geographical regions, where each region corresponds to a continent. Each region has a goal for its annual sales. At the end of the year the actual sales made by each region are compared against the goal for the region. We would like to create a worksheet that will allow us to compare what we were supposed to sell in each region (our goal) with what we actually sold.

(a) Enter the following worksheet with appropriate formulas in the blank cells in the bottom row and right column. Just as a check, the number calculated for Amount Over Goal for Africa should be 3.3, as Actual Sales exceeded the Goal for Africa by $3.3 million.

Annual Sales in $ Millions

Region	Goal	Actual	Amount Over Goal
Africa	24	27.3	
Antarctica	3	19.4	
Asia	20	33.5	
Europe	32	31.2	
North America	25	46.1	
South America	17	11.8	
Total			

(b) Change the Asia Actual sales to 56.7 and the South America Actual sales to 15.1. The numbers in the Total row and Amount Over Goal column should change automatically.

(c) Add formulas in a new column that calculate Percent Over Goal for each of the regions and for the Total. "Percent Over Goal" means the extent to which the goal was exceeded, expressed as a percentage. The Percent Over Goal calculated for Africa should be 13.75. For Europe it should be -2.5. You just need to submit one worksheet as it exists after part (c), rather than a separate worksheet for each part.

2-19. You are thinking of opening an ice cream stand and selling ice cream cones. You plan to sell single-scoop cones and double-scoop cones. You would like to know how much ice cream you would use for various sized cones.

(a) Create a worksheet that allows you to enter three numbers: the height of the cone itself (without any ice cream), the diameter of the cone, and the diameter of the scoop. The output will be two numbers: the number of ounces of ice cream that would be used in a single-scoop cone and the number of ounces of ice cream that would be used in a double-scoop cone.

Assume that the cone is filled with ice cream so the top is level. Assume that each scoop is a perfect sphere. A pint of ice cream fits in a cylindrical container 4 inches high and 3 inches in diameter. The volume of a cone is $V = \pi r^2 h / 3$. The volume of a sphere is $V = 4 \pi r^3 / 3$. The volume of a cylinder is $V = \pi r^2 h$. To obtain the value of π you can use PI( ) in an Excel formula. There are 16 ounces in a pint. Try your worksheet on a cone that is 4 inches high and 2 inches wide with 2.5-inch scoops and on a cone that is 6 inches high and 3 inches wide with 4-inch scoops.

(b) You would like to know the projected cost for each of the ice cream cones. Assume that cones are bought by the gross (144 cones) and ice cream by the gallon (8 pints). Add separate cells for the price of cones per gross and price of ice cream per gallon. Try your worksheet on the above cones with costs of $15 per gross of cones and $4 per gallon of ice cream.

2-20. Create a worksheet to calculate the Break-Even Point for a product. Allow the user to enter three values: a unit Selling Price, the percentage of the selling price required for the Variable Cost of each unit, and the total Fixed Cost. The worksheet should be well-labeled and should contain formulas to calculate automatically two values: the Break-Even Point in units sold and the Break-Even Point in dollar volume sold. The worksheet also may calculate some intermediate values, if you wish. Try your worksheet with the following sets of input values: (a) Selling Price 200, Variable Cost Percent 60, Fixed Cost 40000, and (b) Selling Price 250, Variable Cost Percent 50, Fixed Cost 50000.

2-21. The Body Mass Index (BMI) often is used by scientists and physicians to determine whether a person is underweight or overweight. The BMI is calculated as follows:

Step 1. Divide your body weight in pounds by 2.205 to obtain your weight in kilograms.
Step 2. Divide your height in inches by 39.37 to obtain your height in meters.
Step 3. Square the answer from Step 2.
Step 4. Divide the answer from Step 1 by the answer from Step 3.

A healthy BMI is between 18.5 and 25. The BMI is said to work equally well for both men and women. Create a worksheet to calculate a person's BMI. There should be four values entered into the worksheet: the person's name, the person's weight in pounds, and the person's height in feet and inches. The worksheet should calculate the total height in inches, the values for each of the steps, and then show the resulting BMI.

Try your worksheet on the following people: (a) Jan, 115 pounds, 5 feet 8 inches; (b) Fran, 325 pounds, 5 feet 1 inch; (c) Dana, 240 pounds, 6 feet 4 inches; and (d) Slim, 104 pounds, 5 feet 6 inches. The four inputs for part (a) should be: Jan, 115, 5, 8.

2-22. Kristi has three stocks in her portfolio. Create a worksheet to help her determine how she is doing in the market. The inputs to the worksheet should be the name of each of the three stocks, the number of shares of each she purchased, the price per share at which she purchased each stock, and the current price per share of each of the stocks. Twelve cells for input. The worksheet should calculate the total amount she spent for each of the stocks, the total current value of each of the stocks, the amount gained or lost for each of her stocks, the percentage gained or lost for each of her stocks, and then the same calculations for the portfolio as a whole. Also, your worksheet should calculate the percentage of her current portfolio in each of the three stocks. Your worksheet should work automatically for any inputs.

CHAPTER 3

CHANGING THE APPEARANCE OF CELLS

OBJECTIVES

In this chapter you will learn how to:

- Change the width of columns
- Select ranges of cells
- Set the font, style, and size of text
- Change the alignment of text in cells
- Format numbers
- Place borders around cells
- Change the color of text and cells
- Give your worksheet a three-dimensional shading effect
- Display the formulas in your worksheet

Excel has many ways of changing the appearance of the information in the worksheet, both on the screen and as printed on the page. The general term for changing the appearance of information is **formatting**. Here we are not concerned with the contents of the information, but rather with how it appears. Proper formatting can make a worksheet easier to understand and more visually pleasing.

COLUMN WIDTH

Consider the Price Quote worksheet again. (See Figure 3-1.) Notice that cell B2 contains the text "Price Quote". But this text does not quite fit into the cell. When you start up Excel the columns are all set at the same width. Each cell holds 8.43 characters in the standard Arial 10 point font in Excel. If you type in text that is longer than what will fit in the cell, the computer will display the full text as long as the cell to the right is blank. If you look carefully you will notice that the line between cells B2 and C2 is missing, indicating that the extended B2 is being displayed on top of C2. If cell C2 contained some information, then all of B2 would not be displayed. Rather, only the information that fit within the cell boundaries would show. Similarly, you can see that the entries in B8, B10, and B14 are too long for the cells.

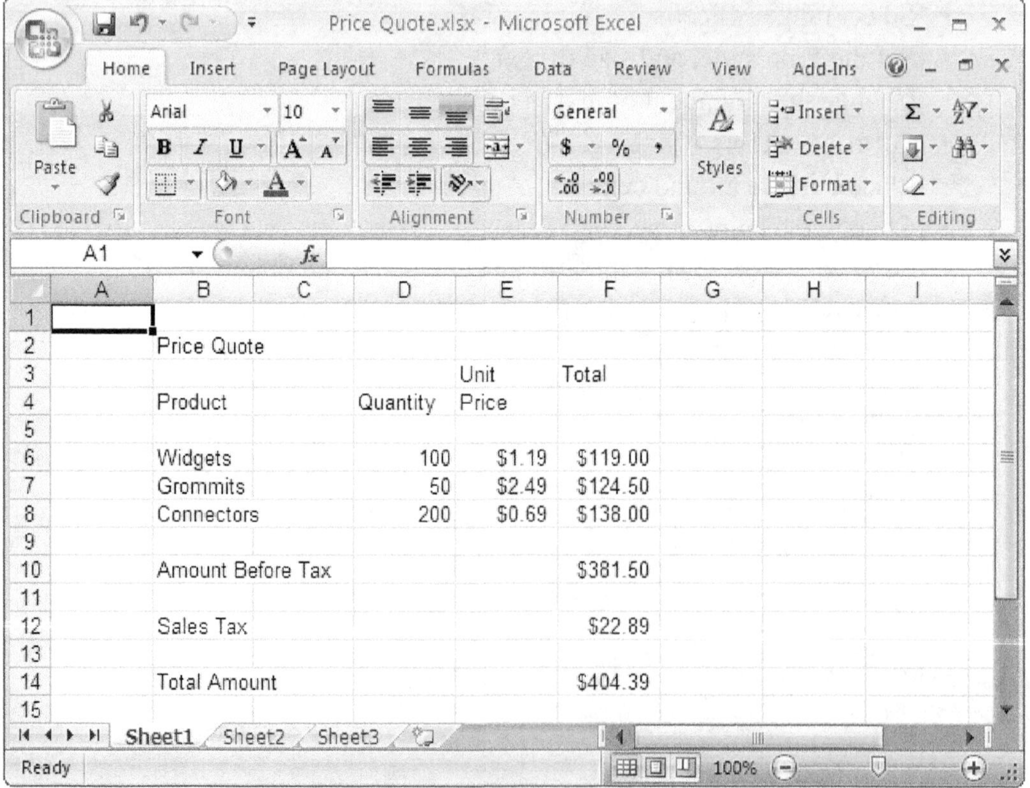

Figure 3-1. The Price Quote worksheet.

It is easy to change the width of the cells in column B so that all of the text fits. Simply move the mouse pointer up to the area right between column head B and C. The mouse pointer shape will change to a vertical line with arrows pointing left and right, as in Figure 3-2. Press the left mouse button, hold the button down, and drag the width of column B to the right to the size you would like. The current width of the column is shown in a box.

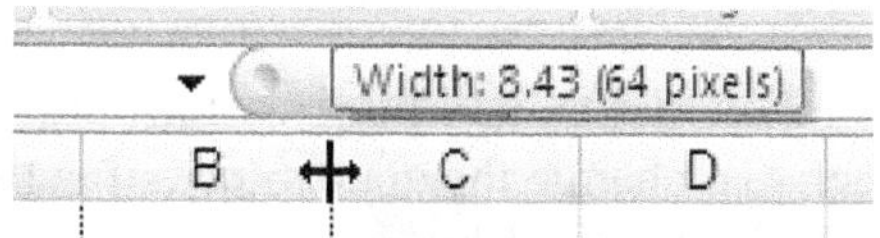

Figure 3-2. When the mouse pointer assumes this shape you can change the width of the column to the left by pressing the left mouse button and dragging.

Alternatively you can double-click when the mouse pointer is in the position in Figure 3-2 and the width of column B will be adjusted automatically.

Now we can move the pointer up to the column head between the C and the D, and drag the pointer to the left to make column C narrower. (See Figure 3-3.)

	A	B	C	D	E	F	G	H	I
1									
2		Price Quote							
3					Unit	Total			
4		Product		Quantity	Price				
5									
6		Widgets		100	$1.19	$119.00			
7		Grommits		50	$2.49	$124.50			
8		Connectors		200	$0.69	$138.00			
9									
10		Amount Before Tax				$381.50			
11									
12		Sales Tax				$22.89			
13									
14		Total Amount				$404.39			
15									

Figure 3-3. The Price Quote worksheet with the widths of columns B and C adjusted.

We can make the rows different heights in the same way, but this technique usually is used only with columns. We can change the row heights automatically by changing the font size of the letters in the cells.

SELECTING CELLS

The characters (letters, digits, and punctuation) are all of the same font, size, style, and color in the worksheet. To change the appearance of cells, we first need to select the cells to be changed. Cells can be selected by dragging across them with the mouse while the left mouse button is pressed. For example, to select the rectangular range of cells from B2 through F14, place the mouse pointer in B2, press down on the button, and drag the mouse to F14. Selected cells are darkened except for the cell in the top left corner of the selection, which is white. In Figure 3-4, the range of cells in B2 through F14 has been selected.

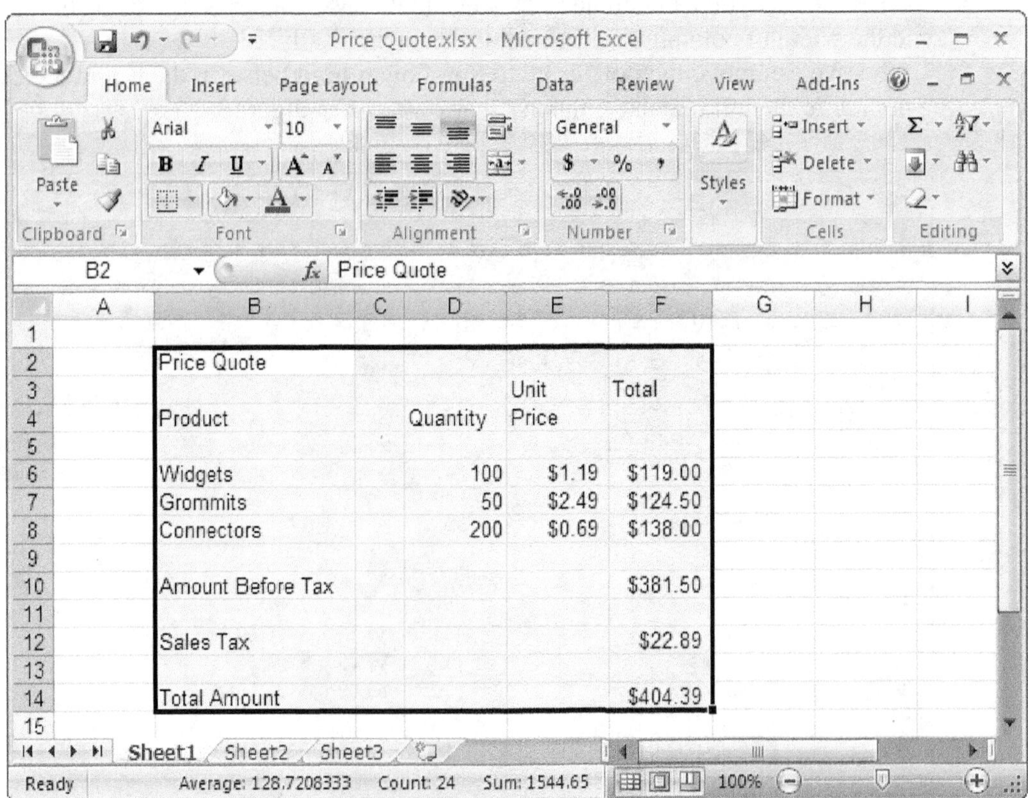

Figure 3-4. The darkened area indicates that the range from B2 through F14 is selected.

It is possible to select a **noncontiguous range** of cells by holding your finger down on the **Ctrl key** ("Control" key) while you do the selection. For example, we could select B12 through B14 by dragging across the cells and then press down on the Ctrl key on the keyboard and with the Ctrl key pressed drag from D6 through F8. This selects two separate areas, as shown in Figure 3-5. This is called **control-clicking**.

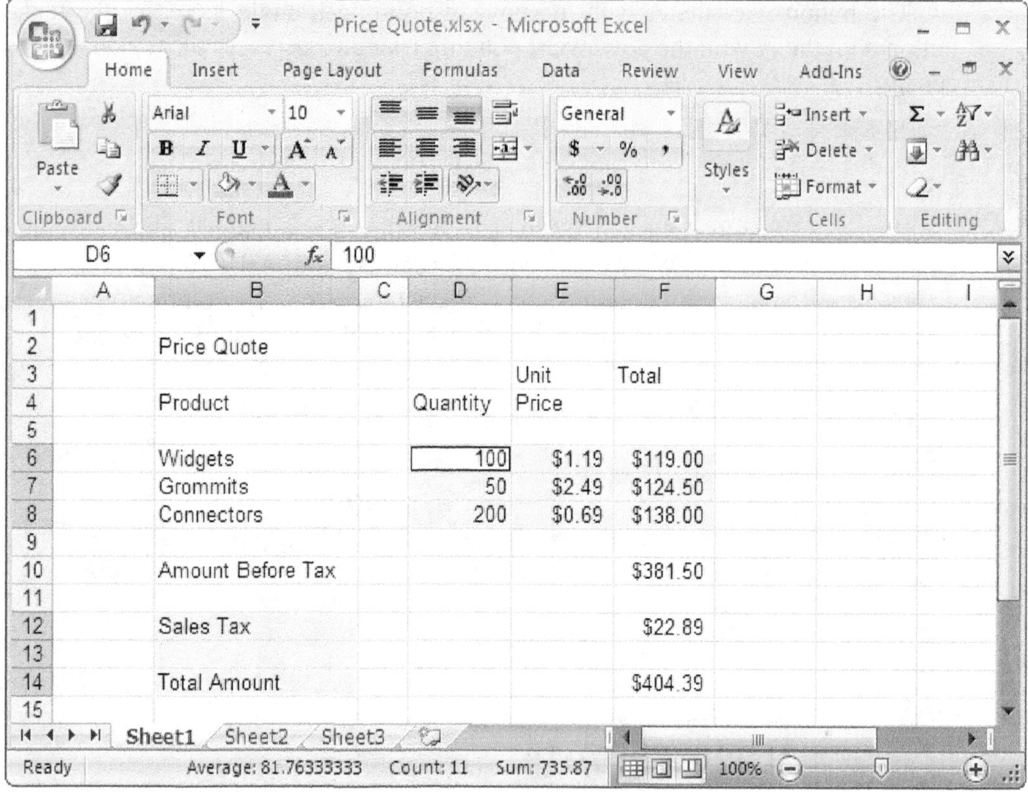

Figure 3-5. Use the Ctrl key ("Control" key) to select multiple areas.

We can select all of the cells in the entire worksheet by clicking on the button above the 1 and to the left of the A, just to the top left of cell A1 in the worksheet.

FORMATTING CELLS

Once cells have been selected they can be formatted by clicking on the appropriate buttons in the Home tab. At the top of the Font group of the Home button are the **Font** and **Size pull-down menus**.

Below these are buttons for making the text in the selected cells appear in **Bold**, *Italics*, and Underlined or, using the tiny triangle pull-down menu just to the right of the U button, Double-Underlined. Pressing a button a second time undoes the formatting on the selected cells.

The button with the A with the upward pointing triangle increases the text size. The button with the A with the downward pointing triangle decreases the text size of the selected cells.

We would like to make cell B2, which contains "Price Quote", more prominent. So we click on B2 to select it. We see that currently cell B2 is in Arial 10 point regular. We select Times New Roman in the Font menu and change the size to 24 point and then click on Bold. The text in cell B2 is changed accordingly to Times New Roman Bold 24. (See Figure 3-6.)

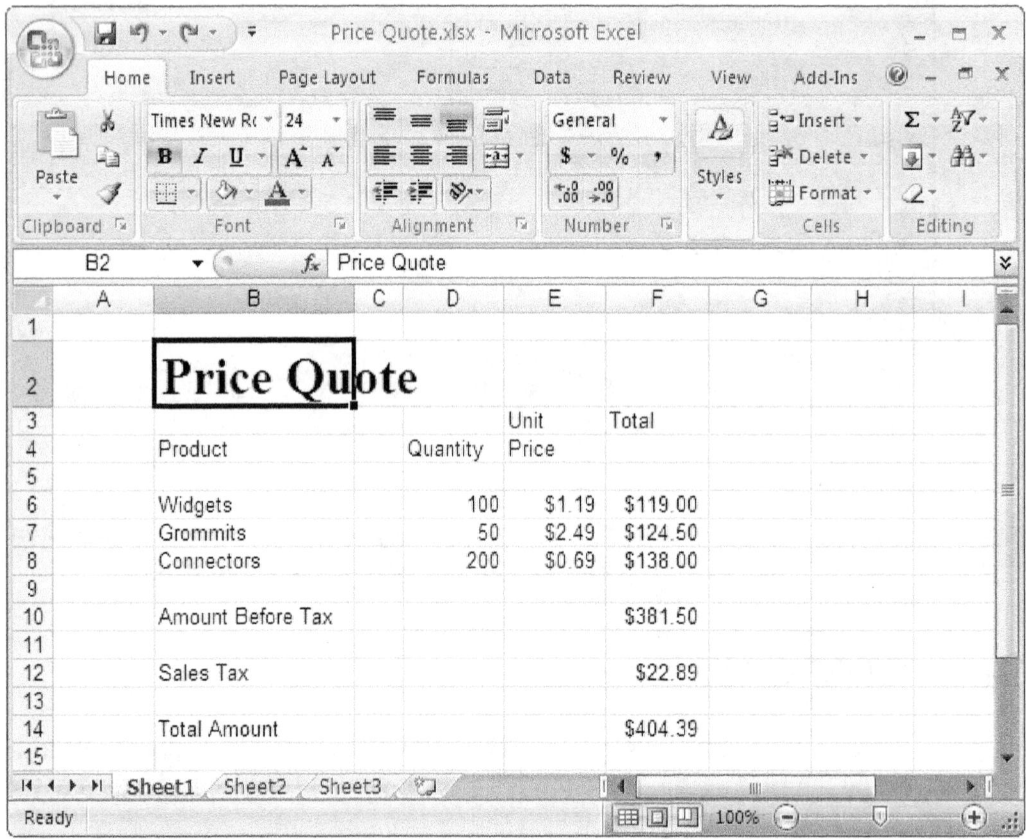

Figure 3-6. Changing the font, size, and style of cell B2.

ALIGNMENT

As you may have noticed, Excel automatically aligns text to the left of each cell and numbers to the right of each cell. This allows the user to see at a glance which cells contain text and which cells contain numbers. However, it also means that numbers usually do not line up under column titles. For example, in the Price Quote worksheet in Figure 3-6, the word "Quantity" in cell D4 is aligned on the left of the cell whereas the numbers below it, in cells D6, D7, and D8, are aligned on the right of the cells. Similarly, the titles "Unit Price" and "Totals" do not line up with the numbers below them. Here, we want to change the alignment of the titles in cells D4, E3, E4, and F4 so they are aligned to the right of the cells like the numbers below them.

If you wish to change the alignment of the text within cells, you can select the cells and then press one of the **Text Alignment buttons** in the Alignment group of the Home tab.

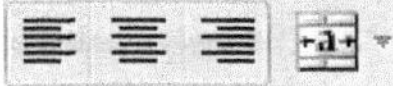

The first Alignment button, the **Align Left button**, causes information in the selected cells to be aligned to the left of the cell. The second button, the **Center button**, causes information to be centered in the cell. The third of these buttons, the **Align Right button**, not surprisingly, causes information to be aligned to the right of the cell.

In the Price Quote worksheet, we can drag across D3 through F4 to select these cells. We then click on the Align Right button and the text is aligned on the right of the cells, as in Figure 3-7.

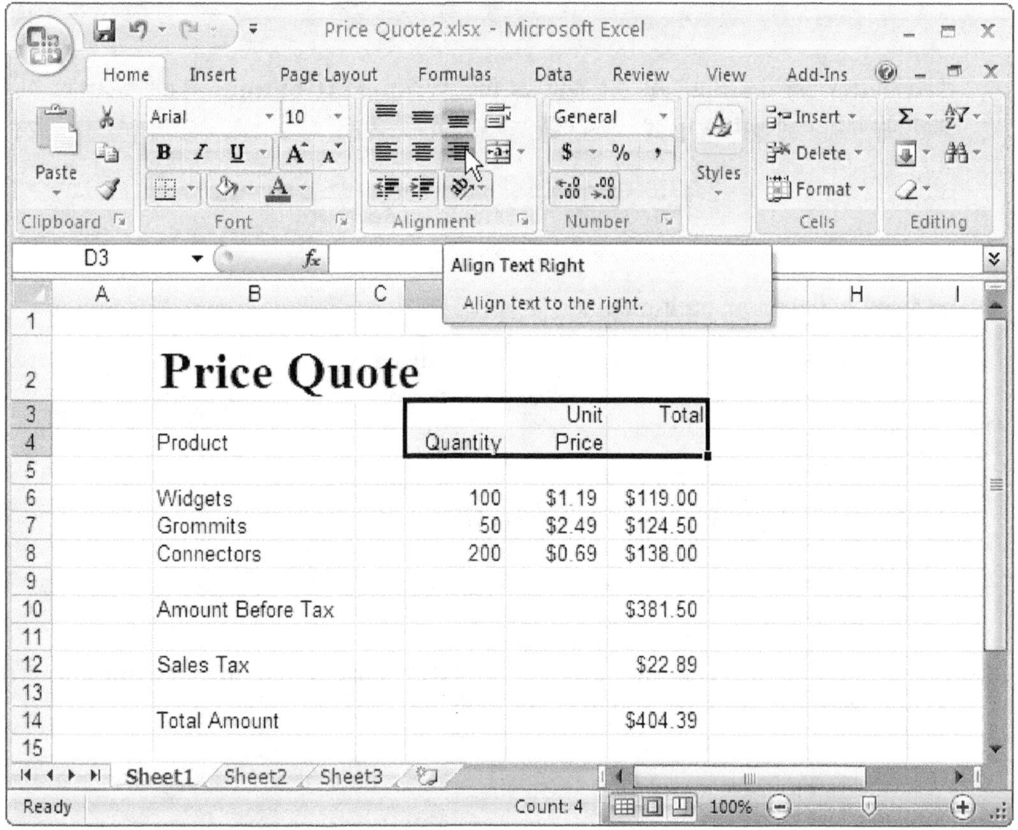

Figure 3-7. Aligning text to the right of the cells.

The rightmost of the Text Alignment buttons in the Formatting toolbar is the **Merge and Center button**. The Merge and Center button allows information to be centered across multiple cells. First, enter information into a cell.

Then, select that cell and several blank cells to the right of the cell and click on the Merge and Center button. The selected cells will be merged. The text will appear centered across the selected cells, though it actually will remain located in the original cell.

To "unmerge" the cells select the cell and click on the button again.

The row of buttons above the horizontal alignment buttons control vertical alignment of the text in cells.

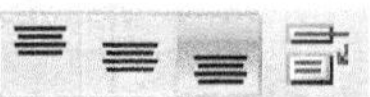

The button on the right of the row is the **Wrap Text button**. This button allows you to change text that is too wide for a cell

to a cell with text on multiple lines

In the bottom row of the Alignment group

the first two buttons control indenting. The rightmost button, the **Orientation button**, is one of my favorites. It allows you to create cells like

with text at an arbitrary angle. Why you might want to do this is a mystery.

HELP!

Excel has a myriad of tabs, buttons, menus, functions, and tools. No one could remember all of the features and details of operating Excel.

Excel has a very extensive **Help system** to assist us. As usual with Excel, there are several ways to access the Help system. The easiest way is simply to click on the **Help button**, the button with a question mark at the top right of the window. Clicking on the Help button brings up the Help window. (See Figure 3-8.) From here you can search for information on any topic of interest.

Alternatively if you are in the middle of an operation and would like some help, you can press function key F1 at any time to obtain help on the feature you are using.

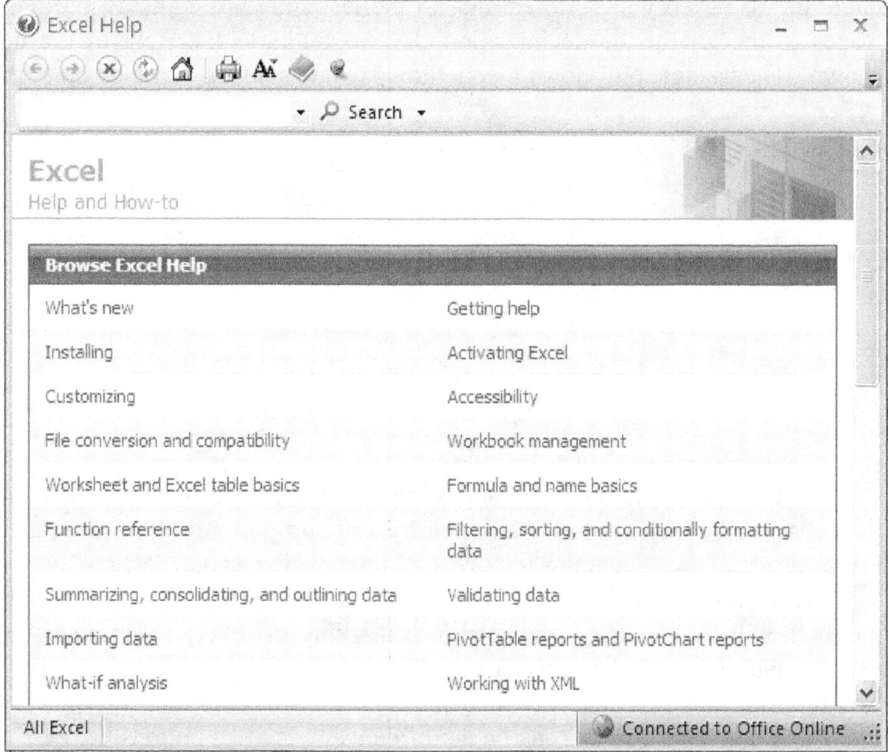

Figure 3-8. The Excel Help window.

FORMATTING NUMBERS

You may have noticed that some numbers in the Price Quote worksheet have dollar signs in front of them and some do not. These numbers have different formats. The important point to remember here is that the format of a cell affects only how the cell is displayed. The format of a cell does not affect the actual contents of the cell. For example, a cell might contain the number 347.4725 and be formatted to appear as $347.47. But the contents of the cell still remain unchanged. If the cell is used in calculations, the number used will be 347.4725 even though the number that appears in the cell is 347.47.

There are a couple of ways to set the **Number format** of a cell. If you type a number into a cell in a particular format, for example if you type $37,405.23, Excel will pick up the numerical format for the cell. Alternatively you can set or change numerical formats by using the buttons and pull-down menus in the Number group of the Home tab.

Three of the most common number formats have their own buttons in the Number group of the Home tab.

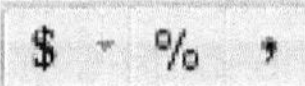

The **Accounting Number Format button** changes the selected cells so that numbers in them are displayed with a dollar sign to the left and with commas marking off every three places to the left of the decimal point. Two digits to the right of the decimal point are shown. The triangle pull-down menu allows you to select a currency other than dollar.

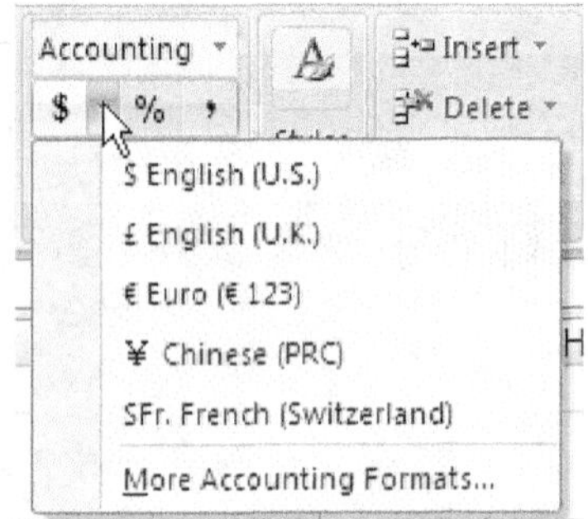

The **Percent Style button** changes the selected cells to Percent format. The contents of the cells will be displayed as multiplied by 100 and will be followed with a percent sign %. For example, if a cell contains 0.0789, it will be displayed as 7.89%.

The **Comma Style button** changes the selected cells to Comma format. Here, the numbers will be displayed with commas marking off every three places to the left of the decimal places. No dollar signs are displayed. This could be considered a "normal" format for numbers.

These and other formats can be modified using the two buttons below

The **Increase Decimal button** increases the number of decimal places displayed in the selected cells by one for each time the button is pressed. For example, if a selected cell contains 304 and displays 304 and this button is pressed twice, the number will be displayed as 304.00.

The **Decrease Decimal button** decreases the number of decimal places displayed in the selected cells by one for each time the button is pressed. For example, if a selected cell displays 304.872 and this button is pressed twice, the number will be displayed as 304.9. The computer rounds off the number displayed but it leaves the actual number stored in the cell unchanged.

If a formatted number is too long to be displayed, then ######### will be displayed in the cell. This is a signal to you that you should widen the column of the cell or decrease the number of decimal places or change the format or the font size.

The Number format buttons displayed in the Number group of the Home tab are only the tip of the iceberg of the Number formats available. To reach the full range of choices for Number formats, click on the arrow button to the right of Number

This yields hundreds of formats. Notice from Figure 3-9 that it is possible to change the way negative numbers are displayed in some formats. (It might be difficult to see without color here, but some of the choices display negative numbers in red.) It also is possible using the Symbol drop-down list to change the currency symbol displayed from $ to £ or € or ¥ or any other symbol.

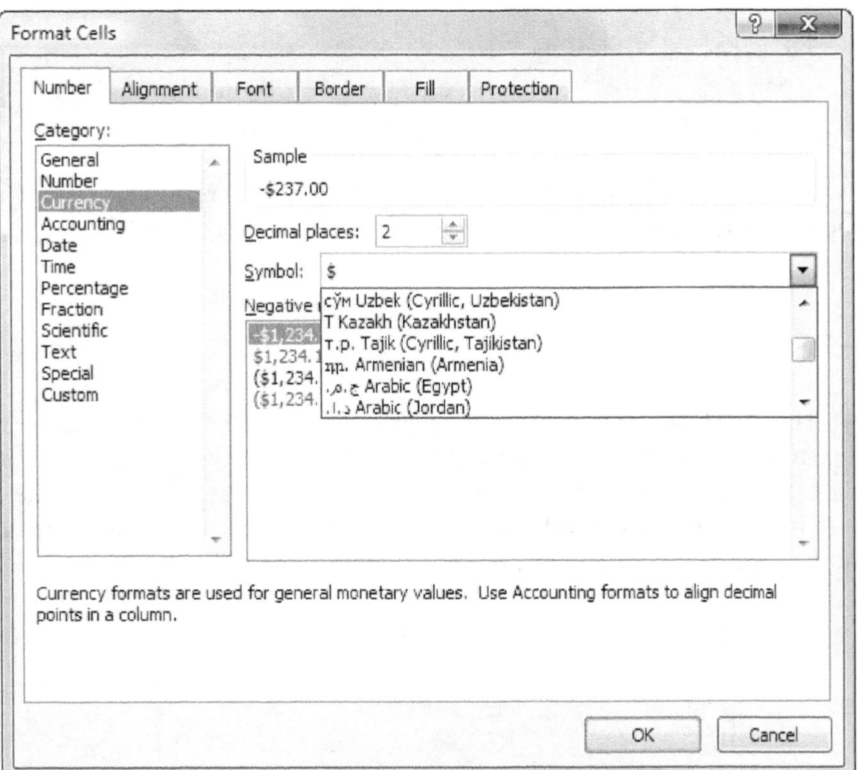

Figure 3-9. Many different formats for numbers are available.

There are many choices of formats for numbers. As you can see in Figure 3-10, there is a **Currency format** for numbers as well as an Accounting format. The numbers in the Price Quote worksheet, as shown in Figure 3-7, actually were displayed in Currency format. The differences between the two formats are illustrated in the worksheet in Figure 3-10. Here negative numbers in Currency format are displayed with a minus sign.

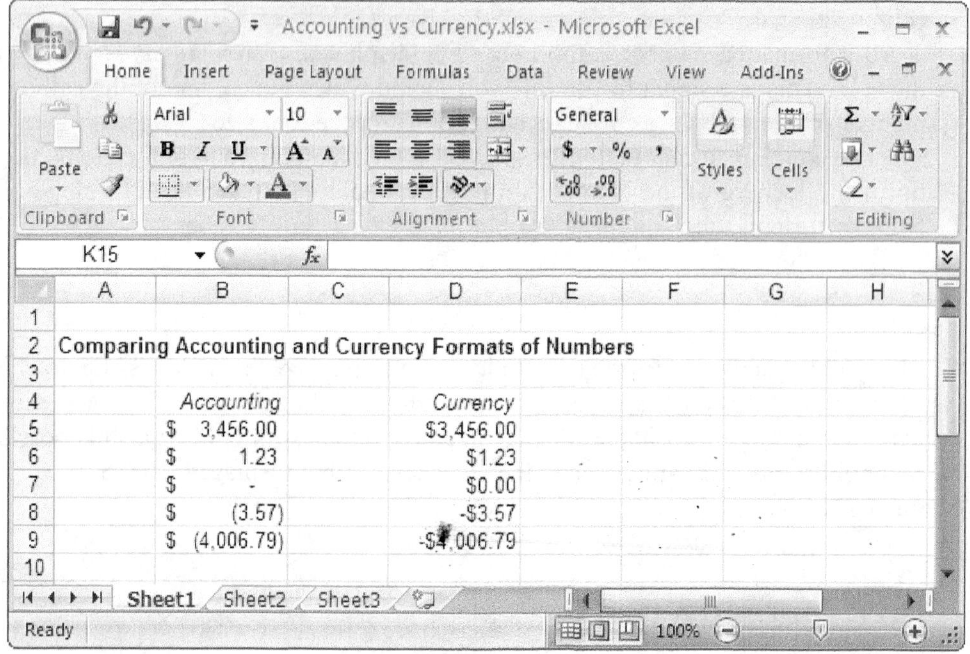

Figure 3-10. Typical Accounting vs. Currency formats.

If you are not satisfied with the choices, you can create your own **Custom format** by clicking on Custom at the bottom of the Category list in Figure 3-9.

BORDERS

The **Borders button** in the Font group of the Home tab allows you to put a border (lines) around selected cells. First select the cells in the worksheet around which you wish to place a border by dragging across them with the mouse. Click on the small downward-pointing triangle on the right of the Borders button. The **Borders menu** pops down with more varieties of borders than you can imagine. Here are some of the choices.

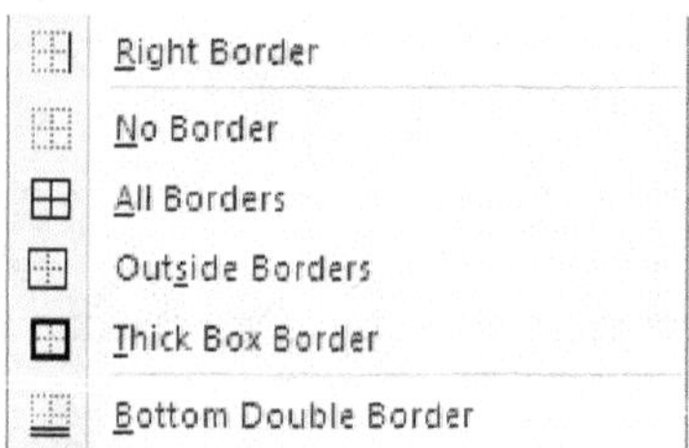

Each of the menu items causes a different type of border to be placed around the selected cells. Note that borders are associated with cells. If the size of the cells changes, for example by changing the column width, the borders automatically are adjusted and redrawn. To undo borders that were previously set, select the bordered cells and then select No Border in the menu.

COLORS

The bottom right two buttons of the Format group of the Home tab let you change the colors of cells.

The **Fill Color button** has a paint can. This button allows you to change the color of the background of the selected cells. Clicking on the small downward-pointing triangle on the right of the button causes the **Color palette** to drop down.

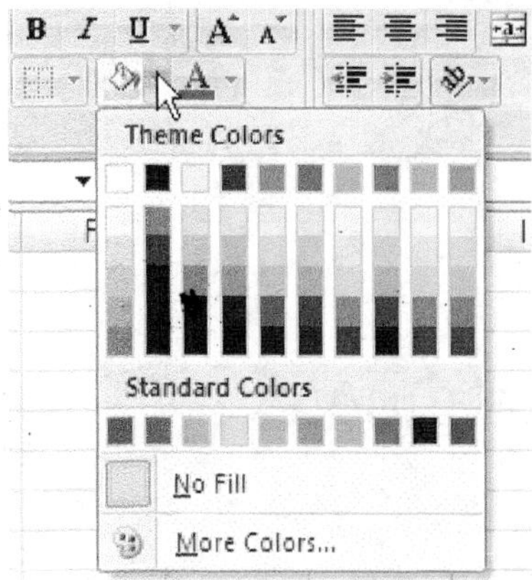

To cause a group of cells in the worksheet to be displayed in yellow, select the cells by dragging across them, click on the right part of the Fill Color button, and then click on yellow in the Standard Colors. Note that the gridlines between the cells no longer show if any of the colors is selected, including white. To return to no fill with the gridlines showing between cells, highlight the cells and select No Fill.

As mentioned earlier, we can select all of the cells in the entire worksheet by clicking on the button above the 1 and to the left of the A just beyond the top left corner of the worksheet. Once all of the cells in the worksheet have been selected we can color all of them by selecting a color in the Color palette. Now the background of the entire worksheet will be a certain color.

The **Font Color button** allows you to change the color of the text that appears in the cell. With this tool you can cause the characters in a cell to be blue or yellow or whatever rather than the normal black. The button works essentially the same as the Fill Color button. Select the cells containing the text you wish to make a different color. Click on the triangle on the right part of the Font Color button. A color palette drops down. Select the desired color for the text from the palette.

It is common in professional worksheets to color all input cells blue. That way the user can tell at a glance which cells are for input and which cells are calculations or descriptions.

Warning! If you make the font color the same as the background color, the text will seem to disappear.

EXAMPLE

We take the Price Quote worksheet. We make the background gray, change the font and size of cell B2, draw some borders, make some cells bold, and make the font size of cells B14 and F14 larger. The result is shown in Figure 3-11.

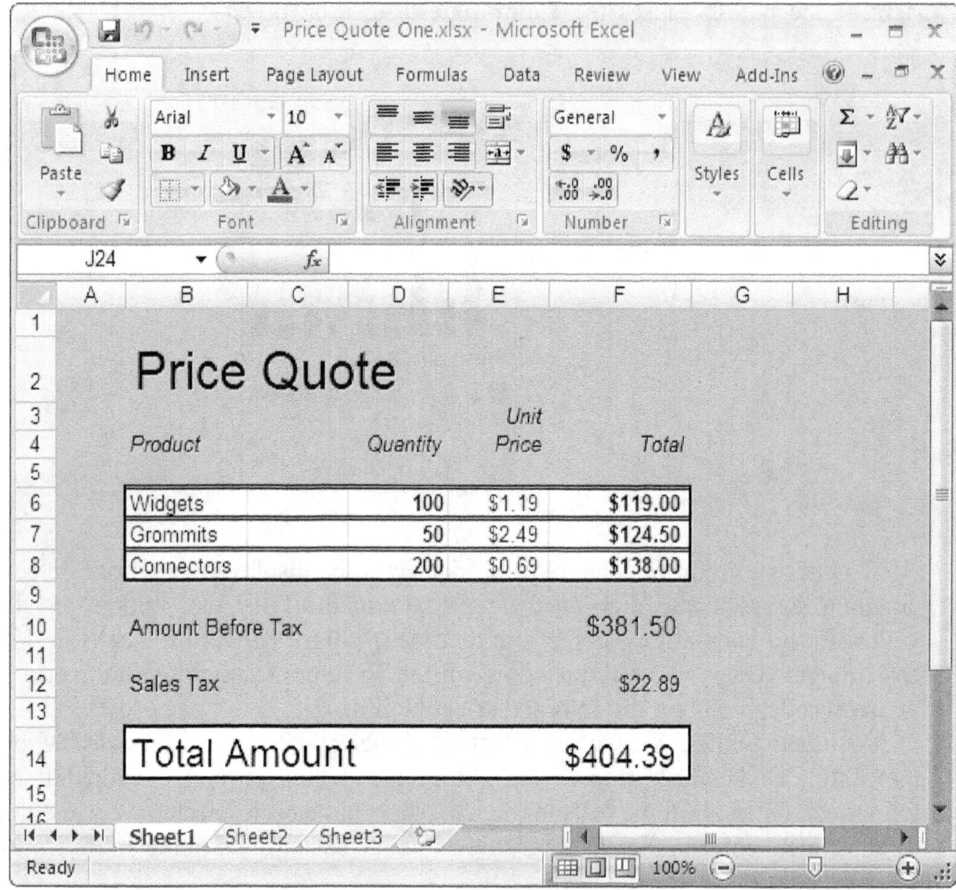

Figure 3-11. One approach to formatting the Price Quote worksheet.

3-D SHADING

It is possible to give your worksheets a three-dimensional effect by the judicious use of colors and borders. An example with the Price Quote worksheet is shown in Figure 3-12.

To begin, select the entire worksheet and color it with some neutral color, for example a medium shade of gray. To format a selection so it appears to be raised, to be above the worksheet, apply white borders on the left and top of the selection and black borders on the right and bottom of the selection. To format a selection so it appears to be sunken, to be below the worksheet, apply black borders to the left and top of the selection and white borders to the right and bottom of the selection.

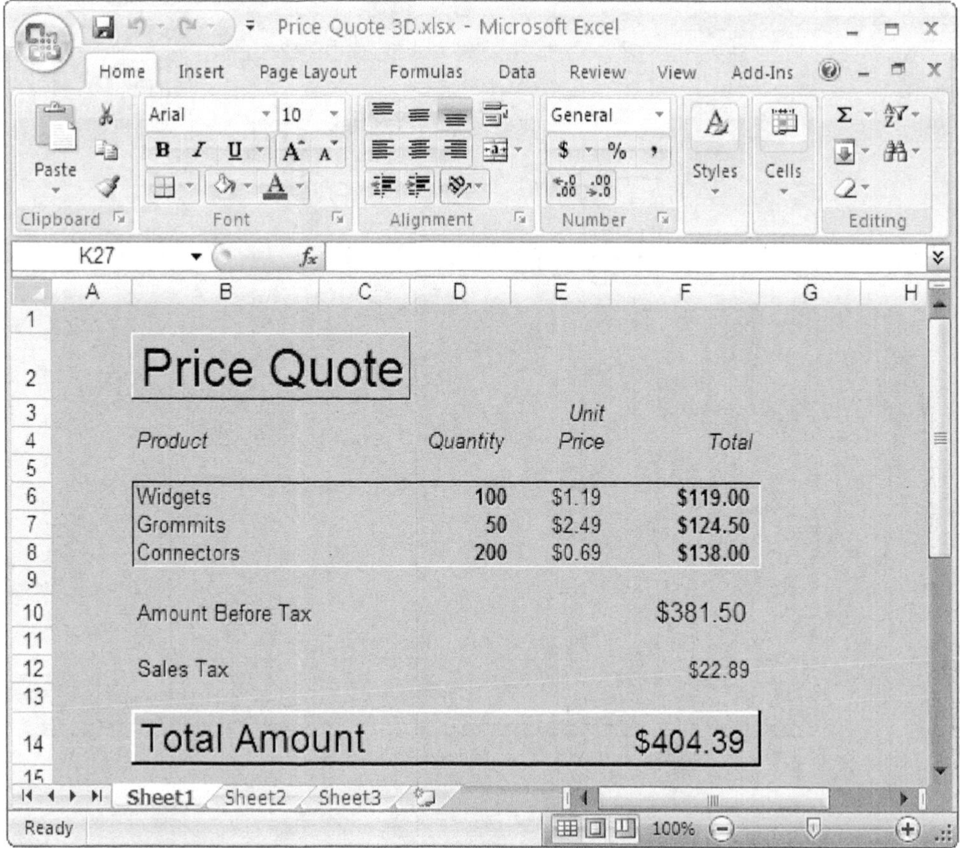

Figure 3-12. Three-dimensional shading of the Price Quote worksheet.

To apply a white border to the top of B2 and C2, we would first select B2 and C2 by dragging across them. Then we select More Borders..., the very bottom selection in the Borders pull-down menu. This gives us full power over the borders. In the Border sheet we have many choices for the borders. (See Figure 3-13.)

We first select the thickness of the line of the border in the Style: section of the Border sheet. The thicker the line, the more pronounced the three-dimensional effect will be. We next click on the white square in the Color: drop-down list. We click on the button with the border line on top of the cell and then click on OK. We will see a white border applied above B2 and C2. The order of selections here matters! In particular, it is important that we select the thickness and the color before selecting the location of the border.

We would use the same technique for each of the other borders. We select B2 and apply a white border to its left. We select B2 and C2 and apply a black border to the bottom of the cells. We select C2 and apply a black border to the right of the cell. This process is tedious, but the resulting worksheet in Figure 3-12 sure looks snazzy (at least to my geeky mind).

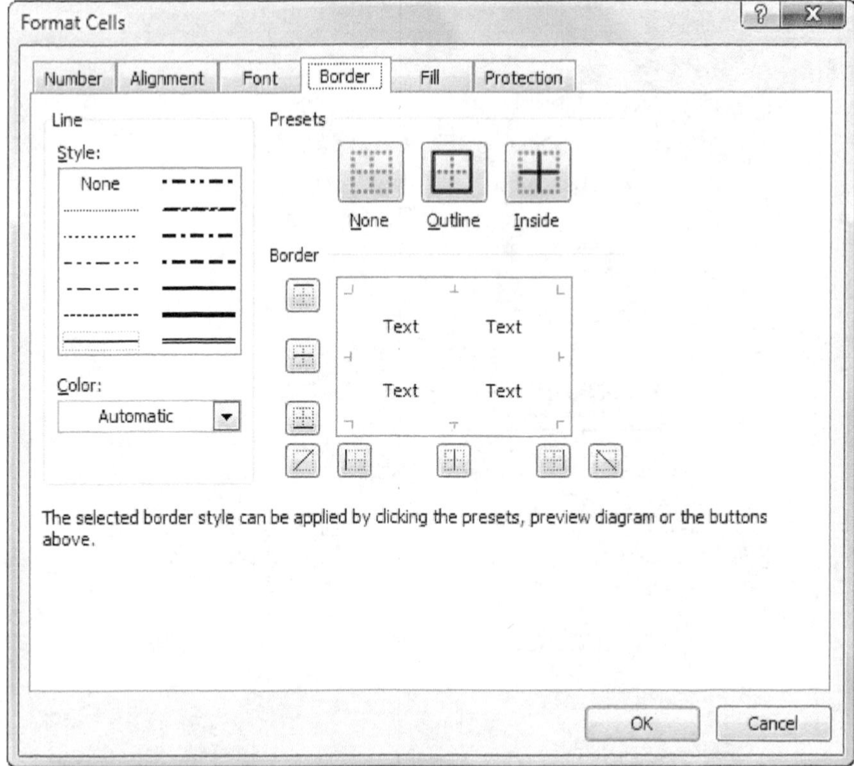

Figure 3-13. The full range of Border options.

THE FORMAT PAINTER BUTTON

If you already have a cell that is formatted in a way that you like, you can capture that format and "paint" it on to other cells using the **Format Painter button**.

The Format Painter button is located in the Clipboard group of the Home tab. To use the Format Painter button: (1) select a cell or range of cells whose format you wish to duplicate, (2) click on the Format Painter button, and (3) click on the cell to which you wish to apply the format or drag across a range of cells to which you wish to apply the format. The format that is captured and then applied includes font, size, style (bold, italics), alignment, borders, and colors.

To apply a format to multiple ranges of cells: (1) select a cell or range of cells whose format you wish to duplicate, (2) double-click on the Format Painter button, (3) click on the cell to which you wish to apply the format or drag across a range of cells to which you wish to apply the format, (4) apply the format to other cells by clicking on them or dragging across them, (5) when you have finished applying the format, click once on the Format Painter button. The Format Painter button will stay depressed during this operation and the cell whose format you have captured will be identified with a dashed line moving around it.

DISPLAYING THE FORMULAS

We can instruct Excel to display the formulas in the cells by going to the Formula tab and selecting Show Formulas in Formula Auditing, as in Figure 3-14.

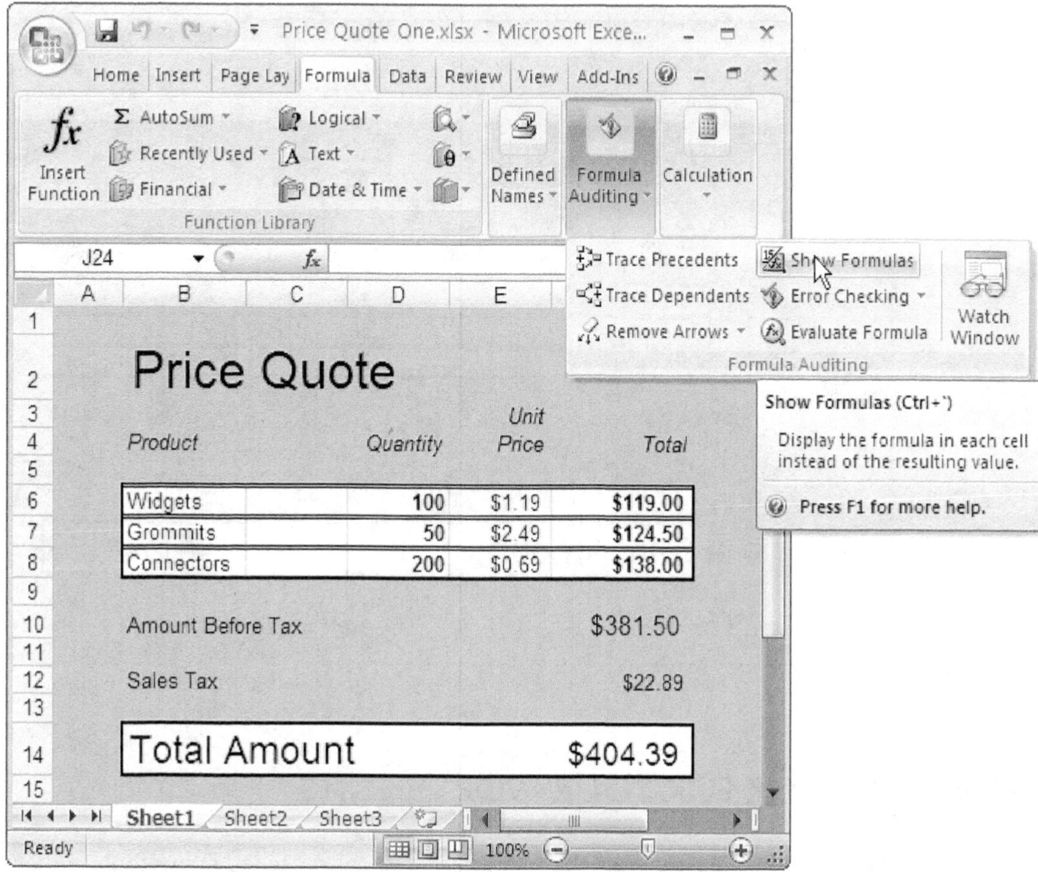

Figure 3-14. Specifying that formulas be displayed in the worksheet.

Show Formulas instructs Excel to display the formulas in the cells rather than the results of evaluating the formulas. The result is shown in Figure 3-15.

This is a very useful way of seeing the formulas that underlie your worksheet. In the worksheet shown in Figure 3-15, we manually changed the column widths so all of the information fits on the screen. Instructing Excel to display the formulas causes the program to change the column widths and cell alignments, not always optimally.

If you print the worksheet in Figure 3-15, the formulas will be printed in the cells. If you are going to print the worksheet with the formulas displayed, you should instruct Excel to print the Column Headings (A, B, C, ...) and Row Headings (1, 2, 3, ...) as well. You can do this by clicking on Print Headings in the Sheet Options group of the Page Layout tab.

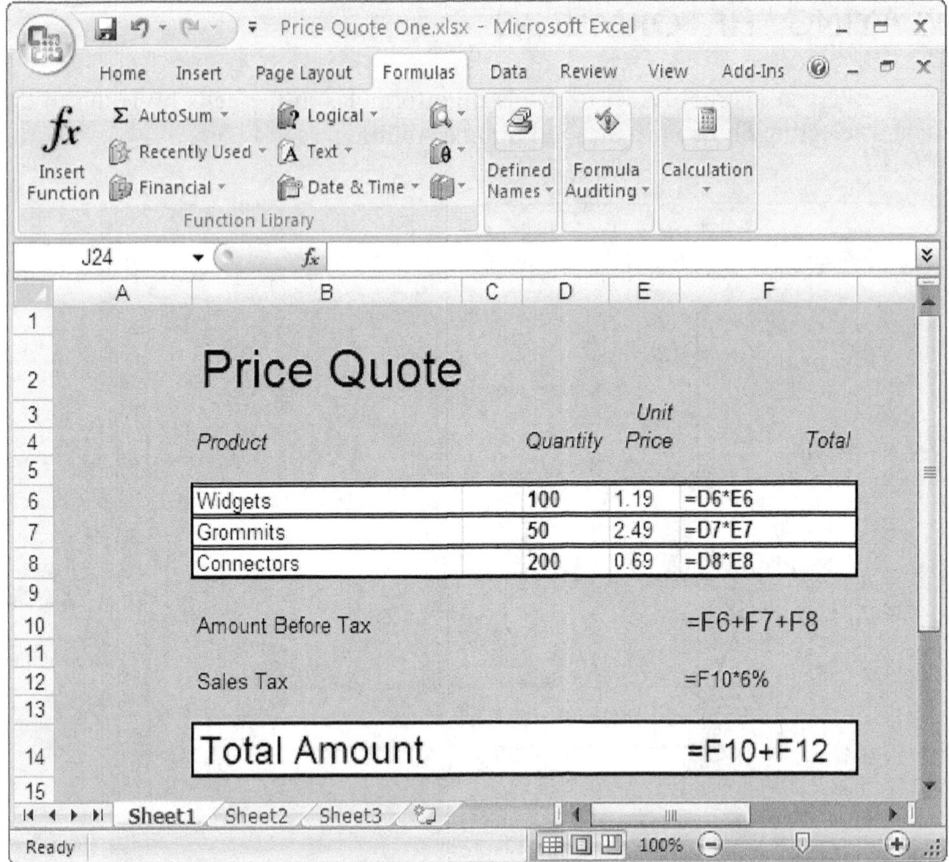

Figure 3-15. The result of Show Formulas and then adjusting the column widths.

FINDING A LOOK FOR YOUR WORKSHEETS

"Beauty lies in the eyes of the beholder." Excel provides many tools for changing the way worksheets appear. Sometimes people just leave the worksheets in the dry, standard style. Sometimes people go wild with an astonishing variety of fonts and colors and borders. The best approach is somewhere in between. You want to highlight the important information in your worksheet. You want the worksheet to be as easy to use and understand as possible. Some companies standardize the appearance of their worksheets. Some people develop their own unique look to their worksheets.

Developing a standard look to your workbooks can be helped along by the **Themes** feature of Excel and other Office 2007 programs. A Theme can be selected in the Themes group of the Page Layout tab. The current Theme affects the standard font and color palette and other features of the appearance of your worksheets.

MINIMIZING THE RIBBON

To the right of the Quick Access toolbar on the top of the screen is the Customize Quick Access Toolbar button, a very long name for a tiny button. Clicking on this button shows the menu in Figure 3-16. The menu allows you to decide which icons you would like to include in the Quick Access toolbar. The final entry in the menu allows you to Minimize the Ribbon, resulting in the Excel window shown in Figure 3-17

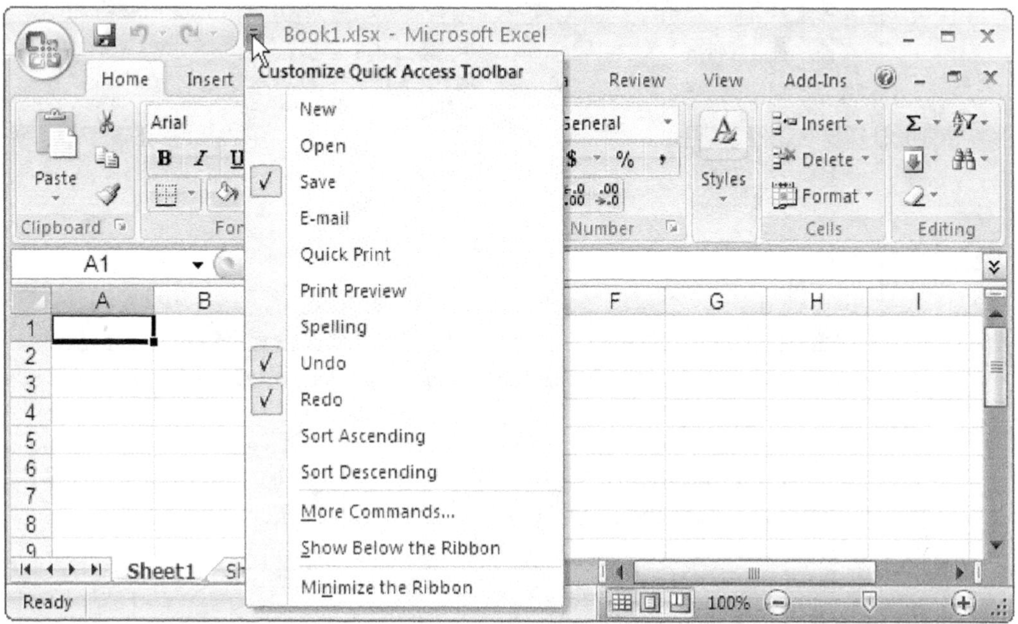

Figure 3-16. The Customize Quick Access Toolbar menu. See the final entry in the menu.

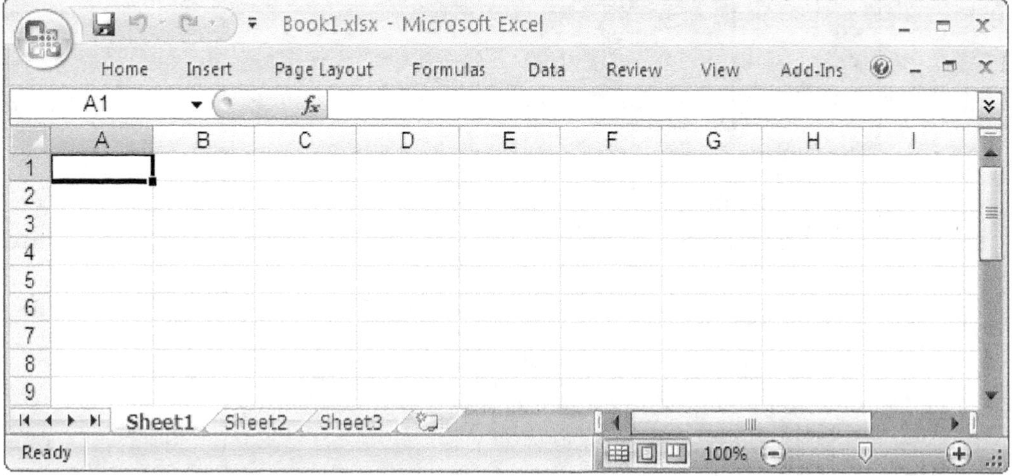

Figure 3-17. Minimizing the Ribbon saves screen space.

The various tabs (Home, Insert, Page Layout, et al.) still appear in Figure 3-17. But the Ribbon isn't taking up space in the window as you work. Future screenshots in this book will have the Ribbon minimized if it isn't relevant.

If the Ribbon is minimized and you click on one of the tabs the Ribbon will appear as a drop down, covering some of the top rows, as in Figure 3-18.

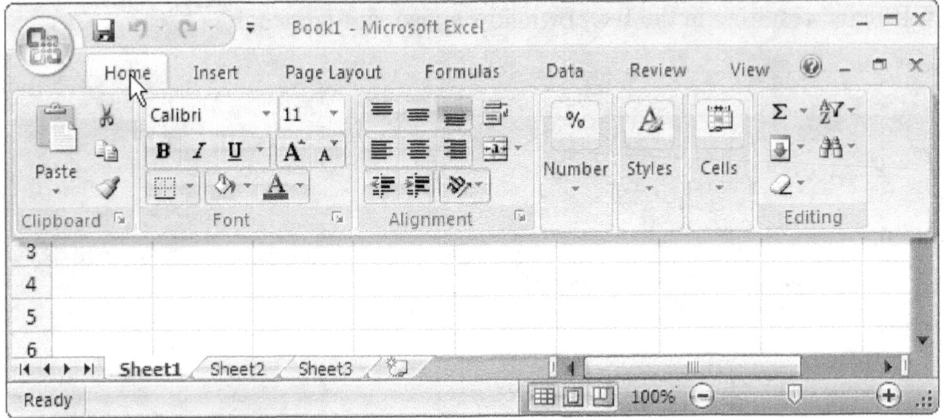

Figure 3-18. If the Ribbon is minimized and you click on a tab the Ribbon drops down.

Also, selecting an area of the worksheet by dragging across it and then right-clicking provides direct access to the operations discussed in this chapter and many more.

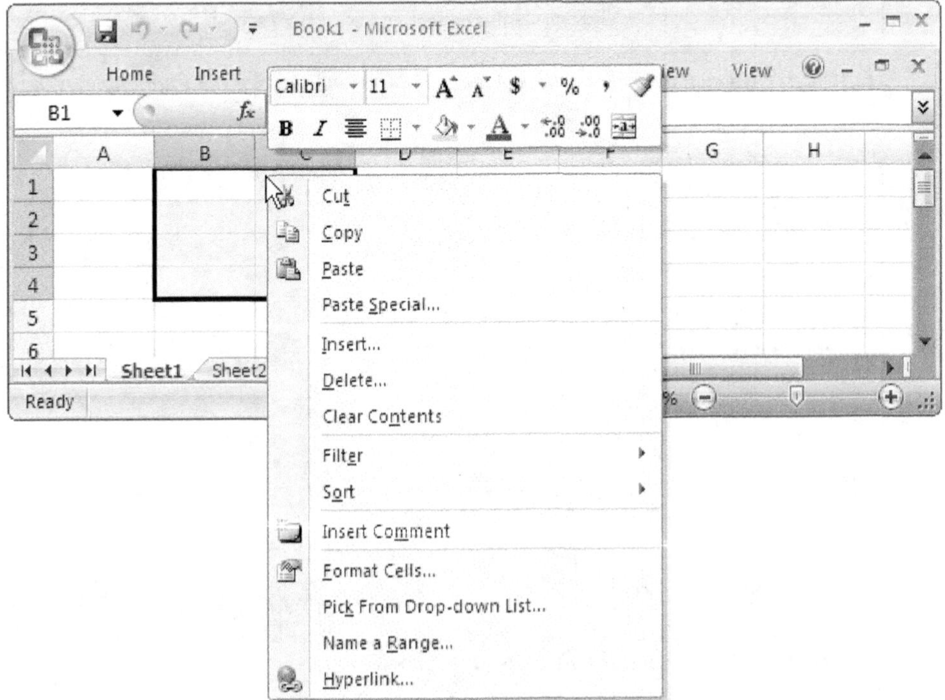

Figure 3-19. Select an area and then right-click to access many relevant operations.

COMPUTER EXERCISES

3-1. Enter the following worksheet, which converts a temperature from Centigrade to Fahrenheit. Widen column B so all of the text shows. Make column A narrow.

CELL	CONTENTS
B1:	*Your Name*
B2:	Exercise 3-1.
B5:	Worksheet to convert temperatures
B7:	Hello
B8:	Please enter the temperature in Centigrade:
C8:	10
B10:	Equivalent temperature in Fahrenheit:
C10:	=(1.8*C8)+32

Cell C10 should show 50, the Fahrenheit equivalent of 10 degrees Centigrade.

(a) Change the format of cell C10 so it shows one decimal place to the right of the decimal point (for example, 50.0). Save the workbook as YourNameExer3_1a (for example, as LeeExer3_1a if your name is Lee).

(b) Color the text in C8 in blue as it is an input cell.

(c) Move to C8. Enter the number 17. The number in C10 should change.

(d) Click on cell B7. Press the Delete (or Del) key. The word Hello should be erased.

(e) Save the workbook on your disk. Save the workbook as YourNameExer3_1e.

(f) Display the formulas in the worksheet rather than the values. Change the column widths appropriately. Save the worksheet as YourNameExer3_1f. Close the workbook and open up YourNameExer3_1e so the result of evaluating the formulas is displayed again in the cells.

(g) Format the worksheet to make it as attractive as possible. Change the fonts and sizes. Draw borders. Color in the cells. Save the workbook as YourNameExer3_1g.

(h) Now take the original worksheet and format it with a completely different look. Perhaps you might use three-dimensional shading if you didn't in the previous part. Save the workbook as YourNameExer3_1h.

3-2. Take a worksheet from the exercises at the end of Chapter 2.

(a) Format the worksheet to make it attractive and easy to understand.

(b) Format the worksheet in a second style.

(c) Which do you prefer? Why?

3-3. Here is a strange one.

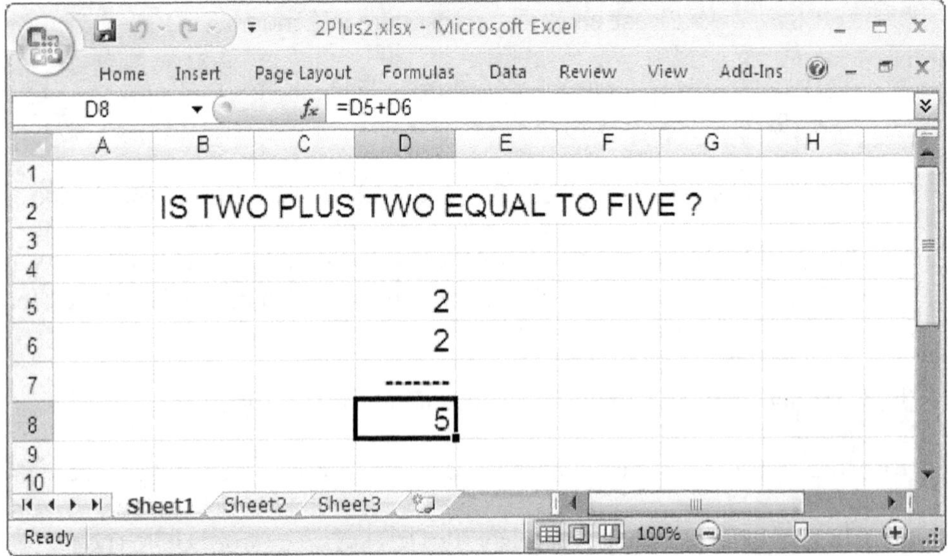

Cell D8 really does contain the formula =D5+D6. Explain exactly how this is possible since 2 + 2 is not equal to 5.

CHAPTER 4

SIMPLE FUNCTIONS AND THE FILL OPERATION

OBJECTIVES

In this chapter you will learn how to:

- Use the SUM, AVERAGE, COUNT, MAX, and MIN functions
- Enter ranges for arguments of functions
- Point to cells in formulas
- Identify and avoid the error of circular reference
- Enter SUM functions automatically with the AutoSum tool
- Use the Function Wizard
- Fill formulas down columns or across rows
- Use Goal Seek to work backwards
- Enter series of numbers using AutoFill

In the first three chapters we have seen how to create, use, and format simple worksheets. The basic idea is that each worksheet is organized as a two-dimensional grid made up of rows and columns. The intersection of each row and column is called a cell. Initially all the cells are blank. We can fill each of the cells with text, numbers, or formulas. The key to Excel is in the formulas. Whenever any cell is changed, all of the relevant formulas are recalculated.

In this chapter we begin to explore how to construct larger, more realistic worksheets. There are two important tools for doing this: built-in functions and the Fill operation. In many ways this is the key chapter of the book. Once you understand how to use built-in functions and the Fill operation you are well on your way to knowing Excel.

BUILT-IN FUNCTIONS SAVE YOU TYPING

Figure 4-1 is a worksheet that shows the monthly sales by group for the first half of the year. The total sales for Africa is in cell H6. What would be the formula in this cell? Clearly, it could be

=B6+C6+D6+E6+F6+G6

Suppose we would like to analyze sales for 60 months. Our formula would have 60 terms. Or, suppose we had 400 regions and would like to find the total sales for January. The formula would have 400 cell addresses and 399 plus signs. We need an easier and shorter way of specifying formulas like this.

Sales by Region.xlsx - Microsoft Excel

Home Insert Page Layout Formulas Data Review View Add-Ins

H6

	A	B	C	D	E	F	G	H
1								
2			SALES SUMMARY BY REGION					
3								
4		JAN	FEB	MAR	APR	MAY	JUN	TOTAL
5								
6	AFRICA	4.6	3.4	4.2	5.4	3.9	4.9	
7	ANTARCTICA	1.1	0.8	0.7	1.3	0.9	1.3	
8	ASIA	43.2	46.4	45.4	47.6	47.1	46.3	
9	EUROPE	32.5	33.7	34.1	33.8	33.5	35.2	
10	LATIN AMERICA	14.7	13.6	13.4	17.5	15.2	18.9	
11	NORTH AMERICA	39.5	41.3	40.8	42.4	38.7	43.5	
12								
13	TOTAL							
14								

Sheet1 Sheet2 Sheet3

Ready 100%

Figure 4-1. A worksheet showing the monthly sales by region.

The best way to add up a list of numbers is to use **SUM**, which is a **built-in function**. The formula in H6 could be

=SUM(B6:G6)

This formula tells Excel that the number that should appear in H6 is the result of adding all the numbers from B6 through G6. Similarly, the formula in cell B13 could be

=SUM(B6:B11)

If we had 400 regions, we could add up all of the sales for January with the formula

=SUM(B6:B405)

Typing this formula clearly is easier than typing out 400 cell addresses and all the plus signs.

Built-in functions can save lots of typing. They help make large worksheets easy to construct.

THE VARIETY OF FUNCTIONS

There are hundreds of built-in functions in Excel. We will discuss five of the more common functions here. Other functions will be discussed in Chapters 11 through 15 and elsewhere in the book.

The most frequently used function by far is SUM. Other common functions include:

AVERAGE	Calculates the average or arithmetic mean of a list of values
COUNT	Counts how many numbers are in a list
MAX	Finds the largest value in a list
MIN	Finds the smallest value in a list

Thus, for the worksheet in Figure 4-1, =AVERAGE(B6:G6) would find the average monthly sales for Africa. The result of evaluating the formula would be 4.4. The formula =MAX(B6:G6) would find the highest monthly sales for Africa, namely 5.4. The formula =COUNT(B6:G6) would count the number of sales figures for Africa, namely 6.

The AVERAGE function is simply the SUM function divided by the COUNT function. The formula =AVERAGE(B6:G6) is exactly the same as the formula =SUM(B6:G6)/COUNT(B6:G6). This is important for understanding how missing values are treated in the AVERAGE function. If the number in F6, the May sales for Africa, was missing and the cell was blank, the average would be computed by adding the remaining numbers and dividing by 5, rather than 6. If one of the cells in the range of an AVERAGE function contains words or letters, it will be ignored (treated as if it is blank) because it does not contain a number. Similarly, any cells in the range of an argument of the SUM function (or MAX or MIN) that are blank or contain words or letters are ignored in the calculations.

Built-in functions not only save typing. They also provide a wide variety of calculations. Some of these calculations are impossible to specify using the normal arithmetic operators. For example, there is no formula using the normal arithmetic operators (+ - * / % ^) for calculating the largest number in a list. SUM saves typing. MAX provides a completely new capability.

ARGUMENTS AND RANGES

The inputs to a function are placed inside the parentheses and are called **arguments**. Multiple arguments in a function are separated by commas. For example, the formula =SUM(C6,3,4*B2) instructs Excel to add up the number in cell C6, the number 3, and the result of multiplying 4 times the number in B2. The SUM function here has three arguments: C6, 3, and 4*B2. The functions SUM, AVERAGE, COUNT, MAX, and MIN can have up to 30 arguments.

The most useful type of argument for these functions is a **range**. The argument in =SUM(B6:G6) is B6:G6, which is a range.

Ranges are very important in Excel. A range normally specifies a rectangular portion of a worksheet. The range B6:G6 consists of a cell address followed by a colon followed by another cell address. The first cell address gives one corner of the range. The second address indicates the diagonally opposite corner of the range. Usually, the first address is the top left corner of the range; the second address is the bottom right corner of the range.

The range B6:G6 is a one cell by six cell horizontal rectangle. The range B6:B11 is a six by one vertical rectangle. The range B6:G11 would contain 36 cells in a rectangle, six cells across from column B through G and six cells down from row 6 through row 11.

What should be the formula in cell H13 in the worksheet in Figure 4-1? This is the grand total of the sales for the six months. There are three choices. The formula could be

=SUM(H6:H11)

This formula would calculate the grand total by adding up the product totals. The formula in H13 could be

=SUM(B13:G13)

This formula would calculate the grand total by adding up the monthly totals. The third possibility is for the formula in H13 to be

=SUM(B6:G11)

This formula would calculate the grand total by adding up the original 36 monthly sales numbers. All three formulas would give the same answer.

How many numbers would be added up in the formula

=SUM(23,C12,B4:B7,47,C2:E5)

There are five arguments:

1. the number 23 -- 1 number
2. the cell C12 -- 1 number
3. the range B4:B7 -- 4 numbers
4. the number 47 -- 1 number
5. the range C2:E5 -- 12 numbers

Thus this formula instructs the computer to add 19 numbers.

Be careful with the commas and the colons. The formula =SUM(B6,G11) instructs the computer to add up 2 numbers, the values in B6 and G11. The formula =SUM(B6:G11) instructs the computer to add up 36 numbers, the values in the rectangular range of cells from B6 through G11.

In Chapter 8 we will see how to specify a three-dimensional range of cells through several worksheets.

POINTING

A convenient way to specify cell addresses in a range is to **point** to them instead of typing them. The idea of pointing is to use the mouse to point to the address that you would like to include in a formula. Pointing is especially useful when specifying a range, because when you point to a range Excel highlights the range on the screen.

To illustrate, consider the worksheet in Figure 4-2. We are in the process of entering the formula for cell H6.

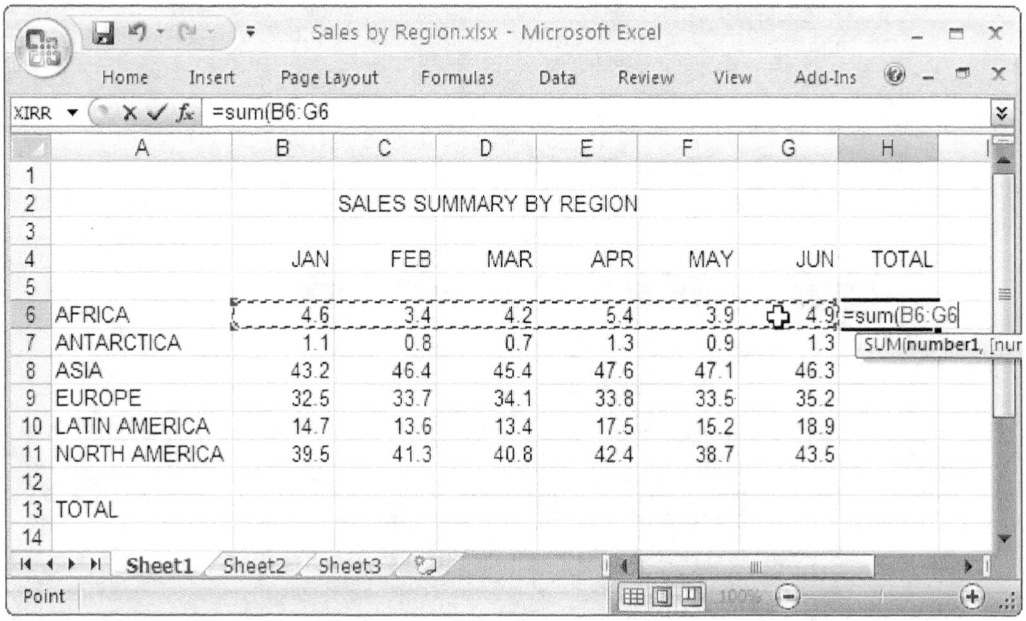

Sales by Region.xlsx - Microsoft Excel

XIRR =sum(B6:G6

	A	B	C	D	E	F	G	H
1								
2			SALES SUMMARY BY REGION					
3								
4		JAN	FEB	MAR	APR	MAY	JUN	TOTAL
5								
6	AFRICA	4.6	3.4	4.2	5.4	3.9	4.9	=sum(B6:G6
7	ANTARCTICA	1.1	0.8	0.7	1.3	0.9	1.3	SUM(number1, [nur
8	ASIA	43.2	46.4	45.4	47.6	47.1	46.3	
9	EUROPE	32.5	33.7	34.1	33.8	33.5	35.2	
10	LATIN AMERICA	14.7	13.6	13.4	17.5	15.2	18.9	
11	NORTH AMERICA	39.5	41.3	40.8	42.4	38.7	43.5	
12								
13	TOTAL							
14								

Sheet1 Sheet2 Sheet3

Point

Figure 4-2. Entering a range of addresses by dragging across the range with the mouse.

We have typed =SUM(and now are entering the range. Instead of typing the addresses of the range we simply drag across the desired range with the mouse (with the button pressed down). Excel automatically fills in the range pointed to in the formula and you can see that as an added aid to the user Excel has placed dashed lines around the range selected. It also lists the arguments of the SUM function in a yellow box below the cell in which we are typing the formula. To complete the formula we type the closing) and press the Enter key.

Pointing is not restricted to ranges. If you want to enter the formula =3*B2+C4, you can type =3*, then point and click on B2, type the +, point and click on C4, and then type the Enter key.

A COMMON ERROR: CIRCULAR REFERENCE

A common error made when entering a formula is to include the address of the cell in the formula itself. An example is shown in Figure 4-3. The formula in H6 should be =SUM(B6:G6). By mistake in H6 we have entered the formula =SUM(B6:H6). This typically occurs when we are pointing to the range and mistakenly extend the range over H6. The formula =SUM(B6:H6) instructs the computer that the value to be shown in H6 is the sum of the numbers from B6 through H6. That is, the computer needs to know the value in H6 in order to calculate the value in H6.

A formula that depends on its own value has a **circular reference**. As you can see, Excel warns you when it encounters a circular reference. There are a few cases where you want a circular reference, but normally it is a mistake that needs to be corrected.

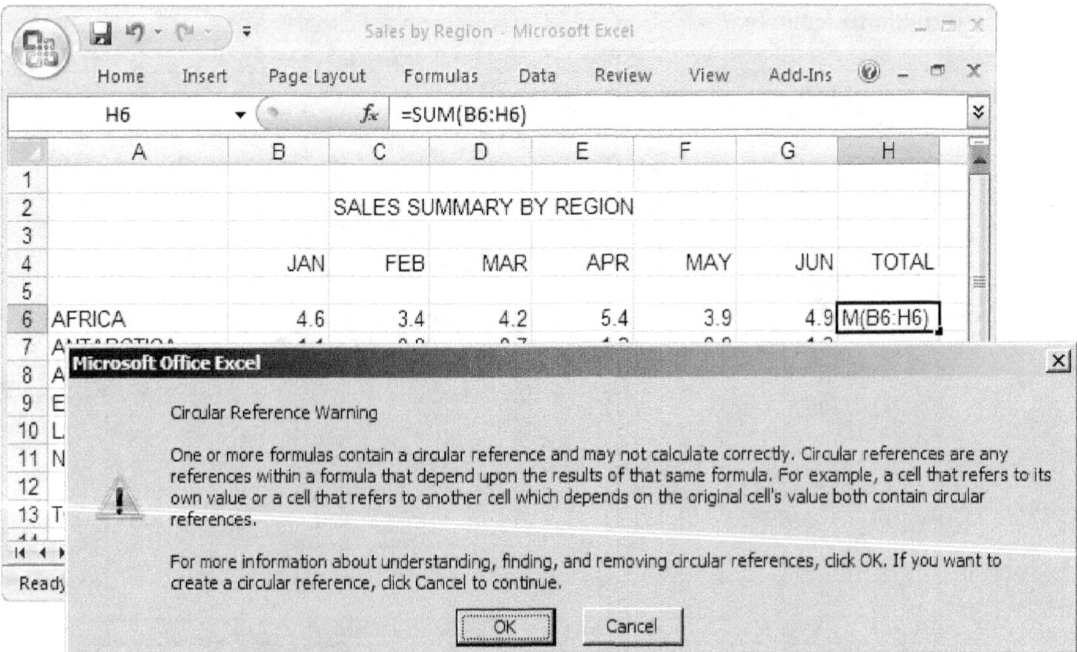

Figure 4-3. A mistake has been made. A circular reference occurs because the cell H6 contains a formula that refers to itself.

OVERUSE OF THE SUM FUNCTION

Sometimes people become so enamored with the SUM function that they use it in every formula. If we want a formula that adds C4 and D6, we can simply use the formula =C4+D6. We could use =SUM(C4,D6) but it is a bit of overkill. Similarly, if we want to multiply the number in F5 by 3, we would write =F5*3. The formula =SUM(F5*3) would work, but the use of the SUM function here is wholly superfluous.

THE AUTOSUM BUTTON

Σ The SUM function legitimately is used so often that Excel provides a special button, the **AutoSum button**, for automatically entering the SUM function.

Simply select the cell in which you want a SUM function (as in Figure 4-1) and then click directly on the AutoSum button in the Editing group of the Home tab. Excel will look at the worksheet and guess what row or column of numbers you want to add up. In the situation in Figure 4-1 if you select H6 and then click on the AutoSum button, Excel will guess that you want the formula =SUM(B6:G6) and this formula automatically will be entered in H6 for your approval.

Σ ▾ If you click on the downward-pointing triangle on the right of the button you will be able to select AVERAGE or COUNT or other functions as a shortcut, as in Figure 4-4.

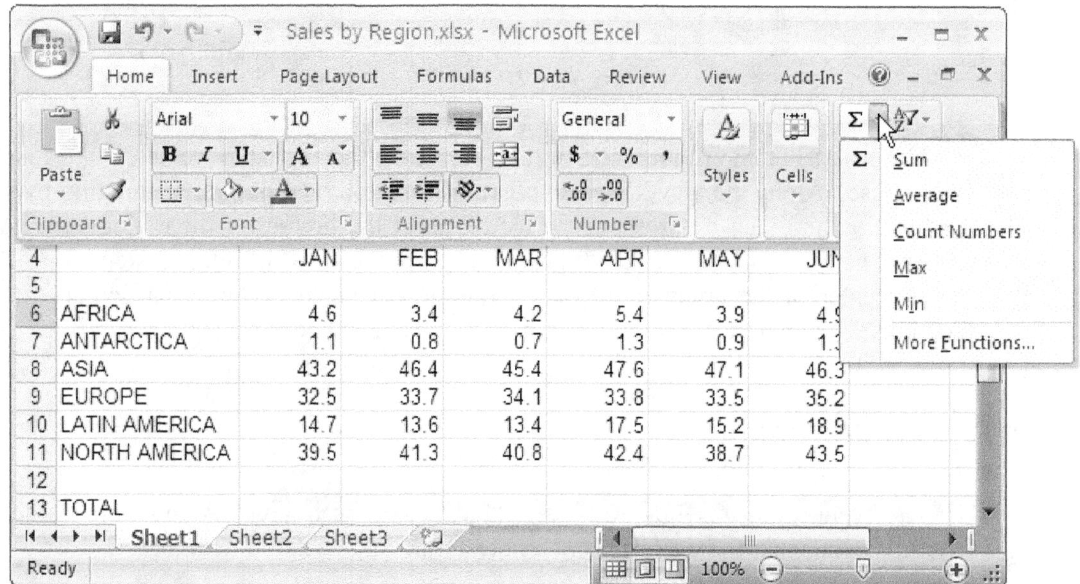

Figure 4-4. Press on the triangle to the right of the AutoSum button for a shortcut to other functions.

THE INSERT FUNCTION TOOL

The **Insert Function** tool helps you enter functions into formulas and find out about their arguments. Selecting H6 and clicking on the Insert Function button, just to the left of the Formula bar, yields the dialog box shown in Figure 4-5.

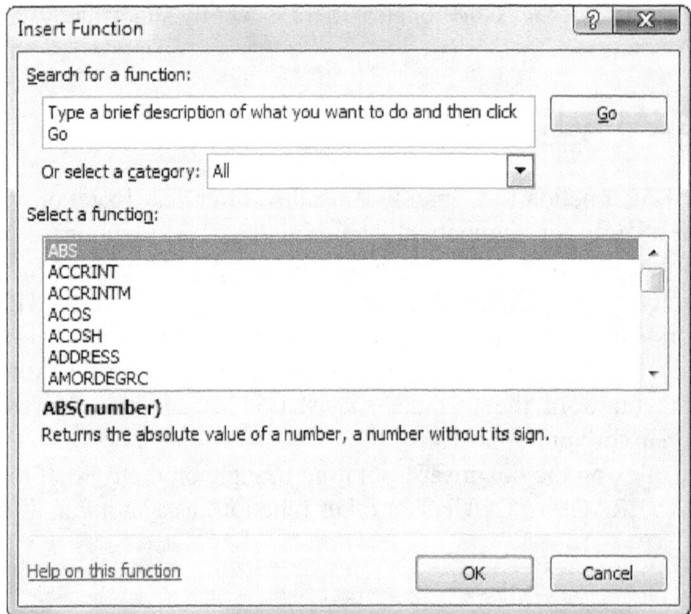

Figure 4-5. Using the Insert Function tool.

The Insert Function tool works in two steps. In the first step we select the function we wish to use. Along the way it's easy to get information on a particular function by selecting the function and then by pressing the Help link at the bottom of the dialog box. After the proper function has been selected, press OK to proceed to the second step. In the second step we enter in the argument(s) of the function selected. This is particularly useful for functions with complicated arguments, as we will see in later chapters.

NESTED FUNCTIONS

The arguments of a function can include other functions. A function inside another function results in a **nested function**. An example of a nested function is

=MAX(SUM(C7:C10),SUM(D7:D10),SUM(E7:E10))

Here the MAX function has three arguments. Each of the arguments is a SUM function. The computer would add up C7 through C10. Then it would add up D7 through D10. Then it would add up E7 through E10. The value calculated by the whole formula would be the largest of these three totals. This is the number that would appear in the cell.

THE FILL OPERATION

Built-in functions with ranges provide an important tool for constructing large worksheets. They allow us to enter a formula that adds up 400 numbers by entering SUM and two addresses. The **Fill operation** allows us to make multiple copies of the formula so we do not have to type it over and over again into a column of cells or row of cells.

Return to our example of tabulating the monthly sales by region. In the worksheet in Figure 4-6 the final formula =SUM(B6:G6) in cell H6 is shown.

Sales by Region.xlsx - Microsoft Excel

Home Insert Page Layout Formulas Data Review View Add-Ins

H6 =SUM(B6:G6)

	A	B	C	D	E	F	G	H
1								
2			SALES SUMMARY BY REGION					
3								
4		JAN	FEB	MAR	APR	MAY	JUN	TOTAL
5								
6	AFRICA	4.6	3.4	4.2	5.4	3.9	4.9	26.4
7	ANTARCTICA	1.1	0.8	0.7	1.3	0.9	1.3	
8	ASIA	43.2	46.4	45.4	47.6	47.1	46.3	
9	EUROPE	32.5	33.7	34.1	33.8	33.5	35.2	
10	LATIN AMERICA	14.7	13.6	13.4	17.5	15.2	18.9	
11	NORTH AMERICA	39.5	41.3	40.8	42.4	38.7	43.5	
12								
13	TOTAL							
14								

Sheet1 Sheet2 Sheet3

Ready 100%

Figure 4-6. We are ready to fill the formula in H6 down the column.

We now would like to enter the formulas to total each of the other regions. The formulas for these cells would be as follows:

H7:	=SUM(B7:G7)
H8:	=SUM(B8:G8)
H9:	=SUM(B9:G9)
H10:	=SUM(B10:G10)
H11:	=SUM(B11:G11)

We could type each of these formulas, although it would be tedious. But suppose we had 400 regions? We would have to type the =SUM formula 400 times. A better solution than typing all of the formulas is to type the first formula and then use the Fill operation.

Once we have entered the formula in cell H6, we can use the Fill operation to tell Excel to fill the formula down the column into the other cells. But notice that we do not want Excel to fill an exact copy of the formula in cell H6 into the other cells. If it did fill an exact copy, then each of the cells from H7 through H11 would contain the formula =SUM(B6:G6) and the number that appeared in each of the cells would be the total for Africa. Rather, Excel has an "intelligent" Fill operation. As Excel fills the formula down the column it automatically adjusts the row numbers in the formula. So =SUM(B6:G6) in H6 becomes =SUM(B7:G7) in cell H7 and =SUM(B8:G8) in cell H8, and so on for each formula that is filled into the cells.

USING THE FILL HANDLE

The simplest way to fill a formula down a column or across a row is to use the **Fill Handle.** The Fill Handle is the small square at the bottom right of the active cell.

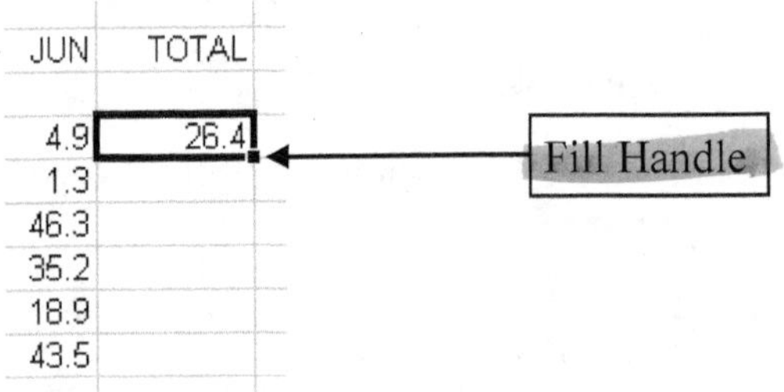

JUN	TOTAL
4.9	26.4
1.3	
46.3	
35.2	
18.9	
43.5	

Fill Handle

If we move the mouse pointer right on top of the Fill Handle, the mouse pointer becomes a thin cross.

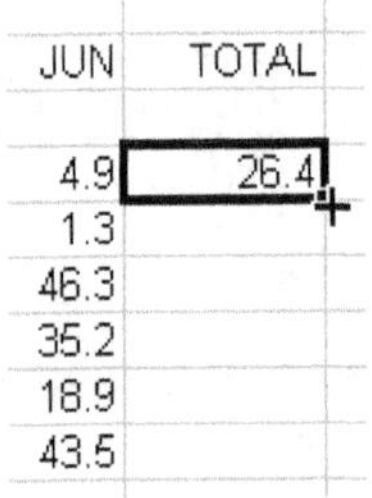

JUN	TOTAL
4.9	26.4
1.3	
46.3	
35.2	
18.9	
43.5	

We press down on the left mouse button and drag down over the cells we would like to fill.

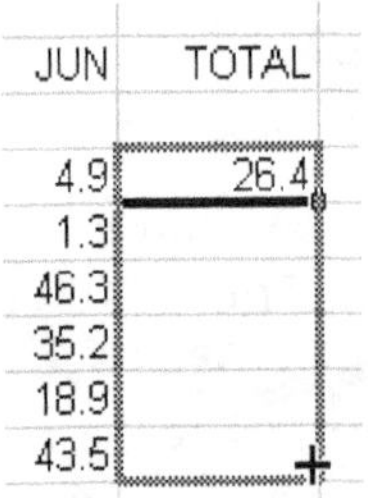

JUN	TOTAL
4.9	26.4
1.3	
46.3	
35.2	
18.9	
43.5	

We lift our finger off the mouse button and the formulas are filled down automatically.

JUN	TOTAL
4.9	26.4
1.3	6.1
46.3	276
35.2	202.8
18.9	93.3
43.5	246.2

We click somewhere else and we are finished. Sure enough, the formula =SUM(B6:G6) was changed as it was filled down the column. (See Figure 4-7.)

Sales by Region.xlsx - Microsoft Excel

Home Insert Page Layout Formulas Data Review View Add-Ins

H8 =SUM(B8:G8)

	A	B	C	D	E	F	G	H
1								
2			SALES SUMMARY BY REGION					
3								
4		JAN	FEB	MAR	APR	MAY	JUN	TOTAL
5								
6	AFRICA	4.6	3.4	4.2	5.4	3.9	4.9	26.4
7	ANTARCTICA	1.1	0.8	0.7	1.3	0.9	1.3	6.1
8	ASIA	43.2	46.4	45.4	47.6	47.1	46.3	276
9	EUROPE	32.5	33.7	34.1	33.8	33.5	35.2	202.8
10	LATIN AMERICA	14.7	13.6	13.4	17.5	15.2	18.9	93.3
11	NORTH AMERICA	39.5	41.3	40.8	42.4	38.7	43.5	246.2
12								
13	TOTAL							
14								

Sheet1 Sheet2 Sheet3

Ready 100%

Figure 4-7. When the formula in H6 is filled down, the addresses in the formula are adjusted automatically.

Now we would like to enter the row of monthly totals in row 13. First we enter =SUM(B6:B11) into cell B13. To fill the formula across the row, we move the mouse pointer on top of the Fill Handle in the bottom right corner of cell B13 until the mouse pointer becomes a thin cross. We press the left mouse button and drag the Fill Handle to the right all the way over to H13. We lift our finger off the mouse button and click somewhere else. We are finished. Row 13 now contains appropriate formulas for calculating the column totals. (See Figure 4-8.)

Sales by Region - Microsoft Excel

E13 =SUM(E6:E11)

	A	B	C	D	E	F	G	H
1								
2			SALES SUMMARY BY REGION					
3								
4		JAN	FEB	MAR	APR	MAY	JUN	TOTAL
5								
6	AFRICA	4.6	3.4	4.2	5.4	3.9	4.9	26.4
7	ANTARCTICA	1.1	0.8	0.7	1.3	0.9	1.3	6.1
8	ASIA	43.2	46.4	45.4	47.6	47.1	46.3	276
9	EUROPE	32.5	33.7	34.1	33.8	33.5	35.2	202.8
10	LATIN AMERICA	14.7	13.6	13.4	17.5	15.2	18.9	93.3
11	NORTH AMERICA	39.5	41.3	40.8	42.4	38.7	43.5	246.2
12								
13	TOTAL	135.6	139.2	138.6	148	139.3	150.1	850.8

Figure 4-8. The formula in B13 has been filled across the row.

FILLING BY DOUBLE-CLICKING

There is an even faster way to fill these formulas down or across. In Figure 4-9, simply point to the Fill Handle in H6 and double-click the left mouse button. The formulas automatically are filled down. This trick works only if the cells to the immediate left or directly above are not empty.

Sales by Region - Microsoft Excel

H6 =SUM(B6:G6)

	A	B	C	D	E	F	G	H
1								
2			SALES SUMMARY BY REGION					
3								
4		JAN	FEB	MAR	APR	MAY	JUN	TOTAL
5								
6	AFRICA	4.6	3.4	4.2	5.4	3.9	4.9	26.4
7	ANTARCTICA	1.1	0.8	0.7	1.3	0.9	1.3	
8	ASIA	43.2	46.4	45.4	47.6	47.1	46.3	
9	EUROPE	32.5	33.7	34.1	33.8	33.5	35.2	
10	LATIN AMERICA	14.7	13.6	13.4	17.5	15.2	18.9	
11	NORTH AMERICA	39.5	41.3	40.8	42.4	38.7	43.5	
12								
13	TOTAL							

Figure 4-9. A shortcut to filling down the formula is to double-click on the Fill Handle.

GOAL SEEK

Goal Seek basically allows us to work backward in a worksheet. Suppose in our Computers course the final grade is determined 40% by homeworks and computer exercises, 15% by each of two exams, and 30% by the final exam. Our scores so far are shown in Figure 4-10.

	A	B	C	D	E
1					
2		Computers Course Grades			
3					
4					*Weighted*
5			*Score*	*Weight*	*Score*
6		Homeworks	95	40%	38.0
7		Exam 1	80	15%	12.0
8		Exam 2	78	15%	11.7
9		Final Exam		30%	0.0
10					
11		Course Grade			61.7

Figure 4-10. Our scores before taking the Final Exam.

We have only the Final Exam to go. Cell C9, which will contain the Final Exam score is blank now, so it counts as 0 in the calculations. We would like to know what score we need to get on the Final Exam to have a final Course Grade of 90.

We could solve this problem by trial and error. That is, we could enter an initial value of, say, 90 as our score for the Final Exam. If the resulting Course Grade was below 90, we could try 100 for the Final Exam. If the resulting Course Grade was above 90, we could try 95 for the Final Exam, and so on. We could continue making closer and closer estimates of the score we need on the Final Exam for our Course Grade to be 90.

Excel automates this trial-and-error process for us. From the worksheet in Figure 4-10 we click on the Data tab. In the Data Tools group we click on the bottom right button, which if the Excel window were wider would say What-If Analysis. In the What-If Analysis pull-down menu, we select Goal Seek, as in Figure 4-11.

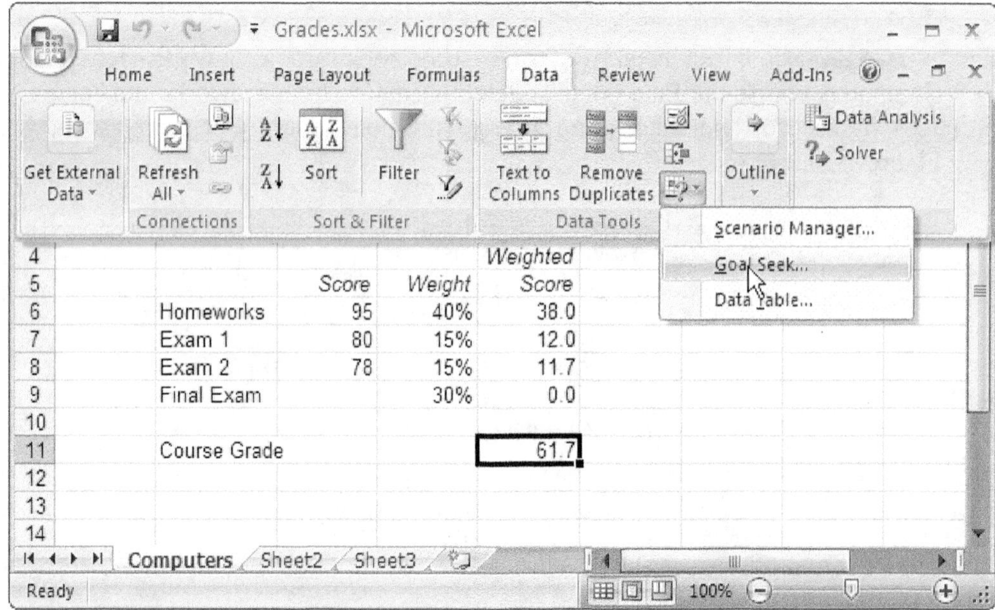

Figure 4-11. Selecting Goal Seek in the What-If Analysis menu of the Data Tools group of the Data tab.

We fill in the Goal Seek dialog box as in Figure 4-12.

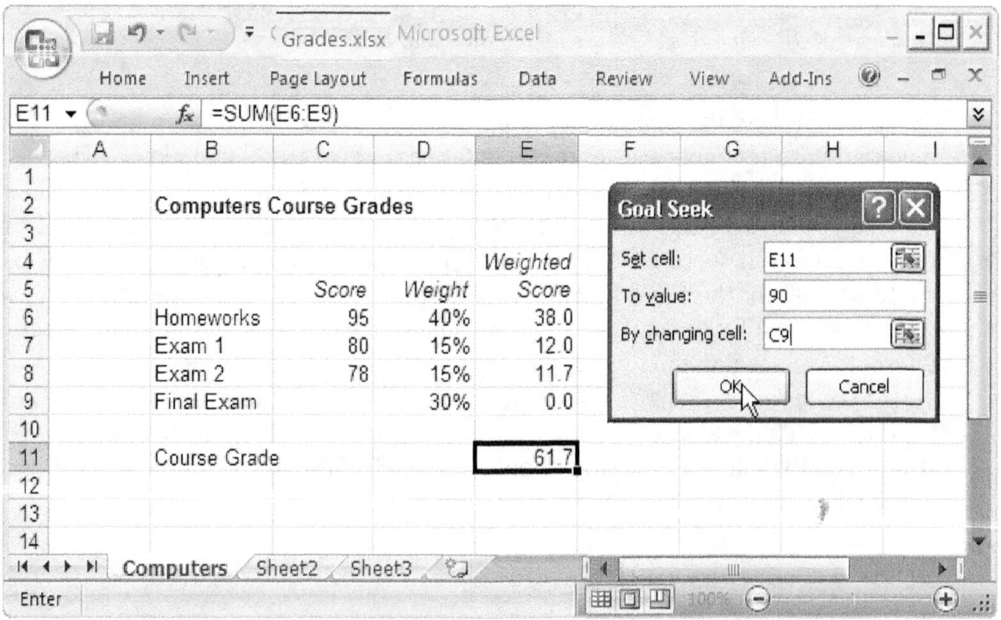

Figure 4-12. We wish to set cell E11 to 90 by adjusting C9.

We tell Excel we would like cell E11 set to 90 by changing cell C9. We can either type in the cell addresses, as here, or point and click on the cells. (If we point and click, Excel displays the addresses with dollar signs, for example E11 is displayed as $E$11. The two mean the same here; the meaning of the dollar signs will be discussed in Chapter 6.) When we click on OK, Excel goes through several iterations of trial and error and then displays the results of its efforts, as shown in Figure 4-13.

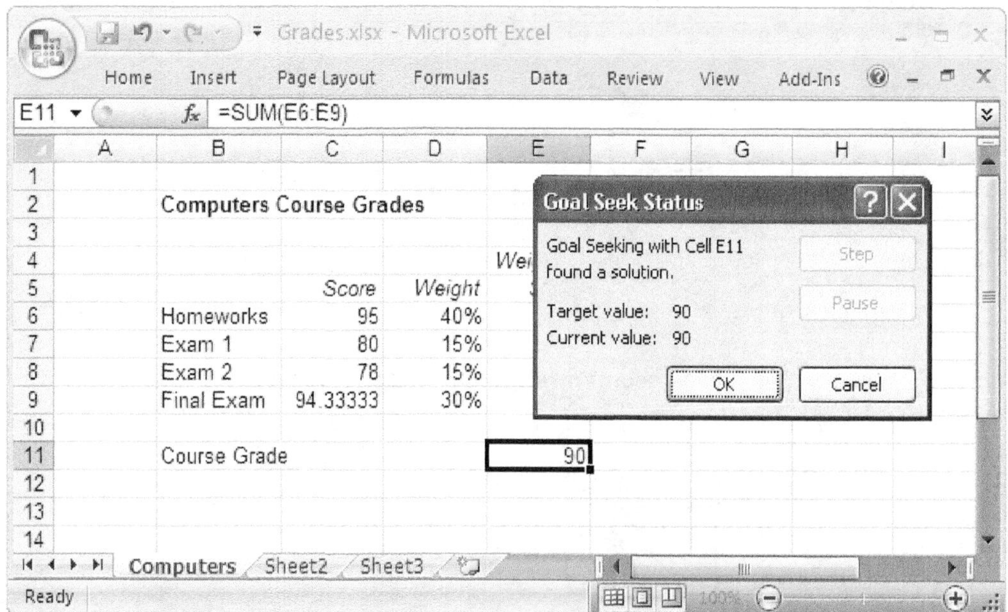

Figure 4-13. The result of Goal Seek. We need a 94.33333 on the Final Exam.

Excel has found a solution. If we receive a score of 94.33333 on the Final Exam, then our Course Grade will be 90. No problem.

AUTO FILL

An interesting feature of Fill allows us to automatically create a series of values. For example, we might want to create a worksheet that has the weeks from 1 through 6 in a column. We could enter a 1 and 2 in successive cells. Then we select the cells by dragging down them.

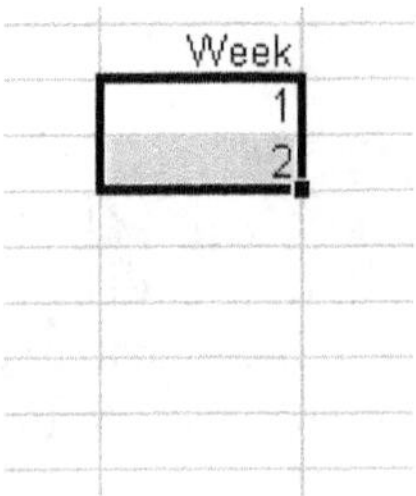

We grab the Fill Handle in the bottom right corner of the selection and drag down four cells.

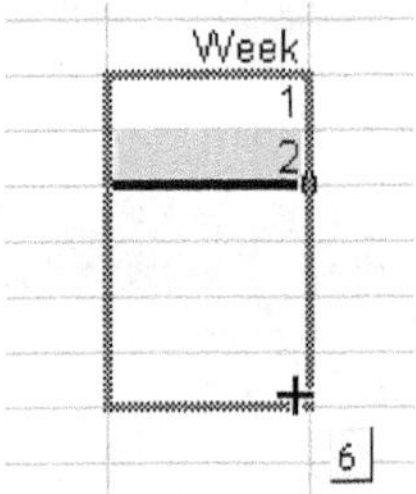

When we let up on the mouse button, Excel automatically fills in the values from 3 through 6.

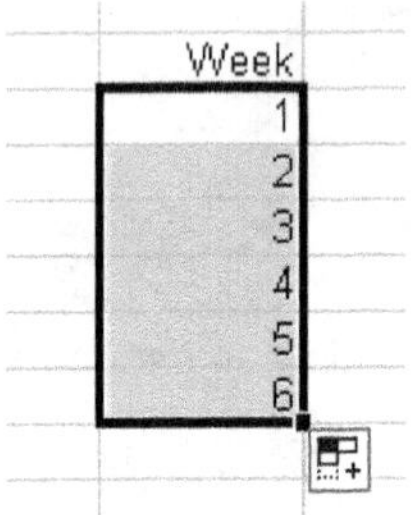

The annoying box at the bottom is the Auto Fill pop-up menu. If you click on it you will have various options. If you ignore it and click somewhere else, eventually the box goes away and the Auto Fill process is complete.

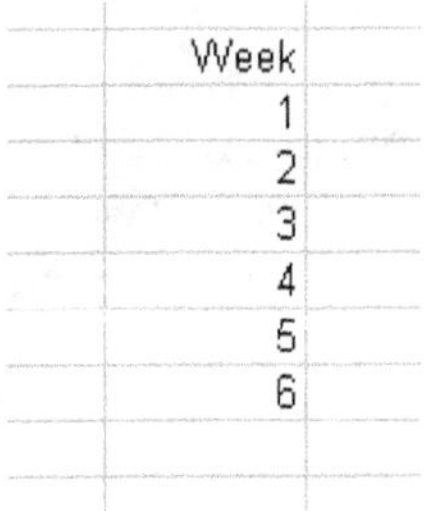

The Auto Fill technique is remarkably flexible. If we had entered 2 and 5 instead of 1 and 2, Excel would have filled in the rest of the series as 8, 11, 14, 17. If we had entered Jan, Feb, Excel would have filled in the month names Mar, Apr, May, Jun. If we had entered in Q1, Q2, Excel would have filled in Q3, Q4, Q1, Q2, because it would interpret Q1 as Quarter 1. If we had entered A, B it would have filled in A, B, A, B. If you would like to enter your own custom series you can do so by clicking on the Excel Options button at the bottom of the Office menu and then clicking on Popular and Edit Custom Lists.

USING AUTO FILL TO FIT A STRAIGHT LINE

Remarkably, Auto Fill automatically will fit a straight line to a series of 3 or more values. For example, if we enter 3, 9, 6, 7 into successive cells, select those cells, and then drag the Fill Handle down four more cells, we will get the sequence 3, 9, 6, 7, 8.5, 9.4, 10.3, 11.2. Excel uses the values entered as the basis for its prediction of the new values.

SUMMARY

Two critical tools for creating larger worksheets are built-in functions and the Fill operation.

Excel provides built-in functions for many types of calculations. The inputs to a function are called arguments. The use of a range as the argument to a built-in function allows calculations to be performed on a large rectangular portion of the worksheet by specifying only the addresses of two of the diagonally opposite corners of the rectangle. For example, the formula =SUM(C101:AA1100) instructs the computer to add up the values of the 25,000 cells in a range 25 columns wide and 1,000 rows down. Ranges can be specified either by typing or by pointing.

The Fill operation allows a given formula to be filled down a column or across a row. For example, to find the sum of each of 1,000 rows of numbers we could enter the formula to sum the top row and then command the computer to fill the formula down through the remaining 999 rows. The Fill operation automatically adjusts the addresses in the new formulas created.

Goal Seek allows us to work backwards in a worksheet, to find the input we need to enter into a cell to obtain a desired output.

The Auto Fill feature allows us to easily create a series of values by entering just the first few values in the series, selecting those values, and then dragging the Fill Handle.

PAPER AND PENCIL EXERCISES

4-1. What is the value of each of the following formulas?

(a) =SUM(4,0,-2)

(b) =MAX(4,0,-2)

(c) =MIN(4,0,-2)

(d) =COUNT(4,0,-2)

(e) =AVERAGE(4,0,-2)

(f) =SUM(MAX(4,0,-2),5,MIN(4,0,-2),6)

(g) =COUNT(MAX(4,0,-2),5,MIN(4,0,-2),6)

(h) =AVERAGE(MAX(4,0,-2),5,MIN(4,0,-2),6)

(i) =AVERAGE(AVERAGE(1,2,3,4),AVERAGE(9,10))

4-2. Consider the following worksheet.

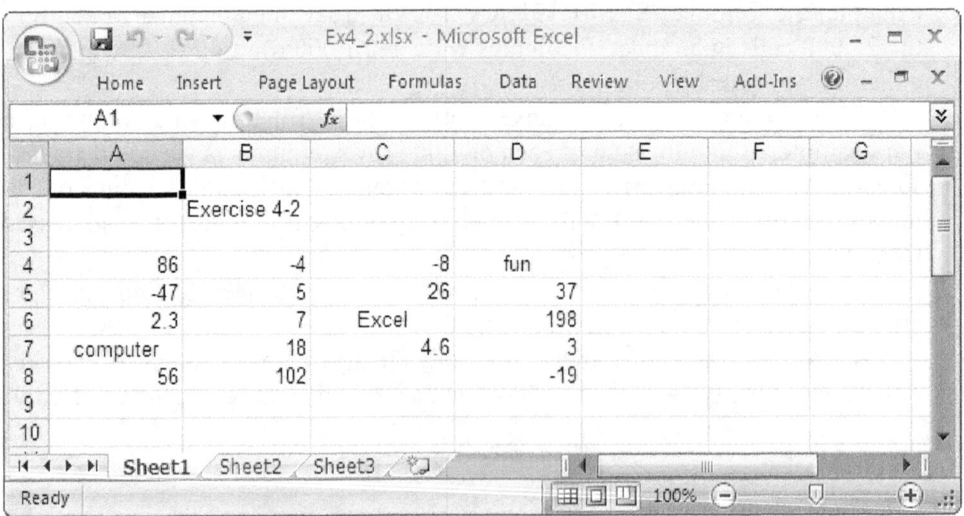

	A	B	C	D	E	F	G
1							
2		Exercise 4-2					
3							
4	86	-4	-8	fun			
5	-47	5	26	37			
6	2.3	7	Excel	198			
7	computer	18	4.6	3			
8	56	102		-19			
9							
10							

What would be the result of evaluating each of the following formulas? Write out your answer on paper. Please do not use the computer. The point of this exercise is to ensure that you understand what functions do.

(a) =SUM(A5:D5)

(b) =COUNT(A5:D5)

(c) =AVERAGE(A5:D5)

(d) =MAX(A5:D5)

(e) =MIN(A5:D5)

(f) =MIN(B7:C8)

(g) =AVERAGE(A3:A7)

(h) =COUNT(A3:A7)

(i) =SUM(AVERAGE(B4:B7),MAX(B4:B7),MIN(B4:B8))

(j) =SUM(3*B4,B4:C7,MAX(A5:C7),2*MIN(A4:B6))

(k) =AVERAGE(SUM(B4:B6),A8,MAX(B6:C8),MIN(B3:C5))

(l) =COUNT(SUM(B4:B6),A8,MAX(B6:C8),MIN(B3:C5))

COMPUTER EXERCISES

4-3. Enter the following worksheet, adding the appropriate formulas. Use the built-in functions and the Fill operation. Test the worksheet by changing some of the numbers and checking the bottom two rows and the right two columns. Format the worksheet appropriately. Save and print the worksheet.

Sales Analysis
Product Line by Season
(All Sales in $ Millions)

Product	Winter	Spring	Summer	Fall	Total	Max
Golf	3.2	6.2	5.7	3.9		
Tennis	4.7	5.2	7.1	2.9		
Skiing	3.7	2.1	1.1	5.2		
Surfing	1.2	2.1	2.9	1.3		
Total						
Average						

4-4. Set up a worksheet to help you track the amount of time you spend on computers this semester. Use the built-in functions and Fill. Enter appropriate values to test the worksheet. Save and print the worksheet.

Hours Spent on Computers

Week	Mon	Tue	Wed	Thu	Fri	Sat	Sun	Total
1								
2								
3								
...								
14								
15								
Total:								
Average:								
Max:								

Maximum number of hours spent in any one day during the semester:

4-5. The following table shows the price of gasoline in several countries in 1990, 1995, 2000, and 2005. These are average prices, including taxes, of a U.S. gallon of unleaded regular gas in U.S. dollars.

Gasoline Retail Prices in Selected Countries
(Average price of unleaded regular gas: U.S. dollars per gallon, including taxes)
Source: U.S. Department of Energy. http://www.eia.doe.gov/emeu/aer/txt/ptb1108.html

	1990	1995	2000	2005
Australia	$ 1.91	1.95	1.94	3.23
Canada	1.87	1.53	1.86	2.87
Germany	2.65	3.06	3.45	5.60
Japan	3.16	4.43	3.65	4.28
Mexico	1.00	1.25	2.01	2.22
South Korea	2.05	2.94	4.18	5.28
Taiwan	2.49	2.23	2.15	2.79
United States	1.16	1.15	1.51	2.30

(a) Add rows at the bottom for average price, maximum price, and minimum price. Use functions and the Fill operation.

(b) Use Auto Fill to show the predicted prices for 2010, 2015, 2020 for each country, assuming a linear trend. Fill the calculation rows out three columns to the right. Format all cells with two places to the right of the decimal point.

4-6. Create a worksheet to calculate the wages for hourly employees.

(a) Start off with a heading, the names of the employees, and the hours worked each day. Try using Auto Fill for the days of the weeks. Type in the numbers of hours worked each day. Use a variety of numbers.

Payroll

Week of

Name	Mon	Tue	Wed	Thu	Fri	Sat	Sun
Abel, Ann							
Jones, John							
Smith, Sam							
Wall, Joan							

(b) Add a column at the end to calculate total hours worked for each employee. Use the SUM function.

(c) Add a column with the hourly wage for each employee. Use a different wage for each employee. Be generous.

(d) Add a column to automatically calculate the gross wages earned for the week.

(e) Add a column for federal tax withholdings of 20%.

(f) Add a column for state tax withholdings of 5%.

(g) Add a column for medical deduction of $12 per week.

(h) Add a column for take-home pay (gross wages minus withholding and deductions).

(i) Add rows at the bottom for the total and the average of each of the columns.
Use the SUM and AVERAGE functions and Fill.

(j) Format appropriate cells with $ signs and to two decimal places to the right of the decimal point.

(k) Format the worksheet so it is as attractive and readable as possible.

4-7. Design and implement a worksheet to keep track of how much time you spend in each of your courses and favorite activities each day during a given week. You should have one row for each of your courses. You should have one column for each of the days of the week (Sun,

Mon, Tue, ...). Add rows for sleeping and eating. Add rows for two other activities that you enjoy and participate in regularly. At the top of the worksheet should be your name and the dates of the week for the numbers in the worksheet.

Enter numbers into your worksheet (you can make them up). Include the time you spend in class for the hours for your courses.

Add a row at the bottom of your worksheet for Total. Use the SUM function and the Fill operation.

Add three columns on the right of your worksheet for Total, Average, and Maximum. Use the built-in functions and the Fill operation.

There are 168 hours in the week. Add a column that gives the percent of the week spent on each course or activity.

Now change some of the numbers in the worksheet. All of the formulas should automatically be recalculated.

4-8. The following table gives hourly compensation costs for production workers in manufacturing in four countries in the Americas.

Hourly compensation costs in U.S. dollars for production workers in manufacturing.
Source: U.S. Bureau of Labor Statistics.
ftp://ftp.bls.gov/pub/special.requests/ForeignLabor/ichccsuppt02.txt

Country	2001	2002	2003	2004	2005
United States	20.52	21.33	22.20	22.82	23.65
Brazil	2.97	2.57	2.74	3.15	4.09
Canada	16.23	16.72	19.53	21.77	23.82
Mexico	2.34	2.49	2.44	2.44	2.63

(a) Add rows at the bottom for average, maximum, and minimum. Use functions and the Fill operation.

(b) Use Auto Fill to show the predicted wages for 2006, 2007, 2008, 2009, and 2010 for each country, assuming a linear trend. Fill the calculation rows out five columns to the right. Format all cells with two places to the right of the decimal point.

4-9. Please do exercise 2-21 on the Body Mass Index (BMI). Use Goal Seek to determine: (a) the weight that would result in a person who is 6 feet 4 inches having a BMI of 22, (b) the lowest healthy weight (BMI of 18.5) for a person who is 5 feet 8 inches, and (c) the highest healthy weight (BMI of 25) for a person who is 5 feet 8 inches.

CHAPTER 5

OPERATIONS ON CELLS

OBJECTIVES

In this chapter you will learn how to:

- Move cells in a worksheet
- Erase a range of cells
- Delete rows and columns
- Insert new rows and columns
- Sort rows of cells
- Attach a comment to a cell
- Use Copy and Paste to move information
- Use the keyboard instead of the mouse
- Copy and Paste from the web
- Get external data from the web
- Link to files and web pages

In this chapter we will discuss some of the more commonly used operations on cells in Excel.

MOVING CELLS

Excel provides an easy way to move a group of cells to another location in the worksheet. First select the range of the worksheet you would like to move by dragging across it with the left mouse button down. Release the button and move the mouse so the mouse pointer is pointing to the very top of the selection. The pointer should change to a white arrow on top of a black figure with arrows pointing in four directions, as in Figure 5-1.

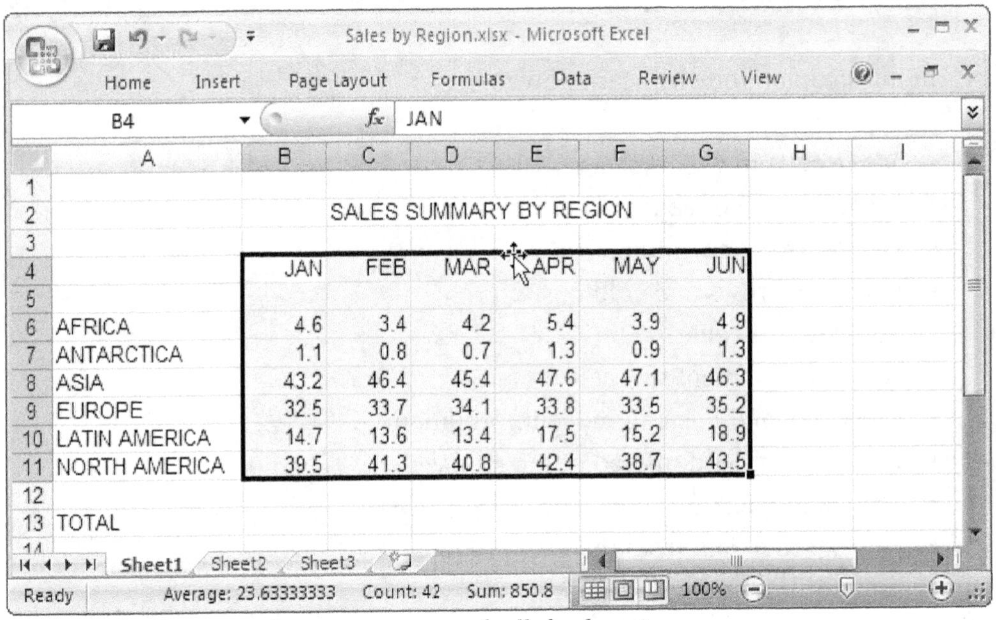

Figure 5-1. Getting ready to move a range of cells by dragging.

Now press the mouse button and drag the selected range to wherever you would like to place it. As you drag, you will see an outline of the range move along with the mouse pointer. Release the mouse button and the selected portion of the worksheet will move. This operation is a form of **drag and drop**. You can force scrolling by dragging the selected cells to the edge of the window.

After you move a range of cells within a complex worksheet, you should look to make sure that all the formulas still work correctly. Excel does its best to adjust all relevant formulas, both the formulas that are moved and the formulas in other cells that refer to the cells that are moved.

If you are unhappy with the results you can Undo the operation.

ERASING A RANGE OF CELLS

The easiest way to erase a range is to select the range by dragging across it and then with the mouse button up move the mouse pointer down to the bottom right hand corner of the range. The pointer will change into a thin cross. Depress the mouse button and drag the mouse back through the range to the top left corner of the range. The range will turn gray as you drag. When you release the mouse button, the contents of the cells will be erased.

Alternatively, you can select the range of cells to be erased by dragging across them and then pressing the Delete key.

Alternatively you can select the range of cells to be erased and then click on the Erase button in the Editing group of the Home tab.

It's best not to use the Cut operation in Excel.

DELETING ROWS AND COLUMNS

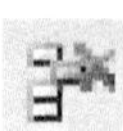

To delete a row, first select the row by clicking on the row number to the left of the worksheet. Now click on Delete in the Cells group of the Home tab, as in Figure 5-2. The entire row will be deleted. All cells below the row will slide up one row.

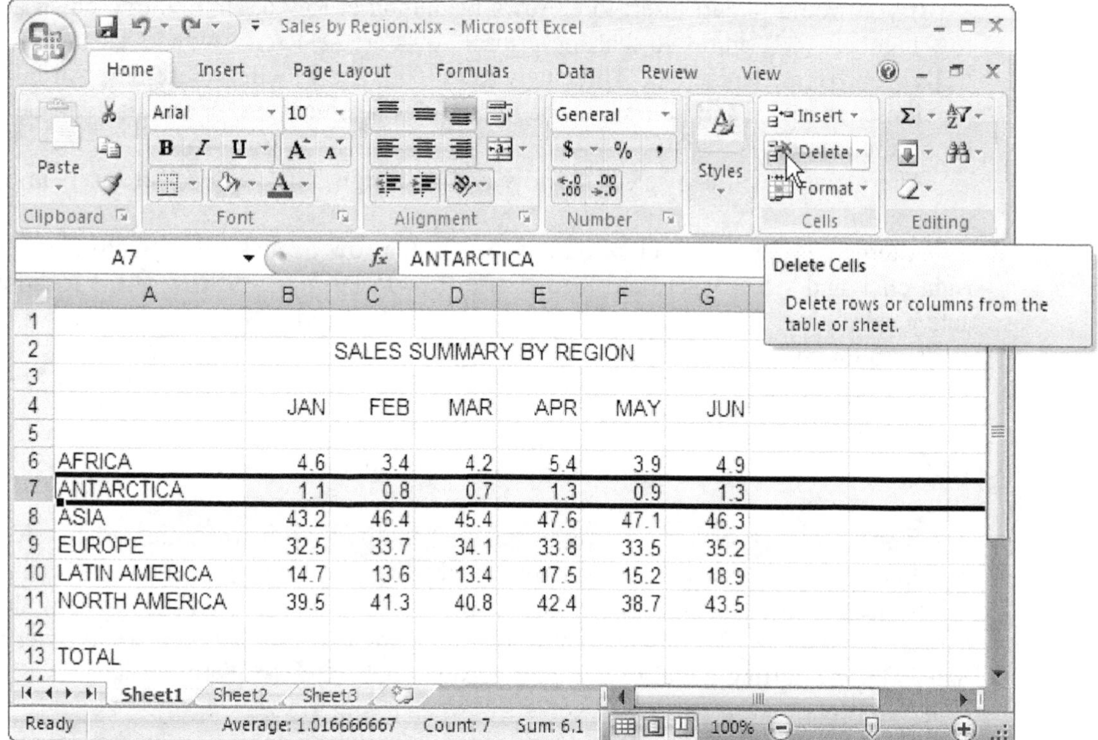

Figure 5-2. Click on the row number to select a row and then click on Delete to delete the row.

Excel adjusts references in formulas as best it can. If you have referred to one of the deleted cells in a formula, the formula might evaluate to #REF!, meaning there is an unresolvable reference in the formula.

To delete multiple rows at once, drag across the row numbers to select the multiple rows and then select Delete in the Cells group of the Home tab.

Alternatively you can select the row and then right click and select Delete in the menu that appears.

Alternatively, you can click on any cell in the row to make it the active cell and then right click and select Delete and then Entire Row to delete the row at the location of the active cell.

Columns are deleted in the same way.

INSERTING ROWS AND COLUMNS

To insert a new row in a worksheet, select the row where you want a new row inserted. For example, if you would like a new row 6 inserted, select the current row 6 by clicking on the row number 6 on the left of the worksheet. Now click on Insert in the Cells group of the Home tab. A new blank row 6 will be inserted. Everything from row 6 down will be moved down one row. References in formulas will be adjusted.

If you would like to insert three rows beginning at row 6, simply drag down across the row numbers 6, 7, and 8 so that these three rows are selected. Now click on Insert in the Cells group of the Home tab. Three new rows (6, 7, and 8) will be inserted. All information previously in row 6 and below will be moved down three rows. Formulas will be adjusted accordingly.

Alternatively you can select the row and then right click and select Insert in the menu that appears.

Alternatively, you can click on any cell in the row to make it the active cell and then right click and select Insert and then Entire Row to insert a new row at the location of the active cell.

Ditto for columns.

SORTING

When we **sort** objects we alphabetize them or put them in numerical order. For example, you might sort the cards in your hand when you are playing gin or Go Fish.

In the worksheet in Figure 5-3 the rows are sorted in alphabetical order by the region names in column A. We might want to rearrange the rows so that they are in order by Total Sales. Before sorting it's always a good idea to save a copy of the worksheet as it's easy to make a mistake and scramble the worksheet when trying to sort.

First we select the entire portion of the worksheet we want to sort by dragging across the cells. In Figure 5-4 we have selected A6:H11. We don't want to include the month names in row 4 or the totals in row 13 in the sort. Nor do we just want to include some of the columns and not the others.

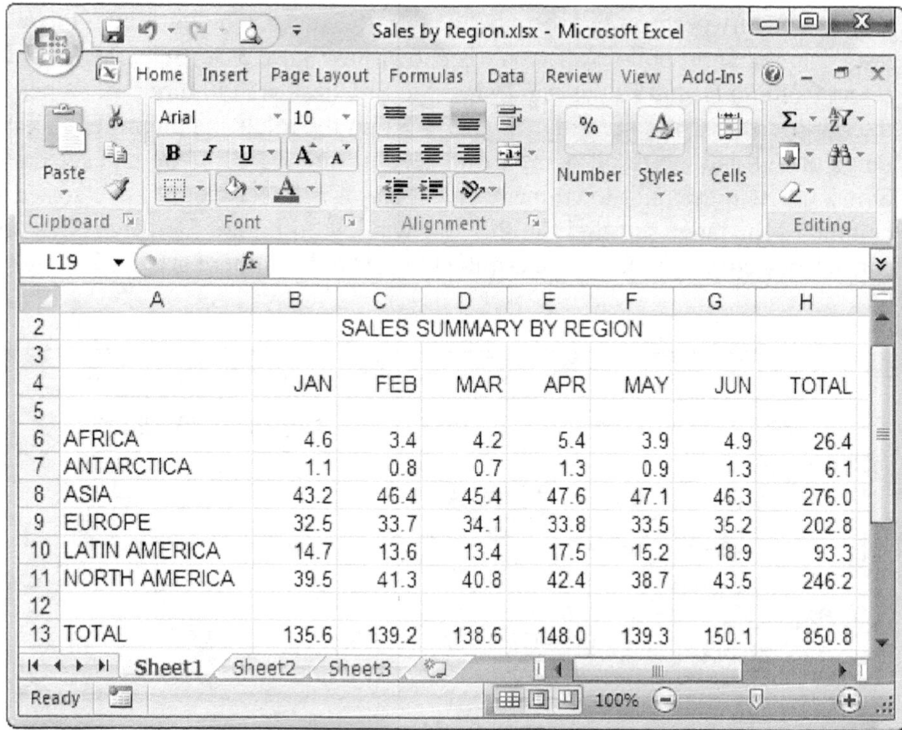

Figure 5-3. The rows are sorted by the region name in column A.

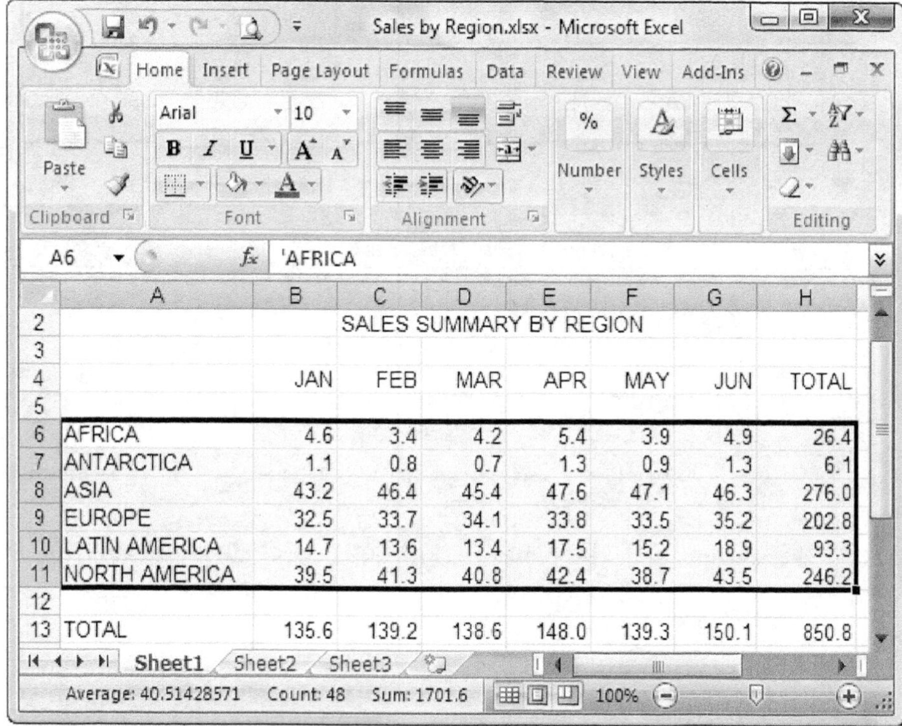

Figure 5-4. Selecting the exact portion of the worksheet to sort.

To actually perform the sort we click on the sort AZ button in the top right of the Home tab. The resulting pull-down menu is shown in Figure 5-5. Select Custom Sort... and then select Column H and Values and Largest to Smallest as in Figure 5-6. When we click on OK the range selected is sorted highest to lowest on the totals in column H. Click away from the range on A1 and the result is the worksheet in Figure 5-7. If we had selected Sort A to Z or Sort Z to A in the pull-down menu in Figure 5-5, Excel would have sorted on the leftmost column of the range selected. In the Sort window in Figure 5-6 if we click on Add Level we can select a column to use to determine the sort order if there are ties in column H.

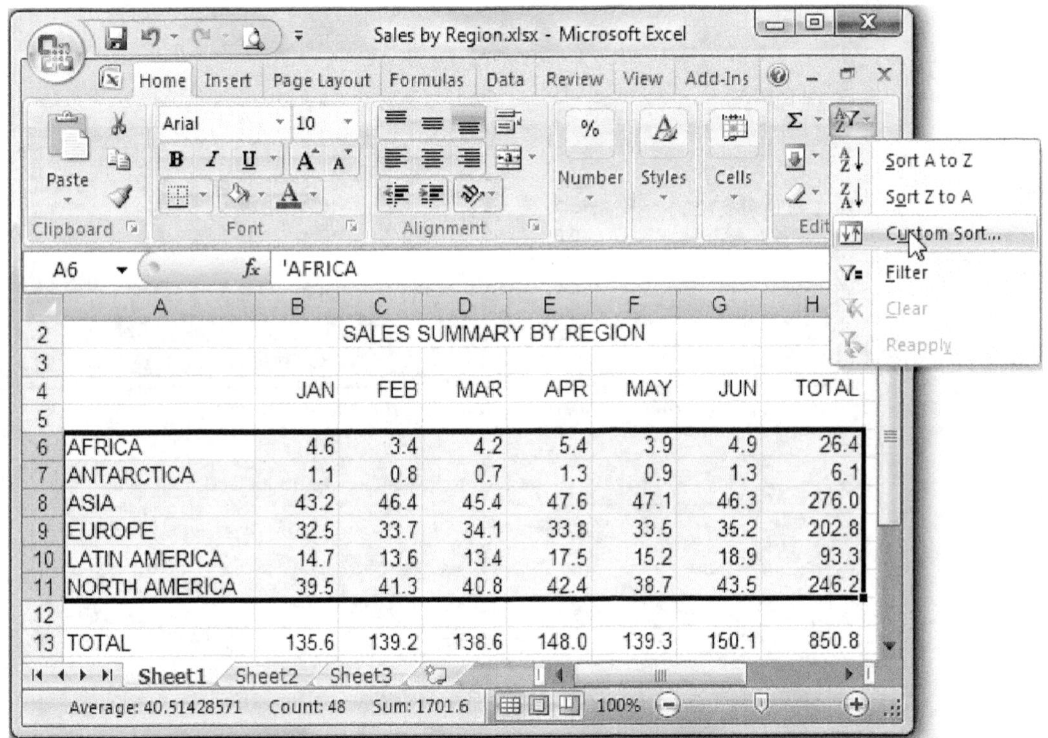

	A	B	C	D	E	F	G	H
2			SALES SUMMARY BY REGION					
3								
4		JAN	FEB	MAR	APR	MAY	JUN	TOTAL
5								
6	AFRICA	4.6	3.4	4.2	5.4	3.9	4.9	26.4
7	ANTARCTICA	1.1	0.8	0.7	1.3	0.9	1.3	6.1
8	ASIA	43.2	46.4	45.4	47.6	47.1	46.3	276.0
9	EUROPE	32.5	33.7	34.1	33.8	33.5	35.2	202.8
10	LATIN AMERICA	14.7	13.6	13.4	17.5	15.2	18.9	93.3
11	NORTH AMERICA	39.5	41.3	40.8	42.4	38.7	43.5	246.2
12								
13	TOTAL	135.6	139.2	138.6	148.0	139.3	150.1	850.8

Figure 5-5. Selecting Custom Sort.

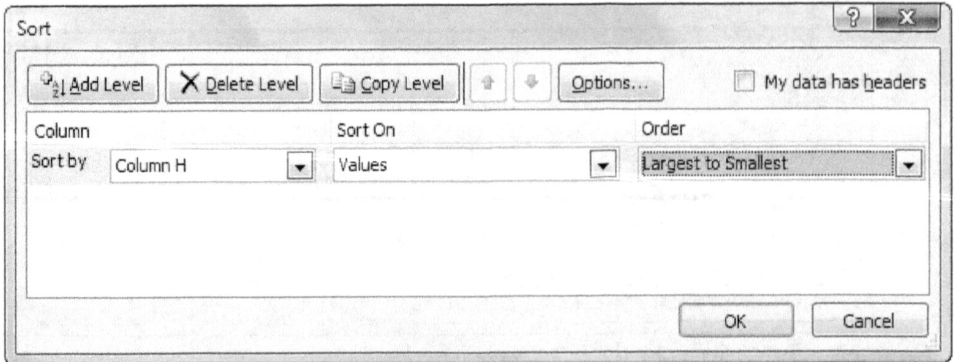

Figure 5-6. Sort on Column H from Largest to Smallest.

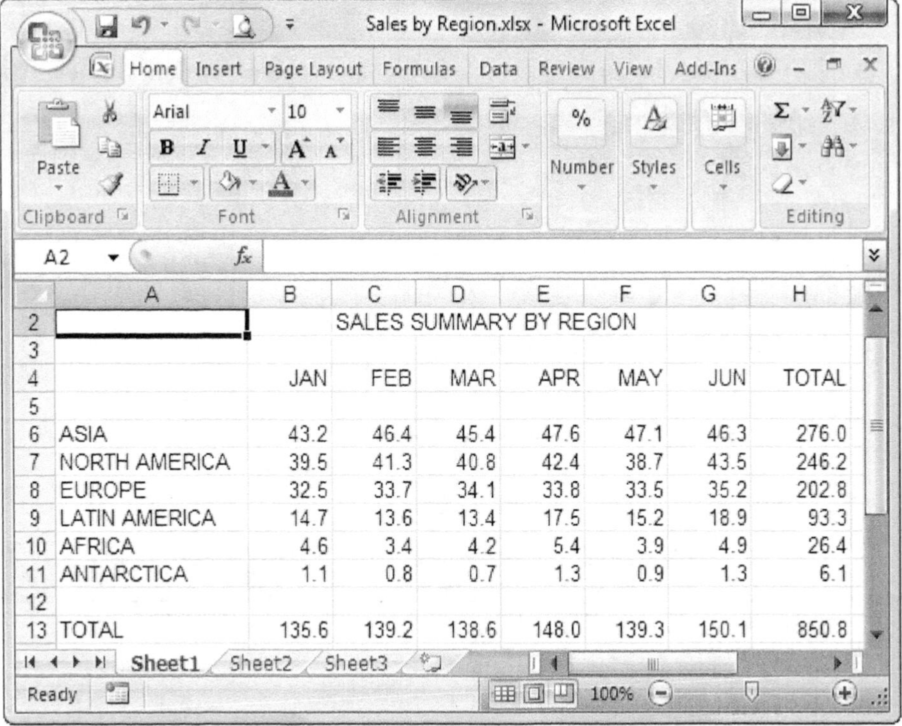

	A	B	C	D	E	F	G	H
2		SALES SUMMARY BY REGION						
3								
4		JAN	FEB	MAR	APR	MAY	JUN	TOTAL
5								
6	ASIA	43.2	46.4	45.4	47.6	47.1	46.3	276.0
7	NORTH AMERICA	39.5	41.3	40.8	42.4	38.7	43.5	246.2
8	EUROPE	32.5	33.7	34.1	33.8	33.5	35.2	202.8
9	LATIN AMERICA	14.7	13.6	13.4	17.5	15.2	18.9	93.3
10	AFRICA	4.6	3.4	4.2	5.4	3.9	4.9	26.4
11	ANTARCTICA	1.1	0.8	0.7	1.3	0.9	1.3	6.1
12								
13	TOTAL	135.6	139.2	138.6	148.0	139.3	150.1	850.8

Figure 5-7. The rows are in descending order by total sales.

ATTACHING A COMMENT TO A CELL

You can attach a **comment** to a cell. For example, if a formula in a cell is particularly complex, you can explain the formula in a comment. If you are making an important assumption about the inflation rate in a worksheet, you can add a comment to the cell with a statement about the assumption.

To attach a comment to a cell, click on the cell and then select New Comment in the Comments group of the Review tab. A yellow box appears with the name of the user. You can retype over the name and then add whatever comment you would like.

Cells that have comments attached are marked in the worksheet with a small red triangle in the top right corner of the cell. To see a comment just let the mouse pointer rest on the cell for a short period of time and the comment will appear, as shown in Figure 5-8.

Attaching comments is an excellent way to provide documentation for your workbook both for yourself and for other people who will be using it.

For people who work jointly on Excel workbooks comments provide an easy way to communicate with each other about the specific contents of various cells in the workbook. To see all of the comments in the workbook at once click on the Show all Comments button in the Comments group of the review tab.

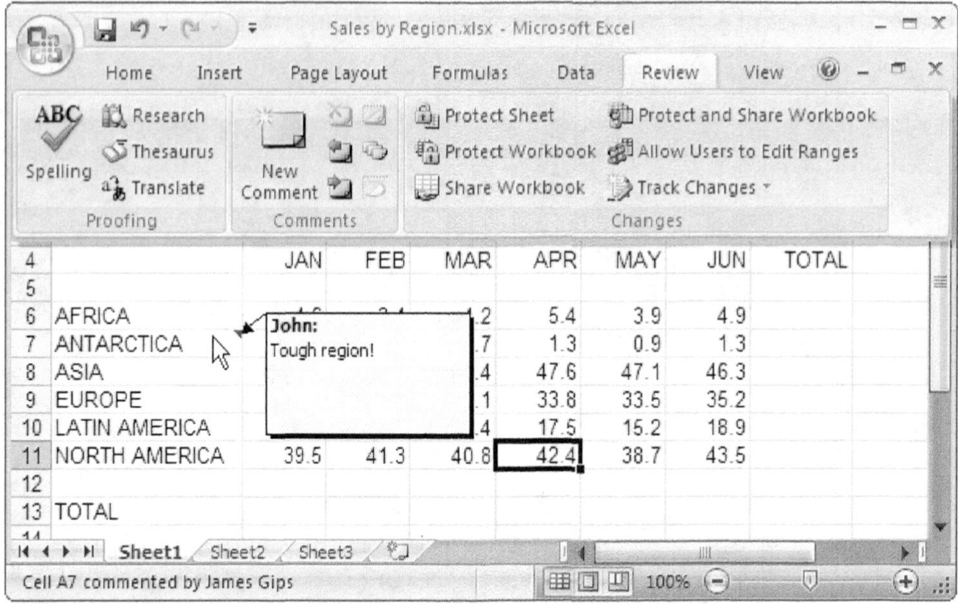

Figure 5-8. A comment in cell A7.

COPY AND PASTE

You may be familiar with the operations of Copy and Paste from other applications, such as word-processing. Copy and Paste is a common method for moving information from one place to another.

The basic idea is that there is a usually hidden part of the computer's memory called the **Clipboard**. The Clipboard holds recent information that was Copied (or Cut).

To Copy information into the Clipboard, first select the information by clicking on it or dragging across it and then click on the **Copy button** in the Clipboard group of the Home tab. Or, after selecting the cell or region to be copied, right click and select Copy from the menu that appears. The copied information is held temporarily in the Clipboard.

To Paste the information from the Clipboard into the worksheet, select the destination cell or range in the worksheet. Then click on the **Paste button** in the Clipboard group of the Home tab or right click and select Paste from the menu that appears.

Copy and Paste can be used to fill a formula down a column. In Figure 5-9, we click on cell H6 and then click on the Copy button to copy the contents of cell H6 into the Clipboard.

We select cells H7:H11 by dragging down them and clicking on the Paste button. The result is shown in Figure 5-10.

The formula from cell H6 has been copied and then pasted down column H. Note that this is an "intelligent" Copy and Paste, so the addresses in the formula have been adjusted. A moving dashed line appears around the most recent cell or range of cells copied into the clipboard.

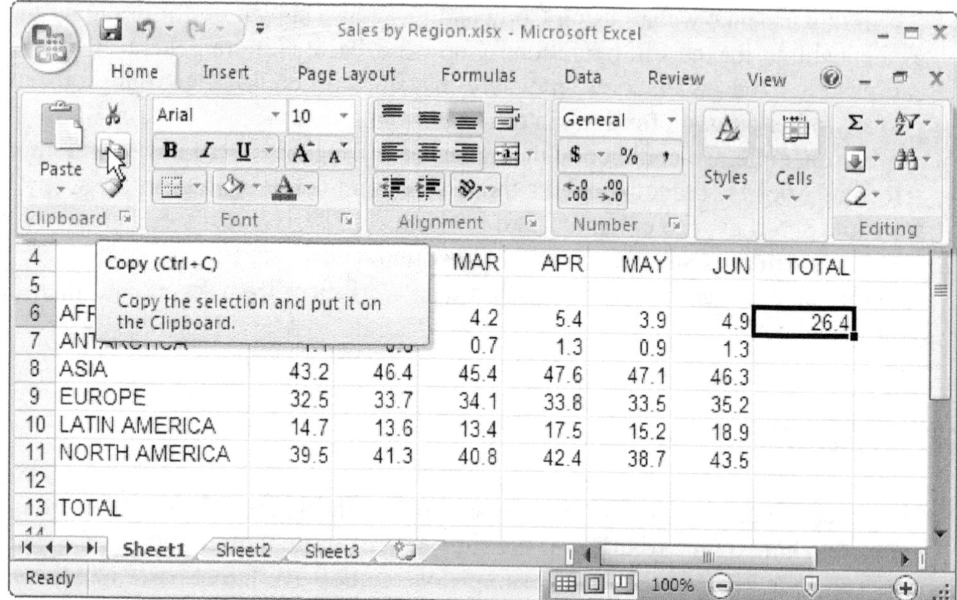

Figure 5-9. Click on cell H6 to select it. Then click on the Copy button to copy the formula in H6 into the Clipboard.

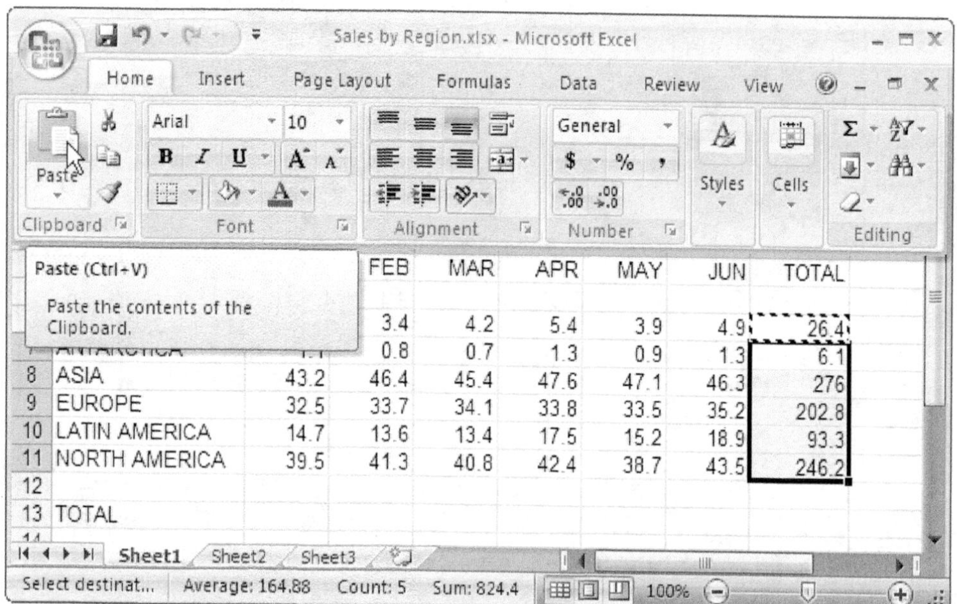

Figure 5-10. Drag down H7:H11 to select these cells. Click on the Paste button. The formula will be pasted from the Clipboard into the cells with the addresses adjusted.

In this instance we are using Copy and Paste as a substitute for dragging the Fill Handle, as a substitute for the Fill operation. Copy and Paste is more general than Fill because you can paste copied information anywhere in your workbook, or into any other workbook, or into any other program for that matter.

For example, we could copy the names of the regions in column A into the Clipboard by selecting A6:A11, dragging across those cells, and then clicking on the Copy button. Next we could scroll over to column T and click on cell T7. Now if we click on the Paste button, the names will be pasted from the Clipboard into cells T7:T12.

Similarly, we could copy a portion of a worksheet from Excel and then paste it into a Word document.

PASTE OPTIONS

When we use the normal Paste operation, as in Figure 5-5, formulas are pasted into the cells. Clicking on the triangle on the right side of Paste button gives us a menu with various options. (See Figure 5-11.) For example, we could have Excel paste just the values into the selected area and not the formulas.

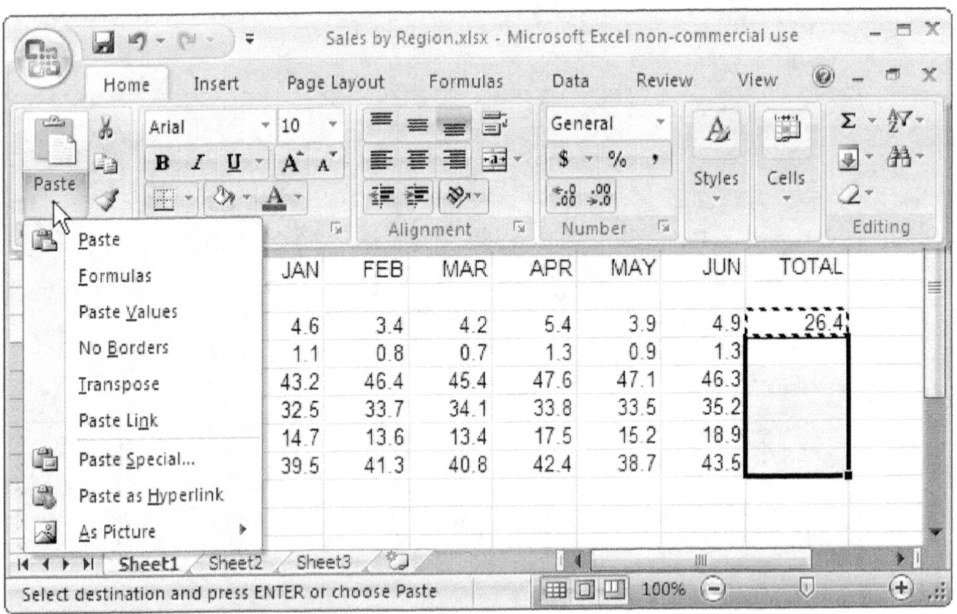

Figure 5-11. The Paste Options menu.

Selecting Paste Special… gives us even more options, as in Figure 5-12.

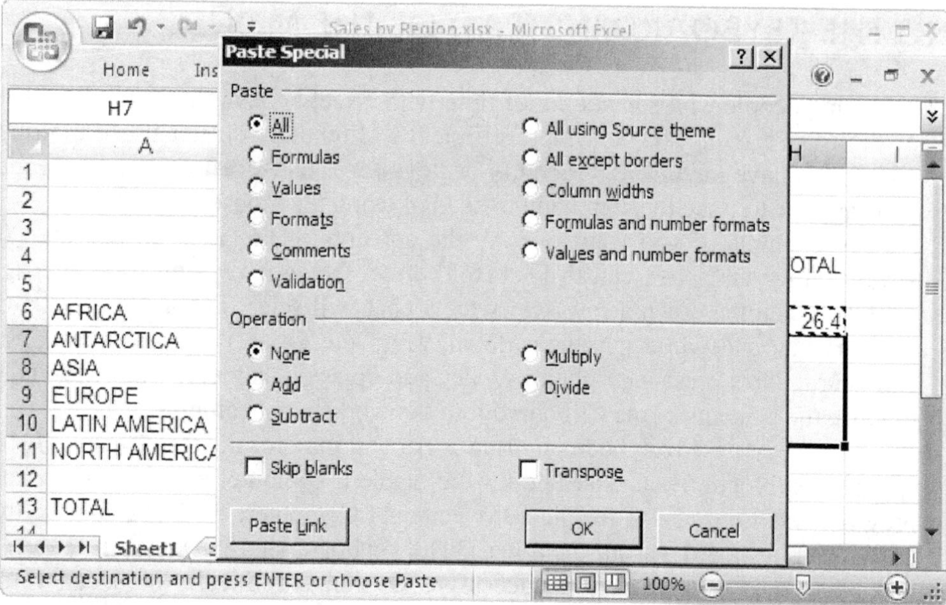

Figure 5-12. Paste Special. The trouble is, Microsoft never gives you enough options.

For example, in another situation we might want to paste the current values in the copied cells, rather than the formulas, but not the formats of the copied cells. And, we might want to add those values into the current values in the cells to which we are pasting. In this case, we would click on Values in the top left column and on Add in the middle left column, as in Figure 5-13.

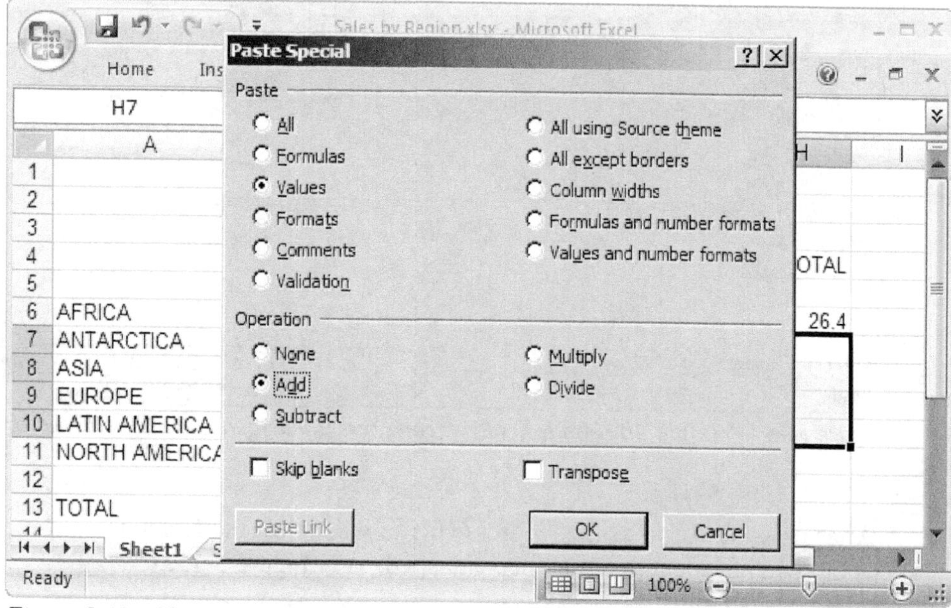

Figure 5-13. Changing options in the Paste Special menu.

USING THE KEYBOARD INSTEAD OF THE MOUSE

Some people who spend a lot of time with Excel believe that using the keyboard instead of the mouse is quicker and more efficient. How can you not use a mouse? Almost all commands have **keyboard shortcuts** or **keyboard accelerators**, keys or sequences of keys you can type to issue the command instead of using the mouse.

For example, if you want to copy the contents of F6:G8 to J4:K6, then use the arrow keys to move the active cell to F6. Hold down the shift key and press the right arrow key once and then the down arrow key twice. That will select F6:J8. Press Ctrl-C (hold down the Ctrl key and while it is held down, press the C key) to Copy the selection into the Clipboard. Now press the right arrow key and up arrow key until you reach J4. Press Ctrl-V to Paste the contents of the Clipboard into the worksheet beginning at J4.

You've just used keyboard shortcuts. As you may recall from Chapter 1, the first major spreadsheet program was VisiCalc for the Apple II computer and the next major spreadsheet program was Lotus 1-2-3 for the IBM Personal Computer. This was before the mouse was used! The keyboard was all there was. The keyboard shortcuts date from over 25 years ago and have been perpetuated in successive versions of Excel. You can find lists of the keystroke combinations for commands by Googling "Excel keyboard shortcuts". But be warned. Some of the keyboard shortcuts that worked in previous versions of Excel may no longer work in Excel 2007.

It's also possible to use the keyboard in conjunction with the tabs and Ribbon in Excel 2007. These are called keyboard accelerators. To get started press the Alt key. You'll see characters appear on the tabs, as in Figure 5-14.

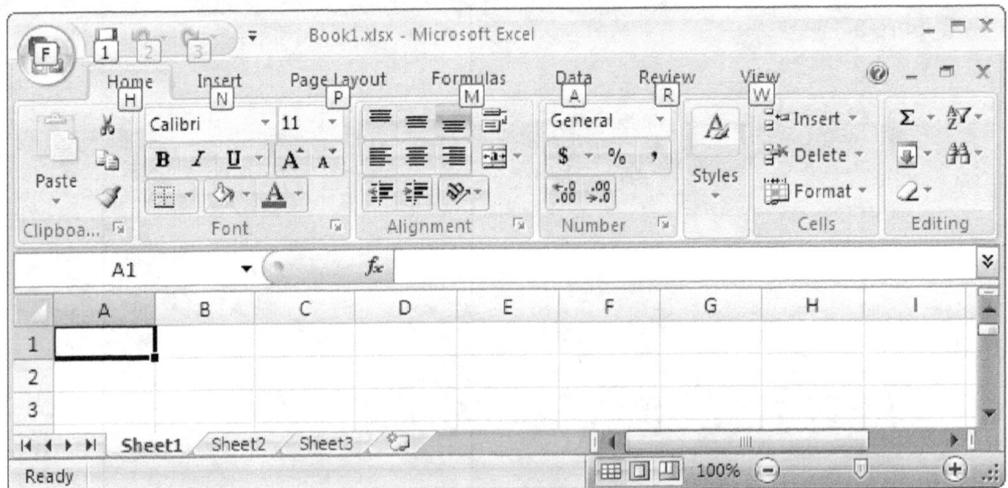

Figure 5-14. Pressing Alt reveals keys you can press to navigate the tabs with the keyboard.

After pressing Alt, if you now press H, you will select the Home tab. The choices in the Home tab will have letters or numbers attached, as in Figure 5-15.

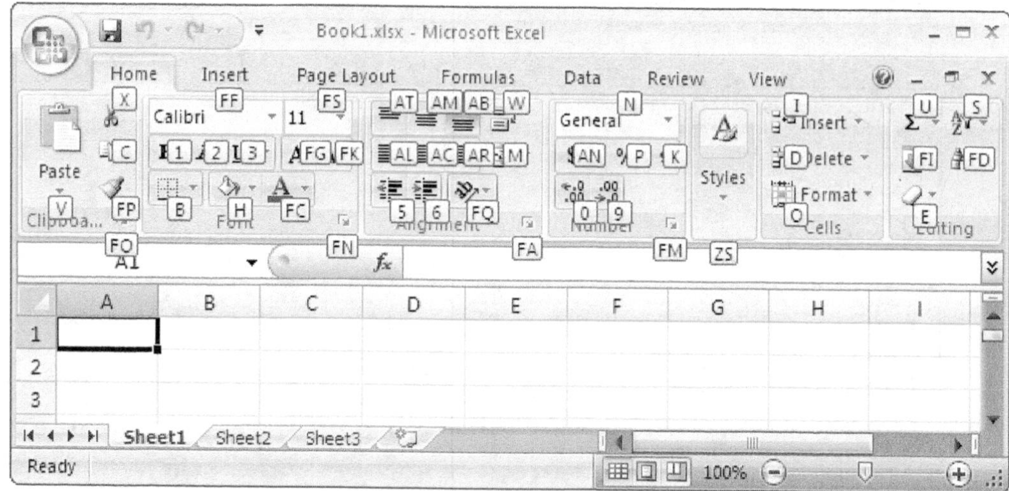

Figure 5-15. Using the keyboard to navigate through the Home tab.

If you press the F key and then the C key you will select the Font Color button. You can use the arrow keys to navigate through the colors that appear. Press the Enter key when you reach the color you want for the text in the cell.

At any time pressing Alt again returns you to the normal mode of using Excel, so that letters you type appear in the cell instead of navigating through the Ribbon and menus.

COPYING AND PASTING FROM THE WEB

Sometimes we find data on the web that we would like to bring into Excel. The general technique is to Copy the data into the Clipboard by first dragging across it in the web browser and then selecting Copy in the browser. Then paste it from the Clipboard into Excel by clicking on a cell in the Excel worksheet and clicking on Paste. The data should be pasted into the worksheet.

That's the theory. Sometimes it works easily in practice, but not always. There are many formats that the original data could be in on the web. If the original data is in Excel or is a table in Word, there should be no problem. If the original data is in a .pdf file and is being viewed in Adobe Acrobat then you will need to click on the Text Select tool in Adobe Acrobat. Then drag across the data to be copied, click with the right mouse button and select Copy, and click in the Excel window and Paste it into your worksheet. Alternatively, the data could be in a table in a webpage or it could be straight text. The best approach is trial and error. Try to Copy and Paste and see what happens.

As an example, suppose we want to analyze how much factory workers in different countries are paid. We find our way to www.bls.gov, the U.S. Bureau of Labor Statistics site. We find the basic data shown in Figure 5-16, which is just what we want. It shows hourly compensation for factory workers in various countries from 1999 through 2005 stated in U.S. dollars.

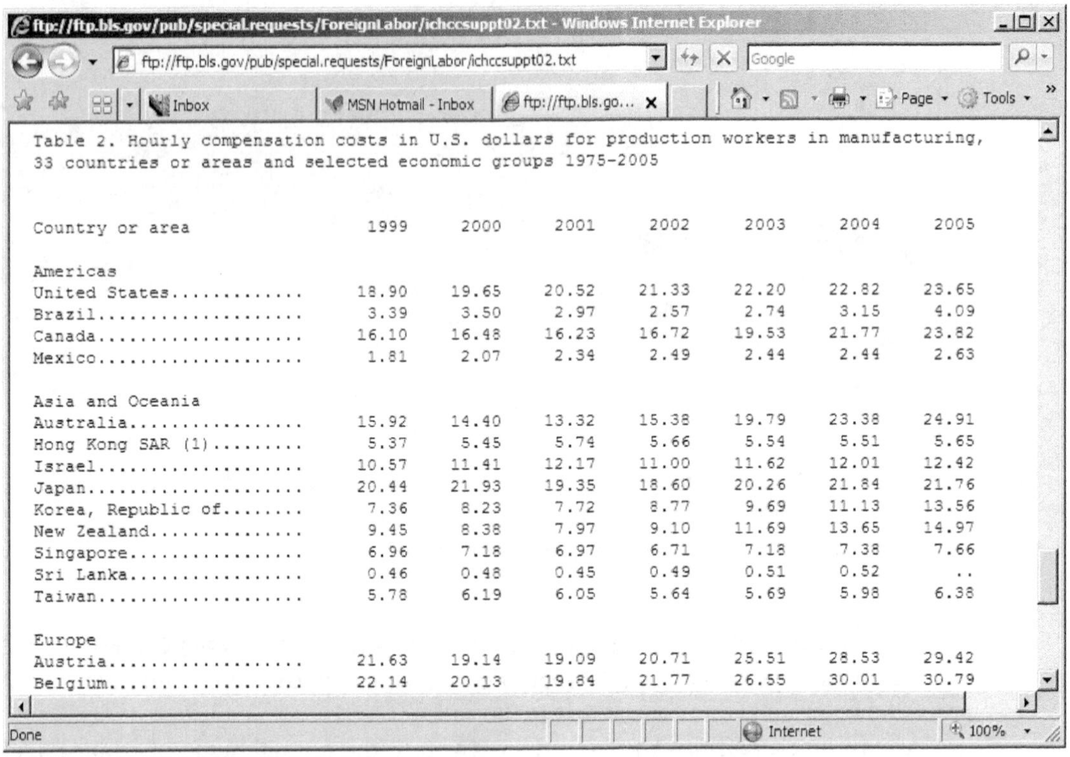
ftp://ftp.bls.gov/pub/special.requests/ForeignLabor/ichccsuppt02.txt - Windows Internet Explorer
ftp://ftp.bls.gov/pub/special.requests/ForeignLabor/ichccsuppt02.txt
Google
Inbox
MSN Hotmail - Inbox
ftp://ftp.bls.go...
Page
Tools
Done
Internet
100%

Table 2. Hourly compensation costs in U.S. dollars for production workers in manufacturing, 33 countries or areas and selected economic groups 1975-2005

Country or area	1999	2000	2001	2002	2003	2004	2005
Americas							
United States............	18.90	19.65	20.52	21.33	22.20	22.82	23.65
Brazil....................	3.39	3.50	2.97	2.57	2.74	3.15	4.09
Canada....................	16.10	16.48	16.23	16.72	19.53	21.77	23.82
Mexico....................	1.81	2.07	2.34	2.49	2.44	2.44	2.63
Asia and Oceania							
Australia.................	15.92	14.40	13.32	15.38	19.79	23.38	24.91
Hong Kong SAR (1).........	5.37	5.45	5.74	5.66	5.54	5.51	5.65
Israel....................	10.57	11.41	12.17	11.00	11.62	12.01	12.42
Japan.....................	20.44	21.93	19.35	18.60	20.26	21.84	21.76
Korea, Republic of........	7.36	8.23	7.72	8.77	9.69	11.13	13.56
New Zealand...............	9.45	8.38	7.97	9.10	11.69	13.65	14.97
Singapore.................	6.96	7.18	6.97	6.71	7.18	7.38	7.66
Sri Lanka.................	0.46	0.48	0.45	0.49	0.51	0.52	..
Taiwan....................	5.78	6.19	6.05	5.64	5.69	5.98	6.38
Europe							
Austria...................	21.63	19.14	19.09	20.71	25.51	28.53	29.42
Belgium...................	22.14	20.13	19.84	21.77	26.55	30.01	30.79

Figure 5-16. Data as it appears in the browser.

We would like to bring the data into Excel to manipulate it. We drag across all the data in the table in the browser (including the data below the window) and copy it into the Clipboard. Then we open a workbook in Excel and paste the data into the worksheet. We obtain the worksheet shown in Figure 5-17. At first glance this worksheet looks OK, but there is a serious problem. All of the data is in column A and it is text. You can see in Figure 5-17 the active cell is in A10 and all of the data for that row is contained in the cell. With all of the data as text in column A, there is no way to refer to individual numbers in formulas. This is a common problem when the original data is simple text, as it is here.

Excel provides a remedy in the form of a **Text to Columns** tool. To use the Text to Columns tool, first select all of the cells with data in column A. Then select click on Text to Columns in the Data Tools group of the Data tab, as in Figure 5-18. The Text to Columns tool shows you the text data, guesses where the column boundaries are, and asks you if it guessed correctly. It usually does. Simply clicking on Next or Finish in each of the three steps produces the worksheet in Figure 5-19.

The worksheet in Figure 5-19 has one number in each cell. The columns can be widened. The worksheet can be formatted. Most importantly, the cells with the numbers can be referred to in formulas so you can analyze the data.

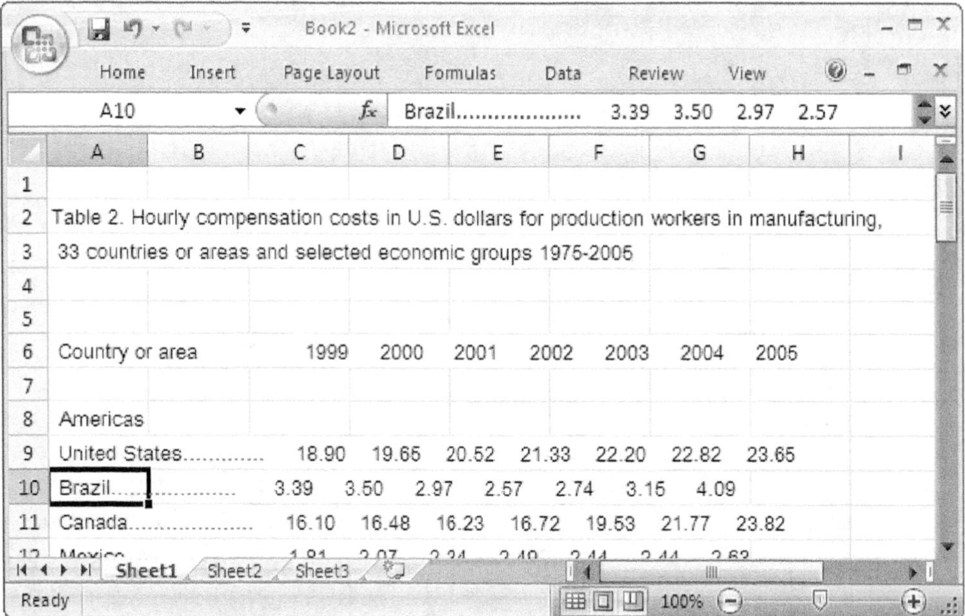

Figure 5-17. After copying and pasting the data into Excel, there is a problem. All of the data is text in column A.

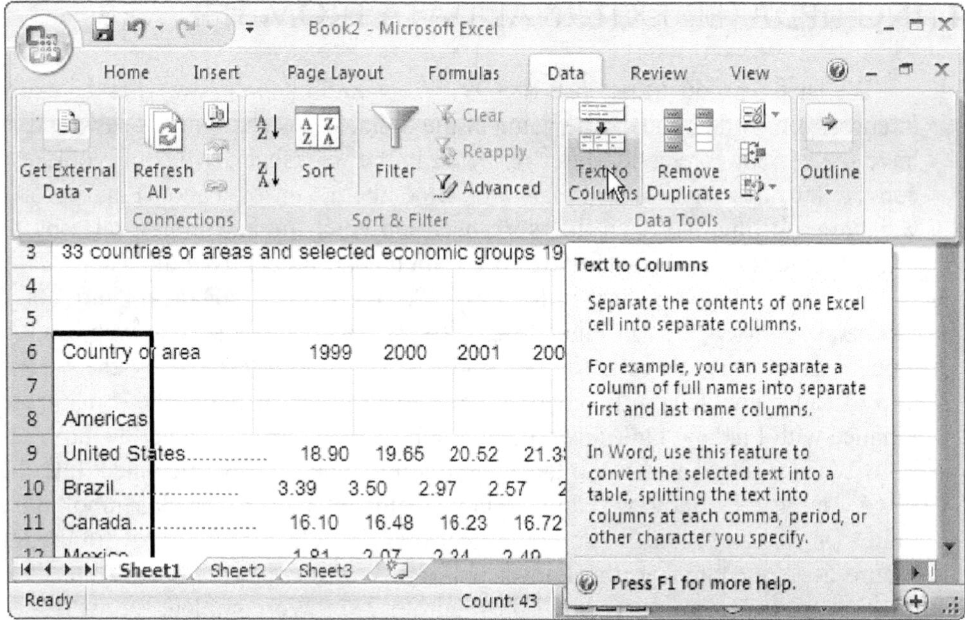

Figure 5-18. First select the data in column A and then click on the Text to Columns tool.

	A	B	C	D	E	F	G	H
1								
2	Table 2. Hourly compensation costs in U.S. dollars for production workers in manufacturing,							
3	33 countries or areas and selected economic groups 1975-2006							
4								
5								
6	Country or	1999	2000	2001	2002	2003	2004	2005
7								
8	Americas							
9	United Sta	18.9	19.65	20.52	21.33	22.2	22.82	23.65
10	Brazil......	3.39	3.5	2.97	2.57	2.74	3.15	4.09
11	Canada....	16.1	16.48	16.23	16.72	19.53	21.77	23.82

Figure 5-19. The Text to Columns tool breaks the text up into separate cells. Now you can widen the columns and format the cells and enter formulas to analyze the data.

GETTING UPDATED EXTERNAL DATA FROM THE WEB

We have a product that costs $89.99. We would like to know what the equivalent cost is in euros, yen, and pounds. The value of the dollar keeps changing. We would like to always have the current conversion rates reflected in the worksheet. We could look up the currency conversion rates on Google Finance or Bloomberg.com or Yahoo Finance or some similar website each time we open the worksheet and enter the conversion rates by hand. Better, Excel provides a way to automatically obtain the latest data from the web.

We set up the worksheet in Figure 5-20. We select the Data tab and then Get External Data and From Web, as in Figure 5-21. Excel now opens a special web browser (!) and we type in finance.google.com for the Address. This is translated by the web browser into http://finance.google.com/finance. The web browser displays the front page of Google Finance with linkable tables marked with a horizontal arrow in a yellow box. (See Figure 5-22.) We can select any of the tables with a horizontal arrow to connect into the worksheet. If we want a stock quote we can type in the company name or stock symbol in the Get quotes field. Or we can browse to any other website. We click on the arrow to the left of Dow in Figure 5-22 and then on the Import button. We tell Excel we want the data to begin at location E2. The result is shown in Figure 5-23. We complete the worksheet by adding formulas to C6:C8, as shown in Figure 5-24.

We can update the worksheet with the latest data from Google Finance (which runs 15 minutes behind real time) by pressing Refresh All in the Data tab, as in Figure 5-25. By pressing the Connections button to the right of Refresh All and then the Properties button we can set the worksheet to update the data automatically as often as we would like. We also can instruct Excel to retrieve the latest data available each time the worksheet file is opened.

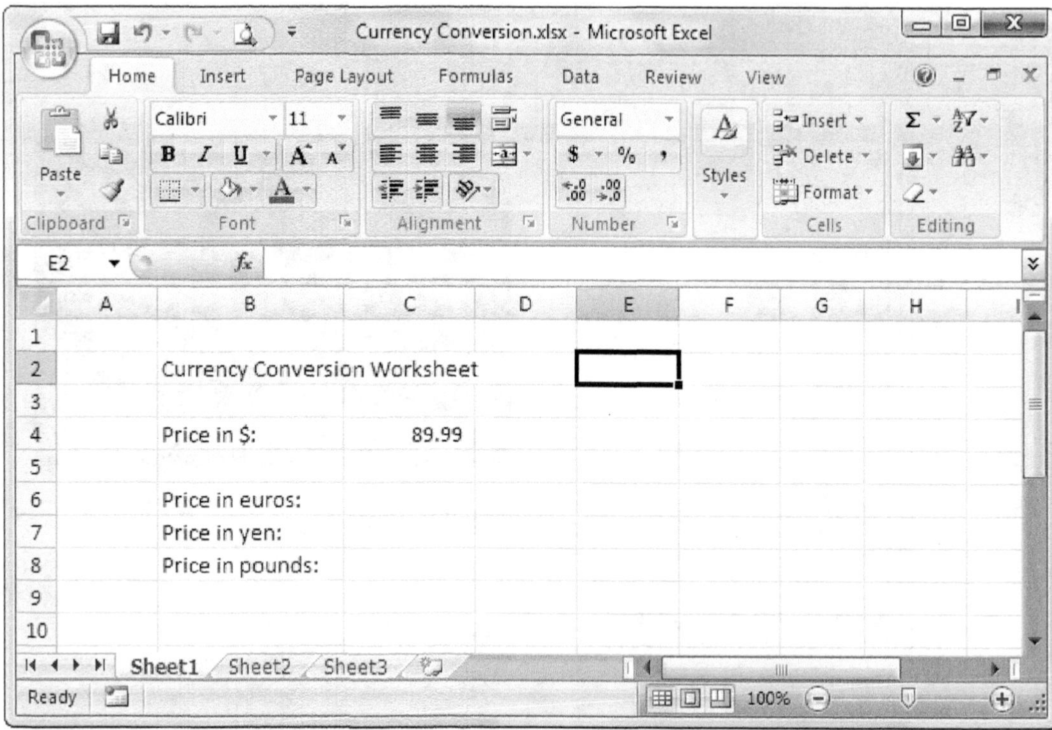

Figure 5-20. Setting up the Currency Conversion worksheet.

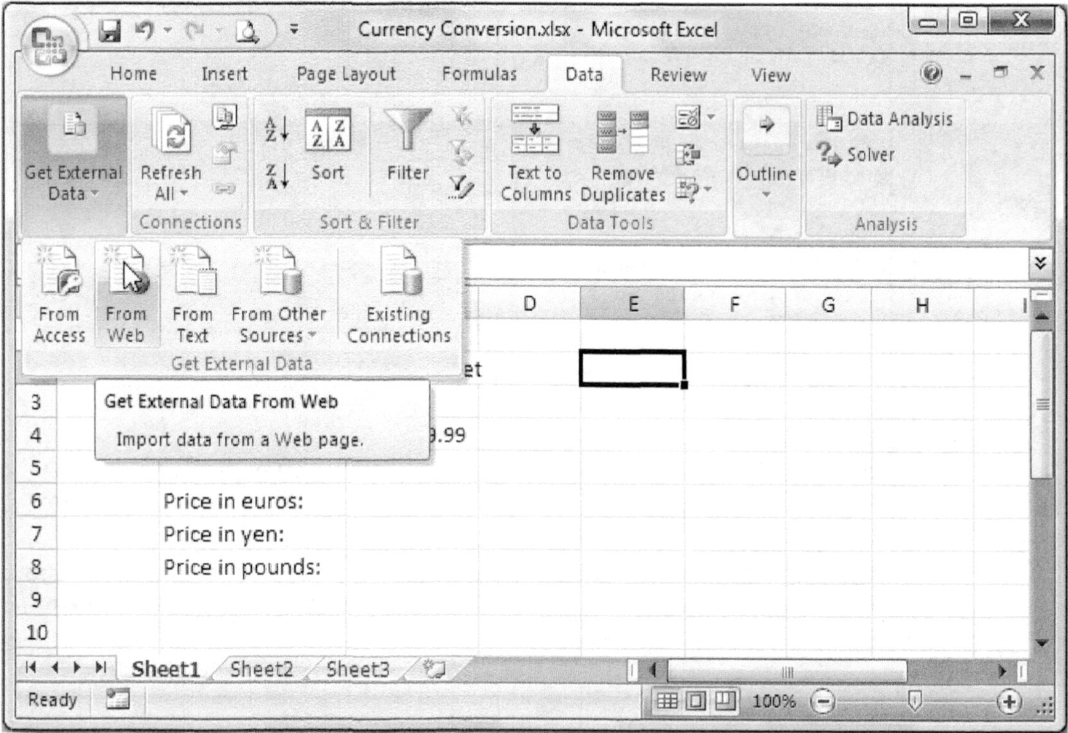

Figure 5-21. Instructing Excel to set up a connection with data on the web.

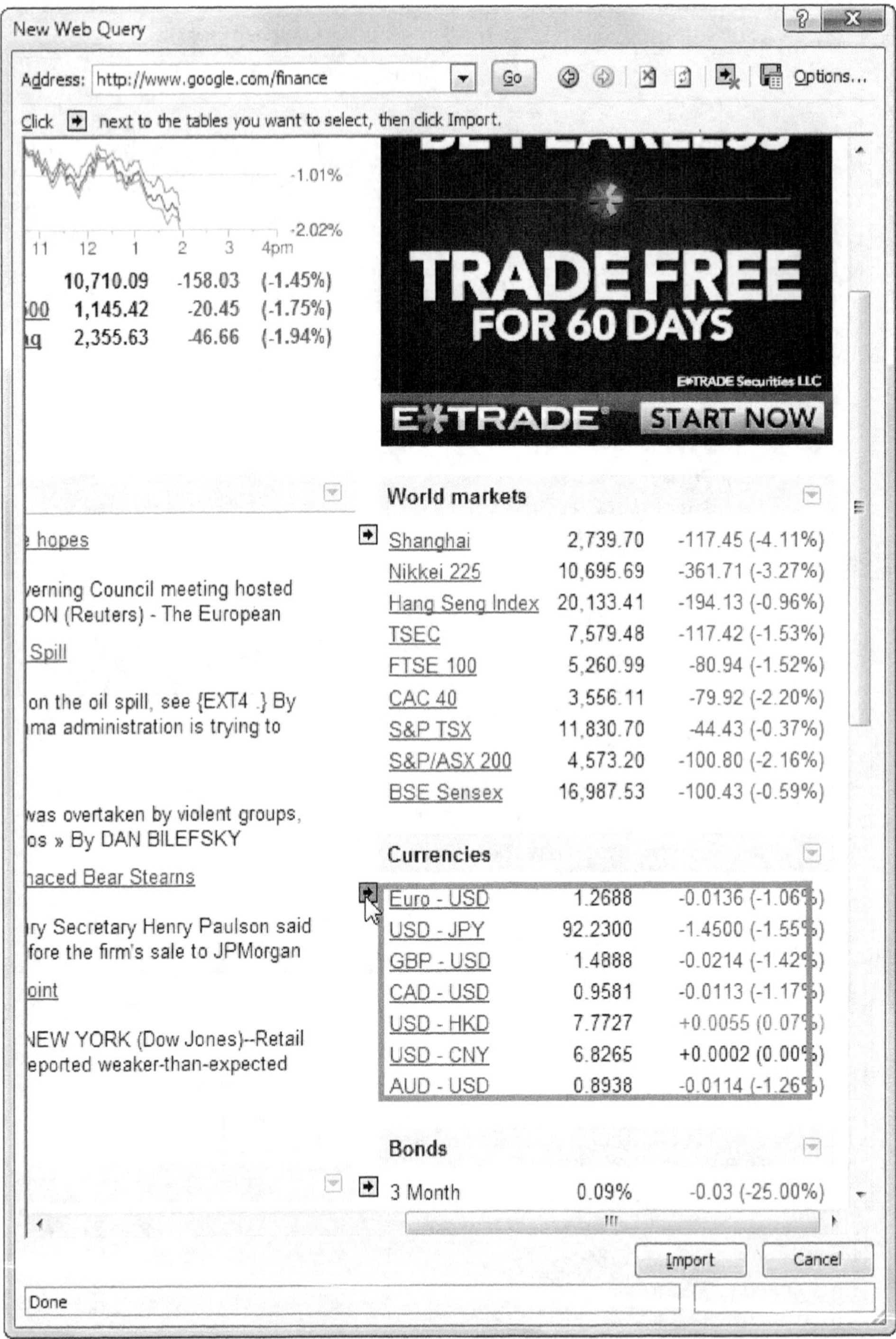

Figure 5-22. Selecting the desired data from the special web browser opened by Excel.

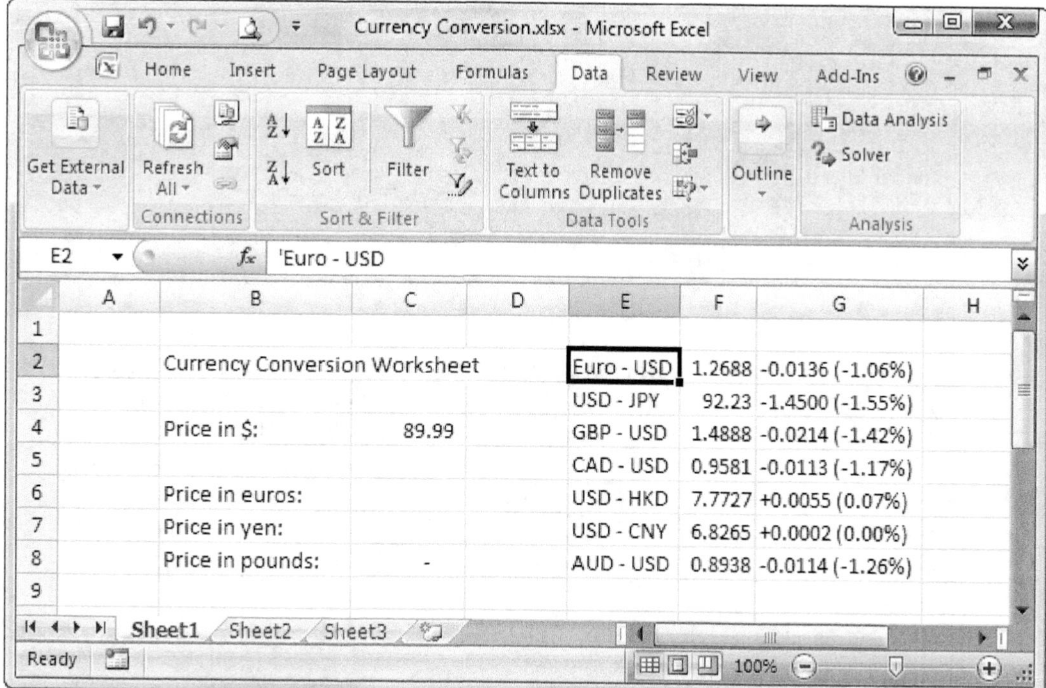

Figure 5-23. A permanent connection has been made between Excel and Google Finance.

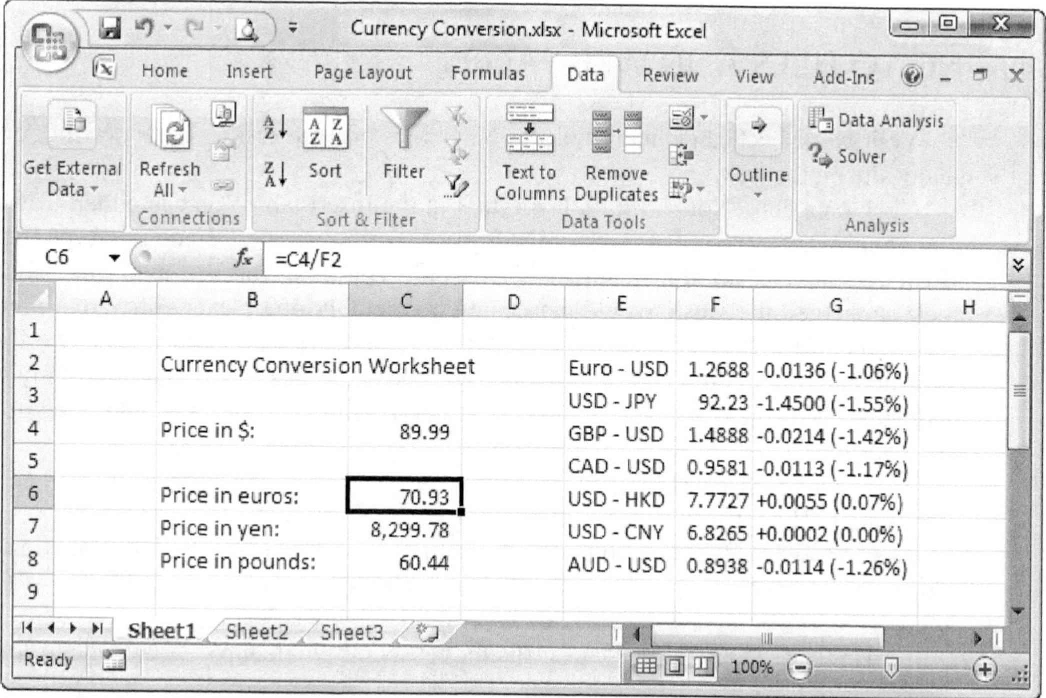

Figure 5-24. The completed worksheet.

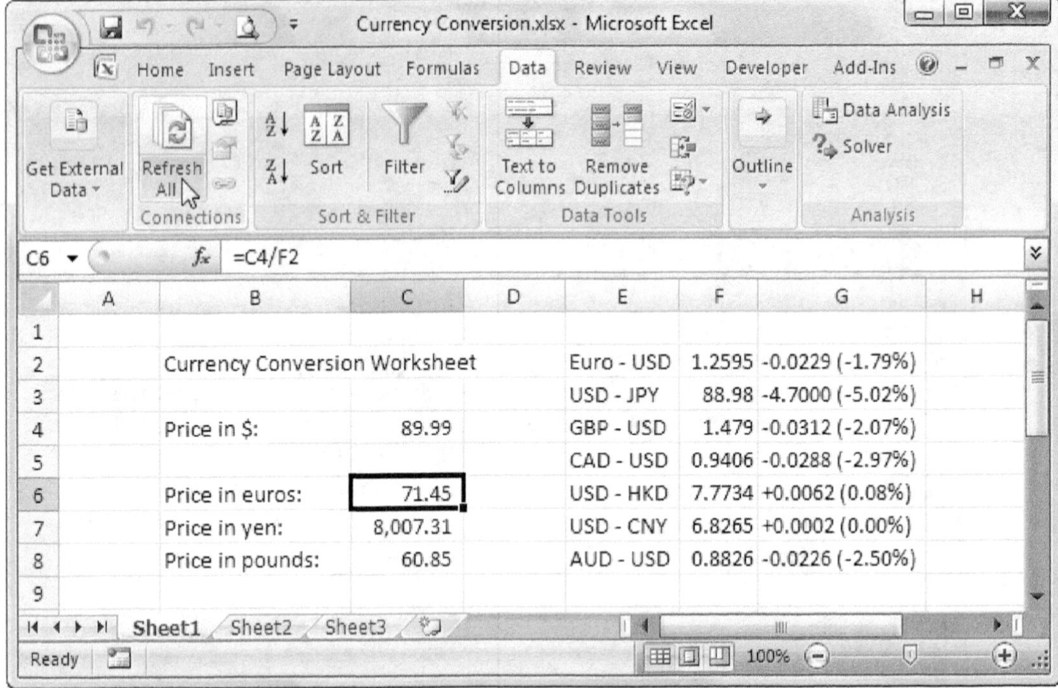

Figure 5-25. Pressing Refresh All updates the values from the web.

LINKING TO FILES AND WEB PAGES

Your worksheet can contain links to other files on your disk or local network or to pages at any site on the web.

Click on a cell. Now click on Hyperlink in the Insert tab. You can either browse for the file you want or type it in directly. For example, I could type in C:\My Music\BeethovensNinthFinale.mp3. This would appear in the cell as a link. Whenever I click on the cell the music would play using my default mp3 player software. You can link to any type of file, for example a movie or a Word document or another Excel workbook.

Alternatively I could type in http://www.cs.bc.edu/~gips. This is a link to my web page at Boston College. Whenever I click on the cell a browser window would open up with the web page in it.

Note that backslashes (\ ) are used for specifying file paths and slashes (/) are used for specifying URLs for web pages.

The **HYPERLINK** function is very useful here. The HYPERLINK function contains two arguments: the link location and a "friendly name". For example, if I put

=HYPERLINK("C:\My Music\BeethovensNinthFinale.mp3","Play Ode to Joy")

in a cell, what will appear is Play Ode to Joy. Clicking on the cell will play the music in the file. Similarly, I could put

=HYPERLINK("http://www.cs.bc.edu/~gips","Click here for a good time")

into a cell, as in Figure 5-26.

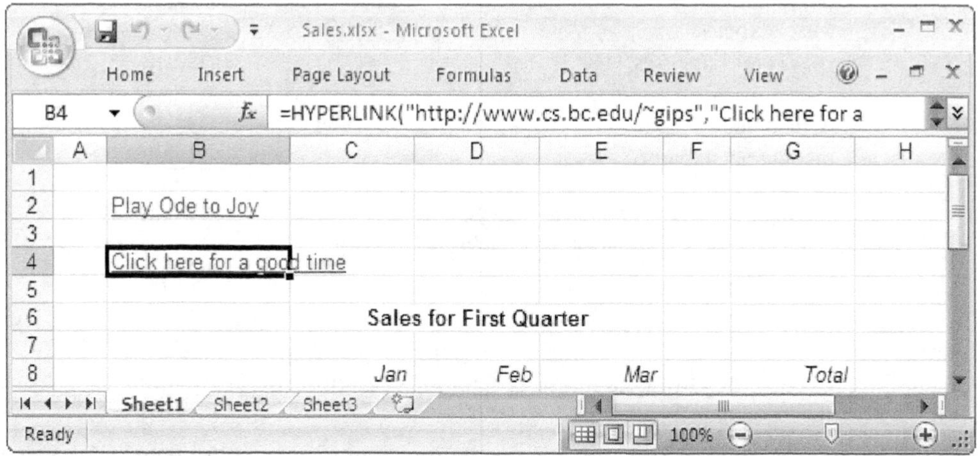

Figure 5-26. A worksheet that will play music and open a web page.

COMPUTER EXERCISES

5-1. We Love Plants, Inc. is a small company in the houseplant care business. People can arrange for the company to come into their apartment or house to care for their plants when they are away on business or on vacation or all-year around. The company has begun offering the same service to businesses and offices.

The most recent Income Statement for the company is as follows.

WE LOVE PLANTS, INC.
Income Statement
For the Year Ended December 31

Revenues:		
Home plant care revenue	$197,329	
Office plant care revenue	65,545	
Total Revenues		$262,874
Expenses:		
Salaries expense	72,488	
Payroll tax expense	9,803	
Rent expense for office	7,800	
Utilities expense	1,377	

Advertising expense	23,103	
Automobile expense	35,292	
Supplies expense	24,550	
Misc. expense	8,500	
Total Expenses		$182,913
Pretax Income		$79,961
Income tax expense		15,992
Net income		$63,969
Earnings per share		$1.60

The company pays 20% in income taxes. There are 40,000 shares of stock.

(a) Create a "template" worksheet for the Income Statement where each of the numbers in the middle column is 0. All of the numbers in the right column should be the results of formulas and should appear as 0 also. The numbers should be formatted as they appear above. Save the worksheet on the disk.

(b) Now fill in the numbers in the middle column. The numbers in the right column should match. Save the worksheet.

(c) Select a rectangular range of cells that includes all of the non-blank cells by dragging across the cells. Move this entire range of cells two columns to the right and one row down.

(d) Erase the first four of the expenses categories and values by selecting the range containing the cells and dragging the Fill Handle back over the range.

(e) Undo the erase.

(f) Delete columns A and B. (They should be empty as the result of the move in part (c).)

(g) Insert a new row in the middle of the expenses. Enter in Insurance Expense 7,300.

(h) Attach the comment "We need to get better control of these." to the cell for Misc. Expense.

(i) Select the information in the two columns of numbers by dragging across it. Then click on the Copy button in the Clipboard group of the Home tab. Click on the cell two columns to the right of the top right cell of the copied range. Now click on the Paste button in the Clipboard group of the Home tab to paste a new copy of the information two columns over. This could be used as the basis for entering in next year's income statement to compare it with this year's.

(j) Erase what was just pasted either by selecting Undo or by erasing the range of cells.

(k) Format the worksheet so that it looks as attractive as possible. Save the worksheet.

(l) Assume that the Expenses remain the same. Use Goal Seek to determine the Total Revenues required for the company to earn $2.00 per share. Save the worksheet under a different name.

5-2. General Electric is a major international company headquartered in Fairfield, CT. General Electric is divided into four segments: Infrastructure (which is divided into Aviation, Energy, Oil & Gas, Transportation), Industrial (Appliances, Lighting, Security, ...), Healthcare (Clinical Systems, Diagnostic Imaging, ...), and NBC Universal (Cable, Film, Network, Parks & Resorts). General Electric has reported their financial results for the first quarter of 2008:

General Electric 1Q '08
(in $ million)

	Revenues	Operating Profit	Operating Profit %
Infrastructure	14,960	2,588	
Industrial	4,110	300	
Healthcare	3,887	528	
NBCU	3,584	712	
Total			

(a) Create a worksheet for the data above. Put in formulas for the right column (Operating Profit as percent of Revenues) and for the bottom Totals row. Use functions and Fill.

(b) Here are the corresponding results for the first quarter of 2007.

General Electric 1Q '07
(in $ million)

	Revenues	Operating Profit	Operating Profit %
Infrastructure	12,202	2,208	
Industrial	4,089	358	
Healthcare	3,895	637	
NBCU	3,484	691	
Total			

Please add this data into your worksheet by Copying the entries from part (a) and then Pasting them below. Change the eight actual values for 2007. The right column and bottom row should be recalculated appropriately by the copied formulas. Change 1Q '08 to 1Q '07.

(c) General Electric is interested in comparing how they did in first quarter 2008 versus 2007. In particular, they are interested in the percentage increases from 2007 to 2008 for the first quarter Revenues and Operating Profit for each segment and for the company as a whole. Please add this to your worksheet by Copying the appropriate cells from part (a) and Pasting them below. Erase any cells that display numeric values. Enter the appropriate formulas for the percentage changes. Use Fill or Copy and Paste. There will be 10 new formulas in all plus appropriate text. As a check, first quarter Infrastructure Revenues were up 22.6% from 2007 to 2008. Be sure to change the descriptive text appropriately.

5-3. We have 1,000 shares of Microsoft, 75 shares of Google, and 800 shares of Apple in our portfolio. Create a worksheet that uses Get External Data From Web to show us at least the current prices of each of our stocks, the current total value of our portfolio, and how much money we have made or lost today since the opening of the stock market. You may have as many other cells as you would like.

CHAPTER 6

RELATIVE VS. ABSOLUTE ADDRESSING

OBJECTIVES

In this chapter you will learn how to:

- Use absolute addressing in formulas
- Create worksheets for "What if" analysis
- Use the Split Bars to split the window
- Name cells and ranges of cells
- Use mixed addressing in formulas
- Use Panes to work with large worksheets

What makes the Fill (or Copy and Paste) operation so powerful in making multiple copies of formulas is that Excel adjusts the addresses in the formulas as it makes the copies. For example, if the formula in H6 is =SUM(C6:G6) and we fill the formula down the column, then the formula in H7 will be =SUM(C7:G7), the formula in H8 will be =SUM(C8:G8), and so on. In Chapter 4, we referred to this as an "intelligent" Fill operation. The Fill operation as described usually works well. However, there are some cases where we do not want the address in the formula to be adjusted as the formula is filled, where changing the address causes an error in the formula. In this important chapter we will examine how to instruct Excel not to change an address in a formula when filling the formula down a column or across a row.

AN EXAMPLE WHERE THE FILL OPERATION SEEMS TO FAIL

We would like to know the proportion of the world's population in each continent. The population for each continent is shown in the worksheet in Figure 6-1.

Population by Continent.xlsx - Microsoft Excel

	A	B	C	D	E	F	G
1							
2		World Population by Continent					
3		(in millions)					
4							
5		Continent	Population	Proportion			
6							
7		Africa	877				
8		Asia	3,879				
9		Europe	727				
10		North America	501				
11		Oceania	32				
12		South America	379				
13							
14		Total					
15							
16							

Figure 6-1. A worksheet for determining the proportion of the world population by continent.

To find the total population on the planet we put the formula

=SUM(C7:C12)

into cell C14. There are approximately 6,395 million people on the planet, of whom 877 million live in Africa. To calculate the proportion of people in Africa, we divide the population of Africa by the total population for the planet. The formula in D7 can be

=C7/C14

as in Figure 6-2. Thus, 0.137, or almost one-seventh, of the world's population lives in Africa.

Population by Continent.xlsx - Microsoft Excel

Home Insert Page Layout Formulas Data Review View Add-Ins

D7 f_x =C7/C14

	A	B	C	D	E	F	G
1							
2		World Population by Continent					
3			(in millions)				
4							
5		Continent	Population	Proportion			
6							
7		Africa	877	0.137138389			
8		Asia	3,879				
9		Europe	727				
10		North America	501				
11		Oceania	32				
12		South America	379				
13							
14		Total	6,395				
15							
16							

Sheet1 Sheet2 Sheet3

Ready 100%

Figure 6-2. To find the proportion of the population in Africa, divide the Africa Population by the Total Population.

Now we would like to Fill the formula down the column to calculate the proportion of the world's population living in the other continents. We click on D7 to select the cell. We move the mouse pointer over the Fill Handle in the bottom right of the cell and drag the Fill Handle down to D12. When we release the mouse button, the formula is filled down into D8:D12. Here is the key point. Filling the formula in D7 down the column yields the worksheet in Figure 6-3.

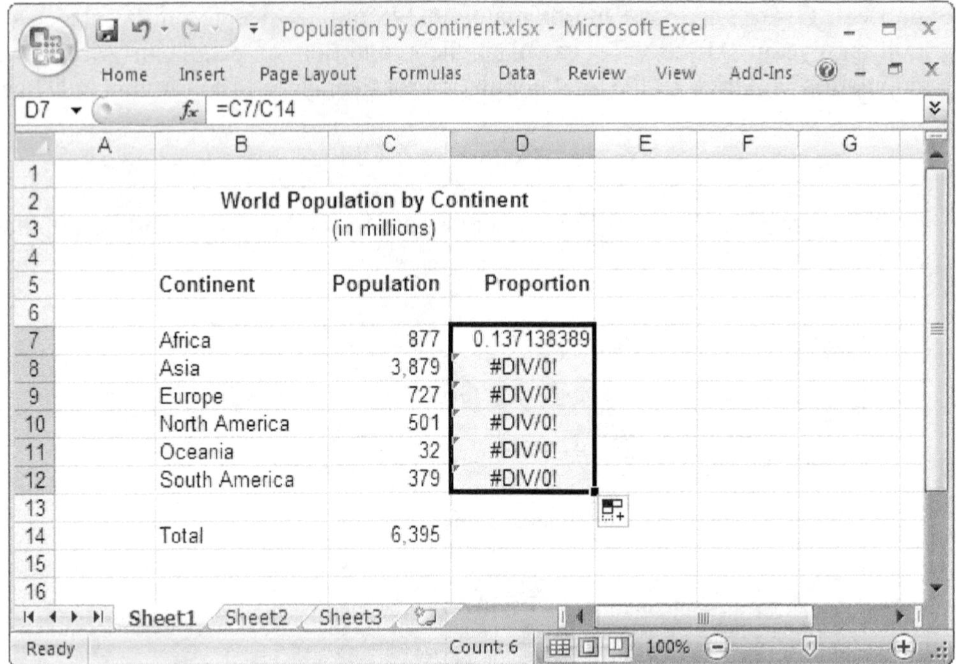

Figure 6-3. Filling down the formula just entered in D7 produces a very instructive error.

What has happened? The cells into which we filled the formula are full of #DIV/0! messages. These are error messages that indicate that we instructed Excel to divide a value by 0. Division by 0 is undefined and, so, produces an error message. What is the source of the problem? If we look at the formula in D8, we see that it is =C8/C15. The C8 is correct. But C15 is a blank cell. In evaluating the formula =C8/C15 the computer divides 3879, the number in C8, by 0, the "number" in C15. Dividing any number by 0 yields the error message.

What should the formula in D8 be? We would like it to be the population of Asia divided by the total population, =C8/C14, rather than =C8/C15. What happened in Figure 6-3? When the formula =C7/C14 in cell D7 was filled down the column, both of the addresses were adjusted by the Fill operation. So =C7/C14 in D7 became =C8/C15 in D8 became =C9/C16 in D9, and so on. We wanted =C7/C14 in D7 to become =C8/C14 in D8 to become =C9/C14 in D9, and so on. That is, we want the Fill operation to adjust the first address C7 in the formula in =C7/C14 but not the second address, C14. The cell address for the total population, C14, should remain unchanged. Excel has an "intelligent" Fill operation but not a brilliant Fill operation. Excel must be told which addresses to adjust and which to keep the same when a formula is filled.

ABSOLUTE ADDRESSING

An address written in the normal way (for example, C14) is adjusted automatically by Excel in a Fill operation and is called a **relative address** or **relative reference**. To instruct

Excel that an address in a formula is not to be changed when filled, the address is written with dollar signs before the column name and row name, for example, as $C$14. An address that is not to be adjusted when copied is called an **absolute address** or **absolute reference**. The dollar signs have nothing to do with money or currency here. For reasons not apparent, the dollar signs were selected to denote an absolute address.

Returning to our example, now we see that the formula in cell D7 should be

=C7/$C$14

When filled down the column, this formula becomes =C8/$C$14 in D8, which becomes =C9/$C$14 in D9, and so on, as in Figure 6-4. The $C$14 is evaluated in the formula just the same as is C14, as the value in cell C14. The only difference in using an absolute address rather than a relative address occurs when the formula is filled or copied and pasted.

Population by Continent.xlsx - Microsoft Excel

Home Insert Page Layout Formulas Data Review View Add-Ins

D10 f_x =C10/$C$14

World Population by Continent
(in millions)

Continent	Population	Proportion
Africa	877	0.137138389
Asia	3,879	0.606567631
Europe	727	0.113682565
North America	501	0.078342455
Oceania	32	0.005003909
South America	379	0.059265051
Total	6,395	

Sheet1 Sheet2 Sheet3

Ready 100%

Figure 6-4. We do not want the reference to cell C14 to be adjusted when the formula in D7 is filled down, so we use absolute addressing.

Why are the terms "relative address" and "absolute address" used? Consider, again, the original formula in cell D7 in Figure 6-2. The formula =C7/C14 in D7 can be interpreted as "Take the number one column to the left and divide it by the number in the cell one column to the left and seven rows down" because the addresses are adjusted when the formula is filled or copied. Hence, the addresses C7 and C14 are "relative addresses". In contrast, the formula =C7/$C$14 in D7 can be interpreted as "Take the number one column to the left and divide it by the number in cell C14" because the address C7 is adjusted as the formula is copied but the address $C$14 remains the same. Hence, the address C7 is relative, but the address $C$14 is absolute.

To complete the example, we format the cells in column D as Percent with one decimal place and add up the percentages in D14 (see Figure 6-5). Note again that formatting a cell, for example as a percentage, only affects the way the cell appears in the worksheet, not the underlying value in the cell. While D10 appears as 7.8%, the value in D10 actually is 0.078342455, the result of dividing 501 by 6,395.

	A	B	C	D
1				
2		World Population by Continent		
3		(in millions)		
4				
5		Continent	Population	Proportion
6				
7		Africa	877	13.7%
8		Asia	3,879	60.7%
9		Europe	727	11.4%
10		North America	501	7.8%
11		Oceania	32	0.5%
12		South America	379	5.9%
13				
14		Total	6,395	100.0%
15				
16				

Figure 6-5. The completed worksheet for the percentage population on each continent.

PETER MINUIT

Absolute addressing is especially important in worksheets where key numbers are put into separate cells. To illustrate this, let's do another example.

Peter Minuit was the director-general of the Dutch West Indies Company's settlements in North America. In 1626 he negotiated a deal with local tribal chiefs and purchased the island of Manhattan from them for bright cloth, beads, and other trinkets valued at 60 guilders, or about $24. Today the island of Manhattan forms the core of New York City and is worth a fortune. But did Peter make such a great deal? Suppose Peter had taken the money and put it into a Money Market Account at the Dutch National Bank. How much would it be worth today? What would be the value of the investment each year from 1626 to 2026?

We need one more piece of information. What interest rate would Peter have received on his money over 400 years? For now, let us assume a constant 3% per year. We will change this assumption later.

Figure 6-6 is a start toward a worksheet that calculates what Peter's investment would be worth. The years from 1626 through 2026 will be in column B. The corresponding value of the investment each year will be in column D.

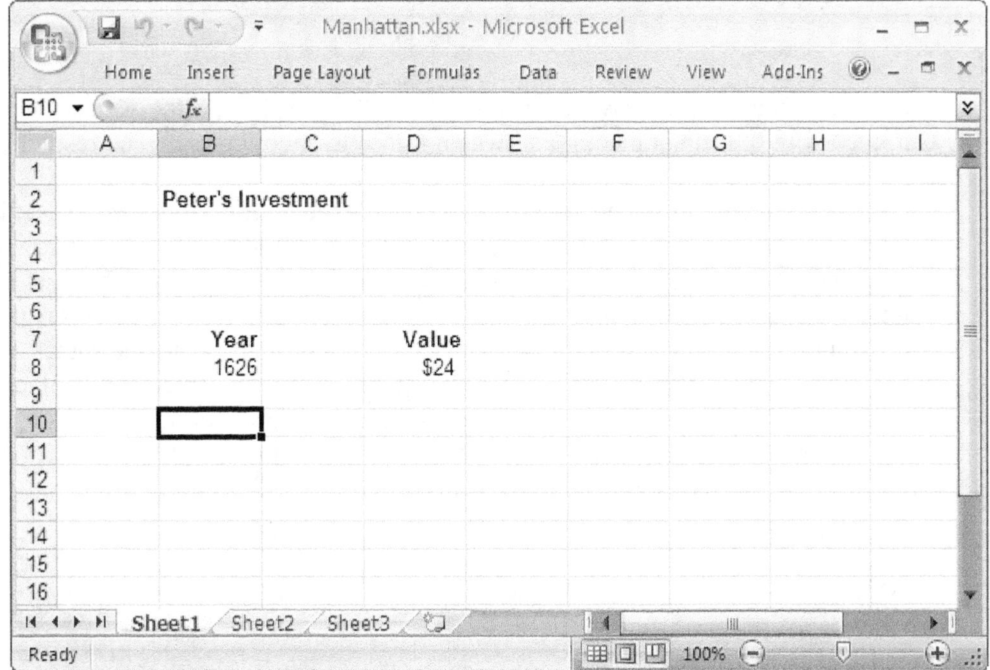

Figure 6-6. Beginning the worksheet to calculate what the value of the $24 would be if Peter Minuit had deposited it in a bank instead of purchasing Manhattan.

How can we obtain the years in column B? We could type each one of them, but who wants to type 400 numbers? We could enter 1627 in cell B9 and then use AutoFill as discussed at the end of Chapter 4. Another solution is to put a formula into B9 and then fill the formula down the column. Each number in column B is to be one greater than the number in the cell above. So in cell B9 we put the formula

=B8+1

We then fill the formula down the column through B408. To do this, we click on B9, grab the Fill Handle in the bottom right of the cell by pressing down on the mouse button, and with the button held down we move the mouse pointer down column B below the bottom of the worksheet, forcing the worksheet to scroll down to B408. The further below the window we move the mouse pointer, the faster it scrolls. We then release the mouse button when we reach B408. Formulas will fill from B9 through B408. The formula in B10 will be =B9+1, the formula in B11 will be =B10+1, and so on. There will be a chain of formulas down the column, each adding one to the value of the cell above. The years from 1626 through 2026 will appear in column B.

How can we obtain the value of the investment each year in column D? We will follow the same technique of entering a formula for the cell in row 9 and then filling the formula down the column. How much money would Peter have in 1627? Peter would have the amount from the previous year plus the interest the money earned during the year. At 3% interest the formula for D9 would be

=D8+D8*3%

We fill the formula from D9 down through D408. We format the values in column D as Currency with 0 decimal places, and widen the cells in column D. The resulting worksheet is shown in Figure 6-7.

Scrolling down to row 398, we can see towards the bottom of the worksheet in Figure 6-8. What would Peter's $24 investment in 1626 be worth today if he received 3% interest per year? About two million dollars. What does two million dollars buy in Manhattan today? A condo, an apartment in a nice building. It appears that Peter was wise in purchasing Manhattan. (Of course, the British fleet took over the city from the Dutch in 1664 and changed the name from Nieuw Amsterdam to New York. If the 60 guilders had been invested in the bank, at least the Dutch still would have had their money. And, in true New York fashion, it is said that the chiefs who "sold" Manhattan to Peter were from the Canarsie tribe in Brooklyn and had no claim to Manhattan.)

Manhattan.xlsx - Microsoft Excel

Home Insert Page Layout Formulas Data Review View Add-Ins

D12 fx =D11+D11*3%

	A	B	C	D	E	F	G	H
1								
2		Peter's Investment						
3								
4								
5								
6								
7		Year		Value				
8		1626		$24				
9		1627		$25				
10		1628		$25				
11		1629		$26				
12		1630		$27				
13		1631		$28				
14		1632		$29				
15		1633		$30				
16		1634		$30				

Sheet1 Sheet2 Sheet3

Ready 100%

Figure 6-7. Calculating the value of the investment assuming a 3% interest rate.

Manhattan.xlsx - Microsoft Excel

D12 f_x =D11+D11*3%

	A	B	C	D	E	F	G	H
383		2001		$1,563,761				
384		2002		$1,610,674				
385		2003		$1,658,995				
386		2004		$1,708,764				
387		2005		$1,760,027				
388		2006		$1,812,828				
389		2007		$1,867,213				
390		2008		$1,923,229				
391		2009		$1,980,926				
392		2010		$2,040,354				
393		2011		$2,101,565				
394		2012		$2,164,612				
395		2013		$2,229,550				
396		2014		$2,296,436				
397		2015		$2,365,330				
398		2016		$2,436,289				

Sheet1 Sheet2 Sheet3

Ready 100%

Figure 6-8. Peter's investment would be worth approximately $2,000,000 at 3% interest.

But what if Peter had received 5% annual interest rate instead of 3%? What would Peter's account be worth now? To answer this question we need to change the worksheet. In particular, we need to change the formulas in column D. The formula in D9 could be changed to

=D8+D8*5%

Then the formula would be filled down to D408. But suppose we then wanted to see what the value of the investment would be if the annual interest rate were 7% or 9% or 11%. In order to change the interest rate we would have to change the formula in D9 and then fill the new formula down the column each time.

A better approach is to put the interest rate in a separate cell and refer to that cell in the formulas in column D. Now if we want to see what would happen with a different interest rate, we would just need to change the number in the cell rather than changing all 400 formulas. This approach is shown in Figure 6-9.

This worksheet illustrates a good general rule: *Any value that you might want to change should be placed in a separate cell, rather than being built explicitly into formulas.*

The Annual interest rate is in cell D5. The formula in D9 is

=D8+D8*$D$5

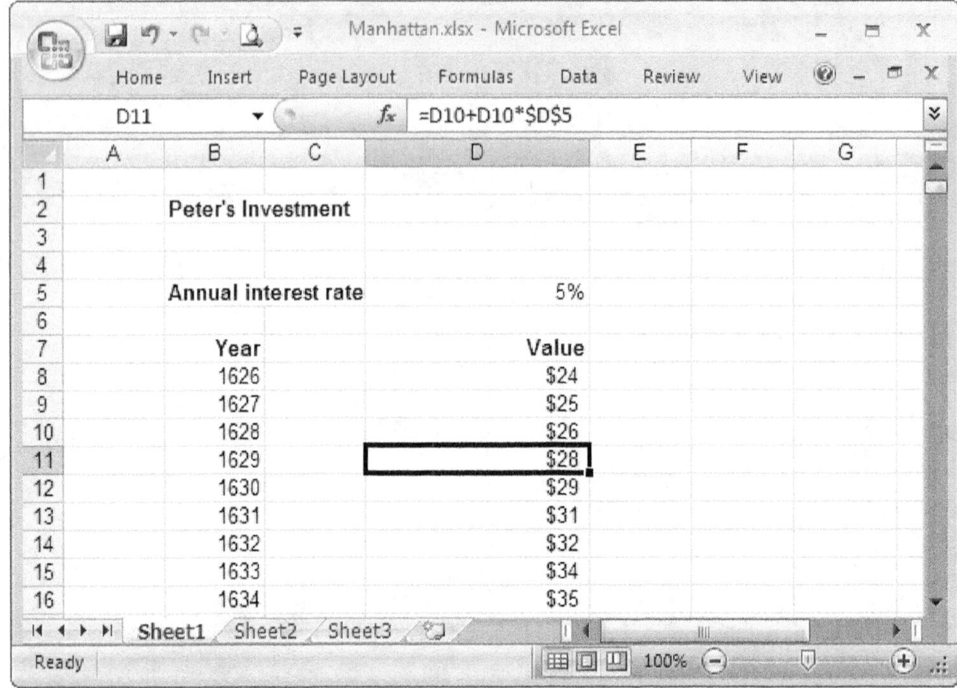

Figure 6-9. A better approach is to place the annual interest rate in a separate cell and refer to the cell in the formulas using absolute addressing.

This formula has been filled from D9 down through D408. We refer to the interest rate as an absolute address ($D$5) so that the address is not adjusted as the formula is filled down the column. In Figure 6-9 the active cell is D11 and indeed we can see that the formula in D11 is

=D10+D10*$D$5

SPLITTING THE WINDOW

Wouldn't it be nice to be able to change the interest rate and be able to see immediately the resulting value of the investment today? Excel has a **Horizontal Split Bar** and a **Vertical Split Bar** (see Figure 6-10). The Horizontal Split Bar is the small horizontal rectangle right above the up scroll arrow. The Vertical Split Bar is the small vertical rectangle to the right of the right scroll arrow.

Dragging the Horizontal Split Bar down allows us to split the window in half. Each portion can be vertically scrolled independently. By scrolling the bottom portion down to row 389 we can see the two portions of the screen shown in Figure 6-11. At 5% interest Peter's $24 investment in 1626 would be worth about $3 billion today. With $3 billion you could buy some major office buildings in Manhattan and a nice hotel or two.

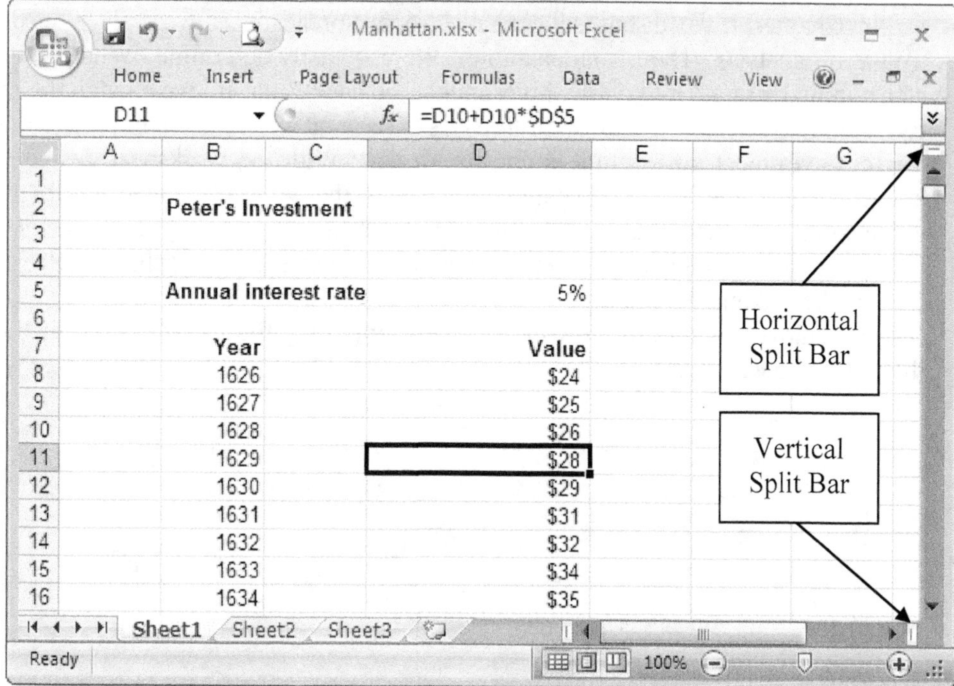

Figure 6-10. The locations of the Horizontal and Vertical Split Bars.

Manhattan.xlsx - Microsoft Excel

Home Insert Page Layout Formulas Data Review View

D11 =D10+D10*$D$5

	A	B	C	D	E	F	G
1							
2		**Peter's Investment**					
3							
4							
5		**Annual interest rate**		5%			
6							
7		**Year**		**Value**			
8		1626		$24			
9		1627		$25			
389		2007		$2,840,103,633			
390		2008		$2,982,108,815			
391		2009		$3,131,214,255			
392		2010		$3,287,774,968			
393		2011		$3,452,163,716			
394		2012		$3,624,771,902			
395		2013		$3,806,010,497			

Sheet1 Sheet2 Sheet3

Ready 100%

Figure 6-11. The Horizontal Split Bar allows the display of two parts of the worksheet.

In Chapter 1 we discussed how electronic spreadsheets were developed to facilitate "What if" analysis. Here is an example. We can easily determine "What if" Peter received some annual interest rate on his investment. To see "What if" we change the number in D5 to the annual interest rate we wish to try. As soon as we enter the new rate, the new values for the investment go rippling down the screen. With the worksheet designed so that the annual interest rate is in a separate cell and with the window divided into two portions, we can change the interest rate to 7% and see almost instantaneously that if Peter had invested $24 in 1626 at 7% annual interest, it would be worth some $4 trillion. (See Figure 6-12.) Now we're talking real money!

To remove the split in the window, we simply drag the Horizontal Split Bar back up to the top of the worksheet.

Manhattan.xlsx - Microsoft Excel

Home Insert Page Layout Formulas Data Review View

D5 f_x 7%

	A	B	C	D	E	F	G
1							
2		Peter's Investment					
3							
4							
5		Annual interest rate		7%			
6							
7		Year		Value			
8		1626		$24			
9		1627		$26			
389		2007		$3,762,101,771,241			
390		2008		$4,025,448,895,228			
391		2009		$4,307,230,317,894			
392		2010		$4,608,736,440,147			
393		2011		$4,931,347,990,957			
394		2012		$5,276,542,350,324			
395		2013		$5,645,900,314,847			

Sheet1 Sheet2 Sheet3

Ready 100%

Figure 6-12. At 7% annual interest rate you might prefer the bank account over Manhattan. What would 9% produce? 11%?

NAMING CELLS

In larger worksheets it is easy to forget which cells contain which quantities. When reading the formulas in a larger worksheet it can be cumbersome to determine which quantities are referred to by cell addresses in the formulas. Excel provides the capability of giving names to cells and ranges of cells and using these names in formulas instead of the cell addresses. It is good practice to name key cells in larger worksheets. For example, in this worksheet we could give cell D5 the name RATE. Then the formula in cell D9 would be

=D8+D8*RATE

rather than

=D8+D8*$D$5

To give cell D5 a name, we first select D5 by clicking on it. Then we click in the Name Box. The Name Box is the box directly above the A column heading. In the Name Box we type the new name of the cell, as in Figure 6-13.

The name can contain up to 255 characters. It should begin with a letter. The name can contain letters, digits, and underscores (_), but not spaces or arithmetic operators or most punctuation characters. Case does not matter in Excel, so RATE is the same as Rate is the same as rate. Select a name that makes sense, one that you will remember.

To use a name in a formula we can simply type the name instead of the cell address. Alternatively, we can select from the list of already defined names by selecting Defined Names in the Formulas tab.

Excel assumes that a name refers to an absolute address. In this case, Excel assumes that the name RATE refers to the absolute address $D$5. So if we use the name in a formula and then fill the formula, the name will continue to refer to the same cell in the filled copies of the formula. (See Figure 6-14.)

The Name Box contains a pull-down menu. (See Figure 6-15.) Just click on the downward-pointing triangle on the right of the Name Box to see the list of all the names that have been given to cells already. If you select a name in the menu the active cell will jump to the cell with that name so you can see which cells are referred to by the various names.

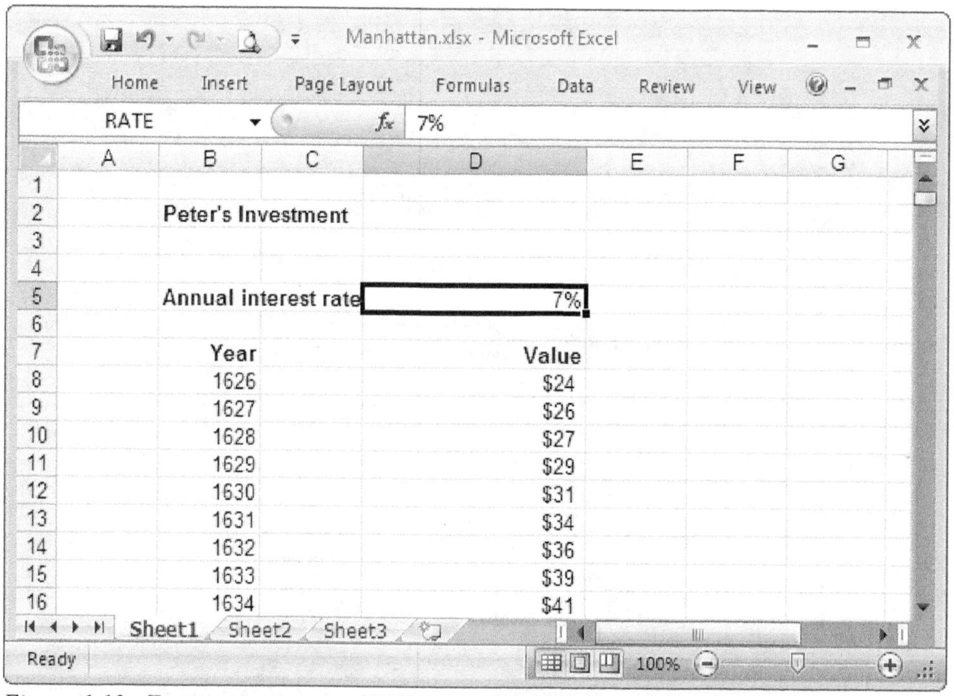

Figure 6-13. To give a name to cell D5, select D5 and then click in the Name Box at the top left of the worksheet and type in the desired name, in this case RATE.

Manhattan.xlsx - Microsoft Excel

Home Insert Page Layout Formulas Data Review View

D12 f_x =D11+D11*RATE

	A	B	C	D	E	F	G
1							
2		Peter's Investment					
3							
4							
5		Annual interest rate		7%			
6							
7		Year		Value			
8		1626		$24			
9		1627		$26			
10		1628		$27			
11		1629		$29			
12		1630		$31			
13		1631		$34			
14		1632		$36			
15		1633		$39			
16		1634		$41			

Sheet1 Sheet2 Sheet3

Ready 100%

Figure 6-14. The name RATE is treated as an absolute reference to the cell D5. The reference is unchanged after the formula is filled down.

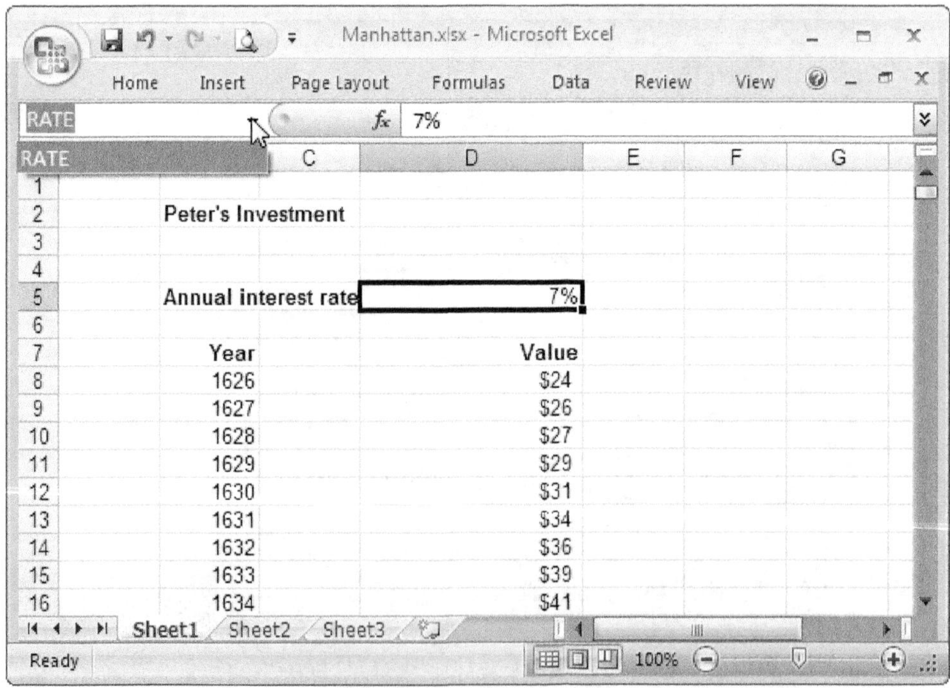

Figure 6-15. Use the Name Box pull-down menu to see the cell names that have been defined already and to find their locations.

Names also can be given to ranges of cells. For example, in the sales-by-region worksheet in the previous chapter we could have selected the range B6:G11 and given it the name SALES. Then instead of the formula =SUM(B6:G11) we could have written =SUM(SALES).

MIXED ADDRESSING

On occasion we might want the column part of the address of a cell in a formula to remain absolute and the row part of the address to be relative. Or we might want the column part of the address of a cell in a formula to be relative and the row part to be absolute. An address in a formula that is to be absolute in one part and relative in the other dimension is called a **mixed address** or **mixed reference**.

The worksheet in Figure 6-16 illustrates a double use of mixed addressing. Each cell in the range B4:M15 is the product of the number in column A for the row and the number in row 3 for the column. Thus the formula in B4 is =$A4*B$3. The body of the table is produced by filling that formula across from B4 through M4 and then filling all of those formulas down from B4:M4 to B4:M15. As a check on your understanding, what would be the resulting formula in, say, cell H8? In the first address in the formula column A is absolute while the row is relative. In the second address in the formula the column is relative while row 3 is absolute. So the formula filled into cell H8 would be =$A8*H$3.

Multiplication Table.xlsx - Microsoft Excel

Home Insert Page Layout Formulas Data Review View Add-Ins

H8 fx =$A8*H$3

	A	B	C	D	E	F	G	H	I	J	K	L	M	N
1	**Multiplication Table**													
2														
3		**1**	**2**	**3**	**4**	**5**	**6**	**7**	**8**	**9**	**10**	**11**	**12**	
4	**1**	1	2	3	4	5	6	7	8	9	10	11	12	
5	**2**	2	4	6	8	10	12	14	16	18	20	22	24	
6	**3**	3	6	9	12	15	18	21	24	27	30	33	36	
7	**4**	4	8	12	16	20	24	28	32	36	40	44	48	
8	**5**	5	10	15	20	25	30	35	40	45	50	55	60	
9	**6**	6	12	18	24	30	36	42	48	54	60	66	72	
10	**7**	7	14	21	28	35	42	49	56	63	70	77	84	
11	**8**	8	16	24	32	40	48	56	64	72	80	88	96	
12	**9**	9	18	27	36	45	54	63	72	81	90	99	108	
13	**10**	10	20	30	40	50	60	70	80	90	100	110	120	
14	**11**	11	22	33	44	55	66	77	88	99	110	121	132	
15	**12**	12	24	36	48	60	72	84	96	108	120	132	144	
16														

Sheet1 Sheet2 Sheet3

Ready 100%

Figure 6-16. A simple worksheet that uses mixed addressing.

PANES

Often in Excel we work with large worksheets with row headings and column headings, like the Multiplication Table worksheet in Figure 6-16, but with many more columns and rows. Sometimes we would like to be able to freeze the row headings and column headings in place and scroll through the rest of the table in the worksheet. We could do this with the Horizontal and Vertical Split Bars discussed earlier in the chapter. An alternative approach is to use Panes.

With the expanded Multiplication Table worksheet shown in Figure 6-17, we click on cell O23, as we would like to freeze all the rows showing above O23 and the columns showing to the left of O23. In the View tab we select Freeze Panes.

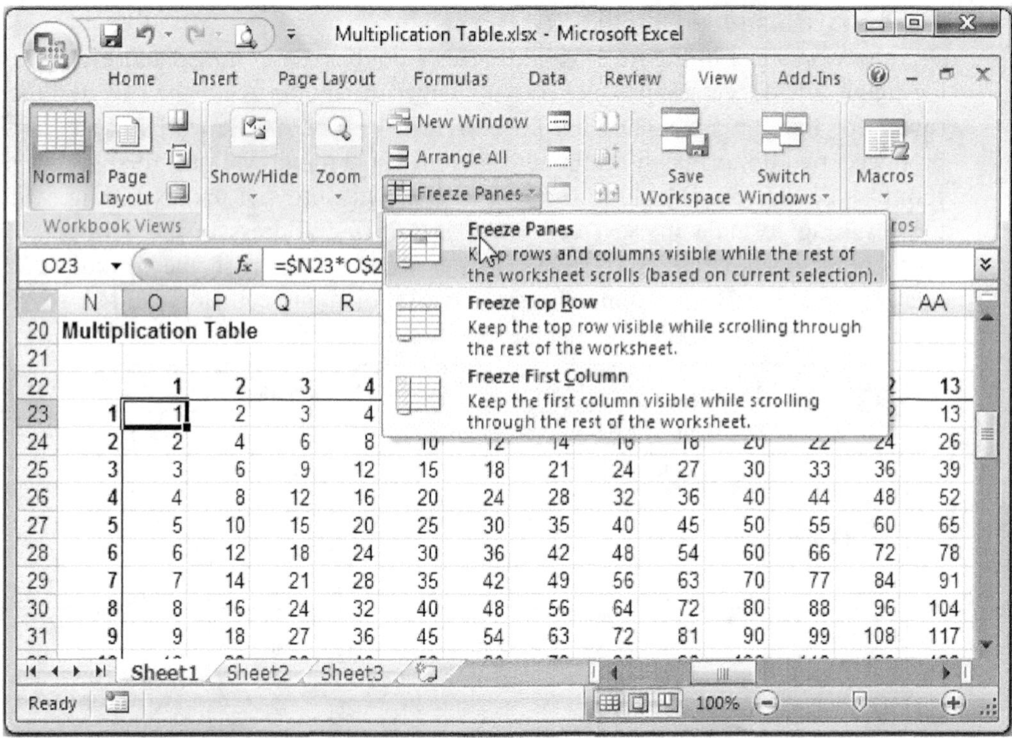

Figure 6-17. Freezing the top three rows and leftmost column so they always are visible.

Now, when we scroll, rows 20 through 22 and column N always remain visible, as in Figure 6-18. To return the display to normal, select Unfreeze Panes, as in Figure 6-19.

Note that only the top rows displayed and leftmost columns displayed can be frozen. Once you Freeze Panes, the Split Bars vanish. You cannot use the Split Bars and Freeze Panes at the same time. Which you employ is a matter of personal preference. Both techniques commonly are used.

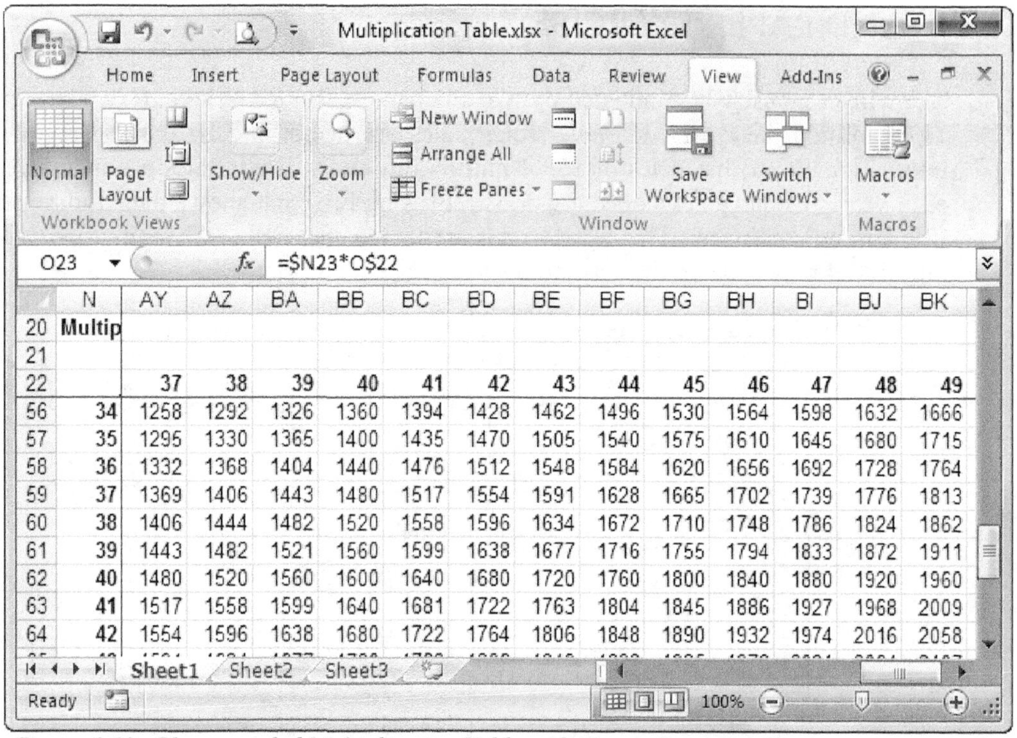

Figure 6-18. The expanded Multiplication Table with Freeze Panes in effect.

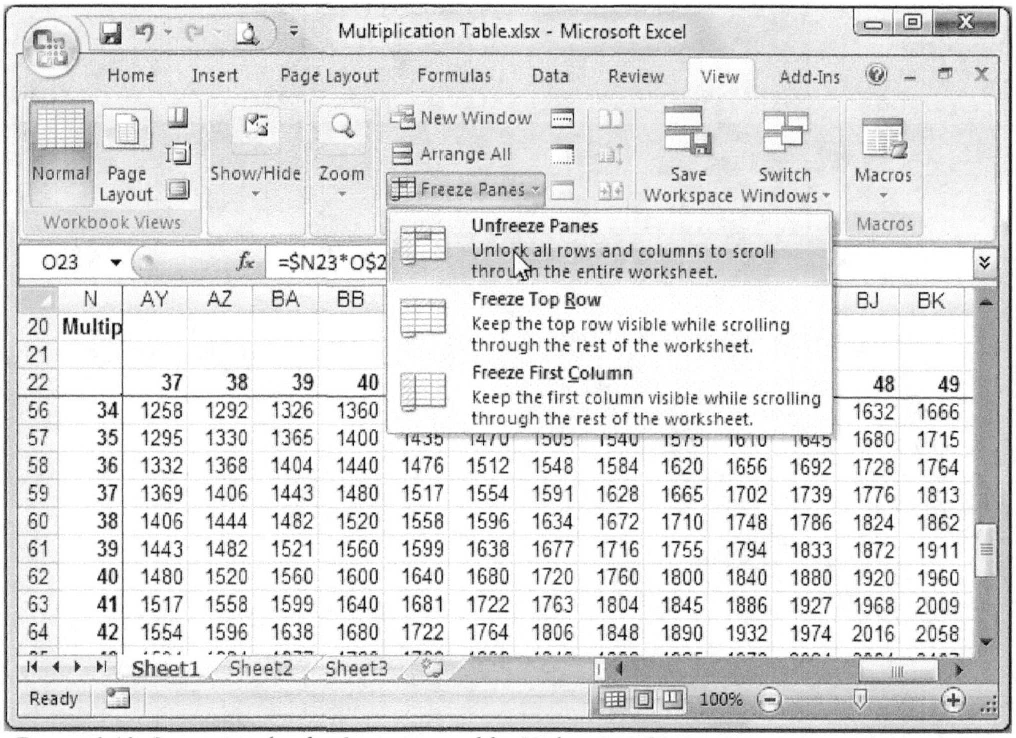

Figure 6-19. Returning the display to normal by Unfreezing the Panes.

PENCIL AND PAPER EXERCISE

6-1. The widget industry is dominated by two companies. United Widget (UW) has total sales of $87.2 million this year. However, their sales are decreasing by 0.8% per year. Widgets International (WI) has sales of $53.4 million this year. Their sales are increasing by 3.2% each year. We have developed a worksheet (using Fill) that shows their future performance if this trend continues. The growth rates are in separate cells. Changing one of the growth rates in C4 or D4 causes the predictions to change appropriately.

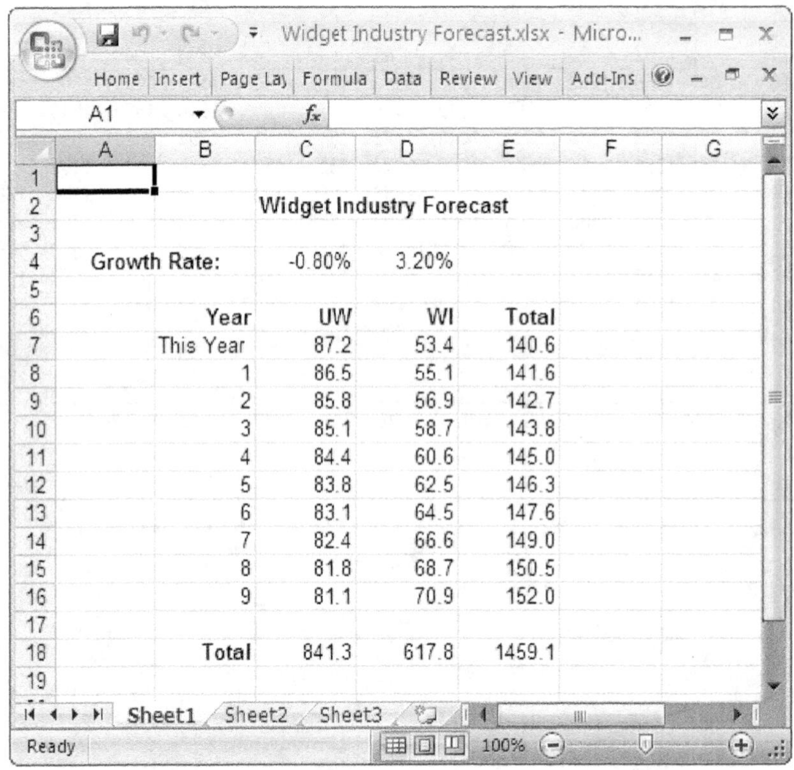

Widget Industry Forecast.xlsx

	A	B	C	D	E
1					
2			Widget Industry Forecast		
3					
4	Growth Rate:		-0.80%	3.20%	
5					
6		Year	UW	WI	Total
7		This Year	87.2	53.4	140.6
8		1	86.5	55.1	141.6
9		2	85.8	56.9	142.7
10		3	85.1	58.7	143.8
11		4	84.4	60.6	145.0
12		5	83.8	62.5	146.3
13		6	83.1	64.5	147.6
14		7	82.4	66.6	149.0
15		8	81.8	68.7	150.5
16		9	81.1	70.9	152.0
17					
18		Total	841.3	617.8	1459.1
19					

What is the formula in each of the following cells?

(a) B12
(b) C12
(c) D12
(d) E12
(e) C18
(f) D18
(g) E18

COMPUTER EXERCISES

6-2. There are eight students in your math class. They all took a quiz. Enter the eight names in one column and eight (different) scores in an adjoining column. At the bottom of the column calculate the class average. Now add a new column that calculates the points above or below the class average for each student. Use the Fill operation. Change one of the scores. Do the class average and all of the points above or below change accordingly?

6-3. The major regions of the earth and their areas in millions of square miles are shown below.

Pacific Ocean	64	Asia	17
Atlantic Ocean	33	Africa	12
Indian Ocean	28	North America	9
Arctic Ocean	5	South America	7
other oceans	9	Antarctica	5
		Europe	4
		Australia	3
		other land	1

(a) Enter this data into a worksheet. Add well-labeled cells for the total area covered by the oceans, the total area covered by land, and the total area of the earth. Name these cells.

(b) Add a column that shows the percentage of the earth covered by each of the 13 regions listed. Use the Fill operation.

(c) Add a column that shows the percentage of the total area covered by ocean that each of the ocean regions occupies. Use the Fill operation.

(d) Add a column that shows the percentage of the total area covered by land that each of the continents occupies. Use the Fill operation.

6-4. You are planning to deposit a fixed amount at the beginning of each year in a bank account for 20 years. Assume that you will earn a constant interest rate on your money. Design and implement a worksheet that will show you how much you will have accumulated at the end of each of the 20 years. You should have separate, well-labeled cells for the amount of your annual deposit and for the interest rate. If you change either of these cells, all the accumulations should change automatically.

Try your worksheet on

(a) a deposit of $5,000 per year and an interest rate of 5% per year,

(b) a deposit of $5,000 per year and an interest rate of 10% per year,

(c) a deposit of $10,000 per year and an interest rate of 5% per year, and

(d) a deposit of $10,000 per year and an interest rate of 10% per year.

(e) How much do you need to deposit each year to have exactly $1,000,000 in 20 years assuming that you earn 8% interest per year? Use Goal Seek.

(f) What annual interest rate would you need to obtain in order to accumulate $1,000,000 at the end of 20 years if you deposit $10,000 per year? Use Goal Seek.

6-5. The cost of a college education has been rising rapidly, as I am sure you are aware. You would like to estimate what it will cost you to put your children through college. First we will need to gather some data and make some assumptions. Find out the current cost of attending your favorite college or university in terms of (1) tuition and (2) all other expenses. If you do not have any children now, assume that your first child will be born five years from now and your second child will be born three years later. Assume that your children will enter college at age 18, that they will attend for four years each, and then graduate with high honors. (Of course they will be model students.) Further we will assume that there will be a single annual rate of increase over the years for tuition and other expenses.

Your worksheet will have a separate section at the top for parameters and data that might be changed. In particular, there should be well-labeled cells for current tuition, current other expenses, and rate of increase. The body of the worksheet should have four columns: year, tuition, other expenses, and total expenses. The values that appear in these columns will depend in part on the values in the input section of the worksheet. At the bottom (or top) of the worksheet there should be a well-labeled output cell that gives the total projected cost of sending your two children to college.

Try your worksheet with an annual rate of increase of 6%. Now change the annual rate of increase to 9%. Do all of the appropriate numbers change? Don't worry. You will have a terrific job. The money you spend on college for your children will be small change.

6-6. The country of Palladia has 3,750,000 people. The birth rate is 1.3%. That is, each year the number of babies born is equal to 1.3% of the people in the country at the beginning of the year. The death rate is 0.7%. Palladia is a wealthy paradise so lots of people are trying to enter from outside. The Minister of Immigration is proposing that 150,000 people be allowed to immigrate into the country each year.

(a) Create a worksheet for the Minister that predicts the population of Palladia for each of the next 10 years. There should be an input area at the top of your worksheet with cells for: starting population, annual birth rate, annual death rate, and annual immigration. Use the numbers above. There should be one row for each year. You can use as many columns as you would like.

(b) Suppose the birth rate is 1.1%, the death rate is 0.9%, and the annual immigration is 100,000.

(c) Suppose the birth rate is 1.0% and the death rate is 0.7%. The Prime Minister would like to see close to 5,000,000 people in the country at the end of 10 years. At what number should the annual immigration quota be set? Use Goal Seek to find a quota that results in a population that is 5,000,000 in 10 years.

6-7. Internet Shopping, Inc. has ambitious plans. This week they have 100,000 visitors to their website. Of their visitors, 2% place orders. These orders average $24.00 each. Thus they are taking orders for $48,000 this week (week 0).

For the next two years they plan to increase the visitors by 3% per week. They expect the percent of visitors who place orders to stay the same. They expect the average amount ordered to increase by $0.15 per week.

Create a worksheet to predict their growth over the next two years. You should have a separate input area with the two growth figures. You should have a row for each week. You should have columns for the week number (0 to 104), the number of visitors, number of shoppers, average amount ordered, and total ordered for each week. Changing either of the numbers in the input area should be reflected in changes in your worksheet.

6-8. Paul and Maria are married. Together they earn a salary of $85,000 per year. Their plan is to save enough money to retire to Bali for the rest of their lives. They believe that if they save $500,000 they should be set for life. Their expenses this year totaled $78,000, including taxes, living expenses, and everything else. They have decided to put the rest in a tax-free mutual fund to save up for their retirement.

Now Paul and Maria would like to do some projections to see when they can retire. They estimate that their salaries should go up by 8% per year. They hope to hold their expenses to an increase of 3% per year. Whatever is left at the end of each year, they will put into the account. They figure they should be able to earn interest of 4% per year on the money in the account, which will be accumulated in the mutual fund.

Your job is to set up a financial planning worksheet for Paul and Maria. You should have a separate input area with well-labeled cells for: current salary, current expenses, annual percentage increase for salary, annual percentage increase for expenses, and annual percentage interest rate earned in the mutual fund. Changing any of these numbers should result in changes throughout the worksheet.

The body of the worksheet should be the forecast for the next 25 years. Each row would represent a separate year. There should be separate columns for: Year, Salary, Expenses, Mutual Fund Interest Earned, Deposit in Mutual Fund, and Mutual Fund End-of-Year

Balance. All funds should accumulate in the mutual fund. You may assume that the deposit in the mutual fund from the difference between salary and expenses occurs at the end of the year.

Please try your worksheet three times: (1) assume the above numbers, (2) assume salary increases by 5% each year while expenses increase at 5% each year and they earn 5% in their mutual fund, and (3) one showing the percentage increase (or decrease) for expenses required if Paul and Maria wish to retire in only 10 years given that their salaries increase by 10% per year and they earn 6% per year in their mutual fund. This latter case can be solved by Goal Seek. For each of these last two cases you should need to change only cells in the input area.

6-9. Compsys is a start-up computer company. This quarter they expect Sales of $550,000. They expect their Sales to grow at a rate of 9% per quarter. Their Cost of Goods Sold is running at 34% of Sales and is expected to stay at that rate. Their Selling Costs are 12% of Sales and are expected to stay at that rate. Their General and Administrative Costs (including Research and Development) are $420,000 this quarter and are scheduled to rise at 2% per quarter.

(a) Design and implement a worksheet to make a 20 quarter income statement projection for Compsys. You should have a separate input area with well-labeled separate cells for each of the numbers above. You should have a separate row for each item in the income statement and a separate column for each quarter. The final row should be for Earnings Before Taxes. Use the Fill operation wherever possible.

In the initial quarters, Compsys should show operating losses (negative Earnings Before Taxes). Under the assumptions stated above, what is the first quarter in which Compsys shows an operating profit (positive Earnings Before Taxes)?

(b) Suppose Sales grow at 12% per quarter. Now in what quarter would Compsys first show an operating profit?

(c) Suppose Sales grow at 9% per quarter and General and Administrative Costs grow at 6% per quarter and Selling Costs are 15% of sales. Now in what quarter will Compsys first show an operating profit?

6-10. The Fibonacci series is named after Leonardo Fibonacci, an Italian mathematician of the thirteenth century. The Fibonacci series is an infinite series of numbers 0, 1, 1, 2, 3, 5, 8, 13, ... The first two numbers in the series are 0 and 1. Subsequent numbers are formed by adding the two previous numbers in the series. The Fibonacci series appears in many unexpected places. Indeed, there is a regularly published journal that is devoted to applications of the Fibonacci series.

What proportioned rectangle is the most aesthetically pleasing? What is the ratio of height to width that people most prefer in a rectangle? Since the Renaissance it has been claimed that The Golden Ratio is the most aesthetically pleasing ratio for a rectangle. The Golden Ratio has been shown to appear often in Western art. The Golden Ratio usually is defined as the proportion that results from dividing a line in two sections such that the ratio of the length of the smaller section to the larger section is the same as the ratio of the length of the larger section to the length of the line as a whole. Another way of computing the Golden Ratio is to take the ratio of successive terms of the Fibonacci series. Thus 0/1, 1/1, 1/2, 2/3, 3/5, 5/8, ... form closer and closer approximations of the Golden Ratio. (So, a 3 x 5 card or a 5 x 8 piece of paper should seem to be aesthetically pleasing rectangles.)

Create a worksheet with three well-labeled columns. The first column should contain the numbers 0, 1, 2, 3, 4, through 20. The second column should contain the successive terms of the Fibonacci series. The third column should contain the successive approximations to the Golden Ratio, displayed as decimal numbers between 0 and 1. Use the Fill operation for all three columns.

6-11. Scientists at the Research Institute for Robotics have created a new type of robot that reproduces itself. The new robot takes two weeks to gather materials and then builds one new robot (exactly like itself) each week for three weeks. The first new robot is activated at the end of week 3, the second new robot is activated at the end of week 4, and the third new robot at the end of week 5. As soon as it is created, each new robot goes through the same cycle of gathering materials for two weeks and then creating three new robots, one per week. And so on for each of the new robots. At the end of the first five weeks of its existence each new robot ceases building new robots but retires and "lives" forever. The scientists plan to build only one robot with their own hands and then set it in motion. Create a worksheet that will tell you how many robots there will be in two years.

6-12. If you have been outside on a cold, windy day, you know that the wind makes it seem colder than it really is. After an extensive study (see Exercise 2-13) the National Weather Service has derived the following wind chill formula:

$$W = 35.74 + 0.6215\,T - 35.75\,(V^{0.16}) + 0.4275\,T\,(V^{0.16})$$

where W is the wind chill adjusted temperature, T is the air temperature in Fahrenheit, and V is the wind velocity in miles per hour.

Create a Wind Chill table that has columns for each temperature from 30 degrees down to -25 degrees in -5 degree increments and rows for wind velocity from 5 mph to 60 mph in 5 mph increments. These values should appear across the top (30, 25, 20, ... -25) and down the left column (5, 10, 15, ... 60) of your table. The body of the table should be the resulting wind chill adjusted temperatures according to the formula. The body of the table should use a single formula that is entered in the cell in the top left corner of the body of the table and then filled across and down.

6-13. To start her new business your aunt plans to take out a loan and pay it back in five annual installments of $50,000. These payments will be made at the end of each of the first five years of operation. She anticipates $180,000 in revenues for the first year and that revenues will grow at 12% per year. She estimates that her (non-loan) expenses for the first year will be $100,000 and will grow at 6% per year.

Design a worksheet that shows her revenues, expenses, loan payments, and pretax income during the first eight years of operation. There should be a separate input area for annual loan payment, initial revenues, initial expenses, annual growth rate for revenues, and annual growth rate for expenses. Changes in any of these values should result in appropriate changes in your worksheet.

(a) Try your worksheet with the above numbers.

(b) Try your worksheet with an annual loan payment of $25,000, initial revenues of $100,000, initial expenses of $50,000, annual growth in revenues of 8%, and annual growth in expenses of 5%.

6-14. Averosas are a new breed of small, furry animal that resemble guinea pigs. They are becoming all the rage as pets. You have decided to earn some extra money by raising averosas in your room. For Christmas you ask Santa Claus to help you out. You must have been good this year because sure enough on Christmas morning under the Christmas tree there is a one-month-old male averosa and a one-month-old female averosa in a cage.

Averosas are quite prolific, and predictably so. They have their first litter at six months of age. Every three months from then on, each female has a litter of on average four baby averosas (assume two males and two females). Of course, these babies will go through the same breeding cycle. At the end of each quarter (three months) you plan to sell all the averosas that have reached two years of age to the local pet stores. This is how you will make your fortune. You won't have any expenses because your roommate works in a restaurant and you figure your roommate can bring home the leftovers from the salad bar to feed the animals. This sounds like a great scheme but your roommate would like to know (1) how many averosas will be born in your room each quarter and, more important, (2) how many averosas will be living in the room each quarter! You would like to know (3) how many averosas you'll be able to sell at the end of each quarter so you can plan what to do with all the money you'll earn. Incidentally, your roommate will be (somewhat) relieved to learn that averosas don't smell too bad if their cages are cleaned often.

Set up an Excel worksheet to answer these three questions. Assume you will have the averosa colony for the next five years. Of course you will use the Fill operation wherever possible. Use several columns. Label all columns clearly. Assume the quarter ends at January 1, April 1, July 1, and October 1. Assuming everything goes as planned, what is the total number of averosas you will have owned during the five years? What is the maximum number of averosas that will be in your room at any one time? How long will it be before your roommate leaves?

CHAPTER 7

COMMON OPERATIONS

OBJECTIVES

In this chapter you will learn how to:

- Have Excel validate inputs
- Protect cells from being changed
- Conditionally format cells
- Create text boxes
- Add shapes, clip art, pictures, and SmartArt

In this chapter we look at some common operations in Excel.

VALIDATING INPUTS

In worksheets we often want the values of cells to be limited, for example to years between 2000 and 2020 or to numbers between -0.05 and +0.35 or to names in a certain list. Excel provides a very useful Data Validation tool in the Data tab. (See Figure 7-1.)

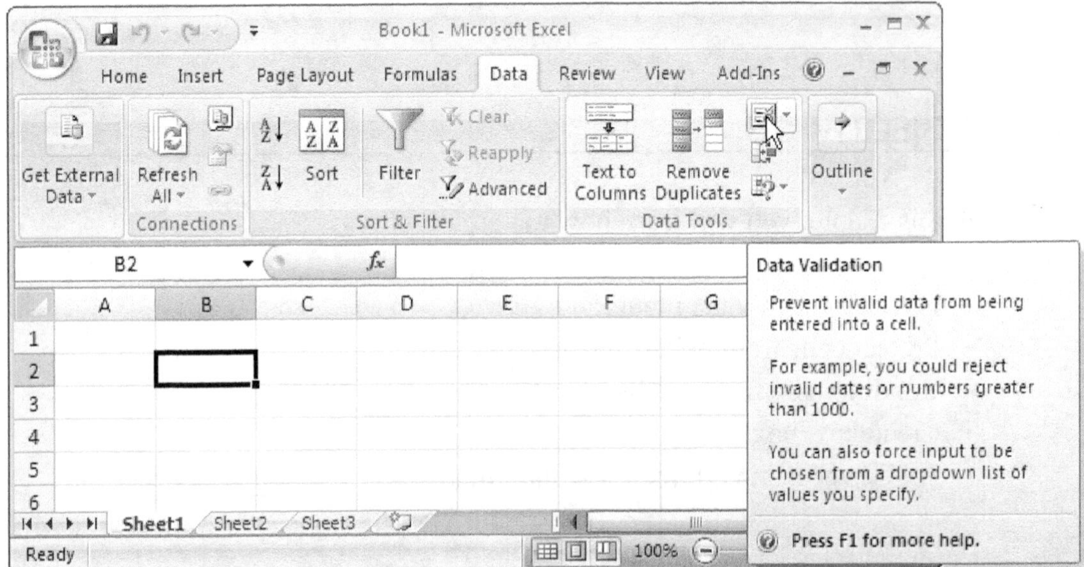

Figure 7-1. Starting Data Validation for B2.

Clicking on the Data Validation tool brings up the Data Validation window. As you can see in Figure 7-2, the Data Validation window allows you to select the type of input that should be allowed for the cell, the allowable range of possible inputs, an input message that will appear when the cell is selected, and an error message that will appear if the user enters an invalid value. After entering in the type of input allowed and the allowable range, we enter suitable text in the Input Message tab and the Error Alert tab.

In Figure 7-3, the user has ignored the input message ("Starting Year: Please enter a year between 2000 and 2020.") that appeared when the cell was selected and thus is confronted with the official looking error message.

It also is possible to specify a list of items that are allowed to appear in the cell, as in Figure 7-4. Conveniently these items appear in a dropdown menu when the cell is selected, as in Figure 7-5. Note that the user still can type an entry into the cell. But if it is not one in the list specified, the Error Alert appears. Note also that the allowable items can be taken from the worksheet itself. In this case the Source in the Settings tab of the Data Validation window in Figure 7-4 would be the address of the range of cells that contain the allowable entries.

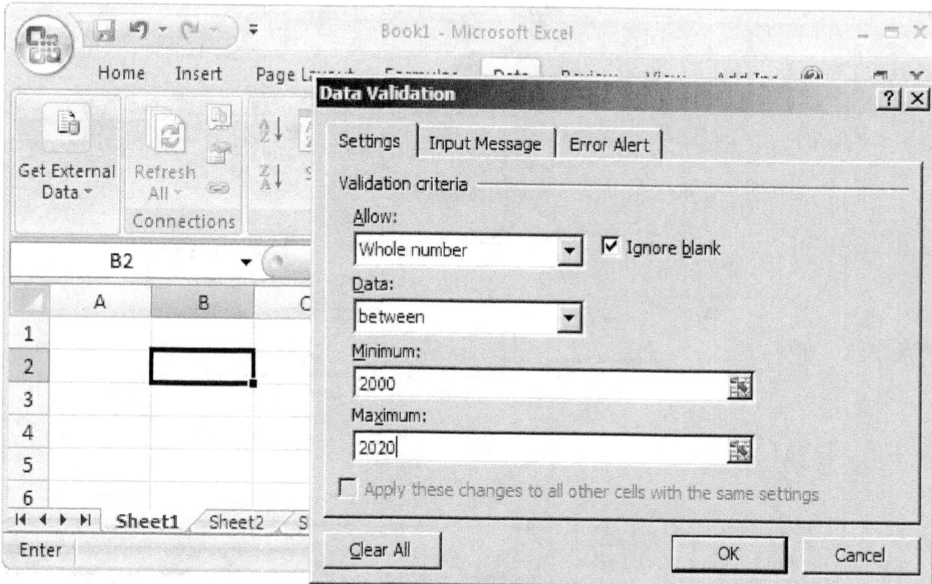

Figure 7-2. The Data Validation entry window. Subsequent entries are made in the Input Message tab and Error Alert tab.

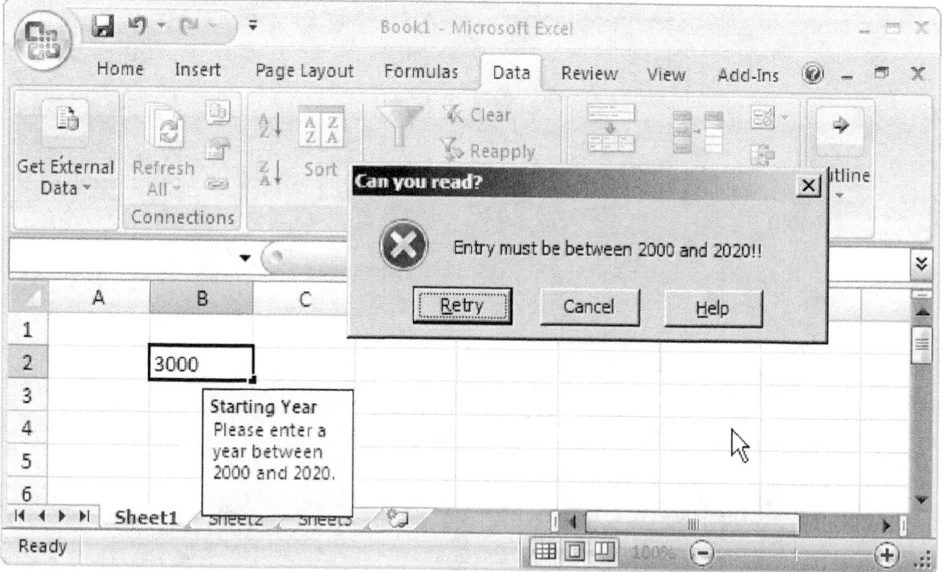

Figure 7-3. The user tries to enter an illegal value into the cell. The message below the cell is from the Input Message tab and appears when the cell is selected. The error message is specified in the Error Alert tab and appears if the validation criteria are not met.

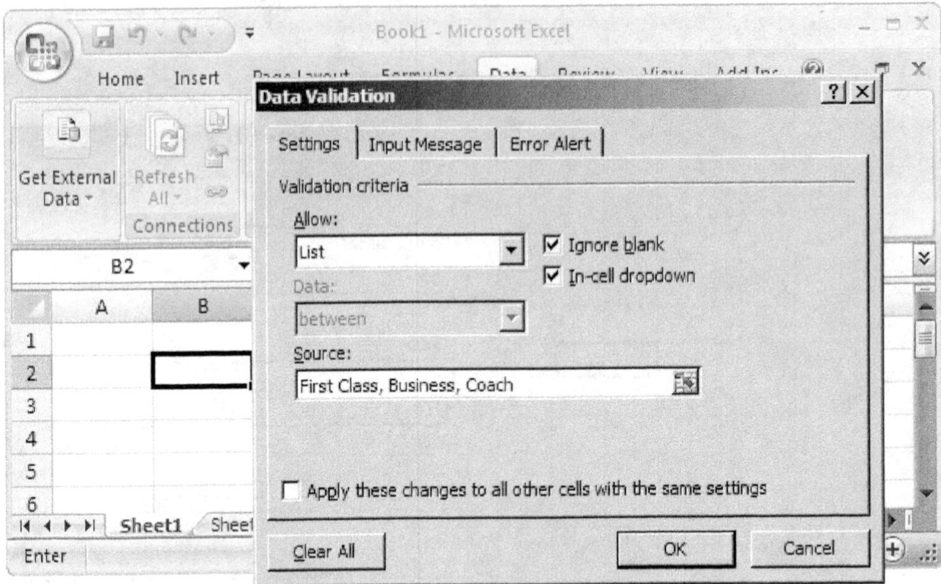

Figure 7-4. Specifying a list of items that can appear in the cell.

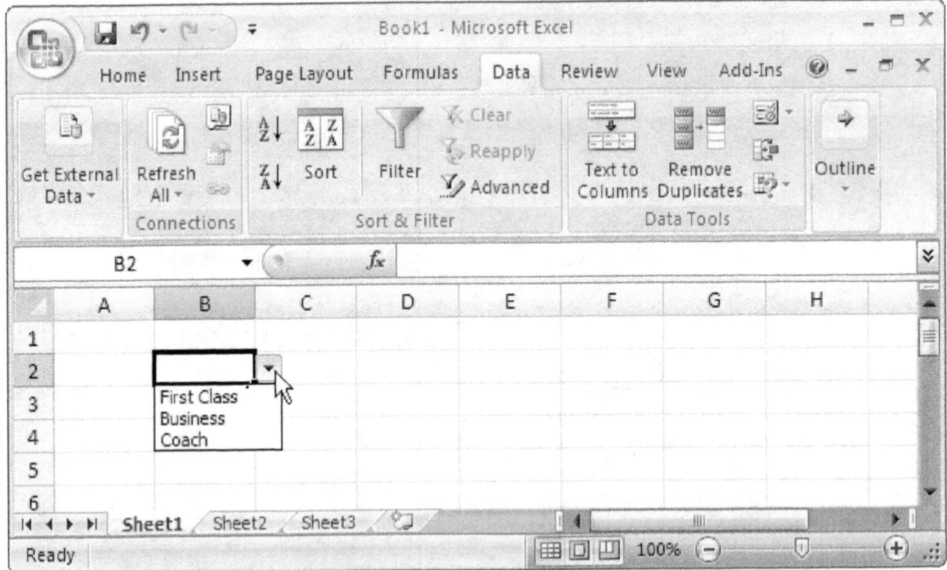

Figure 7-5. A dropdown menu appears when the cell is selected.

CELL PROTECTION

Cell protection is an important capability of Excel that should be used with almost all worksheets. Cell protection prevents the user from inadvertently changing or erasing cells in a worksheet. There are two steps to protecting cells in a worksheet. First we specify which cells should *not* be protected. Then we turn on the protection for the worksheet.

The first step is to inform Excel which cells we wish to be able to change, which cells should be **unlocked**. For example, in the Price Quote worksheet shown in Figure 2-1 or in Chapter 3, only cells D6:D8 should be left unlocked because these are the only cells we wish the user to be able to change.

To cause the cells D6:D8 to be unlocked, we select D6:D8 by dragging across them and then select the Font button in the Font group of the Home tab. We click on the Protection tab and click to *clear* the Locked box in the dialog window, and obtain the situation in Figure 7-6. Thus, cells D6:D8 will be the only cells in the worksheet that are *not* locked.

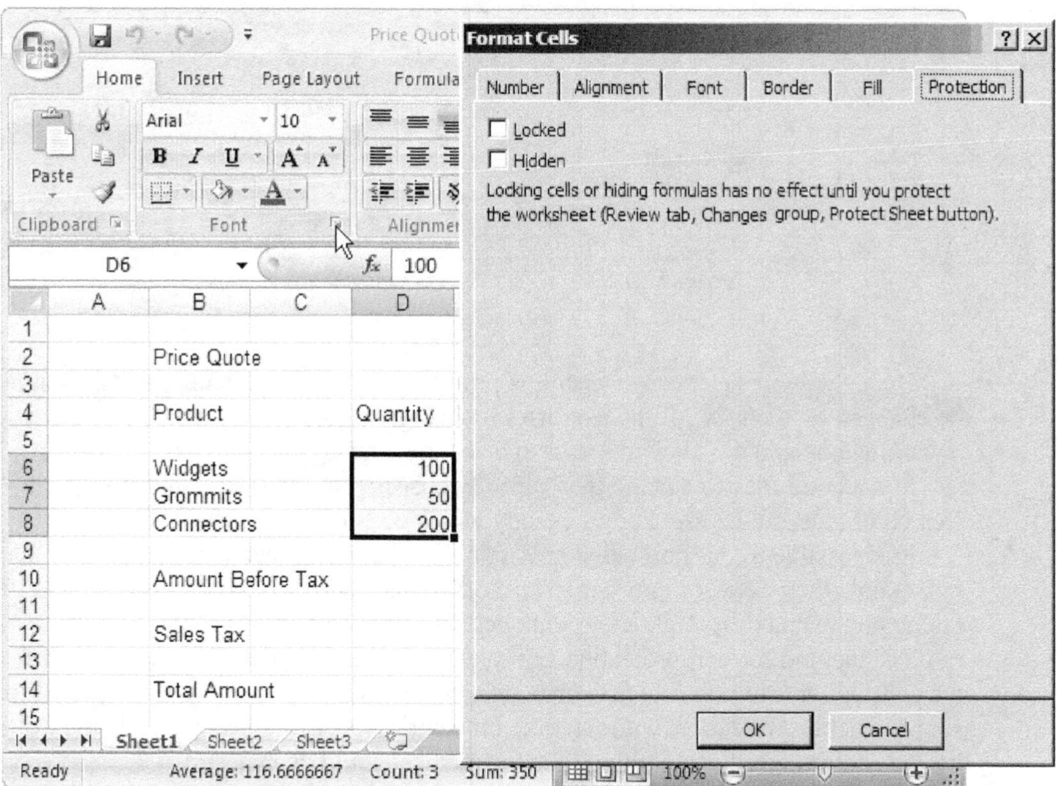

Figure 7-6. The first step is to click off Locked for the cells we want the user to be able to change. The mouse pointer indicates the button to click to obtain the Format Cells window.

The second step in the process is to enable (turn on) the cell protection for the worksheet. This is accomplished by clicking Protect Sheet or Protect Workbook in the Changes group of the Review tab, as shown in Figure 7-7.

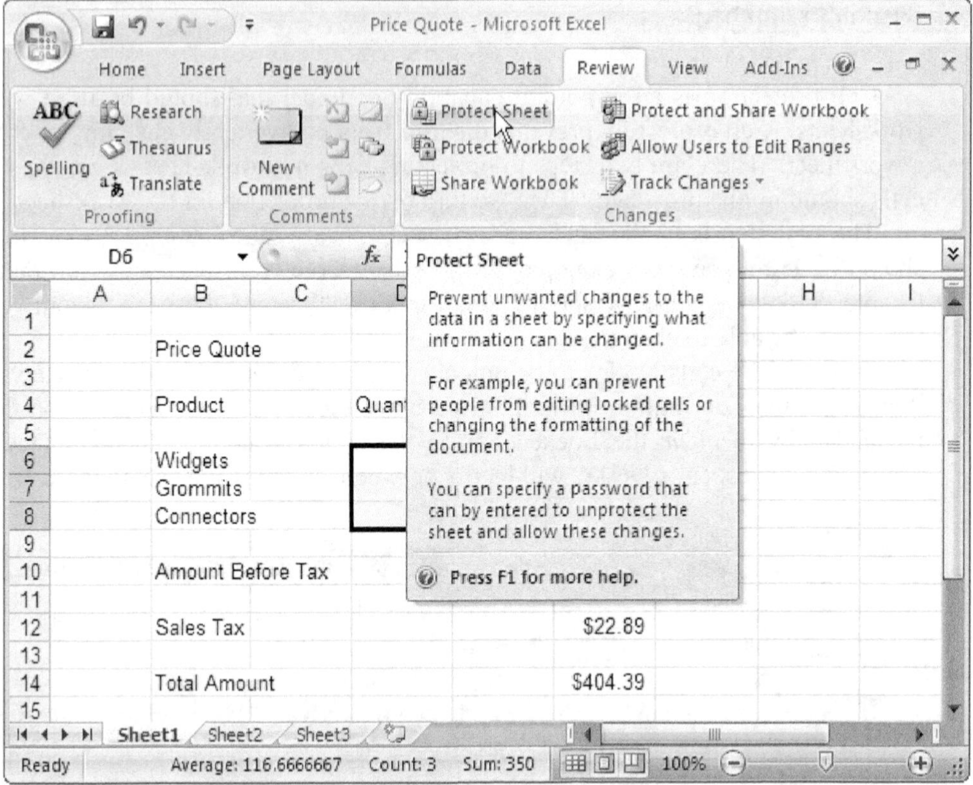

Figure 7-7. The second step is to protect the worksheet or workbook.

Once the worksheet or workbook is protected then only the cells that are not locked can be changed by the user. If the user tries to change one of the locked cells Excel will display a warning box and not allow the user to make the change.

It is a good idea to change the color of cells that are unlocked, for example to make the font color blue, so the user knows exactly which cells can be changed.

It is possible to put **password** protection on the worksheet or workbook, so that the user must know the password in order to turn off protection. A password can be specified in the dialog box that appears right after you click on Protect Sheet or Protect Workbook.

The method for cell protection can take time to get used to. Basically, you first unlock the cells you want to be able to change. Then you enable (turn on) the cell protection. If you simply enable protection without first unlocking specific cells, then all the cells will be locked and protected and nothing in the worksheet could be changed.

Cell protection is especially useful when a workbook you create is going to be used by naive users. Only certain cells are meant to be input cells. These cells are unlocked. The other cells contain formulas that you have worked hard on, and you don't want the users mangling them with inputs. These cells are all locked and protected.

CONDITIONAL FORMATTING

Conditional Formatting allows you to change the format of cells based on the values in the cells. For example, consider again the Real Estate worksheet from Figure 1-3. Suppose we want to conditionally format the number of bedrooms in each house. We select B5:B100. Then we click on the Styles button in the Home tab and select Conditional Formatting. In Figure 7-8 we have selected Data Bars and Blue Data Bar. A conditional "data bar" format appears in the selected cells where the width of the bar depends on the value in the cell.

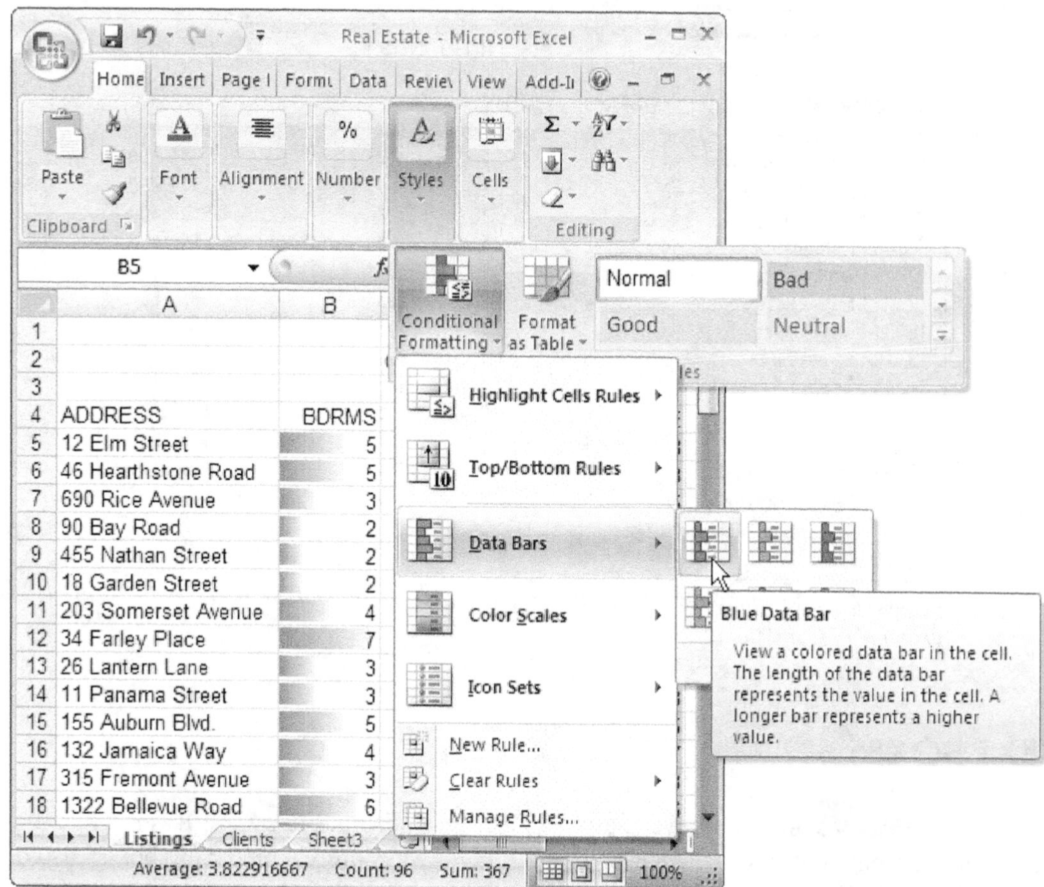

Figure 7-8. The format of each cell in B5:B100 is conditional on the value in the cell.

Alternatively, the cells could have different colors depending on their values or various icons (checks and X's and so on) could appear in the cells. For example checks could appear in the cells with more than 4 bedrooms and X's in the cells with under 3 bedrooms, as in Figure 7-9.

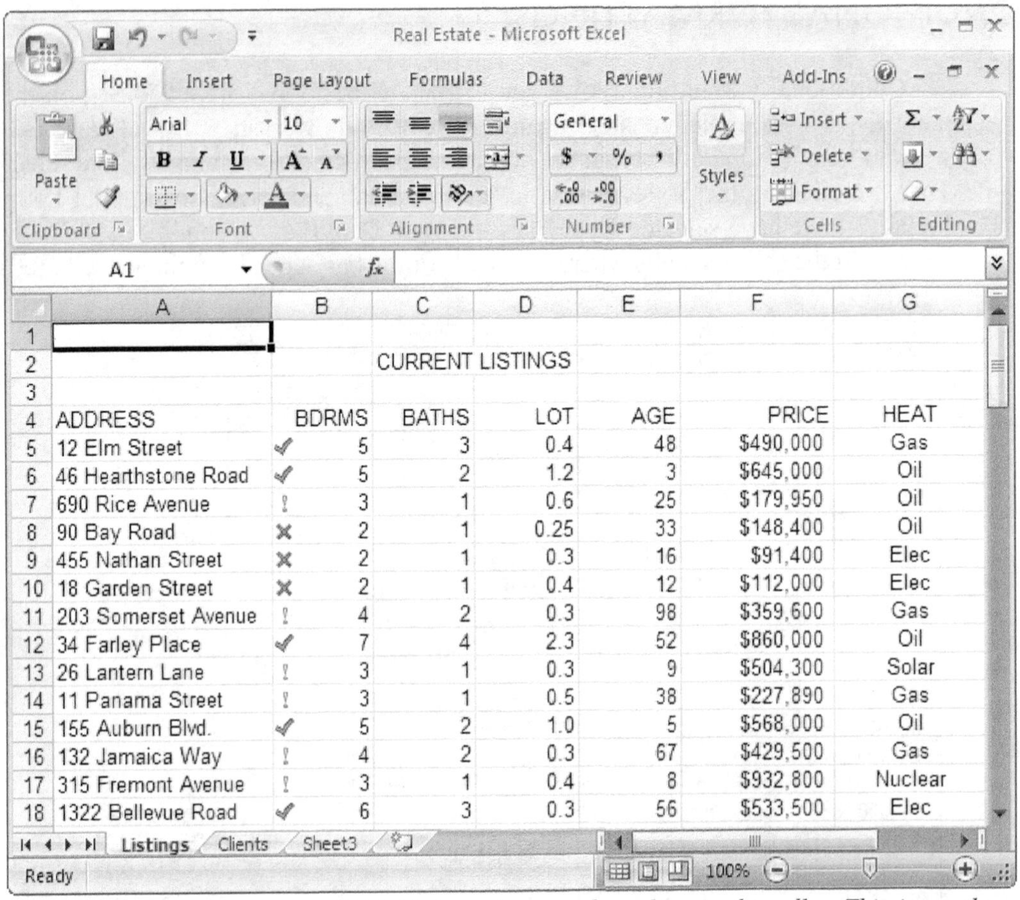

Real Estate - Microsoft Excel

	A	B	C	D	E	F	G
1							
2			CURRENT LISTINGS				
3							
4	ADDRESS	BDRMS	BATHS	LOT	AGE	PRICE	HEAT
5	12 Elm Street	✓ 5	3	0.4	48	$490,000	Gas
6	46 Hearthstone Road	✓ 5	2	1.2	3	$645,000	Oil
7	690 Rice Avenue	! 3	1	0.6	25	$179,950	Oil
8	90 Bay Road	✗ 2	1	0.25	33	$148,400	Oil
9	455 Nathan Street	✗ 2	1	0.3	16	$91,400	Elec
10	18 Garden Street	✗ 2	1	0.4	12	$112,000	Elec
11	203 Somerset Avenue	! 4	2	0.3	98	$359,600	Gas
12	34 Farley Place	✓ 7	4	2.3	52	$860,000	Oil
13	26 Lantern Lane	! 3	1	0.3	9	$504,300	Solar
14	11 Panama Street	! 3	1	0.5	38	$227,890	Gas
15	155 Auburn Blvd.	✓ 5	2	1.0	5	$568,000	Oil
16	132 Jamaica Way	! 4	2	0.3	67	$429,500	Gas
17	315 Fremont Avenue	! 3	1	0.4	8	$932,800	Nuclear
18	1322 Bellevue Road	✓ 6	3	0.3	56	$533,500	Elec

Figure 7-9. Icons appear in B5:B100 depending on the values in the cells. This is another example of Conditional Formatting.

TEXT BOXES

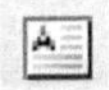

Text boxes float above the worksheet in a separate **drawing layer**. Text boxes differ from Comments (see Chapter 5) in that they always are visible. Text boxes also differ from borders (Chapter 3) that can be added around cells in a worksheet. Text boxes are independent of cells.

A text box is added to a worksheet by clicking on the Text Box button in the Text group of the Insert tab and then by dragging the mouse pointer across the area of the worksheet where you would like the text box to appear initially. (The text box later can be moved anywhere.) After the blank text box appears you can click inside it and start typing.

Once you have added and selected a text box, a new Drawing Tools tab appears above the Format tab on top of the window. (See Figure 7-10.) The Drawing Tools Format tab allows a staggering variety of shapes, colors, fills, and effects, as can be seen in Figure 7-11.

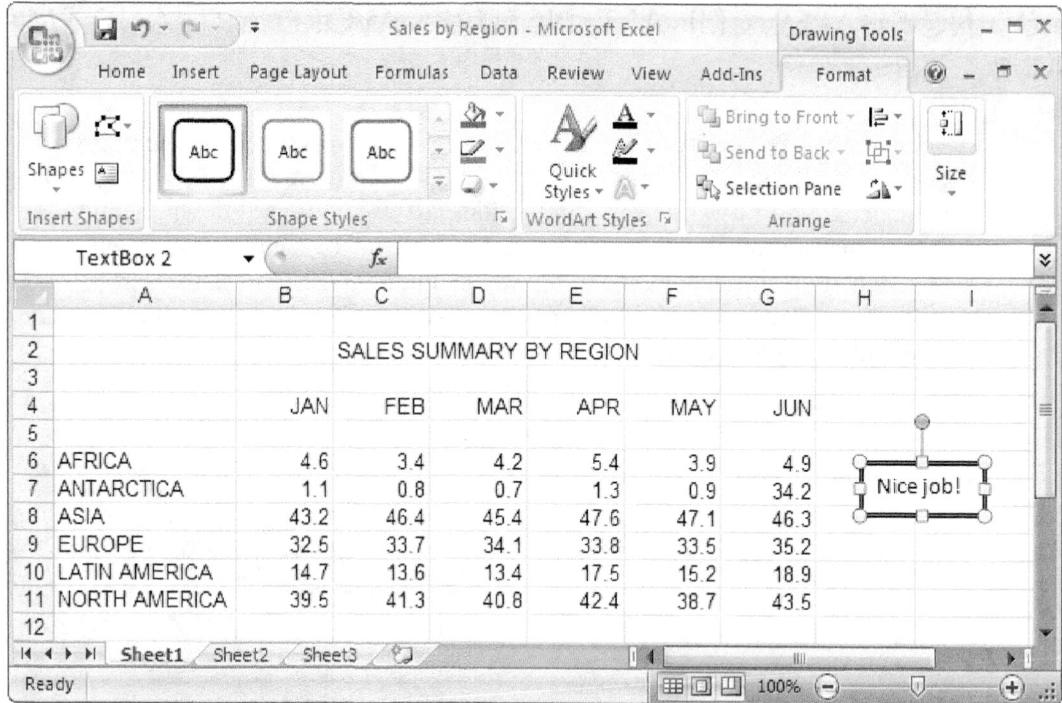

Figure 7-10. When a text box is entered and selected the Drawing Tools tab appears.

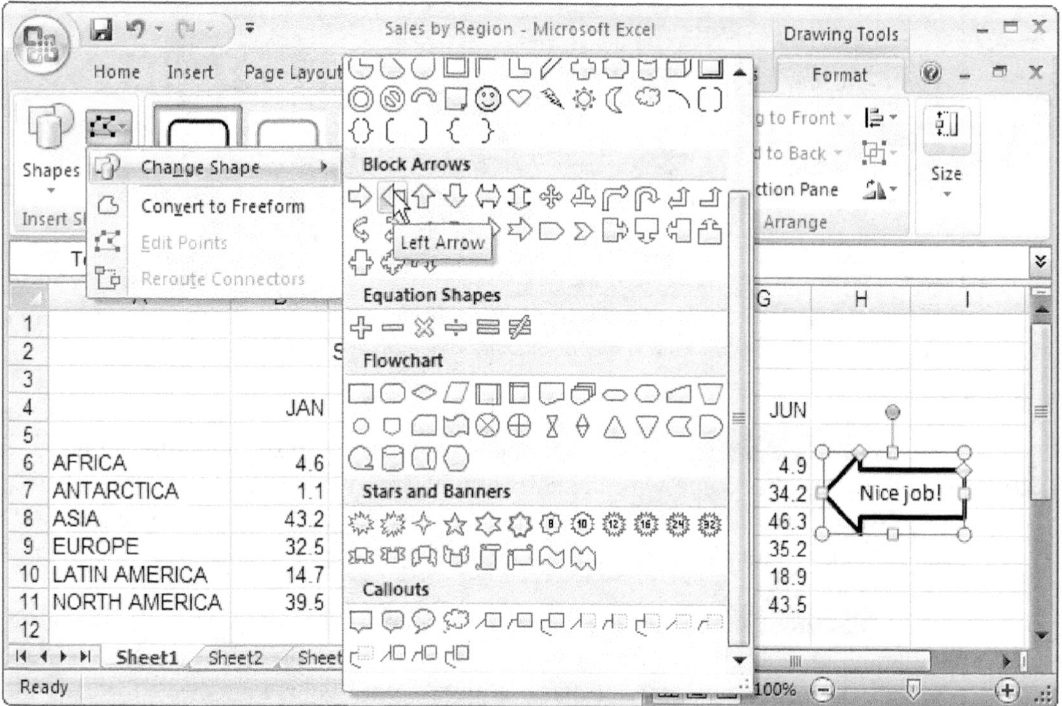

Figure 7-11. The Drawing Tools Format tab allows for a phenomenal variety of shapes and styles.

ADDING SHAPES, CLIP ART, PICTURES, WORD ART, AND SMART ART

Shapes can be added to the drawing layer of a worksheet by clicking on the **Shapes** button in the Illustrations group of the Insert tab. In Figure 7-12 a Down Ribbon shape has been added. No Fill was selected in the **Shape Fill** button pull-down menu in the Drawing Tools Format tab; otherwise you would not be able to see the underlying cell. A smiley face was added from the Shapes menu shown in Figure 7-12, above the scroll. Note that by default the smiley face and all other shapes have a fill color. Here the fill color is white. Hence you can't see the cells beneath the smiley face.

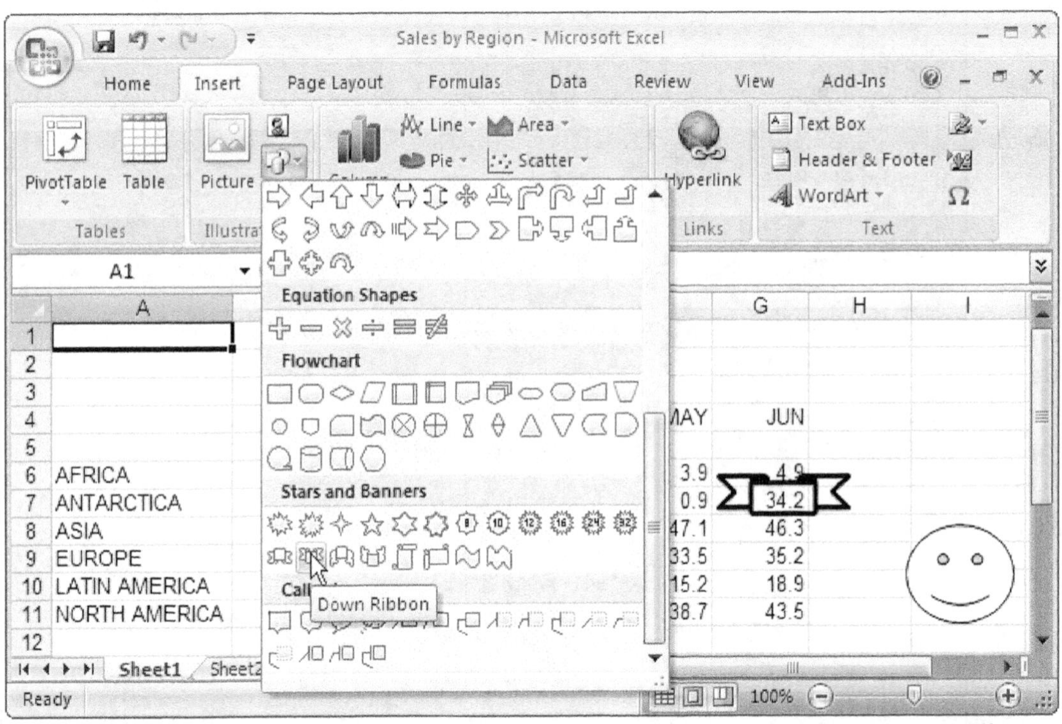

Figure 7-12. A Down Ribbon has been placed in the drawing layer over the cell in G7. No Fill was selected in the Shape Fill button menu. A smiley face also was added.

The **Clip Art** button in the Illustrations group of the Insert tab allows you to place drawings that come with the software, or are available in Microsoft's files on the web, in the drawing layer on top of the worksheet. When I searched for "book" in the Clip Art collection, the drawing at right was one of the first selections found.

The **Picture** button in the Illustrations group of the Insert tab allows you to insert a photograph or other picture from your disk onto the drawing layer on top of your worksheet. Alternatively, you can Copy and Paste a picture onto your worksheet, for example, off the web. All pictures can be selected, moved, and resized, as can all of the other drawing objects on the drawing layer.

The **WordArt button** allows us to make drawings out of words to place in the drawing layer above the worksheet. An example is given in Figure 7-13. There are a large variety of styles and formats for WordArt.

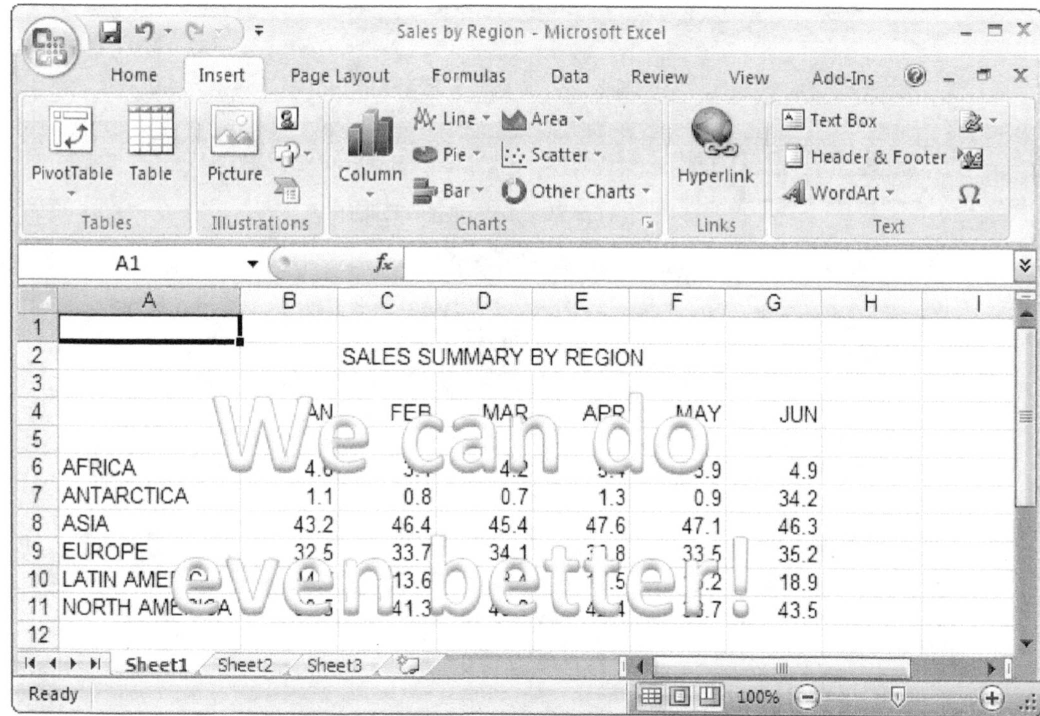

Figure 7-13. An inspiring WordArt message overlays the worksheet.

Finally, the **SmartArt** button in the Illustrations group of the Insert tab allows us to insert a customizable Smart Art graphic on the worksheet. We can select from a wide variety of SmartArt graphic templates, as shown in Figure 7-14. An example of a customized SmartArt graphic is shown in Figure 7-15.

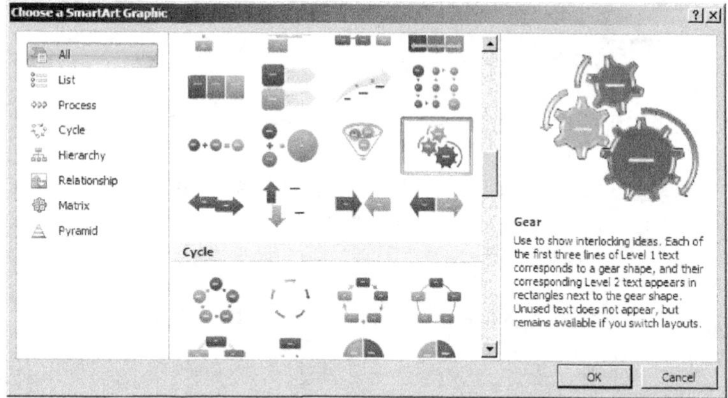

Figure 7-14. Some of the SmartArt templates available.

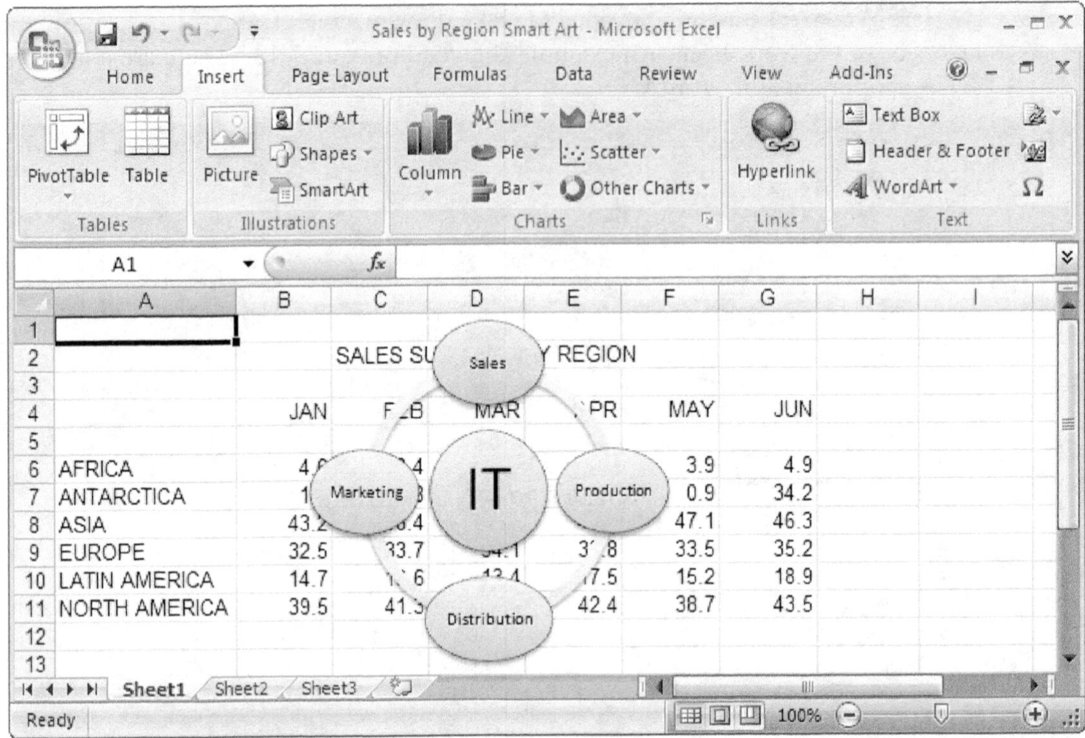

Figure 7-15. A SmartArt graphic. Any text can be entered into the circles (ellipses).

COMPUTER EXERCISE

7-1. Please enter the following worksheet.

Stock Portfolio - Microsoft Excel

	A	B	C	D	E
1					
2		Stock Portfolio			
3					
4		Stock	Shares	Price	Total
5					
6		Dell	500	$ 26.22	$ 13,110
7		IBM	100	$ 106.87	$ 10,687
8		Microsoft	500	$ 31.11	$ 15,555
9					
10		Total			$ 39,352

Be sure to align the column headings (Shares, Price, and Total) on the right sides of the cells and enter the formulas for column E for the Totals for E6, E7, E8, and E10. Format the cells as shown.

(a) The stocks were purchased for the following amounts: Dell 36.74, IBM 92.40, and Microsoft 27.86. Add a new column that lists the purchase price for each. Add a column that shows our total original investment in each stock and a column that indicates the amount of money we have gained (or lost) on each stock since we purchased it. Finally, add another column that indicates the percentage gain or loss from the purchase price. Your formulas should work whatever the values in the cells. Format the numbers in this column as percentages with two decimal places.

(b) Add validation to the cells for the current prices per share so that a user must enter a positive number or be given an error message. Test the validation by trying to enter a negative current share price for IBM.

(c) Spend some time formatting the worksheet so it looks nice. Include different colors or shades for different cells. Include different fonts of different sizes and styles.

(d) Conditionally format the cells that contain the amount of money gained or lost on each stock with different colors. Now conditionally format the cells that contain percentage gains or losses with appropriate icons. Test the conditional formats by entering various current prices.

(e) Add a text box. Add a shape or two. Add some WordArt. Add an appropriate clip-art picture or photograph, perhaps one of Michael Dell or Thomas J. Watson or Bill Gates. Add a SmartArt graphic.

(f) Protect the worksheet so that only the cells that contain current prices per share can be changed. Try changing one of the other cells. Can you?

(g) Change the current share prices. Do all the features and formulas work?

CHAPTER 8

WORKBOOKS WITH MULTIPLE WORKSHEETS

OBJECTIVES

In this chapter you will learn how to:

- Move between worksheets
- Insert new worksheets
- Make a duplicate copy of a worksheet
- Modify multiple worksheets at the same time
- Use cells from other worksheets in formulas
- View multiple worksheets and workbooks
- Link to data in other workbooks

So far, we have been doing all of our work on a single worksheet. An Excel workbook holds multiple worksheets, just as a printed book has multiple pages. Using multiple sheets can make many problems easier to solve in Excel.

MOVING BETWEEN WORKSHEETS

An Excel workbook starts out with three worksheets and can contain as many worksheets as will fit in memory. Initially, the worksheets are named Sheet1, Sheet2, and Sheet3. To move to another worksheet simply click on the appropriate **worksheet tab** at the bottom of the window. In Figure 8-1, we have clicked on the tab for Sheet3. You can tell we are working in Sheet3 because its tab is white. Usually we can see at most six sheet tabs at a time. We can scroll so that other sheet tabs are visible using the four buttons to the left of the sheet tabs at the very bottom left of the window.

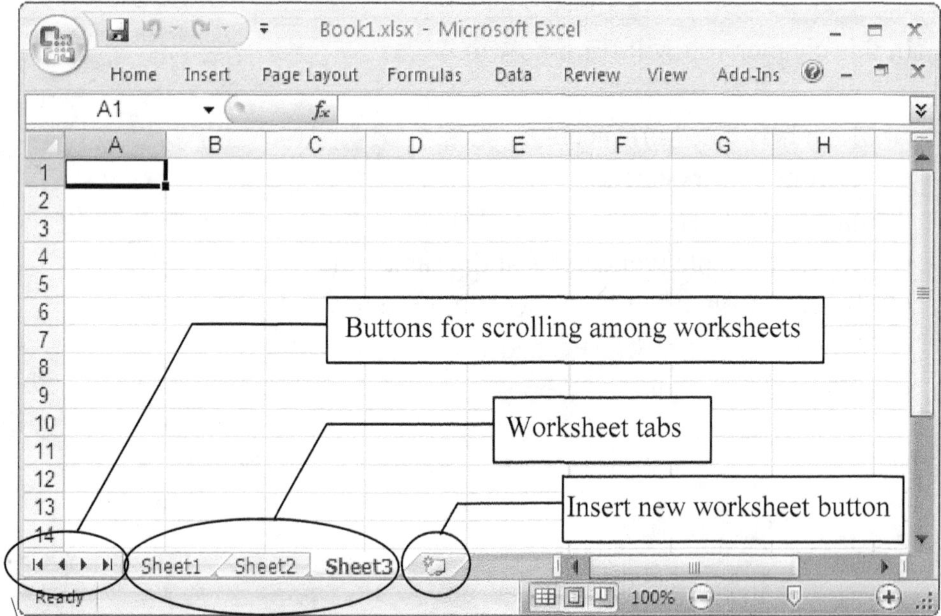

Figure 8-1. Select a different worksheet by clicking on the tab at the bottom of the window.

|◀ instructs Excel to scroll left all the way to the first worksheet tab.

◀ instructs Excel to scroll left one worksheet tab.

▶ instructs Excel to scroll right one worksheet tab.

▶| instructs Excel to scroll right all the way to the last worksheet tab.

USING MULTIPLE WORKSHEETS

Audio International is a small but exclusive chain of stores that sells and installs top-of-the-line audio equipment. AI carries four types of products: home audio, automobile audio, personal audio, and commercial audio equipment. AI has stores in Beverly Hills, Dubai, Geneva, and Shanghai. Each quarter the stores send their sales data to world headquarters for compilation. For convenience, all stores report their sales in millions of U.S. dollars. We would like to create a workbook for keeping track of AI's sales for the year. A simple worksheet for keeping track of the sales in the quarter is shown in Figure 8-2.

	A	B	C	D	E	F	G
1							
2				Audio International			
3							
4		Q1		Sales in $ Millions			
5							
6			Automotive	Home	Personal	Commercial	Total
7		Beverly Hills	2.3	4.2	0.6	1.5	8.6
8		Dubai	3.7	5.1	0.2	1.7	5.0
9		Geneva	1.4	1.8	0.5	1.3	10.7
10		Shanghai	3.0	3.8	0.6	3.8	11.2
11		Total	10.4	14.9	1.9	8.3	35.5

Figure 8-2. Audio International's sales for the first quarter.

Now the second quarter's sales are in and we would like to enter them. The best place to do this is on the next worksheet. First let's name the current worksheet. To change the name of the current worksheet, just double-click on the sheet tab, where it says Sheet1. The current name is selected. You can type in the new name.

We type in Q1 and the sheet is renamed Q1. The next step is to copy the information from the first sheet to the second sheet. One approach is to use Copy and Paste. We select the range A1:G11 by dragging across it. Now we right click and select Copy from the menu or click on the Copy button or type Ctrl-C. This copies the range into the Clipboard. Now click on the tab for Sheet2 at the bottom of the window. Click on cell A1 of Sheet2 to select the cell. Right click and select Paste from the menu or simply click on the Paste button or type Ctrl-V. The range will be copied into Sheet2 beginning at A1, as in Figure 8-3.

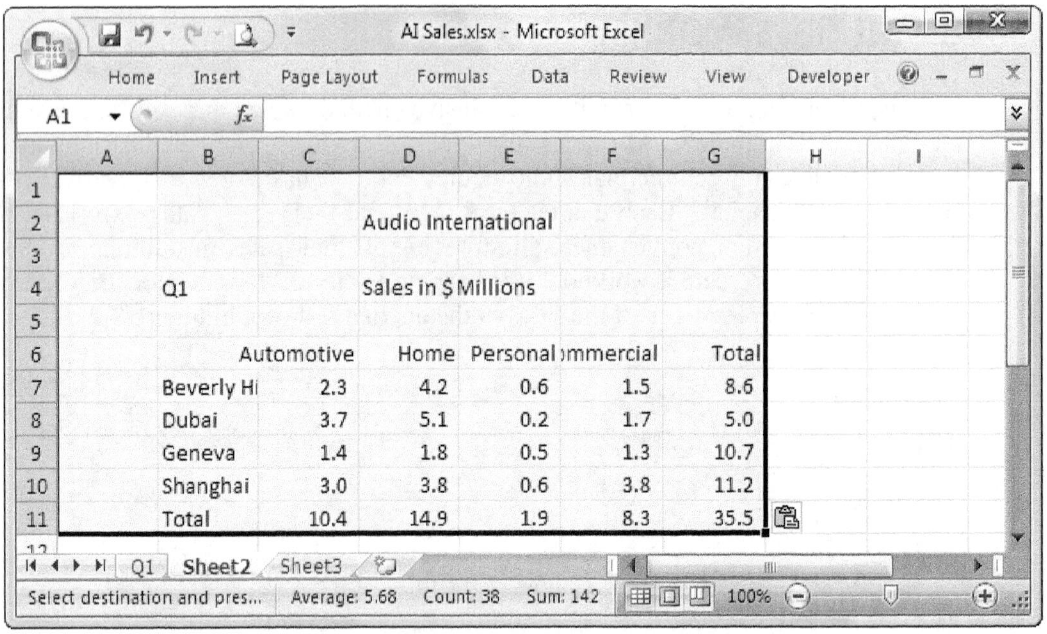

Figure 8-3. *The result of copying and pasting from sheet Q1 to sheet Sheet2.*

The Copy and Paste operation sort of worked, but notice that the column-width information was not transferred. Let's take another approach. We delete this entire worksheet by right clicking on the Sheet2 tab and selecting Delete in the menu. This command doesn't just erase the worksheet. It tears the entire worksheet out of the workbook. (Or we could have just pressed the Undo button.)

A better approach to duplicating the Q1 worksheet is to right click on the Q1 sheet tab and select Move or Copy… from the menu. This yields the dialog box in Figure 8-4. The name of the workbook we are working on is AI Sales.xls. We click on the Create a copy box at the bottom of the dialog box because we want to make a second copy of the worksheet rather than just moving it. We click on Sheet3 because we want the new copy to appear just before Sheet3. (Notice that there is no Sheet2 because we just deleted it.)

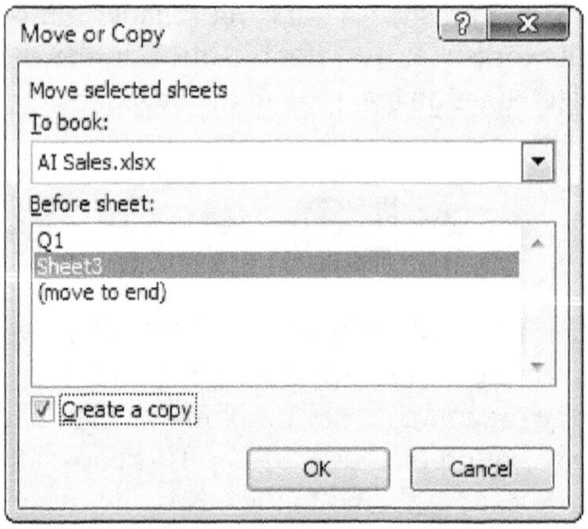

Figure 8-4. *Making a copy of a worksheet.*

Click on OK and an exact duplicate of the worksheet Q1 appears with the name Q1(2), meaning the second copy of worksheet Q1. We double-click on the sheet tab and name the new worksheet Q2. Now we go in and change cell B4 to Q2 and enter in the sales figures for the second quarter. An even better approach might have been to create a copy of the sheet with no sales figures filled in and then used that to make the new quarterly sales worksheets.

As the third and fourth quarter sales figures come in, we copy the prior quarter's worksheets into new worksheets called Q3 and Q4 and fill in the appropriate sales figures. We now have a workbook with four worksheets.

We decide that we would like to insert a first sheet and make it a cover sheet for the workbook. We move to worksheet Q1 by clicking on the Q1 tab. To insert a new worksheet in front of Q1 we right click on the Q1 tab and select Insert and then Worksheet. We name this worksheet Cover by double-clicking on the new tab. We enter information into the worksheet and format it.

WORKING WITH MULTIPLE SHEETS AT THE SAME TIME

We decide to jazz up the worksheets themselves. We'd like to place boxes, adjust the fonts, and so on. We would like the changes to take place on all four quarterly worksheets at once. We want to avoid formatting the worksheet for Q1 and then repeating the formatting for worksheet Q2 and so on. The secret is to select multiple sheets before doing the formatting.

There are two ways to select multiple sheets at once.

If you hold your finger down on the Ctrl or Control key while you click on the sheet tabs, you can select Q1, and then Q2, and then Q3, and finally Q4. Using **Ctrl-clicking** you can select whichever sheets you would like one at a time.

Alternatively, if you would like to select a sequence of sheets, you can click on the first sheet tab Q1 and then hold your finger down on the Shift key and click on sheet tab Q4. All of the sheets from Q1 through Q4 will be selected. This is **Shift-clicking**.

Now whatever actions we perform on worksheet Q1 will be performed simultaneously on worksheets Q2, Q3, and Q4. After we are finished we click once on an unselected sheet tab (Sheet3) to undo the group selection and then click back on worksheet Q3 to see the result in Figure 8-5.

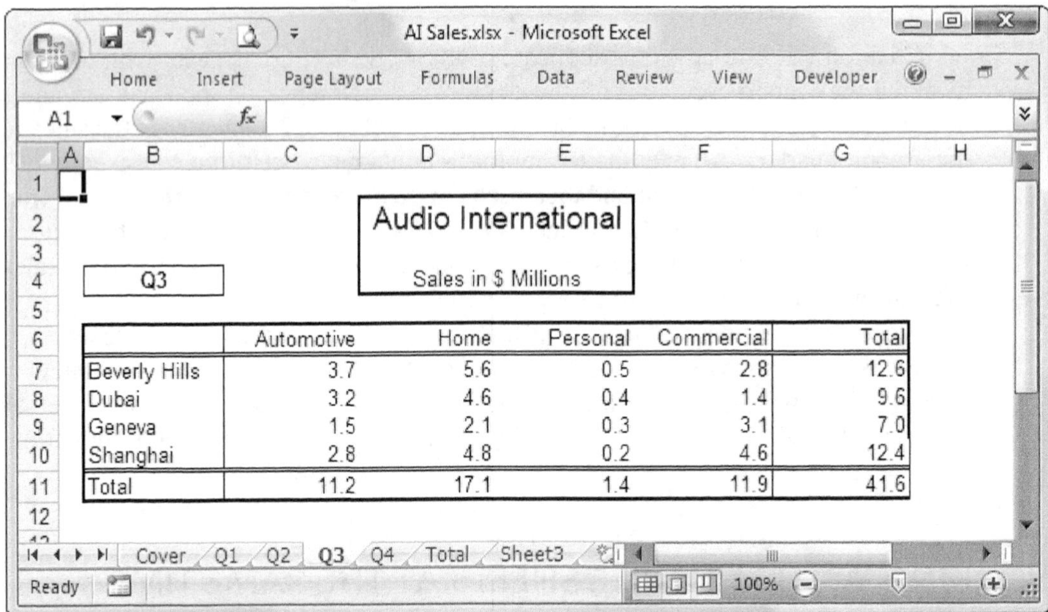

	Automotive	Home	Personal	Commercial	Total
Beverly Hills	3.7	5.6	0.5	2.8	12.6
Dubai	3.2	4.6	0.4	1.4	9.6
Geneva	1.5	2.1	0.3	3.1	7.0
Shanghai	2.8	4.8	0.2	4.6	12.4
Total	11.2	17.1	1.4	11.9	41.6

Figure 8-5. The result of formatting all four worksheets at once.

CALCULATIONS ACROSS WORKSHEETS

We would like a Totals worksheet that adds up the quarterly figures. We make a copy of worksheet Q4 and place it before the next sheet. We name the new sheet Totals. We enter Total for the Year in B4. We clear the data values in C7:F10 from the worksheet by selecting them and then dragging the Fill Handle back and up across them.

We are ready to enter the formulas into the body of the worksheet, into cells C7:F10. We want cell C7 in the Totals sheet to be the sum of C7 in the Q1, Q2, Q3, and Q4 worksheets. So we click on C7 in the Totals worksheet to activate it. We type in =SUM(and then we click on sheet tab Q1, hold our finger down on the Shift key, and click on sheet tab Q4. Thus far we have selected the four sheets Q1:Q4 in the formula. Now we click on cell C7 in sheet Q1 and then type the closing parenthesis and the Enter key. The formula in C7 in sheet Totals is

=SUM('Q1:Q4'!C7)

This formula instructs Excel to add four numbers together, the numbers in C7 in sheet Q1, C7 in sheet Q2, C7 in sheet Q3, and C7 in sheet Q4. The worksheet names usually are included within apostrophes (') in a formula. A range of worksheets is indicated by the colon (:). The names of the worksheets are separated from the addresses of the cells within the worksheets by the exclamation mark (!).

We now can fill this formula across row 7 in sheet Totals by dragging the Fill Handle at the bottom right of C7 across to F7. If we want to keep the existing formatting in place, including the existing borders, then we need to use the pop-up Fill menu that appears and select Fill Without Formatting, as in Figure 8-6.

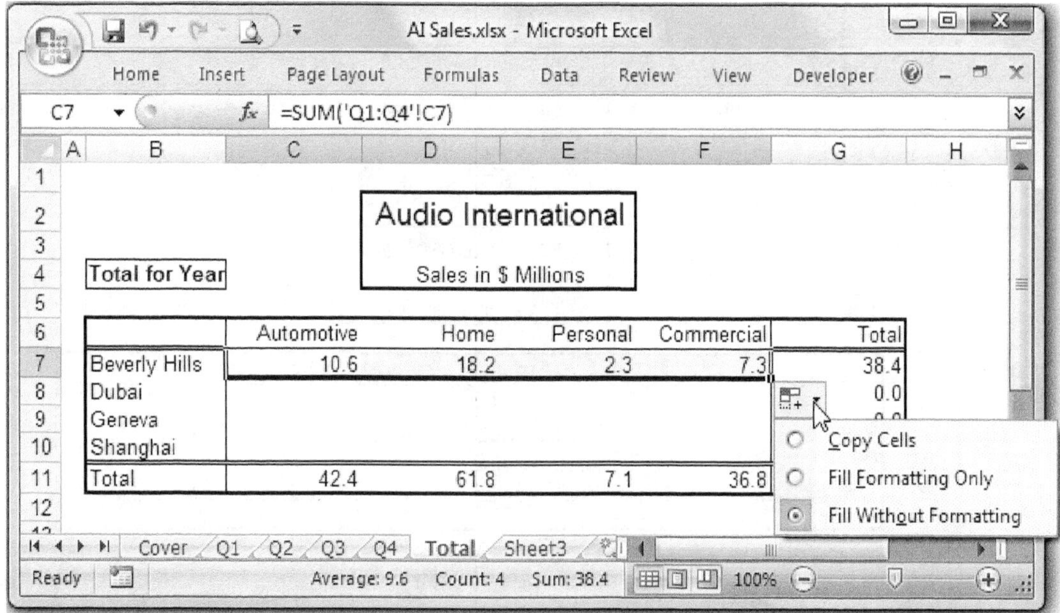

Figure 8-6. Filling the formula in C7 across the row and then preserving the existing formatting, in this case the borders.

With C7:F7 still selected, we drag the resulting Fill Handle at the bottom right of F7 down to F10. Again we select Fill Without Formatting in the Fill pop-up menu and click on D9 to unselect the range. The resulting worksheet is shown in Figure 8-7. You can see that the formula in cell D9 of the Totals worksheet adds up the four corresponding cells in worksheets Q1, Q2, Q3, and Q4.

There are several possible formulas for cell G11 in the Totals worksheet, for example

=SUM(G7:G10)

or

=SUM(C11:F11)

or

=SUM('Q1:Q4'!G11)

or

=SUM('Q1:Q4'!C7:F10)

This last formula would instruct Excel to add up a 4 x 4 x 4 cube of cells, 64 cells, the cells in the range C7:F10 on sheets Q1, Q2, Q3, Q4. The four SUM formulas given should all result in the same values.

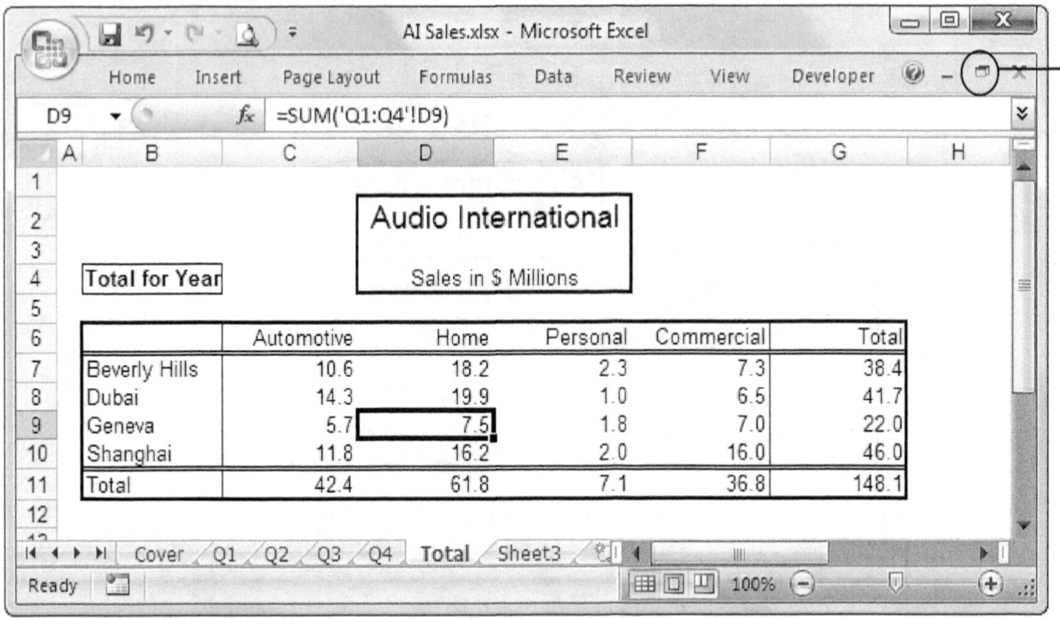

Figure 8-7. Calculating the sum of cells through four worksheets.

VIEWING MULTIPLE SHEETS AND WORKBOOKS

It is possible to view several worksheets at once. First select New Window in the Window group of the View tab. Each time you select New Window you will create a new worksheet window. But they are all windows within the Excel framework window. If the current Excel worksheet window is maximized within Excel, all you'll see is that one worksheet window. You'll need to press the Restore Window button in order to allow the current worksheet window to be resized. Then drag the bottom right corner of the worksheet window (the triangle of dots) to resize the worksheet window. Now you should be able to see two or more worksheet windows at once. Within each of these worksheet windows you can scroll or select other worksheets. The window will be named something like AI Sales.xlsx:2, meaning it's the second view of the AI Sales workbook. See, for example, Figure 8-8.

You also can view multiple workbooks at once. Simply start a new workbook with an old one open or open a second workbook. Each workbook will appear in a different window within Excel.

You gain even more flexibility by starting up Excel multiple times. Now you have multiple Excel windows, each with different workbooks. This is convenient for copying information from one workbook into another.

The exact behavior of multiple workbooks with multiple windows depends on the version of the operating system you are using and the version of Excel. You should be able to select among the different windows that are open by using the Excel task button(s) at the very bottom of your Windows display window.

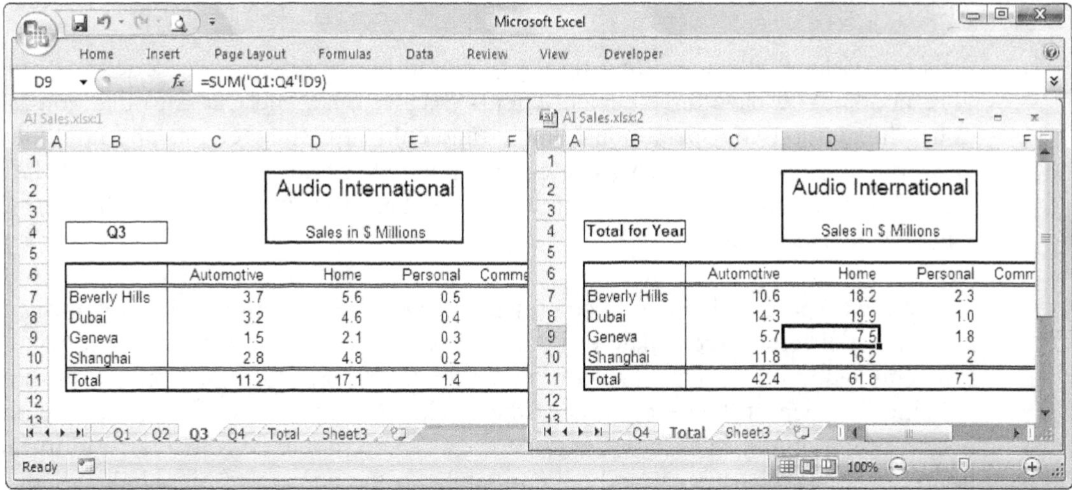

Figure 8-8. Viewing windows of two different worksheets of the same workbook.

LINKING WORKBOOKS

In addition to viewing multiple workbooks at the same time, it is possible to link two open workbooks. That is, it is possible to instruct Excel to obtain a value from a cell in another open workbook. For example, in a cell we could enter the formula

=[Sales]Sheet1!$H$7

This formula tells Excel that the value that is to appear in the cell is the value in H7 in the worksheet called Sheet1 of the Excel workbook called Sales. Thus, to refer to a cell in another workbook, put the name of the workbook file in square brackets [ ].

We also can point to the cell to which we wish to link. For example, if we are working in a workbook called US_Sales and in cell D8 we would like to refer to cell E15 in a workbook called Atlanta, we can open up the Atlanta workbook within Excel, click on D8 in US_Sales, type the = sign to begin a formula, and click on the cell in Atlanta whose value we want to appear in D8 in US_Sales. The link will be entered in the formula in cell D8. We press the Enter key to enter the formula.

=[Atlanta.xlsx]Sheet1!$E$15

An important issue is when linked data is updated. If the Atlanta sales are changed and saved and then you open US_Sales without Atlanta being open, will the data in US_Sales be updated automatically? The answer used to be "Yes" but now with security concerns it's not necessarily. The safest approach is to have US_Sales and Atlanta open at the same time. Then you can be sure the data from Atlanta in US_Sales is up to date.

COMPUTER EXERCISES

8-1. As a professional at a consulting firm, you would like to set up a workbook to keep track of your hours. You have three current clients (Acme, Beta, and Carlisle) that you bill by the hour. In addition you spend non-billable time cultivating new clients and non-billable time at work on other tasks, such as attending internal meetings and staring out the window (though you usually like to be thinking about a client's problem when you're staring out the window, so the time is billable).

Set up a workbook to help you keep track of your time and billing. Each worksheet should represent a different week. There should be five rows: one for each different client, one for time cultivating new clients, one for "nonproductive" time spent at work. You should have columns for each of the seven days of the week. Entries will be filled in for the number of hours spent each day in each of the categories. There should be row totals for the number of hours spent in each category and column totals for the number of billable hours, the number of non-billable hours, and the total number of hours you worked each day.

You bill your clients at $350 per hour. This value should be entered into a separate cell in the worksheet, because it is subject to change (upwards). You should have cells for the dollar amounts to be billed each client each day and for the week. The final cell should give the total amount to be billed for the week.

Your firm bills its clients every four weeks. You should have a worksheet in your workbook for each week in the cycle. Each of these worksheets should have the week number. After these weekly worksheets you should have a Totals worksheet that lists all useful totals, including the total accumulated hours for the cycle for each category, the total amount to be billed each client for the cycle, and the total amount billed for the cycle.

8-2. Design and create a workbook to keep track of the payroll for hourly employees. Each worksheet will correspond to a different week. You have six employees. List them in a column. Each employee makes a different amount per hour. List the hourly pay for each employee in a new column. Now add a column for each of the seven days of the week. In these columns enter the number of hours worked by each employee each day that week. To the right add columns that give the total number of hours worked by each employee and the gross pay for each employee. The federal government asks you to deduct 20% of gross pay for federal income taxes. Your state or province asks you to deduct 5% of gross pay for state income taxes. Add columns for these. Social Security deduction is 6.2% of gross pay. The deduction for medical insurance is $20 per week. Add columns for these. Each employee's take home pay is the gross pay minus the deductions. Add a column for take home pay. Add a row to total all of the columns. Add appropriate cells with headings for the worksheet.

Now use the worksheet you just created for one week's payroll to create a workbook for a month (four weeks). You should have an initial worksheet that gives a title and other information. There should be one worksheet for each week. Employees may work different hours from week to week. The final worksheet should be the totals for the four weeks. There should be six worksheets in all.

8-3. Design and create a workbook to keep track of how you spend your time. Each worksheet will correspond to a different day. There should be columns for each 6 hour period: night (midnight to 6 AM), morning (6 AM to noon), afternoon (noon to 6 PM), and evening (6 PM to midnight). The rows will correspond to your most common activities. For example, there might be rows for studying, going to class, sleeping (we'll assume no overlap in the activities), eating. You select at least six activities and a row for miscellaneous activities. The cells will contain the number of hours spent during each time period on each activity. Add cells with formulas for totals and averages for each row and for totals for each column. The columns should each add up to 6, the number of hours in each period.

Create a worksheet for one day. Then make copies for a full week. At the top of each worksheet give the date for the data in the worksheet and the day of the week. Fill in data for all of the worksheets. You can make up the data if you wish. Add a title worksheet at the front. Add a worksheet at the end for the weekly sums of the values and another worksheet for the weekly averages of the values and a third worksheet for the weekly maximums of the values. The final workbook should consist of eleven worksheets. Changing any of the data values should cause changes to ripple through the calculations in the worksheet that was changed and the three summary worksheets at the end of the workbook.

8-4. Design and create a workbook to keep track of a stock portfolio. You own shares in five different companies:

Shares	Company	Purchase Price	Current Price
1000	Allied Networks	34.50	38.75
3500	Bionic Controls	8.25	56.50
9000	Cortical Connections	2.75	1.75
2000	United Housing	15.75	18.50
500	Energy Management	78.25	83.00

Create a workbook with multiple worksheets that allows you to keep track of your portfolio over the next 10 business days. During those 10 days the price of the shares will change, but you can assume that you will neither purchase nor sell any shares. Once the workbook is set up, you will enter in only 50 values, the closing price of each of the stocks on each of the days. All other cells should be protected and calculated automatically.

The workbook will tell you for each day the total value of each stock holding, the change from the previous day in both dollar amount and percent, and the change from original purchase price in both dollar amount and percent. There also will be cells that tell you the highest price of each stock over the 10-day period and the highest value of your portfolio over the 10-day period.

There are several ways to organize the workbook in terms of what appears on each worksheet. The exact organization is up to you.

8-5. Where does all the money go? Create a workbook to help keep track of weekly expenses. Each worksheet will correspond to one week's worth of expenses. In each worksheet you should have columns corresponding to the days of the week (Mon, Tue, ...). You should have rows for at least five different categories on which you spend money. Fill in values. (You can make up the numbers.) You should have sums and averages for the rows and columns. Now create a workbook for five weeks, with one sheet for each week. At the beginning add a colorful title worksheet. At the end you should have worksheets for overall totals and for overall averages. The workbook should consist of eight worksheets.

8-6. To raise money for a service trip your organization is considering holding a concert on campus. You figure fixed expenses for the band and for the facility are $2,000. Variable expenses are $2 per person who attends. The facility holds a maximum of 500 people. You are considering charging $10 per ticket.

(a) Create a worksheet to determine the financial results at different numbers of ticket sales. You should have a data entry area with cells for fixed expenses, variable expenses per ticket, price per ticket, and number of tickets sold. The main body of the worksheet should have columns for number of tickets sold, total revenues, fixed expenses, variable expenses, total expenses, and profit. There should be 501 rows for ticket sales from 0 through 500.

(b) You would like to explore other possible assumptions. Make another worksheet with a copy of the worksheet from (a). Put text on the top of the first worksheet that says "Original assumptions." Change the name of the worksheet in the original worksheet tab appropriately. In the new copy of the worksheet, change the fixed expenses to $4,000. All the values in the table should change. Add a label to the top of the worksheet and change the worksheet tab appropriately.

(c) Make a new copy of the original worksheet. Change the amount charged per ticket to $12. Add a label to the top of the worksheet and change the worksheet tab appropriately.

(d) Make a new copy of the original worksheet. Change the variable expenses per ticket to $4. Add a label to the top of the worksheet and change the worksheet tab appropriately.

CHAPTER 9

THE PROBLEM-SOLVING PROCESS

OBJECTIVES

In this chapter you will learn:

- The process of developing workbooks
- Common forms of documentation for workbooks

In the first eight chapters we looked at the basics of creating Excel workbooks. Now it is time to step back and look at the process of using Excel to help solve problems. This process usually involves five phases.

1. PROBLEM DEFINITION

What is the problem to be solved? What are we trying to accomplish? What information would we like to have? It is very important that you understand the problem before trying to solve it. You do not want to spend hours developing and perfecting a workbook that solves the wrong problem; that is of little use.

2. DESIGN

Is Excel the right tool to use to solve the problem? Sometimes people become so enamored with Excel that they try to use the program to solve problems that would be better solved by other means. There is an old saying "To a person with a hammer, everything looks like a nail." Excel is a powerful and useful tool, but it is not the solution to every problem. If a calculation is to be performed only once, sometimes it is easier just to do the calculation by hand, to use paper and pencil and a calculator. For problems that are better solved using the computer, several different types of computer software are available. Many problems are better solved using, say, a database program rather than Excel or by using some specialized software. For example, if you would like the computer to help you keep the accounting books of a small business, you could create custom Excel workbooks, but you might save a lot of time and trouble by just buying a small business accounting program.

Once you decide that Excel is the right tool to use, it is best to design the workbook on paper first. What are the inputs? What information needs to be provided? What are the outputs? What are we trying to learn? What should be the format of the outputs? Are there any special printed reports that need to be produced? What should they look like? How do you get from the inputs to the outputs? Are there any key formulas to be developed? Could you perform the calculations by hand given enough time and a calculator? You want to be sure that there is nothing mystical in your workbook design, no key steps that need to be calculated but that you do not know how to specify.

As we saw in the Peter Minuit example in Chapter 6, an important principle for designing effective workbooks is that any number that might be changed should be placed into a separate cell. Do not put numbers that might be changed, like interest rates, directly into formulas. Rather put them into separate cells and always refer to these cells in the formulas. All of the numbers that might be varied should be placed together in a separate, well-labeled input area of the workbook.

In designing a workbook you might have four separate areas: introduction, input, calculations, and output. The introduction contains a description of the workbook, the name of the developer, the date, instructions to the user, and documentation. The introduction might encompass the entire first sheet of the workbook. The input area contains all of the cells that will be entered by the user. In a worksheet for "What if" analysis, the input area would contain all of the assumptions, all of the numbers that might be varied. The calculations area contains the formulas. The calculation area often is by far the largest section of the workbook. The output area pulls the results of special interest out of the calculations area. The output area might be located next to the input area for easy viewing.

3. IMPLEMENTATION

Normally it is best to have the worksheets designed on paper before proceeding to the computer. Implementation should be straightforward. It is useful to name the important cells and ranges and to use these names in the formulas. Names should remind you of the contents of the cell or range. If a formula is going to be filled, be careful about using relative, mixed, or absolute addressing. Think about whether the address is relative, whether it is to be adjusted as it is replicated, or whether the address is absolute, always referring to the same cell or range of cells. Use the cell protection capability of Excel to protect all of the cells except the input cells from being changed by mistake. Put the input cells in blue so they can be easily distinguished from the other cells. Use Validation to make sure the each input is of the right type and a reasonable value.

It is customary to store a frequently used workbook as a template. A template is a workbook where all of the input values are set to zero. The user would retrieve the template workbook from the disk or network, enter in the input values, and save the filled-in workbook on the disk under a new name. The template would remain on the disk or network unchanged.

4. TESTING

Beginners often expect their Excel workbooks to work correctly the first time. Sometimes they do, but even the best planned and designed workbooks often contain errors. It is best to assume that a new workbook is full of errors and then test it extensively to make sure it is correct. Testing a workbook involves working out the numbers ahead of time with pencil, paper, and calculator before trying them on the computer. It is important that the workbooks be tested on a wide variety of inputs, on typical inputs and on extreme inputs.

There are several types of errors in Excel workbooks that can be uncovered. There can be errors in your understanding of the problem. Sometimes you create a workbook and then realize that you did not quite understand the problem. The workbook might "work" but it does not produce the answers you need. In this case, you would need to go back to step 1 to reanalyze the problem. There can be errors in your design of the workbook. You might have used an erroneous formula. You might have built a number that needs to be changed into a formula in a worksheet. You might not have foreseen some condition that might occur. In this case, you would need to go back to step 2 to modify your design for the workbook. There can be errors in your implementation of the workbook. You might have a number that is too large for the width of the column. You might forget to use absolute addressing where it is required. You might have made an error in typing a formula or pointing to an address. These errors in step 3 can be corrected right on the computer.

5. DOCUMENTATION

Documentation is the part of the problem-solving process that involves making the workbook understandable by people, rather than just by the computer. Documentation includes external paper and electronic documentation as well as instructions within the workbook itself. In a sense, documentation includes everything in a workbook except for the numbers and the formulas themselves. Documentation should not be an afterthought but rather an integral part of the entire development process.

The extent of the documentation required depends on the uses to which your workbook will be put.

If you are the only person who will ever use your work, then you should provide yourself with sufficient text, comments, and instructions so that the workbook will be understandable to you six months in the future.

If the workbook is being handed in as an assignment, your instructor will determine the level of documentation required. Certainly you should include your name, the date, and the assignment number. You should indicate any extra assumptions you have made and explain any tricky aspects of your work.

A workbook produced for class generally is seen by just two people—yourself and the person who grades the assignment. In industry there often are several people who use and modify the workbooks you will create.

In industry, workbooks often are used by people other than the creator of the workbooks. These people may have only a superficial understanding of Excel and its operation. Therefore it is important to include explicit instructions with your workbooks in these situations. The instructions should include where the data should be entered, how and where to save the work, and how to produce reports. Important instructions are best included as text in the worksheets themselves as well as in a separate file. Instruction files can easily be separated from the workbooks or lost altogether. The cell protection capabilities should be used so that only input cells can be modified easily. Data validation should be used as much as possible.

In industry, workbooks often are modified by people other than the person who creates them. You create an Excel workbook as part of your job and then you are rapidly promoted twice. Someone else is hired for your old position. This person inherits your work. Can this person make sense of your workbooks? Where did these data come from? What is this formula? What are the assumptions underlying this worksheet? What happens at the end of the year? Here you would like the work to be transparent, self-explanatory. List assumptions for the workbooks. List sources for data. Explain unusual formulas. Give explicit instructions. Put yourself in the place of the person who will succeed you. Could you understand this workbook the way it is written if you hadn't developed it yourself?

With important workbooks in industry it is customary to create a full documentation packet. The documentation packet could include:

- a description of the problem the workbook is designed to solve
- a general discussion of the workbook, its design and operation
- full, detailed instructions for a novice user
- full documentation for someone who will modify the workbook, including any

assumptions, a discussion of formulas, any pitfalls or possible errors in the workbook, and features that might be added
- a full printout of the worksheets with values displayed
- a full printout of the worksheets with formulas displayed
- two semi-sealed CDs containing the workbook and documentation to be used for emergency backup.

Electronic versions of the documentation packet should be produced as well and stored on the network.

Most people provide much too little documentation for their workbooks. The reason is simple. It takes a long time and a lot of effort to produce good documentation. It can take as long to document a workbook as it does to identify the problem, design the workbook, implement the workbook, and test the workbook all combined. A little extra effort with documentation can save users of your workbook many hours of work.

COMPUTER EXERCISES

9-1. Your courses each have different requirements—different types of assignments, quizzes, exams, etc. Create a workbook to keep track of all of the grades you receive. Every grade should appear in the workbook along with a description of what it is for, and the date received. You probably will want a different worksheet for each course. Your workbook should calculate your average in each class, if possible using the weighting system of the instructor. In the workbook all cells should be protected except for the input cells. Go through the process of problem definition, design, implementation, testing, and documentation.

9-2. Create a workbook to help keep track of a checking account. There should be separate entries for each check, deposit, ATM withdrawal, electronic transfer, debit card charge, and service charge. These entries should include the date, the amount, the check number (if any), the payee (if any), and the purpose. The workbook should keep track of the balance in your account and should help you check for errors in the statement you receive from the bank each month. Go through the process of problem definition, design, implementation, testing, and documentation.

9-3. Create a workbook that helps you budget income and expenses for each month. Include separate entries for income and expense items. Allow for both budgeted and actual income and expenses. You may use fictional data if you wish. Go through the process of problem definition, design, implementation, testing, and documentation.

9-4. If you have a car, how much does it cost to operate? Create a workbook that will allow you to track operating expenses for your car for a year. Your workbook should allow you to record money spent for gas, oil, repairs, insurance, registration, and any other expenses. For each expense, you should record the date, the odometer mileage, the payee, a description of the expense, and an amount. The workbook should calculate subtotals for each type of expense, the total amount of money spent, the cost per mile and the cost per day to drive your car. Go through the process of problem definition, design, implementation, testing, and documentation.

9-5. Perhaps you belong to a group, such as a campus organization or a church group, that is considering undertaking an activity, for example a picnic or a dance or a raffle. Create a workbook that will allow you to model the financial aspects of the activity. You might have cells for the number of tickets sold and the price of the tickets and for any other revenue variables and for each of the different expense variables. The workbook should allow you to try out different scenarios. For example, what would happen if all of the tickets are sold? What would happen if only 20 tickets are sold? What would be the financial consequences if it rains on the day of the picnic? In the workbook all cells should be protected except for the input cells. Go through the process of problem definition, design, implementation, testing, and documentation.

CHAPTER 10

CHARTS AND TRENDLINES

OBJECTIVES

In this chapter you will learn how to:

- Create charts
- Decide which type of chart to use
- Chart data in noncontiguous areas of your worksheet
- Chart multiple sets of data
- Create separate chart sheets
- Use trendlines to forecast the future

Charts have visual impact. People often see relationships more easily in charts than they do in tables of numbers. An important part of Excel is the ability to turn tables of numbers into pie charts, bar charts, and other types of charts. Charting is easy, useful, and fun.

FUNDAMENTALS OF CHARTING[1]

Before beginning a chart it is best to ask yourself what is the purpose of the chart. Are you trying to discover some pattern or relationship hidden in the data? Are you trying to convey some particular message about the data? Are you just looking for a colorful visual to spice up the monotony of a long report composed mostly of text and tables?

The mechanics of creating a chart in Excel are quite simple. In Excel, charts are made from ranges of numbers in a workbook. Basically we need to specify (1) the cells that contain the values to be charted and (2) the type of chart we want drawn.

Excel has many different types of charts, as shown in Figure 10-1.

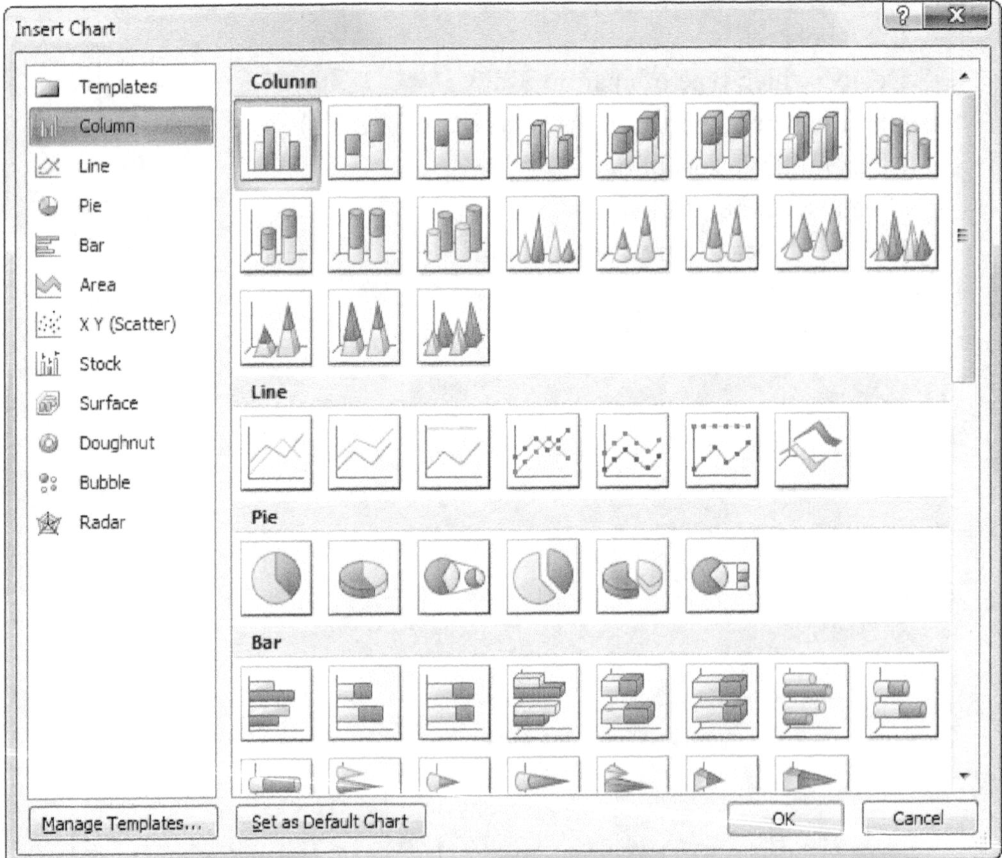

Figure 10-1. Some of the different types of charts available in Excel..

[1] With thanks to Prof. Howard Straubing for urging me to discuss the design of charts as well as the mechanics of charting. This chapter is rewritten for the Sixth Edition.

WHEN TO USE DIFFERENT TYPES OF CHARTS

How can we decide which type of chart to use for our data? In his book *The Say it with Charts Complete Toolkit* (McGraw-Hill, 2007), Gene Zelazny emphasizes that the type of chart that we should use depends on the nature of the comparison we are trying to make. Gene Zelazny is the long-time Director of Visual Communications at McKinsey & Company, the well-known consulting firm. If you are interested in visual communication I urge you to obtain a copy of Zelazny's excellent book. Zelazny distinguishes five common kinds of comparisons: component comparison, item comparison, time series comparison, frequency distribution comparison, and correlation comparison, and discusses the best types of chart to use for each.

Component comparisons emphasize the relative sizes of parts of a whole as percentages. For example, we have four divisions in our company and we want a chart that illustrates the relative sales of each as percentages of the total sales of the company. A component comparison can be effectively illustrated in a **Pie chart**.

In item comparisons we are interested in the relative sizes of different items, for example the Gross National Product of various countries or the weights of different candy bars. An item comparison usually is best illustrated in a horizontal **Bar chart**. The items in the bar chart usually are sorted from largest to smallest before being charted.

A time series comparison shows the changes in a value over time. An example would be the revenue of our company each year for the last ten years. A time series comparison usually is best illustrated by a **Column chart** or a **Line chart** or a **Scatter Chart** where time is along the horizontal axis and the value being charted is along the vertical axis.

A frequency distribution comparison shows the number of items that fall into various numeric or category ranges. For example we might want to know how many pitchers in the major leagues had 0 wins last year or 1 win or 2 wins, and so on. Frequency distributions usually are shown in Column charts or Line charts.

A correlation comparison shows the relationship between two variables. For example if we were in the Admissions Office we might want to know whether students who enter with higher SAT scores tend to have higher college GPAs. We could take all of the college seniors and plot their SAT scores along the horizontal axis and GPAs along the vertical axis. We would have one point on the chart for each senior. A Correlation comparison is shown in a **Scatter chart**.

Let's work through some examples that illustrate these.

CREATING CHARTS

The worksheet from Figure 6-1 with the population by continent is shown in Figure 10-2. We would like to create a chart illustrating the sizes of the population of each continent. Note that all the continents are given in the worksheet. Since the sum of the populations given adds up to 100% of the population of the world, this qualifies as a component comparison. A Pie chart is appropriate. If we had just listed the populations of five countries, say the United States, Ghana, Italy, Chile, and South Korea, then it would make no sense to use a Pie chart as the countries are not all the components of any larger whole.

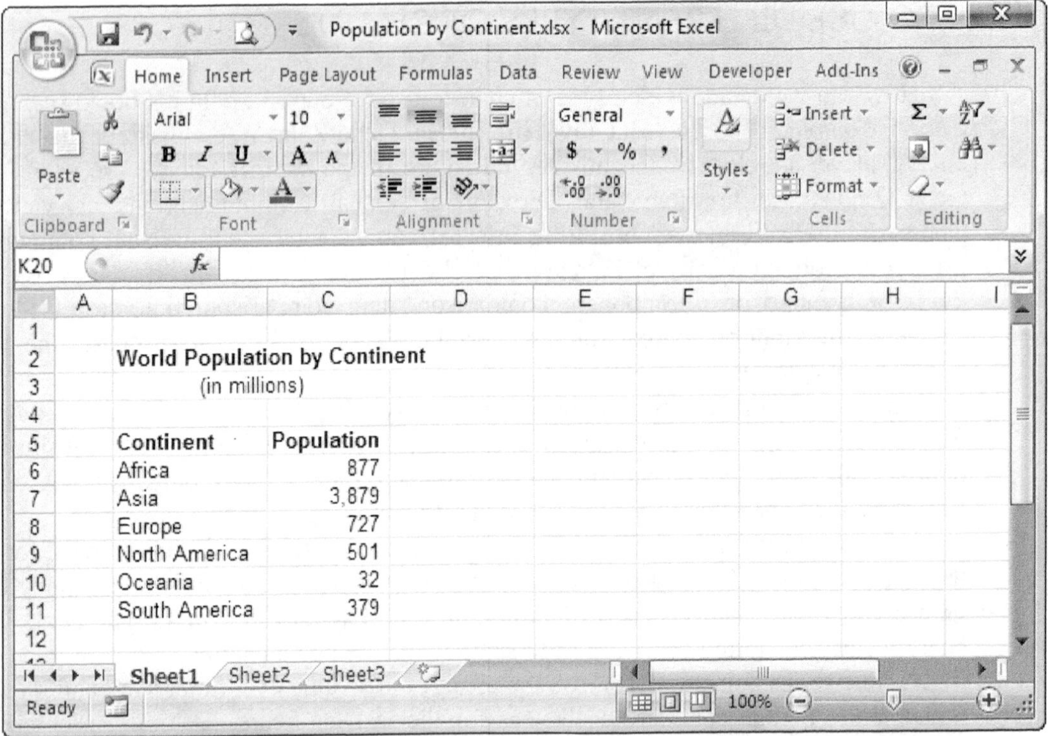

Figure 10-2. Data to be charted.

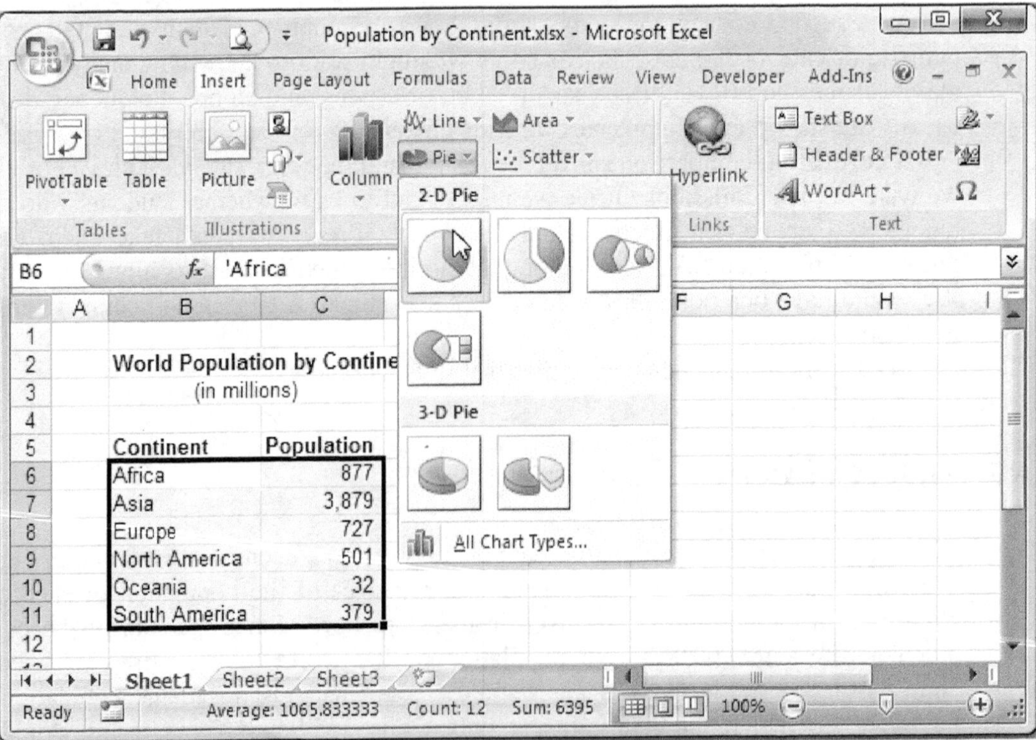

Figure 10-3. First select the data to be charted and then the type of chart.

Charting in Excel used to be complicated, but with each release Microsoft has made it easier. First, we specify the range of cells to be charted. We drag across B6:C11 to select the data to chart. Next we select the type of chart. We click on the Insert tab and on Pie in the Charts area and then on the first type of 2-D Pie chart as in Figure 10-3. A chart appears right on top of the data. We drag the chart to a different part of the worksheet. Whenever we click on a chart or one of its parts, a Chart Tools tab appears in the ribbon, as in Figure 10-4. The Chart Tools tab allows us to adjust many, many different aspects of the chart.

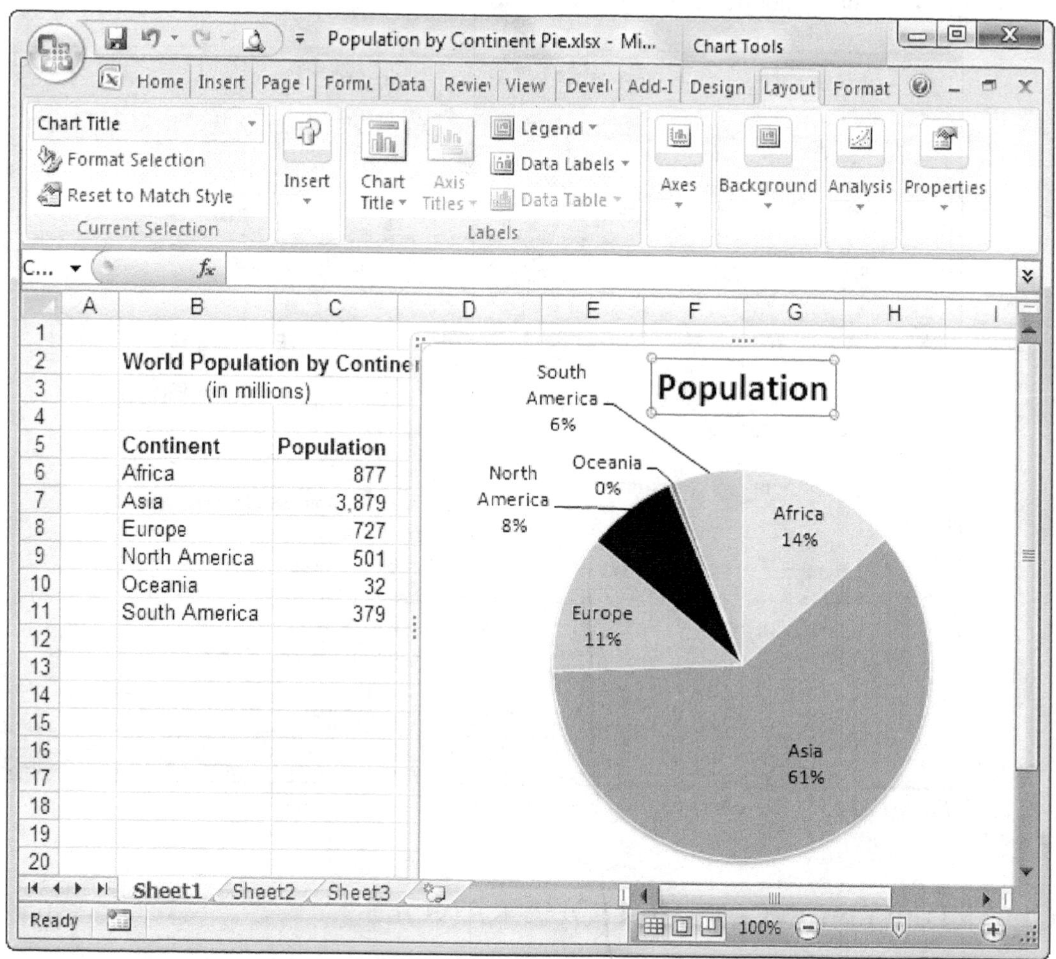

Figure 10-4. A Pie chart emphasizes the relative proportional sizes of parts of a whole.

It's important to keep the chart as simple and easy to understand as possible. For example, while a 3-D Pie chart might seem snazzier than a 2-D Pie chart, it often obscures the underlying data.

The chart is dynamic. That is, if the underlying data in the worksheet is changed the sizes of the slices in the chart automatically are changed accordingly.

Excel draws the slices of the Pie chart in the order that you list the data, beginning at "12:00" and working its way clockwise around the chart. The order here in the worksheet and thus in the chart is alphabetical. Zelazny suggests that if you want to emphasize one of the components its slice should be drawn just to the right of the 12:00 line and in the most contrasting color possible. Zelazny also suggests that a Pie chart should have no more than six slices.

The same data could be treated as an item comparison and be charted as a Bar chart, as in Figure 10-5. Here we have sorted the data by Population before charting it.

The Pie chart emphasizes that these values add up to 100% of the world's population. The Bar chart emphasizes the relative sizes of items that are comparable but may or may not be all of the components of a whole.

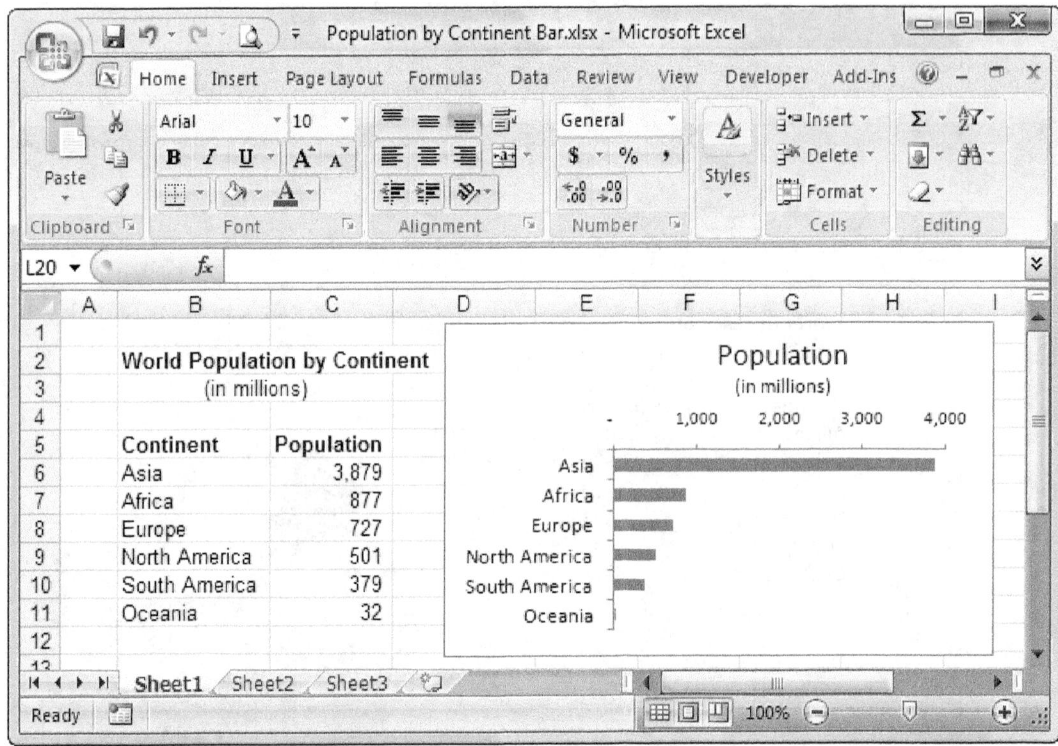

Figure 10-5. A Bar chart emphasizes the relative sizes of items.

CHARTING NONCONTIGUOUS RANGES

Often we want to chart noncontiguous areas of a worksheet, areas that are not next to each other. For example, in the worksheet in Figure 10-6 we might want to chart the Total Sales by year. The years are in row 5. The Total Sales are in row 15. One approach is to drag across from B5 to G5, hold your finger down on the Ctrl key, and drag from B15 to G15. As described in Chapter 3, this is called control-clicking and allows you to select noncontiguous areas in the worksheet. The result is shown in Figure 10-6.

Now that the values to be charted are selected we can click on Insert and then on Charts and then on Column and then on the simplest 2-D Column chart. This is time series data, the third type of comparison, so a Column chart is appropriate. We fiddle with the details of the chart and the result is shown in Figure 10-7

Apple Sales Column.xlsx - Microsoft Excel

Home | Insert | Page Layout | Formulas | Data | Review | View | Developer | Add-Ins

B15 f_x 'Total Sales

Apple Sales by Product Line (in $ millions)

Source: Apple 10-K filings

	2005	2006	2007	2008	2009
Mac Desktops	3,436	3,319	4,023	5,622	4,324
Mac Portables	2,839	4,056	6,313	8,732	9,535
iPod	4,540	7,676	8,305	9,153	8,091
iTunes and other music	899	1,885	2,496	3,340	4,036
iPhone	-	-	630	6,742	13,033
Peripherals	1,126	1,100	1,303	1,694	1,475
Software and Service	1,091	1,279	1,508	2,208	2,411
Total Sales	13,931	19,315	24,578	37,491	42,905

Sheet1 Sheet2 Sheet3

Ready Average: 14825.5 Count: 11 Sum: 148255 100%

Figure 10-6. Noncontiguous ranges B5:G5 and B15:G15 have been selected.

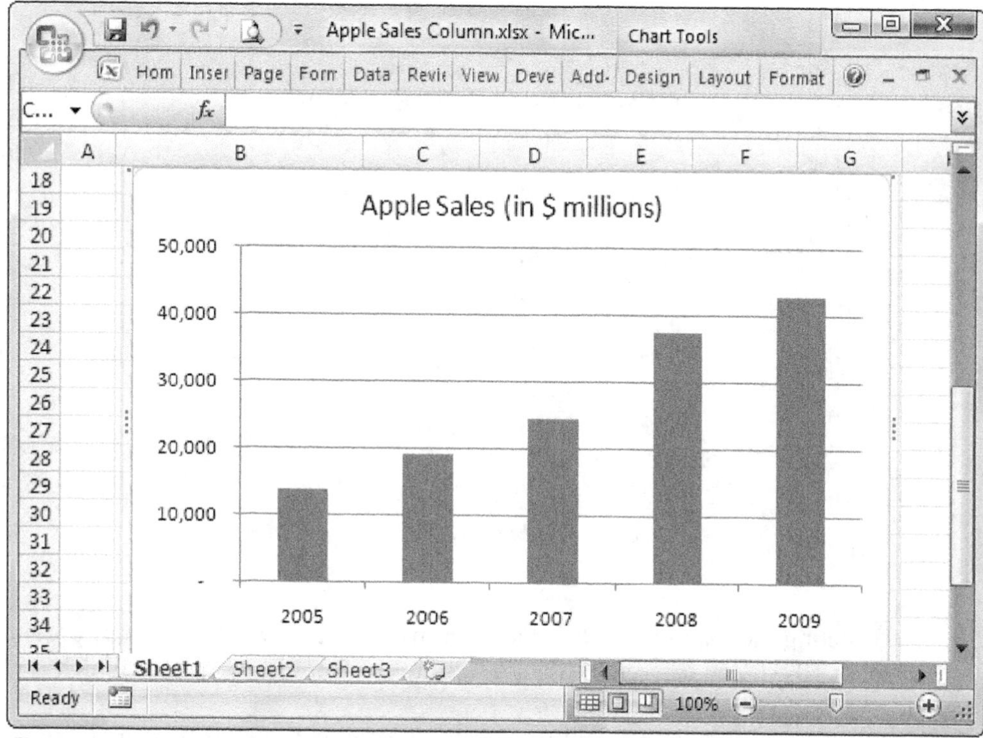

Figure 10-7. A Column chart for the time series data.

A Column chart or a Line chart works for time series data if the data are from consecutive time periods, for example every day for a month or every year for 20 years. If the data are not from consecutive time periods, for example if there are missing data or the data are from, say 1980, 1995, 2000, 2001, 2005, 2008, then a Scatter chart should be used.

Another approach to charting different ranges of data from a workbook in a single chart is to set up a special area in a worksheet that contains just the data to be charted in just the order you want. The cells in this area can be copied and pasted from different sections of the workbook, or they can contain simple formulas (=C3) that refer to the values to be charted. It is important that the selected area contains just the data to be charted and that no blank rows or columns are included.

MULTIPLE SETS OF DATA IN THE SAME CHART

The worksheet in Figure 10-8 shows the height distribution of males and females in the United States according to a national survey. This is frequency distribution data, the fourth type of comparison, so it is appropriate to display it as a Column chart or as a Line chart according to Zelazny.

Height Distribution.xlsx - Microsoft Ex...

Adult Human Height Distribution (USA)

Source: http://psychology.wikia.com/wiki/Body_height

Height	Female	Male
4ft 11in	4.60%	0.00%
5 ft 0in	5.10%	0.20%
5ft 1in	8.00%	0.30%
5ft 2in	11.20%	0.90%
5ft 3in	13.60%	1.70%
5ft 4in	14.60%	3.30%
5ft 5in	13.50%	5.50%

Figure 10-8. Frequency distribution of heights by gender.

Selecting the data in B5:D25 and then inserting a 2-D Column chart produces the chart in Figure 10-9. You can see the data as a Line chart in Figure 10-10. Which is easier to read and understand?

A Histogram Tool for automatically creating frequency distributions from data is described in Chapter 17.

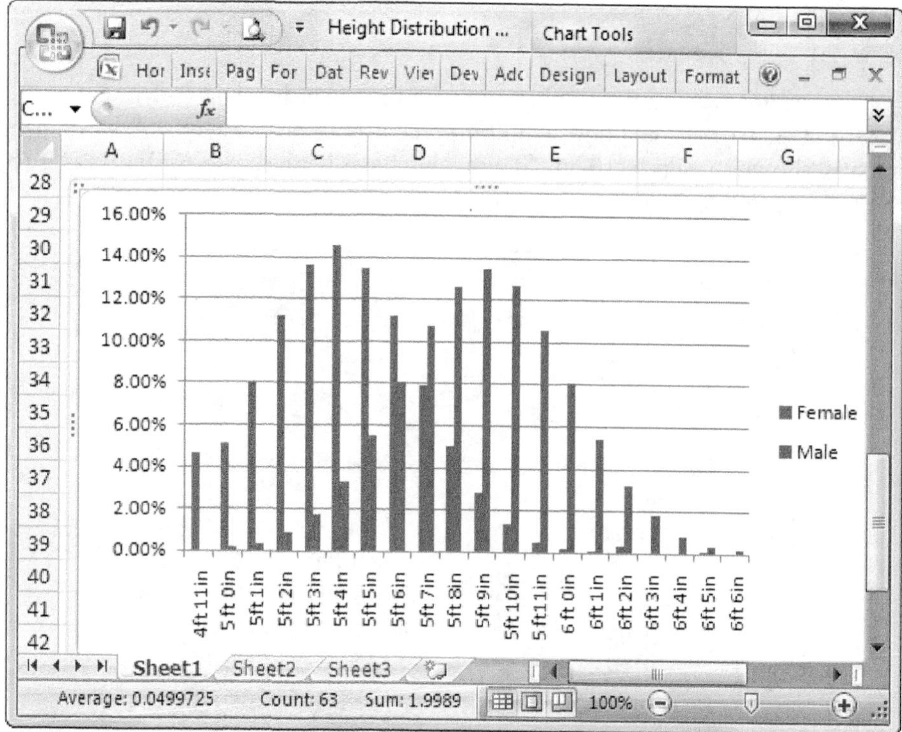

Figure 10-9. A Column chart for frequency distribution data.

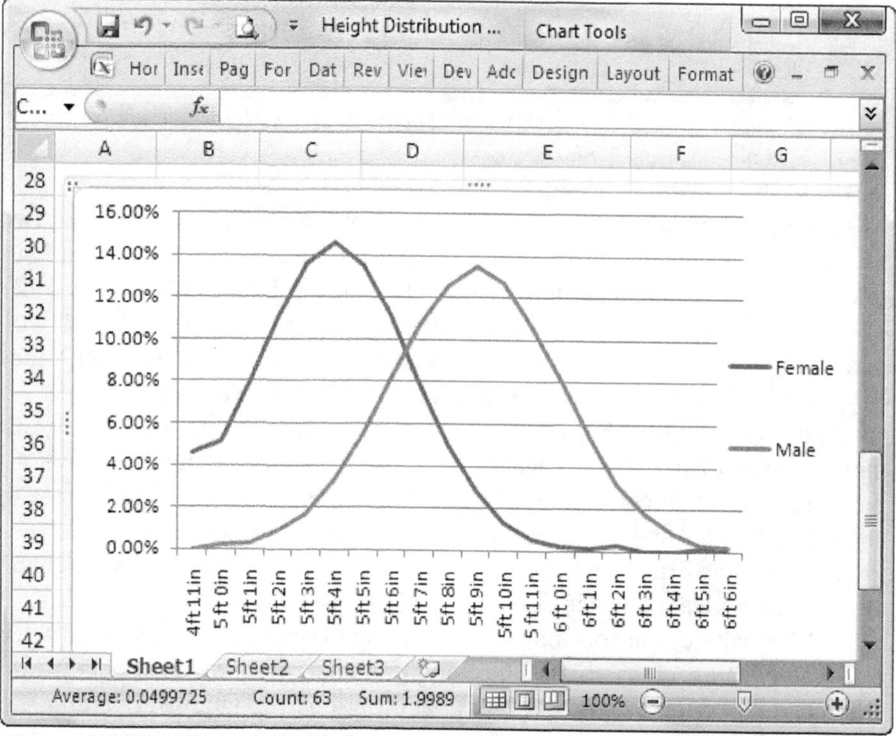

Figure 10-10. A Line chart for the same data.

SCATTER CHARTS

Do Major League Baseball teams with high salaries tend to win games? It's easy to find total player payroll data and winning percent data on the web. A worksheet with the 2009 data is shown in Figure 10-11. The teams have been sorted by Payroll. (The full data is at http://www.masteringexcel.com/MLB2009.xls.)

MLB2009.xlsx - Microsoft Excel

Major League Baseball 2009 Payroll vs. Winning Percentage

Team	Payroll	PCT
Yankees	201,449,189	0.636
Mets	149,373,987	0.432
Cubs	134,809,000	0.516
Red Sox	121,745,999	0.586
Nationals	60,328,000	0.364
Pirates	48,693,000	0.385
Padres	43,734,200	0.463
Marlins	36,834,000	0.537

Figure 10-11. Payroll and winning percentage for Major League Baseball teams.

This is a correlation comparison, looking at the relationship between two variables, so a Scatter chart is the right chart to use. We select the data in C5:D34 and have a Scatter chart drawn. A few adjustments in the formatting of the Scatter chart yields the chart in Figure 10-12. Note that if you hover the mouse on top of a point Excel will show you the underlying data. Looking in the list of data reveals that the team with the high payroll of $149,373,987 and the winning percentage of .432 is the New York Mets.

In the worksheet in Figure 10-13 a line has been fitted to the data by Excel. There is an upward slant to the line so teams with higher salary do tend to have a higher winning percent. The actual correlation is 0.2182, which is not huge. Fitting lines to data in Scatter charts is discussed and explained in the section on trendlines below.

Scatter charts are very useful. They are the only type of Excel chart that allows for arbitrary numerical values in the horizontal axis as well as the vertical axis.

This concludes our tour of the five common types of comparisons discussed by Zelazny. His whole approach is to use the simplest chart possible to convey information. Excel provides lots of fancy types of charts and options for fancy formatting. These should be resisted unless they make the data more understandable. Simpler usually is better.

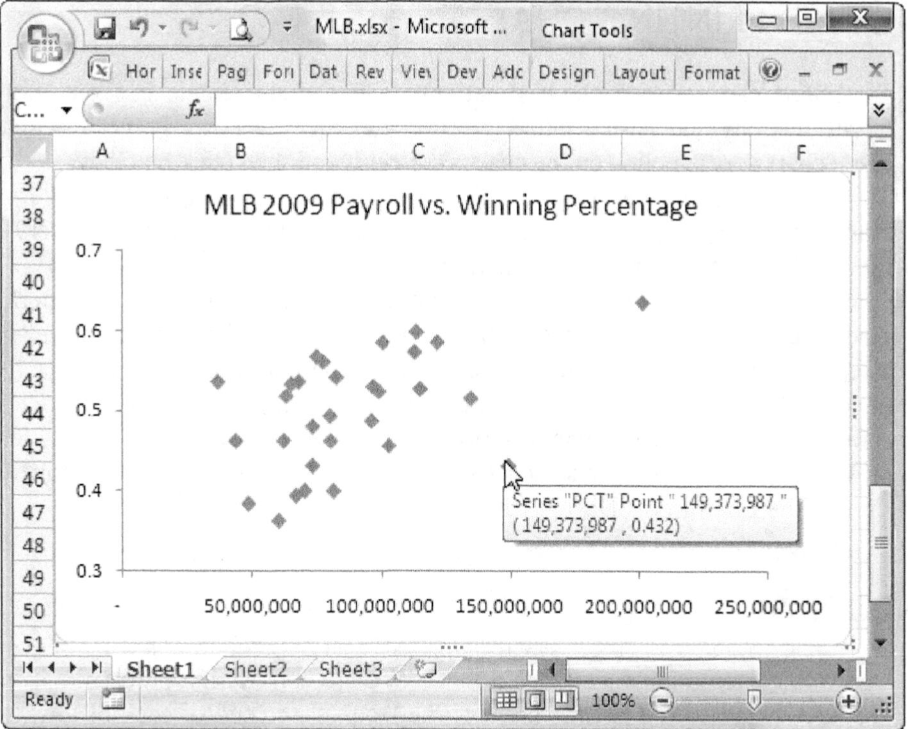

Figure 10-12. Scatter chart of the Major League Baseball team data.

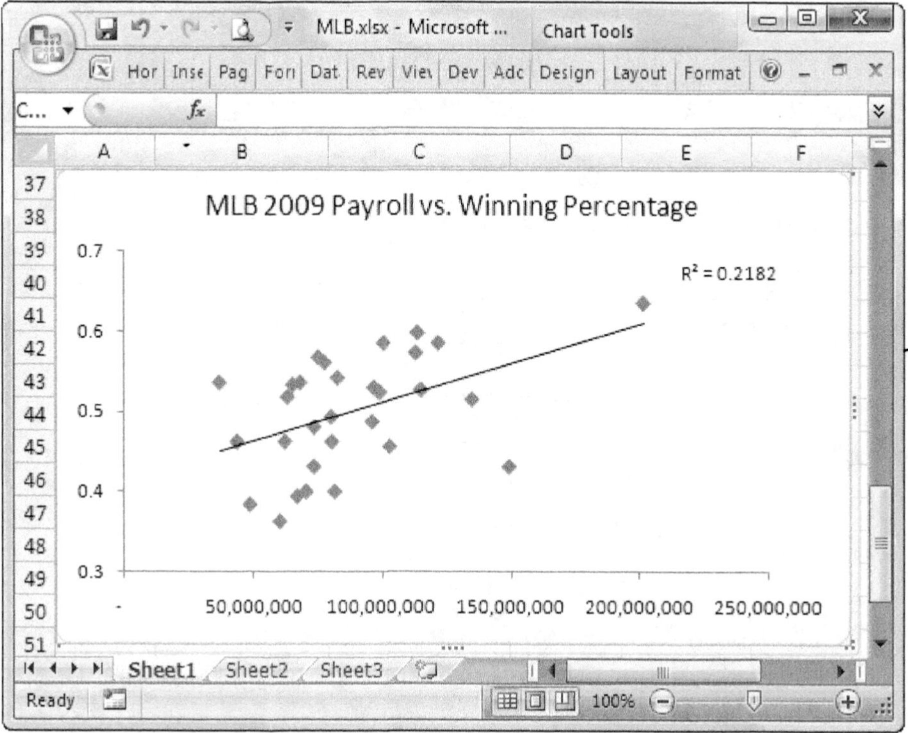

Figure 10-13. There is a positive correlation between payroll and winning

USING AND PRINTING CHARTS

Charts can have various destinations. They might remain in Excel workbooks. They might be Copy and Pasted into a Word document or a PowerPoint presentation. To Copy just a chart you can click on the chart to select it and then click on Copy.

A chart that will be used in a PowerPoint presentation usually should be even simpler than a chart that will be included in a report as the viewer might have very limited time to look at the chart during the presentation.

Charts can be designed for viewing on the computer or in a printed report. We have been placing the charts on worksheets. If the chart is going to be printed it usually is best to have a separate **chart sheet** devoted to the chart. A chart sheet does not contain rows or columns or cells. It just contains a single chart. The text in chart sheets can be difficult to read on the screen, but chart sheets generally print in the right size and proportions for a report. To move a chart to its own chart sheet select the chart and then click on Move Chart at the far right of the Chart Tools Design tab.

TRENDLINES

Audio International has gone public. We are considering purchasing some of its stock. We have obtained the closing price of the stock at the end of each of the 25 weeks since it was issued and entered the data into the worksheet in Figure 10-14.

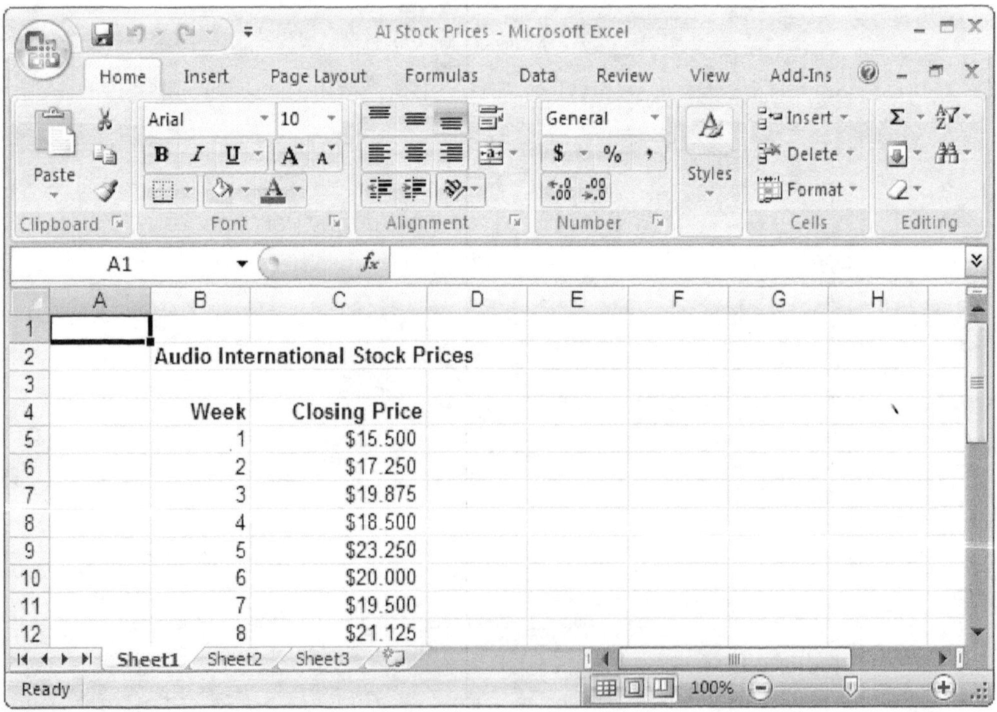

Audio International Stock Prices

Week	Closing Price
1	$15.500
2	$17.250
3	$19.875
4	$18.500
5	$23.250
6	$20.000
7	$19.500
8	$21.125

Figure 10-14. Audio International goes public.

First, we would like to chart the stock so we can see what the change in price looks like. We select B4:C29 and click on Charts in the Insert tab and select a Scatter chart. (Trendlines only work on Scatter charts.) After a few manipulations, the result is shown in Figure 10-15.

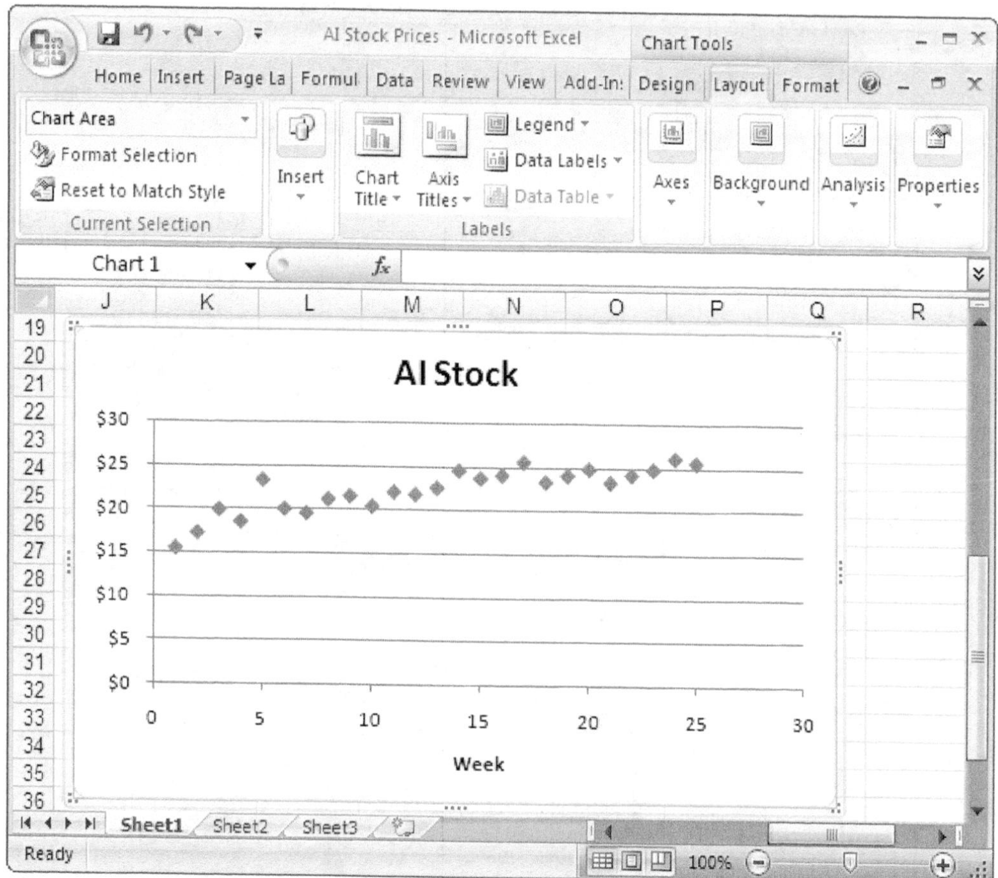

Figure 10-15. A chart of the stock prices.

That is the past. We are thinking of investing, so we are interested in forecasting the price of the stock for future weeks. One of the nicest features of Excel is that it will automatically compute and display **trendlines**. Trendlines are a way of using the past data to suggest what the future data will be.

To obtain a trendline, first we click on the chart to select the chart. Then we go to the pull-down menu at the top left of the Chart Tools Layout tab. (The menu says Chart Area in Figure 10-15). Select "Series: Closing Price" in the pull-down menu. Many of the points in the chart will have X's around them to show the series of data is selected. Now click on Trendline in the Analysis group of the Chart Tool Layout tab. At the bottom of the resulting pull-down menu (Figure 10-16), select More Trendline Options.

The idea is that Excel will fit a trendline of the type we select to the existing data. There are half a dozen different types of trendlines based on common forms of equations. See Figure 10-17 for the Trendlines Options… window.

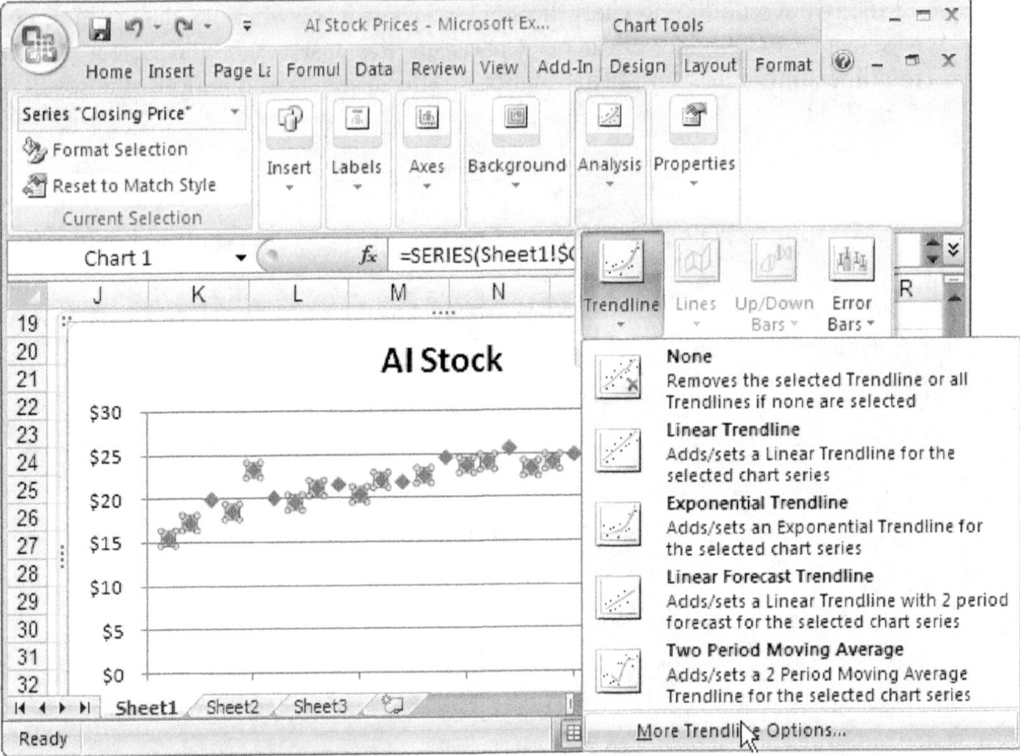

Figure 10-16. Adding a trendline.

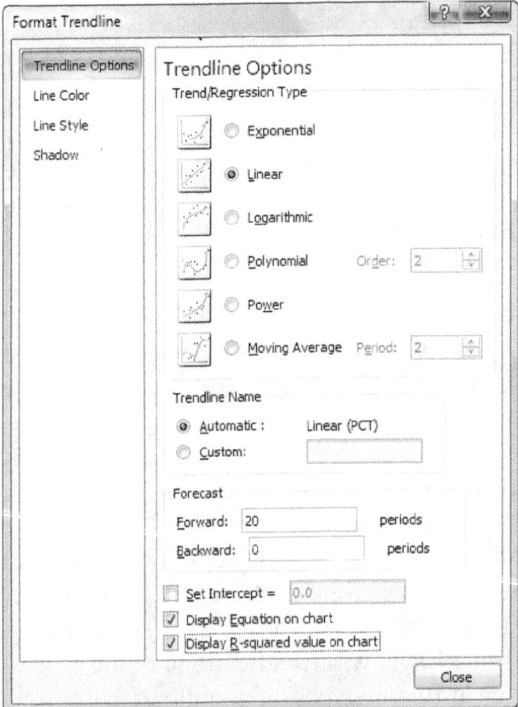

Figure 10-17. Trendline Options.

The nicest part is that Excel will do all of the math for us automatically. We select Linear, which means we want Excel to fit a straight line to the data. We enter 20 in the Forecast Forward box. We want Excel to predict the prices for 20 weeks into the future. We also click on the Display Equation and on the Display R-squared value. (There is no extra charge.) We click on Close and the result is shown in Figure 10-18.

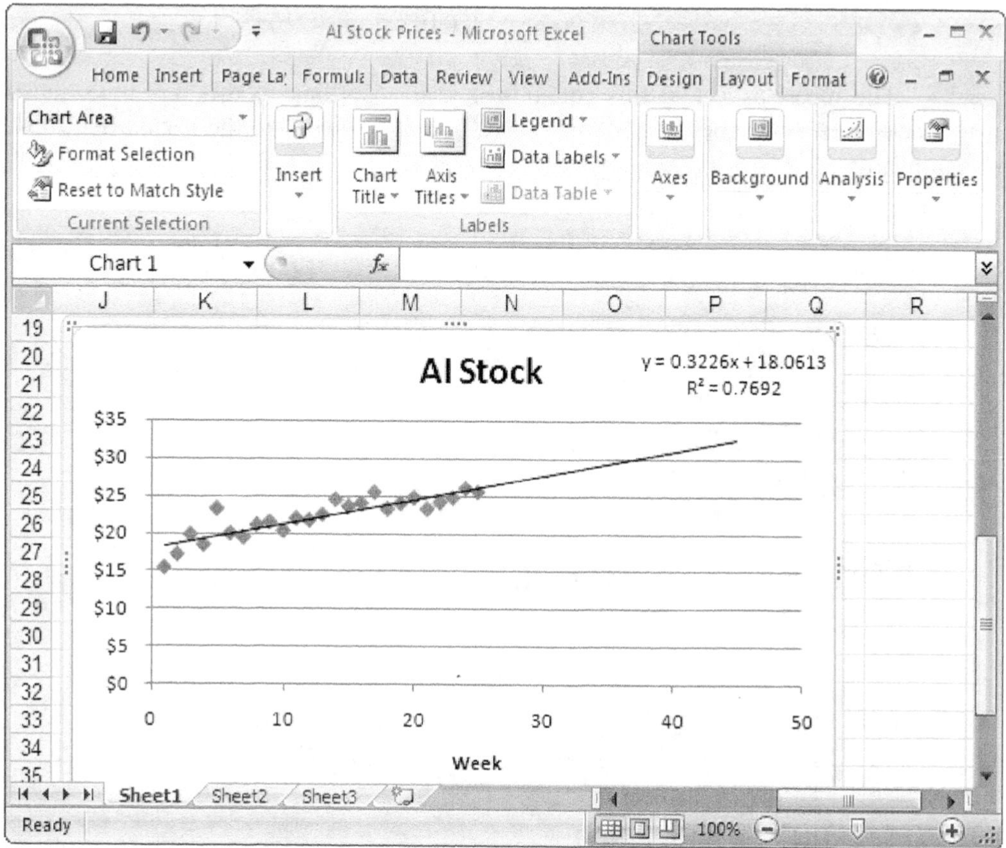

Figure 10-18. The linear trendline for the stock price data.

Excel has fitted a straight line to the data and has displayed the line for 20 weeks into the future. If the trend holds true, the price of the stock should be over $32 in 20 weeks (at week 45). On the top right of the window is a text box that displays the equation and the R-squared value. The equation is

$$y = 0.3226x + 18.0613$$

Here x is the week. The equation gives the formula that Excel found for predicting the price of the stock (y) given the week number (x). The R^2 value is 0.7692. R is the correlation between the values predicted by the equation and the actual values. The square of R is used as an indication of the goodness of fit of the line to the data. If all of the data points were right on the line and there was no deviance at all, the R^2 value would be 1. If the data values were randomly scattered and the line does not fit at all, the R^2 value would be 0.

If you are unhappy with the straight line trendline, you can select exponential, logarithmic, polynomial, power, or moving average. For example, fitting a polynomial of order 3 to the data gives us the trendline shown in Figure 10-19. (Order 3 means that 3 is the highest exponent of x in the polynomial equation.)

We have improved the R^2 value to 0.8248. The equation that Excel found is

$$y = 0.0009x^3 - 0.0482x^2 + 1.0210x + 15.7298$$

The nicest aspect of this equation is that according to this trendline, in 20 weeks the stock price should be over $48 per share! And, it looks like the trend after 20 weeks is ever upwards!

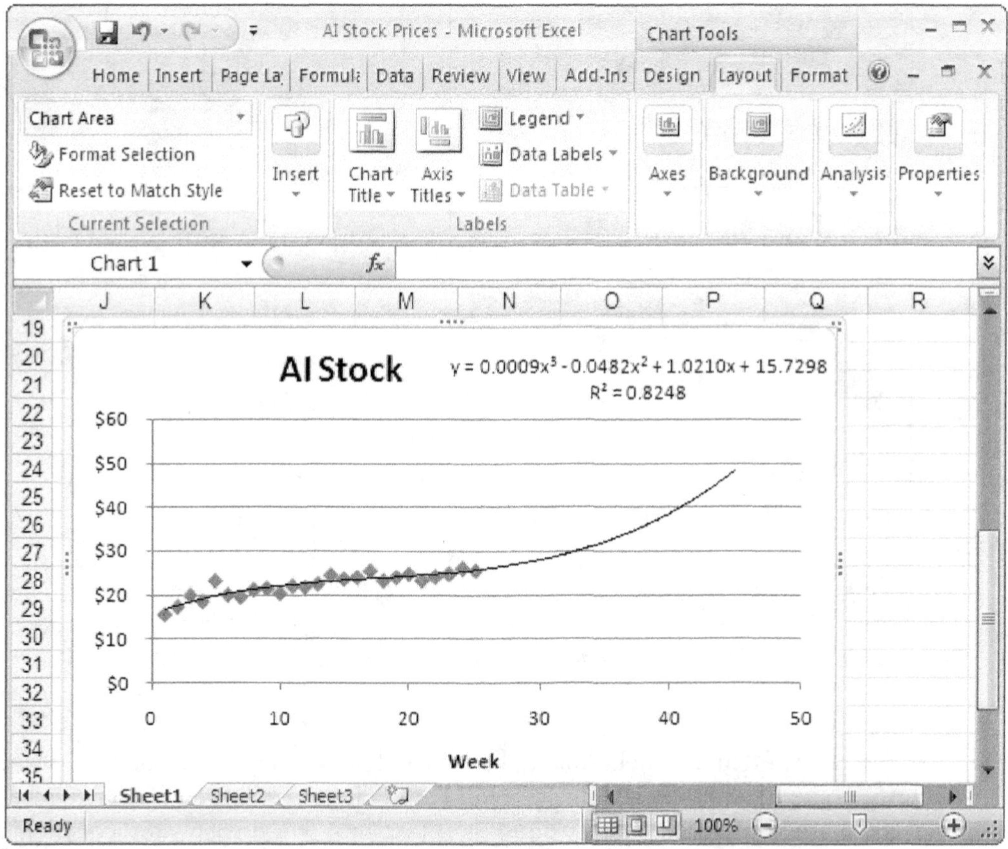

Figure 10-19. Fitting a polynomial equation of order 3 greatly improves the performance predicted for the stock price.

To determine what the trendline predicts for a longer period of time, we click on the trendline in the chart to select it and then right-click and select Format Trendline… from the pull-down menu that appears. We change the number of Forward Units requested from 20 to 40. We click on OK. The resulting chart is shown in Figure 10-20. According to the trendline, the stock will rise to over $130 in just 40 more weeks!

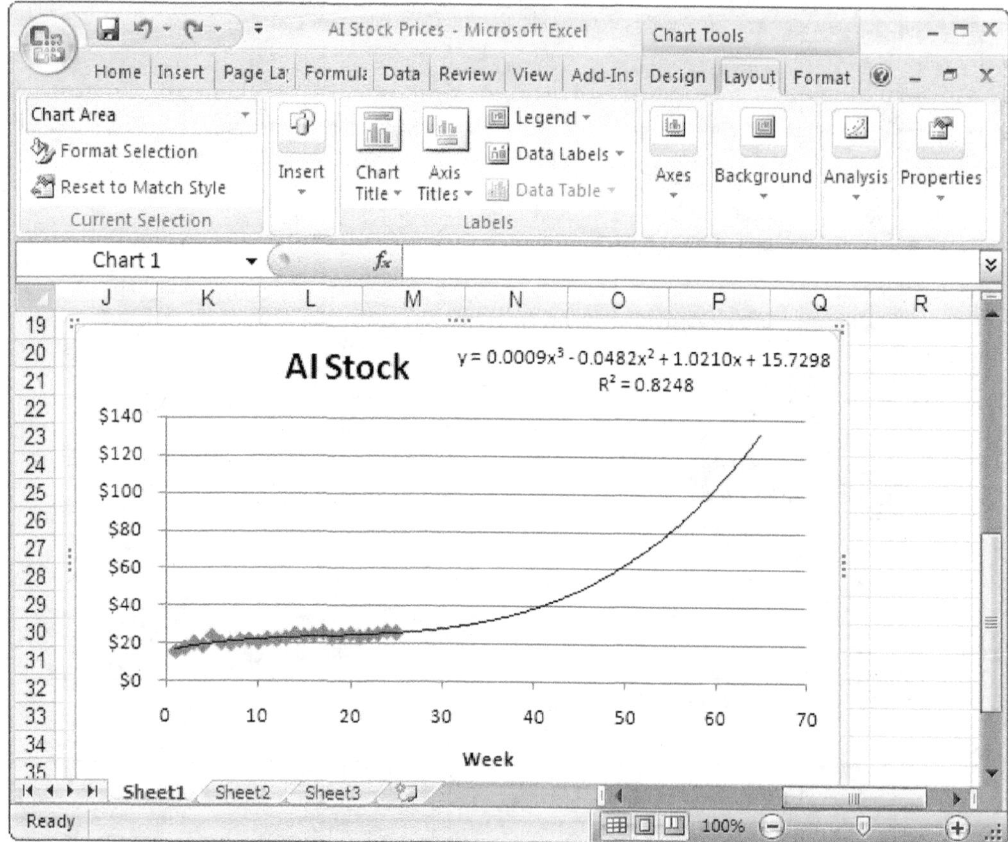

Figure 10-20. By week 60 we will be wealthy!

We'll make a fortune! *Caveat emptor.* Buyer beware. Trendlines based on past performance are not always good predictors of the future, as many people have discovered to their dismay.

3-D CHARTS

Excel does have the capability of drawing three-dimensional charts. Let's try out the Apple historical sales by product line data. The original data are shown again as a table in Figure 10-21. The data are shown in a 3-D Column chart in Figure 10-22. It took awhile to get all the product lines and years to show in the chart. Which is easier to read and to use to perceive trends?

There are some instances where 3-D charts are helpful. For example, Excel was used to produce the 3-D Column chart in Figure 10-23 that shows where people looked on the television screen as they watched television shows. The chart makes it easy to see that people usually look at the center of the screen and rarely at the edges. (Source: S. A. Brasel and J. Gips, "Points of View: Where Do We Look When We Watch TV?", *Perception*, December 2008.)

Apple Sales Tbl.xlsx - Microsoft Excel

Apple Sales by Product Line (in $ millions)

Source: Apple 10-K filings

	2005	2006	2007	2008	2009
Mac Desktops	3,436	3,319	4,023	5,622	4,324
Mac Portables	2,839	4,056	6,313	8,732	9,535
iPod	4,540	7,676	8,305	9,153	8,091
iTunes and other music	899	1,885	2,496	3,340	4,036
iPhone	-	-	630	6,742	13,033
Peripherals	1,126	1,100	1,303	1,694	1,475
Software and Service	1,091	1,279	1,508	2,208	2,411
Total Sales	13,931	19,315	24,578	37,491	42,905

Figure 10-21. Apple sales data as a table.

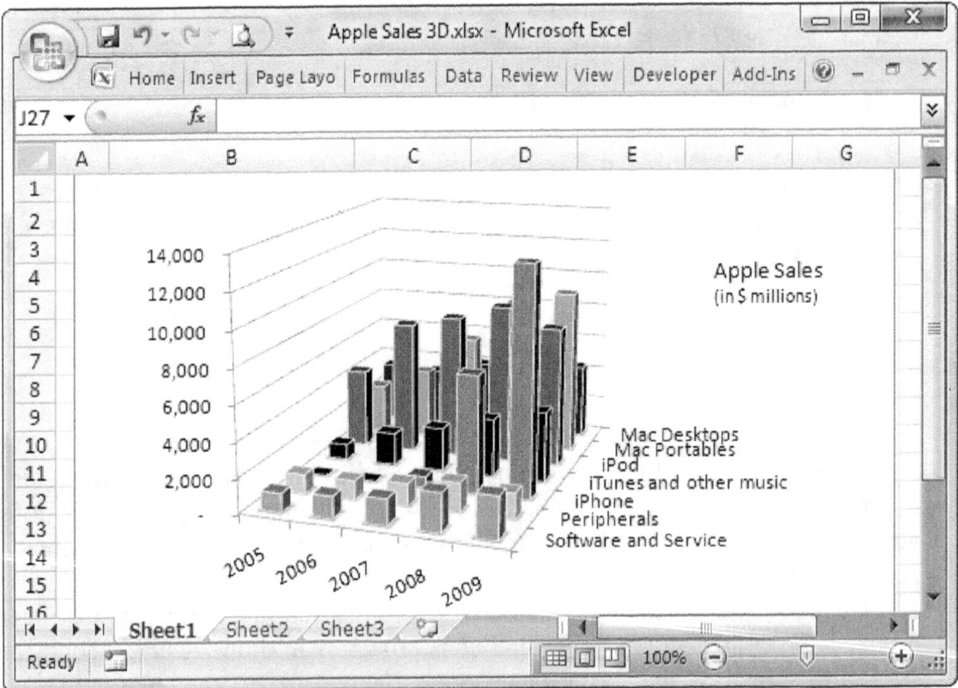

Figure 10-22. Apple sales data as a 3-D Column chart.

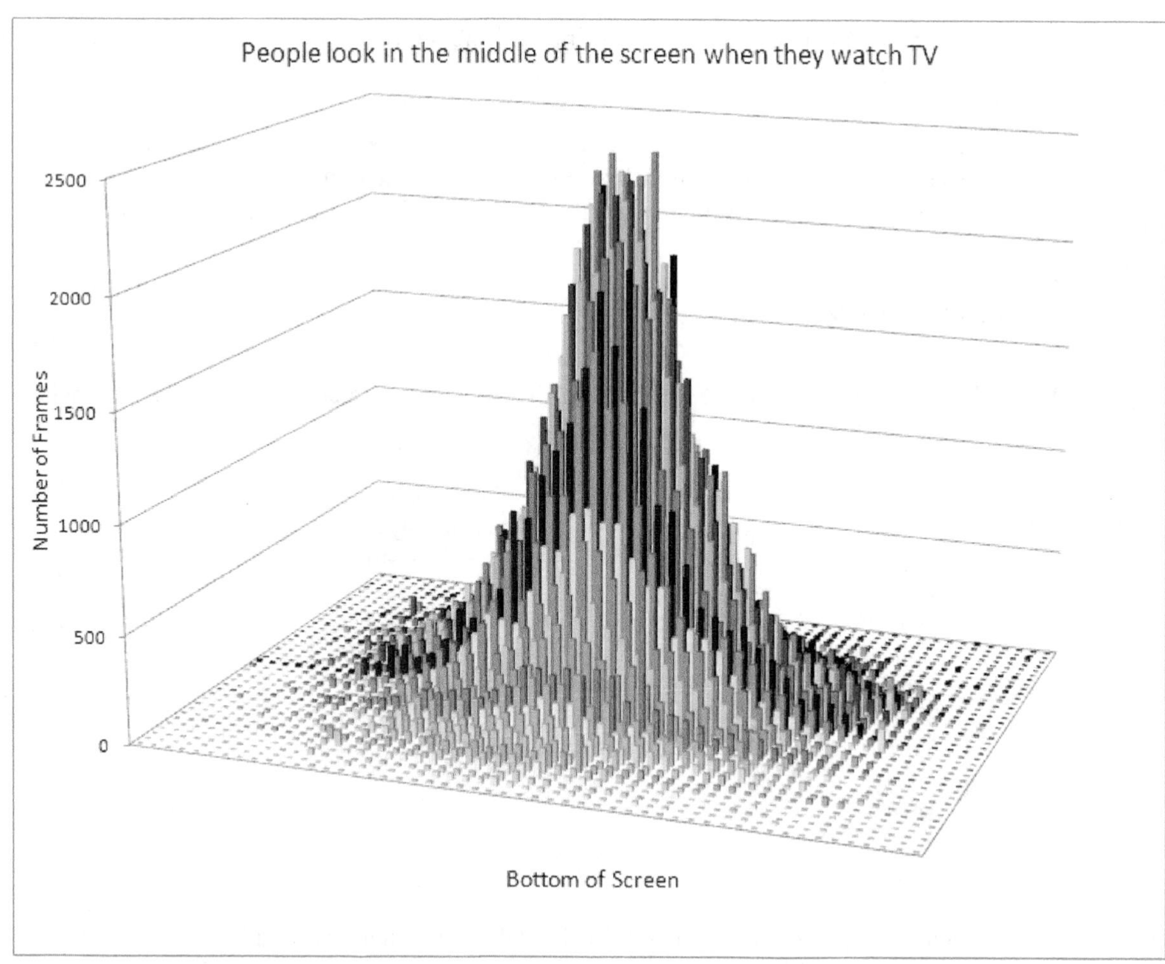

Figure 10-23. 3-D Column chart of the location of over 378,000 gaze points on a television screen.

PAPER AND PENCIL EXERCISE

10-1. For each of the following sets of data list the types of comparisons that could be made according to the five common comparison types, the types of charts that could be used, the type of chart you would use, and why.

(a) The total number of searches yesterday at Google, Yahoo!, Bing, Baidu, and Yandex.

(b) The number of people who apply for admission each year from 1995 to the present.

(c) The total number of A's, A-'s, B+'s, etc. given out in all undergraduate courses combined in an academic year.

(d) The number of billionaires in China, Japan, Mexico, Russia, and the United States.

(e) The number of years of schooling and the annual salary of every 40 year old who is an employee at General Electric.

(f) The number of entering students who arrive with a Macintosh bought through the university program, a Macintosh bought elsewhere, a Windows computer bought through the university program, a Windows computer bought elsewhere, no computer, and other.

COMPUTER EXERCISES

10-2. The following worksheet was used in Exercise 4-3. Either enter the worksheet with formulas or retrieve the worksheet from your disk.

Sales Analysis
Product Line by Season
(All Sales in $ Millions)

Product	Winter	Spring	Summer	Fall	Total	Max
Golf	3.2	6.2	5.7	3.9		
Tennis	4.7	5.2	7.1	2.9		
Skiing	3.7	2.1	1.1	5.2		
Surfing	1.2	2.1	2.9	1.3		
Total						
Average						

Produce four appropriate charts for the data. The charts should be of different types. All of the charts should be as understandable as possible and should be clearly identified with titles, legends, and so on.

10-3. Produce a well-labeled Line chart that illustrates the difference in obtaining fixed annual compound interest rates of 5%, 10%, and 15% on an investment of $100,000 over the course of 10 years. Your chart should show three curves: the value of the investment growing at 5% per year, 10% per year, and 15% per year. You first should create a worksheet with all of the values to be charted.

10-4. Create a worksheet that keeps track of your major living expenses over the past five months. Include at least four different categories of expenses (for example room and board, school, transportation, clothing, and misc.). Fill in numbers. You may use fictional numbers if you wish. Calculate row and column totals. Create four appropriate and informative charts from the data. All of the charts should be as understandable as possible and should be clearly identified with titles, legends, and so on.

10-5. The world population is estimated as follows:

Year	Population
1	200,000,000
1650	500,000,000
1850	1,000,000,000
1930	2,000,000,000
1975	4,000,000,000
2000	6,080,000,000

In the year A.D. 1, at the time of Jesus, there were fewer people in the entire world than there are in the United States today.

(a) Enter these values in a worksheet. (You may want to enter the populations in millions of people and leave off the six rightmost 0's.) Draw a Scatter chart of the population. The years should be the X axis values.

(b) Fit a trendline to the data. You choose the best type of trendline to use. Display the equation. Have Excel draw the trendline out past the year 2100. What will be the world population in the year 2100 according to the trendline? Does the trendline appear reasonable to you, to be a reasonable fit to the data? What do you think accounts for this?

(c) Create your own formula to fit the data. Your formula should be some function of the year and should yield the best possible approximation to the population in that year. Create a new column in your worksheet that shows the prediction made by your formula for each of the years in your worksheet. Now add the years 2010, 2020, through 2100 and your predictions for those years. Create a Scatter chart that has the years as the X axis values and both the actual population and your calculated population as data values. Does your formula appear to match the data? How does your trendline compare with the trendline calculated by Excel?

10-6. Obtain a recent financial statement or Annual Report for your college or university or for a company or organization with which you are familiar.

(a) Use the financial data to prepare four charts that best capture the most important points to be made about the financial situation of the organization. Your charts should be well thought out, well-labeled, and self-explanatory.

(b) Produce charts that use trendlines to show the future course of the organization if trends continue.

(c) Produce a written report on the financial health of the organization. Include your charts.

10-7. You have been asked to make a presentation to the United States Congress about the United States government's finances and its trends. Enter the data and then fill in formulas for the Total Receipts, Total Outlays, and Deficit.

U.S. Government Receipts and Outlays in Billions of Dollars
Source: http://www.whitehouse.gov/omb/budget/Historicals/ as of March 2010

	1980	1985	1990	1995	2000	2005	2010 (est.)
Receipts							
Individual Income Taxes	244	335	467	588	1,004	927	936
Corporate Income Taxes	65	61	94	151	207	278	157
Social Insurance Taxes	158	265	380	484	653	794	876
Excise Taxes	24	36	35	58	69	73	73
Other	26	37	56	63	92	81	124
Total Receipts							
Outlays							
National Defense	134	253	299	272	294	495	719
Social Security	119	189	249	336	409	523	721
Income Security	87	128	147	223	253	346	686
Medicare	32	66	98	157	197	298	457
All Other Government	166	181	275	293	413	626	951
Interest	53	129	184	234	223	184	187
Total Outlays							
Surplus (Deficit)							

(a) Use the worksheet to prepare four charts that best capture the most important historical and present points to be made about the U.S. budget. Your charts should be well thought out, well-labeled, and self-explanatory.

(b) Create a chart that shows the deficit or surplus over the six time periods and then uses a trendline to forecast what the deficit or surplus would be up through 2025 if the trend continues.

(c) Prepare the text of your testimony. State in English the important points that your charts illustrate.

(d) Create a PowerPoint presentation to accompany your testimony. Include the charts in the presentation along with other appropriate screens.

10-8. From finance.google.com (or from elsewhere) obtain a series of prices for an individual stock or for the Dow Jones Industrial or some other standard average. In finance.google.com enter in a company name or stock symbol and then click on Get Quotes and on Historical Prices. Then click on Download to Spreadsheet and Save. The data will be downloaded to your disk as a .csv file (comma separated values file), which can be opened with Excel. Create a chart of the data. Fit an appropriate trendline to the data. What does the trendline predict for the future?

10-9. The following data on the prevalence of smoking among adults is from the World Health Organization (Source: http://www.who.int/tobacco/en/atlas40.pdf).

Country	Males	Females
Brazil	38.2%	29.3%
Canada	27.0%	23.0%
France	38.6%	30.3%
Japan	52.8%	13.4%
Russian Federation	63.2%	9.7%
United States	25.7%	21.5%

(a) Create a chart that presents the data as clearly as possible.

(b) Create a workbook with five worksheets. The last four worksheets should have different ways of presenting the data in charts or tables. The first worksheet should have a paragraph that indicates which worksheet you think best presents the data and why.

10-10. Key data for measuring historical global temperature change comes from ice core samples. Scientists drill deep into the ice in a location that has been frozen for hundreds of thousands of years and extract a long cylinder of ice. The farther down the cylinder, the older the ice. By looking at the characteristics of the sample at different depths, scientists can estimate the temperature of the surface at the time the ice was formed.

Two commonly used sets of ice core data are from Greenland and from Vostok, Antarctica. Both sets of data are available for free from the National Climatic Data Center of the National Oceanic and Atmospheric Administration of the U.S. Department of Commerce. The Greenland data is at http://www.ncdc.noaa.gov/paleo/metadata/noaa-icecore-2475.html. The Vostok data is at http://www.ncdc.noaa.gov/paleo/metadata/noaa-icecore-2453.html and then in file deutnat.txt. The Greenland data extends back almost 50,000 years. A copy of the complete Greenland Temperature Reconstruction and Accumulation data file has been placed at http://www.masteringexcel.com/greenland.doc. The Vostok data extends back over 400,000 years. A copy of the complete Vostok Ice Core Deuterium and Temperature data file has been placed at http://www.masteringexcel.com/vostok.txt.

(a) Download the Greenland data file either from masteringexcel.com/greenland.doc or from the government site. Open the file in Word or Notepad or your browser. Scroll down. The first data set consists of two columns, the age of the sample in thousands of years before the present and the estimated temperature in central Greenland at that time in degrees Centigrade. Select all of this first set of data (and the explanation at the top if you would like). Copy and Paste the data into a new Excel worksheet. The last entry should be 49.981 and -39.9694, meaning that 49.981 thousand years ago it was -39.964° Centigrade in central Greenland. Notice that the data probably are all contained in one column instead of two. If so, use the Text to Columns tools, as explained in Chapter 5, to separate the data into two columns. Now create two new columns to be charted, the first with the number of years ago expressed as a negative number (and multiplied by a thousand) and the other with a copy of the temperature data. So the last entry should become -49981 and -39.964.

Create three Greenland Scatter charts: one of the temperatures over the last 500 years, one of the temperatures over the last 5,000 years, and one of all of the available temperature data going back 50,000 years. It's probably best to use a Scatter Chart with Smooth Lines. Label the charts appropriately. An even longer range picture can be seen from the Vostok data.

(b) Download the Vostok data from http://www.masteringexcel.com/vostok.txt or from the government site. Copy and Paste the 3310 rows of data into a new worksheet in the same Excel workbook. Use the Text to Columns tool if necessary. There are four columns of data. The second column gives the age of the sample in years and the fourth column gives the estimated temperature as a deviation from the present. Create two new columns to be charted. The first column with the number of years ago expressed as a negative number and the second with the temperature deviation from the present as given. So the final row of data should be -422766 and 0.23, meaning that 422,766 years ago the temperature in Vostok was 0.23 degrees warmer than the present. Now create a Scatter Chart with Smooth Lines of all of the data. Label the chart appropriately. Label the worksheets.

Note that neither set of data contains temperature readings for the last century. The Intergovernmental Panel on Climate Change (http://ipcc.ch) estimates that the temperature rose 0.7° Centigrade between 1900 and 2008. (http://www.ipcc.ch/graphics/syr/fig1-1.jpg)

(c) The two data sets were created separately. Of course Greenland and Antarctica are on opposite ends of the planet. How do the two data sets compare? Copy the Greenland data to a third worksheet. Copy the most recent 50,000 years of the Vostok data to the worksheet. Create a Scatter chart of the Greenland data and below it a Scatter chart of the last 50,000 years of the Vostok data. Do they seem to be in alignment?

CHAPTER 11

LOGICAL FUNCTIONS

OBJECTIVES

In this chapter you will learn how to:

- Use IF functions to select between alternatives
- Create logical tests using comparison operators
- Use nested IF functions to select among multiple alternatives
- Implement complex conditions using the AND, OR, and NOT functions

Sometimes we would like a cell to display one of two or more alternative values. If you sell over $2 million you receive a bonus of $1,000, otherwise you receive no bonus. People caught driving at a speed over 80 miles per hour owe a fine of $200; people caught driving between 66 and 80 owe $90; otherwise, no fine. In this chapter we will look at functions that are designed to solve the problem of making decisions and selecting among alternatives.

THE IF FUNCTION

For orders under $100 there is a $5 Shipping charge. For orders of $100 or more there is no charge for Shipping. The total of the order is in cell D35 of a worksheet. What formula will calculate the Shipping charge?

The solution is to use an **IF** function, as follows:

=IF(D35<100, 5, 0)

The IF function always has three arguments:

=IF(logical_test, value_if_true, value_if_false)

The first argument is a **logical test**. A logical test is an expression that evaluates to **TRUE** or **FALSE**. In this case the logical test is D35<100. If D35 is less than 100 then the logical test is TRUE, otherwise the logical test is FALSE. Logical tests usually contain one or more of the following **comparison operators**:

operator	meaning
<	less than
<=	less than or equal to
=	equal to
>=	greater than or equal to
>	greater than
<>	not equal to

Note that the operators <= >= <> are formed by two consecutive keystrokes.

The second argument in an IF function is the value of the IF function if the logical test is TRUE. The third argument is the value of the IF function if the logical test is FALSE. That is, the result of evaluating an IF function is always either the second argument or the third argument. If the first argument is TRUE then the IF function evaluates to the second argument. If the first argument is FALSE then the IF function evaluates to the third argument.

In the example, if the value in D35 is 34, then the condition (the logical test) in the IF function is TRUE and the value of the IF function is 5. If the value in cell D35 is changed to 200, then the condition becomes FALSE and the value of the IF function changes to 0.

The second and third arguments in the IF function can be any formula. For example, suppose orders under $100 are charged 5% for shipping. Then the formula would be

=IF(D35<100, 5%*D35, 0)

A cell can contain just a logical test. That is, a cell could contain the formula =D23<>4 or a cell could contain =X17>(0.8*Q55). In this case, Excel would show either TRUE or FALSE in the cell. TRUE and FALSE are called **logical values**.

ANOTHER EXAMPLE

Salespeople who sell at least $2,000,000 are entitled to a free trip to Hawaii. The names of the salespeople and their sales figures are listed in the worksheet in Figure 11-1.

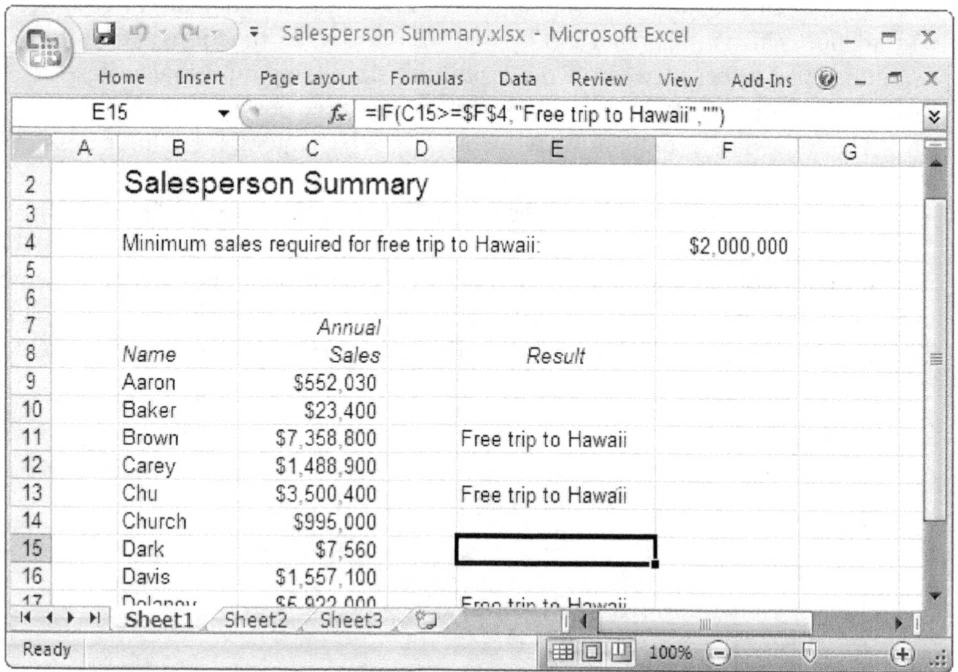

Figure 11-1. People with sales of at least $2,000,000 are entitled to a free trip to Hawaii.

What formula should be entered into cell E9 (and filled down) so that the cell contains "Free trip to Hawaii" if the person is eligible and appears blank otherwise? The answer is

=IF(C9>=$F$4, "Free trip to Hawaii", "")

The second and third arguments of the IF function are character strings that are enclosed in quotation marks. Thus if the logical test C9>=$F$4 is TRUE then the result of evaluating the function is the text "Free trip to Hawaii". If the condition C9>=$F$4 is FALSE the result of evaluating the function is the text that contains nothing, that is blank.

Text must be enclosed in quotation marks. The formula =IF(C9>=$F$4, Free trip to Hawaii, "") will not work. If the quotation marks were absent from the second argument then Excel would attempt to interpret Free trip to Hawaii as the name of a cell. Since no cell has that name (and indeed because the phrase contains a space it would be an illegal name anyway), if you try to leave the quotes off, the computer would display #NAME? in the cell, an error message meaning it does not recognize a name.

NESTED IF FUNCTIONS

Suppose that salespeople who sell under $100,000 are to be fired. Now there are three choices for the cells in column E. Cell E9 should contain “Free trip to Hawaii” if cell C9 contains a value of at least $2,000,000. Cell E9 should appear blank if cell C9 contains a value between $100,000 and $2,000,000. Cell E9 should contain “Fired” if cell C9 is under $100,000. This is illustrated in Figure 11-2. So far, IF functions have allowed us to create formulas that select between two possibilities depending on a logical test. In this example, we need a formula that allows us to select among three possibilities.

The following formula in E9 will correctly select among these three possibilities:

=IF(C9>=$F$4, "Free trip to Hawaii", IF(C9<$F$5,"Fired",""))

The formula contains nested IF functions. This means that one IF function contains another IF function as an argument. The formula can be read as follows: If C9 is greater than or equal to F4 then this cell should show “Free trip to Hawaii”. Otherwise, if C9 is less than

Salesperson Summary.xlsx - Microsoft Excel

Home Insert Page Layout Formulas Data Review View Add-Ins

E14 =IF(C14>=$F$4,"Free trip to Hawaii",IF(C14<$F$5,"Fired",""))

	A	B	C	D	E	F	G
1							
2		Salesperson Summary					
3							
4		Minimum sales required for free trip to Hawaii:				$2,000,000	
5		People who sell under this amount are fired:				$100,000	
6							
7			*Annual*				
8		*Name*	*Sales*		*Result*		
9		Aaron	$552,030				
10		Baker	$23,400		Fired		
11		Brown	$7,358,800		Free trip to Hawaii		
12		Carey	$1,488,900				
13		Chu	$3,500,400		Free trip to Hawaii		
14		Church	$995,000				
15		Dark	$7,560		Fired		
16		Davis	$1,557,100				

Sheet1 Sheet2 Sheet3

Ready 100%

Figure 11-2. People with sales of under $100,000 are fired. Now there are three possibilities.

F5 then this cell should show "Fired", otherwise this cell should appear blank. The only way the cell will appear blank is if both conditions are FALSE. What are the arguments here? The outer IF function has three arguments:

1. The logical test: C9>$F$4
2. The value if the condition is TRUE: "Free trip to Hawaii"
3. The value if the condition is FALSE: IF(C9<$F$5,"Fired","")

The inner IF function is the third argument. It, too, clearly has three arguments:

1. The logical test: C9<$F$5
2. The value if the condition is TRUE : "Fired"
3. The value if the condition is FALSE: ""

Thus the inner IF function is nested within the outer IF function. The key to working with nested IF functions is to remember that IF functions always should have exactly three arguments. Nested IF functions are evaluated from the outside in.

YOU TRY

A worksheet for tabulating the results of the Eagles hockey season is shown in Figure 11-3. We would like the cells in column G to say "Win" if the Eagles won, "Tie" if the number of points each team scored was equal, and "Lose" if the Eagles lost. What should be the formula in G7? Write out your answer before continuing.

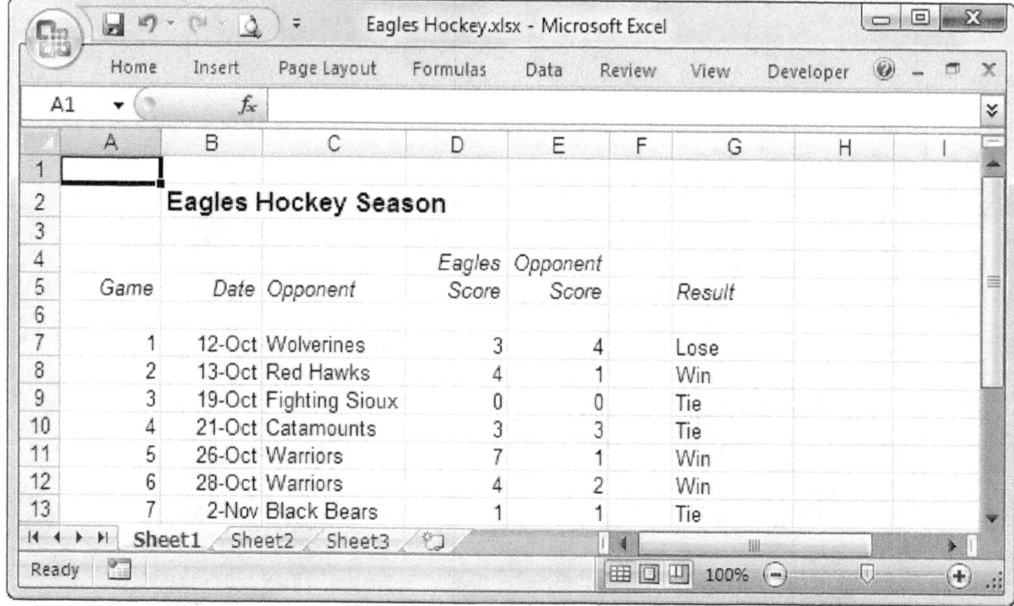

Eagles Hockey Season

Game	Date	Opponent	Eagles Score	Opponent Score		Result
1	12-Oct	Wolverines	3	4		Lose
2	13-Oct	Red Hawks	4	1		Win
3	19-Oct	Fighting Sioux	0	0		Tie
4	21-Oct	Catamounts	3	3		Tie
5	26-Oct	Warriors	7	1		Win
6	28-Oct	Warriors	4	2		Win
7	2-Nov	Black Bears	1	1		Tie

Figure 11-3. What formula has been placed in G7 and filled down?

There are several possible correct answers. A good solution would be

=IF(D7>E7, "Win", IF(D7=E7,"Tie","Lose"))

Here the computer first checks to see if D7 is greater than E7. If that logical test is TRUE then the answer is “Win” and the evaluation is over. If D7 is not greater than E7 then the computer evaluates the third argument, the inner IF function. Now the computer checks the first argument of the inner IF function. The computer checks to see if D7 equals E7. If D7 does equal E7 then the answer is “Tie”. If the first condition is FALSE and then the second condition is FALSE then the answer is “Lose”.

With nested IF functions Excel always makes its way from the outside in.

We could rearrange the order, for example, by checking for a tie first:

=IF(D7=E7, "Tie", IF(D7>E7,"Win","Lose"))

There are four other similar rearrangements that would work.

Suppose we want the cells in column G to contain the name of the team that won (or the word “Tie”) as in the worksheet shown in Figure 11-4. What formula would you put in cell G7 and then fill down?

Eagles Hockey.xlsx - Microsoft Excel

Eagles Hockey Season

Game	Date	Opponent	Eagles Score	Opponent Score	Result
1	12-Oct	Wolverines	3	4	Wolverines
2	13-Oct	Red Hawks	4	1	Eagles
3	19-Oct	Fighting Sioux	0	0	Tie
4	21-Oct	Catamounts	3	3	Tie
5	26-Oct	Warriors	7	1	Eagles
6	28-Oct	Warriors	4	2	Eagles
7	2-Nov	Black Bears	1	1	Tie
8	9-Nov	Warriors	3	3	Tie
9	10-Nov	Wildcats	2	5	Wildcats
10	16-Nov	Minutemen	1	1	Tie
11	17-Nov	Minutemen	2	3	Minutemen
12	23-Nov	Huskies	3	4	Huskies
13	30-Nov	Terriers	6	2	Eagles

Figure 11-4. We would like the name of the winner to appear in column G or the word “Tie” if there is a tie. What is the formula in G7?

Here, what we would need to do is to change two of the arguments, as follows:

=IF(D7>E7, "Eagles", IF(D7=E7,"Tie",C7))

The cell C7 contains the name of the opponent. Of course, when this formula is filled down, the row numbers of C7, D7, and E7 will be adjusted accordingly.

If we wanted to choose among four alternatives, we would need three nested IF functions. There can be up to 64 nested IF functions in a formula. Again, each IF function should have three arguments. Any of these arguments can be other IF functions.

LOGICAL FUNCTIONS AND, OR, NOT

At the Tropical Resort there are 600 guest rooms. The guest rooms are classified as suites, doubles, or singles. Some face the beach, some face the pool, and some face inland (the parking lot). The resort manager has decided to charge $259 per night for suites that face the beach. All other rooms will be $179 per night. The worksheet in Figure 11-5 shows a list of the guest rooms. Each cell in column E should contain the price of the room. What formula should appear in cell E6 and then be filled down?

Clearly, we want to use an IF function here as there are two alternatives. The IF function would have the basic form

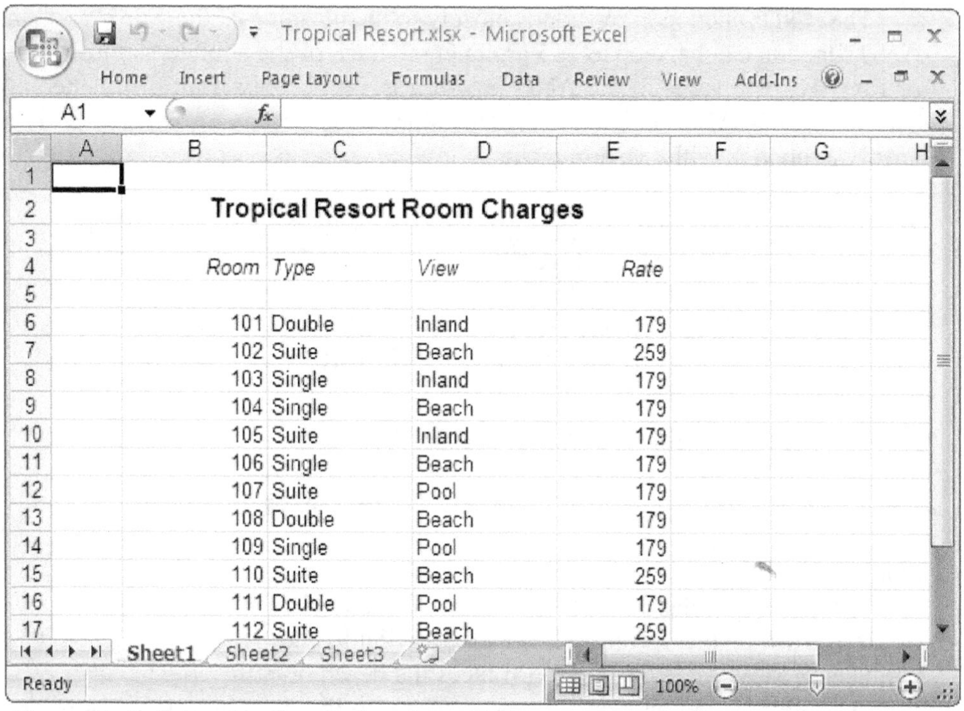

Tropical Resort.xlsx - Microsoft Excel

Tropical Resort Room Charges

Room	Type	View	Rate
101	Double	Inland	179
102	Suite	Beach	259
103	Single	Inland	179
104	Single	Beach	179
105	Suite	Inland	179
106	Single	Beach	179
107	Suite	Pool	179
108	Double	Beach	179
109	Single	Pool	179
110	Suite	Beach	259
111	Double	Pool	179
112	Suite	Beach	259

Figure 11-5. Suites that face the beach are $259 per night. All other rooms are $179 per night. What formula has been placed in E6 and filled down?

=IF(logical_test, 259, 179)

Now we need to fill in the logical test. There are two parts to the logical test, both of which must be TRUE for the logical test as a whole to be TRUE. That is, in order for the room to cost $259 the room both must be a suite and must face the beach.

First, we can check whether a cell contains a specific label with a logical test like C6="Suite". This logical test will be TRUE if C6 contains the word "Suite" and FALSE otherwise.

Excel provides the **AND** function for the purpose of testing whether two or more logical values are all TRUE. The completed formula would be

=IF(AND(C6="Suite",D6="Beach"), 259, 179)

The logical test is AND(C6="Suite",D6="Beach") This logical test will be TRUE only if both C6 contains the word "Suite" and D6 contains the word "Beach".

The AND function sometimes is called a **Boolean function**. (George Boole was an English mathematician who developed key ideas of symbolic logic. His best known book is *The Laws of Thought*, which was published in 1854.) Boolean functions work on arguments that are logical values, that are TRUE or FALSE, just the way that arithmetic functions, like SUM and AVERAGE, work on arguments that are numbers. The value produced by a Boolean function also is a logical value (just the way that the value produced by an arithmetic function is a number). An AND function always evaluates to TRUE or FALSE.

The AND function corresponds closely to the meaning of the word "and" in English. An AND function can have up to 255 arguments. Each of the arguments must evaluate to TRUE or FALSE. The value of the AND function is TRUE only if all of its operands are TRUE. The value of an AND function is FALSE if any of its arguments is FALSE. For example, for an AND function with two arguments:

Function	Value
AND(TRUE,TRUE)	TRUE
AND(TRUE,FALSE)	FALSE
AND(FALSE,TRUE)	FALSE
AND(FALSE,FALSE)	FALSE

So, for example, the value of

=AND(2+2=4,3+3=5)

would be FALSE.

There are two other Boolean functions: **OR** and **NOT**.

If we wrote the formula =IF(OR(D6="Suite",E6="Beach"), 259, 179) then a room would cost $259 if it is a suite or if it faces the beach or both.

The OR function also corresponds closely to the meaning of the word "or" in English. An OR function can have up to 30 arguments. Each of the arguments must evaluate to TRUE or FALSE. The value of the OR function is TRUE only if any of its operands is TRUE. The value of an OR function is FALSE only if all of its arguments are FALSE. For example, for an OR function with two arguments:

Function	Value
OR(TRUE,TRUE)	TRUE
OR(TRUE,FALSE)	TRUE
OR(FALSE,TRUE)	TRUE
OR(FALSE,FALSE)	FALSE

So, for example, the value of

=OR(2+2=4,3+3=5)

would be TRUE.

The NOT function transforms TRUE into FALSE and FALSE into TRUE.

Function	Value
NOT(TRUE)	FALSE
NOT(FALSE)	TRUE

The NOT function can have only a single argument. The NOT function also follows normal English usage. I hold a black belt in the martial arts. Not!

ANOTHER EXAMPLE

Suppose the manager decides that suites that face the beach will be $259. All other suites will be $189. Doubles that do not face inland will be $189. All other rooms will be $149. (See Figure 11-6.)

Now we have three possibilities. The formula for cell E6 could have the form

=IF(logical_test1, 259, IF(logical_test2,189,149))

We need to fill in the logical tests. Logical_test1 is the same as before, namely

AND(C6="Suite",D6="Beach")

The tough one is logical_test2. Logical_test2 consists of an OR of two parts. The first part of logical_test2 is

D6="Suite"

The second part of logical_test2 is

AND(C6="Double",NOT(D6="Inland"))

Tropical Resort 2.xlsx - Microsoft Excel

Home Insert Page Layout Formulas Data Review View Add-Ins

E6 =IF(AND(C6="Suite",D6="Beach"), 259, IF(OR(C6="Suite", AND(C6="Double",NOT(D6="Inland"))), 189, 149))

	A	B	C	D	E	F	G	H
1								
2		**Tropical Resort Room Charges**						
3								
4		*Room*	*Type*	*View*	*Rate*			
5								
6		101	Double	Inland	149			
7		102	Suite	Beach	259			
8		103	Single	Inland	149			
9		104	Single	Beach	149			
10		105	Suite	Inland	189			
11		106	Single	Beach	149			
12		107	Suite	Pool	189			
13		108	Double	Beach	189			
14		109	Single	Pool	149			
15		110	Suite	Beach	259			
16		111	Double	Pool	189			
17		112	Suite	Beach	259			

Sheet1 Sheet2 Sheet3

Ready 100%

Figure 11-6. Suites that face the beach are $259 per night. All other suites are $189, as are all doubles that do not face inland. All other rooms are $149. (Note that this button controls whether the formula is displayed in one line or multiple lines.)

So the entire formula would be

=IF(AND(C6="Suite",D6="Beach"), 259, IF(OR(C6="Suite",
AND(C6="Double",NOT(D6="Inland"))),189,149))

Alternatively, the formula could be written

=IF(AND(C6="Suite",D6="Beach"), 259, IF(C6="Suite",189,
IF(AND(C6="Double",NOT(D6="Inland")),189,149)))

Here we have treated the two parts of logical_test2 separately. Another nested IF has been added to accommodate this extra condition. This formula resembles the original statement of the problem on the previous page. Do you see how these two formulas are equivalent? If not, you might take a few minutes to work through the two formulas by writing out the arguments for each of the IF functions and applying the formulas to the examples in Figure 11-6.

TESTING IF FUNCTIONS

Testing worksheets that contain IF functions presents a challenge. Consider the worksheet for salespeople in Figure 11-2. The worksheet basically contains one nested IF function that has been filled down column E. To test this worksheet you should try Annual Sales values of (1) a number more than $2,000,000 (for example $5,000,000), (2) the number $2,000,000 exactly, (3) a number between $2,000,000 and $100,000 (for example $995,000), (4) the number $100,000 exactly, and (5) a number below $100,000 (for example $23,400). You also should try varying the value in C9 (the top cell in the column) and the value in C89 (the bottom cell in the column) and the value in a cell between just to be sure that the formula was filled down correctly. You also should try changing the threshold values in F4 and F5.

IF functions with complicated conditions require careful testing. Worksheets with many independent IF functions require very extensive testing to make sure that they are correct. It is quite possible and common for a worksheet with IF functions to work correctly most of the time but to fail when certain relatively unlikely conditions are true.

PENCIL AND PAPER EXERCISES

11-1. Consider the following worksheet:

Ex11_1.xlsx - Microsoft Excel

	A	B	C	D	E	F	G	H
1								
2		Exercise 11-1						
3								
4	86	-4	-8	fun				
5	-47	5	26	37				
6	2.3	7	Excel	198				
7	computer	18	4.6	3				
8	56	102		-19				
9								

What would be the result of evaluating each of the following formulas? Assume that no errors will result from the formulas.

(a) =IF(B5>6,"Yes","No")

(b) =IF(B4<D6,C5,A6)

(c) =IF(SUM(B4:B7)>=D5,A4,"Nope")

(d) =B5<A5

(e) =(2*B6)>(C4+10)

(f) =IF(B7=12,47,IF(C4<D7,59,B7))

(g) =IF(C4=26,IF(B5=19,2,4),IF(A8=56,6,8))

(h) =AND(A8>B7,D6<B6)

(i) =IF(AND(K25<10,K25>20),A4,B7)

(j) =IF(OR(K25>10,K25<20),A4,B7)

(k) =IF(AND(OR(B6=7,C6="Excel"),NOT(B7>20)),44,33)

(l) =IF(OR(NOT(B5<6),D7>3),A7,IF(AND(C4=2*B4,D8>D7),C6,D4))

(m) =IF(D5="D5",D5,"D5")

11-2. What is the result of evaluating each of the following formulas?

(a) =IF(AND(6>3,8>2,2>7),"Mastering","Excel")

(b) =IF(OR(1>3,8>2),"yes",5)

(c) =IF(OR(AND(4>2,2>3),OR(4>7,4>5)),7,9)

(d) =IF(AND(6>3,4>7),IF(5>2,8,7),IF(5>3,3,9))

(e) =IF(SUM(3,5,7)=MAX(11,19,15),23,IF(NOT(OR(4=5,MIN(4,1,3)=1)), IF(4>2,6,7),9))

11-3. The ages of John, Juan, and Wan are in cells D4, D5, and D6. Give the Excel equivalents of the following conditions. I have answered (a) to give you the idea. Each of the parts is independent of the others.

(a) Juan is at least 18 years old. *Answer: (D5>=18)*

(b) Wan is not more than 55.

(c) John is at most 23.

(d) Juan is not 37.

(e) Both Wan and John are under 25.

(f) John is between 19 and 23, inclusive.

(g) At least one of the people is over 21.

(h) No one is over 65.

(i) Everyone is over 17.

(j) Juan and Wan are under 22 but John is not.

(k) Exactly one of the people is 20.

(l) Wan is within three years of Juan.

(m) John is the oldest and Juan is the youngest.

(n) John and Wan are not over 21.

11-4. We are creating a worksheet to select stocks for our clients. We have gathered some of the relevant data in the following worksheet. The P/E Ratio is the closing price divided by this year's earnings.

	A	B	C	D	E	F	G
1							
2		**Our Stock Recommendations**					
3							
4	Stock	Earnings	Earnings	Earnings	Closing	P/E	We
5		2 yrs ago	Last yr.	This yr.	Price	Ratio	Recommend
6							
7	AA Electronics	$3.47	$3.59	$3.83	$48.50	12.7	
8	Ardvark Intl.	$0.69	$1.24	$0.53	$15.75	29.7	
9	Abaco	$4.23	$5.89	$5.92	$33.25	5.6	
10	Abandon Mines	$0.12	$0.15	$0.23	$2.25	9.8	
11	Abernathy	$1.27	$1.31	$0.96	$21.00	21.9	

What formula would go into cell G7 and be filled down for each of the following recommendations? Each of the cells in column G should contain "Buy", "Hold", "Sell", or appear blank. When no recommendation is made, the cell should appear blank. I have answered part (a) just to give you the basic idea. Each part is independent of the others.

(a) Buy if the P/E Ratio is below 10. *Answer: =IF(F7<10,"Buy","")*

(b) Buy if the earnings have increased this year.
Sell if the earnings have decreased this year.

(c) Buy if the earnings have increased for each of the two years and the P/E Ratio is below 10.
Sell if the earnings have decreased for each of the two years.

(d) Buy if this year's earnings are up over 20% from last year and this year's earnings are up over 30% from 2 years ago or if the P/E ratio is below 8.
Sell if this year's earnings are down over 20% from last year or if the P/E ratio is above 20.
Hold otherwise.

11-5. In determining whether they are to receive a bonus, each of our 5,000 employees has been rated between 1 and 100 on each of three factors.

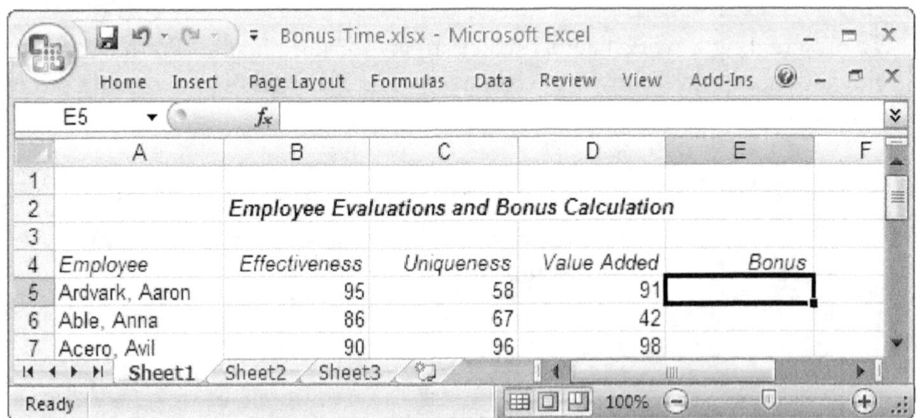

	A	B	C	D	E
1					
2		*Employee Evaluations and Bonus Calculation*			
3					
4	*Employee*	*Effectiveness*	*Uniqueness*	*Value Added*	*Bonus*
5	Ardvark, Aaron	95	58	91	
6	Able, Anna	86	67	42	
7	Acero, Avil	90	96	98	

Give the formula that can be entered in E5 and filled down to fulfill each of the following. Each employee's bonus depends on that employee's ratings. Each of the four parts below is independent of the other parts. You may use extra cells.

(a) If all the ratings are 90 or above then the person receives a bonus of $20,000.
Otherwise if all the ratings are 80 or above the person receives $10,000.
Otherwise no bonus.

(b) If at least one of the ratings is above 90 and none of the factors are below 80 the person receives a bonus of $20,000.
Otherwise if at least one of the ratings is above 80 the person receives $10,000.
Otherwise no bonus.

(c) If at least two of the ratings are above 90 the person receives a $20,000 bonus.
Otherwise no bonus.

(d) If all three of the ratings are within 5 points of each other the employee receives a $20,000 bonus.
Otherwise no bonus.

COMPUTER EXERCISES

11-6. At Hill University students who register for at least 12 credits are considered Full-Time students and pay $4,320 tuition. Students who register for less than 12 credits are considered Part-Time students and pay $360 per credit. Create a worksheet that allows you to enter a student's name and the number of credits for which he or she is registering. The worksheet should then display (1) the status of the student (Full-Time or Part-Time) and (2) the amount of tuition owed. Try your worksheet on the following three students: Maria 15 credits, John 6 credits, and Yu 12 credits.

11-7. At the Downtown Theater: Orchestra seats are $40, Mezzanine seats are $30, and Balcony seats are $20. Children (under 12) are half price. Seniors (65 or over) receive a $5 discount. Create a worksheet that allows you to enter the location of the ticket desired and the age of the person and gives you the price of the ticket. If the person types in an illegal seat location the worksheet should so inform the user. You can use as many cells as you would like. Try your worksheet for Orchestra for an 88-year-old, Mezzanine for a 7 year-old, Backstage for an 18 year-old, and Orchestra for a 21 year-old.

11-8. A company evaluates new graduates for positions according to three criteria. If the candidate has a Grade Point Average (GPA) of at least 3.3, the candidate receives 1 point. On the interview, candidates who score 7 or 8 (out of 10) receive 1 point; candidates who score 9 or 10 receive 2 points. The company gives an aptitude test as well. A candidate who scores above 85 gets 1 point.

The company adds up the points to obtain a candidate's rating. A candidate who receives a rating of 0, 1, or 2 points is not given a job offer. A candidate who receives 3 points is given an offer as a Junior Salesperson. A candidate who receives 4 points is given an offer as a fast-track Manager in Training. Create a worksheet that allows the Human Resources Department to enter in a candidate's name, GPA, interview score, and aptitude score and determines the employment decision.

11-9. Leary, Lebowsky, and Li are running for mayor.

(a) Create a worksheet that has the names of the candidates and next to the names the number of votes each receives. Now create another cell with a formula that gives the name of the winner, for example "Li wins!" You may assume there are no ties.

(b) Modify your worksheet so it allows for two-way ties ("Leary and Li tie!") or even for a three-way tie.

(c) Lopez has entered the race. Now there are four candidates. Create a worksheet that has the names of the candidates and next to the names the number of votes each receives. Now create another cell with a formula that gives the name of the winner, for example "Li wins!" You may assume there are no ties.

11-10. An employee is eligible for retirement if he or she satisfies at least one of the following three criteria:

(i) the employee has worked here for at least 40 years
(ii) the employee is 65 or over
(iii) the employee has worked here for at least 30 years and is 60 or over

(a) Create a worksheet that allows a person to enter in his or her age and the number of years worked here. A cell in the worksheet should respond either "Congratulations! You are eligible for retirement!" or "Back to work."

(b) Add a cell that will indicate how many years it will be until the employee is eligible for retirement if he or she is not now eligible. You may use extra cells in your worksheet.

11-11. At the county courthouse speeders pay a fine of $50 plus $5 for every mph above the speed limit. Anyone caught driving 90 mph or over pays an extra $200. Create a worksheet that will allow you to enter a driver's name, the speed limit on the road where the driver was caught, and the driver's speed. If the driver's speed did not exceed the speed limit, then the worksheet should display "Sorry! No fine." Otherwise the worksheet should display the fine owed.

Try your worksheet on the following five tickets: Alicia, Speed Limit 40, Driver's Speed 55; Bob, Speed Limit 55, Driver's Speed 97; Carlos, Speed Limit 65, Driver's Speed 65; Darlene, Speed Limit 25, Driver's Speed 28; Ernie, Speed Limit 45, Driver's Speed 17.

11-12. The Tigers and the Warriors are playing a three-game playoff for the league championship. Whoever wins the most games wins the championship. If any team wins the first two games, the third game is not played.

(a) The games cannot end in a tie. The scores are in a worksheet as below. Cell C8 must have a formula that determines the winner. You can use extra cells if you would like.

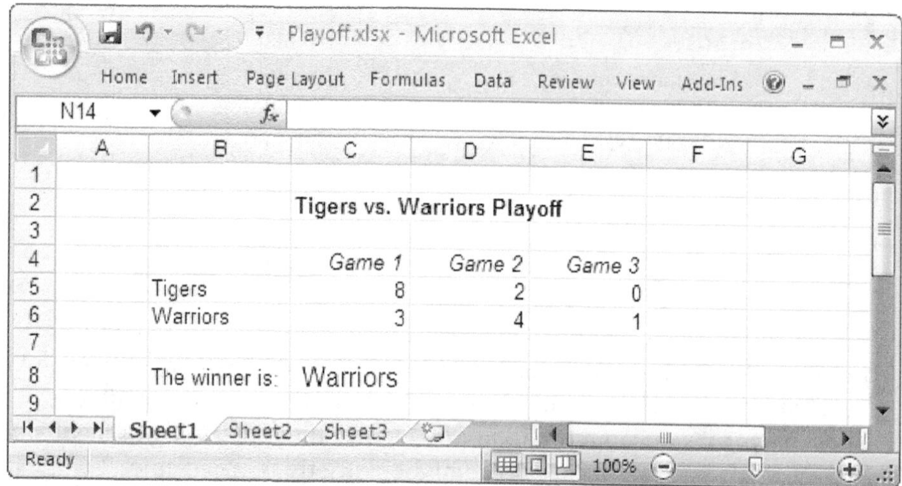

(b) The games can end in a tie and so can the championship. Modify your worksheet accordingly. Be sure to cover all possibilities, for example two ties and one win or one win by each team and a tie.

11-13. Some of us are fortunate to have lived in two years that are palindromes. Most people live in at most one. A year is a palindrome if it reads the same backwards as forwards. So 1991 and 2002 are palindromes but 2009 is not.

(a) Create a worksheet that gives in column B a list of all of the four-digit years that are palindromes, beginning with 1001 in B6 and extending on down in ascending order. You may use other columns as well, but the final answer for the row must be in column B. Furthermore, all rows below row 7 must be the result of filling the cells in row 7 down the worksheet. You may not use Auto Fill.

(b) Create a similar worksheet for all five-digit years that are palindromes, beginning with 10001 in B6.

11-14. Salespeople receive $10,000 base salary plus a commission of 2% of sales. Anyone who sells over $3 million receives a free vacation in Tahiti. Anyone who sells over $5 million receives an additional $5,000 bonus. At the end of the year salespeople are rated as follows: under $2 million "Dud", $2 million through $5 million "Star", over $5 million "Superstar". Create a worksheet that allows you to enter a salesperson's name and annual sales amount and then calculates the following:

Salesperson Summary

Name:	(input)
Annual sales:	(input)
Base salary:	$10,000
Commission:	(formula)
Bonus:	(formula)
Total pay:	(formula)
Free vacation?	(formula)
Status:	(formula)

11-15. The administration and faculty at New Ivy University have thought long and hard about their admission criteria. They have decided to forget about activities, athletics, parents who are alumni, interviews, recommendations, etc. in deciding which high school students should be admitted. NIU is going to decide admission strictly on academics. Only standardized test scores and grades will count.

Applicants will not have to write essays. All they will have to submit are five numbers: three test scores (Critical Reading SAT score, Mathematics SAT score, and Writing SAT score), rank in graduating class, and number of students in graduating class. SAT test scores always range from 200 to 800.

The following criteria are used in deciding admissions:

1. If an impossible number is submitted, the applicant is refused admission.
2. If any test score is 800, the applicant is accepted.
3. If any of the test scores is below 300, the applicant is refused admission.
4. If the test scores average above 650 and the applicant is in the top quarter of the graduating class, the applicant is accepted.
5. If any two of the test scores are below 400 or the applicant is in the bottom quarter of the graduating class, the applicant is refused admission.
6. Otherwise the applicant is put on the waiting list.

These criteria are applied in order. Thus, any impossible number disqualifies an applicant. If the five numbers are valid, then any test score of 800 means acceptance, regardless of the other numbers. If the first two criteria do not hold, then check the third criterion. And so on.

For this exercise you are to create a worksheet to decide whether an applicant is admitted. Your worksheet should be designed to accept the information for a single applicant. Thus a visiting high school senior could enter the information into your worksheet and find out the admission decision. In your worksheet you should have a different cell for each criterion. Then you should combine all six criteria into a final decision of either "Accepted", "Denied Admission", or "Waiting List".

Try your worksheet on each of the following 11 applicants:

Student	Reading SAT	Math SAT	Writing SAT	Rank	Class Size
A	520	480	460	103	298
B	640	120	800	3	137
C	260	300	800	492	506
D	590	600	720	352	440
E	590	800	740	193	160
F	660	680	240	53	800
G	580	700	560	120	410
H	320	520	380	42	77
I	420	290	450	10	240
J	460	520	420	-15	137
K	600	720	920	210	982

11-16. The number 371 is a "special" number because the sum of the cubes of the digits that compose it is equal to the number itself:

$$3^3 + 7^3 + 1^3 = 3*3*3 + 7*7*7 + 1*1*1 = 27 + 343 + 1 = 371$$

This is very unusual. Most numbers are not "special". For example, 502 is not "special" because $5^3 + 0^3 + 2^3 = 125 + 0 + 8 = 133$ rather than 502.

Create a worksheet that will find the highest three-digit "special" number. (Three-digit numbers are 100, 101, 102, ... 998, 999.) The answer should be calculated by the worksheet and appear automatically in an appropriately labeled cell at the top of the worksheet. This cell must have a formula in it, not just the answer typed in. All cells must have formulas in them and the same formulas must have been filled down for all 900 rows. Do not use Auto Fill. There are a couple of approaches to this problem. One uses the MOD function; others do not require learning new functions.

11-17. The Game of Life was invented by the Cambridge mathematician John Conway in the 1960s. The Game of Life takes place on an infinite two-dimensional grid. Each cell in the grid is either dead or alive. Each cell has eight neighbors, the cells that touch its sides or corners.

If a cell is alive it will survive into the next time period (next generation) if it has two or three neighbors that also are alive. If a cell is alive and has four or more neighbors that are alive, it will die of overcrowding. If a cell is alive and has zero or one neighbor that is alive, it will die of exposure.

If a cell is dead it will remain dead in the next generation unless exactly three of its neighbors are alive. In this case, the cell will be "born" in the next generation.

The rules are applied simultaneously to all cells from one generation to the next. We begin the game at Generation 1 with some configuration of living cells specified by the user. Each subsequent generation is determined by the rules established by Conway. The living cells can flourish and expand or stay the same or die off.

For example, suppose we start with the following configuration:

	A	B	C	D	E	F	G	H	I	J	K	L	M	N
1														
2			Generation						1					
3														
4														
5														
6														
7					1	1	1	1						
8														
9														
10														

Applying Conway's rules, cell E7 dies because it has only one living neighbor. Cell F7 survives because it has two living neighbors. Cell G7 survives. Cell H7 dies. New cells are born at F6, G6, F8, and G8 because all were dead but have three living neighbors. No other cells are born. The result is the following configuration:

	A	B	C	D	E	F	G	H	I	J	K	L	M	N
1														
2			Generation						2					
3														
4														
5														
6						1	1							
7						1	1							
8						1	1							
9														
10														

Applying the rules to these cells we get the following configuration:

	A	B	C	D	E	F	G	H	I	J	K	L	M	N
1														
2			Generation						3					
3														
4														
5														
6						1	1							
7					1			1						
8						1	1							
9														
10														

This configuration is stable. All of the living cells have two or three neighbors so all survive. No new cells are born. So the next generation looks the same as the previous generation.

	A	B	C	D	E	F	G	H	I	J	K	L	M	N
1														
2			Generation						4					
3														
4														
5														
6						1	1							
7					1			1						
8						1	1							
9														
10														

The colony is immortal. It stays the same forever.

Implement the Game of Life in Excel. Living cells should be represented by 1's. Dead cells should appear blank. (Hint: You might want to represent dead cells by 0's but not display the 0's by clicking on the Excel Options button at the bottom of the Office menu, clicking on Advanced, and clicking off the Show a zero in the cells that have zero value box.) You should use at least a 20 x 20 universe and draw a box around the universe. The universe should be surrounded by a blank row or column on all four sides so nothing leaks at the edges of the universe. At the top of each universe you should display the generation number.

The top left of the first sheet in the workbook should be a special universe for the user to enter in the initial configuration of 1's into Generation 1. The rest of the workbook should be protected from being changed. Any initial configuration of 1's should be acceptable. It is up to you how to design the rest of the workbook. You might want to use a separate worksheet for each generation. Or you might want to do all of the work in one worksheet. Or you might want to have one area of a worksheet where the universe changes over time. In this case you might want to turn off Automatic Recalculation by clicking on the Excel Options button at the bottom of the Office menu, clicking on Formulas, and then clicking on

Manual under Calculation Options. Then the formulas recalculate the next generation only when you press F9. The design of the workbook is up to you.

Be sure that the rules are applied only to cells in one generation to obtain the configuration of cells in the next generation. The workbook should be easy to use and should accurately portray the progress of life in the universe over at least a dozen generations, and preferably more, for any initial configuration.

(a) Try your workbook with the preceding initial configuration, with the three initial configurations that follow, and with three new initial configurations of your choice. For each of the initial configurations determine the ultimate fate of the inhabitants, for example whether the colony lives and expands forever, is stable, or dies off.

	A	B	C	D	E	F	G	H	I	J	K	L	M	N
1														
2			Generation						1					
3														
4														
5														
6														
7					1		1							
8					1	1	1							
9					1		1							
10														

	A	B	C	D	E	F	G	H	I	J	K	L	M	N
1														
2			Generation						1					
3														
4														
5														
6														
7					1	1	1							
8					1	1	1							
9					1	1	1							
10														

	A	B	C	D	E	F	G	H	I	J	K	L	M	N
1														
2			Generation						1					
3														
4														
5														
6					1									
7						1								
8				1	1	1								
9														
10														

(b) Determine the ultimate fate of the following initial configuration. You may need to modify your workbook. (Remember that the universe in the Game of Life is as large as necessary, as is the number of generations.)

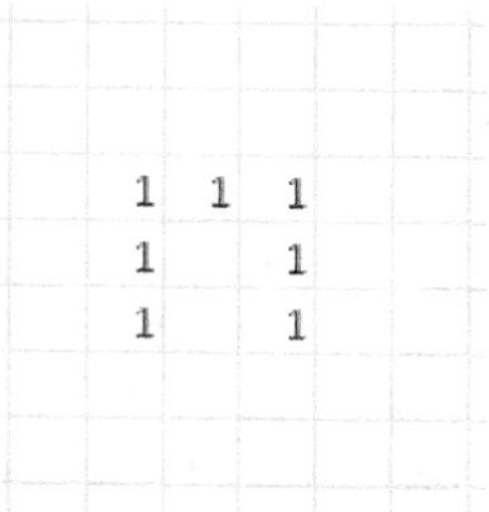

(c) Find an original initial condition where the colony grows in number and expands forever.

11-18. The portion of Interstate 90 that crosses Massachusetts is known as "The Massachusetts Turnpike" or "The Mass. Pike" or just "The Pike". On The Pike

> "Any individual convicted of a violation of the maximum speed limit in violation of 730 CMR 7.08(6)(c) is subject to punishment by a fine of $50.00. Where such conviction is for operating a motor vehicle at a rate of speed exceeding ten miles per hour over the speed limit, an additional fine of $10.00 for each mile per hour in excess of the ten miles per hour is assessed, to a maximum fine of $500.00. "

"Between the New York State border and Interchange 14 in Weston, eastbound, and from Interchange 15 in Newton to the New York State border, westbound" the normal speed limit is 65. Elsewhere the normal speed limit is 55. Lower maximum speed limits can be posted as conditions dictate. All fines are doubled in a posted "Construction Zone". In addition to the fine, a $50.00 assessment is added which goes to the Head Injury Fund established by the state.

Create a worksheet to assess penalties for speeding on The Pike. The inputs should be the speed limit at the location, the speed of the driver, and whether it was in a Construction Zone. The output should be the total owed, including fines and assessment. Be sure to check if the driver is not in fact exceeding the speed limit (then no fine or assessment: case dismissed). Also be sure to check that the fine is not over $500 (or $1,000 in a Construction Zone.) Your worksheet should be as informative to the user as possible. Your worksheet should handle one speeding incident.

11-19. A number is a palindrome if it reads the same forwards as backwards. Examples of palindromes include: 3, 44, 606, 1771, 24042. Examples of numbers that are not palindromes include: 57, 228, 4125, 78047.

a) Create a worksheet that has as input one number, a year between 1000 and 9999 inclusive, and as output a statement about whether or not the year is a palindrome. If the number entered is not in the range 1000 through 9999, an error message should be displayed. You may use as many extra cells as you would like. Hint: You may want to look at the MOD and INT functions.

b) If the number entered is not a palindrome, your worksheet should display the next year that is a palindrome. For example if the number entered is 2009 the worksheet should display 2112. If the number entered is 8432 the worksheet should display 8448. If the number entered is 4996 the worksheet should display 5005.

c) Create a worksheet that has as input one number, a year between 0 and 99,999 inclusive, and as output a statement about whether or not the year is a palindrome. If the number entered is not in the range 0 through 99,999, an error message should be displayed. You may use as many extra cells as you would like.

11-20. Create a worksheet that allows the user to enter 25 numbers. Have the worksheet calculate the mean and standard deviation of the numbers. You can use the STDEV function. In the column to the right of the original numbers have the worksheet automatically list just the numbers that are within one standard deviation of the mean. (The cells in the column corresponding to numbers that are at least one standard deviation from the mean should be blank.) In the next column to the right have the worksheet display just those numbers that are between one and two standard deviations of the mean. In the next column have the worksheet display those numbers that are more than two standard deviations from the mean. Finally, have the worksheet calculate and display (a) how many numbers are within one standard deviation of the mean, within one and two standard deviations of the mean, and greater than two standard deviations of the mean, and then (b) give the percentages for each of the three categories. All the calculations should change if any of the 25 numbers in the data change.

11-21. Bollinger Bands is an analytical technique developed by John Bollinger in the 1980's that is used by some traders to determine when to buy and sell stocks, commodities, and currencies. There are several variations on Bollinger Bands, one of which is given here. You might want to Google "Bollinger Bands" and read up on it.

The idea for Bollinger Bands is to construct three "Bands" or lines or boundaries given the historical daily closing prices for a stock. The Middle Band is the 20 day moving average for the stock. This is calculated at the end of each day by taking the average of the closing price for the most recent 20 days (skipping weekends and holidays when the market is closed, but including the current day). Next calculate the standard deviation for the same most recent 20 day period (you can use the STDEV function). The value at the end of each day for the Upper Band is the 20 day moving average plus two standard deviations. The value at the end of each day for the Lower Band is the 20 day moving average minus two standard deviations.

To illustrate this, I went to Google Finance (finance.google.com), entered in IBM and then clicked on Historical Prices to obtain a year of IBM's stock prices. I then clicked on Download to Spreadsheet. Google Finance downloaded a .csv file (comma separated values file) to my computer's disk. Google Finance is not officially released as of this writing so this might change. In Excel 2007 I opened the file with no problems and obtained the most recent year's daily data on the prices of shares of IBM in the worksheet in Excel.

Each row of the worksheet gives the data for a different day. I then set up columns to calculate the 20 day moving average for each day (the average of the most recent 20 days' closing stock prices) for the previous 100 days and the standard deviation of the same 20 day periods. I set up columns to calculate the value for the Upper Bollinger Band (moving average plus two standard deviations) and the Lower Bollinger Band.

IBMStockData.xlsx - Microsoft Excel

Home Insert Page Layout Formulas Data Review View Add-Ins

H4 =AVERAGE(E4:E23)

	A	B	C	D	E	F	G	H	I	J	K	L
1	IBM Stock Prices											
2								20 day		20 day		
3	Date	Open	High	Low	Close	Volume		moving avg		STDev	Upper	Lower
4	10-May-07	103.82	105.11	103.71	104.68	8959800		99.90		3.74	107.37	92.43
5	9-May-07	103.93	104.75	103.7	104.38	8408086		99.45		3.67	106.79	92.10
6	8-May-07	102.42	103.39	102.21	103.29	5972400		98.99		3.60	106.19	91.79
7	7-May-07	102.76	103.17	102.4	103.16	5620878		98.65		3.49	105.63	91.66
8	4-May-07	102.75	103.03	102.25	102.96	5469734		98.32		3.35	105.02	91.62
9	3-May-07	101.75	103	101.35	102.8	7318750		98.00		3.19	104.37	91.62
10	2-May-07	102.8	103.14	102.13	102.22	7045178		97.67		3.00	103.67	91.67

IBMStockData

Ready 100%

Then I graphed the closing prices and the three Bands with time on the horizontal axis and price on the vertical axis for the last 100 days. (See the following graph.)

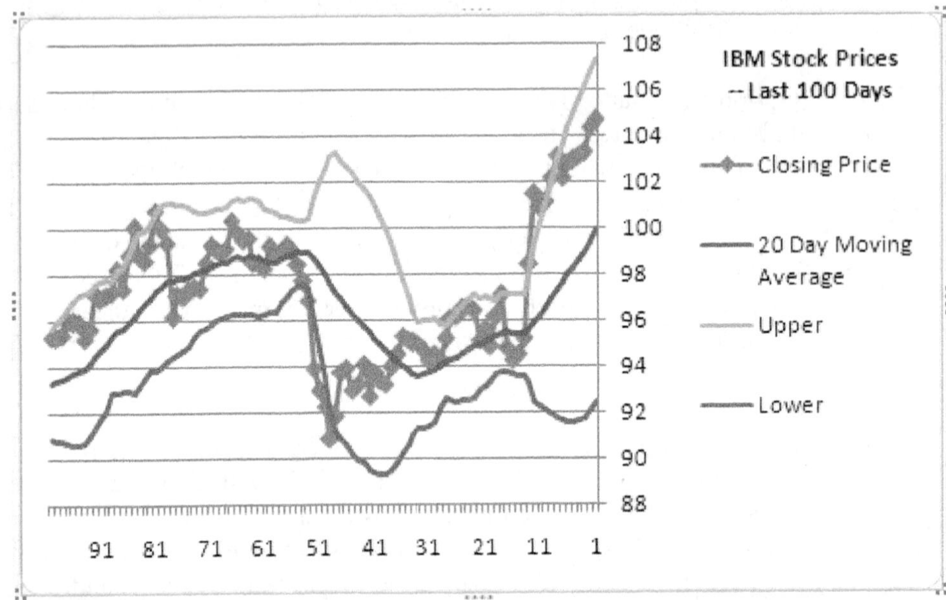

IBM Stock during this 100 day period started at near $95, went up over $100, dropped to almost $90, and closed above $104. So far, so good.

Now comes the controversial part, the rules for buying and selling. These vary from strategy to strategy, but here is a simple set of rules:

Buy Signal: "A trader buys when the price has fallen below the Lower Bollinger Band."

Sell Signal: "A trader sells when the price goes above the Upper Bollinger Band."
This can be viewed as an attempt to operationalize "Buy Low, Sell High".

a) Download a year's worth of data from Google Finance or elsewhere for your favorite stock. Open the data in Excel. You're mainly interested in the Closing Price for each day. In separate columns calculate the 20 day moving averages, the 20 day standard deviations, the Upper Band values, and the Lower Band values. Skip the calculations for the earliest 20 days of the year as you don't have the necessary prior data in your worksheet. Your worksheet should resemble the one on the previous page.

b) Graph the values, as above, for all available data.

c) Use IF functions to issue Buy and Sell orders in a column according to the above rules.

d) Test how well the rules do with your stock data. The Buy and Sell orders can be interpreted in several ways. A straightforward way of interpreting them is: You start off with no shares. If you don't have any stock and see a Buy order then buy 10,000 shares at the next day's Opening Price (given in the Google Finance data). If you already own 10,000 shares and see a Buy order, ignore it. If you don't own any shares and see a Sell order then ignore it. If you already own 10,000 shares and see a Sell order then sell the shares at the next day's Opening Price. You must sell all shares at the very end. Put formulas in your spreadsheet to automate these rules for buying and selling and to calculate when you buy and sell stocks and how much money you make or lose each for Sell transaction. The outcome for the year (the total money you made or lost) should appear at the top of the worksheet in some newly inserted rows. Your worksheet should work for any data values.

e) Make duplicates of the worksheet and then download data for other stocks or other years. Copy and Paste the data into the duplicated worksheets. Enter the name of the stock into each worksheet of data. The formulas and graph should automatically apply to the new data. Your workbook should have several worksheets.

f) Put a new page in front of your workbook. On the page write a brief report indicating your findings. How much money did you make or lose on each set of data? What do you think of this trading scheme?

g) Through reading on the web and by thinking about it create a different Buy and Sell strategy. Note there is a class of radically different strategies to the one given above called "Bollinger Band Breakout" strategies. You might want to figure out and mark on the graph what the optimal dates would be for buying and selling. Decide on a definite strategy. Of course your strategy can only look at current and past data. No fair having it look into the future! Add clearly labeled columns to your workbook to test your strategy. Write the Buy and Sell rules out in English. How does your strategy work using historical data for different stocks in different years? Do you consistently make money with this strategy? Fully write up the strategy and the results. *Please note: This is an exercise in Excel and by no means an endorsement of this type of trading.*

CHAPTER 12

FUNCTIONS RELATED TO IF

OBJECTIVES

In this chapter you will learn how to:

- Use COUNTIF to count the cells that meet some criteria
- Use SUMIF to add cells meeting some criteria
- Create lookup tables
- Use VLOOKUP for inexact and exact matches
- Catch error conditions with the IFERROR function
- Do two-dimensional lookups with INDEX and MATCH
- Add Form Controls to your worksheet

In this chapter we discuss the use of several functions that are related to the IF function to solve problems involving the selection of different values.

THE COUNTIF FUNCTION

The countries of the world are listed in order of Gross Domestic Product per Capita in the worksheet in Figure 12-1. That is, each country is listed, followed by the continent, the Gross Domestic Product for the country in $1,000,000,000, the population of the country, and the average Gross Domestic Product per person in the country.

GDP.xlsx - Microsoft Excel

F8 =D8*1000000000/E8

Countries of the World by Gross Domestic Product per Capita

(Source: The CIA Factbook, https://www.cia.gov/cia/publications/factbook/index.html)

		Country	Continent	GDP in $ billions	Population	GDP per Capita
7	1	Luxemburg	Europe	32.6	474,413	$ 68,716
8	2	Bermuda	North America	4.5	65,773	$ 68,417
9	3	Jersey	Europe	5.1	91,084	$ 55,992
10	4	United Arab Emirates	Asia	129.4	2,602,713	$ 49,717
11	5	Equatorial Guinea	Africa	25.69	540,109	$ 47,564
12	6	Norway	Europe	207.3	4,610,820	$ 44,959
13	7	Ireland	Europe	177.2	4,062,235	$ 43,621
14	8	United States	North America	12,980	298,444,215	$ 43,492
230	224	Congo, Republic of the	Africa	44.6	62,660,551	$ 712
231	225	Burundi	Africa	5.744	8,090,068	$ 710
232	226	Comoros	Africa	0.441	690,948	$ 638
233	227	Malawi	Africa	8.038	13,013,926	$ 618
234	228	Somalia	Africa	5.023	8,863,338	$ 567
235	229	East Timor	Asia	0.37	1,062,777	$ 348

Figure 12-1. GDP and population of the countries of the world.

We are interested in calculating various statistics about the countries of the world. For example, suppose we would like to have a cell that reports the total number of countries in Europe. There are several approaches to solving this problem, but an easy approach involves the use of the **COUNTIF** function. In a cell we could type the formula

=COUNTIF(C7:C235,"=Europe")

This formula instructs Excel to count up all of the cells in the range C7:C235 that contain the word "Europe". In fact, we could omit the = sign and enter the formula

=COUNTIF(C7:C235,"Europe")

The COUNTIF function has two arguments, a range and the criterion. The criterion is written in quotes. The value returned by the function is the number of nonblank cells in the range that meet the criterion.

As another example, suppose we want to have a cell that gives the number of countries that have a GDP above $100 billion. Since in the worksheet GDP's are given in billions of dollars, we could use the formula

=COUNTIF(D7:D235,">100")

This would return the number of values in D7:D235 that are greater than 100.

THE SUMIF FUNCTION

Now suppose we want to find the total GDP for Asia. To solve this problem we could use the formula

=SUMIF(C7:C235,"Asia",D7:D235)

The **SUMIF** function has three arguments: the range of the cells to be tested, the criterion to be used in the test, and the range that contains the cells to be summed. In this case, for each cell in the range C7:C235 that contains the word "Asia" the number in the corresponding cell in the range D7:D235 will be added into the total that is calculated by the function.

If we want a cell that calculates the total number of people who live in countries that have under $1,000 GNP per capita, we could enter the formula

=SUMIF(F7:F235,"<1000",E7:E235)

This worksheet basically is organized as an Excel table. There are many operations that can be performed with this data, as we will see in Chapter 16.

USING IF FUNCTIONS IN EXTRA COLUMNS

Suppose we would like to have the largest GDP of any country in Africa appear in a cell at the bottom of the worksheet. Well, you might say, let's just use the MAXIF function. Unfortunately, there is no MAXIF function in Excel.

One approach is to use an extra column to pull out the GDP of the countries that are in Africa. (See Figure 12-2.)

GDP Africa.xlsx - Microsoft Excel

Home Insert Page Layout Formulas Data Review View Add-Ins

G237 f_x =MAX(G7:G235)

	A	B	C	D	E	F	G
1							
2		**Countries of the World by Gross Domestic Product per Capita**					
3	Source: The CIA Factbook, https://www.cia.gov/cia/publications/factbook/index.html						
4							
5				*GDP in*		*GDP per*	*Africa*
6		*Country*	*Continent*	*$ billions*	*Population*	*Capita*	*GDP*
7	1	Luxemburg	Europe	32.6	474,413	$ 68,716	
8	2	Bermuda	North America	4.5	65,773	$ 68,417	
9	3	Jersey	Europe	5.1	91,084	$ 55,992	
10	4	United Arab Emirates	Asia	129.4	2,602,713	$ 49,717	
11	5	Equatorial Guinea	Africa	25.69	540,109	$ 47,564	25.69
230	224	Congo, Republic of th	Africa	44.6	62,660,551	$ 712	44.6
231	225	Burundi	Africa	5.744	8,090,068	$ 710	5.744
232	226	Comoros	Africa	0.441	690,948	$ 638	0.441
233	227	Malawi	Africa	8.038	13,013,926	$ 618	8.038
234	228	Somalia	Africa	5.023	8,863,338	$ 567	5.023
235	229	East Timor	Asia	0.37	1,062,777	$ 348	
236							
237			Maximum GDP of any country in Africa:				576.4
238							

Sheet1 Sheet2 Sheet3

Ready 100%

Figure 12-2. Using IF in an extra column to select the GDP of African countries.

Here, cell G7 contains the formula

=IF(C7="Africa",D7,"")

which has been filled down column G. Thus the cells in column G contain the GDP for each country in Africa and are blank for each country not in Africa. In cell G237 we place the formula

=MAX(G7:G235)

so that cell G237 contains the highest GDP of any country in Africa, namely the GDP of South Africa.

This technique of using an extra column containing IF functions is useful for solving many different problems.

THE VLOOKUP FUNCTION

It often is convenient to express a multi-way selection in a table. For example, we might have a tax rate table which indicates that if you earned so much money, then your tax rate is such and such. Or, we might give volume discounts, where the more you purchase, the lower the price. This could be expressed in a volume discount table that indicates how much you must purchase to qualify for the different discounts. Excel provides the special function **VLOOKUP** especially for making selections by looking up values in a table.

The VLOOKUP function has three arguments. The first argument is the number you want to look up. The second argument is the location of the **vertical lookup table**. The third argument indicates which column in the table contains the answer, the value to be returned by the function.

Suppose that the photocopy center charges are based on the number of photocopies ordered, as follows:

Photocopy Prices

Number Of Copies	Price Per Page
1 to 19	.06
20 to 99	.05
100 to 499	.04
500 to 999	.035
1000 or more	.03

In cell C15 we have the number of copies. We would like the price per page to appear in cell C17. What formula should go into cell C17?

We could solve this problem using a nested IF function. The cell would contain the formula

```
=IF(C15<20,.06,IF(C15<100,.05,IF(C15<500,.04,IF(C15<1000,.035,.03))))
```

This formula works, but it is cumbersome and does not indicate the price table explicitly in the worksheet. If the price changes we would need to find and change the formula. An alternative approach to solving this problem uses a vertical lookup table and VLOOKUP function, as in Figure 12-3.

The formula in cell C17 is

```
=VLOOKUP(C15,E20:F24,2)
```

This formula instructs the computer to look up the number in cell C15 in the vertical lookup table located in cells E20 through F24. The value of the function will be the corresponding value in the second column of the vertical lookup table (column F).

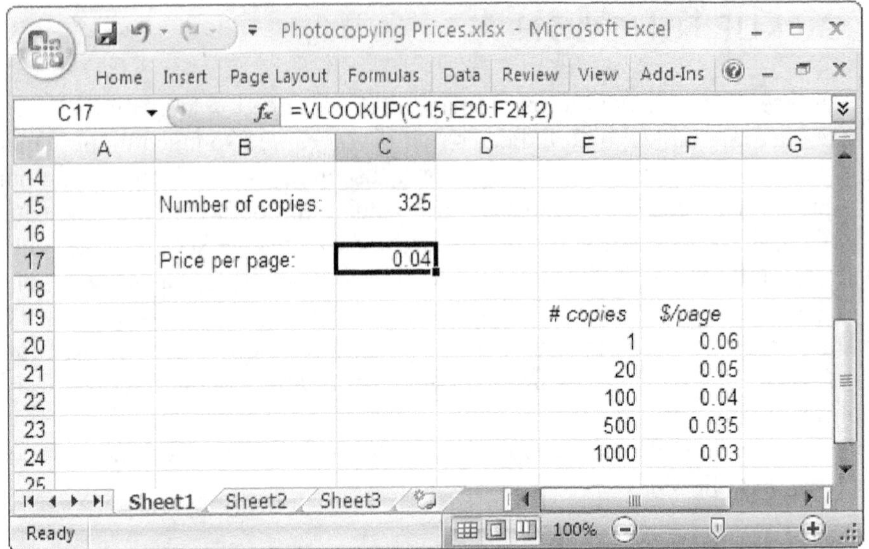

Figure 12-3. Using the lookup table in E20:F24 to find the price per page for the number of copies in C15.

A vertical lookup table has a definite organization. The values in the first column normally are in ascending order. The computer takes the number in C15 and compares it to the top left cell in the lookup table. If the number in the cell is less than C15, the computer proceeds to the next cell down. The computer keeps chugging down the left column until it finds a number that is greater than the value in C15. At that point it goes up one cell and over to the column in the vertical lookup table indicated by the third argument. The third argument is called the **column index**. This may sound confusing at first, but it works well.

In the example in Figure 12-3, the number to be looked up in the table is 325. The computer compares 1 with 325. 1 is less than 325 so the computer moves down a cell. 20 is less than 325 so the computer moves down another cell. 100 is less than 325 so the computer moves down a cell. At last, 500 is greater than 325. The computer moves up one cell. This is the row with the answer. Then it moves over to the second column in the vertical lookup table (because the third argument in the VLOOKUP function is 2). Finally the computer returns the number 0.04. The number 0.04 is the result of evaluating the VLOOKUP function in cell C17.

Suppose the number in cell C15 is 700. The result of evaluating the VLOOKUP function in C17 would be 0.035.

Suppose the number in cell C15 is 5000. The result of evaluating the VLOOKUP function in C17 would be 0.03. If the number to be looked up is larger than any number in the first column of the table, then the computer stops at the last row in the table.

Suppose the number in cell C15 is -25. The result of evaluating the VLOOKUP function would be the error message #N/A, which stands for "No value available." If the number to be looked up is less than the first value in the table, then the computer indicates an error.

Suppose the number in cell C15 is 100. The result of evaluating the VLOOKUP function in C17 would be 0.04. In this case the first number in the column that would be larger than the number we are looking up would be 500. The computer would then go up one cell and over to column F.

A major advantage of using a lookup table is that the numbers in the table are visible in the worksheet. The person using the worksheet can see the table rather than having the values hidden inside a nested IF formula. If the pricing policy changes, we can change the numbers in the table rather than trying to edit a complicated formula. For example, if the price per page for 100 to 499 copies is raised to $0.045, the number in cell F22 can be changed to 0.045. In the worksheet in Figure 12-3 the result of evaluating the formula in C17 would become 0.045.

What is the purpose of the third argument, the column index? Suppose we had two classes of customers, regular and preferred, and two sets of rates. The regular customers are "walk-ins", anyone who walks in the door. The preferred customers pay us an annual fee for special service and prices. We could assign regular customers a code of 2 and preferred customers a code of 3. Now we could determine the rate by making the code be the column index, as in the worksheet in Figure 12-4.

Prices.xlsx - Microsoft Excel

Home Insert Page Layout Formulas Data Review View Add-Ins

C17 fx =VLOOKUP(C15,E20:G24,C12)

	A	B	C	D	E	F	G
12		Customer type	3				
13		(2=regular, 3=preferred)					
14							
15		Number of copies:	35				
16							
17		Price per page:	0.045				
18							
19					*# Copies*	*$/page*	
20					1	0.06	0.05
21					20	0.05	0.045
22					100	0.04	0.035
23					500	0.035	0.03
24					1000	0.03	0.025

Sheet1 Sheet2 Sheet3

Ready 100%

Figure 12-4. The lookup table with two types of customers.

We entered the Customer Type in C12 and used that entry as the column index in the formula in C17

=VLOOKUP(C15,E20:G24,C12)

Note that we extended the lookup table over to column G in the formula. We could be fancier and have the person type in "regular" or "preferred" and then use an IF function to determine the column index.

This same technique would work for income tax tables where there are different rates for single taxpayers, married taxpayers filing jointly, and so on.

Warning! If a formula containing a VLOOKUP function is to be filled down a column, be sure that the table location is expressed as an absolute address. Otherwise, the address of the table will change as the formula is filled. This is a common but subtle error when using lookup functions.

It often is useful to name a lookup table as well as the other key cells. The formula in C17 could be

=VLOOKUP(COPIES,PRICE_TABLE,CLASS_CODE)

There is an **HLOOKUP** function that is similar to VLOOKUP. It works horizontally, scanning across the top row of a **horizontal lookup table**.

USING VLOOKUP FOR EXACT MATCHES

In the preceding example we wanted to look up a number in a range of values. Sometimes we want only an exact match. Suppose we have a list of the players on a team and their numbers. We would like to create a worksheet that an announcer can use to quickly find the name of a player given his number. We could create the worksheet shown in Figure 12-5.

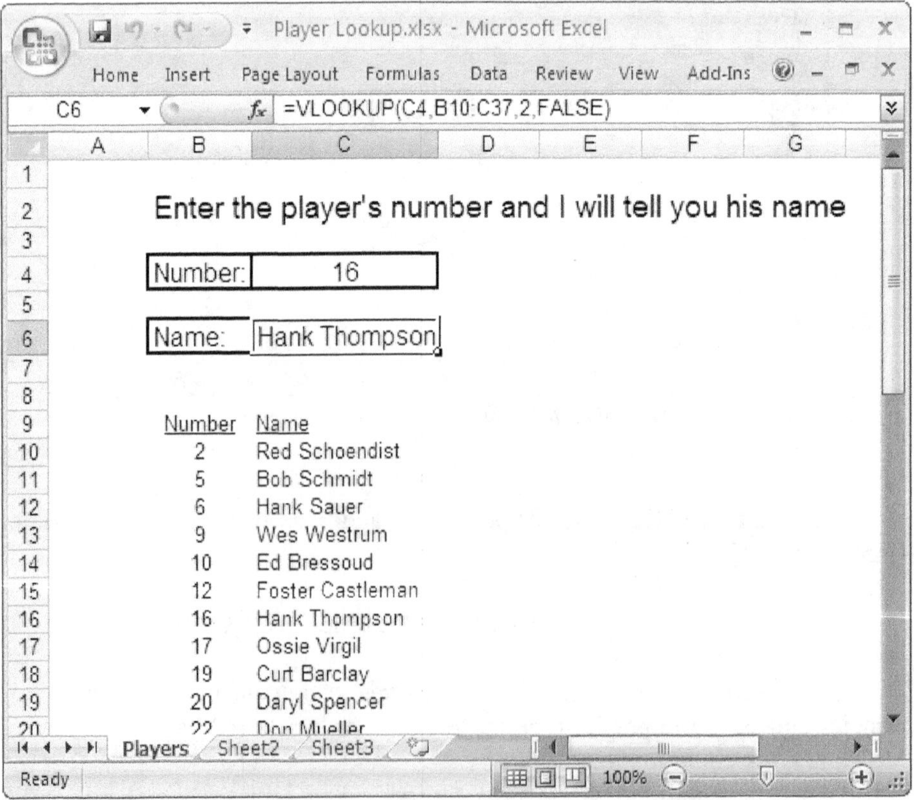

Figure 12-5. When we look up the number of a player we want an exact match.

Here we enter a number into the cell in C4. The computer automatically displays the name of the player in cell C6. The formula in C6 is

=VLOOKUP(C4,B10:C37,2,FALSE)

In this formula we are instructing Excel to look up the value in cell C4 in the first column of the vertical lookup table in B10:C37 and return the corresponding value in the second column, column C, of the table.

The VLOOKUP function call contains a fourth argument, namely FALSE. The VLOOKUP function has an optional fourth argument, which is either TRUE or FALSE.

If the fourth argument is omitted, as in the photocopy example in the previous section, the fourth argument is assumed to be TRUE. If the fourth argument is omitted or TRUE, then we are instructing Excel that we want an approximate match and that Excel should find the correct range in the first column of the lookup table in which the value occurs. If the fourth argument is FALSE, as it is in this example, we are instructing Excel that we require an exact match.

For example, if we enter 7 for the player's number, and there is no number 7 in the first column of the lookup table because no player wears the number 7, we don't want the name of the player who wears number 6. We want an indication that we entered an erroneous number. In fact, if we were to enter the number 7 in cell C4 in the worksheet in Figure 12-5, we would get the error message #N/A (no value available) in cell C6.

Note that if we are requiring an exact match in a VLOOKUP function by including FALSE as the fourth argument, then the entries in the left column of the lookup table do not need to be in ascending order. If an exact match is required, as in the worksheet in Figure 12-5, the values in the left column of the lookup table can be entered in any order.

THE IFERROR FUNCTION

We could check for the potential error in the worksheet in Figure 12-5 and insert our own error message by using the Excel function **IFERROR**. The function IFERROR is very convenient. It has two arguments. The first argument is a formula and the second argument is what to do if the formula results in an error. We can embed the VLOOKUP function into the IFERROR function and intercept the #N/A error message before it appears, as in Figure 12-6.

The formula in cell C6 now is

=IFERROR(VLOOKUP(C4,B10:C37,2,FALSE), "No such player!")

This formula instructs Excel that if the value of the VLOOKUP function is an error (for example, #N/A) then Excel should display the message "No such player!" in the cell. Otherwise, Excel should display the result of the VLOOKUP function, the name of the player.

The IFERROR function is useful in many circumstances, not just with VLOOKUP.

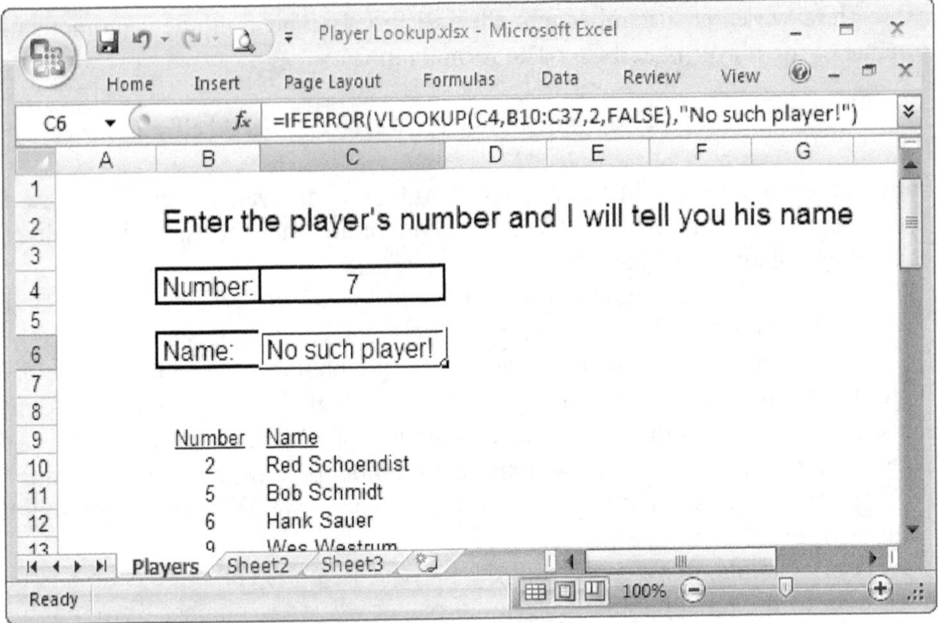

Figure 12-6. "No such player!" is more meaningful than "#N/A".

COMBINING VLOOKUP AND DATA VALIDATION

At the beginning of Chapter 7 we discussed Data Validation. One of the features of Data Validation is the ability to limit the values of a cell to the contents of a range of cells. In the player lookup example in Figures 12-5 and 12-6 we could limit the entries for the player's number in C4 to the list of valid numbers in B10:B37, thereby eliminating the possibility of an erroneous entry.

Starting with the worksheet in Figure 12-5, we click on cell C4 and then click on the Data tab and Data Validation. We select List and then for Source we drag across B10:B37, resulting in the Data Validation Settings for C4 in Figure 12-7.

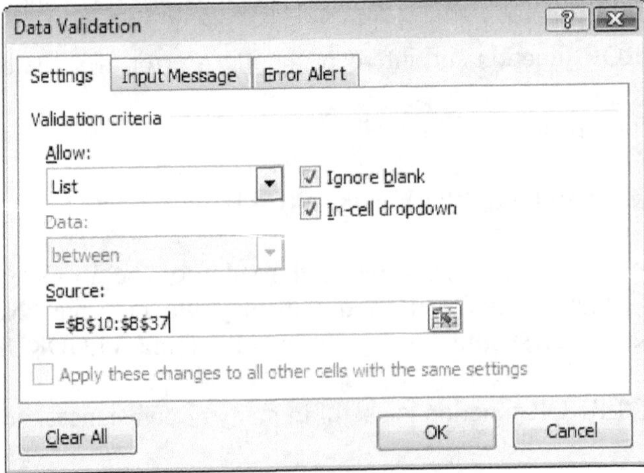

Figure 12-7. Restricting possible player numbers.

Now C4 becomes a dropdown list with only the valid player numbers. (See Figure 12-8).

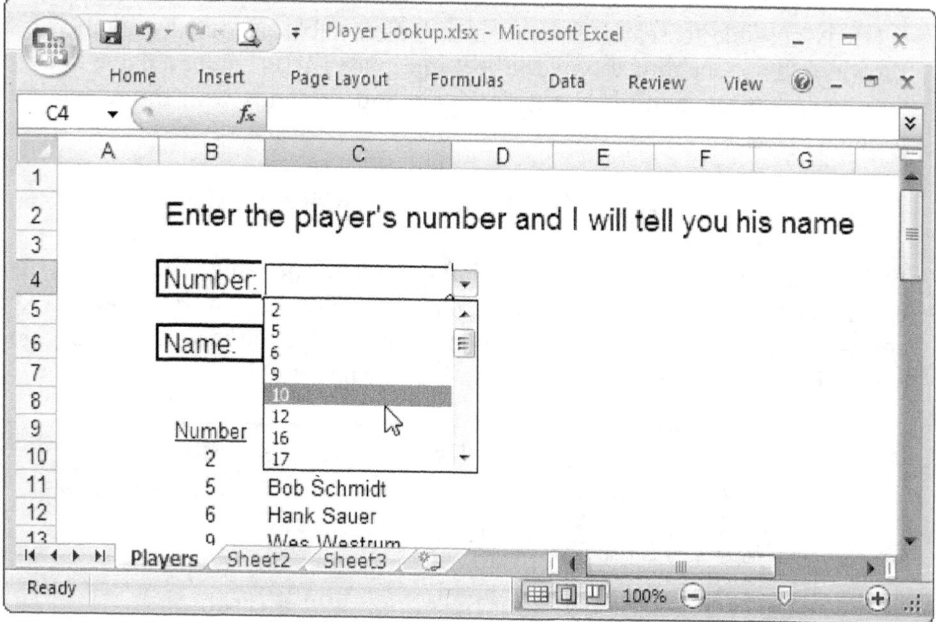

Figure 12-8. The player number must be an entry in the list.

If we click off the box for "In-cell dropdown" in Figure 12-7 then no dropdown list will appear. We must type in the number by hand. If the number does not match one of the numbers in the selected range B10:B37 an error box appears, as in Figure 12-9.

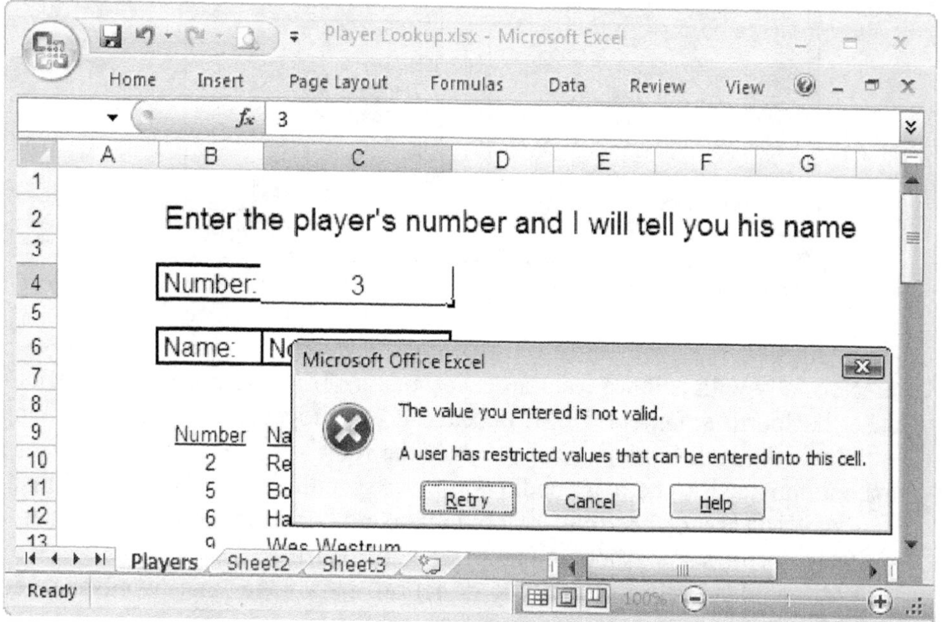

Figure 12-9. Entering a non-existent player number produces an error message.

LOOKING UP TEXT

It is possible to search for text in a lookup table as well as numbers. An example is shown in the phone directory worksheet in Figure 12-10. Enter a name in C6. The computer then looks up the name in the table below and responds with the telephone number. The formula in C8 is

=VLOOKUP(C6,B11:C405,2,FALSE)

Excel looks up the value in C6 in the left column of the table in B11:C405. When it finds an exact match (because the fourth argument is FALSE) in B11:B405, Excel returns the corresponding value in column C, column 2 of the lookup table. If it does not find an exact match, Excel will return #N/A, as when looking up numbers.

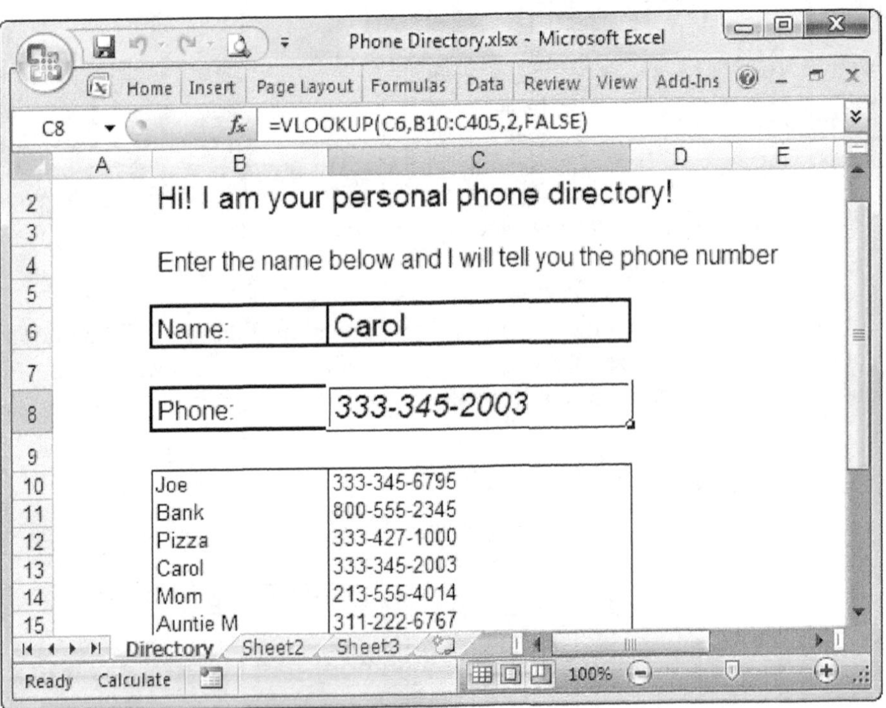

Figure 12-10. Looking up text in a personal phone directory.

Normally with text we want an exact match. If we do not want an exact match, we can make the fourth argument TRUE or leave it off altogether. If we are looking up the range within which a cell falls, in other words if the fourth argument is missing or TRUE, then the first column needs to be in ascending order. Ascending order for text is alphabetical order.

Excel is **case insensitive** in looking up text in a lookup table. That is, looking up "CAROL" is the same as looking up "Carol" or "carol".

We could use the IFERROR function in C8 in this worksheet combined with VLOOKUP. Similarly we could use Data Validation.

TWO-DIMENSIONAL LOOKUPS WITH INDEX AND MATCH

We have been using VLOOKUP to do one-dimensional lookups. Suppose we have a large array of values, as in Figure 12-11, and we would like to do a two-dimensional lookup.

Parts.xlsx - Microsoft Excel

B5 =INDEX(D7:ABC353204,MATCH(B2,B7:B353204,0),MATCH(B3,D6:ABC6,0))

	A	B	C	D	E	F	G
1	*Please enter the city and part number and I will tell you the inventory*						
2	City:	Adelaide					
3	Part Number:	0007-34A					
4				**Inventory of Parts**			
5	Inventory:	785					
6				0007-26A	0007-29C	0007-34A	0008-19F
7		Abidjan	Côte d'Ivoire	35	33	404	46
8		Accra	Ghana	5	40	21	29
9		Adana	Turkey	22	22	84	33
10		Addis Abeba	Ethiopia	33	64	656	30
11		Adelaide	Australia	19	34	785	48
12		Agra	India	26	16	566	3

Worldwide Inventory | Parts Key | Sheet3

Figure 12-11. A two-dimensional array of data.

We would like to be able to enter in the city and the part number and find the inventory of the part in that city. A solution is given in Figure 12-12.

Parts.xlsx - Microsoft Excel

	A	B	C	D	E	F	G
1							
2							
3							
4				**Inventory of Parts**			
5							
6				0007-26A	0007-29C	0007-34A	0008-19F
7		Abidjan	Côte d'Ivoire	35	33	404	46
8		Accra	Ghana	5	40	21	29
9		Adana	Turkey	22	22	84	33
10		Addis Abeba	Ethiopia	33	64	656	30
11		Adelaide	Australia	19	34	785	48
12		Agra	India	26	16	566	3

Worldwide Inventory | Parts Key | Sheet3

Figure 12-12. A two-dimensional lookup using the INDEX and MATCH functions.

The solution combines the use of the **INDEX** and **MATCH** functions. The INDEX function has three arguments:

=INDEX(array, row index, column index)

Here an **array** is a two-dimensional range. Of course, two-dimensional ranges always are rectangular. If we enter in the formula

=INDEX(D7:ABC353204,4,3)

the value would be the entry in the fourth row of the range D7:ABC353204 and the third column. The fourth row of the range is row 10. The third column of the range is column F. So the value of the formula would be 656, the value in F10.

The order of the arguments in the INDEX function seems counterintuitive to me. We indicate the address of a cell by column followed by row, as in F10. But the arguments are in the order row index followed by column index. If you don't like it (and I don't) you can try writing Bill Gates at bill@microsoft.com.

Note that the second and third arguments of the INDEX function, the row index and the column index, must be at least 1. If either value is 0 or less you will get a #VALUE! error. A row index of 1 corresponds to the top row of the range indicated in the first argument. A column index of 1 corresponds to the left column of the range indicated in the first argument.

Thus

=INDEX(D7:ABC353204,1,1)

would evaluate to the top left value of the range indicated in the first argument. In the worksheet in Figure 12-11 or Figure 12-12, that would be 35, the value in D7.

We can use the MATCH function to find the correct row index and column index. MATCH looks for a value within a one-dimensional range. If the third argument is 0 the match must be exact. The formula

=MATCH("Agra",B7:B353204,0)

would evaluate to 6, as "Agra" is the sixth entry in the list. If we entered the name of a city that isn't in the list or misspelled a city name, Excel would return the error message #N/A as a value. MATCH always returns either an integer value of 1 or more or #N/A.

Thus

=MATCH(B2,B7:B353204,0)

finds the row index of the city and

=MATCH(B3,D6:ABC6,0)

finds the column index of the part number and

=INDEX(D7:ABC353204,MATCH(B2,B7:B353204,0),MATCH(B3,D6:ABC6,0))

finds the inventory in the range D7:ABC353204 that corresponds to the given city and part number. Cool, huh?

CATCHING AND PREVENTING ERRORS IN INDEX AND MATCH

Suppose we enter a city that is not in the list, as in Figure 12-13, or misspell the city name?

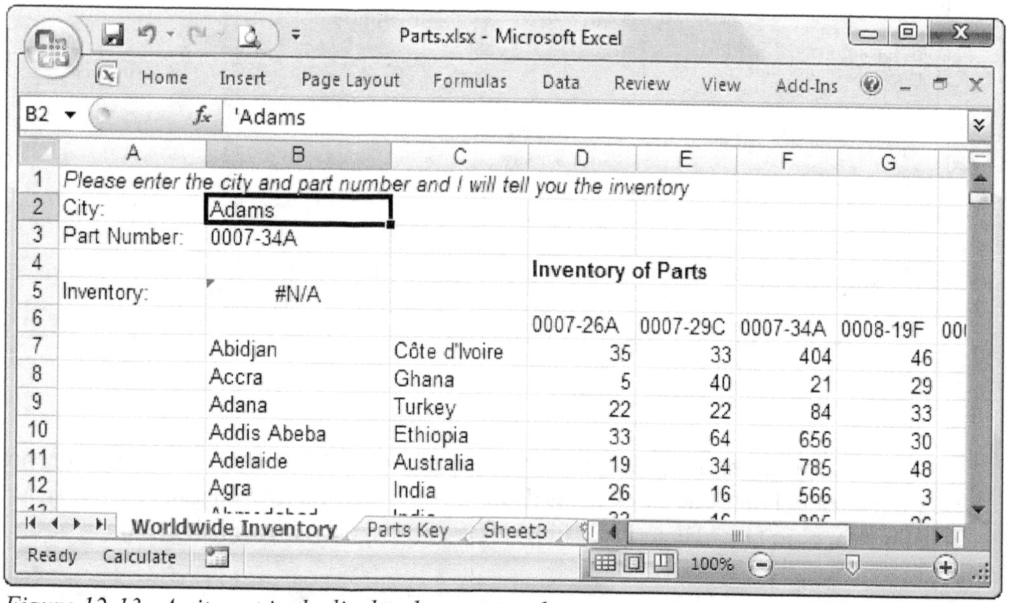

Figure 12-13. A city not in the list has been entered.

The result of the formula in B5 is #N/A. This is not as helpful as it could be. We could put formulas in C2 and C3 and change the formula in B5 so the worksheet is more helpful.

In C2 we put the formula

=IFERROR(MATCH(B2,B7:B353204,0),"ERROR: CITY NOT IN LIST")

In C3 we put the formula

=IFERROR(MATCH(B3,D6:ABC6,0),"ERROR: PART NUMBER NOT IN LIST")

Now C2 holds either the correct row index for the city or an error message. C3 hold either the correct column index of the part number or an error message.

In B5 we can change the formula to

=IFERROR(INDEX(D7:ABC353204,C2,C3),"ILLEGAL ENTRY")

The resulting worksheet is shown in Figure 12-14.

Parts.xlsx - Microsoft Excel

Home Insert Page Layout Formulas Data Review View Add-Ins

B2 f_x 'Adams

	A	B	C	D	E	F	G
1	Please enter the city and part number and I will tell you the inventory						
2	City:	Adams	ERROR: CITY NOT IN LIST				
3	Part Number:	0007-34A	3				
4				Inventory of Parts			
5	Inventory:	ILLEGAL ENTRY					
6				0007-26A	0007-29C	0007-34A	0008-19F
7		Abidjan	Côte d'Ivoire	35	33	404	46
8		Accra	Ghana	5	40	21	29
9		Adana	Turkey	22	22	84	33
10		Addis Abeba	Ethiopia	33	64	656	30
11		Adelaide	Australia	19	34	785	48
12		Agra	India	26	16	566	3

Worldwide Inventory | Parts Key | Sheet3

Ready 100%

Figure 12-14. Adding error messages.

Alternatively, we could prevent errors by using Data Validation to create a dropdown list in B2 to restrict choices to cities in B7:B353204 and a dropdown list in B3 to restrict choices to part numbers in D6:ABC6. (See Figure 12-15.)

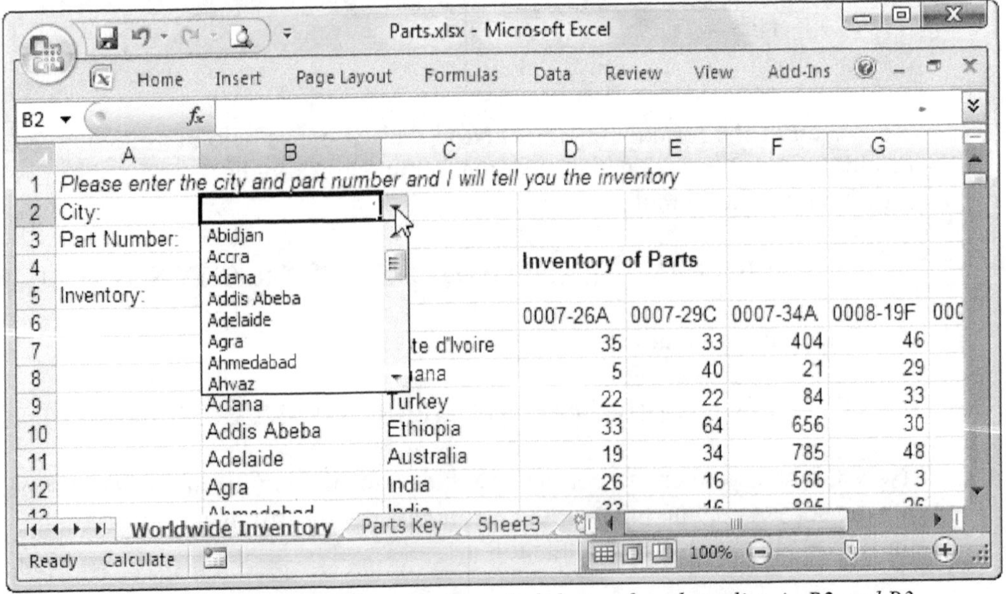

Figure 12-15. Preventing errors by using Data Validation dropdown lists in B2 and B3.

FORM CONTROLS[2]

Hidden away in Excel is a different approach to allowing the user to interact with the worksheet. **Form Controls** enable the user to enter values using **Scroll Bars**, **Option Buttons**, **Check Boxes**, and other familiar interface devices.

The Thrills and Chills Amusement Park has two types of admission prices: admission only and admission plus all rides. The prices are based on the age of the person. Children under 2 and adults 100 or older are admitted free. In the worksheet in Figure 12-16 we use two Form Controls for input: a Scroll Bar (slider) to specify the age and Option Buttons (radio buttons) to specify the type of admission.

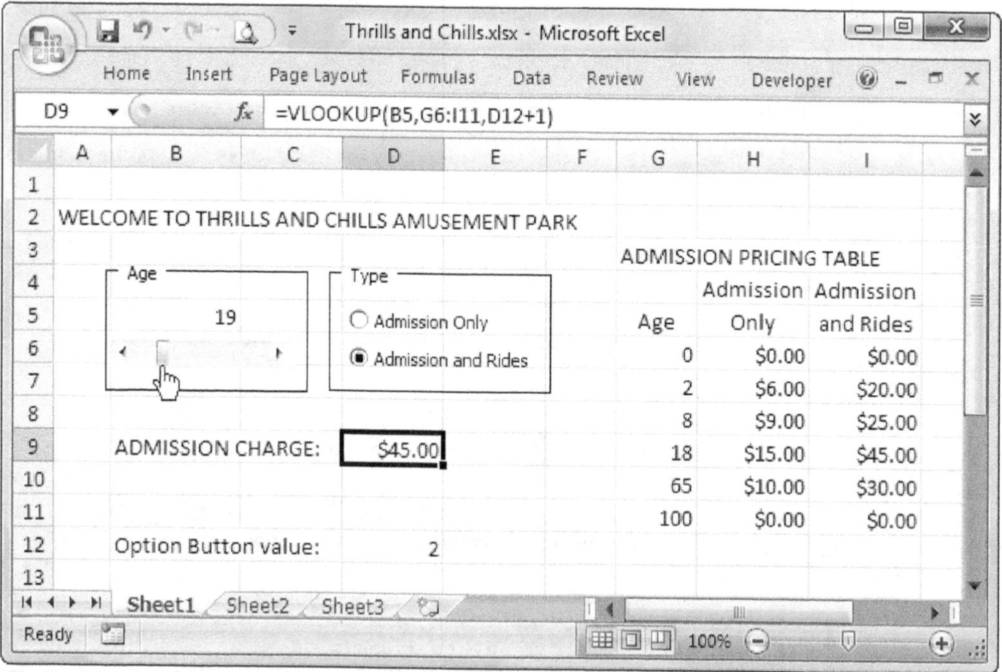

Figure 12-16. Using a scroll bar and option buttons to input values to a worksheet.

Form Controls float on top of the worksheet like a graphic, but each can link to a cell you specify in the worksheet. Moving the Scroll Bar changes the value in the cell B5. Clicking an Option Button changes the value in D12. The current value in D12, 2, indicates that the second Option Button is selected. The formula in D9 uses the values in B5 and D12 to find the admission charge in the lookup table.

If you look carefully at the tabs in the Ribbon in the worksheet in Figure 12-16, you'll notice that a new tab, Developer, now appears. The Developer tab has to be present for you to be able to add Form Controls to a worksheet. To show the Developer tab, click on the Office button at the top left of the Excel window. At the bottom of the Office menu click on the Excel Options button. In the Excel Options window, click on Popular and then on Show

---

[2] With thanks to Prof. Edward Sciore.

Developer tab in the Ribbon, as in Figure 12-17. Now the Developer tab will be visible in the Ribbon. In the Developer tab click on Insert and the Form Controls will be displayed, as in Figure 12-18.

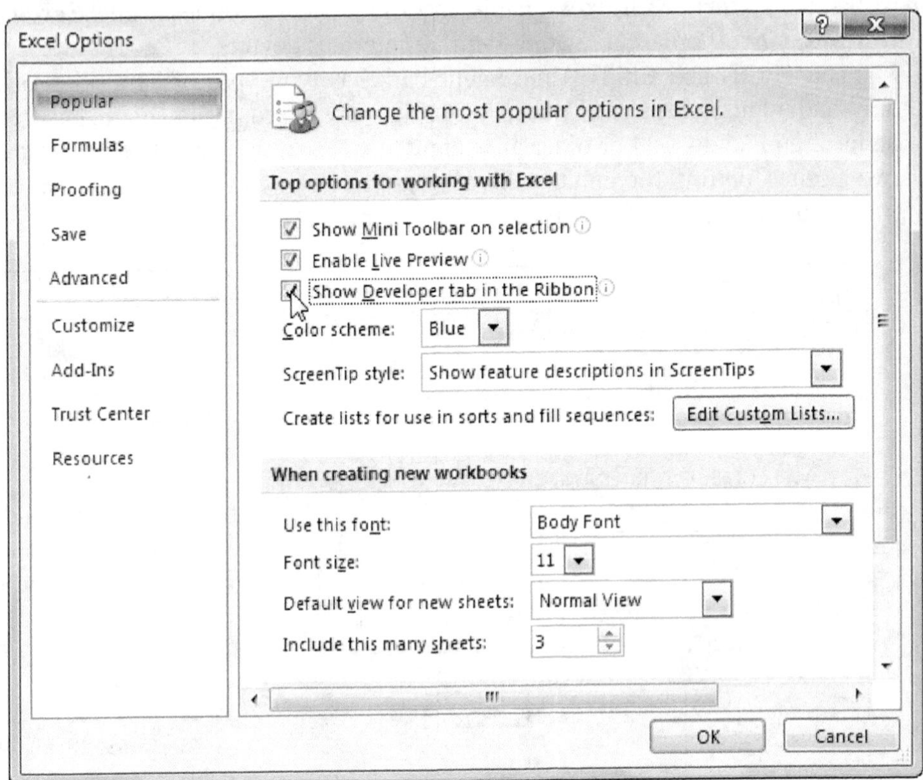

Figure 12-17. How to show the Developer tab in the Ribbon.

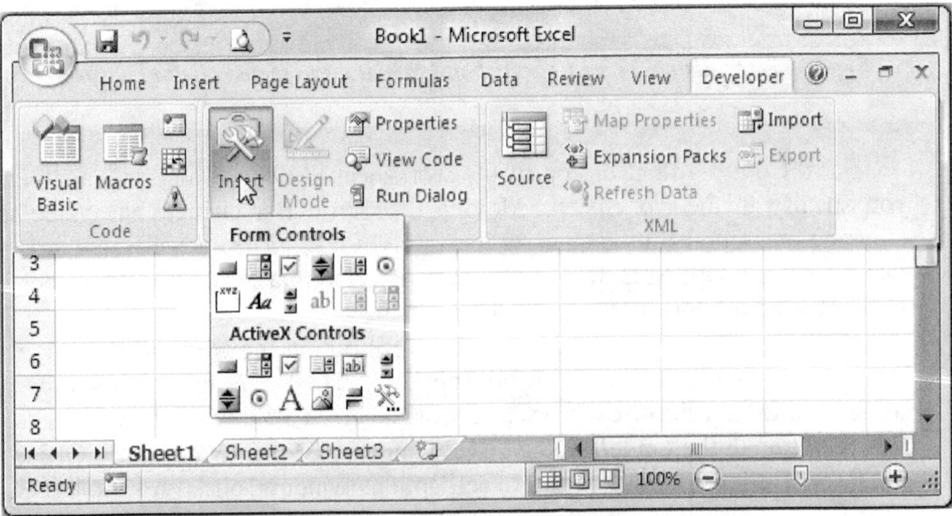

Figure 12-18. Form Controls are found in the Developer tab.

In the worksheet in Figure 12-16 we used the Scroll Bar, the Option Button, and the Group Box. These are indicated in Figure 12-19.

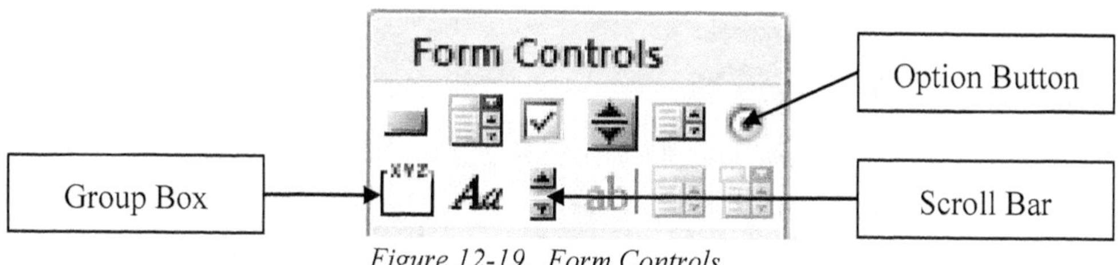

Figure 12-19. Form Controls.

To create the worksheet in Figure 12-16, we click on the Option Button in Form Controls (*not* ActiveX Controls) and then click the mouse button and drag where we want the Option Button to appear in the worksheet. (See Figure 12-20.)

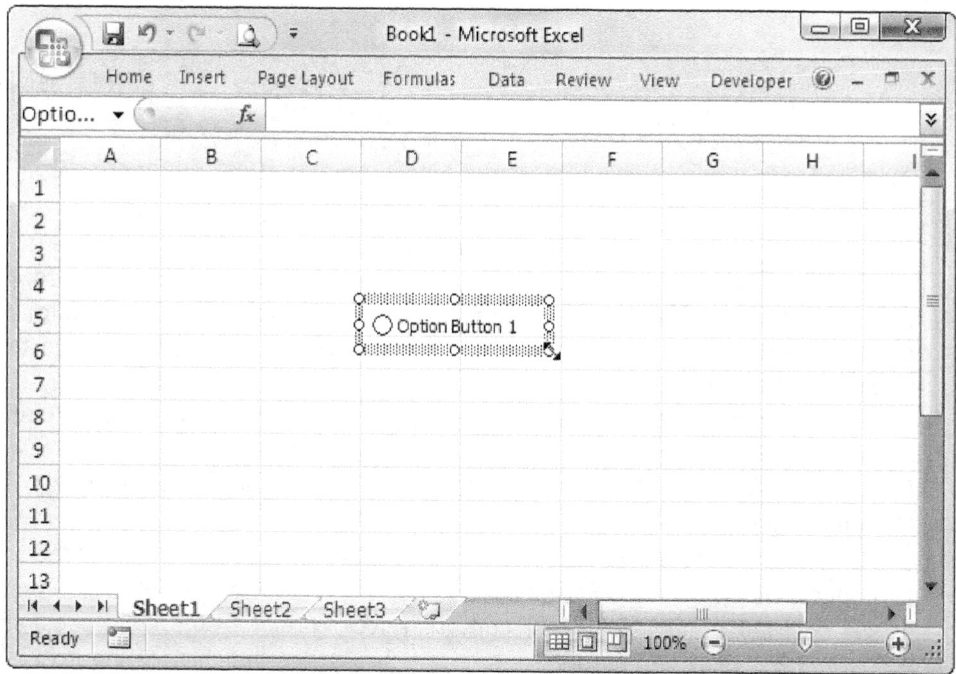

Figure 12-20. Adding an Option Button to a new worksheet.

The Option Button is not in a cell, but rather floats above the worksheet. We select the text in the Option Button and change it to Admission Only. We add another Option Button below it and change the text to Admission and Rides. We right click on the first Option Button and select Format Control... from the menu that appears. In the Format Control window we select the Control tab and then enter D12 as the Cell link, as in Figure 12-21.

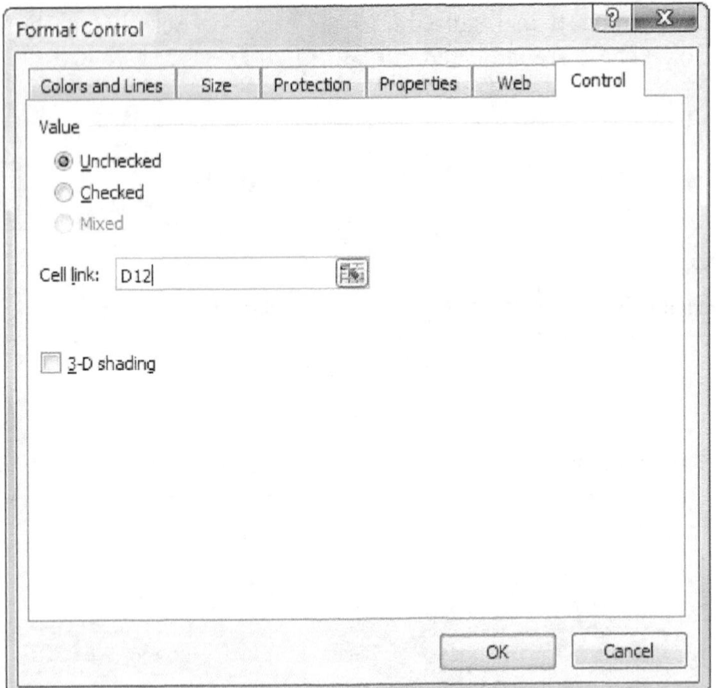

Figure 12-21. Linking the first Option Button to cell D12.

We repeat this process with the second Option Button linking it also to D12 but this time clicking on Checked. Select Group Box in Form Controls and drag the Group Box around the two Option Buttons. This informs Excel that these two Option Buttons are grouped together so that only one of the Option Buttons can be selected. Change the text of the Group Box to Type.

A common mistake is to squeeze the Group Box in so that part of an Option Button is outside the Group Box. If the Option Buttons act independently, be sure that both Option Buttons are linked to the same cell and enlarge the Group Box so there is no doubt the Option Buttons are fully inside.

Now click on the Scroll Bar in the Form Controls section of Insert in the Developer tab. Drag horizontally across the worksheet to the left of the Option Buttons. Right click on the Scroll Bar and in the menu that appears select Format Control… The Format Control window will appear. In the Control tab set the values as indicated in Figure 12-22, including typing in B5 as the Cell link.

Add a Group Box around the Scroll Bar section. This Group Box serves no purpose except to make the worksheet easier to understand and look more consistent.

Enter in the text and values and the formula in D9 to obtain the worksheet in Figure 12-16. The same worksheet is shown in Figure 12-23 with different inputs.

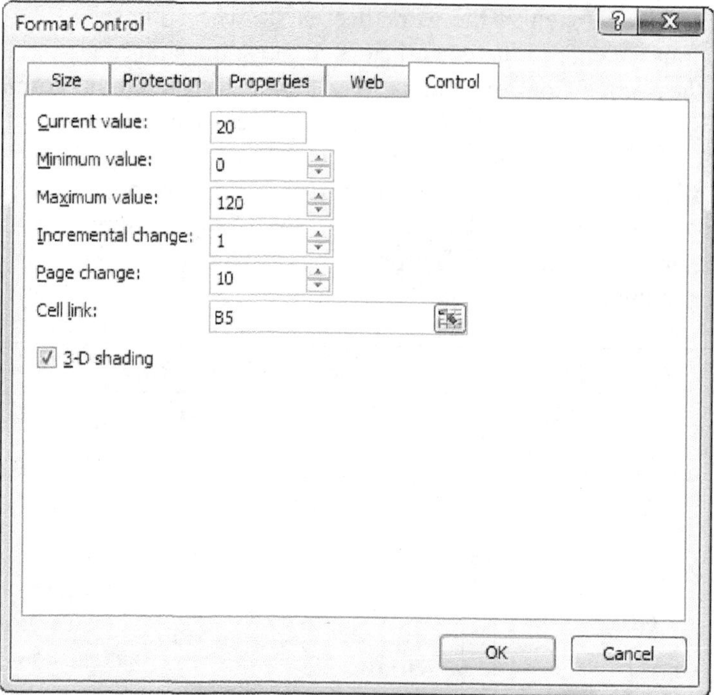

Figure 12-22. Formatting the Scroll Bar for Age.

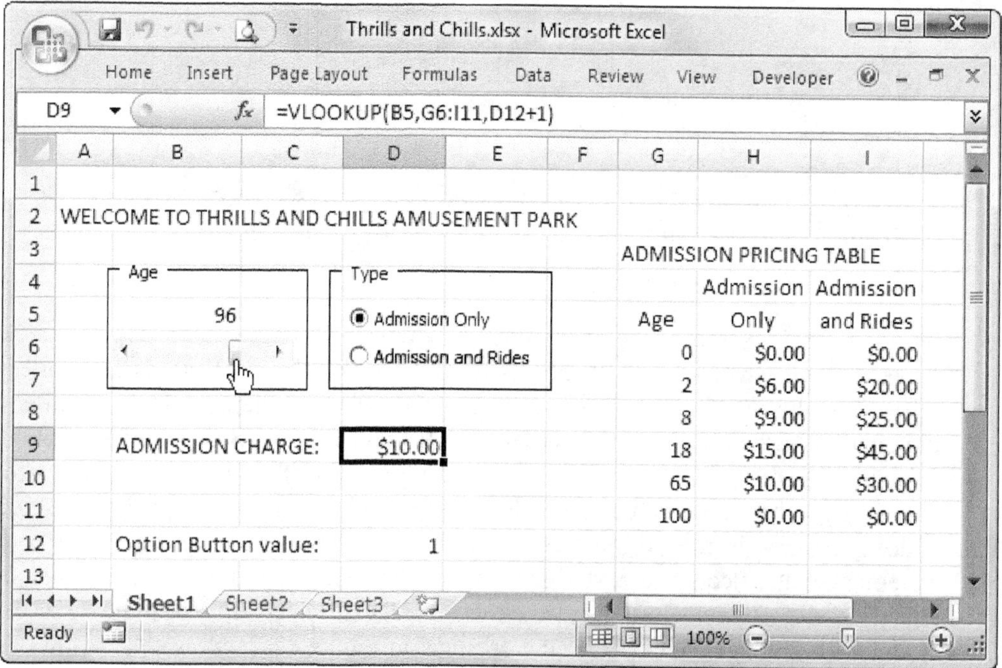

Figure 12-23. The amusement park admission charge worksheet with different inputs.

An alternate version of the worksheet is shown in Figure 12-24. Here, we use a Check Box to input whether to include all rides in the admissions charge. The Check Box is linked through the Format Control window to cell D12. To obtain the Format Control window for a Check Box, right-click on the Check Box and select Format Control... in the resulting pop-up menu. D12 now takes on the value of TRUE or FALSE depending on whether or not Include all Rides is checked. A **Spin Button** is used to input the Age. The Spin Button has an up and down arrow. Clicking on the arrows changes the number in B5, as specified in the Format Control for the Spin Button. The VLOOKUP function in D9 adjusts the column index depending on the value in D12.

D9 =VLOOKUP(B5,G6:I11,IF(D12,3,2))

WELCOME TO THRILLS AND CHILLS AMUSEMENT PARK

Age: 5

Type: Include all Rides

ADMISSION CHARGE $20.00

Check Box value: TRUE

ADMISSION PRICING TABLE

Age	Admission Only	Admission and Rides
0	$0.00	$0.00
2	$6.00	$20.00
8	$9.00	$25.00
18	$15.00	$45.00
65	$10.00	$30.00
100	$0.00	$0.00

Figure 12-24. The amusement park worksheet using a Spin Button and Check Box.

As a final example, the worksheet in Figure 12-25 contains a pie chart that varies depending on which Option Button is checked. The Option Buttons are linked to cell G1 through the Format Control window. The values of E5:E8 depend on the number in G1. The pie chart is based on the values in cells B5:B8 and E5:E8. So, changing the Option Button selected changes G1 which changes the numbers in E5:E8 which changes the sizes of the pie slices. The Chart Title is the value displayed in cell E3. To accomplish this, select the Chart Title, type an = in the Formula Bar and click on E3 in the worksheet. E3 contains an IF statement that selects the text displayed in the cell depending on the value of G1. So, changing the Option Button selected changes G1 which changes the text in E3 which changes the Title of the chart. The worksheet in Figure 12-26 shows the result of clicking on the 2009 Option Button.

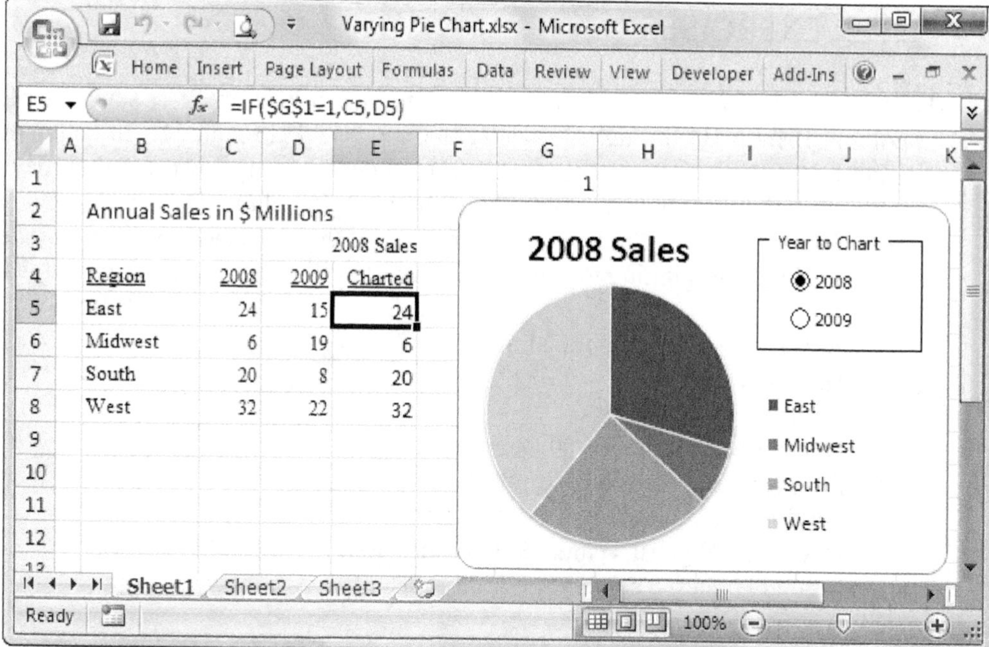

Figure 12-25. The sales charted depend on which Option Button is selected. Here the 2008 Sales are charted.

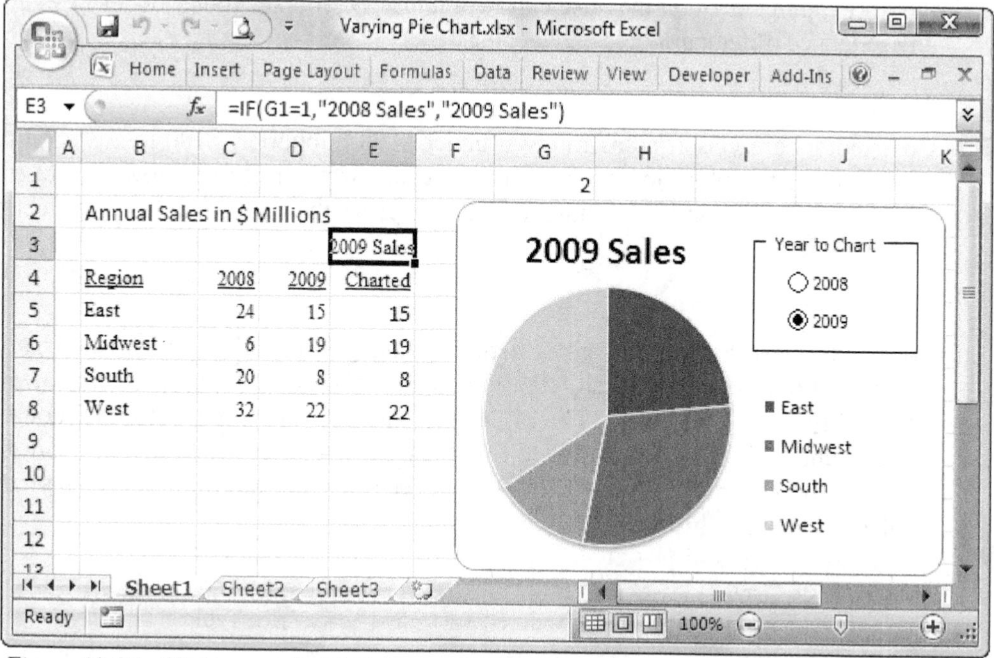

Figure 12-26. Clicking on the 2009 Option Button causes the 2009 Sales to be charted.

COMPUTER EXERCISES

12-1. The Weather Bureau would like a worksheet to help it keep track of some simple statistics. In column B from B8 through B38 enter the numbers 1 through 31. In column C from C8 through C38 enter the highest temperature recorded for your town for each day during the last month. (You can make up these temperatures.) In column D from D8 through D38 put Sunny, Cloudy, Rain, or Snow. In the top lines of the worksheet put appropriate titles and column headings. Beginning in cell B40 and continuing down put the following labels:

Average Temperature for Month
Highest Temperature
Number of Sunny Days
Number of Days above 50 Degrees
Average Temperature of Rainy Days
Highest Temperature of a Rainy Day
Day of the Highest Temperature of the Month
Second Highest Temperature of Month

Widen column B appropriately. Your task is to enter formulas so that the appropriate statistics are calculated automatically in C40 through C47. The Day of the Highest Temperature of the Month would be 23 if the highest temperature of the entire month occurred on the twenty-third of the month. In case of a tie, select the latest day. Do not use the Sort command. You may use extra columns. Of course, your worksheet should work for any sequence of temperatures and weathers.

12-2. Contributors are classified as follows: under $100 Supporter, $100 to $399 Patron, $400 to $999 Fellow, $1,000 or more Blue Chip. Create a worksheet that allows you to enter a name and a contribution and then automatically displays the contributor's classification. Use a lookup table.

12-3. (a) Create a worksheet that gives a price quote. You will enter an item name and the quantity of that item purchased. Your worksheet should look up the item name in the Price Table to find the Unit Price. Then it should calculate the Total Before Discount. Look up this amount in the Discount Table to find the discount percent. Then your worksheet should calculate the Discount Amount, the Total After Discount, add in 6% sales tax, and give the final Total Due for the order.

Price Quote			
		Price Table	
Item:	*(Input)*		Unit
Quantity:	*(Input)*	Item	Price $
		Connectors	3.98
Unit Price:		Grommits	15.99
Total Before Discount:		Hasps	0.35

Discount %:	Widgets	8.79
Discount Amount:		
Total After Discount:	Discount Table	
Sales Tax:		
	Amount $	Discount
Total Due:	0	0%
	100	5%
	500	10%
	1000	15%

Try your worksheet three times, on the following orders: 100 Connectors, 2000 Widgets, 300 Faranges.

(b) Create a new workbook that allows the customer to order some quantity of each of the items at once. The discount should be applied to the total amount ordered. Try your workbook on one order of 30 Connectors, 0 Grommits, 50 Hasps, 5 Widgets.

12-4. Concert tickets are priced as follows:

	22 and under	over 22
Premier tickets	$65	$90
Floor tickets	$50	$70
Balcony tickets	$30	$30
Standing Room	$15	$20

(a) Create a worksheet that allows a person to enter in an age and a ticket location (Premier, Floor, Balcony, Standing Room) and automatically gives the price of the ticket. Use VLOOKUP.

(b) If the user enters an illegal ticket location the worksheet should put an appropriate error message in the cell.

12-5. On the Allied Student Cell Phone plan: If you use 60 minutes or less in a month you pay $17.99 in usage charges. If you use between 60 and 120 minutes you pay the $17.99 plus $0.25 per minute for each minute over 60 in usage charges. If you use more than 120 minutes you pay $29.99 plus $0.15 per minute for each minute over 120 in usage charges. In addition there is a $7 processing charge per month. Then there is an 8% sales tax on all charges. Create a worksheet that allows you to enter the minutes used and then shows you the usage charge, the processing charge, the tax, the total charge, and the average total cost per minute. Try your worksheet with inputs of 10 minutes, 100 minutes, and 5000 minutes.

12-6. In the country of Freedonia, the national currency is the royal. Single people pay no taxes on the first 1,000 royals, 10% on any income between 1,000 and 3,000 royals, 20% on any income between 3,000 and 10,000, and 30% on any income over 10,000. Married people filing jointly pay no taxes on the first 1,000 royals, 8% on any income between 1,000 and 3,000, 15% on any income between 3,000 and 10,000 and 25% on any income in excess of 10,000 royals. So, for example, a single person with an income of 5,000 royals would pay 200 royals for the income between 1,000 and 3,000 and 400 for the income between 3,000 and 5,000 for a total tax bill of 600 royals.

(a) Create a worksheet to calculate the tax owed given marriage status and income. The worksheet also should show the actual percentage of income owed in taxes. In the example given the 600 royals owed represent 12% of income.

(b) Create a similar worksheet using Form Controls.

12-7. At the Royal Pizza Parlor, pizzas are priced as follows:

	Small	Medium	Large
Triple Cheese	$7.95	8.95	10.95
Pepperoni	8.95	10.45	11.95
Goat Cheese and Fig	11.95	14.95	17.95
Sausage and Pepper	9.45	10.95	12.45
The Works	10.00	12.00	14.00
Cola	0.95	1.25	1.75

(a) Create a worksheet that allows a person to enter a type and a size and learn the price of the pizza. Use VLOOKUP.

(b) Create a worksheet that allows a person to enter a type and a size and learn the price of the pizza. Use INDEX and MATCH.

(c) Give an appropriate error message if the person enters a type or size that the Parlor does not carry. Use Data Validation.

(d) Create a worksheet that allows a customer to enter up to six different pizzas (or drinks) with quantities and then calculates the total bill for the customer. For example the customer might order 2 Medium Sausage and Pepper, 4 Large The Works, and 6 Large Cola.

12-8. The SoKo Cell Phone Company offers five anywhere/anytime plans. Plan A is $9.99 per month and each minute is $0.50. Plan B is $19.99 per month with the first 100 minutes free and each minute in excess of 100 costing $0.40. Plan C is $39.99 per month with the first 250 minutes free and each minute over 250 costing $0.30. Plan D is $79.99 per month with the first 1,000 minutes free and each minute in addition costing $0.20. Plan E is $159.99 per month with unlimited calls at no extra cost.

Create a worksheet that allows a person to enter in a name, the plan letter, and the number of minutes used in a month. The worksheet should calculate the total bill for the month. You may use as many cells as you like in your design.

Try your worksheet on: John A 7 minutes, Luis B 80 minutes, Carla B 120 minutes, Shruti C 300 minutes, Omar D 1200 minutes, Dawn E 2400 minutes, and Kzyki E 12 minutes.

12-9. In your History course there are three hour exams, a paper, and a final exam. Each of these is graded between 0 and 100. In determining the final grade, the professor has decided to drop each student's lowest hour exam grade. The two highest hour exam grades will count 1/6 each, the paper will count 1/3, and the final exam will count 1/3 in determining the overall average for the course. The final letter grade for the course will be based on the overall average, as follows: below 60 is an F, 60 to 65 is a D, 65 to 75 is a C, 75 to 80 is a B-, 80 to 90 is a B, 90 to 95 is an A-, 95 and above is an A.

(a) There are 10 students in the course. Create a worksheet that automatically calculates and displays the overall average and final letter grade for each student. Enter 10 names and sets of grades that fully test the formulas in the worksheet. You should enter a name, three hour exam grades, a paper grade, and a final exam grade for each student. Everything else should be calculated automatically.

(b) In deciding the Grade Point Average, an A is worth 4 points, a B is worth 3 points, a C is worth 2 points, a D is worth 1 point, and an F is worth 0 points. An A- is worth 3.666 points and a B- is worth 2.666 points. Add formulas to your worksheet so that the course Grade Point Average is calculated and displayed. For example, the average grade for the 10 students in the course might be 2.8.

(c) To further encourage students to work hard on their papers, the professor has decided that whoever receives the highest grade on the paper will receive at least an A- in the course whatever the student's grades on the exams. Modify your worksheet so that the student who receives the highest grade on the paper automatically receives at least an A-.

12-10. The sum of the series 1/1 + 1/2 + 1/3 + … never converges. Thus if you add enough terms you can reach any value. For example it takes 4 terms of the series to reach 2 as 1 + 1/2 + 1/3 + 1/4 is 2.08333333 and 11 terms for the series to reach 3.

Create a worksheet that allows the user to enter in a number between 1 and 12. The worksheet should tell the user how many terms of the series must be summed to reach the input number and the value of the sum of the series for that many terms. For example, if the number entered is 3, the answers given should be 11 and 3.019877. If the number entered is 10.5 the answers given should be 20,490 and 10.50004. If the user does not enter a number between 1 and 12 an appropriate error message should be displayed. Hint: Pre-compute the values in a long table and look up the answers.

12-11. Verizon's six America's Choice cell phone plans are given below.

Verizon America's Choice Plans			
Plan	Monthly Minutes	Monthly Access	Additional Minutes
A	450	$39.99	$0.45
B	900	$59.99	$0.40
C	1350	$79.99	$0.35
D	2000	$99.99	$0.25
E	4000	$149.99	$0.25
F	6000	$199.99	$0.20

A customer signs up for a plan. If the customer signs up for plan D, he or she gets 2000 free minutes per month and has to pay $99.99 per month no matter what. If the customer uses 2000 minutes or less for the month there is no additional charge. If the customer uses over 2000 minutes the customer must pay $0.25 for each additional minute beyond the 2000.

Create a worksheet that has two input cells: the Plan letter and the number of minutes used for the month. The worksheet should then show the Monthly Access fee for the plan, the number of excess minutes (if any), the cost for the excess minutes (if any), and the total amount owed for the month. You may have extra cells as well. The table above should be part of the worksheet. Changing relevant values in the table should result in changes to the answers provided by your worksheet.

12-12. People in the U.S. with income consisting of salary and some interest income can complete Form 1040. Obtain a copy of Form 1040EZ at www.irs.gov. Implement the form in Excel. Include the tax tables as part of your workbook. The only numbers entered by the user should be the numbers requested in steps 1, 2, 3, 5, 7, 8, 9 of the form.

12-13. Use the data in Exercise 10-8 to produce a worksheet like the one in Figure 12-12 that enables a user to enter a Country and a Year and that tells the user the corresponding hourly compensation for production workers.

(a) Use INDEX and MATCH. Invalid entries should produce a #N/A error message.

(b) Use IFERROR combined with INDEX and MATCH to produce a better error message.

(c) Use Data Validation to produce dropdown lists for the two input cells.

(d) Use Data Validation to produce error messages for invalid entries but no dropdown lists.

12-14. The World Series is won by whichever team wins 4 games first. Create a worksheet to like the one below to calculate the World Series winner given the scores of the games so far.

	A	B	C	D	E	F	G	H	I
1									
2									
3		**World Series**							
4									
5		**Teams**	**Game 1**	**Game 2**	**Game 3**	**Game 4**	**Game 5**	**Game 6**	**Game 7**
6									
7		Boston Red Sox	4	2	7				
8									
9		Houston Astros	6	0	1				
10									
11									
12		Winner:	No winner yet						

	A	B	C	D	E	F	G	H	I
1									
2									
3		**World Series**							
4									
5		**Teams**	**Game 1**	**Game 2**	**Game 3**	**Game 4**	**Game 5**	**Game 6**	**Game 7**
6									
7		Boston Red Sox	4	2	7	3	10	4	
8									
9		Houston Astros	6	0	1	6	9	2	
10									
11									
12		Winner:	Boston Red Sox						

Cell C12 should have the name of the winner from B7 or B9 or "No winner yet" depending on the scores. Note that there can be no ties in the games. A maximum of 7 games is played. Cells B7:I9 are input cells. Changing those cells (including the names of the teams) should change the answer in C12.

You may use as many extra cells below row 12 or to the right of column I as you would like, but they should be well-labeled.

12-15. Do Problem 11-18 using Form Controls.

12-16. The following data was used in Exercises 4-3 and 10-2.

Sales Analysis
Product Line by Season
(All Sales in $ Millions)

Product	Winter	Spring	Summer	Fall
Golf	3.2	6.2	5.7	3.9
Tennis	4.7	5.2	7.1	2.9
Skiing	3.7	2.1	1.1	5.2
Surfing	1.2	2.1	2.9	1.3

(a) Create a worksheet with this data that displays the sales for one Season for all Product Lines in a pie chart. The particular Season charted should be selected and changeable by clicking on one of four Option Buttons.

(b) Create a worksheet that allows you to chart the sales of any two Product Lines across the four Seasons in a 3-D Column chart. For example, you could chart Tennis vs. Skiing. The design of the selection controls is up to you.

12-17. Data on stock prices can be obtained easily from websites such as Google Finance (finance.google.com). At the site type in Microsoft and then click on Get Quotes and then Historical Prices. Enter the dates Oct 1, 2007 and Oct 1, 2009 and click on Update:

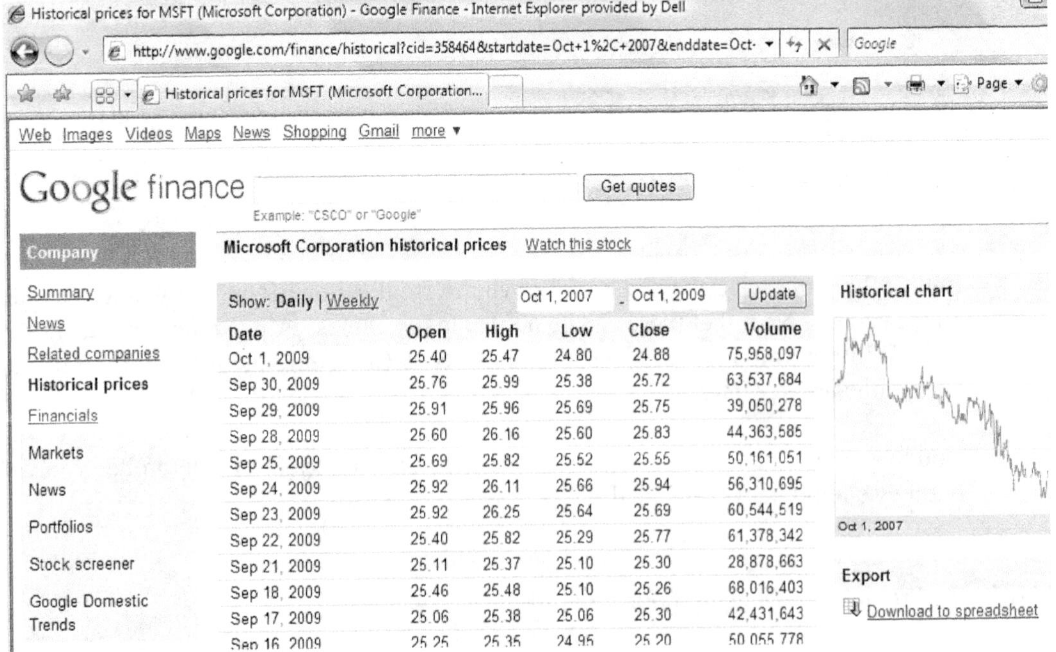

Date	Open	High	Low	Close	Volume
Oct 1, 2009	25.40	25.47	24.80	24.88	75,958,097
Sep 30, 2009	25.76	25.99	25.38	25.72	63,537,684
Sep 29, 2009	25.91	25.96	25.69	25.75	39,050,278
Sep 28, 2009	25.60	26.16	25.60	25.83	44,363,585
Sep 25, 2009	25.69	25.82	25.52	25.55	50,161,051
Sep 24, 2009	25.92	26.11	25.66	25.94	56,310,695
Sep 23, 2009	25.92	26.25	25.64	25.69	60,544,519
Sep 22, 2009	25.40	25.82	25.29	25.77	61,378,342
Sep 21, 2009	25.11	25.37	25.10	25.30	28,878,663
Sep 18, 2009	25.46	25.48	25.10	25.26	68,016,403
Sep 17, 2009	25.06	25.38	25.06	25.30	42,431,643
Sep 16, 2009	25.25	25.35	24.95	25.20	50,055,778

Now click on Download to spreadsheet, shown at the bottom right of the screen shot beneath the Historical chart. Select Save and rename the file and select a folder on your disk. The data is downloaded as a .csv (comma separated values) file. The file can be opened in Excel. When you open the .csv file in Excel, Excel should either read it in correctly or automatically run the Text Import Wizard.

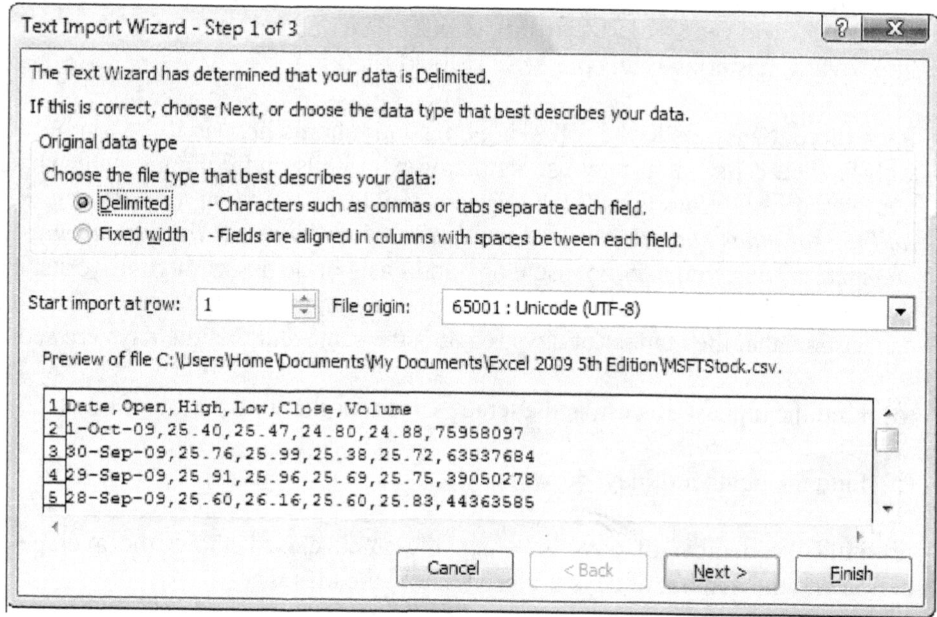

Select Delimited and click on Next. Then select Comma and click on Next. Select Finish. Widen Column A as necessary and the worksheet should look like:

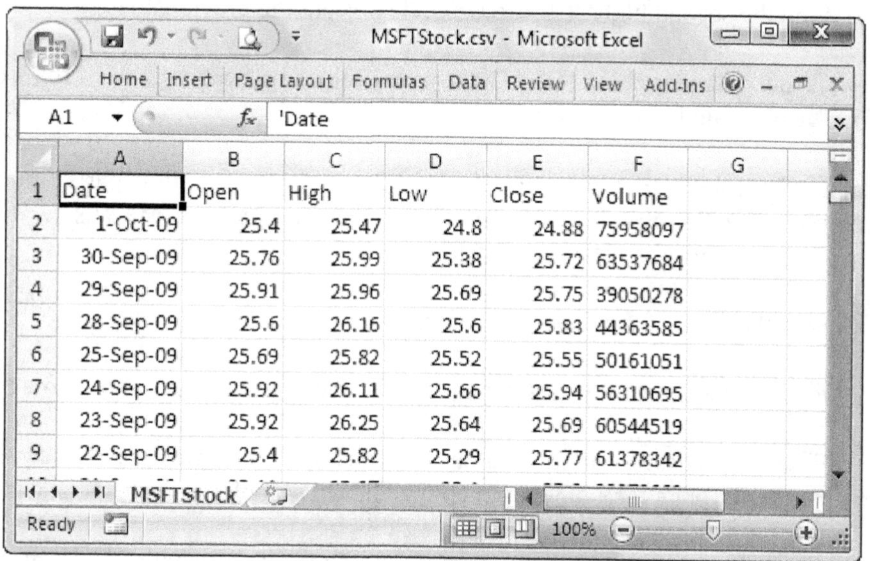

Insert some extra rows at the top. Enter the name of the stock. Select Save As and save the file as a regular .xlsx file instead of as a .csv file. Now we're ready. The worksheet contains the date, the stock price at the Open of the day, the High, Low, and Close stock prices for the day, and the Volume, the total number of shares bought and sold, that day.

For this assignment you should use the stock and dates assigned by your instructor. (Note that the two years of Microsoft stock data above are available on the web at http://www.masteringexcel.com/MSFTStockData.xls.)

Each of your answers to the following questions should appear at the top of the worksheet in well-labeled cells. You may use as many extra cells and columns with whatever formulas you would like. *However all the answers should be based on formulas on the existing data and the formulas should work automatically to yield correct answers if any of the data are changed.* (Thus, you may not use Copy and Paste or do a Sort in your worksheet as changing the original data then would not result in correct automatic calculation of the answers.) You can assume that the number of days remains the same and that the days are sequential.

(a) Find the highest, lowest, and average Close for the time period of the data.

(b) Find the number of days (rows) of data.

(c) Find the number of days in which the stock closed above the average for the entire period and the number of days it closed below the average.

(d) Add columns to the right for the dollar change from the previous Close to the Close and the percentage change from the previous Close to the Close. Find the highest Close percentage change from the previous day.

(e) Find the second highest Close percentage from the previous day.

(f) Create a Scatter chart of the Close over time and a Scatter chart of the Volume over time. The Date should be the X axis.

(g) Find the Date of the highest Close. As with all the other parts, this should be done completely with formulas. If any of the data is changed, the answer at the top of the worksheet should change as appropriate.

(h) Find the Date of the lowest Volume.

(i) Find the most recent Dates the Close was above the average and below the average.

(j) Find the highest Volume for a day in which the Close was above the previous Close and the highest Volume for a day in which the Close was below the previous Close.

(k) Find the average percentage change in Close on days with above average Volume and the average percentage change in Close on days with below average Volume.

CHAPTER 13

DATES AND TIMES

OBJECTIVES

In this chapter you will learn how to:

- Use serial numbers to represent dates and times
- Enter dates and times into a worksheet
- Write formulas to perform calculations on dates and times
- Format cells as dates and times

The calendar we use was developed over 2,000 years ago by Julius Caesar and improved slightly by Pope Gregory XIII in 1582. We are so used to the system of 12 months per year and 28, 29, 30, or 31 days per month and leap days almost every fourth year that we don't think twice about it. Still, it is difficult to perform calculations in the calendar system. How many days is it until Christmas? A payment was due on November 27. When will the payment be 60 days overdue? How many days have you been alive? Not surprisingly, the calculations are difficult in the same way that doing arithmetic with Roman numerals is difficult.

Similarly, we are used to the division of the day into 24 hours (usually expressed as 12 hours AM and 12 hours PM), the hour into 60 minutes, and the minute into 60 seconds. But calculations using this time notation system are awkward too. How many minutes are there between 9:38 AM and 3:22 PM? A movie that is 2 hours and 27 minutes long begins at 8:46 PM. When will the movie end? How many seconds are there in a day?

The capabilities provided in Excel simplify date and time calculations. The secret lies in the use of serial numbers to represent dates and times.

SERIAL NUMBERS

In Excel, each day beginning at January 1, 1900 is assigned a sequential **serial number**. January 1, 1900 is serial number 1. January 2, 1900 is serial number 2. February 1, 1900 is serial number 32. January 1, 1901 is serial number 367. November 15, 2008 is serial number 39767. December 31, 2078 is serial number 65380.

Time of day is represented by a fraction of a serial number. The serial number 39767.5 is noon on November 15, 2008. The serial number 39767.75 is 6:00 PM on November 15, 2008. The serial number 39767.6650694444 is 3:57:42 PM on November 15, 2008. Strictly speaking, the serial number 39767 is actually 12:00 midnight at the beginning of November 15, 2008.

Can you see how serial numbers make date and time calculations easier? To determine the number of days between two dates just subtract one serial number from the other.

AN ERROR IN EXCEL

As you may have noticed, there is a minor error in assigning serial numbers. The serial number 60 is assigned to February 29, 1900. But that day never existed! There was no leap day in 1900, because 1900 was not a leap year. Years ending in 00 are not leap years unless they are divisible by 400. Thus, all dates after February 29, 1900 are assigned serial numbers one greater than they should be. If you think about it, this error is only rarely consequential. Calculations of the length of time between a date in January or February 1900 and a date in March 1900 or later are off by a day. All other calculations are unaffected. Still, in such a well-designed program any known error is worth noting, if only for some future trivia question. Actually, the developers of Excel are not responsible for the error. This dating system was used in Lotus 1-2-3 and adopted by Excel as is so that Excel would be compatible with Lotus 1-2-3.

A SECOND DATE SYSTEM

To correct the error, but add to the confusion, there is a second date system that sometimes is used in Excel, especially on Macintosh computers. This date system begins at January 1, 1904 rather than January 1, 1900. In this system, all of the serial numbers correspond to dates four years later. You can determine which date system you are using by clicking on the Excel Options button at the bottom of the Office icon button pull-down menu. Then select Advanced and scroll down, as indicated in Figure 13-1. If the 1904 Date System box is checked, you are using the **1904 Date System**. If the box is blank, you are using the **1900 Date System**. Just for consistency, if you are using dates in your workbook, I suggest that at the beginning of your session in Excel you look to make sure that the box is not checked and that you are employing the standard 1900 Date System.

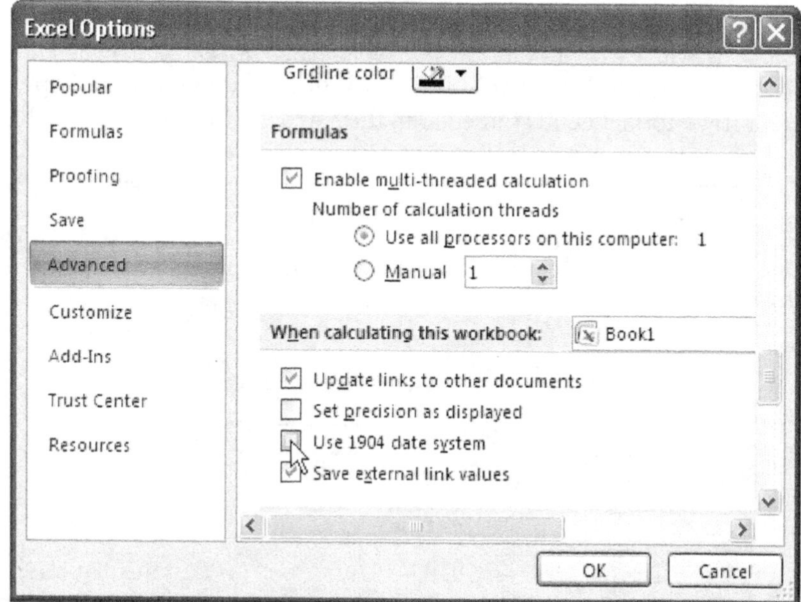

Figure 13-1. How to switch between date systems.

ENTERING DATES INTO THE WORKSHEET

How can we calculate how many days there are between September 23, 2008 and January 14, 2009? The short answer is to subtract the serial number for September 23, 2008 from the serial number for January 14, 2009. But how can we determine the serial numbers for those dates?

If we enter a date into a cell in the proper format, the computer recognizes the entry as a date and automatically converts the date into the corresponding serial number, as in Figure 13-2. Here we have typed 23-Sep-08 into cell D4 and 14-Jan-09 into cell D5. Excel recognizes these as dates and automatically converts them into serial numbers.

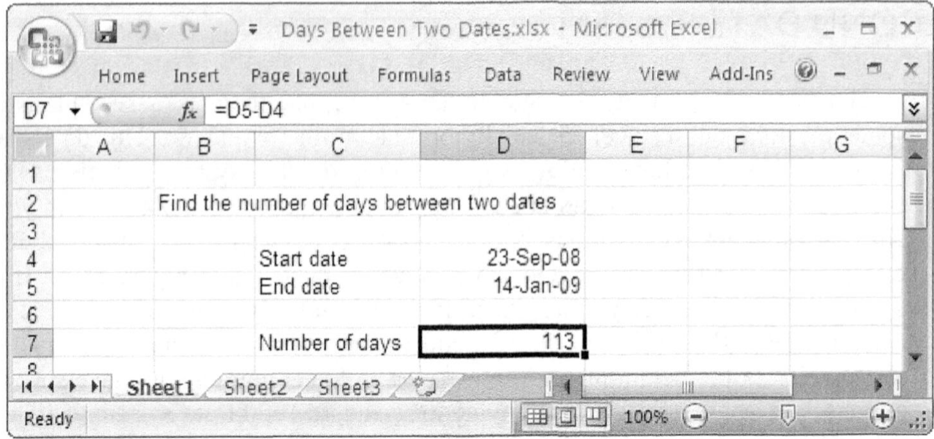

Figure 13-2. To find the number of days between two dates, enter them and subtract.

The value of cell D4 actually is 39,714, the serial number for September 23, 2008, as is apparent if we format cell D4 in comma format, as in Figure 13-3.

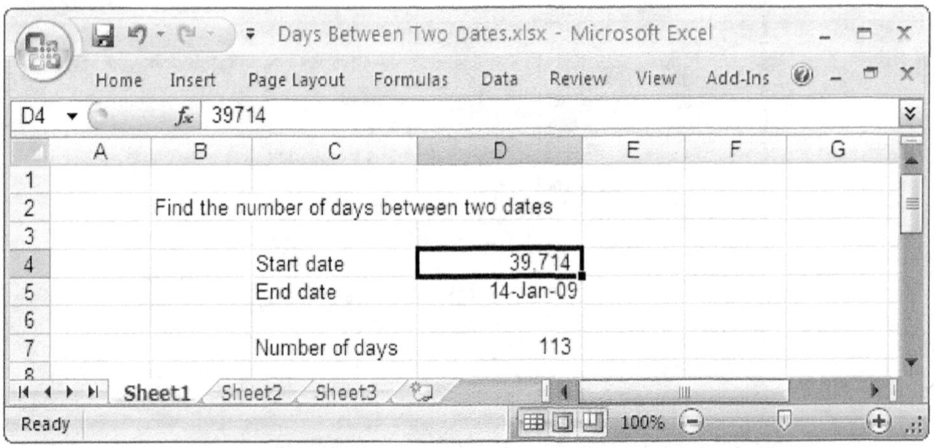

Figure 13-3. A number can be formatted to appear as a number or as a date.

We have to be very careful here. The date has to be typed in just right. For example, if we type a space before the date, the computer will not recognize the entry as a date. Rather, the entry will be taken as text, as in Figure 13-4. Here, Excel is trying to subtract a label from a number, which yields the #VALUE! error message. You can tell that cell D4 now contains text because the entry is aligned to the left of the cell rather than to the right of the cell. Recall that Excel automatically aligns text on the left of the cell and numbers on the right of the cell, just so you can tell which cells contain text and which contain numbers.

What are the allowable formats for dates? It depends to some extent on the settings in Regional and Language Options in the computer's Control Panel. Different countries have different formats for dates. For a computer set to English (United States) Excel will recognize each of the following entries as a date:

September 23, 2008
23-Sep-08
9/23/08
Sept 23, 08
9-23-08

and automatically will convert the entry into the equivalent serial number. If you enter

9/23
9-23
September 23
23-Sep

or variants into a cell, the computer will interpret it as September 23 of this year.

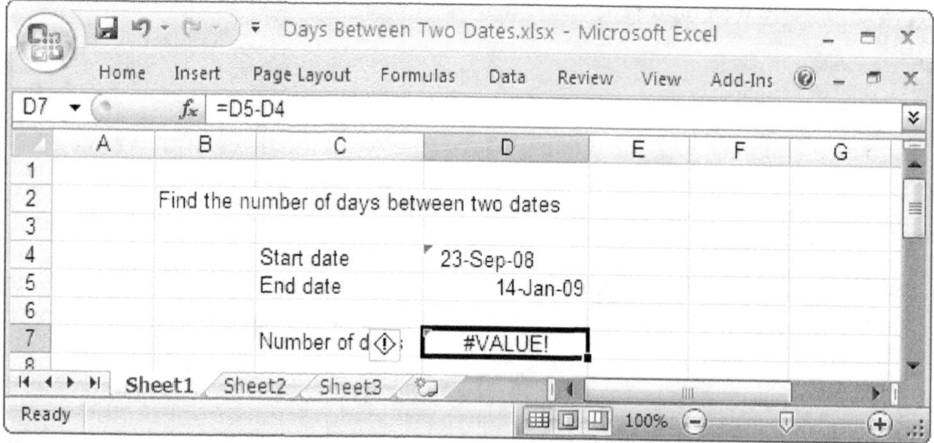

Figure 13-4. If we type a space before the date then the entry is regarded as text.

USING DATES DIRECTLY IN FORMULAS

In the example in Figure 13-2, we entered the dates into cells and then used the cell addresses in the formula =D6-D4. Suppose we want to do the calculation in a single formula. If we type the formula

= 14-Jan-09-23-Sep-08

into a cell, we get a #NAME? error. Why? Excel interprets the dashes as minus signs. Excel tries to subtract the contents of the cell named Jan from the number 14, but there is no cell with the name of Jan so we get the #NAME? error.

To do the date arithmetic directly in a formula, we need to place quotes around the dates:

= "14-Jan-09" - "23-Sep-08"

Now Excel will interpret the text in the quotes as dates, automatically convert these dates into their equivalent serial numbers, and perform the subtraction, yielding the value 113, the number of days between the two dates.

Off to the side of the cell is a warning that it's better not to specify years by only two digits. The problem is by "48" we could intend 1948 or 2048. My copy of Excel 2007 takes "14-Jan-29" to mean January 14, 2029 and "14-Jan-30" to mean January 14, 1930. Thus

= "14-Jan-30" - "23-Sep-29"

is taken to mean

= "January 14, 1930" - "September 23, 2029"

You can see why that causes trouble. So it's better to use 4 digits for years.

Similarly we could type

= "1/14/2009" - "9/23/2008"

into a cell and get 113, the number of days between the dates. But typing

= 1/14/2009 - 9/23/2008

will result in the value of -0.000159318, the result of the calculation with numbers rather than dates, as the "dates" in this last formula are not in quotes.

THE TODAY FUNCTION

The computer has a **system clock** which keeps track of the current date and time. This clock has its own battery so it stays current (excuse the mild pun) even when the computer is shut down. It also can check the date and time over the internet if you're connected.

Excel can access the system clock using the **TODAY** function. If we enter the formula

=TODAY( )

into a cell, the cell will contain the serial number for today. The computer automatically will format this number as a date, so today's date will appear in the cell. The parentheses following TODAY are necessary to indicate this is a function and not the name of a cell. The function will be recalculated whenever all the other formulas are recalculated. The TODAY function will give you the current date rather than the date the worksheet was created.

THE DATE FUNCTION

The **DATE** function has three arguments: a year, a month number, and a day of the month. The result of evaluating the date function is the corresponding serial number. The formula =DATE(2009,1,14) calculates the serial number for January 14, 2009, which is 39827. Thus the following formula also calculates the number of days between September 23, 2008 and January 14, 2009:

=DATE(2009,1,14) - DATE(2008,9,23)

Entering this formula into a cell in Excel yields an answer of 113.

DATE FORMATS

Excel has several built-in formats for dates. If you specify a date format for a cell that contains a number, Excel takes the number as the serial number of a date, and displays the corresponding date. The formats are specified by clicking on the Format Cells button in the Number group of the Home tab. In Figure 13-5 some of the formats available for English (United States) are shown.

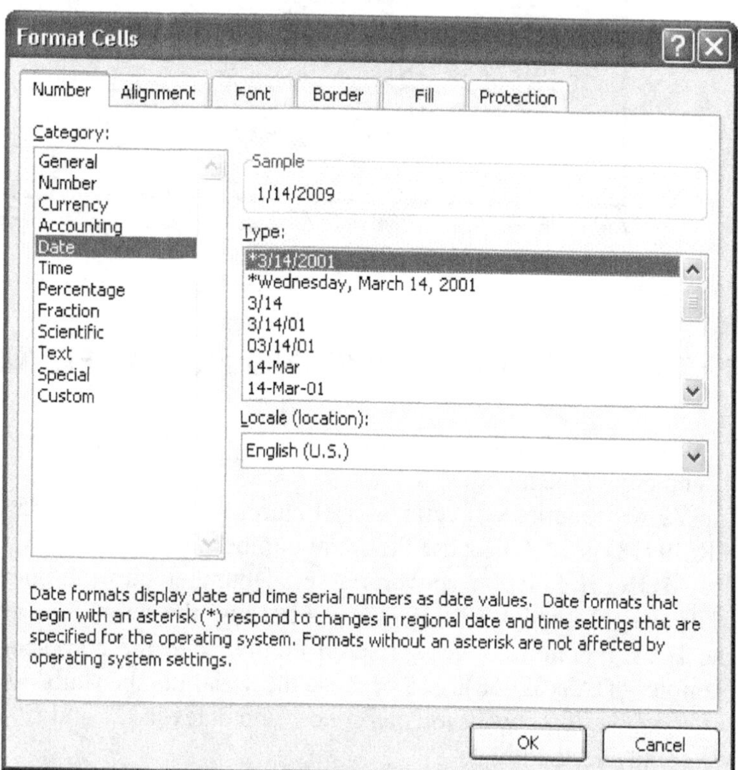

Figure 13-5. Various date formats are available.

If you would like to use a different language or calendar system, Microsoft tries to accommodate you. Notice the Locale pull-down menu. This has well over a hundred choices. If you are preparing a worksheet for clients in Saudi Arabia and would like the date in Arabic, some of the date formats and calendars available are shown in Figure 13-6.

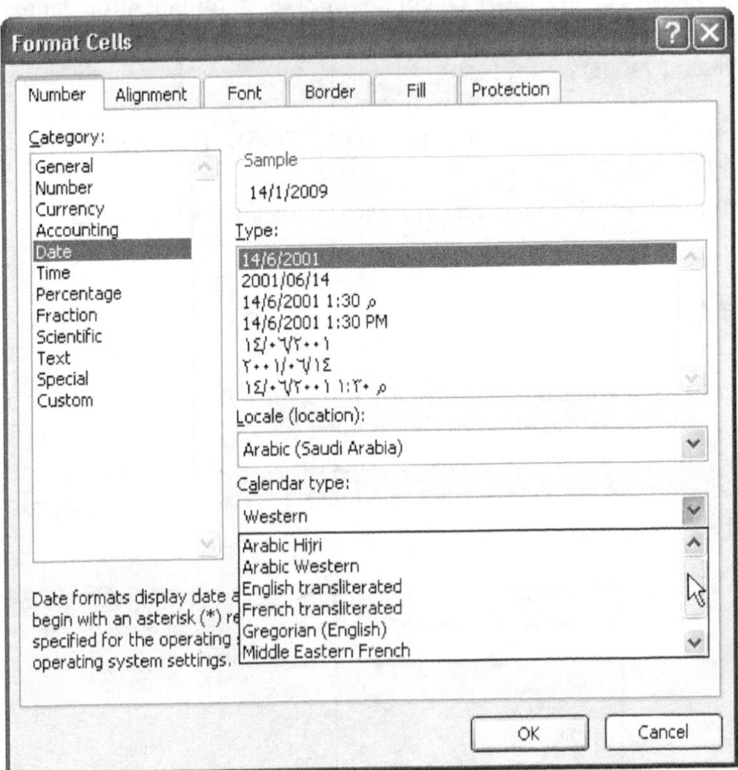

Figure 13-6. Alternative date formats and calendars for Arabic (Saudi Arabia).

DATE FUNCTIONS FOR CONVERTING FROM SERIAL NUMBERS

There are three date functions that convert a serial number into the corresponding year, month, and day of the month.

The **YEAR** function converts a serial number into the corresponding year. For example, =YEAR(39918) is 2009 because the serial number falls in 2009.

The **MONTH** function converts a serial number into the corresponding month of the year. For example, =MONTH(39918) is 4 because the serial number falls in April.

The **DAY** function converts a serial number into the corresponding day of the month. For example, =DAY(39918) is 15 because the serial number falls on April 15, 2009.

For example, if we want to determine if the dates in C7 and C9 are in the same calendar year we could check with

=IF(YEAR(C7)=YEAR(C9), "Same year", "Different years")

EXAMPLE: HOW MANY DAYS UNTIL JULY 1?

Our organization uses a July 1 budget year. Budgets begin and end at midnight (at the beginning) of July 1. We would like to be able to calculate how many days are left before our current budget expires. If the current budget year ends on July 1, 2009, we could write the formula in one of two ways:

="1-July-2009" - TODAY( )

or

=DATE(2009,7,1) - TODAY( )

The only problem is that each year we would have to adjust the year in the quotes or in the first argument in the DATE function by hand. How could we write the formula so it always works automatically whatever the current year? As a first try we could substitute the current calendar year for the 2009 in the preceding formula, as follows:

=DATE(YEAR(TODAY( )),7,1) - TODAY( )

Here, YEAR(TODAY( )) evaluates to the current calendar year, to 2009 if this is 2009. This formula works if the current month is January through June, if we are in the same calendar year as the budget end. However, if this were October then the above formula would be incorrect. If the month were July through December, the formula would evaluate to a negative number because

=DATE(YEAR(TODAY( )),7,1)

would yield the serial number of the July 1 in the current calendar year, of the previous July 1 rather than the next July 1.

To solve this problem we could use an IF function where the condition is TRUE if today's month is before July and FALSE if today's month is July or after.

=IF(MONTH(TODAY( ))<7,(DATE(YEAR(TODAY( )),7,1)-TODAY( )),
(DATE(YEAR(TODAY( ))+1,7,1)-TODAY( )))

If the month is before July, the computer calculates the serial number of July 1 of this year minus today's serial number. Otherwise, if the month is July or after, the computer calculates the serial number of July 1 of next year minus today's serial number.

HOURS, MINUTES, AND SECONDS

Serial numbers represent days. The fractions of a serial number represent fractions of a day. For example, 0.5 represents 12 hours. An hour is 0.0416666667, which is 1/24. A minute is 0.0006944444, which is 1/(24*60). A second is 0.0000115741, which is 1/(24*60*60) of a day.

Midnight is 0. 6:00 AM is 0.25. Noon is 0.5. 7:30 PM is 0.8125. 11:58:23 PM is 0.998877314814815.

The same types of built-in functions and display formats are provided for times as are provided for dates.

THE NOW FUNCTION

The **NOW** built-in function evaluates to the serial number for the date and time right now according to the system clock. The value of the formula

=NOW( )

changes each time the worksheet is evaluated. So, for example, if it is 8:00 AM on December 25, 2008, the value of NOW( ) is 39807.333333333.

You can force the NOW function (and all other formulas in the worksheet) to be re-evaluated by pressing function key F9, the recalculation key. Pressing F9 will update the current time and date.

To obtain just the current time we can use both the NOW( ) and TODAY( ) functions together. For example, if we wish the worksheet to greet the user we could enter the following formula into a cell:

```
=IF( (NOW( ) – TODAY( )) < 0.5, "Good morning", IF ( (NOW( ) – TODAY( )) < 17/24,
        "Good afternoon", "Good evening" ))
```

Thus if it is before noon then Excel wishes the user “Good morning”. Otherwise if it is before 5 PM (which is 17/24 through the day), Excel wishes the user “Good afternoon”. Otherwise Excel wishes the user “Good evening”.

TIME FORMATS

There are several formats for displaying times in Excel. (See Figure 13-7.) The time formats are specified by clicking on the Format Cells button in the Number group of the Home tab.

When a cell is displayed strictly in a time format, the digits to the left of the decimal point in the number in the cell are ignored. Only the fractional part of the number is used to determine what is displayed. Thus a cell with the number 65.59 would appear the same as a cell with the number 42051.59 if the cells have the same time format. Both would be displayed as 2:09:36 PM, the time that is 0.59 through the day. There are some time formats that display both the date and the time represented by the serial number in the cell.

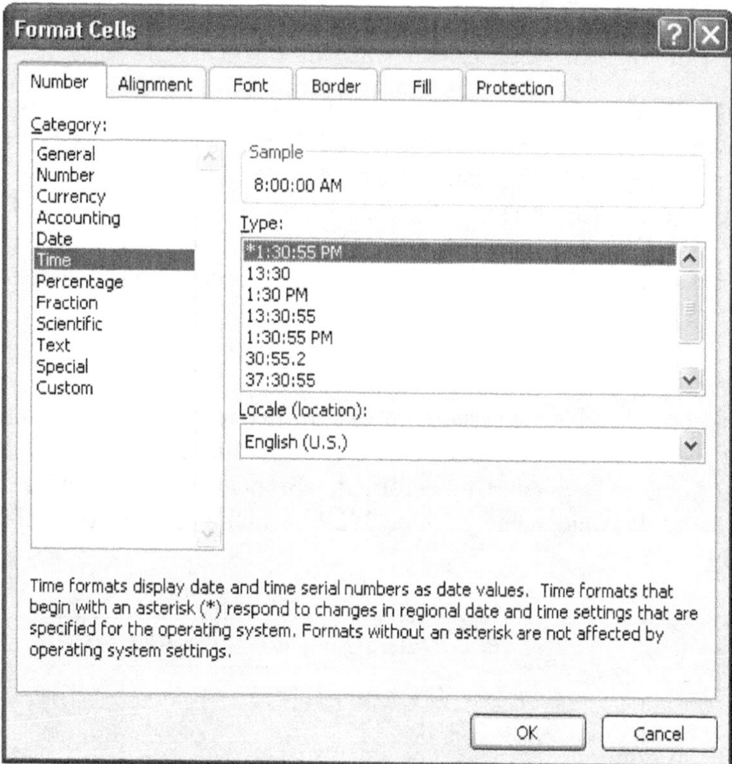

Figure 13-7. Time formats.

ENTERING A TIME INTO A CELL OR FORMULA

As with a date, a time can be entered directly into a cell. If you type 9:52 into a cell, Excel will interpret the entry as a time. The cell will contain the serial number for 9:52 AM, namely 0.4111111111. The cell will be formatted as a time, so 9:52 will appear in the cell, just as you typed it.

The **TIME** function has three arguments: the hour based on a 24-hour clock, the minute, and the second. The result of evaluating the TIME function is the equivalent serial number. For example, =TIME(19,12,0) evaluates to 0.8, as 7:12 PM is 80% through the day.

The movie began at 8:46 PM. The movie is 2 hours and 27 minutes long. When will the movie be over? A formula for determining the answer is

= "8:46 PM" + "2:27"

which yields the value 0.967361111111111 in the cell. Displaying this cell in a time format gives you the answer 11:13 PM. Another possible formula to use is

=TIME(20,46,0) + TIME(2,27,0)

which also yields 11:13 PM.

EXAMPLE: TESTING THE ENGINES

United Engines performs extensive tests on their products. They would like a worksheet to allow them to enter the starting date and time of a test and the number of hours for the test and then display the ending date and time for the test.

The worksheet is shown in Figure 13-8. The date at the start of the test is entered into cell C4. The time at the start of the test is entered into cell C5. The number of hours the test is to run is entered into cell C7. Cells F4 and F5 both have the same formula:

= C4 + C5 + C7/24

This formula adds the serial number for the date of the start plus the serial number of the time of the start plus the number of days that the test is to run. Cell F4 is given a date format. Cell F5 is given a time format. Both F4 and F5 contain the same formula and, hence, the same value, namely 39985.32292, which is the serial number for 7:45 AM on June 21, 2009.

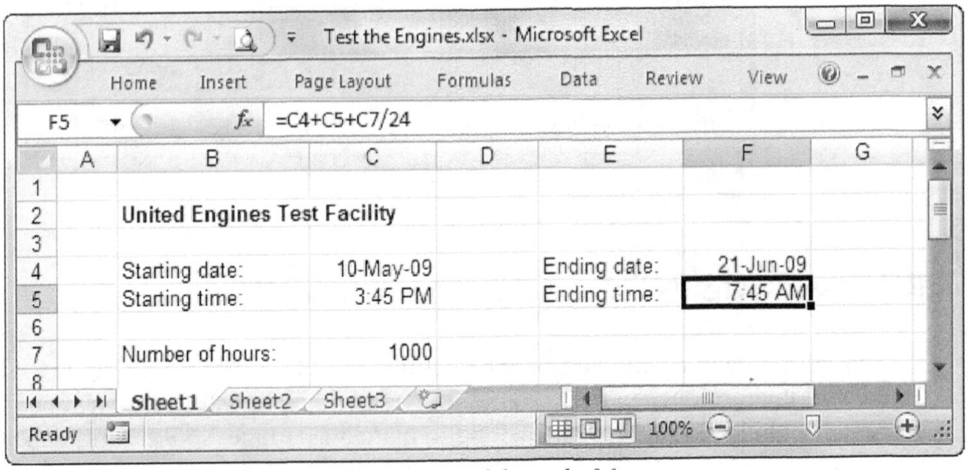

Figure 13-8. Calculating the date and time of the end of the test.

TIME FUNCTIONS FOR CONVERTING FROM SERIAL NUMBERS

There are three time functions that convert a serial number into the corresponding hour, minutes, and seconds.

The **HOUR** function converts a serial number into the corresponding hour of the day. For example, =HOUR(39827.847) is 20 because the serial number falls between 8 PM and 9 PM.

The **MINUTE** function converts a serial number into the corresponding minute of the hour. For example, =MINUTE(39827.847) is 19 because the serial number falls between 8:19 PM and 8:20 PM.

The **SECOND** function converts a serial number into the corresponding second of the minute. For example, =SECOND(39827.847) is 41 because the serial number falls closest to 8:19:41 PM.

The serial number 39827.847 corresponds to 8:19:41 PM on January 14, 2009, to the nearest second.

PENCIL AND PAPER EXERCISE

13-1. Write down the formula that calculates each of the following quantities. Then identify the type of format in which the cell is to be displayed. You may use the computer to check the formulas. (You do not need to write down the result of evaluating each formula. You just need to write down the formula itself and the format in which the answer will be displayed.) I have answered part (a) just to give you the general idea.

(a) The date that is 90 days after December 23, 2008.
Answer: *The formula is* *="23-Dec-2008" + 90*
Format the answer as a date.

(b) The number of days Franklin D. Roosevelt was President of the United States. FDR was inaugurated on March 4, 1933. He died in office on April 12, 1945.

(c) The date that is 1000 days from today.

(d) The date that was 1000 hours ago.

(e) The number of days until the year 2015.

(f) The date of serial number 10000.

(g) The serial number for April 3, 2046.

(h) The year for serial number 500000.

(i) The date of the 200th day of 2009.

(j) The number of days you have been alive.

(k) The number of hours between 11:52AM on 05-Nov-08 and 8:07AM on 25-Dec-08.

(l) The time 1000 hours from now.

(m) The hours:minutes:seconds between 6:46:32 AM and 10:23:15 PM.

(n) The number of minutes in the entire 21st century.

(o) The exact time 60% through the day.

(p) The time and date 100,000 minutes after 4:12 PM on November 12, 2008.

COMPUTER EXERCISES

13-2. Use the TODAY function to create the following worksheet. Your worksheet should work automatically whatever the day. It should work during leap years and non-leap years.

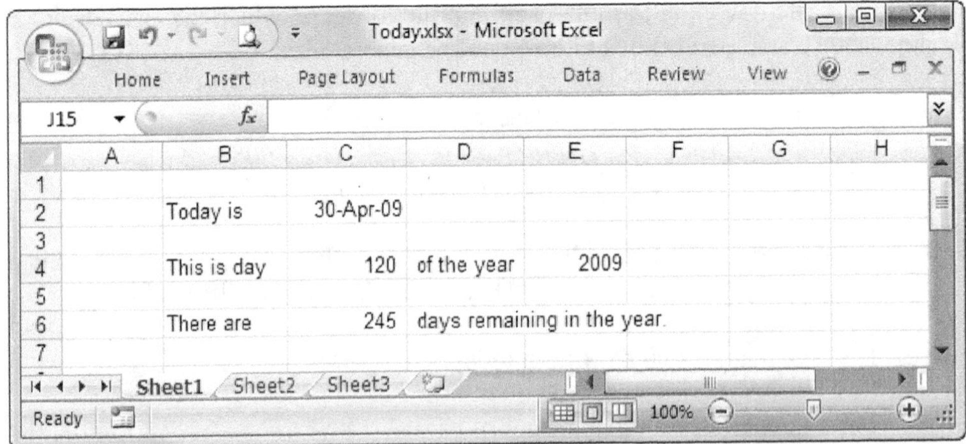

13-3. The local department store has hired you to create a well-labeled worksheet that displays in four cells the number of days, hours, minutes, and seconds from now until Christmas. The worksheet should be updated automatically each time it is opened. To update the worksheet once it is opened, press F9, the Recalculation key.

13-4. Create a worksheet that allows you to enter in any date into a cell and then in separate cells gives the date 30, 60, 90, and 120 days from the entered date.

13-5. John loves riding on roller coasters. His lifetime dream is to set the world endurance record for riding a roller coaster and have his achievement be recorded in the *Book of World Records*. Now John has his chance. The local amusement park is excited about supporting John for the publicity his great accomplishment will bring. According to the book, the current record is 503 hours. The amusement park would like John to break the record at 8:00 PM on July 4. Create a worksheet to determine the date and time he should begin.

13-6. NASA has commissioned you to create a worksheet for Mission Control. The design is given below. The time and date of launch will be entered as shown in C5 and D5. The worksheet should display the current time and date automatically. The elapsed length of the mission so far should be calculated and displayed in two ways: (1) in terms of days in C10 and then hours, minutes, and seconds in E10 and (2) in terms of hours and fractions of hours in C12. To update the display, you will need to press F9, the Recalculation key.

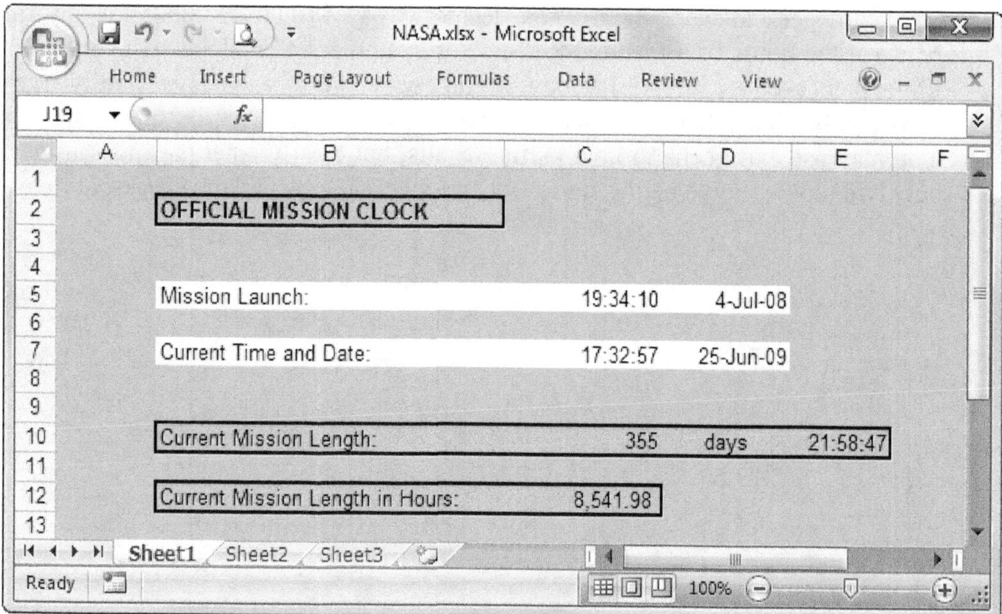

13-7. You have been hired by Club 2020 to design and implement a worksheet for the "greeter" at the door to use to determine whether people are old enough to enter. Create a well-labeled worksheet that allows the greeter to enter into a cell the person's birth date as listed on the person's driver's license. In a separate cell should appear either "Welcome" if the person is at least 21 years old or "Sorry, you are underage" otherwise. Use TODAY and IF.

13-8. You have taken a part-time job as manager of the Happy Hamburger Stand. The Stand is open from 6 AM to 11 PM. Employees work all different odd schedules. Employees are paid at the rate of $8.00 per hour from the moment they check in to the moment they check out. So, for example, an employee who checked in at 6:00 PM and checked out at 9:15 PM would earn $26.00 for the day.

(a) Create a well-labeled worksheet that accepts two entries, the check-in time and the check-out time, as inputs. The worksheet should show the number of hours the employee worked and the amount of money the employee is to be paid for the day. No other inputs are allowed.

(b) The Stand is so popular under your management that you decide to stay open until 3 AM. Create a second worksheet that accepts check-in and check-out times between 6 AM and 3 AM. Again, the worksheet should show the total number of hours the employee worked and the amount of money the employee is to be paid for the day. Still, the only two cells used for input should be the entries for the check-in time and the check-out time.

(c) The Stand is doing a booming business at dinnertime, but you are finding it difficult to hire employees to work then. You decide to pay $10.00 per hour for any time worked between the hours of 5 PM and 8 PM. For example, an employee who checked in at 6:00 PM and checked out at 9:15 PM now would earn $30.00 for the day. Modify your worksheet accordingly. Your third worksheet should work for any check-in time and check-out time. You may use extra cells to hold partial results, but clearly label the final answer. Still, the only two inputs should be the entries for the check-in time and the check-out time.

CHAPTER 14

FINANCIAL FUNCTIONS

OBJECTIVES

In this chapter you will learn how to:

- Create worksheets to solve problems involving the time value of money
- Use the PMT function to calculate loan payments
- Use the Function Wizard to assist you in entering functions
- Use the PV, RATE, NPER, and FV functions to analyze financial situations
- Make investment decisions using IRR, NPV, and XIRR

Excel often is used to help analyze financial problems.

A basic concept in finance is the **time value of money**. The value of money changes over time because of the potential of earning interest on the money. Which is more valuable, $1,000 today or $1,001 two years from now? The $1,000 today is more valuable because with almost no risk you could put the $1,000 in the bank, earn interest, and have over $1,050 two years from now.

Furthermore, if you leave the money in the bank, the interest compounds. During the second year you earn interest not just on the amount you deposited in the bank but also on the interest that you earned the first year. Suppose you decide to start saving for a down payment for a house. You open an account that pays 3% per year. Every year you put $2,500 into the account. How much money will you have in four years? How long will it be before you have $20,000?

Suppose you have $10,000 that you would like to invest for four years. The bank will guarantee you 6% interest per year. Your cousin has this great idea for starting a business. If you invest the $10,000 with her, she promises to pay you $2,000 after one year, $3,000 after two years, $4,000 after three years, and $5,000 at the end of four years. Which investment would pay the higher rate of interest? In making the decision of what to do with your money you may decide to invest in the bank because it is much less risky or you may decide to invest with your cousin because she is family, but at least you ought to be able to figure out how the options compare in terms of the rate of return on your money.

The calculations in financial analyses can be quite complex. A lot of money can be riding on making the correct calculations. To help in this important application area, several financial functions are provided in Excel. These functions facilitate many calculations involving the time value of money.

CALCULATING LOAN PAYMENTS WITH THE PMT FUNCTION

Wouldn't it be fun to drive around town in a bright red Ferrari 599 GTB Fiorano with a nice throaty V12 engine? I know it's not environmentally correct, but 612 hp and 0-60 in 3.4 seconds? Perfect for Boston winters. Here is a new one advertised for only $295,500. Not bad. I can scrape up $3,000. My buddy just got an auto loan at 9% annual interest. Maybe I could take out a loan and then pay it back over four years. I wonder what the monthly payment would be on a $292,500 loan.

When borrowing money for an automobile loan or for the mortgage for a house or condo, the money usually is paid back in equal monthly payments. Part of these payments cover the interest that is owed. Part of the payments go to paying off the principal. The principal of a loan is the amount of money that was borrowed. After each payment, the amount owed on the principal is decreased. After the final payment the loan is paid off. The formula for calculating the fixed monthly payment is built into the **PMT** function.

The PMT function has five arguments (inputs): the periodic interest rate, the number of periodic payments, the present value, the future value, and the type:

PMT(rate, nper, pv, fv, type)

When using the PMT function, or any financial function, the first step is to decide on the period. All figures must be expressed in terms of a common period of time. If the payments are to be made each month, then the period would be a month. This means that the first argument to the PMT function, the interest rate to be paid, must be stated as the monthly interest rate. The second argument, nper, would be the number of monthly payments to be made, the number of periods of the loan.

How much would the monthly payment be for the Ferrari?

The interest rate is 9% per year. The monthly interest rate would be 9%/12 or 0.75%. This could be written in the formula either as 0.75% or as .0075.

We would make monthly payments for four years, for a total of 48 monthly payments.

The present value of the loan would be the principal, the amount borrowed, which would be 292500. Here, we need to be careful not to include a dollar sign or any commas. If we put in a dollar sign, Excel will think it's the beginning of an absolute address and give us an error message. If we include a comma to mark off the thousands, Excel will think the comma is separating two different arguments.

The future value is the amount of money that will be exchanged at the end of the loan. Here, the future value would be 0 as the loan will be all paid off after 48 months. In some cases there is a "balloon payment", an amount to be paid off at the end of the loan period. This would be included as the future value.

Finally, the type of the loan is either 0 or 1. The type is 0 if the payment is due at the end of each month. The type is 1 if the payment is due at the beginning of each month. Normally the bank would require you to make your first payment at the end of the first month and subsequent payments would be due at the end of each succeeding month, so the type would be 0.

The formula for calculating the monthly payment for the Ferrari would be

```
=PMT(0.75%, 48, 292500, 0, 0)
```

Entering this formula into a cell yields the answer ($7,278.87). The parentheses mean this is a negative number. That is, each month we would need to pay the finance company $7,278.87. Taxes and insurance and gas and tune-ups are extra. You know, I've always wanted an eight-year-old Chevy.

One of the tricky parts of using financial functions in Excel is the sign of the number. A positive number represents money you are receiving, cash coming into your wallet. A negative number represents money you are paying, cash going out of your wallet. In this example we are receiving $292,500 from the bank at the beginning of the transaction of the loan so the present value would be +292500. Each month we are paying money to the bank out of our wallet so the monthly payment is represented in Excel as a negative number.

The last two arguments in the PMT function are optional, in the sense that if they are 0, you can leave them off. Thus, we could write the formula

```
=PMT(0.75%, 48, 292500)
```

Rather than entering the numbers for the loan directly into the formula, we could put them into separate cells and refer to the cells in the formula, as in the worksheet in Figure

14-1. The advantage of this approach, of course, is that to change the specifics for the loan, we would just need to change the numbers in the cells rather than going in and editing the formula. Also, these numbers show on the worksheet and in a printout of the worksheet. Most lending institutions state the interest rate and the length of the loan in years so the worksheet in Figure 14-1 is designed accordingly. The interest rate and length of the loan are converted to monthly figures in the formula. The actual data in the worksheet in Figure 14-1 show the figures for a $400,000 mortgage at 7% per year over 30 years.

Note that a balloon payment would be entered as a positive number in C7. It would be money out of our pocket at the end of the loan period, negative cash flow for us. The balloon payment is converted to a negative number in the formula in C10 by placing a minus sign before the entry for C7 in the fourth argument in the formula.

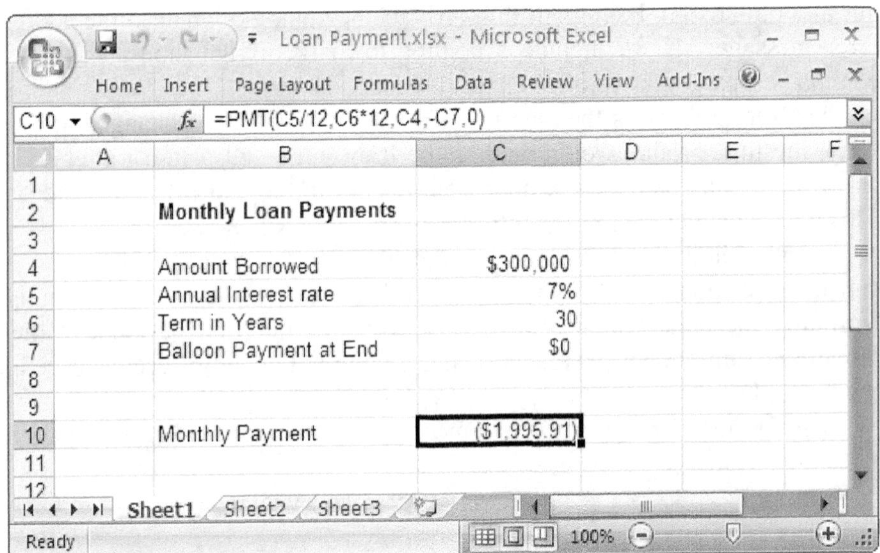

Figure 14-1. A worksheet for calculating the monthly payment for a loan. In this case, the loan is for $300,000 for 30 years.

USING THE INSERT FUNCTION TOOL

The Insert Function tool was introduced in Chapter 4. It is especially useful with financial functions in specifying the arguments. The Insert Function button is just to the left of the Formula bar.

The first step is to select the function you wish to use. You either type the name of the function in the top box or you can select the category of functions in the pull-down menu and then find the function in the list below, as in Figure 14-2. The list of arguments and a brief description of the function is shown at the bottom of the dialog box. You can ask for Help to find out all about the function if you wish. Click on OK once you have identified the correct function.

Insert Function

Search for a function:

Type a brief description of what you want to do and then click Go

Go

Or select a category: Financial

Select a function:

ODDFPRICE
ODDFYIELD
ODDLPRICE
ODDLYIELD
PMT
PPMT
PRICE

PMT(rate,nper,pv,fv,type)

Calculates the payment for a loan based on constant payments and a constant interest rate.

Help on this function

OK Cancel

Figure 14-2. Find and select the function.

The second step of the Insert Function tool is the Function Argument dialog box, shown in Figure 14-3. The dialog box gives you the arguments and their order. It is critical that the arguments be in the correct order in the formula. To enter cell addresses in the arguments, either you can type the addresses or you can click on the cells themselves. If the cells you need to refer to are hidden by the dialog box window, you can drag the window to one side and scroll through the worksheet. Or, if you click on the button to the right of the argument box, the Function Arguments window temporarily will roll up out of your way. The result of evaluating the function is shown at the bottom of the dialog box. The optional Help facility really is helpful here and explains the functions and their arguments. Click on OK in the dialog box of Figure 14-3 and you have the formula in Figure 14-1.

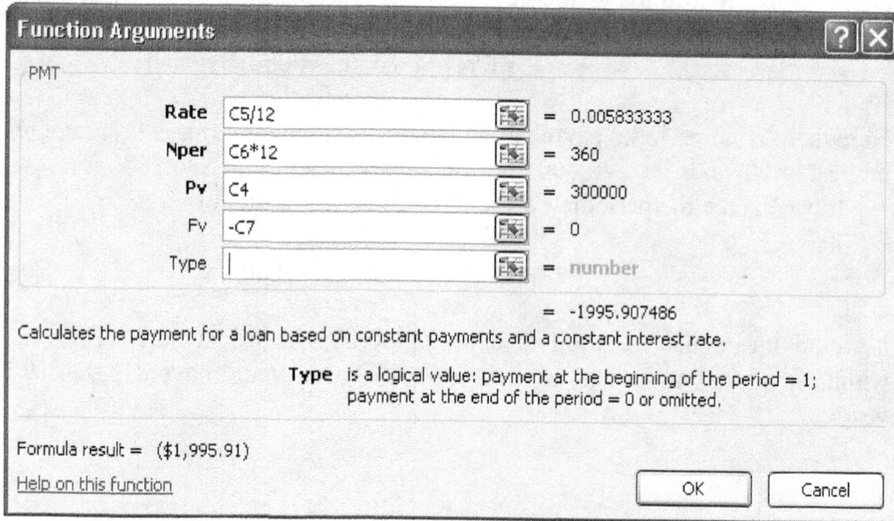

Figure 14-3. The Insert Function tool shows and explains the list of arguments.

CALCULATING FUTURE VALUES USING THE FV FUNCTION

I have $40,000 to invest right now. Each year I plan to invest $5,000 more. I figure I can earn 8% per year on my investment. How much will I have accumulated in 10 years?

To solve this problem we would use the **FV** function. The FV function calculates the future value of an investment assuming constant periodic payments and a constant interest rate throughout the life of the investment. The FV function has five arguments:

FV(rate, nper, pmt, pv, type)

Again, the first step is to determine the time period involved in the investment. Since all of the information is stated in years, we will use a time period of a year. So, the rate and number of periods will be stated in terms of years.

The annual rate is 8%. The number of years of the investment is 10. The annual payment is $5,000 out of our wallet, so we'll enter -5000 into the formula for pmt. The present value is -40000, our initial investment. We plan to make our annual investment at the end of each year. That is, the first payment of $5,000 will be made one year from now rather than right now. So the type of the investment is 0 rather than 1.

Using the FV function to solve the problem of the future value of our investment, we get the formula

=FV(8%, 10, -5000, -40000, 0)

Entering this formula into Excel tells us we will have accumulated $158,789.81 after 10 years. We have deposited a total of $90,000 (that is, $40,000 initially and $50,000 over 10 years) so the remaining $68,789.81 is the amount we have earned in interest.

Suppose we are uncertain about being able to make the $5,000 deposit each year. We just want to see what an initial deposit of $40,000 would earn in 10 years at 8% if we left it alone. Now the formula would be

=FV(8%, 10, 0, -40000, 0)

Here there is no periodic payment, so the third argument, pmt, is 0. Excel tells us that at 8% interest in 10 years the $40,000 investment would turn into $86,357.

If we change the periodic payment to +5000, as in the formula

=FV(8%, 10, 5000, -40000, 0)

it would mean that we want to deposit $40,000 in an account earning 8% per year and withdraw $5,000 at the end of each year. Here we would have $13,924.19 at the end of 10 years.

THE BASIC IDEA OF THESE FINANCIAL FUNCTIONS

These investments (or loans) have five basic parameters:

pv	the value or cash flow at the beginning of the investment
rate	the interest rate per time period
nper	the total number of time periods
pmt	the payment that is made each time period
fv	the value or cash flow at the end of the investment

Given any four of these parameters, there is a financial function to calculate the fifth. For the PMT function we know the present value, the interest rate, the number of periods, and the future value. PMT tells us the amount of the periodic payment. For the FV function we know the present value, the interest rate, the number of periods, and the periodic payment. FV tells us the future value of the investment.

THE NPER FUNCTION

My goal is to become a millionaire, to accumulate 1,000,000 dollars. I have $100,000 saved up in an investment earning 10% per year. If I deposit $25,000 additional each year, how many years until I have the $1,000,000?

The **NPER** function has five arguments:

NPER(rate, pmt, pv, fv, type)

Filling in the arguments

=NPER(10%, -25000, -100000, 1000000, 0)

we find it will take 13.4 years until I am a millionaire!

Suppose by some good fortune I find myself with a million dollars. I decide to put it in a safe investment at 5% per year and retire to a tropical island. I figure I will need $80,000 per year to live the tropical lifestyle to which I would like to become accustomed. How many years will it be until I run out of money?

This is still a problem for NPER. Entering the formula

=NPER(5%, 80000, -1000000, 0, 1)

yields an answer of 18.5 years before I run out of money. The fifth argument, the type, is 1 because I want that first withdrawal right away and each subsequent withdrawal at the beginning of the year.

Suppose I could earn 10% per year on my money. The formula

=NPER(10%, 80000, -1000000, 0, 1)

yields an answer of #NUM!. This is an error message. In this case it means that there is no such number. If you think about it, at 10% interest per year I will be earning more than I am spending so I can withdraw $80,000 per year forever and my investment will continue to increase in value! NPER has no value; the number of periods the investment will last is infinite.

THE RATE FUNCTION

Suppose we have $20,000 to invest and we would like to grow it into $50,000 in five years. What interest rate would we need to receive?

The **RATE** function has six arguments:

RATE(nper, pmt, pv, fv, type, guess)

The final argument, the guess, is optional. The guess is the user's guess about what is the correct answer. There is no algebraic formula for calculating the rate, so the computer does it iteratively, by trial and error. The guess is the starting point for the computer's attempts to find the correct answer. If the user leaves off the guess, the computer automatically will begin with a guess of 10%.

To solve this problem we enter

=RATE(5, 0, -20000, 50000, 0)

and the computer informs us we will require an annual interest rate of 20.11%.

If we had wanted to grow the $20,000 into $5,000,000 in five years, then we would enter

=RATE(5, 0, -20000, 5000000, 0)

Now the computer evaluates the formula to #NUM!, meaning it couldn't come up with an answer. The problem is that the computer started with a guess of 10% but the required rate is much higher. If we instruct the computer to begin with a guess of 100% per year

=RATE(5, 0, -20000, 5000000, 0, 100%)

then the formula evaluates to 202%, meaning we need to receive more than 200% interest each year. We must triple our money each year to achieve this rather ambitious objective.

We need to enter a number for the guess in the RATE function if the final answer is not close to 10%.

THE PV FUNCTION

Mike is hoping to spend 18 months on a Greek island programming the great new computer game (and tasting a little ouzo). Mike figures he will need $3,000 per month to live and $800 at the end of the period for transportation home. How much money would Mike need to deposit initially in an account paying 6% interest per year to be able to withdraw $3,000 per month for 18 months and have $800 left at the end?

The **PV** function has five arguments:

PV(rate, nper, pmt, fv, type)

The formula would be

=PV(6%/12, 18, 3000, 800, 1)

Here the time period is the month so we divide the annual interest rate by 12. The formula evaluates to ($52,507.20), meaning Mike must now deposit $52,507.20 in the account to be able to make the desired withdrawals.

MAKING INVESTMENT DECISIONS USING IRR

Let's return to the investment decision we posed in the beginning of the chapter. You have $10,000. The bank will pay you 6% interest per year if you deposit your $10,000 there for four years. Your cousin says that if you invest the $10,000 in her new business she promises to pay you $2,000 after one year, $3,000 after two years, $4,000 after three years, and $5,000 at the end of four years. Which investment would pay the higher rate of interest? Here we have periodic (annual) payments being made, but the payments are not equal. This frequently is the case in proposed investments in business. Thus the set of five functions just discussed (PMT, FV, NPER, RATE, PV) would not pertain here, because they require all of the periodic payments to be the same.

A different set of functions in Excel is designed to help analyze situations where there is an arbitrary stream of cash flows.

The **IRR** function is used to calculate the interest rate returned on an investment involving various positive and negative payments that are made on a regular basis. The IRR function calculates "internal rate of return". The use of the IRR function to calculate the internal rate of return for the investment in your cousin's business is shown in the worksheet in Figure 14-4.

The cash flows are listed explicitly in column D. As usual in Excel, any investments you make, money you pay out, are entered as negative numbers. Any returns on your investment, money you receive, are entered as positive numbers. Using the IRR function in the worksheet we can see that investing in your cousin's business under the terms proposed would result in a rate of return of 12.83%. The bank is paying only 6% so you would receive a higher rate of return from your cousin.

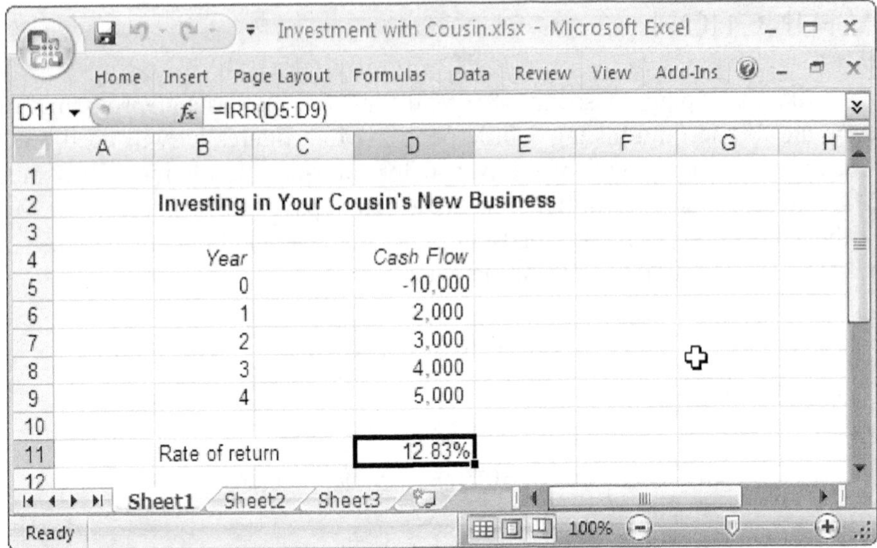

Figure 14-4. Using the IRR function to calculate the rate of return on an investment in your cousin's business, assuming she pays you back as promised.

The IRR function has two arguments:

IRR(cash flows, guess)

The first argument to the IRR function is the range of addresses where the series of cash flows is located on the worksheet. The cash flows should be in sequential cells, either down a column or across a row. The period of time from one cash flow to the next must be the same. The resulting rate of return is for that period. That is, if the time between each payment in the cash flows is one year, then the result of evaluating IRR will be an annual rate of return. If the time between each payment in the cash flows is one month, then the result of evaluating IRR will be a monthly rate of return. Note that in the worksheet in Figure 14-4, the year numbers in column B are there just to help make the worksheet understandable by people. The numbers in column B are not used by the computer in the IRR calculations.

The IRR function assumes that the initial cash flow in the range occurs right now and not at the end of the first period. The initial cash flow usually is negative and represents an initial investment.

There must be at least one negative number (representing an amount invested) and one positive number (representing an amount received) within the cash flows. Otherwise you'll get the dreaded #NUM! error message, because there would be no rate of return.

It is possible to list the cash flows explicitly within the function argument by putting them within curly brackets { }. Thus, we could do the entire calculation using the formula

=IRR({-10000,2000,3000,4000,5000})

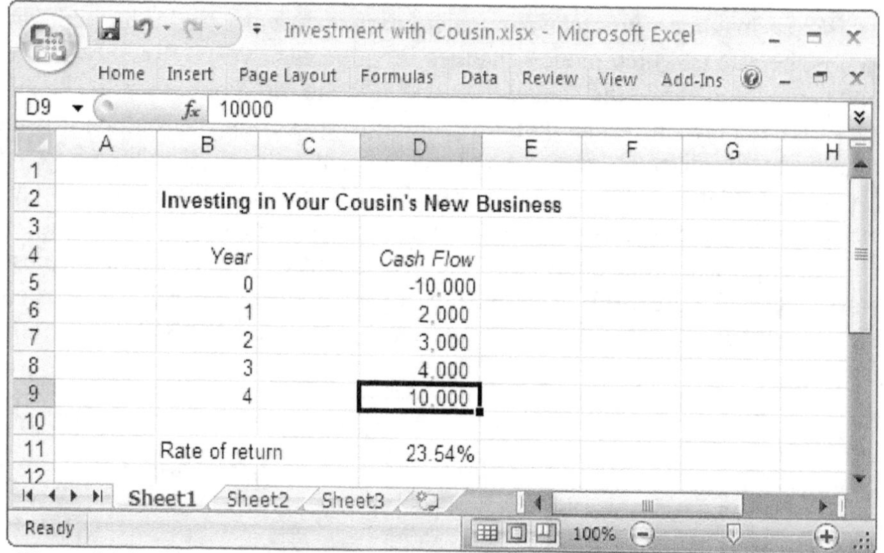

Figure 14-5. Your cousin is so successful and grateful to you for the loan that she pays you back $10,000 in year 4.

Of course, the advantage to using the worksheet in Figure 14-4 is that it is easy to play "What if" by changing one of the values in the cells. Suppose your cousin is so successful in her business and so grateful for your investment that she decides to give you $10,000 at the end of year 4 instead of the $5,000. Now, what would be the annual rate of return on your investment? To find out we can just change the number in D9 to 10,000, as in Figure 14-5. The internal rate of return of the series of cash flows -10,000, 2,000, 3,000, 4,000, 10,000 is 23.54%.

If at the end of the second year you would need to invest another $2,000 rather than receiving $3,000, you would change the number in D7 to -2,000.

The second argument is the guess. IRR is basically an extended version of the RATE function that works when the payments throughout the investment are of different amounts. Just as with the RATE function, there is no closed algebraic formula for calculating the IRR. The computer uses trial and error and begins with the guess. Entering a guess is optional. If none is included by the user, the computer assumes a guess of 10%.

NET PRESENT VALUE

An alternative approach to analyzing an investment in terms of its internal rate of return is to calculate its **net present value**. In a present value calculation you state future cash flows in terms of their value in today's dollar. If money earns 10% per year, then $500 today would be worth the same as $550 a year from now. So the present value of $550 a year from now using a **discount rate** of 10% would be $500. Similarly, the present value of $605 two years from now using a discount rate of 10% would be $500. (1.10 * 500 is 550. 1.10 * 550 is 605.) The net present value of an investment is the total value of each of the cash flows for the investment stated in terms of today's dollars.

When making a present value calculation, you must use a discount rate. The discount rate is the rate at which money changes in value each year. Roughly speaking, the discount rate is the interest rate the bank will pay or it is the inflation rate in the economy.

If the net present value of an investment is greater than zero, then it is a good investment relative to the discount rate. If the net present value is less than zero, then it is a poor investment relative to the discount rate. Or, alternatively, if you are comparing the merits of two potential investments, you would select the investment with the higher net present value.

A net present value analysis of the investment in your cousin's business is shown in the worksheet in Figure 14-6. The net present value of the investment is calculated by finding the present value of the future cash flows and subtracting the $10,000 initial investment.

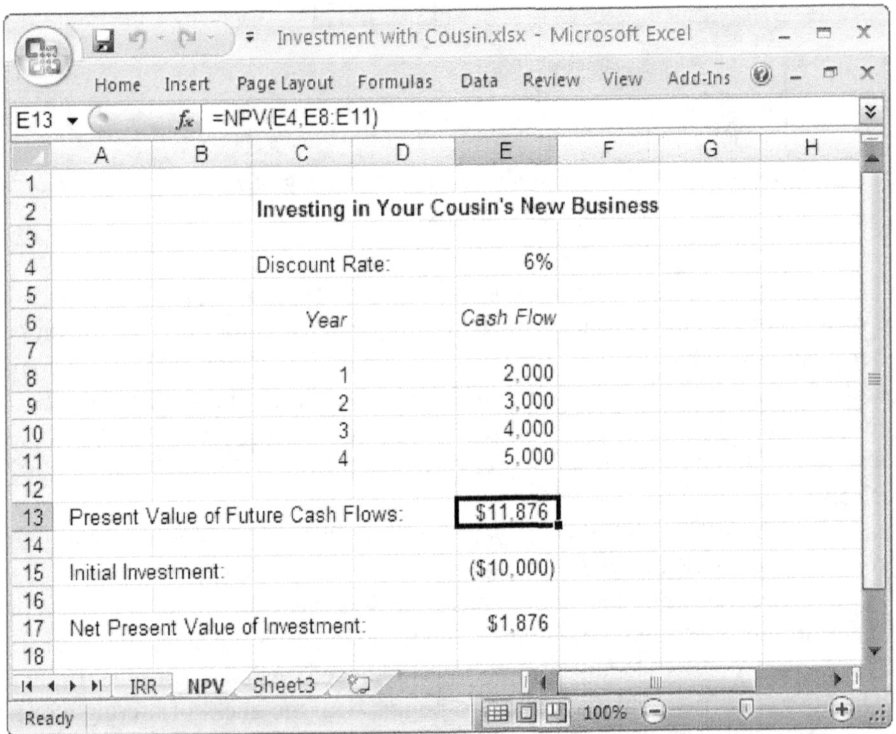

Investment with Cousin.xlsx - Microsoft Excel

Home Insert Page Layout Formulas Data Review View Add-Ins

E13 =NPV(E4,E8:E11)

	A	B	C	D	E	F	G	H
1								
2			Investing in Your Cousin's New Business					
3								
4			Discount Rate:		6%			
5								
6			Year		Cash Flow			
7								
8			1		2,000			
9			2		3,000			
10			3		4,000			
11			4		5,000			
12								
13	Present Value of Future Cash Flows:				$11,876			
14								
15	Initial Investment:				($10,000)			
16								
17	Net Present Value of Investment:				$1,876			
18								

IRR NPV Sheet3

Ready 100%

Figure 14-6. Analysis shows a positive net present value of $1,876 using a 6% discount rate. The investment would make you $1,876 in today's dollars.

The **NPV** function is used to calculate the present value of a stream of possibly varying future cash flows.

NPV(discount rate, cash flows)

The first argument is the discount rate, the rate at which money changes value each period. After the discount rate comes the future cash flows. These arguments can be the addresses of the future cash flows in the worksheet, as in the function used in cell E13 of the worksheet in Figure 14-6.

=NPV(E4,E8:E11)

Or, unlike in the IRR function, the cash flows can be listed explicitly as a sequence of arguments in the NPV function (without the curly brackets). So, we also could perform the calculation in one formula

=NPV(6%,2000,3000,4000,5000) - 10000

The NPV function is similar to the PV function discussed earlier. However, where the PV function assumes that the cash flow each period is a constant, the NPV function allows for different amounts each period. If in each year you would receive $4,000, then you could use the PV function. If, as is the case in the current example, the cash flows are not the same from year to year, you would use NPV to calculate the present value.

In the worksheet in Figure 14-6 we use a discount rate of 6% because that is the rate the bank would pay. The net present value for the investment is calculated by taking the present value of the future cash flows and subtracting the initial investment required. In cell E17 we see that the net present value of the investment is $1,876. Investing in your cousin's business would be worth $1,876 more in today's money than investing the money in the bank at 6% interest.

Unlike the IRR function, the NPV function assumes that the first of the cash flows occurs at the end of the first period rather than right away. Note that the NPV function is somewhat misnamed. The NPV function does not calculate the net present value of an investment. Rather, the NPV function calculates the present value of a series of possibly different future cash flows that occur at fixed intervals. The net present value is then calculated by subtracting any initial investment that might be made right now.

The IRR function and the NPV function are closely related. The NPV function is used in the series of calculations made for the IRR function. Indeed, if we use the internal rate of return of the investment as the discount rate, then the net present value of the investment will be 0.

INVESTMENTS WITH ARBITRARY DATES FOR CASH FLOWS

All of the investment scenarios we have looked at so far have money that exchanges hands monthly or annually or at some other fixed time period. Of course, there are many investment scenarios where the cash flows occur on arbitrary dates.

Suppose we are considering a takeover of a company. We estimate it will cost us $10,000,000 to buy the company outright. Our target date for the acquisition is January 1, 2011. Our analysis tells us that the company is worth more if each of the three divisions is sold off separately. We figure to sell the first division September 1, 2011 for $3,000,000, the second division April 1, 2012 for $4,000,000, and the third division July 1, 2012 for $6,500,000. At that point, the company is totally sold off.

We create the spreadsheet in Figure 14-7 to calculate the annual rate of return on the investment.

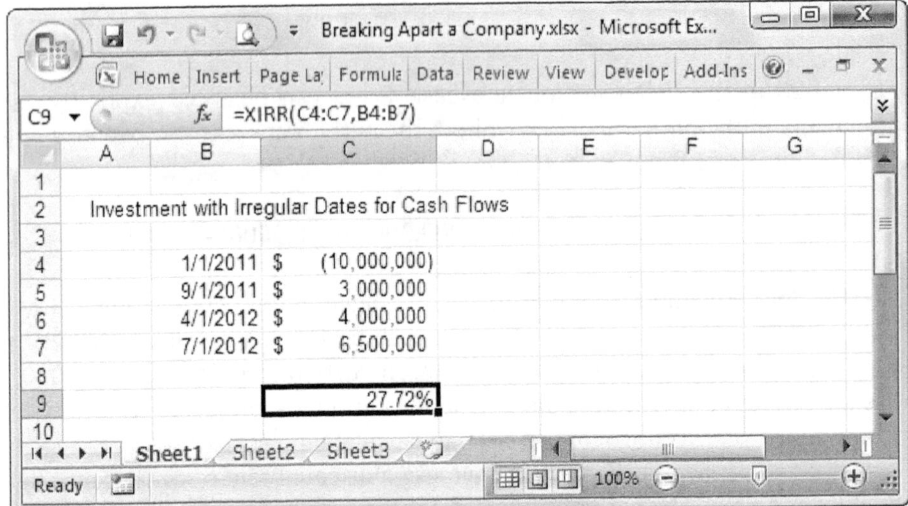

Figure 14-7. The XIRR function allows for arbitrary dates.

The **XIRR** function has three arguments, with the third being optional:

XIRR(cash flows, dates, guess)

With the XIRR function the dates are explicitly stated and XIRR always returns the annual interest rate. Recall from Chapter 13 that dates are represented internally as numbers, and that there are pre-defined date formats for numbers. When using XIRR you need to be careful that the dates you enter are recognized by Excel as dates and are not just text that resembles dates. Recall that dates (and numbers) are automatically right justified in the cells while text is automatically left-justified. If you enter a date and it appears left-justified you should be suspicious. (See Figure 14-8.)

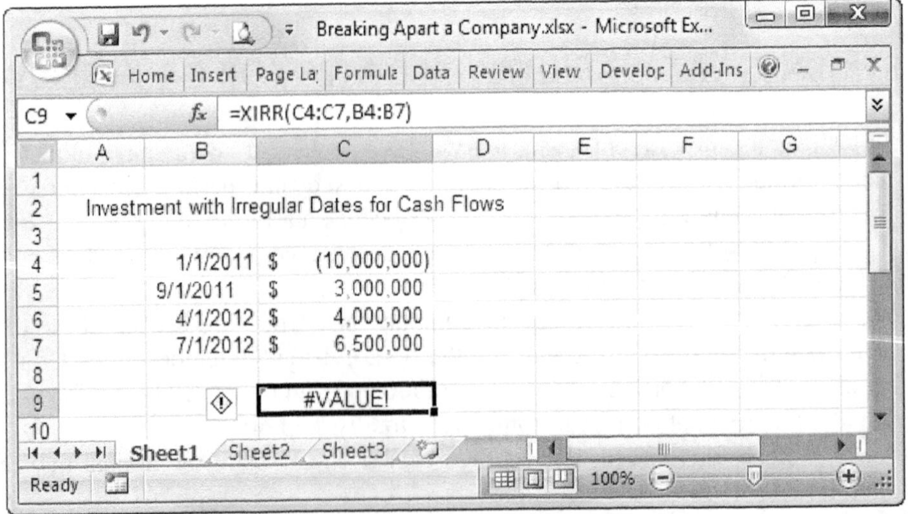

Figure 14-8. The entry in B5 is really text, not an official date. Note that it is left-justified.

Spreadsheets with the XIRR function allow you to do "What if" analysis on the dates of cash flows, as well as the amounts. For example, we could see the effect on the rate of return of delaying the final payment by a month.

There also is an XNPV function for calculating present values for cash flows with arbitrary dates.

WINNING THE LOTTERY

We now have covered several financial functions available in Excel. All of the functions are designed to facilitate analyses involving the time value of money. These calculations take practice so let's do one more example.

Many states have lotteries. Typically you pay $1 to select the numbers that you think will be drawn. If you select all the numbers correctly you win a fortune! But do you? Suppose you have selected your numbers and the day after the drawing you learn that they have drawn your numbers and you have won $1,000,000! You are a winner! You head down to the state lottery office to collect your million dollars. But at the office you learn that the lottery commission does not give you the million dollars all at once. Rather they pay the money to you in 20 equal annual payments. You receive $50,000 now and $50,000 per year at the end of each of the next 19 years.

How much have you really won? Clearly that last $50,000 payment 19 years from now is not going to be worth very much if inflation picks up. It is legal to sell your winning ticket. There are companies that will pay you cash now for a winning ticket. Suppose someone offered you $100,000 right now for your ticket (and all the winnings). Would you take it? No, your winnings are worth more than $100,000 even though they are spread out over 20 years. Suppose the person offered you $900,000 right now for your ticket. Yes, $900,000 today is worth more than $1,000,000 paid out in 20 equal annual payments.

How can we figure out how much your lottery winnings would be worth in terms of today's money? What we are asking for is the present value of the winnings. There are three functions that calculate present value, XNPV, NPV and PV. The XNPV function calculates the present value of a series of possibly unequal future cash flows that occur at arbitrary dates. The NPV function calculates the present value of a series of possibly unequal future cash flows that occur periodically. The PV function calculates the present value of a series of equal, periodic cash flows. The lottery winnings are paid in equal amounts each year so PV is the function to use. A worksheet to calculate the present value of winning the lottery is shown in Figure 14-9.

The formula in C12 calculates the present value using the PV function. The final argument of the PV function is the type. In this case the type is 1 because the first payment is made right now, at the beginning of the first period.

Assuming a discount rate (inflation rate) of 5%, the present value of 20 annual payments of $50,000 each is $654,266.04. Another way of looking at the problem is that you would have to deposit $654,266.04 in an account earning 5% per year to be able to withdraw $50,000 today and $50,000 at the end of each of the next 19 years. So if you believe the discount rate to be 5% for the next 20 years, you might want to accept an offer of $700,000 for your winnings and decline an offer of $600,000.

Figure 14-9. The present value of winning $1,000,000 in the lottery paid out in 20 annual payments. This is the amount it would be fair to pay for 20 equal annual payments of $50,000 assuming a discount rate of 5%.

Of course, our analysis has not taken into account the income taxes you would have to pay on your winnings.

Look at the situation from the state's point of view. The state can take a million dollars and put it in the bank. If they earn 5% per year, they would make $50,000 per year in interest, which they pay you. At the end of the 20 years the state would still have its $1,000,000 intact.

OTHER FINANCIAL FUNCTIONS

Understanding the time value of money is critical to being able to analyze many financial situations. The financial functions of Excel provide important tools. We have looked at just the basic financial functions. There are dozens of additional financial functions built into Excel.

PENCIL AND PAPER EXERCISES

14-1. Write down the formula that calculates each of the following quantities. You may use the computer to try your answers. You need only write down the formula. You do not need to calculate the result of evaluating the formula.

(a) The monthly payment on a 30 year mortgage for $4,500,000 at 8% per year.

(b) The value of your Tiger Woods sports card in 30 years if it is worth $20.00 today and increases in value by 9% per year.

(c) The annual rate of increase in the value of a house that was purchased for $59,000 in 1983 and sells for $232,000 today.

(d) The value of your retirement account in 50 years if you deposit $2,400 each year and receive 6% annual interest on your money.

(e) The value of your retirement account in 50 years if you deposit $200 per month for 50 years and receive 6% annual interest on your money.

(f) The annual interest rate you must receive to triple your money in 10 years.

(g) The monthly interest rate you are paying to Joe the Shark if you borrow $10,000 today and pay back $1,000 each month for 11 months and then pay back $10,000 a year from now.

(h) The amount of money you would need to accumulate to be able to retire for the rest of your life on $100,000 per year if your money earns 10% per year.

(i) The number of months a new company could last if it raised $2,000,000 and had a burn rate (spending rate) of $60,000 per month, assuming it kept its cash in an account earning 5% per year.

(j) There are two major companies in the widget market. United Widgets had sales of $20 million last year and is expected to grow at the rate of 4% per year. Widgets International had sales of $14 million last year. Give a formula that will indicate the annual rate at which Widgets International must grow to catch up to United Widgets in seven years.

(k) The year in which the country of Corinth will reach 8,000,000 people given that it has 3,488,710 people today and its population is increasing by 2.4% per year. For example, your formula might tell us that Corinth will reach 8,000,000 people in the year 2025.

(l) The rate of increase required for Corinth to reach a population of 8,000,000 in the year 2025 given that it has a population of 3,488,710 today.

14-2. Evaluate each of the following by hand. The idea here is for you to learn how these functions really are calculated. If you get stuck you can check your answer on the computer, but eventually you should be able to do these problems and other problems like them without a computer or calculator.

(a) =FV(10%,1,0,-2000)

(b) =FV(10%,2,0,-2000)

(c) =FV(10%,1,-500,-2000)

(d) =FV(10%,1,-500,-2000,1)

(e) =FV(10%,2,-500,-2000)

(f) =FV(10%,2,500,-2000)

(g) =PMT(0%,5,-2000,7000)

(h) =NPER(5%,0,-1000,1102.50)

(i) =NPER(5%,-1050,1000,0)

(j) =PV(10%,2,0,4840)

(k) =RATE(5,100,-2000,1500)

(l) =RATE(2,0,8000,-8160.80)

14-3. Write down the formula that calculates each of the following quantities. You do not need to calculate the result of evaluating the formula.

(a) No one quite knows how Carpathian frogs were introduced into Lake Canuga, but they are taking over the habitat and destroying the local species in the process. There are 10,000 Carpathian frogs there now. Baby frogs are born at the rate of 5% per month. 200 of the frogs die each month. Give a formula that will calculate how many Carpathian frogs there will be in five years if this continues.

(b) We would like to have $1,000,000 in ten years. We have $700,000 now in an account. We are withdrawing $100,000 a year from the account at the beginning of each year. What annual interest rate would we need to achieve our goal?

(c) We estimate the amount of capital needed to buy and open a very nice bed and breakfast to be $700,000 and to be increasing by 3% per year. We currently have an account with

$400,000, which is earning 8% per year. How much would we need to deposit at the end of each year to be able to buy and open the bed and breakfast in seven years?

(d) You would like to have $1,000 next Christmas to buy presents. Your plan is to deposit a certain amount of money on the 3rd of each month in an account earning 0.25% per month. You plan to open your account on January 3 with your first deposit. You plan to make your last deposit on November 3 (11 deposits in all). You will close the account on December 2 after you receive the interest for the month. How much do you need to deposit each month?

(e) If I invest $63,000 today in a bond, the state will pay me $100,000 in seven years. My cousin says that if I loan him the money for five years he will give me double the annual compounded interest rate that the state will. He promises to pay it all off in one payment at the end of five years. How much would my cousin owe me in five years?

(f) The OhMy computer virus currently infects 250,000 computers. It is infecting 1.5% new computers per day. The only known way to destroy the virus is to wipe out the hard drive (or take a sledgehammer to the computer). 1,000 people per day are doing this. If this continues, how many computers will be infected with the virus in 180 days?

(g) Ten years ago your parents bought $10,000 worth of Trans-National Systems, Inc. stock. At the end of each year they invested another $2,000. Today the stock is worth $54,000. Give a formula that determines what annual interest rate they made on their money.

(h) There are 200,000,000 of the new dollar coins in circulation now. Each year 5% are removed from circulation for one reason or another (by collectors or are lost). The government plans to add 100,000,000 new coins at the end of each year. Give a formula that determines how many years it will be until there are 1,000,000,000 in circulation.

(i) There are 100 million traditional phones. The number is increasing by 2% per year. There are 30 million cell phones. The number is increasing by 20% per year. A number between 2010 and 2100 is in D5. Give a formula that determines whether there will be more traditional phones or cell phones in the year given in D5.

(j) Your uncle is losing 10% of his hair each year. If this started when he was 20, how old will he be when he only has 1% left?

(k) The U.S. national debt is $7 trillion ($7 million million) dollars. If we reduce the debt by $1 billion dollars per day, how many years will it take to reduce the debt to zero? Most of the debt is in the form of government issued bonds that pay 3%/year.

(l) XWeb stock sells for $10/share today and is increasing at the rate of 20% per month. It can't keep up this rate of increase for long. You estimate that it will continue to increase at that rate until the price reaches $100 per share, and then begin a long slow decline of 1% per month. Based on these assumptions, what will the stock be worth 3 years from now? Assume that by the end of the three years it has reached $100 and begun its decline.

COMPUTER EXERCISES

14-4. The Friendly Mortgage Company offers your choice of 10-year, 20-year, and 30-year home mortgages all at the same interest rate. Create a worksheet that will allow you to enter the amount of the mortgage and the annual interest rate. For each type of loan the worksheet should calculate: (a) the monthly payment, (b) the total amount paid back to the mortgage company, and (c) the total amount of interest paid. That is, your worksheet should have two cells of input and nine cells of output.

14-5. As Division Manager you have $20,000,000 to invest in a new project. The Excelsior Project Team says that if you invest with them the company will receive returns of $8,000,000 after a year, $10,000,000 after two years, and $12,000,000 after three years. The Indela Project Team says that if you invest with them the company will receive nothing for the first two years and then $34,000,000 at the end of the third year. Create a worksheet that determines which project team offers the better financial return on the investment. The answer "Excelsior project" or "Indela project" should appear in a cell.

14-6. Your broker suggests that you buy a zero coupon bond ("zero") with a face value of $20,000 maturing in 10 years that sells today for $6,237. That is, you pay $6,237 today and receive $20,000 10 years from now. You would like to find out the yield, the effective annual interest rate you would receive, on the zero.

(a) Create a worksheet for analyzing zeros that allows you to enter the face value, the time to maturity, and the current price. The output should be the yield. Of course, your worksheet should work for any inputs.

(b) Create a similar worksheet that allows you to enter the face value, the actual maturity date, and the current price. The output should be the yield. Use the TODAY function.

14-7. You are presented with a proposal for a project. The bottom line is that it is claimed that if you invest $20 million in a project this year, you will receive $5 million, $18 million, and $12 million over the following three years.

(a) Set up a worksheet that will tell you both the net present value of this project assuming a 12% discount rate and the internal rate of return for this project.

(b) You decide that most likely the project will cost $24 million this year and return $4 million, $14 million, and $10 million over the next three years. What would be the net present value and internal rate of return?

14-8. The "Rule of 72" is a very convenient rule of thumb for performing mental calculations on the effect of compound interest. The rule indicates the approximate doubling time for money at a given interest rate or the approximate interest rate required to double your money in a certain period of time. The Rule of 72 states that to find the time required to double an investment at a given interest rate, divide the interest rate into 72. Equivalently, the Rule of 72 states that to find the interest rate required to double your money in a certain number of years, divide the number of years into 72. For example, the rule states that investments at 6% double in 12 years. Investments at 9% double in 8 years. Investments at 18% double in 4 years.

How is this helpful? What will a $20,000 investment at 14% be worth in 10 years? At 14% the doubling time is approximately 5 years. So in five years the investment will double in value to $40,000. In five more years the investment will double again to $80,000. So, $80,000 is the approximate answer.

For this exercise you are to check the validity of the Rule of 72. Create a worksheet with three columns and 72 rows plus column headings and titles. In the first column should be interest rates from 1% through 72%. In the next column should be the actual time for money to double at this interest rate as calculated using the NPER function. In the third column should be the amount of time for money to double at this interest rate predicted using the Rule of 72. Is the Rule of 72 reasonably accurate?

14-9. The Director of New Business Development has come to you with an interesting proposal. The Home Products Division of International Industries is for sale. The best estimate is that the Home Products Division will earn $4 million next year, $5 million the following year, $6 million the third year, and that in the fourth year you will be able to sell it for $30 million. Your company expects to earn 20% per year on its investments.

(a) Create a worksheet that will tell you a fair price to pay today for the Home Products Division.

(b) On negotiation, International Industries says that they will accept 1/3 of the total payment today, 1/3 in a year, and 1/3 in two years. Create a worksheet that allows you to enter in a total payment and then assigns the payments to the various years and gives you the rate of return on the investment. Have a cell at the top that tells you whether or not you achieve your goal of a 20% return.

(c) If you assume the correctness of the estimates in (a) and the results of the negotiations in (b) what would be a fair price to pay to earn 20% on your money?

(d) Suppose you can sell the Division only for $20 million instead of $30 million? Now what would be a fair price to pay?

14-10. You are considering purchasing a new car. The price would be $18,239. You would pay $2,000 now and the rest monthly in a four-year loan. The automobile dealership is offering a sales promotion where either (a) you will receive a $1,000 rebate check right now and the annual interest rate on the loan will be 11.9% or (b) the annual interest rate on the loan will be 1.9% but there is no rebate. Create a worksheet to compare the two options by calculating the present value of each of the options, assuming an 8% discount rate. Which is the better deal? Write a paragraph to justify your answer.

14-11. Mobile Power is a startup company. They are out on the capital market looking for funding. They are willing to sell you 20% of the stock in their company for an investment of $500,000. According to their business plan they expect to lose money for the first two years. Then their big product will kick in and they expect to make money in the third and fourth year. These funds will be plowed back into the company for expansion. They then expect to be acquired by a major company for $10,000,000 in the fifth year. At this point you would cash out and receive 20% of the proceeds. Create a worksheet to analyze this venture in terms of the rate of return and the net present value of your investment. Since this is a very risky venture and you would buy in towards the beginning, you would expect a return of at least 30% per year on your money. Does Mobile Power seem like a reasonable investment opportunity?

14-12. A loan amortization table shows the effect of each payment on the amount of principal still owed. A worksheet for constructing loan amortization tables for 48-month loans is shown below. The worksheet has two input cells: (1) the principal of the loan (the original amount borrowed) and (2) the annual interest rate. All other numbers in the worksheet are calculated. Changing either or both of these input numbers will create a new amortization table.

Note that in the table, the amount of interest owed each month is the monthly interest rate times the amount of the principal still owed at the beginning of the month. The amount of the payment that goes to reducing the principal is the amount of the payment that is left over. If all of the calculations are correct, then the principal owed at the end of the forty-eighth month should be 0.

(a) Duplicate the worksheet. Try it on the loan indicated and then on a $53,000 loan at 12% and on a $4,000 loan at 2.9%.

(b) Construct a similar worksheet for 36-month loans. Try the worksheet on the same three sets of data.

(c) Construct a worksheet that produces an amortization table for any term loan of from one to five years (60 monthly payments). The worksheet should have three input cells: the principal of the loan, the annual interest rate, and the number of years for the loan. This is a bit tricky. While you might have 60 rows of formulas, the table should only appear to have one row for each month of payment. All rows below the final payment should appear blank.

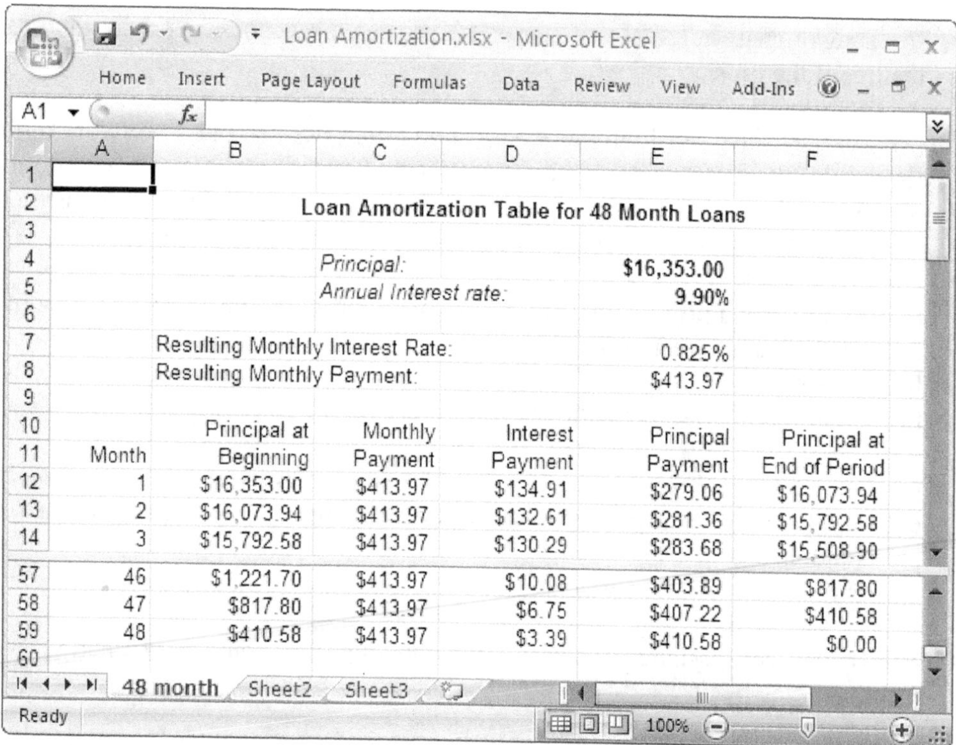

Loan Amortization.xlsx - Microsoft Excel

Loan Amortization Table for 48 Month Loans

Principal:	$16,353.00
Annual Interest rate:	9.90%
Resulting Monthly Interest Rate:	0.825%
Resulting Monthly Payment:	$413.97

Month	Principal at Beginning	Monthly Payment	Interest Payment	Principal Payment	Principal at End of Period
1	$16,353.00	$413.97	$134.91	$279.06	$16,073.94
2	$16,073.94	$413.97	$132.61	$281.36	$15,792.58
3	$15,792.58	$413.97	$130.29	$283.68	$15,508.90
46	$1,221.70	$413.97	$10.08	$403.89	$817.80
47	$817.80	$413.97	$6.75	$407.22	$410.58
48	$410.58	$413.97	$3.39	$410.58	$0.00

14-13. You have been asked to analyze the proposed Skopi Project. Initial investment in the project would be $100 million, which would be spent on planning, design, and construction. This phase would take three years. It is proposed that in year 0, $10 million would be spent. In year 1, $30 million would be spent. In year 2, $60 million would be spent.

Revenues would be generated beginning in year 3. In year 3, revenues would be $10 million. In year 4, revenues would be $30 million. In years 5 through 13, revenues would be $60 million per year. In year 14, revenues would be $30 million. At the end of year 14, the project would be scrapped. In year 15, the project would return $20 million in the scrap value of the equipment.

Expenses would be as follows: Annual operating expenses for years 3 through 14 are figured at $12.5 million for raw materials, $10 million for maintenance and repairs, $5 million for labor, and $2.5 million for other expenses.

(a) Develop a worksheet that figures out the internal rate of return of this project. You should have a separate input area with separate cells for each of the assumptions. You should have columns for each of the years from 0 through 15. You should have separate rows for each of the revenue and expense items and for the total revenues and total expenses. The bottom row should be annual cash flow. You should have a separate well-labeled cell for the rate of return. Sketch the worksheet on paper before entering it into the computer. Have your worksheet calculate the internal rate of return using the preceding assumptions.

(b) Draw a chart in Excel that shows the projected revenues, expenses, and cash flow over the life of the project.

(c) Next try some sensitivity analysis. You might want to put a copy of the full worksheet for each of these scenarios on a different sheet. Suppose revenues for years 5 through 13 are only $40 million. What would be the internal rate of return? Suppose construction costs are $100 million in year 2? Suppose labor costs are double those expected?

(d) Put together a professional report on your analysis of the project. The company expects at least a 14% rate of return on its money. What is your recommendation on this project? Include appropriate copies of worksheets and graphs in your report. To what parameters is the rate of return most susceptible?

(e) Put together a 15-minute presentation on your analysis of the Skopi Project suitable for delivery to the Executive Committee of your company. Use PowerPoint to prepare the presentation.

14-14. You have been assigned the task of comparing two sources of energy for a proposed manufacturing plant.

(a) Build a worksheet that determines the more economical of the two choices by comparing the present value of the expenses associated with each choice. A basic design for the worksheet and some projected data are given below. You may fill in whatever intermediate calculations you wish, but be sure to label these cells clearly. The bottom row of the worksheet should use an IF function to indicate whether Electricity or Fuel Oil is a more economical choice.

COMPARISON OF ENERGY SOURCES

	Electricity		Fuel Oil	
Unit Cost	$0.160	per kwh	$1.45	per gallon
Setup Cost	$15,000		$25,000	
Annual Consumption	700,000	kwh	125,000	gallons
Annual Maintenance	$3,000		$2,000	
Number of Years	8		8	
Discount Rate	0.12		0.12	
Present Value:				
More Economical Energy Source:				

(b) There is some uncertainty in the prices that can be negotiated in a long-term supply contract for the energy sources. Listed below are three possible scenarios. Create a new worksheet for each scenario, having your worksheet determine which choice would be more economical. To do this, you should be able to change just the values in the appropriate cells at the top of your worksheet. All other calculations should then be done automatically by the computer.

THREE UNIT COST SCENARIOS

Scenario	Electricity		Fuel Oil	
1 (original)	$0.160	per kwh	$1.45	per gallon
2	$0.195	per kwh	$1.75	per gallon
3	$0.125	per kwh	$1.15	per gallon

(c) Write a brief but professional report giving your recommendation on the energy source to select. Include appropriate copies of your worksheets.

14-15. Mary and John have been married for three years. They both work. Their salaries total $95,000 per year. They currently are paying $1,800 per month rent plus utilities. Between savings and wedding gifts they have managed to accumulate $58,000, which they have in a money market account.

Mary and John are thinking about buying a house. They have done some looking and after much dispute have settled on a suburban house that costs about $220,000. Annual real estate taxes would be about $2,800. They are asking the age-old questions: Can we afford it? Will we be better off financially 10 years from now if we buy the house instead of continuing to rent?

Your task is to design and implement a worksheet that will analyze the financial implication over the next 10 years of buying versus renting.

The issue of home ownership is a complicated one in this society. You can make some assumptions:

- Assume a fixed rate mortgage for 80% of the purchase price of the home. Mary and John will pay 20% of the price as a down payment when they purchase the home. Find out the prevailing mortgage rate by checking in the local newspaper or by calling a bank. John and Mary would use the $58,000 for the down payment, closing costs, and moving expenses.

- Assume that everything (house values, rents, real estate taxes, salaries) goes up with inflation. Have a separate cell for the inflation rate.

Of course, if they buy, Mary and John would no longer get the interest they now receive from the $58,000 in the money market account.

An important aspect of home ownership in the United States can be the income tax advantage. If Mary and John buy their own home, then real estate taxes and the interest (but not the principal) they pay on their mortgage are deductible for income tax purposes. You will need to find out what income tax bracket Mary and John are in, assuming no other dependents.

From a financial point of view would Mary and John be better off buying a house or continuing to rent? Write a professional report for Mary and John. Include appropriate parts of the worksheet and a chart or two.

14-16. Boston College is considering literally raising the roof of Conte Forum and adding 1,000 new "nosebleed" seats. The university would like to accommodate another 1,000 students at the games. They plan to sell the additional tickets to 16 home basketball games and 14 home hockey games at $10 each for the first year. They estimate that any extra expenses (cleaning, overhead) will be offset by increased concession sales. They figure they'll be raising ticket prices by 5% per year. They estimate the useful life of the addition at 20 years. At that point Conte Forum will need a major renovation or be torn down and replaced. To finance the addition the university will issue a 20 year bond at 6% per year interest (this is just like taking out a loan at 6% annual interest).

(a) Create a worksheet to determine the maximum amount BC should pay today for the addition in order to at least break even. There should be five input cells: number of seats being added, initial per seat ticket price, number of games per season, annual growth of ticket price, and annual interest rate for the bond. There should be a separate output cell with the break even cost for the addition.

(b) Assume that ticket prices rise by 6% per year and that the annual interest rate paid on the bond is 4%. Now what would be the break even cost for the project?

14-17. John is 25 years old and is making $80,000 this year. Of course he is unsure what the future holds, as are we all. But he thinks a middle of the road scenario is that he will receive a 5% raise each year for 35 years and retire at age 60. He is considering going back to school full-time next year for an MBA. It takes two years to receive an MBA. During that time he would earn no salary. Also he would need to borrow $100,000 to pay for the MBA. He could obtain a loan at 6% annual interest that he would need to pay back during the first 10 years after he finishes his MBA. The loan would not begin accumulating interest until he finishes his studies. He figures that the first year he is back working after his MBA his starting salary would be $105,000. He assumes he then would receive a 5% raise each year until he retires at age 60.

(a) Create a worksheet to help John determine whether he would be better off financially going back for his MBA or not. You should have separate input cells for: John's current salary, the total cost of an MBA, the interest rate for the loan, the rate for the increase of John's salary without an MBA, the salary of John's first position after his MBA, the rate for the increase of John's salary with an MBA, the annual discount rate for the next 35 years.

Have cells that calculate the Net Present Value of John's future earnings under each of the two scenarios. Assume a 4% discount rate. You may assume that the loan is paid back in equal annual payments. Also, you should have a cell at the top of the worksheet that uses an IF to state which scenario is better.

(b) John learns he might be able to receive a graduate assistantship during his MBA. Then the MBA would cost $60,000 instead of $100,000. Also he thinks that because of the contacts he would make in the MBA program his annual salary increase with the MBA might be 6% instead of 5% but his starting salary after the MBA program might be $100,000 for the first year. Have your worksheet calculate the NPVs using these assumptions. Under these assumptions is it financially better for John to go back to school for his MBA or not?

14-18. As a Financial Analyst for General Enterprises you have been asked to take a look at the proposed new Track It! product. The champions of Track It! propose that the company invest $10,000,000 total in the new product: $3,000,000 in Year 1 and $7,000,000 in Year 2 in expenses to ramp up. The first units will be manufactured and sold in Year 3. They expect to sell 100,000 units in Year 3 at $90 per unit, for $9,000,000 in revenues in Year 3. They expect to have ongoing $3,000,000 per year in fixed expenses beginning in Year 3 and $30 per unit in variable expenses. Thereafter they expect the number of units sold to increase by 10% per year for 3 years (Year 4, 5, 6) and then decrease by 20% per year for 4 years (Year 7, 8, 9, 10). They expect the sales price per unit and the fixed expenses to remain constant throughout the life of the product but they expect to be able to decrease the unit expenses by 2% per year through efficiencies. The Track It! product will be discontinued at the end of Year 10. Other products may be introduced to complement or replace Track It! over the next 10 years but that is outside the scope of this analysis.

(a) Develop a worksheet that calculates the internal rate of return for Track It! You should have a separate input area with separate cells for each of the assumptions. You should have columns for each of the years from 1 through 10. You should have separate rows at least for each of the revenue and expense items and for the total revenues and total expenses. The bottom row should be annual cash flow (total revenues minus total expenses). You should have a separate well-labeled cell at top for the calculated rate of return. Sketch the worksheet on paper before entering it into the computer. Have your worksheet calculate the internal rate of return using the preceding assumptions.

(b) Draw a chart in Excel that shows the projected revenues, expenses, and cash flow over the ten years.

(c) Copy the full worksheet onto a different sheet. You investigate the numbers in depth. You believe that $11,000,000 will be required in Year 2 to get to production rather than $7,000,000. Also you believe the product will need to be sold at $83 per unit to meet sales goals and that the initial variable expenses actually will be $34 per unit. All other assumptions seem reasonable. Now what would be the rate of return for Track It!?

(d) Create a brief but professional report in Word on your financial analysis of Track It! The company expects at least a 14% rate of return on its money. What is your recommendation on this project? Include appropriate copies of worksheets and charts in your report.

(e) You will be given 7 minutes in front of the Executive Committee to make a presentation on your financial analysis of Track It! Create a full PowerPoint presentation on your analysis. Be sure to include relevant tables and charts.

CHAPTER 15

RANDOM NUMBERS AND SIMULATION

OBJECTIVES

In this chapter you will learn how to:

- Use RAND to generate random numbers
- Create worksheets to simulate probabilistic situations
- Simulate situations with multiple possible outcomes using lookup tables
- Model queuing problems
- Generate random integers

One way of dealing with the complexities of the world is to build a model to simulate a situation or environment. The model then can be tested and manipulated. These results can be used to predict what will happen in the world. An airplane company wants to know how a proposed new plane will fly, so it builds a model and places the model in a wind tunnel and runs tests. Or, it creates a computer program that allows engineers to specify the plane on the screen and then mathematically simulate the plane flying under different conditions.

Of course, the effectiveness of using a model to predict what really will happen depends on how well the relevant aspects of the situation are captured in the model. One certainly can imagine an airplane whose design worked great on the computer but that crashes when it is first flown. There is a saying in the computer field, "Garbage In, Garbage Out," or "GIGO". If you put nonsense into the computer, you will get nonsense out. Don't believe everything that comes out of the computer. Just because "the computer says" something doesn't mean it is right.

People have attempted to create computer models for all kinds of situations. There are computer models of the weather. Enter in the temperature, wind velocity, and so on at many different locations on the earth. The computer predicts what the weather will be like tomorrow or next week. There are computer models of the economy. Suppose we raise the income tax rate. What will be the effect on the economy a year from now or five years from now?

We have seen how Excel can be used as a simulation tool. "What if" analysis is a form of computer simulation. To predict the profitability of a new enterprise, create an Excel worksheet to model the projected finances and try it out under different scenarios.

Some situations are best modeled probabilistically. One third of the time this will happen; two thirds of the time something else will happen. These situations can be modeled on the computer with the use of **random numbers**. Simulations that make use of random numbers often are called **Monte Carlo simulations**. Monte Carlo is a city on the Mediterranean Sea that is the site of a well-known gambling casino.

In this chapter we will discuss random numbers in Excel and their use in simulations.

THE RAND FUNCTION

Random numbers are generated in Excel using the **RAND** function. The RAND function has no arguments. The value of the RAND function is a number between 0 and 1 (but not including 1). The user cannot predict what this number will be. An example of a worksheet with 10 random numbers is shown in Figure 15-1.

The value of each call to the RAND function is calculated out to 15 digits to the right of the decimal point. Only nine decimal places of each number are displayed in each random number in Figure 15-1. To see the full numbers, select the cells, right click to see the contextual menu, and click on the Increase Decimal button.

When entering the RAND function into a formula you must include the parentheses

=RAND( )

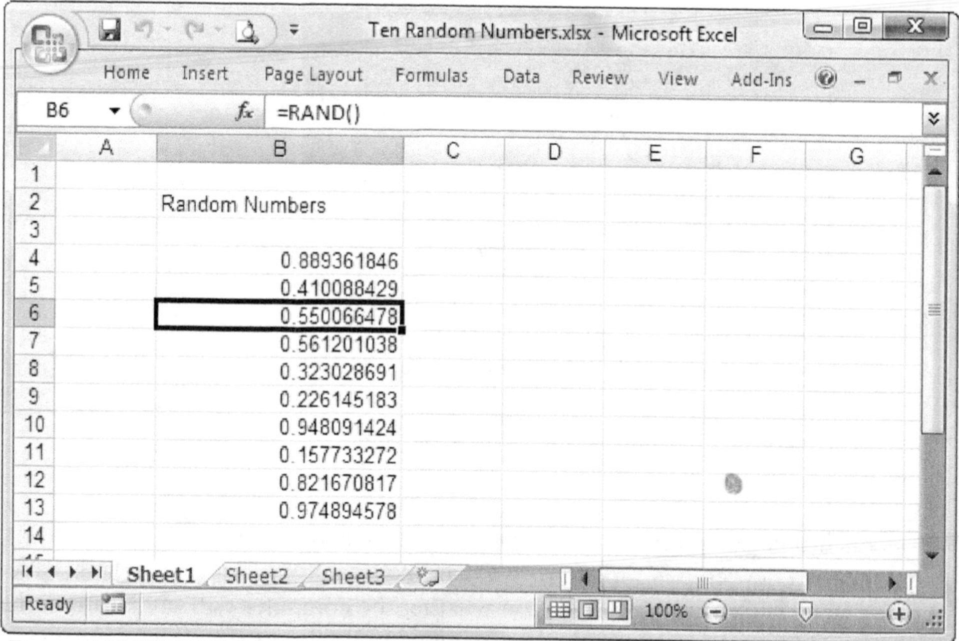

Figure 15-1. Generating ten random numbers.

even though there is nothing placed between them. If you enter =RAND with no parentheses, Excel will expect RAND to be the name of a cell so you will get a #NAME? error message.

The RAND function is a strange beast. Each time the worksheet is recalculated, the value of each RAND changes! You can force a recalculation at any time by pressing function key F9 on the keyboard.

FLIPPING COINS

Suppose we want to simulate flipping a coin in Excel. Each time we recalculate the worksheet (by pressing F9), the computer flips the coin again. The computer will say Heads or Tails, but we won't know in advance which it will be. We would like Heads and Tails each to occur 50% of the time.

To accomplish this, we will use random numbers generated by the RAND function. We would like half the possible numbers produced by RAND to be Heads and the other half of the numbers to be Tails. Thus, we check the random number against 0.5. If the random number is less than 0.5, we call the result Heads. Otherwise, we call the result Tails. The formula is

=IF(RAND( ) < 0.5, "Heads", "Tails")

The worksheet is shown in Figure 15-2.

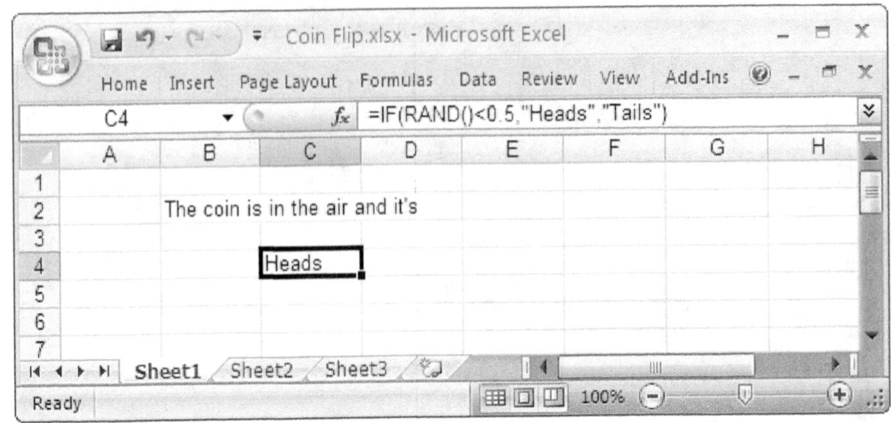

Figure 15-2. Simulating the flip of a fair coin.

Each time we press F9 a new random number between 0 and 1 is produced by RAND and hence a new coin is flipped with equal likelihood of a Heads or a Tails. We have no way of knowing before each recalculation whether the computer will say Heads or Tails.

Should we check if the random number is less than 0.5 or less than or equal to 0.5? Since 0 is a possible random number but 1 is not, it seems fairer for 0.5 to count as a Tails. Actually, there are so many possible random numbers that the probability of exactly 0.5 being generated is too small to worry about!

Suppose that we would like to rig the worksheet so that 70% of the time the flip comes out Heads and only 30% of the time the flip comes out Tails. We could change the formula, as follows

=IF(RAND( ) < 0.7, "Heads", "Tails")

Now 70% of the random numbers (all the numbers between 0 and 0.7) will result in Heads and only 30% of the random numbers (all the numbers from 0.7 to 1) will result in Tails.

Suppose we would like three possible outcomes. We would like Heads 49% of the time, Tails 48% of the time, and 3% of the time we would like the outcome to be Coin rolls away.

The first step is to divide up the numbers from 0 to 1 into three segments that correspond to the desired outcomes. We assign the numbers from 0 to 0.49 to correspond to Heads. (This is 49% of the numbers.) The numbers from 0.49 to 0.97 will correspond to Tails. (This is 48% of the numbers.) The numbers from 0.97 to 1 correspond to Coin rolls away. (This is 3% of the numbers.) This is illustrated in Figure 15-3.

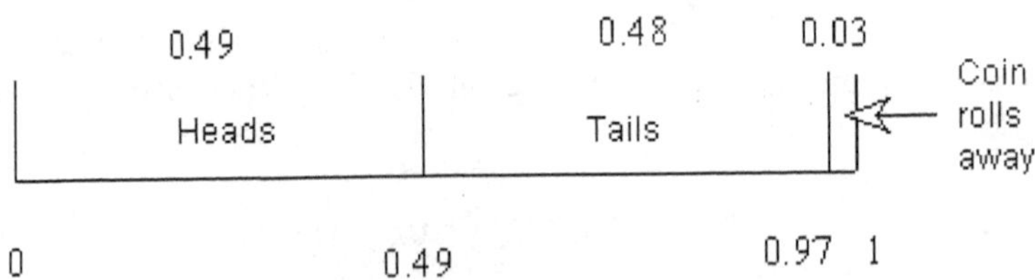

Figure 15-3. Dividing up the number line from 0 to 1 so that 49% of the numbers correspond to Heads, 48% of the numbers correspond to Tails, and 3% of the numbers are Coin rolls away.

To implement this distribution in the worksheet we might first think of writing a formula like

=IF(RAND( )<.49,"Heads",IF(RAND( )<.97,"Tails","Coin rolls away"))

This formula is the right idea but it has a subtle error. The problem is that each time the RAND function is called, it returns a different value. Thus the two calls to RAND in the preceding formula will return different random numbers and the desired probabilities will not be obeyed.

The remedy is to place the call to RAND in a different cell, for example G4, and then refer to that cell in the formula, as in

=IF(G4<.49,"Heads",IF(G4<.97,"Tails","Coin rolls away"))

This solution is shown in Figure 15-4. Now the same random number is used in both places in the formula. To flip another coin, press F9 to recalculate the worksheet. This generates another random number in G4 and another result in C4. If you would like, the actual random number can be placed in a cell off the screen or on another sheet so it does not show.

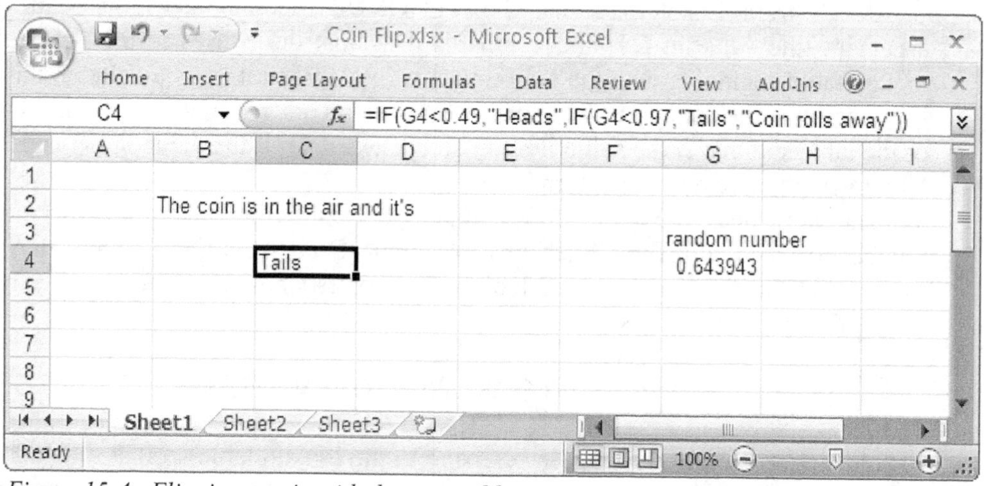

Figure 15-4. Flipping a coin with three possible outcomes.

An alternative to using the nested IF function is to use a lookup table. Lookup tables have the advantage of showing the cutoff points for the random numbers explicitly in the worksheet. An equivalent worksheet for flipping coins that uses a lookup table is shown in Figure 15-5. To determine the outcome of the coin flip, the random number in G4 is looked up in the table in G9:H11. The key formula, in C5, is

=VLOOKUP(G4,G9:H11,2)

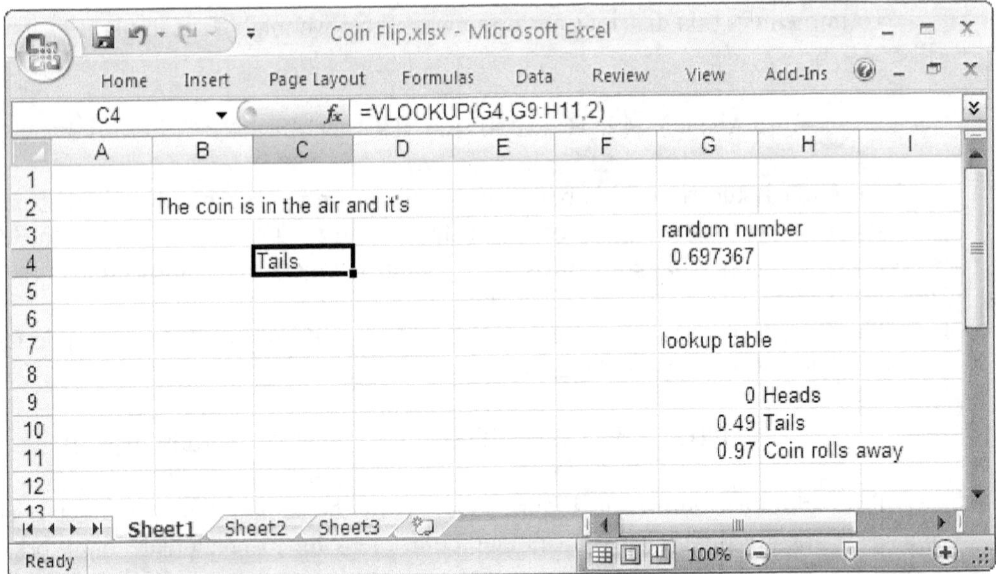

Figure 15-5. Flipping a coin with three possibilities using a lookup table.

Recall from Chapter 12 that the VLOOKUP function takes the value of the first argument (the value in G4) and compares it against the entries in the first column of the lookup table beginning with the first entry (in G9). When it finds a value in the column that is greater than the number it is looking up, it goes up one row and over to the second column of the table and that is the value it returns. For example, if the value in G4 is 0.7840133, the VLOOKUP function would return Tails.

The worksheet in Figure 15-6 simulates ten coin flips. Here we use a new random number for each coin flip. Each cell in column C contains the formula =RAND( ). The formulas in the cells in column E look up the corresponding random number in the lookup table. The formula in E7 is

=VLOOKUP(C7,$G$9:$H$11,2)

Absolute addressing is used when referring to the lookup table so that the addresses do not change when the formula is filled down column E. Alternatively, we could name the table in G9:H11 Outcomes and use the formula

=VLOOKUP(C7,Outcomes,2)

It is important to use ten different random numbers in this worksheet, one for each coin flip. If we use only one random number and refer to it ten times, then all of the coin flips would come out the same.

Each time we press the recalculation key F9, ten more coin flips are simulated.

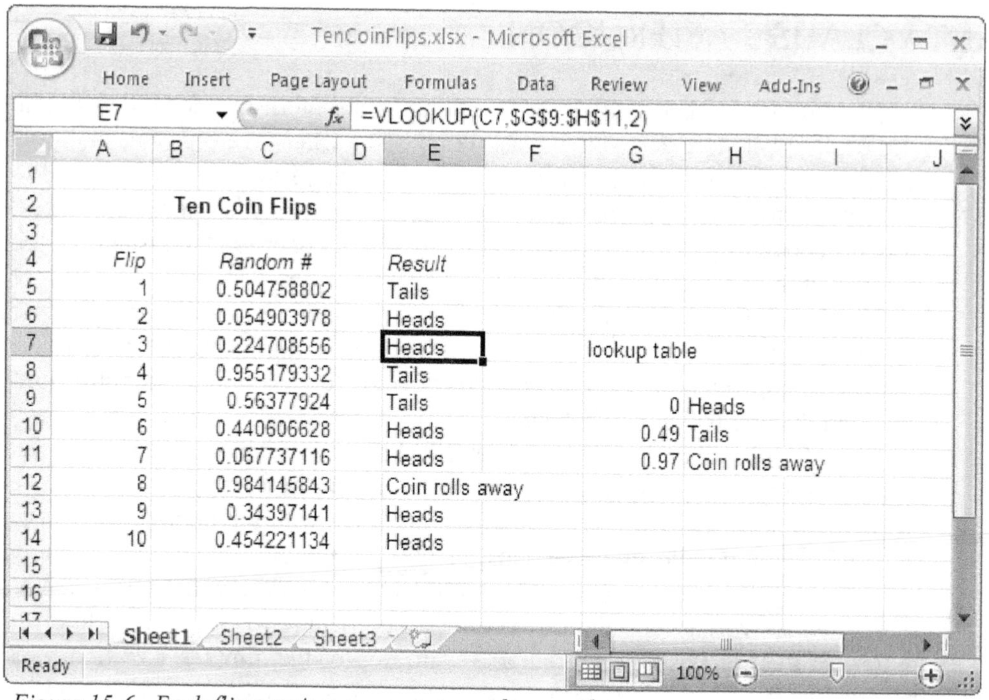

TenCoinFlips.xlsx - Microsoft Excel

E7 =VLOOKUP(C7,$G$9:$H$11,2)

	A	B	C	D	E	F	G	H
1								
2		Ten Coin Flips						
3								
4	Flip		Random #		Result			
5	1		0.504758802		Tails			
6	2		0.054903978		Heads			
7	3		0.224708556		Heads		lookup table	
8	4		0.955179332		Tails			
9	5		0.56377924		Tails		0	Heads
10	6		0.440606628		Heads		0.49	Tails
11	7		0.067737116		Heads		0.97	Coin rolls away
12	8		0.984145843		Coin rolls away			
13	9		0.34397141		Heads			
14	10		0.454221134		Heads			

Figure 15-6. Each flip requires a separate random number.

QUEUING PROBLEMS

A common application for Monte Carlo simulation is in queuing problems. A **queue** is a waiting line. People form a queue for a bus or when waiting to cash a check in a bank or to pay for their groceries in a supermarket. In particular, a queue is a line where the first people to arrive in the line are the first to be served. That is, a queue is what people think of as a "fair" waiting line. (A **stack** is a line where the first to arrive are the last to be served. This occurs, for example, if people are lined up for the bus and the bus stops so that the door opens at the end of the line. The last person on line would be the first on the bus.) In some situations there is one large master queue (for example, in most banks). In some situations there are multiple queues (for example, in most supermarkets).

People have studied queuing problems for years. How many tollbooths should be built at the entrance to the bridge? If too few are built, the traffic will back up too far. Widening the highway for tollbooths is expensive. If too many tollbooths are built, money will be spent unnecessarily. How many checkout registers should be built in the supermarket? At a busy intersection, for how long should the green light be on in each direction? How should tasks be divided up on an assembly line? All of these are problems involving queues.

One approach to solving queuing problems is to model the process on the computer. Once the basic model is set up, we can change some of the assumptions and see what the results would be in the model. We can do "What if" analysis with queuing models just as we can with financial models. Of course, the usefulness of the results depends on the fidelity with which the relevant portions of the world have been captured in the model.

SANTA CLAUS'S AFTERNOON

It is late November and you are working as an intern in a local department store. The rival department store across town has set up Santa Claus in a big chair in their store and has invited parents to bring their children in to meet him. Their promotion seems to be working well. Your store manager has asked you to do the same in your store. To make the idea even more attractive to parents, you plan to hire a photographer to take instant photographs of the children sitting on Santa's lap.

You have limited space in the store. The department next to the area where Santa will sit is Fine Jewelry, and the manager of the department does not want a long line of screaming kids winding through the department. You decide to try a quick computer simulation to see how long the line is likely to become.

Santa Claus will be in the store from 2 PM to 5 PM each afternoon. You figure that with each kid sitting down, pulling Santa's beard, saying he or she has been good, and telling Santa what he or she wants for Christmas, and then with the photographer taking a picture, Santa can serve a child in 30 seconds, or two per minute. How many children will arrive each minute? You decide to visit the rival department store with your watch and a pad and to use their arrivals as an estimate for your store. After observing for a while you decide that in 10% of the minutes no children arrive, in 20% of the minutes 1 child arrives, in 30% of the minutes 2 children arrive, in 30% of the minutes 3 children arrive, and in 10% of the minutes 4 children arrive.

Now we need to translate this into an Excel model. Each row in the model will correspond to a different minute with Santa. We will draw a new random number each minute and use the random number to determine the number of children who arrive using the preceding distribution. For simplicity, we will assume that all children arrive right at the beginning of each minute. The number of children who see Santa each minute will depend on the number of people still waiting from the previous minute and the number of arrivals. If no children are there, then Santa has the minute off. If there is only one child there, then Santa will see the one child. If there are two or more children, then Santa will see two children that minute and any remaining children will wait in line.

The worksheet for the simulation is shown in Figure 15-7.

In column A the times are listed from 2:00 PM through 4:59 PM. This was accomplished by typing 2:00 PM into A6, 2:01 PM into A7, selecting A6 and A7, and then dragging the Fill Handle down to A185. The result was that AutoFill correctly filled in the minute-by-minute sequence of times.

Column B contains the random numbers. Each cell in B6:B185 contains the formula

=RAND( )

The number of children who arrive at the beginning of each minute is calculated in column C using the lookup table in G7:H11. The lookup table is set up so that there is a 10% chance that no children arrive, a 20% chance that 1 child arrives, a 30% chance that 2 children arrive, a 30% chance that 3 children arrive, and a 10% chance that 4 children arrive. This is illustrated in Figure 15-8.

Santa Claus - Microsoft Excel

E7 =E6+C7-D7

Santa Claus's Afternoon

	A	B	C	D	E	F	G	H
4	*Time*	*Random#*	*Arrivals*	*Served*	*Queue*			*Number of*
5	start				0			*Arrivals*
6	2:00 PM	0.1837	1	1	0			*per Minute*
7	2:01 PM	0.9150	4	2	2		0.0	0
8	2:02 PM	0.8426	3	2	3		0.1	1
9	2:03 PM	0.2455	1	2	2		0.3	2
10	2:04 PM	0.2264	1	2	1		0.6	3
11	2:05 PM	0.0721	0	1	0		0.9	4
183	4:57 PM	0.1788	1	2	7			
184	4:58 PM	0.5238	2	2	7			
185	4:59 PM	0.2947	1	2	6			
186								
187	Total arrivals		362					
188	Longest length of line:				18			
189								

Day 1 | Day 2 | Sheet2 | Sheet3

Figure 15-7. A minute-by-minute simulation of Santa's afternoon.

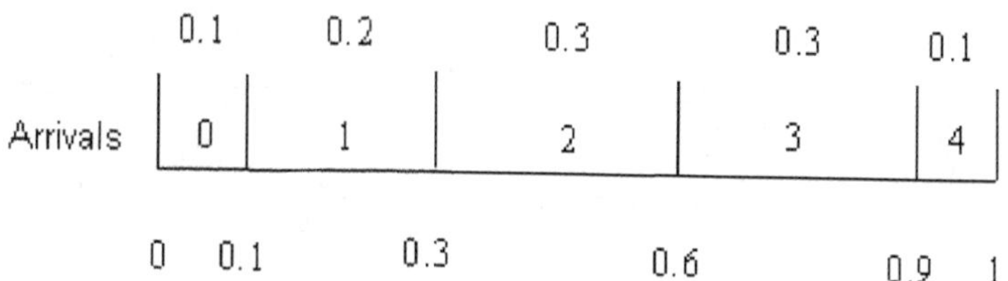

Figure 15-8. Dividing the numbers between 0 and 1 so that 10% correspond to 0 arrivals, 20% correspond to 1 arrival, 30% correspond to 2 arrivals, 30% correspond to 3 arrivals, and 10% correspond to 4 arrivals.

The formula in C6 is

=VLOOKUP(B6,$G$7:$H$11,2)

The formula has been filled from C6 down to C185. This generates the number of children who arrive each minute.

Remember that we are estimating that Santa Claus can see at most two children per minute. In any minute the number of children available for Santa to see is the number of children already waiting in line plus the number of children who just have arrived. Thus, the formula in D6 for the number of children served is

=MIN(E5+C6,2)

This formula is then filled down to D185. This formula might require a little thought. Recall that MIN returns the smallest of its arguments. Suppose there are 4 children waiting in line and 1 child arrives. The number of children Santa can see that minute is =MIN(4+1,2), which is =MIN(5,2), which is 2.

Finally, column E contains the queue, the length of the line each minute. Here we set E5 to 0, assuming that the line would be 0 when Santa begins, though it certainly is possible that people might show up at 1:55 PM to see Santa at 2:00 PM. The length of the line each minute will be the length of the line the previous minute plus the number of arrivals minus the number of children who see Santa. So the formula in E6 is

=E5+C6-D6

This formula is filled down column E.

At the end of the day in Figure 15-7 we see that there are 6 children waiting in line and that the longest the line has been is 18 children. A total of 362 children have arrived to see Santa during the three hours.

To simulate another day we would press F9 again. A new set of random numbers would appear. For each minute a new set of arrivals would be generated, Santa would see children, and the line would grow or shrink. The worksheet determines the total number of children seen and the longest length of the line during the day.

Santa Claus - Microsoft Excel

D7 | fx =MIN(E6+C7,2)

	A	B	C	D	E	F	G	H
1								
2			Santa Claus's Afternoon					
3								
4	*Time*	*Random#*	*Arrivals*	*Served*	*Queue*			*Number of*
5	start				0			*Arrivals*
6	2:00 PM	0.9014	4	2	2			*per Minute*
7	2:01 PM	0.6324	3	2	3		0.0	0
8	2:02 PM	0.2873	1	2	2		0.1	1
9	2:03 PM	0.5378	2	2	2		0.3	2
10	2:04 PM	0.4039	2	2	2		0.6	3
11	2:05 PM	0.1666	1	2	1		0.9	4
183	4:57 PM	0.4315	2	2	27			
184	4:58 PM	0.0879	0	2	25			
185	4:59 PM	0.2617	1	2	24			
186								
187	Total arrivals		377					
188	Longest length of line:				40			
189								

Day 1 | Day 2 | Sheet2 | Sheet3

Ready 100%

Figure 15-9. Another busy day for Santa.

We also could copy the worksheet over to a new sheet, as in Figure 15-9, and accumulate a number of different simulations. We then could compute statistics on the simulation of a month's worth of days.

What can we conclude? Under these assumptions the system is saturated. Santa would be worked at full capacity and there would be quite long lines. (Thirty children waiting in line with their parents can cause some disturbance in a small area.) The manager of the Fine Jewelry department has reason to be concerned. You should think about ways to improve the situation. Perhaps the visits with Santa could be speeded up a bit or Santa could be hired for more hours to dissipate the demand or a second Santa could be hired or you could go to a reservation system. Forewarned is forearmed.

This exercise was somewhat fanciful and simple-minded, but Monte Carlo simulation has proved useful in understanding a wide variety of queuing problems. In more sophisticated simulations we might model a probabilistic distribution for serving people as well as for arrivals. For example, some children might come with long lists of toys they want and take more time with Santa. Parents who arrive might leave if the line is too long. The probability distribution for arrivals might change as the day progresses. For example, more people might arrive right after school lets out. We might have multiple lines and multiple servers. All of these situations and more could be modeled by expanding the worksheet.

GENERATING RANDOM INTEGERS USING RANDBETWEEN

The RAND function generates random numbers between 0 and 0.99999... (to 15 decimal places). In some situations it is useful to be able to generate a random set of integers instead. For example, we might want to simulate the rolling of a die by generating the integers 1, 2, 3, 4, 5, 6, with equal probability. Excel provides the function **RANDBETWEEN** to generate random integers.

RANDBETWEEN has two arguments

=RANDBETWEEN(BOTTOM,TOP)

The first argument gives the bottom of the range of random integers to be generated. The second argument gives the top of the range of random integers.

For example,

=RANDBETWEEN(1,6)

will generate random integers between 1 and 6 inclusive with equal probability.

The formula

=RANDBETWEEN(50,60)

will evaluate to one of the 11 integers between 50 and 60 inclusive with equal probability each time the spreadsheet is recalculated.

ROLLING A PAIR OF DICE 100,000 TIMES

From playing Monopoly and other board games, and from trips to the casinos, we are interested in the probabilities of different outcomes when we roll a pair of dice. We set up the worksheet in Figure 15-10. In column A we have the number of the roll. In columns B and C we simulate rolling each die. The formula in each of the 100,000 cells in B5:C100004 is

=RANDBETWEEN(1,6)

The worksheet uses 200,000 different random integers. In column D we have the total that would result for the roll. In column G we summarize the 100,000 rolls using the COUNTIF function. The formula in G3 is

=COUNTIF($D$5:$D$100004,F3)

Since F3 contains the number 2, this formula counts all of the occurrences of 2 in the range D5:D100004.

When constructing this worksheet it is useful to turn off Automatic Calculation. This is done in the Calculation group of the Formulas tab in Calculation Options. By selecting Manual Calculation, the workbook will be recalculated only when F9 is pressed.

In the worksheet in Figure 15-10 we see that the most common combination is a 7 and that it occurs about one-sixth, of the time.

100000 rolls of a pair of dice.xlsx - Microsoft Excel

Home Insert Page Layout Formulas Data Review View Add-Ins

G6 =COUNTIF($D$5:$D$100004,F6)

	A	B	C	D	E	F	G	H
1								
2	**Rolling a pair of dice 100,000 times**					*Value*	*Occurrences*	*Percent*
3						2	2,881	2.88%
4	*Roll*	*Die 1*	*Die 2*	*Total*		3	5,534	5.53%
5	1	6	3	9		4	8,377	8.38%
6	2	3	4	7		5	11,100	11.10%
7	3	1	2	3		6	13,688	13.69%
8	4	2	6	8		7	16,692	16.69%
9	5	6	5	11		8	13,949	13.95%
10	6	3	4	7		9	11,117	11.12%
11	7	1	4	5		10	8,298	8.30%
12	8	5	6	11		11	5,543	5.54%
13	9	6	1	7		12	2,821	2.82%
14	10	6	6	12				
100003	99,999	6	4	10				
100004	100,000	1	1	2				

Sheet1 Sheet2 Sheet3

Ready Calculate 100%

Figure 15-10. Simulating 100,000 rolls of a pair of dice.

PENCIL AND PAPER EXERCISE

15-1. Write out on paper how to use RAND or RANDBETWEEN to generate each of the following distributions. Show all formulas and tables.

(a) 50% I win
50% You win

(b) 80% I win
20% You win

(c) 55% I win
30% You win
15% Tie

(d) 35% I win
25% You win
30% Tie
10% Rained out

(e) 32% I win
22% You win
25% We both win
15% We both lose
6% Rained out

(f) 50% 1
50% 2

(g) 25% 7
25% 8
25% 9
25% 10

(h) the years (integers) from 2000 through 2099 with equal likelihood

(i) the (integer) temperatures from -37 through 120 degrees with equal likelihood

(j) the integers 2, 4, 6, 8 with equal likelihood

(k) the numbers 3.0, 3.1, 3.2, ... 4.9 with equal likelihood

(l) the numbers -0.0012, -0.0014, -0.0016, … -0.0026 with equal likelihood.

.60 .30

COMPUTER EXERCISES

15-2. Create an Executive Decision Maker. The user will type in a decision that needs to be made. For example, "Should we launch a takeover bid for IBM?" or "Should I ask Pat out for dinner?" Your worksheet should respond with one of the following answers with the frequencies indicated.

60%	Go for it!
30%	No. The time is not right.
10%	Please gather more information.

15-3. The Eagles and the Warriors are playing for the championship. Each team has an equal likelihood of scoring 0, 1, 2, 3, or 4 goals. Create a worksheet to simulate the number of goals each scores and the winner of the game (Eagles, Warriors, or Tie). Each time you press F9, the recalc key, a new game should be simulated.

15-4. For each day in the month of January, the probabilities are

.19	that it will snow
.36	that it will be cloudy
.30	that it will be sunny
.15	that it will rain

Create a worksheet that uses RAND to "predict" the weather for the month of January. Each time F9 is pressed, the worksheet should show a different prediction. The worksheet should look like:

I Predict

January	1	Cloudy
January	2	Rain
January	3	Cloudy
...		
January	30	Snow
January	31	Sunny

15-5. Create a worksheet that will simulate the random selection of a single card from a deck of cards. A deck of cards has 52 cards, 13 face values in each of four suits. The face values are: 2, 3, 4, 5, 6, 7, 8, 9, 10, Jack, Queen, King, and Ace. The suits are: Clubs, Diamonds, Hearts, and Spades. Each time the worksheet is recalculated a new card will be selected as if from a new deck. Each of the 52 cards should have an equal chance of being selected. Your worksheet can have more cells than shown in these examples.

	A	B	C	D
1				
2		The card selected is the		
3				
4		9	of	Diamonds
5				

	A	B	C	D
1				
2		The card selected is the		
3				
4		Queen	of	Clubs
5				

15-6. Create an automated Fortune Teller. The user will type his or her name and the computer will tell the person's fortune. You should have at least eight possible fortunes, for example: "You will become the ruler of your country" or "You will have ten children" or "You will be the first person to land on the sun". Each time a person types in a name, one of the fortunes should be displayed. If the cell with the person's name is blank, then the cell that shows the fortune should be blank. As soon as a name is entered, a fortune should appear. The fortunes themselves should not be visible on the worksheet. Put them off to the side or on another worksheet.

15-7. The Super Cherry slot machine has three wheels that spin independently when the handle is pulled. For each wheel the probabilities are 20% that a Cherry will appear, 30% that a Plum will appear, 25% that an Ace will appear, and 25% that a Seven will appear. For each pull of the handle you put in a bet of $1. If you get three Cherries you win your bet back plus $25. If you get any two Cherries you win your bet back plus $2. If you get one Cherry you get your bet back. Otherwise you lose your bet of $1. You start with a stake of $100. Create a worksheet to simulate a session of 100 spins. You should have 100 rows, one for each spin. You should have columns at least for the spin number (1 through 100), each of the three wheels, the amount you win or lose on the spin, and the amount of money you have at the end of the spin. Each time you press F9 (recalc) you should get a different set of spins and results according to the above probabilities.

15-8. Our soccer team has 12 games scheduled. The coach figures that for each game the probabilities are:

Our Score	Opponent's Score
10% the team scores 0 goals	35% the opponent scores 0 goals
20% the team scores 1 goal	10% the opponent scores 1 goal
40% the team scores 2 goals	10% the opponent scores 2 goals
20% the team scores 3 goals	10% the opponent scores 3 goals
10% the team scores 4 goals	35% the opponent scores 4 goals

Note that the probabilities for the team's goals are independent of the probabilities for the opponent's goals.

Create a worksheet that "predicts" the season. You should have one row in the main body of your worksheet for each game. You should have columns for at least: game number (1 through 12), random number for us, number of goals we score, random number for them, number of goals they score, and the result of the game for us (win, lose, draw). At the bottom of the worksheet show the predicted record for the season: the number of wins, losses, and draws.

15-9. Your stockbroker suggests you buy 1,000 shares of International Electronics. The stock currently is selling at $38.75 per share. From research on the web you discover that the stock is quite volatile and that, based on recent past data, in

21% of the weeks it goes up $1.00
17% of the weeks it goes up $0.50
10% of the weeks it remains unchanged
35% of the weeks it goes down $0.50
17% of the weeks it goes down $1.00

(a) Create a worksheet to simulate the price of the stock and the value of your portfolio for 100 weeks assuming the preceding distribution. You should have 100 rows in the main part of your worksheet, one for each week. You should have separate columns for the week number, a random number, the price change that week, the closing price of the stock that week, and the value of your portfolio. Have separate cells at the top of the worksheet for the resulting High, Low, and Close for the stock price over the 100 weeks, indicating the highest price the stock reaches, the lowest price the stock reaches, and the closing price after 100 weeks. Have a separate cell that shows the amount of money you would have made (or lost) on the investment. Finally, have a cell containing either "I made money at the end of 100 weeks" or "I lost money at the end of 100 weeks" or "I was even at the end of 100 weeks". Run your simulation several times. Based on the past history data and your simulations, is this a good investment?

(b) Construct a chart with the number of the week along the X axis and the price of a share of stock along the Y axis. Press F9 repeatedly to see the result of different simulations.

(c) On telling your broker your findings she suggests that you employ the following strategy: Buy the 1,000 shares of stock now. Put in a Sell order for the stock at $43.75 or at 100 weeks, whichever comes first. That way if the stock reaches $43.75 you will sell out and achieve a profit of $5 per share. Otherwise you will sell out at the end of 100 weeks and take whatever profit or loss results. On inquiry your broker tells you that there will be a commission cost to you of $79 for purchasing the stock and another $79 for selling the stock. Create a worksheet like the worksheet in part (a) for simulating your broker's strategy. Run the simulation 10 times and record the consequences of using this investment strategy.

(d) Prepare a brief report in Word on this investment strategy. Include copies of appropriate worksheets and charts. Would you make money or lose money on average using this strategy? How much on average? Should you invest?

15-10. The game of Rock-Paper-Scissors is played by two people. At the count of three each person puts out either a closed fist (Rock), a flat hand (Paper), or two fingers (Scissors). The winner is decided as follows: Rock breaks Scissors. Paper covers Rock. Scissors cuts Paper. If both players make the same selection, it is a tie.

(a) Create a worksheet so you can play Rock-Paper-Scissors against the computer. There will be a cell for you to enter in your choice (Rock, Paper, or Scissors). There will be another cell where the computer makes its choice. The computer should choose among the three alternatives randomly. Each choice should be equally likely. (No fair having Excel peek at the person's choice in this formula!) A third cell should indicate the outcome: "You win", "I win", or "Tie". Test your worksheet until all nine possible combinations are tried.

(b) What happens in your worksheet if the person misspells the entry? Modify your worksheet so it says "Illegal entry." in this case.

(c) Create a workbook that allows you to play the computer 25 times. The workbook should automatically keep track of the number of times you win, it wins, and there is a tie. There are a couple of approaches to solving this problem. One approach is to have a single worksheet that automatically accumulates the results. This is a bit tricky as it will involve circular references where the cells refer to themselves in their formulas. A second approach involves having 25 sheets with the Rock-Paper-Scissors worksheet. The twenty-sixth sheet would have the summary statistics. You might want to set Excel to manual recalculation.

15-11. The Zing snack company is known for its high-caffeine, high-sugar snacks. Their vending machine near the computer lab has two kinds of snacks: Coffee Zings cost $1.00 each and Joltin Zings cost $1.50 each. Each morning at 10 AM the Zing delivery person stops by and fills the vending machine so it has its capacity of 150 Coffee Zings and 100 Joltin Zings.

Every ten minutes the probabilities are 35% no one buys a Coffee Zing, 30% one person buys a Coffee Zing, 25% two people buy a Coffee Zing, 10% three people buy a Coffee Zing. Every ten minutes the probabilities are 45% no one buys a Joltin Zing, 30% one person buys a Joltin Zing, and 25% two people buy a Joltin Zing. Once the machine runs out of Coffee Zings no more Coffee Zings can be purchased. Once the machine runs out of Joltin Zings no more Joltin Zings can be purchased.

Create a worksheet to simulate the operation of the vending machine over the course of one day beginning at 10 AM. For each ten-minute period show at least the number of Coffee Zings purchased, the number of Joltin Zings purchased, the number of Coffee Zings remaining in the vending machine and the number of Joltin Zings remaining in the vending machine. For the day we would like to know: how many Coffee Zings were sold, how many Joltin Zings were sold, how many minutes the machine was out of stock of Coffee Zings, how many minutes the machine was out of stock of Joltin Zings, and how much money was taken in for the day. There should be separate well-labeled cells at the top of the worksheet for each of these values.

15-12. There is 1 minute 50 seconds left to go in the championship football game. Our team is down by 5 points. We recover the ball on the opponent's 45-yard line. We have no time-outs left. There is enough time on the clock for exactly eight plays. Coach figures that on each play these are the probabilities:

20%	Gain 7 yards.
10%	Gain 15 yards.
10%	Gain 25 yards.
10%	Gain 3 yards.
10%	Sack. Lose 10 yards.
10%	Interception.
28%	Incomplete. No gain or loss.
2%	Gain 60 yards.

(a) Simulate the rest of the game. If you cross the goal line you win. If you don't make it to the goal line or there is an interception, you lose. Have a single cell at the top that gives the result of the game, either win or lose. Don't worry about first downs.

(b) Do worry about first downs. If you go four downs without a net gain of 10 yards after any down you lose.

15-13. Persistent Telemarketing, Inc. has offered you a commissioned part-time job. They will give you 500 names and telephone numbers. You are to telephone these people and sell them disposable cell phones on behalf of a well-known telephone company. The customer will receive a cell phone in the mail. The phone has a fixed number of built-in anywhere, anytime minutes. The customer pays in advance and then throws away the cell phone when the minutes run out. There are four different plans that you will be offering with different amounts of minutes allowed under each plan: $300, $400, $600, and $1000. Persistent Telemarketing will pay for all of your telephone calls and will give you a 10 percent commission on all of your sales.

You speak to a friend who has done this. She tells you that 20% of the time she reaches a person on the first call. 15% of the time she reaches a person on the second call. 10% of the time she reaches a person on the third call. She said that she never makes more than three calls to a person so 55% of the time she never reaches a person at a given number.

If she connects to a person she said that 85% of the time she doesn't make a sale. 8% of the time she connects to a person she sells the $300 plan. 4% of the time she connects to a person she sells the $400 plan. 1% of the time she connects with the person she sells a $600 plan. 2% of the time she connects with a person she sells the $1000 plan.

Assume that to make a call and not reach someone takes 15 seconds. If someone answers and the person does not buy a plan assume it takes an average of 45 seconds. If someone answers and the person does purchase a plan, assume it takes an average of 5 minutes to make the sale and obtain and record all of the information.

You would like to estimate how much money you might make if you take this job, how many phone calls you will make, and how much time you will spend. Create a worksheet to simulate this job. You should have a row for each of the 500 people you'll be given. You should have a cell in each row for at least: the prospect number (1 to 500), how many calls it takes to reach the person (1, 2, 3, never), how much you sell to the person ($0, $300, $400, $600, $1000), how much you make in commission for the person, and how much time you spend on each person.

On the top of the worksheet you should have well-labeled cells with: (a) the total number of calls made, (b) the total number of sales pitches (answered calls) made, (c) the total number of sales made, (d) the total amount of commission made, (e) the total time spent, and (f) the expected dollars per hour you will make.

15-14. Create a worksheet to simulate the Brady family finances for five years under the following assumptions:

- Their monthly income varies. In any given month the probabilities are 10% they make no money, 25% they make $1,000, 25% they make $2,000, 25% they make $3,000, and 15% they make $4,000.

- Their expenses generally (85% of the time) are $1,800 per month, but in a given month there is a 10% chance their expenses are $3,000 and a 5% chance their expenses are $5,000.

- All funds accumulate in their bank account. Currently they have $3,000 in the account. When the account is positive they make 0.25% per month interest on the funds. If their account goes below $0 they have to pay 1.5% per month interest on the debt. Again, this all accumulates in the account. Assume that all income and expenses occur at the end of the month.

(a) Your worksheet should have a row for each month. There should be columns at least for: month number, income, expenses, interest, and balance. You can have as many additional cells as you wish.

(b) At the top of your worksheet please show the maximum amount in the bank account, the minimum amount in the bank account, the number of months they were in debt, and the total of the interest for the five years.

(c) Create a chart that has the month number along the X axis and dollars along the Y axis and plots the Brady family bank account over the 5 years.

15-15. Jack is taking a vacation at a tropical resort. The first evening he visits Land's End, an open-air bar, which is located on the end of a narrow pier, over the water. It's beautiful there but unfortunately he has a bit too much to drink. Jack needs to make his way back to the hotel. The pier is 60 steps long but only eight steps wide.

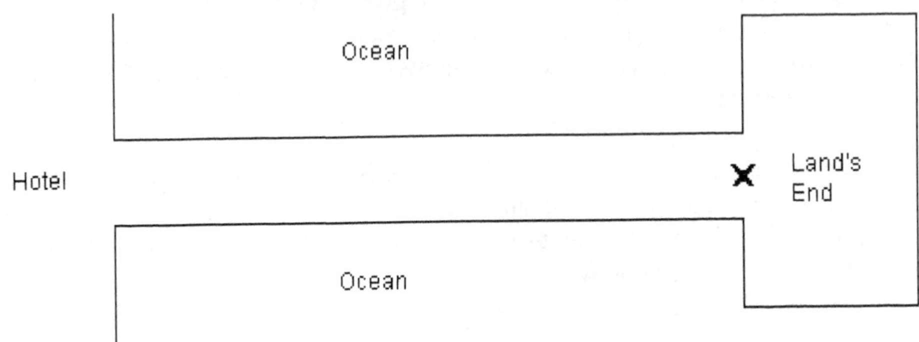

In the diagram Jack is at the X. He is headed towards the hotel. Each time he takes a step, there is a 70% chance he steps forwards, towards the hotel. There is a 10% chance he stumbles a step backwards. There is a 10% chance he takes a step to his left, towards the ocean. There is a 10% chance he takes a step right, towards the ocean.

If Jack ever makes it back to the hotel the people there will look after him and see him to his room. If he ever ends up 5 steps to the right or 5 steps to the left, he will fall into the ocean. Once he is in the ocean his voyage is over. After 100 steps if Jack is still on the pier he will collapse.

Create an Excel worksheet to simulate Jack's random walk back to the hotel. There should be 100 rows in your worksheet, one for each potential step. At the top of the worksheet there should be a cell that gives Jack's final result: either "Hotel" or "Ocean" or "Collapse on pier". Try your worksheet 10 times by pressing F9, the recalc key.

15-16. So that people feel they are getting more value for all of the taxes they pay, the United States government has decided to hold a giant national lottery. Everyone in the country automatically is entered. Once a month a Social Security number will be selected at random. Whoever has that Social Security number will be given $10,000,000 tax free.

You have been hired to create the worksheet that will generate the random Social Security number. Social Security numbers have the form 012-34-5678. Each of the billion possible Social Security numbers should be equally likely to be selected in your worksheet.

For you to receive full payment for your work the government contract officer insists that all 0's in the Social Security number selected appear in your worksheet and that the dashes appear in their usual places in the number.

15-17. The tortoise and the hare are having a race. Whoever can travel the most distance in an hour wins. For the tortoise, each minute the probabilities are 25% he rests and doesn't move, 30% he travels forward 1 foot, 35% he travels forward 2 feet, and 10% he travels forward 3 feet. For the hare, each minute the probabilities are 10% he moves backward one foot, 65% he doesn't move, and 25% he moves forward 5 feet.

(a) Create a worksheet to simulate the race. You should have a row for each minute. You should have columns at least for: minute number, tortoise position, hare position, who is ahead. You may use other columns and cells as you wish. At the top of the worksheet give the winner for the simulation (or possibly it's a tie). Also at the top please give the total number of minutes during which the hare is behind where he started.

(b) Create a chart that has minutes along the X axis and position in feet from the starting line along the Y axis. The chart should show the positions of the tortoise and the hare during the race. Pressing F9 to simulate a new race should cause the chart to be updated automatically.

15-18. In the game of Roulette, you bet on a number. The croupier spins the ball around the spinning Roulette wheel and the ball falls randomly in a slot with a number. If you bet on the number in which the ball falls you win 35 times your bet. If a number comes up that is different from the one on which you bet, you lose your money.

(a) Create a worksheet to simulate a session of 100 spins at the Roulette table where you bet \$10 on the same number each time. The possible numbers are 0 through 36. You will enter the number on which you bet in a cell at the top of the worksheet. You will have rows for 100 spins. Each row will show at least the spin number (1 through 100), the number that comes up on the wheel (0 to 36), the amount you win or lose, and your cumulative earnings so far. At the top of your worksheet there should be a cell with the final result for your earnings for the session.

(b) Create a chart that has the number of the spin (from 1 to 100) along the X axis and dollars along the Y axis and that shows the progression of your cumulative earnings during the course of your session.

(c) In most casinos these days there is an additional number, 00 (double zero). You can bet on 00 and it is equally likely to come up on the wheel, so there are 38 possible outcomes. The payoff is still 35 to 1. Modify your worksheet to allow for 00 both in the betting and on the wheel.

(d) You begin with \$300. If you drop down to \$0 you are bankrupt and cannot keep betting. If you ever reach \$1,000 you leave the table and cash in your chips. The subsequent rows of the simulation can appear in your worksheet, but the outcomes in the rows should say either "Bankrupt" or "Big Winner" if you reach either of the limits. The result also should appear at the top of your worksheet. Run the simulation 10 times. Out of the 10 times how many times did you go bankrupt? How many times did you walk away a big winner?

15-19. The game of Chuck-a-Luck is popular at carnivals and fairs and also is played in casinos. Chuck-a-Luck is played with three large dice tumbling over in a cage. You can bet on various outcomes. We will assume for a minute that each bet is for \$1. Here are three of the more popular bets available:

Triple. If any number comes up on all three dice you win \$30.

High. You win \$1 if the total of the three dice is 11 or more, except you always lose if it is a triple.

Low. You win \$1 if the total of the three dice is 10 or under, except you always lose if it is a triple.

Create a worksheet to allow a person to play Chuck-a-Luck on the computer. The person should be able to place bets for any amount on Triple, High, and Low. The worksheet should show the values of the three dice, how much the person wins or loses on each bet, and the total amount won or lost for the tumble.

You should turn off the Automatic Recalculation of formulas by selecting Manual Recalculation in Calculation Options in the Calculation group of the Formulas tab. Now the dice will be rolled only when F9, the recalculation key, is pressed.

15-20. The number $\pi = 3.14159...$ is the ratio between the circumference and the diameter of a circle. This problem is concerned with using random numbers to approximate π.

Consider the shaded quarter circle below and the 1 by 1 quadrant in which it is inscribed.

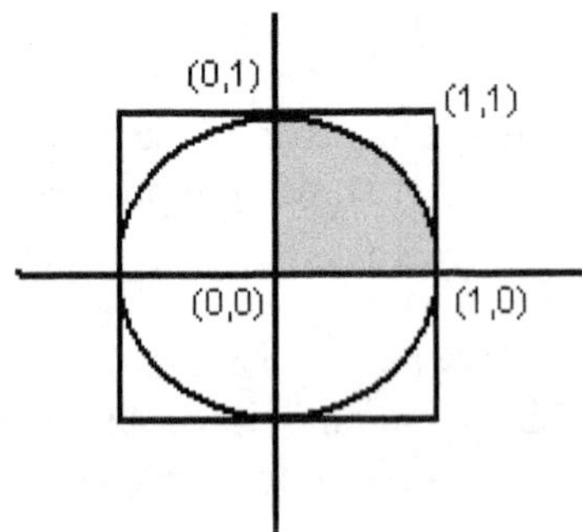

The shaded part has area $\pi/4$. Now consider N randomly generated points within this quadrant. (Like throwing darts N times in the quadrant.)

Let K be the number of such points that fall within the shaded part. Recall that Pythagoras' Theorem tells us that any point (x,y) with the property that $x^2 + y^2 < 1$ is within the shaded part.

Since the points are generated randomly, the ratio K/N approximates the ratio of the area of the shaded part to the area of the entire quadrant (i.e., $(\pi/4)/1$ or simply $\pi/4$). Therefore, 4*(K/N) is an approximation of π. Note that the quality of this approximation improves as N grows large.

Create an Excel worksheet that generates 100,000 random (x,y) points within the 1 by 1 quadrant, and displays the approximate value for $\pi = 4 * K / N$ at the top of the worksheet.

15-21. Create a worksheet that simulates a child's peg box toy. A peg box toy is a box with a glass front, a hole in the middle of the top surface, and pegs positioned as shown by the dark underlines in the following worksheet:

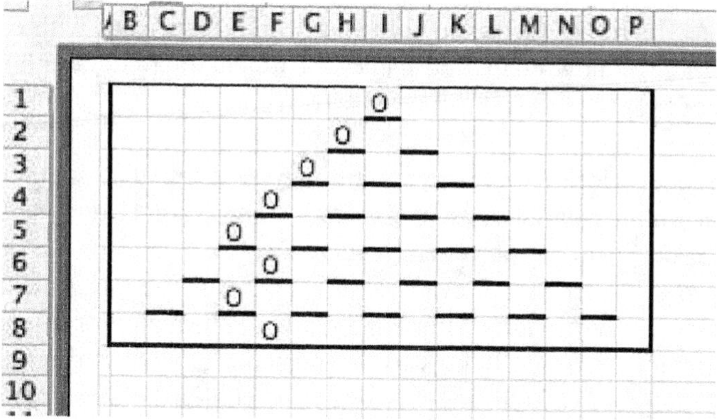

The toy allows for a ball to be dropped into the box through the hole in the top. The ball will hit a peg positioned just below the hole. Half the time the ball will fall to the left from the peg and half the time the ball will fall to the right. The ball will continue to hit pegs as it falls through the box to the bottom.

Your simulation should depict the course the ball would take as it falls through the box. When the worksheet is recalculated, a new simulation of the falling ball should appear.

15-22. Mary and John are applying for the same job. Both know they want the job and will accept it if offered. Mary is interviewing first. There is a 30% chance that Mary will be offered the job at the end of her interview and a 70% chance the decision will be deferred. If John is interviewed there is a 50% chance that John will be offered the job, a 30% chance that Mary will be offered the job, and a 20% chance that the company will offer the job to neither candidate but keep searching. Create a worksheet to simulate the situation. There should be a cell at the top of your worksheet with the name of the new employee: Mary, John, Neither. Your worksheet can have as many other cells as you wish.

15-23. Four brothers -- David, Jonathan, Kevin, and Manny -- have inherited a pair of season tickets to the Red Sox. There are 81 regular season home games. After much discussion, they decide that who will go to which game will be left up to chance. On the odd games (games 1, 3, 5, ...) two of the four of them will go together. For each odd game they'll put the four names in a hat and select one name at random and then the second name at random from the remaining three names. For the even games one of the four of them will be given both tickets and be able to bring a guest. The brother who gets the pair of tickets for each even game also will be selected at random by putting the four names in a hat and selecting one at random for each game.

(a) Implement their plan in a worksheet. You can have the odd games on the left and the even games a couple of columns over on the right. For each game you should show at least the game number and the names of the brothers who will be attending in separate cells (two for each odd game and one for each even game). No brother should be systematically favored. At the top of the worksheet you should have rows with each of the four names and cells that indicate how many odd games each gets to attend and how many even games each gets pairs of tickets to attend.

(b) The brothers decide that it doesn't quite seem fair that one person can have many more tickets than another by the luck of the draw. There are 41 odd games for a total of 82 tickets so it would be fair if two brothers receive 21 tickets and two brothers receive 20 tickets to the odd games. There are 40 even games so it would be fair if each brother receives 10 pairs of tickets for the even games. Implement a worksheet similar in appearance to the one above that will randomly assign tickets to brothers but always will result in the total numbers of tickets for the season indicated. No brother should be systematically favored. There are several ways to accomplish this.

As always, you can use as many extra cells or columns as you wish.

15-24. Some dice problems, with thanks to Prof. Fred J. Rispoli.

(a) Consider the following game. A player rolls one die. If the outcome is 3, the player wins $3. If the outcome is 2 or 6 the player wins $1. If the outcome is 1, 4, or 5 the player loses $2. Construct a simulation of this game. There should be separate cells for the number rolled and for the amount of money the player wins (or loses). Test your simulation by typing the F9 key repeatedly to see if you are obtaining the correct output.

(b) A player rolls one die. If the outcome is 3 or 5, the player wins $2. If the outcome is 1, 2, 4, or 6 the player must pay $1. Construct a simulation of this game. There should be separate cells for the number rolled and for the amount of money the player wins (or loses). Test your simulation by typing the F9 key repeatedly to see if you are obtaining the correct output.

(c) A player rolls two dice. If the outcome on both dice is the same (doubles) the player wins \$5. If the sum of the two dice is 7 or 11, the player wins \$3. If neither of these occurs, the player must pay \$1. Construct a simulation of this game. There should be separate cells at least for each of the numbers rolled and for the amount the player wins (or loses). You may have additional cells as you wish. Test your simulation by typing the F9 key repeatedly to see if you are obtaining the correct output.

(d) A player rolls three dice. If the same number comes up on all three dice, the player wins \$3. If the same number comes up on any two of the dice, the player wins \$1. Otherwise, the player loses \$1. Construct a simulation of this game. There should be separate cells at least for each of the numbers rolled and for the amount the player wins (or loses). You may have additional cells as you wish. Test your simulation by typing the F9 key repeatedly to see if you are obtaining the correct output.

(e) A player selects a number between 1 and 6 and an operator rolls three dice. If the number chosen by the player comes up on all three dice the player wins \$5, If the number selected comes up on two dice, the player wins \$2, If the number selected by the player comes up on one of the dice, the player wins \$1. Otherwise, if the number does not appear, the player loses \$2. Construct a simulation of the game. There should be a single input cell for the player to select a number. There should be separate cells at least for the numbers rolled and for the amount the player wins (or loses). You may have additional cells as you wish. Test your simulation appropriately.

(f) Estimate the expected outcome for the game in part (a) above by creating a worksheet that simulates 100,000 games, that is 100,000 rolls of a die. Each game should be independent from the others. There should be at least 100,000 rows in your worksheet, one for each game. The worksheet should have no input cells. There should be columns at least for the game number, the roll, and the amount won or lost. At the top of the worksheet should be a well-labeled cell with the average amount won or lost per game. Each time you press F9, 100,000 more games should be simulated and the average result should appear at the top. Does this look like a good game to play for money? Enter your answer at the top of the worksheet and your reason.

(g) Estimate the expected outcome for the game in part (b) above by creating a worksheet that simulates 100,000 games, that is 100,000 rolls of a die. Each game should be independent from the others. There should be at least 100,000 rows in your worksheet, one for each game. The worksheet should have no input cells. There should be columns at least for the game number, the roll, and the amount won or lost. At the top of the worksheet should be a well-labeled cell with the average amount won or lost per game. Each time you press F9, 100,000 more games should be simulated and the average result should appear at the top. Does this look like a good game to play for money? Enter your answer at the top of the worksheet and your reason.

(h) Estimate the expected outcome for the game in part (c) above by creating a worksheet that simulates 100,000 games, that is 100,000 rolls of a pair of dice. Each game should be independent from the others. There should be at least 100,000 rows in your worksheet, one for each game. The worksheet should have no input cells. There should be columns at least for the game number, the rolls, and the amount won or lost. At the top of the worksheet should be a well-labeled cell with the average amount won or lost per game. Each time you press F9, 100,000 more games should be simulated and the average result should appear at the top. Does this look like a good game to play for money? Enter your answer at the top of the worksheet and your reason.

(i) Estimate the expected outcome for the game in part (d) above by creating a worksheet that simulates 100,000 games, that is 100,000 rolls of a set of three dice. Each game should be independent from the others. There should be at least 100,000 rows in your worksheet, one for each game. The worksheet should have no input cells. There should be columns at least for the game number, the rolls, and the amount won or lost. At the top of the worksheet should be a well-labeled cell with the average amount won or lost per game. Each time you press F9, 100,000 more games should be simulated and the average result should appear at the top. Does this look like a good game to play for money? Enter your answer at the top of the worksheet and your reason.

(j) Estimate the expected outcome for the game in part (e) above by creating a worksheet that simulates 100,000 games, that is 100,000 rolls of a set of three dice. Each game should be independent from the others. There should be at least 100,000 rows in your worksheet, one for each game. The worksheet should have one input cell, the number selected. The same number should be used in all 100,000 games. There should be columns at least for the game number, the rolls, and the amount won or lost. At the top of the worksheet should be a well-labeled cell with the average amount won or lost per game. Each time you press F9, 100,000 more games should be simulated and the average result should appear at the top. Does this look like a good game to play for money? Enter your answer at the top of the worksheet and your reason.

(k) For the game in part (e) above does it matter which number is selected? That is, is it better to select one number rather than another? If so which number is best? Construct a worksheet simulation to demonstrate your hypothesis. Include your answer as to whether it matters which number is selected and your answer as to which and why and how your worksheet demonstrates your answer.

15-25. Cornerstone Hedge Fund believes that the stock of International Ventures is in a very volatile period but in any day it is as likely to go up as down. In particular they believe that each day there is equal likelihood that the stock will gain or lose anywhere between \$1.00 and -\$1.00. So it might change \$0.73 that day or it might change -\$0.26 or \$0.39 all with equal probability.

(a) Create a worksheet to simulate the stock over 250 days (approximately one year). The stock of International Ventures currently sells for $20.00 per share. Each day the stock will go up or down, depending on a random number. Of course, each day the movement is relative to the opening price for the day rather than the opening price for the simulation. You can assume the opening price for the day is the same as the closing price for the previous day. You can treat the probabilities for daily stock change as a discrete distribution with 201 possible values ranging from +1.00 through -1.00 (including 0.00). Or you can treat the probabilities for daily stock change as a continuous distribution ranging between +1 and -1 (or between +0.99999... and -1.00000... Since random numbers are calculated to 15 decimal places the lack of +1.00000000000000 really wouldn't matter.) Your worksheet should have one row for each day and columns for day number, opening price, daily change, and closing price.

(b) Your boss has devised a strategy he thinks might take advantage of the volatility. Put in an open Buy order for 100,000 shares at $19 per share. If the stock drops to $19 per share or lower, you will buy 100,000 shares at exactly $19 per share. As soon as you purchase the shares put in an open Sell order at $21 per share. Then if the stock reaches $21 per share or higher, you will automatically sell the 100,000 shares at exactly $21 per share, making $200,000. (Brokerage fees can be ignored.) Your boss's strategy says you should continue doing this as many times as possible and he thinks that the strategy should work for the next 250 business days. So at any time you will either be holding 100,000 shares of International Ventures or 0 shares. If at the end of the 250 days, you are holding 100,000 shares you will sell them at the closing price for day 250. Note that on average the stock is not predicted to go up or down, so this is a pure volatility play. Each buy and sell cycle before day 250 you lock in $200,000 in gains.

Before the Fund invests using this strategy he would like you to simulate the strategy in Excel. Add a column for the action that day (either "Buy", "Sell", or blank), and for the number of shares held at the close of the day (0 or 100,000). At the top of the simulation add well labeled cells for the number of times you bought and sold and for the amount of money you made or lost using the strategy. Also you should add cells for the alternative strategies (Strategies 2 and 3) of buying at beginning of the first day (at $20 per share) and selling at the end of the last day and also of not buying the stock at all and making (and losing) $0 on the stock. Add a cell that determines which of the three strategies did best.

(c) Now do some sensitivity analysis. Modify the workbook so it works through the simulation 100 different times. There are several ways to do this, including copying and pasting the simulation 100 times down the worksheet, putting 100 worksheets in the workbook, using a two dimensional data table.

At the top of the main worksheet show the average number of times the stock was bought or sold each 250 day simulation, the percent of simulations you made money using the strategy, the average amount made or lost, the most that was made in any simulation, and the most that was lost in any simulation. Compare these to the two other strategies. Add a sentence or two about whether you think the Fund should follow the proposed investment strategy.

(d) Try the strategy on real stock data. Instructions for downloading stock data from Google Finance are available as part of exercise 11-21 and exercise 12-17. Download the data for a year for your favorite stock. The opening price for the stock is used to set the Buy Price and the Sell Price for the year. Under this strategy the Buy Price is set at 5% below the opening price for the year. The Sell Price is set at 5% above the opening price for the year. So if the opening price is $20, the Buy Price would be $19 and the Sell Price would be $21. Assume you begin with no shares. If the stock goes below the Buy Price you will buy 100,000 shares at the Buy Price. If the stock subsequently goes above the Sell Price you will sell the 100,000 shares at the Sell Price. Enter and fill formulas so the process automatically repeats as in (b) for the entire year. If you are holding shares at the end of the year they should be sold automatically at the closing price for the year. At the top of the worksheet add well labeled cells for the number of times you bought and sold and for the amount of money you made or lost for the stock during the year using the strategy. Compare these to the alternative strategies of buying at beginning of the first day (at $20 per share) and selling at the end of the last day and also of not buying the stock at all and making (and losing) $0 on the stock. You should be able to Copy and Paste the prices for any stock into the worksheet and have it work automatically. Which of the three strategies makes the most money?

CHAPTER 16

DATA MANAGEMENT WITH TABLES

OBJECTIVES

In this chapter you will learn how to:

- Work with large amounts of data organized as tables
- Sort the data into alphabetical or numerical order
- Find the data that match certain criteria using Filters
- Create a Totals row for a table
- Summarize the data using PivotTables

A major use of computers is for data management, for handling large amounts of data. Airline reservations, personnel, accounts payable and receivable, inventory, and payroll all can involve large amounts of data and all profitably have been automated. A special type of software, called database management systems, has been developed for data management. There are database management systems for large computers and for personal computers and for all types of computers in between. Whereas a word processor can be considered a computerized typewriter and an electronic spreadsheet can be considered a computerized calculator and ledger paper, a database management system can be considered a computerized filing cabinet.

Excel has some powerful and useful data management features. We are going to explore these capabilities in this chapter. But before we begin, it is important to point out that Excel is not considered a database management system itself. The major difference is that the data management facilities in Excel are designed to work with a single set of data, whereas a database management system can work with multiple sets of data and their interactions.

Microsoft does provide a database management program, Access, with many versions of Office. It is possible to move sets of data back and forth between Access and Excel. It also is possible to create sets of data within Excel itself. In either case, a set of data that is used in Excel usually is in the form of a **table**.

WHAT IS A TABLE?

A table is a range of data that is organized so that all of the information about a single person, object, or transaction occupies a single row and so that each column contains information of the same type. ("Tables" were called "Lists" in previous versions of Excel.) The top row of the table contains the name of the data in the corresponding column. For example, each row might be the data for a different employee and there might be columns for last name, first name, date of birth, date of hire, title, and so on. Or, each row might correspond to a different book in the bookstore and there might be columns for title, author, publisher, list price, number in stock, and so on.

Consider the following situation. The owner of the Tri-Valley Auto Dealership decides that he would like to learn more about his customers and about which type of customers are purchasing which types of vehicles so he can segment his advertising better. He decides to keep some simple data on each of his customers and the type of vehicle each has purchased. Since setting up this worksheet, he has sold 12 vehicles, as shown in Figure 16-1.

Here, each row corresponds to the information about a different vehicle that was sold and the customer who purchased it. Column A contains the day of the sale. Column B contains the type of vehicle. The dealership offers three basic models: a family sedan, a sports utility vehicle (SUV), and a convertible. Column C shows the purchase price of the vehicle. And so on.

In database terminology, in a table in Excel, a row corresponds to a **record** and a column corresponds to a **field**. The table itself is contained in A4:E16 of the worksheet. Row 4 contains the names of the columns. Note that a table can have only one row of names at the top. This is called the **Header** row. Each name in the Header row of the table must be unique. None of the cells in the Header row of the table should be blank.

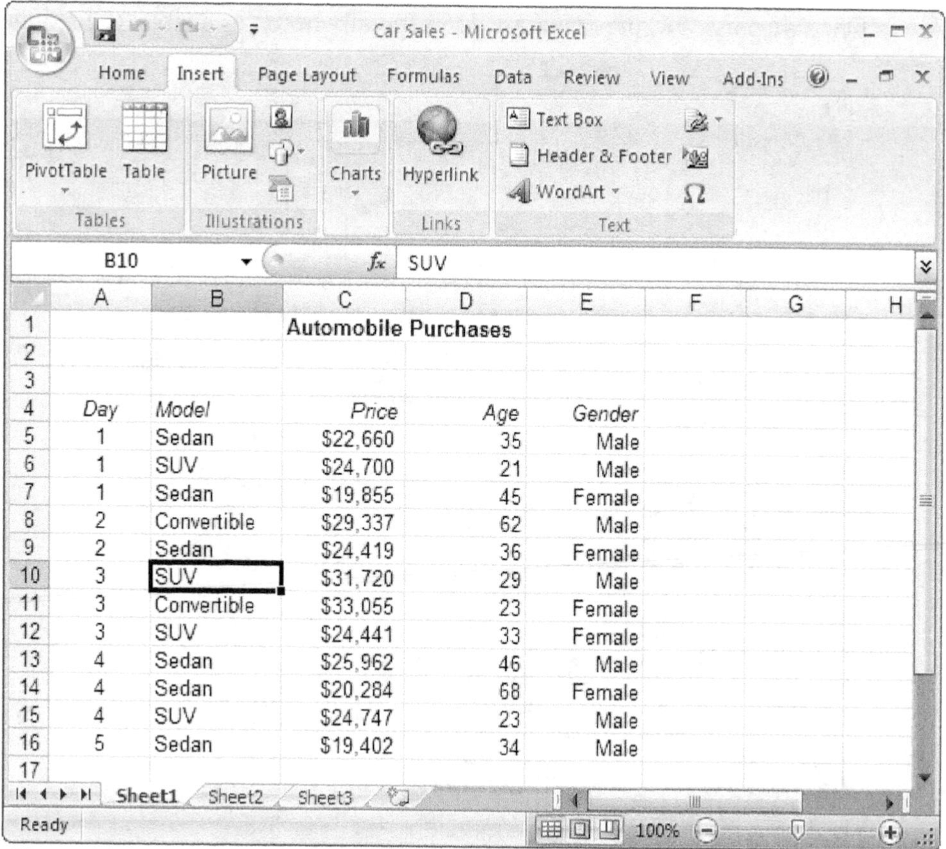

	A	B	C	D	E
1			Automobile Purchases		
2					
3					
4	*Day*	*Model*	*Price*	*Age*	*Gender*
5	1	Sedan	$22,660	35	Male
6	1	SUV	$24,700	21	Male
7	1	Sedan	$19,855	45	Female
8	2	Convertible	$29,337	62	Male
9	2	Sedan	$24,419	36	Female
10	3	SUV	$31,720	29	Male
11	3	Convertible	$33,055	23	Female
12	3	SUV	$24,441	33	Female
13	4	Sedan	$25,962	46	Male
14	4	Sedan	$20,284	68	Female
15	4	SUV	$24,747	23	Male
16	5	Sedan	$19,402	34	Male
17					

Figure 16-1. A set of data.

But A4:E16 is *not yet* an official table in Excel 2007. To make the range into an official table click on a cell in the table, as in Figure 16-1, and then click on Table in the Tables group of the Insert tab. Once you do, the Create Table dialog box appears, as in Figure 16-2. Excel has looked around the active cell to find blank rows and columns and has guessed correctly the boundaries of the table. If it guesses wrong you can correct it. A header row for the table is the row at the top that provides unique names for the columns. The top row of A4:E16 does contain unique names for the Header row.

Figure 16-2. The Create Table dialog box.

Once we press OK, the range A4:E16 officially becomes a table. (See Figure 16-3.)

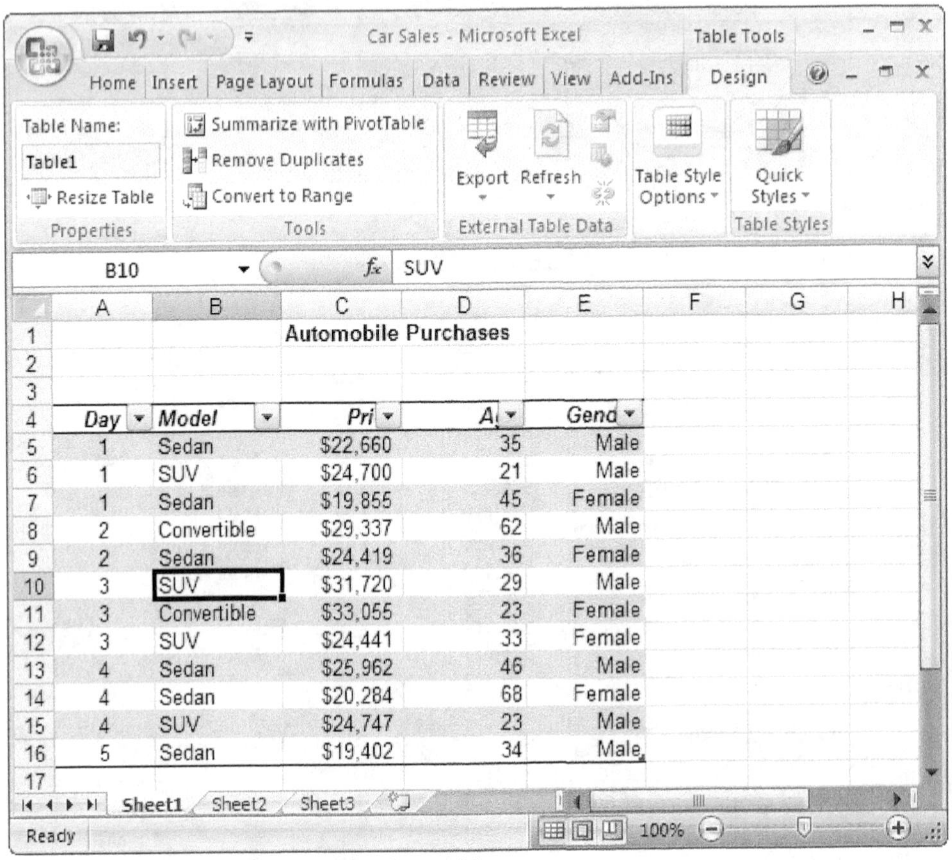

	A	B	C	D	E
1			Automobile Purchases		
2					
3					
4	Day	Model	Pri	A	Gend
5	1	Sedan	$22,660	35	Male
6	1	SUV	$24,700	21	Male
7	1	Sedan	$19,855	45	Female
8	2	Convertible	$29,337	62	Male
9	2	Sedan	$24,419	36	Female
10	3	SUV	$31,720	29	Male
11	3	Convertible	$33,055	23	Female
12	3	SUV	$24,441	33	Female
13	4	Sedan	$25,962	46	Male
14	4	Sedan	$20,284	68	Female
15	4	SUV	$24,747	23	Male
16	5	Sedan	$19,402	34	Male
17					

Figure 16-3. Now A4:E16 is officially a table.

The first thing you probably notice is that a table typically has banded rows, rows with alternating colors. Clicking on Quick Styles in the Table Styles group of the newly appeared Table Tools Design tab gives you dozens of options for the colors of the bands.

The second aspect of an official table in Excel 2007 is that the cells in the Header row are partially obscured by the down arrows indicating pull-down menus. You can use these arrows to sort the rows and to filter (select) rows according to certain criteria.

SORTING TABLES

When we sort a table we move around the rows if necessary so that the entries in a particular column are in alphabetical or numerical order. The records in the automobile table already are sorted by day. We could sort them many other ways.

To sort the rows in a table, click on the arrow next to the cell in the Header row for the column which is to be the basis of the sort. For example if we want to sort the rows in the Automobile table on Age then click on the down arrow to the right of the cell that contains

Age in the Header row of the table, as in Figure 16-4. Select Sort Smallest to Largest.

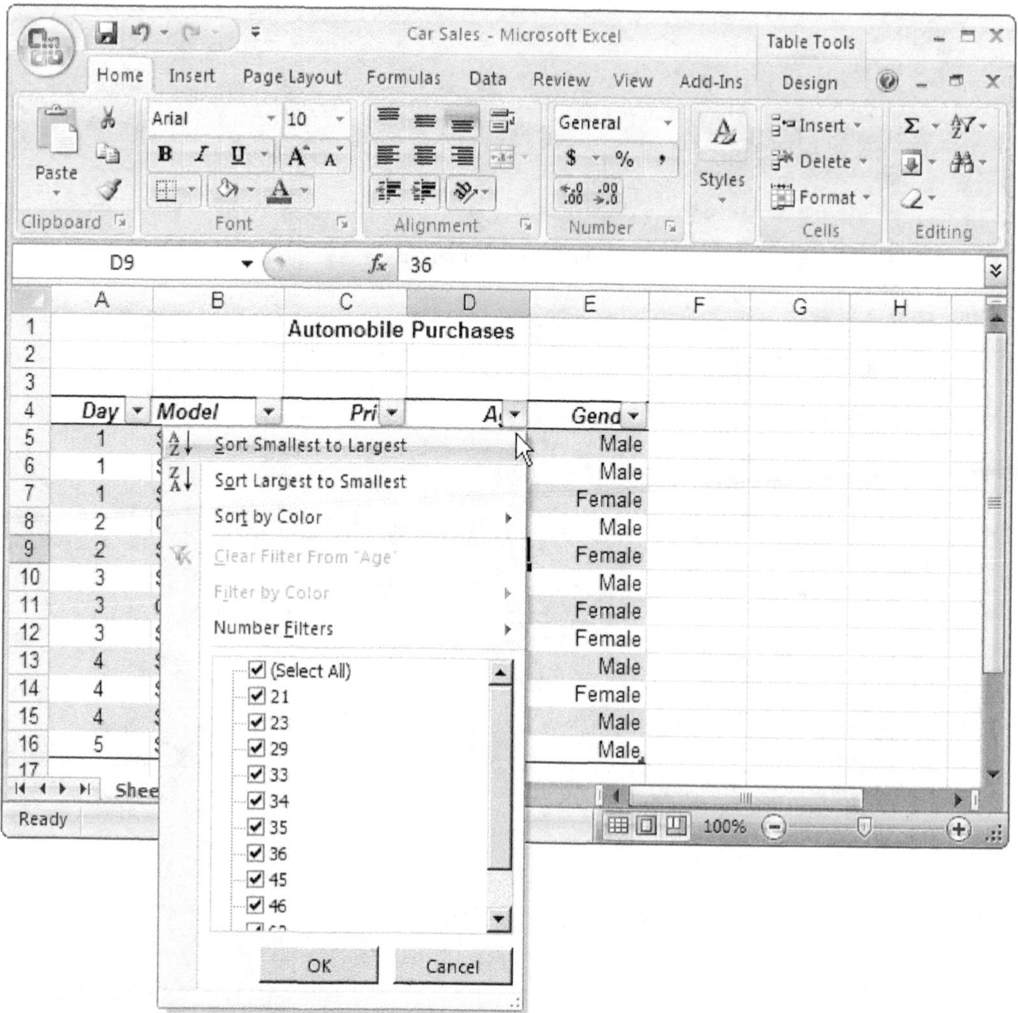

Figure 16-4. Sorting the rows of a table.

When we select Sort Smallest to Largest in the Age pull-down menu, the rows in the table automatically are rearranged so that they are sorted in order by Age, as in Figure 16-5.

Note that within the sort, prior order of the rows still holds. So where there is a tie in the Age, the previous order of the rows determines which row is first. In the example in Figure 16-5, there are two purchasers of age 23. Within those purchasers, the one who purchased on day 3 appears before the one who purchased on day 4, because before the sort on Age, the table was sorted by day of purchase. If you would like the rows to be sorted by Model and within Model the ties to be broken by Gender, first sort on Gender and then sort on Model.

An alternative to using the Age pull-down menu is to click on a cell in the Age column and then click on the Sort & Filter icon in the Editing group of the Home tab.

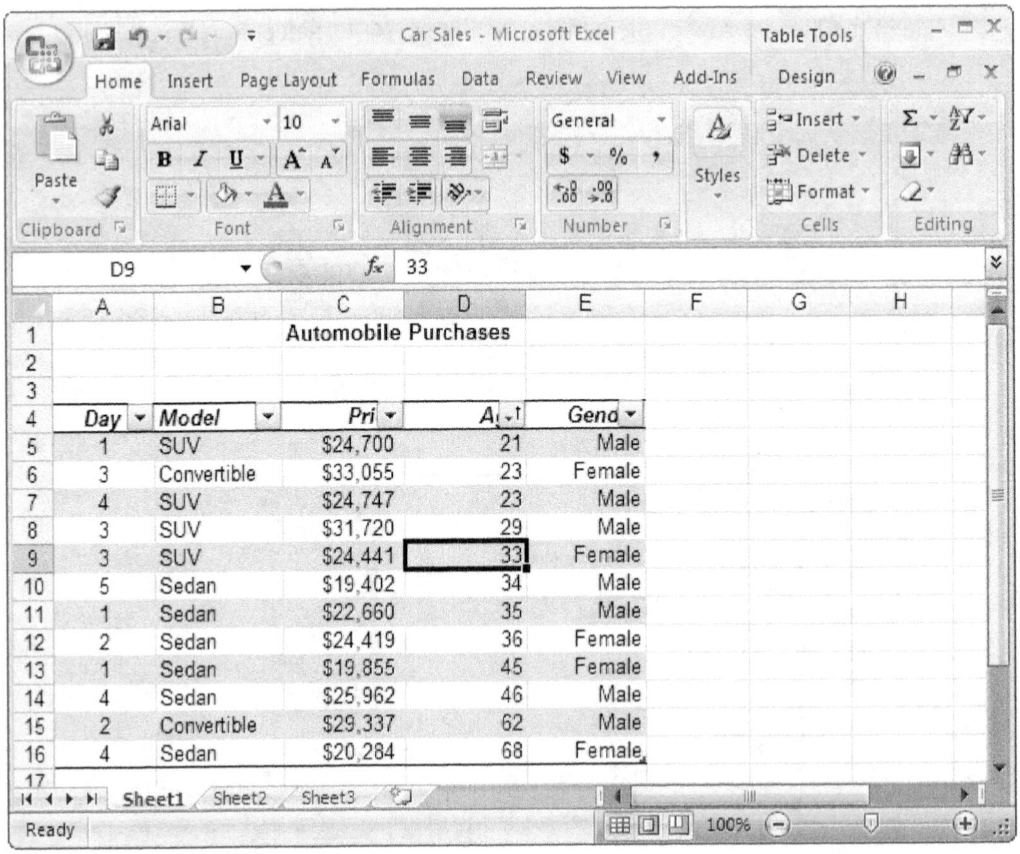

Automobile Purchases

Day	Model	Price	Age	Gender
1	SUV	$24,700	21	Male
3	Convertible	$33,055	23	Female
4	SUV	$24,747	23	Male
3	SUV	$31,720	29	Male
3	SUV	$24,441	33	Female
5	Sedan	$19,402	34	Male
1	Sedan	$22,660	35	Male
2	Sedan	$24,419	36	Female
1	Sedan	$19,855	45	Female
4	Sedan	$25,962	46	Male
2	Convertible	$29,337	62	Male
4	Sedan	$20,284	68	Female

Figure 16-5. The rows sorted by Age.

FINDING RECORDS WITH FILTERS

The table in our worksheet contains 12 records. It is possible for a table to have a million records (limited by the number of rows in a worksheet and the amount of memory in your computer). We might want to find records that match certain criteria. For example, we might want to find all of the sedans that were purchased by females. Or, we might want to find all the vehicles that were purchased for over $25,000 by people under 25. The easiest approach to finding records in a table is through the use of **Filters**. The Filters are in the pull-down menus in the Header cells below the Sort selections.

If we want to see only the records of sedans purchased by females, we filter the table in two stages. First we find the vehicles purchased by females. Then we find which of those vehicles are sedans. (We could filter in the other order.)

Working with the table in figure 16-6, click on the arrow to the right of Gender and you can see the choices. In the Gender pull-down menu we click off the check mark for (Select All) and then click on the check mark for Female. (See Figure 16-6.)

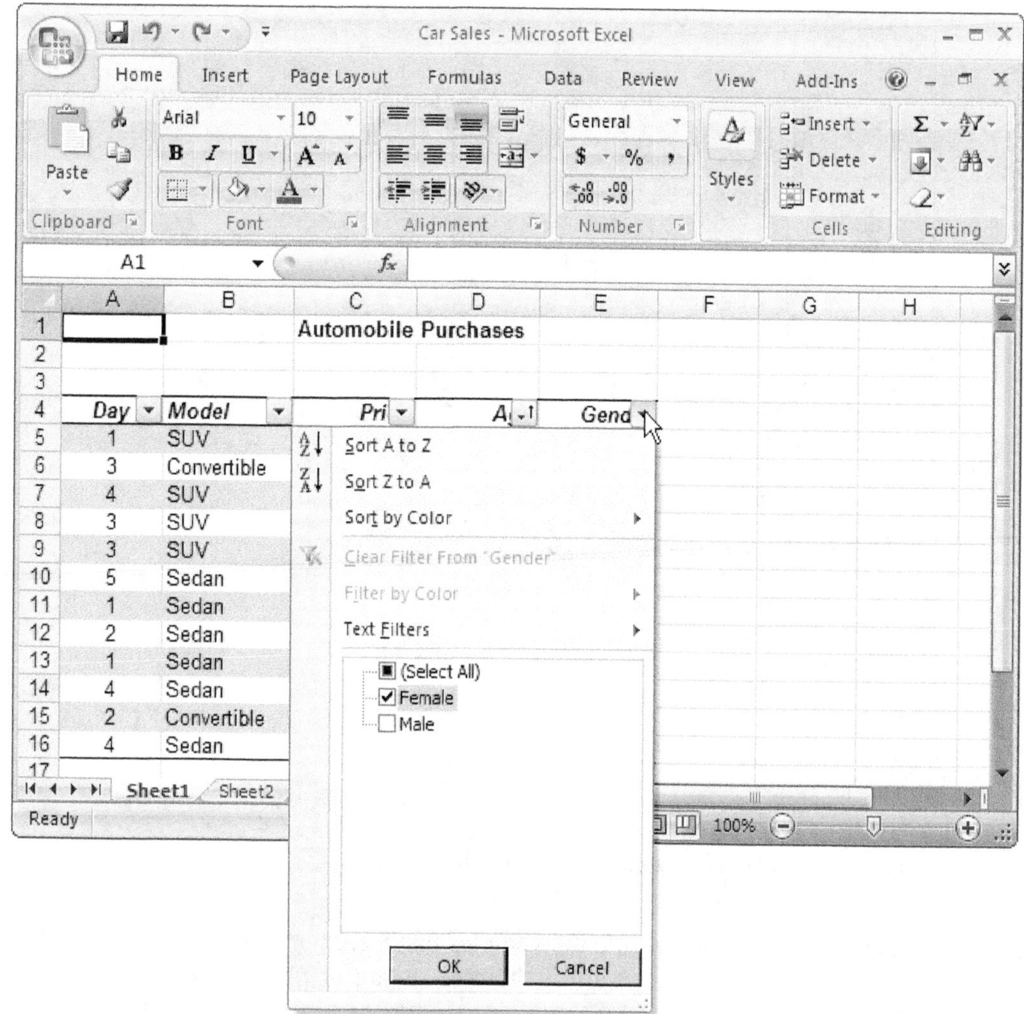

Figure 16-6. Selecting just the vehicles purchased by females.

When we click OK the result is that only the records of the vehicles purchased by females are shown. Rows in the table that do not have the word Female in column E are hidden. In the worksheet in Figure 16-7 you can see that rows 5, 7, 8, 10, etc. are not shown. Note the Filter symbol (the funnel) by the Gender pull-down menu and the Sort symbol (the thin arrow) by the Age pull-down menu.

Now to show just the sedans purchased by females, we click on the Model pull-down menu in cell B4 and select Sedan. Only the records for sedans purchased by females will be shown. All other records will be hidden.

To unhide (display) the rows, we can reverse the process. Click on (Select All) in the Model pull-down menu and then (Select All) in the Gender pull-down menu. All of the records will be displayed.

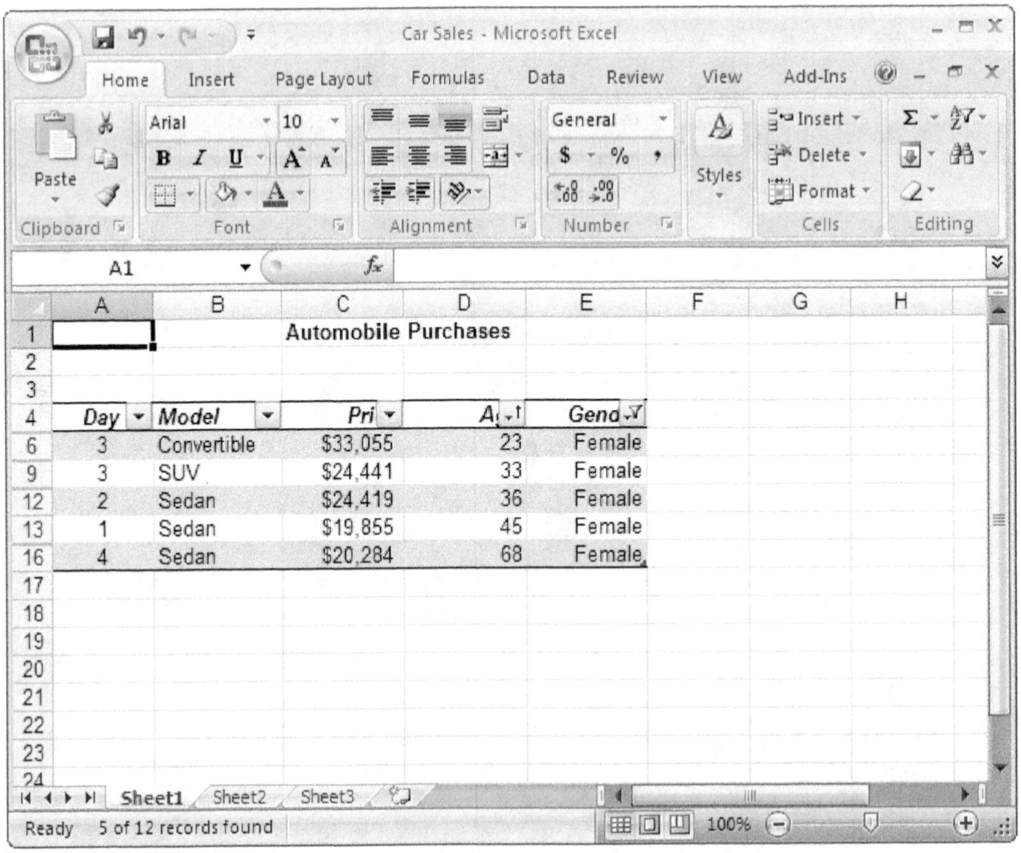

	A	B	C	D	E
1			Automobile Purchases		
2					
3					
4	Day	Model	Pri	A	Gend
6	3	Convertible	$33,055	23	Female
9	3	SUV	$24,441	33	Female
12	2	Sedan	$24,419	36	Female
13	1	Sedan	$19,855	45	Female
16	4	Sedan	$20,284	68	Female

Ready 5 of 12 records found

Figure 16-7. The vehicles purchased by females.

As another example, to find the vehicles that were purchased for over $25,000 by people under 25, we first make sure all of the records are displayed again. Then we go into the Price pull-down menu in cell C4 and select Number Filters and then Greater Than... in the resulting sub-menu. We then see the Custom AutoFilter dialog box and type in 25,000, as in Figure 16-8.

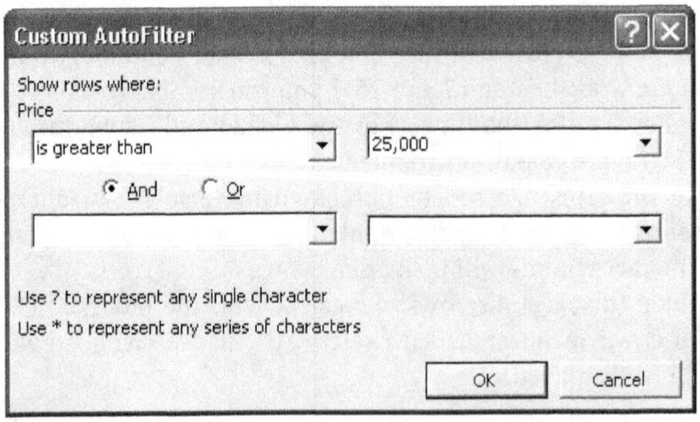

Custom AutoFilter

Show rows where:
Price

is greater than | 25,000

And Or

Use ? to represent any single character
Use * to represent any series of characters

OK Cancel

Figure 16-8. Finding the vehicles that sold for more than $25,000.

When we click on OK only the records for the vehicles with price greater than $25,000 are displayed.

To display just the records of the vehicles that were purchased for over $25,000 by people under 25, we would repeat the process for Age and select Number Filters and then Less Than... in the Age pull-down menu and then type in 25 and press OK. The record for that nice convertible will be the only record in the table displayed.

A special feature in the Number Filters is the **Top 10** Filter. This Filter allows you to select, for example, the records of the 10 vehicles with the highest prices or the records of the three vehicles sold to the youngest people. The dialog box for Top 10 allows you to change the selection to Top 5 or Bottom 3 or whatever.

Notice that the Custom AutoFilter dialog box has room for two criteria for the field. This allows us to select the vehicles priced greater than 25,000 and less than 40,000. Or, we could select the vehicles with Model equal to Sedan or equal to Convertible.

Filters hide rows, but the rows still are there in the worksheet. If you do calculations on a column, the hidden values will be included in the calculation. For example, if in cell C18 in the worksheet in Figure 16-8 we put the formula =SUM(C5:C16), all vehicle prices will be included in the calculation, not just the vehicle prices of the records that are showing. To calculate, for example, the total price or average price of just the vehicles purchased by females, we need to use another technique.

ADDING THE TOTAL ROW TO A TABLE

A Total Row is a special feature of a table that allows you to take the sum or average of just the values in a table that are displayed after filtering. The Total Row always occurs at the bottom of a table.

To add a Total Row, click in a cell in the table and then select Table Style Options in the Table Tools Design tab. Click on Total Row. A new row appears at the bottom of the table. (See Figure 16-9.)

The values calculated by the cells in the Total Row can be changed to Average or Count or many other functions. If you click on one of the cells in the Total Row, a pull-down menu appears, as in Figure 16-10, allowing you to select the function you would like calculated. You also can change the text that appears in the left cell of the Total Row. For example, in Figure 16-10 you could change the contents of A17 from "Total" to "Average" to indicate you are calculating averages.

You can insert new rows into the table or delete rows from the table. If you do, the table automatically is adjusted and the Total Row calculations are updated.

To convert a table in a worksheet back to a normal range of data, click on a cell in the table and then click on Convert to range in the Tools group of the Data Tools Design tab. The banded formatting will stay. The Total Row will still work, but you won't be able to filter out rows without converting the range back to a table.

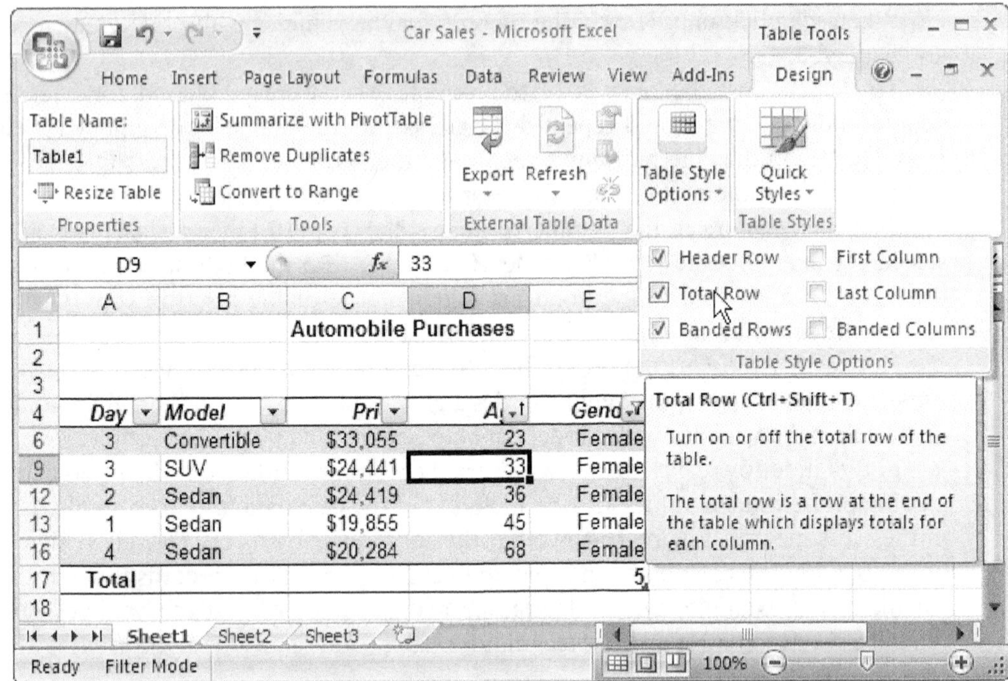

Figure 16-9. Adding a Total Row to the table.

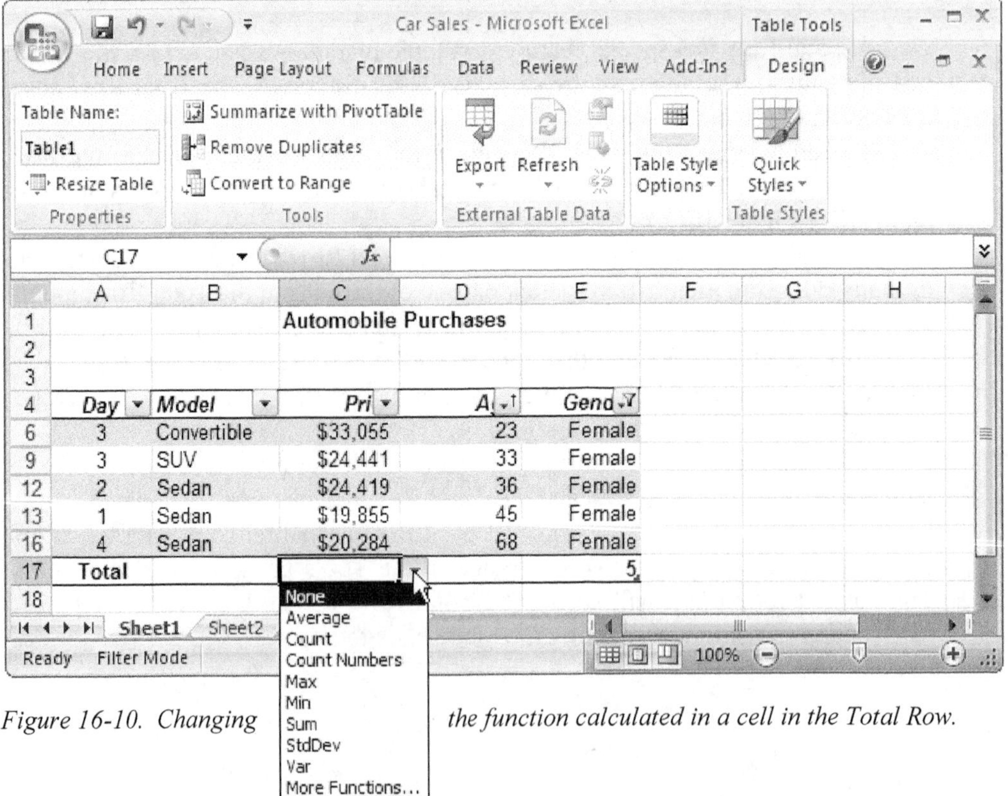

Figure 16-10. Changing the function calculated in a cell in the Total Row.

PIVOT TABLES

An Excel table can have hundreds of thousands of rows of data. Often it is difficult to see patterns with all of the data. What we need is a summary of the data. A **PivotTable** is a summary of a table of data.

We begin again with the original table of data on the vehicles sold and their purchasers in Figure 16-3. With the active cell somewhere in the table we click on Summarize with PivotTable in the Tools group of the Table Tools Design tab. This calls up the Create PivotTable window in Figure 16-11. Table1 is the name of the vehicle purchase table.

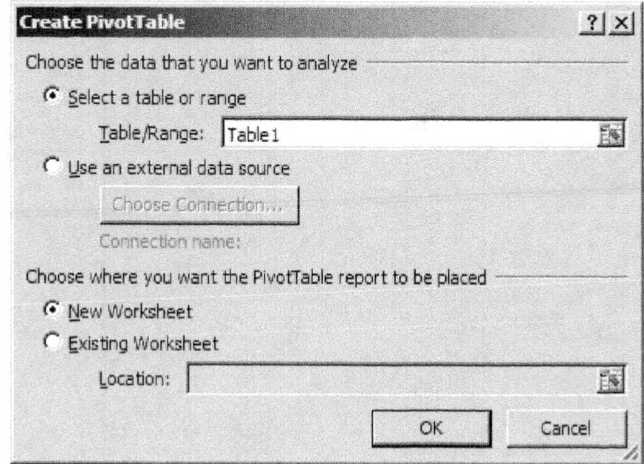

Figure 16-11. Creating a Pivot Table in a new worksheet.

Clicking OK brings up my candidate for the strangest and most obscure window in Excel, but also one of the most powerful, the PivotTable Layout window in Figure 16-12.

The different fields (columns) in the table are shown on the right side in the PivotTable Fields List pane. The idea is to drag those fields into the proper areas below so that we can create the pivot table we would like to see to summarize the data in the table.

For example, suppose we are interested in learning the average ages of: the females who purchased convertibles, the females who purchased sedans, the females who purchased SUVs, the males who purchased convertibles, the males who purchased sedans, and the males who purchased SUVs. That is, we want the data summarized in a Model by Gender pivot table that shows the Average Age. In terms of the pivot table, we want Model to be the Rows, Gender to be the Columns, and Average Age to be the Values.

To specify this in the window in Figure 16-12, we drag Model from the Field List into the Row Labels area below. We drag Gender from the Field List into the Column Labels area below. We drag Age from the Field List into the Values area below.

The result is the window in Figure 16-13. We're halfway there. Miraculously, Excel has automatically constructed the report we see on the new Sheet4. There are no formulas in the cells in Sheet4. The PivotTable is being created by the PivotTable tool as we make changes in the PivotTable Field List pane.

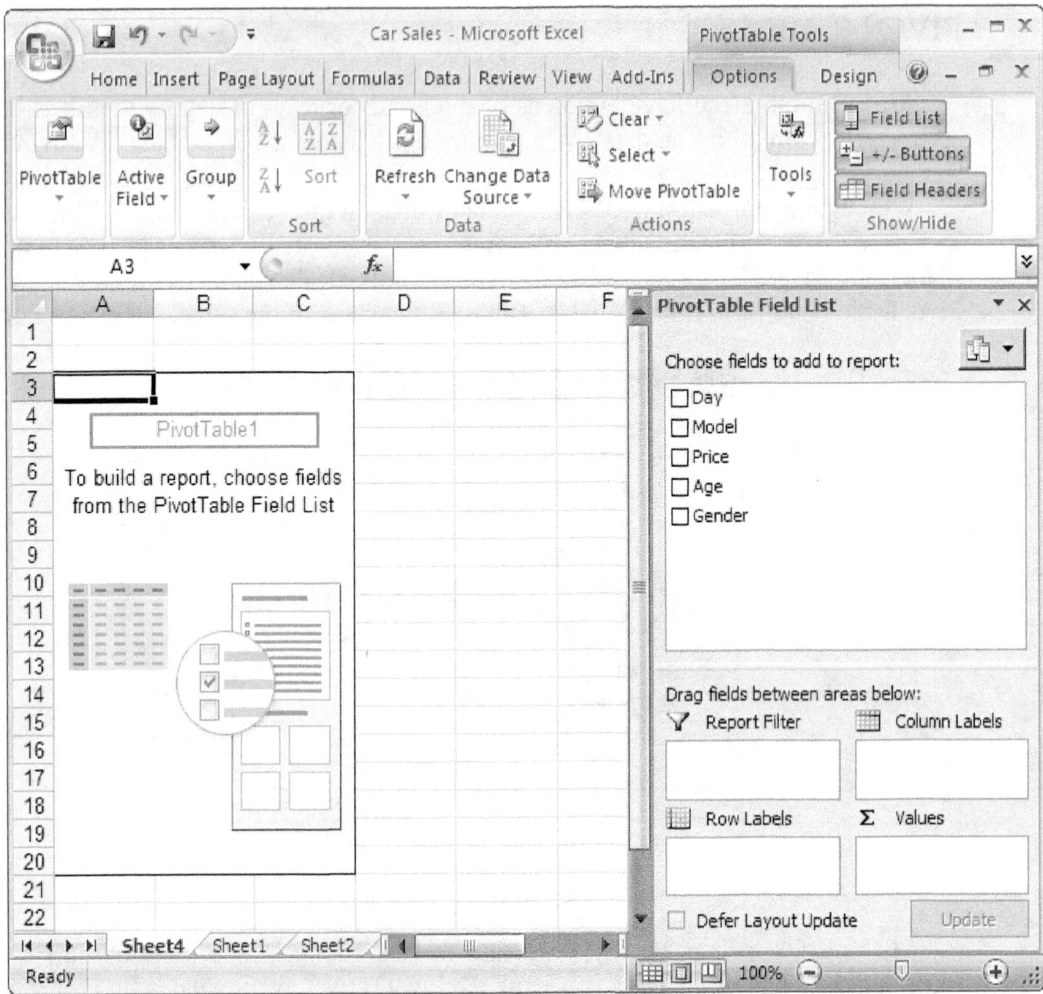

Figure 16-12. This window is key for setting up the PivotTable.

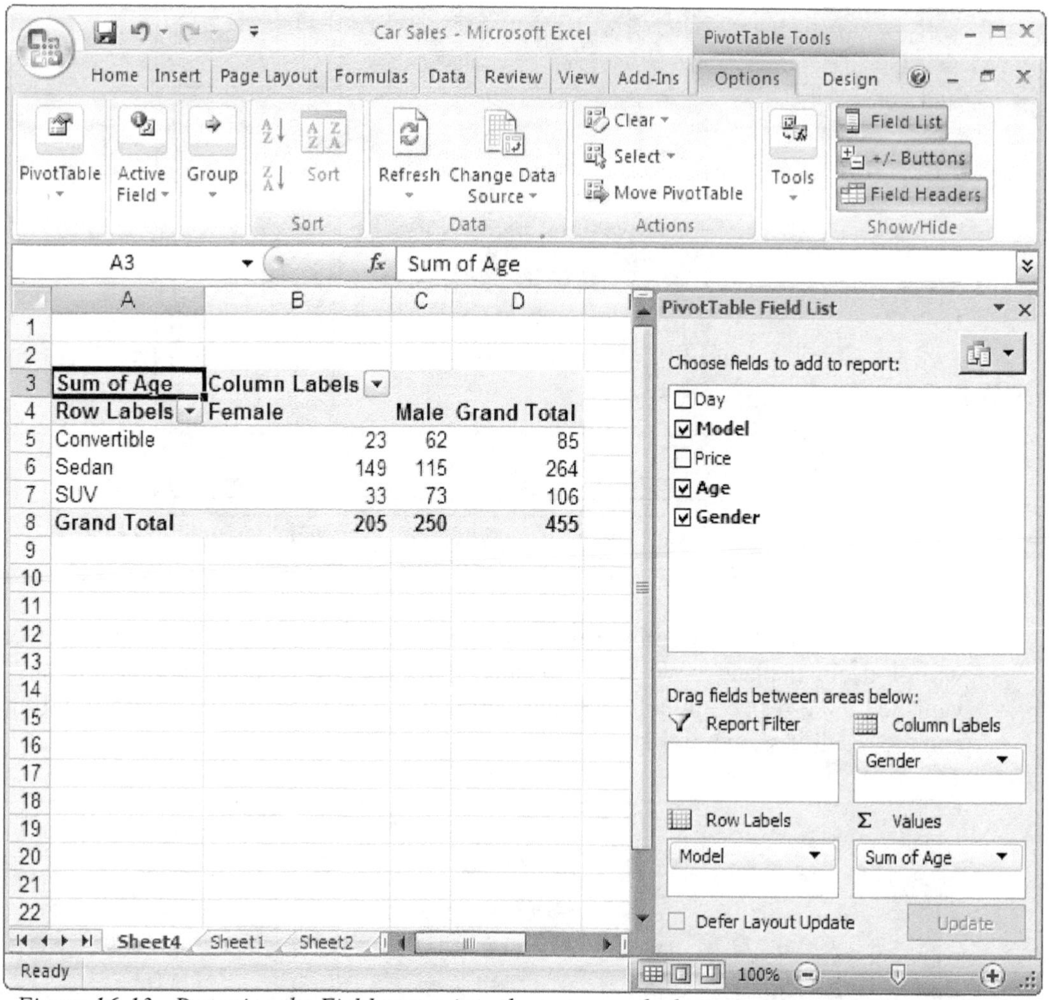

Sum of Age	Column Labels		
Row Labels	Female	Male	Grand Total
Convertible	23	62	85
Sedan	149	115	264
SUV	33	73	106
Grand Total	**205**	**250**	**455**

Figure 16-13. Dragging the Field names into the areas on the bottom right is the first step in the construction of the PivotTable.

We would like to see the average age and the Pivot Table shows the Sum of Age. So we click on the small triangle to the right of Sum of Age in the values area of the PivotTable Field List pane

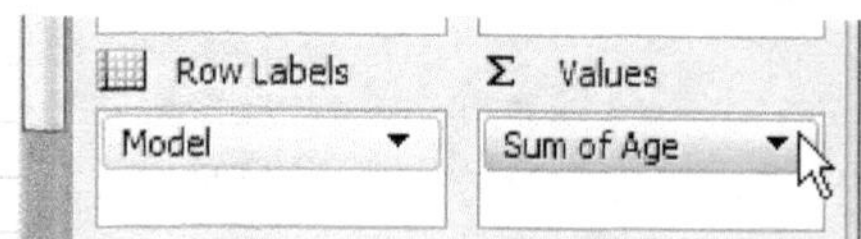

and then on Value Field Settings in the resulting menu. That yields the Vale Field Settings window in Figure 16-14.

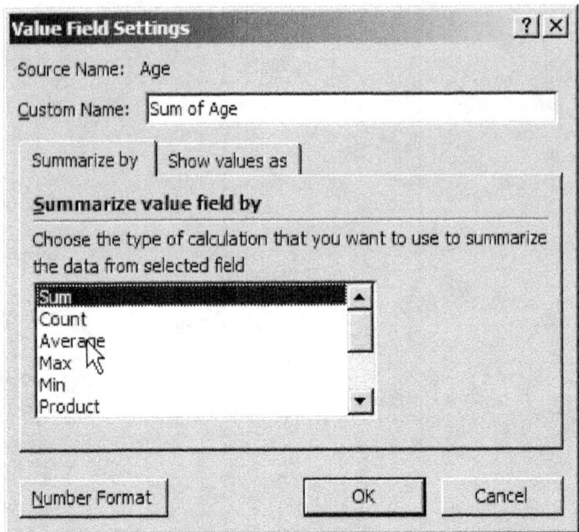

Figure 16-14. Changing what is calculated in the PivotTable.

We click on Average in the window. We click on Number Format and select Number with 1 decimal place. We click on one of the cells outside the PivotTable and the pane vanishes. We resize the columns and window and change some of the formatting and text and the result is shown in Figure 16-15.

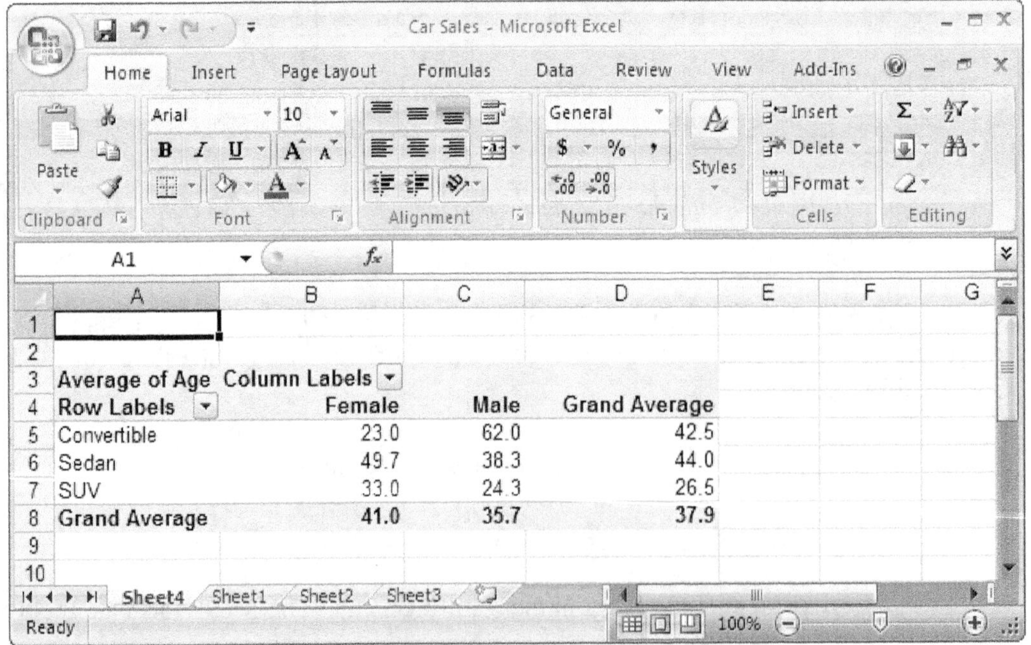

Figure 16-15. The PivotTable provides a very useful summary of the data.

In the pivot table we see the data summarized for us just as we requested. This is a Model by Gender analysis. Each cell in the table indicates the average age of the purchasers. For example, B6 tells us that the average age of the females who purchased sedans is 49.7. Note that the cells in the pivot table contain numbers and not formulas. If any of the values are changed or if new rows are added, we must call up the PivotTable tool again to generate an updated PivotTable. However, we can **drill-in** to the data by double-clicking on one of the cells. For example, if we double-click on cell B6 we automatically get the table in new worksheet Sheet5 shown in Figure 16-16.

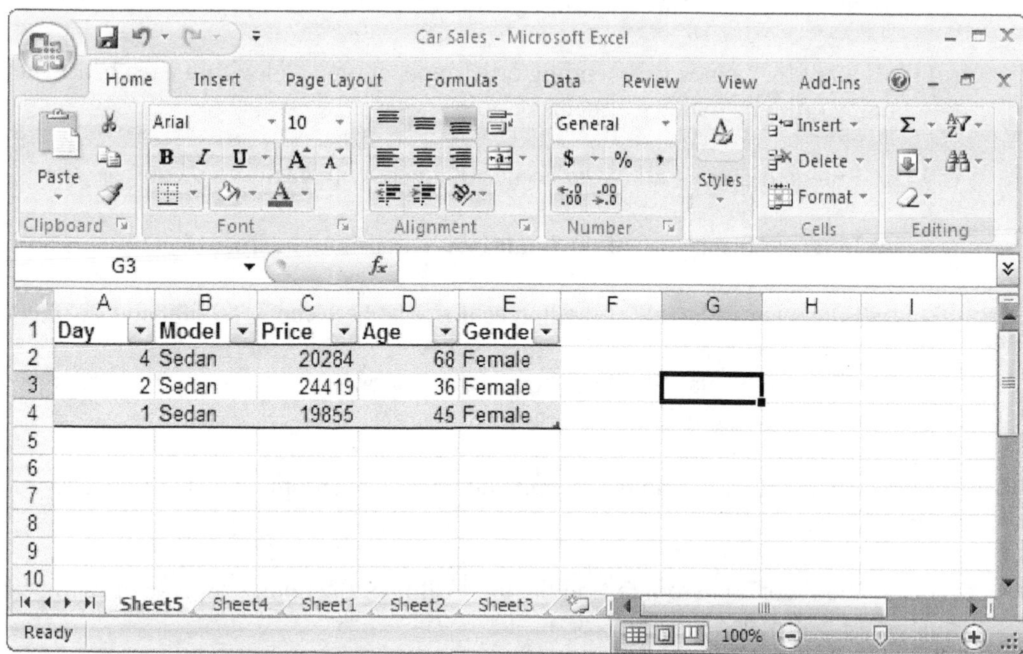

Figure 16-16. Double-clicking on cell B6 in the worksheet in the previous figure causes Excel to show the data that determine the cell.

With the PivotTable tool we could summarize the data in many different ways simply by dragging different fields over to the different locations in the Layout dialog box. In this example we have only 5 columns and 12 rows of data. We could have 50 columns and 120,000 rows of data to summarize.

In this case we might want a more detailed analysis. For example, we might want to be able to separate out the analysis by days. We could drag the Day field over to the Report Filter area. This would enable us to create PivotTables to analyze the data for all the days together or for each day separately.

COMPUTER EXERCISES

16-1. Enter the real estate worksheet in Figure 1-3 (in Chapter 1).

(a) Change the range of the data into a table.

For each of the following begin with the original table from (a).

(b) Sort all of the homes in descending order by price.

(c) Sort all of the homes in ascending order by heat type and within each heat type in descending order by number of bedrooms.

(d) Use Filters to display all of the homes that heat with gas.

(e) Use Filters to display all of the homes with 4 or more bedrooms.

(f) Use Filters to display all of the homes that cost between $150,000 and $250,000.

(g) Use Filters to display all of the homes that are on a lot of at least 0.75 acres, heat with oil, and cost under $300,000.

(h) Use a Total Row to find the average number of bedrooms, lot size, age, and price of homes for sale.

(i) Use the PivotTable tool to find the total value of the homes for sale of each heat type and number of bedrooms.

(j) Use the PivotTable tool to find the average value of the homes for sale of each heat type and number of bedrooms.

(k) Use the PivotTable tool to find the average age of the homes for sale of each heat type and number of baths.

(l) Double-click on one of the entries in the PivotTable in (k) to see the underlying data.

16-2. Susan is a consultant with three different clients: Allied Electronics (AE), Dynamic Solutions (DS), and International Networks (IN). She bills her clients by the hour. She is very busy and tends to switch her attention from one client to another throughout the day. Her principal activities are talking on the phone, having meetings, and working on her computer. In order to be sure that each client is billed fairly, she constantly keeps Excel open on her computer and quickly makes an entry for each period of time she spends as shown:

Client	Minutes	Activity
DS	10	phone
IN	27	computer
DS	8	phone
DS	42	meeting
AE	12	phone
...		

(a) Enter the preceding information into a worksheet. Make it into a Table.

(b) Make 20 more entries into the Table.

(c) Use a Filter to display only the meetings.

(d) Use Filters to display all the phone calls for AE that exceeded 5 minutes.

(e) Display all of the entries sorted by activity and within each activity sorted by time.

(f) Display all of the entries sorted by client and within each client by activity and within each activity by time.

(g) Use the Total Row to display the total amount of time spent on client IN.

(h) Find the average amount of time of a telephone call.

(i) Use the PivotTable tool to display a summary of the total amount of time spent on each activity for each client.

(j) Double-click on one of the entries in the PivotTable in (i) to see the underlying data.

16-3. Create a Table of use to you. Some suggestions for topics: (i) companies in an industry, (ii) summer job prospects, (iii) classmates or professors or roommates or people from high school, (iv) books or video games or music or movies, or (v) people you meet.

(a) Design the system. Decide what information to include. Be sure to include at least five fields (columns) total, including at least two numeric fields.

(b) Enter at least ten rows. Make it a table.

(c) Sort the data on one of the columns.

(d) Change the information in two of the rows.

(e) Add four new rows.

(f) Sort the rows on a different column.

(g) Use a Total Row to display averages or totals for the numeric fields.

(h) Use a Filter to display only some of the records.

(i) Display all of the records.

(j) Use a Filter to display a different set of records.

(k) Display all of the records again.

(l) Use the PivotTable tool to create a pivot table. This will work best with fields with limited entries.

(m) Double-click on one of the entries in the PivotTable to see the underlying data.

CHAPTER 17

ANALYZING DATA USING THE ANALYSIS TOOLPAK

OBJECTIVES

In this chapter you will learn how to:

- Use add-ins
- Access the Analysis ToolPak
- Obtain descriptive statistics on data
- Create histograms of data
- Calculate correlations
- Perform t-tests on data
- Calculate linear regressions

People use Excel to solve a wide variety of problems. One of the most popular applications of Excel is to analyze data. The **Analysis ToolPak** provides additional capabilities for analyzing data.

The Analysis ToolPak is an **add-in** program. An add-in program is a program you can add to Excel to increase its capabilities. Microsoft includes the Analysis ToolPak with your purchase of Excel.

GETTING ACCESS TO THE ANALYSIS TOOLPAK

Possibly the Analysis ToolPak already has been added into Excel on the computer you are using. To determine if this is the case, look in the Data Tab. If there is an Analysis group with a Data Analysis command (look ahead to Figure 17-3), then the Analysis ToolPak has been added and you're all set. You can skip the rest of this section.

If Data Analysis... is not present, then the Analysis ToolPak needs to be added in to Excel. Click the Office icon button and then click on the Excel Options button at the bottom of the Office menu. Click on Add-Ins on the left side. You should see a screen like the one in Figure 17-1.

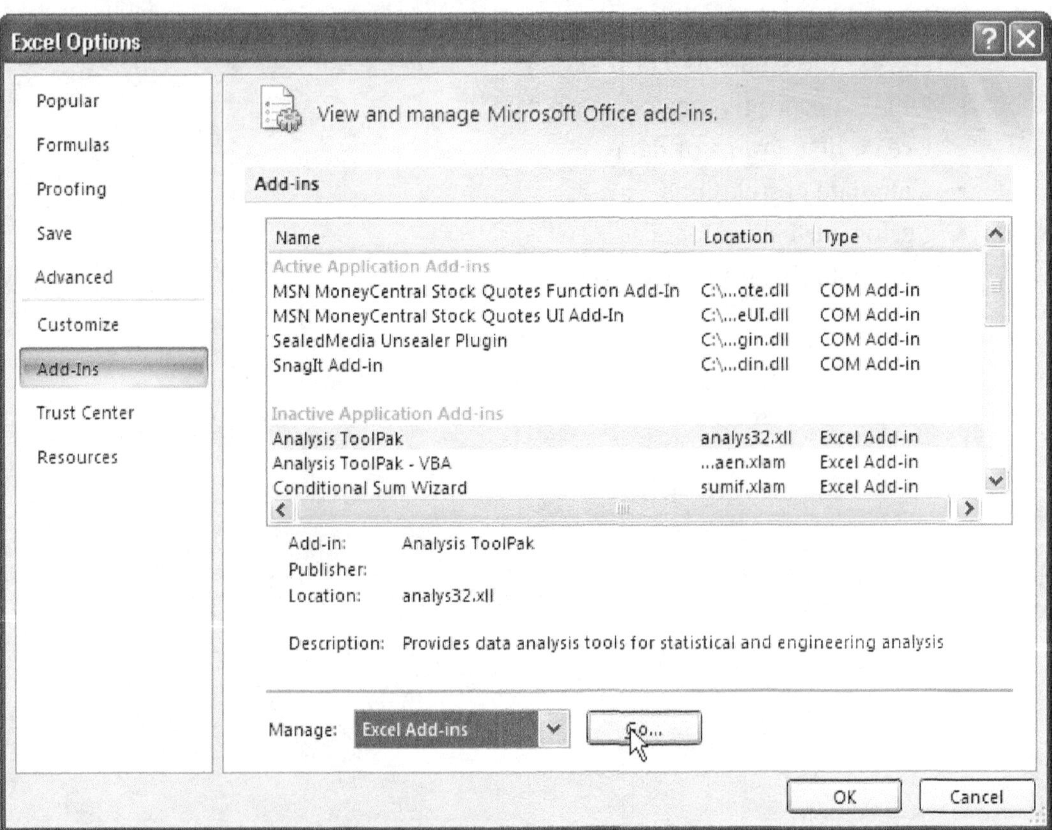

Figure 17-1. Adding in the Analysis ToolPak.

With Excel Add-Ins selected in the Manage box, click on the Go button. You should see the Add-Ins window. Click on the box next to Analysis ToolPak, as in Figure 17-2, and click on OK. (Note: Be sure to use the version titled Analysis ToolPak rather than Analysis ToolPak - VBA. This latter version adds capabilities to Visual Basic in Excel.) With perhaps another click on Yes, the Analysis ToolPak should be installed and added to Excel.

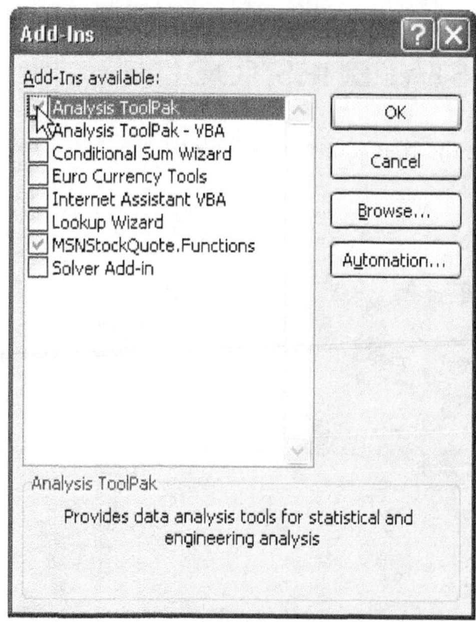

Figure 17-2. Adding in the Analysis ToolPak.

If you have been successful you can see the Data Analysis selection in the Analysis group of the Data tab, as in Figure 17-3.

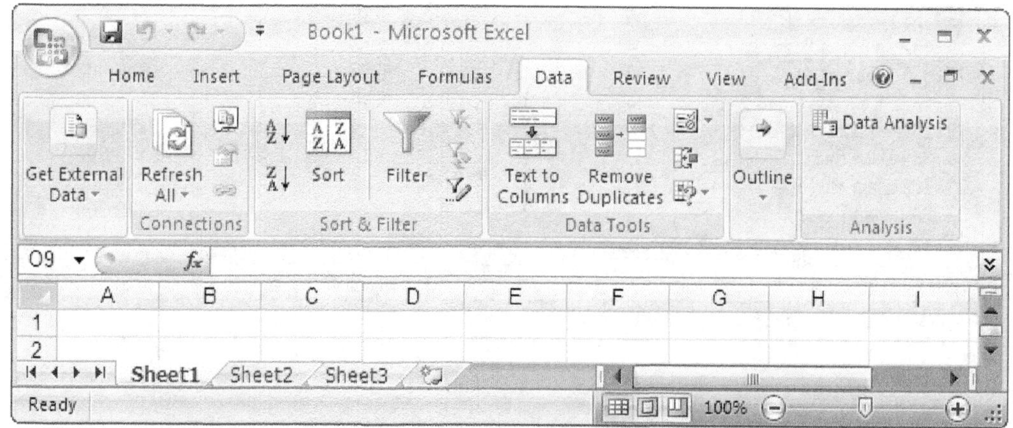

Figure 17-3. Happiness is the Data Analysis selection appearing in an Analysis group of the Data tab.

WHAT IS IN THE ANALYSIS TOOLPAK?

The Analysis ToolPak adds 19 statistics tools to Excel. These are not traditional functions, but rather tools that analyze data in a worksheet and produce a table of output based on the analysis. These tools are very useful in solving statistical problems.

THE DESCRIPTIVE STATISTICS TOOL

Consider again the real estate worksheet in Figure 17-4.

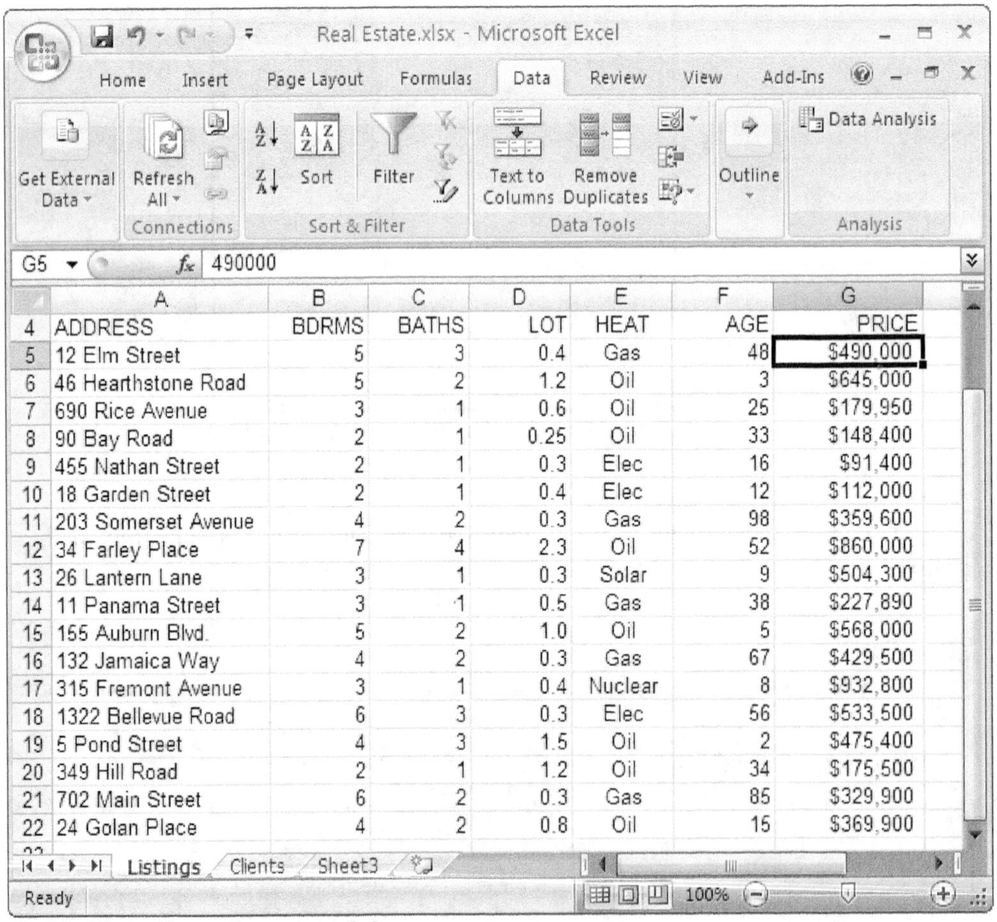

	A	B	C	D	E	F	G
4	ADDRESS	BDRMS	BATHS	LOT	HEAT	AGE	PRICE
5	12 Elm Street	5	3	0.4	Gas	48	$490,000
6	46 Hearthstone Road	5	2	1.2	Oil	3	$645,000
7	690 Rice Avenue	3	1	0.6	Oil	25	$179,950
8	90 Bay Road	2	1	0.25	Oil	33	$148,400
9	455 Nathan Street	2	1	0.3	Elec	16	$91,400
10	18 Garden Street	2	1	0.4	Elec	12	$112,000
11	203 Somerset Avenue	4	2	0.3	Gas	98	$359,600
12	34 Farley Place	7	4	2.3	Oil	52	$860,000
13	26 Lantern Lane	3	1	0.3	Solar	9	$504,300
14	11 Panama Street	3	1	0.5	Gas	38	$227,890
15	155 Auburn Blvd.	5	2	1.0	Oil	5	$568,000
16	132 Jamaica Way	4	2	0.3	Gas	67	$429,500
17	315 Fremont Avenue	3	1	0.4	Nuclear	8	$932,800
18	1322 Bellevue Road	6	3	0.3	Elec	56	$533,500
19	5 Pond Street	4	3	1.5	Oil	2	$475,400
20	349 Hill Road	2	1	1.2	Oil	34	$175,500
21	702 Main Street	6	2	0.3	Gas	85	$329,900
22	24 Golan Place	4	2	0.8	Oil	15	$369,900

Figure 17-4. The real estate worksheet.

This worksheet lists the homes for sale in a certain town. We are interested in calculating various statistics about the ages and prices of the homes. What is the average age? The standard deviation of the prices? We could calculate each of the statistics in a separate cell by including the appropriate formula. Or, we can use the **Descriptive Statistics**

tool in the Analysis ToolPak. We click on Data Analysis in the Analysis group of the Data tab. Then we select Descriptive Statistics, as in Figure 17-5, and click on OK.

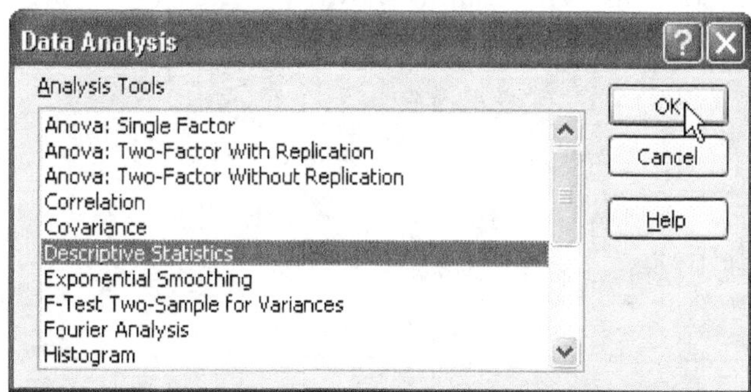

Figure 17-5. Select Descriptive Statistics in the Data Analysis dialog box.

Excel displays the Descriptive Statistics dialog box (Figure 17-6). We click in the Input Range box and drag across F4:G22 to specify the location of the variables for which we wish to calculate descriptive statistics. We select Columns because the data are organized one variable per column. We notify Excel that the first row in the input range contains descriptive labels that can be used as the names of the variables. We inform Excel that we would like the output of the Descriptive Statistics tool to be placed in a new ply (worksheet). Alternatively we could have the output placed somewhere in this worksheet or in a new workbook. It is important to check off the Summary Statistics box of the Descriptive Statistics dialog box so that Excel will calculate the full set of statistics.

Descriptive Statistics
Input
Input Range: $F$4:$G$22
Grouped By: Columns / Rows
Labels in First Row
Output options
Output Range:
New Worksheet Ply:
New Workbook
Summary statistics
Confidence Level for Mean: 95 %
Kth Largest: 1
Kth Smallest: 1
OK
Cancel
Help

Figure 17-6. The Descriptive Statistics dialog box.

When we click on OK, the computer goes to work and calculates the descriptive statistics for the two columns. The results are placed beginning in A1 in a new worksheet. We widen the columns. The result is shown in Figure 17-7.

Real Estate.xlsx - Microsoft Excel

D7 f_x 242710.273104762

	A	B	C	D
1	AGE		PRICE	
2				
3	Mean	33.66666667	Mean	412946.6667
4	Standard Error	6.807819418	Standard Error	57207.35999
5	Median	29	Median	399700
6	Mode	#N/A	Mode	#N/A
7	Standard Deviation	28.88313165	Standard Deviation	242710.2731
8	Sample Variance	834.2352941	Sample Variance	58908276671
9	Kurtosis	-0.056177025	Kurtosis	-0.039105744
10	Skewness	0.878819995	Skewness	0.634496268
11	Range	96	Range	841400
12	Minimum	2	Minimum	91400
13	Maximum	98	Maximum	932800
14	Sum	606	Sum	7433040
15	Count	18	Count	18
16				

Figure 17-7. Descriptive statistics for Age and Price.

We see that the mean age of the homes for sale is 33.67 and that the median age is 29. The standard deviation of the price is $242,710.

There are two important points. First, the computer doesn't care whether or not the statistics are meaningful in this situation. It just follows its program and produces the output. It is up to you, the intelligent and knowledgeable user, to decide how to interpret the calculations and whether they make any sense. Second, notice that the cells in the output area do not contain formulas. They simply contain values, as you can see with cell D7 in Figure 17-7. The Descriptive Statistics tool deposits the numbers there once, when it is called. If you change the original data, the statistics are *not* recalculated automatically. Each time you want the statistics to be recalculated you must invoke the Descriptive Statistics tool all over again. This is an important difference between using tools and using formulas in cells.

USING THE HISTOGRAM TOOL

The **Histogram tool** allows us to see the distribution of values in a variable. Suppose we would like to examine the distribution of the prices of the homes. First we enter in **bin ranges** in the worksheet. That is, we inform Excel of the break points for the ranges for the histogram. We would like to see how many houses cost under $100,000, how many cost between $100,000 and $200,000, and so on. We enter $0, $100,000, $200,000, ... into cells I6:I16. We click on Data Analysis in the Analysis group of the Data tab. We select Histogram (see Figure 17-5 again) and click OK. Excel displays the Histogram dialog box. We fill in G4:G22 for the Input Range for the Histogram tool and I6:I11 for the Bin Range, as in Figure 17-8.

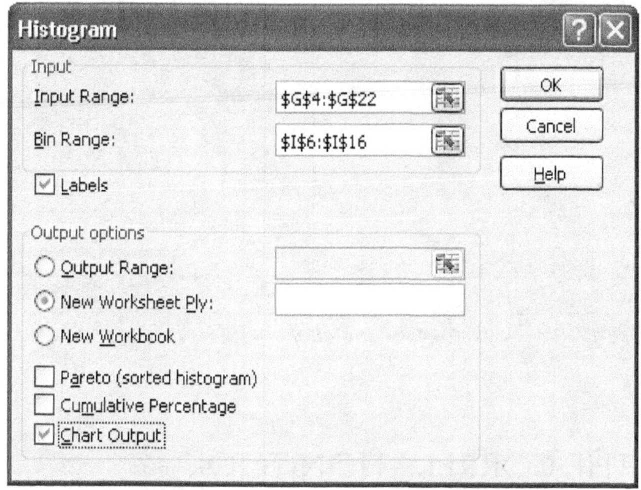

Figure 17-8. The dialog box for the Histogram tool.

In the Histogram dialog box we click on Labels because the top cell of the Input Range contains a label. We click on Chart Output at the bottom of the dialog box to request that the Histogram tool automatically chart the results.

Clicking on OK after filling in the entries, as shown in Figure 17-8, automatically produces a new worksheet with the histogram and a chart. We make the chart larger by dragging on the handle in the bottom right corner. The result is shown in Figure 17-9.

The histogram in Figure 17-9 is to be understood as saying there is 1 home with price under $100,000, 4 homes with prices between $100,000 and $200,000, 1 home with price between $200,000 and $300,000, and so on. The numbers in column A of the table and along the horizontal axis of the chart are the highest values of the bins. (The bins work the opposite of the lookup tables discussed in Chapter 12.) The chart is a regular Excel chart that floats above the worksheet. We can select the chart by clicking on it and then make changes in the chart, as discussed in Chapter 10. For example, we could change the wording of a title or the maximum value of the vertical axis.

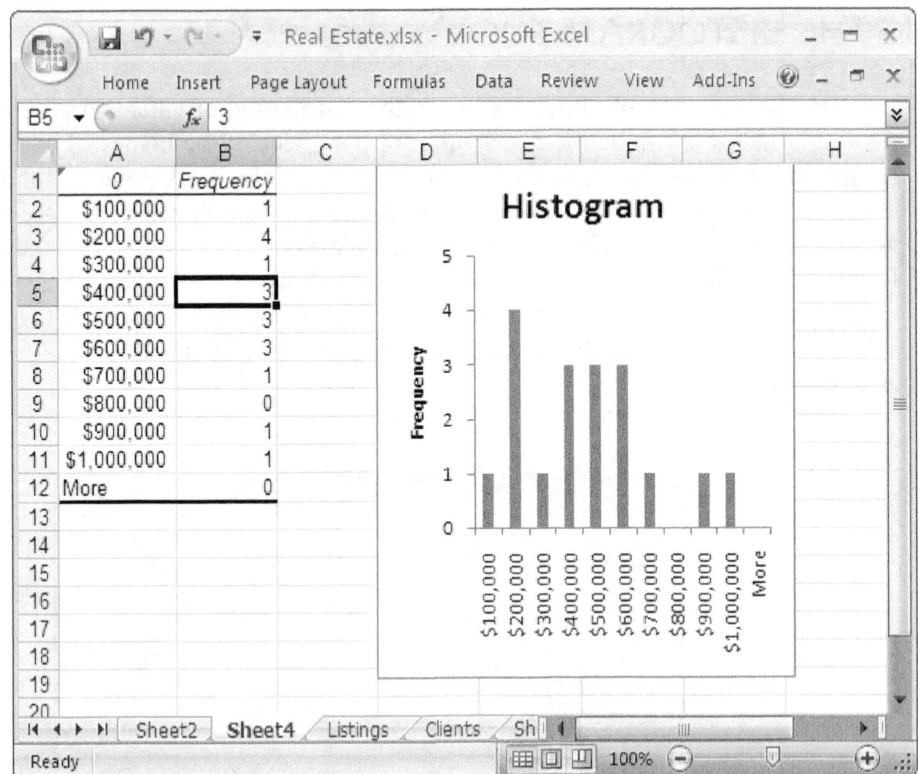

Figure 17-9. The histogram and chart of home prices produced by the Histogram tool.

USING THE CORRELATION TOOL

The tools we have examined so far have treated each variable, each column of data, separately. Suppose we are interested in understanding the interactions between the variables. For example, we might be curious as to how the variables correlate. Do homes with many bedrooms tend to be old? Do expensive homes tend to have large lots? The **Correlation tool** will help us answer these questions.

The Correlation tool, like most of the tools in the Analysis ToolPak, works only on numeric values. With the Correlation tool all of the data must be contiguous (next to each other). The Heat data in column E of the Real Estate worksheet consist of text rather than numbers. (See Figure 17-4 again.) Before we can use the Correlation tool we need to get the Heat data out of the way. So we select E4:E22 and then move it over to the blank column H by grabbing it at the top of the selected area and dragging it over. Now column E is blank. We select F4:H22 and drag it over to the left one column. The heating column now is in G4:G22 on the right of the data; all of the numeric values are contiguous in the range B4:F22.

In the Correlation tool dialog box in Figure 17-10 we specify that we want to correlate the five variables in columns B, C, D, E, and F. We request a new worksheet with the correlation outputs.

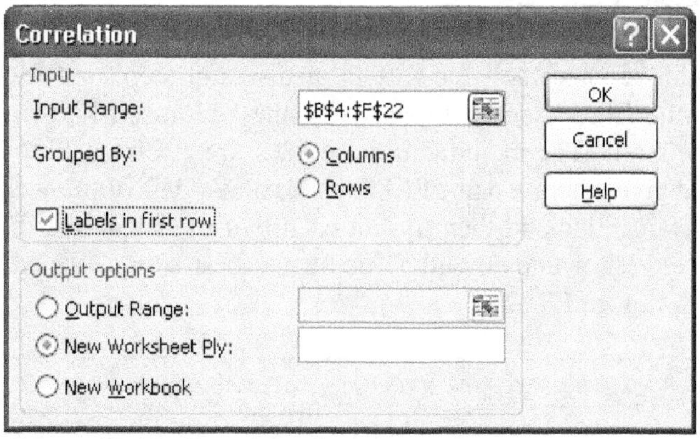

Correlation

Input

Input Range: $B$4:$F$22

Grouped By: Columns / Rows

Labels in first row

Output options

Output Range:

New Worksheet Ply:

New Workbook

OK · Cancel · Help

Figure 17-10. Specifying the correlations.

From the output of the Correlation tool in Figure 17-11 we can see that the number of bathrooms correlates very highly (0.86) with the number of bedrooms. The price of the home correlates highly with bedrooms, baths, and lot size, but not at all with the age of the home.

Notice, again, that the cells in the correlation matrix contain numbers rather than formulas. Changing the original data will not cause the correlation matrix values to be changed automatically. Rather, we would need to run the Correlation tool each time we change the data.

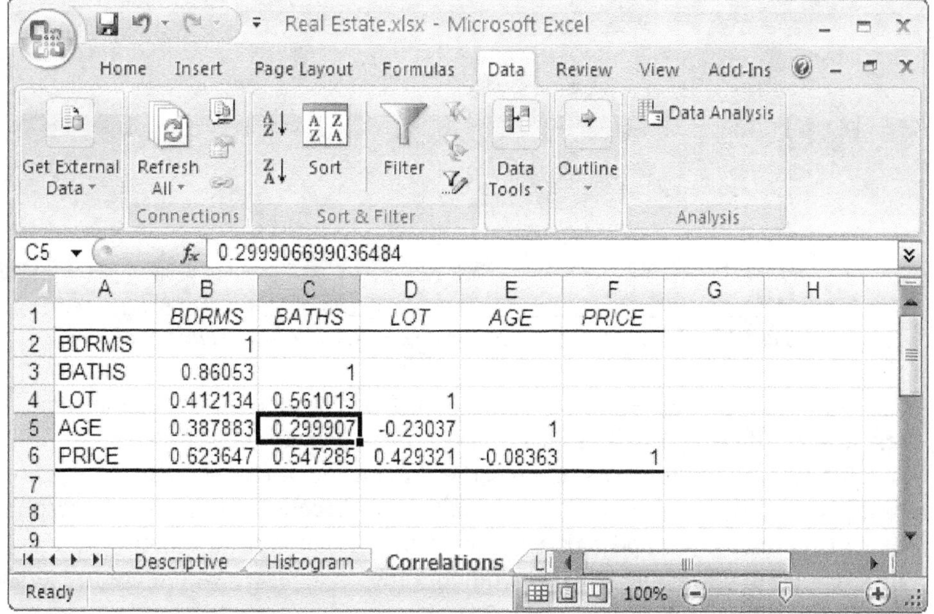

Figure 17-11. The correlations between the variables.

USING A t-TEST TOOL

Elite athletic shoes sell for $29.99 at discount stores. The manufacturer would like to know how the Elite shoes compare with the $119 well-known brand available at upscale stores at the mall. The manufacturer decides to perform a simple test. He recruits a dozen students and gives them a pair of Elite shoes and a pair of the well-known shoes in their size. The students examine and then try out each pair of shoes. He then asks each student to rate the shoes between 1 and 5, with 5 being the best score. These scores are recorded in the worksheet in Figure 17-12.

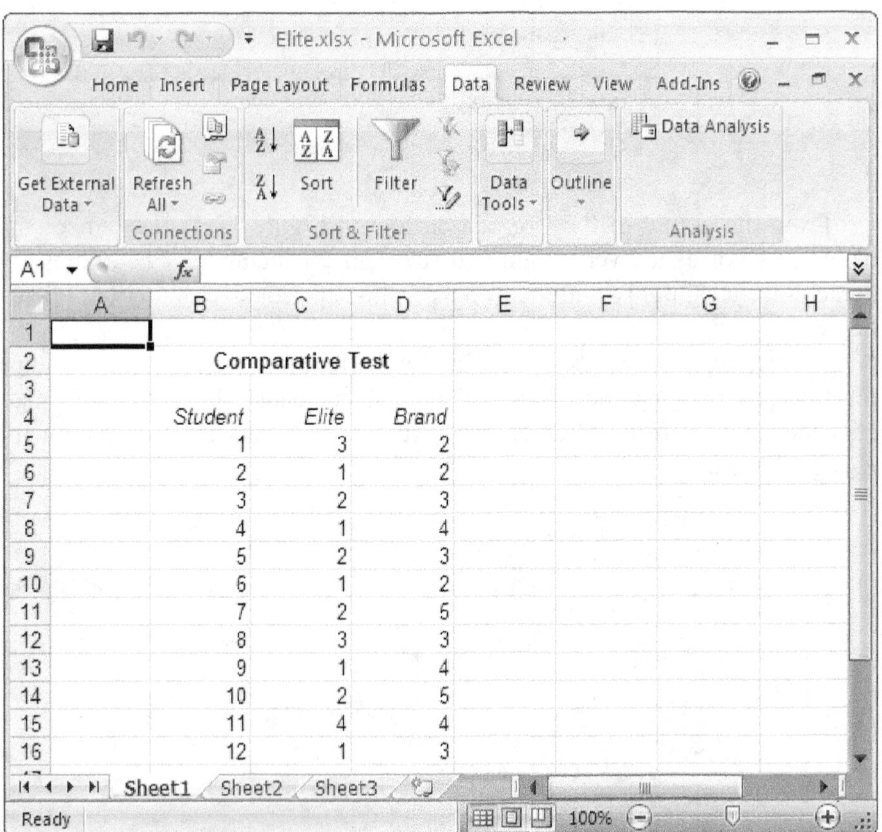

Comparative Test

Student	Elite	Brand
1	3	2
2	1	2
3	2	3
4	1	4
5	2	3
6	1	2
7	2	5
8	3	3
9	1	4
10	2	5
11	4	4
12	1	3

Figure 17-12. The raw data for the comparison of two brands of athletic shoes.

We would like to test the hypothesis that people rate the shoes the same. To do this we test to see if there is no difference between the means of the scores.

A **t-test** is used to determine whether the means of two sets of samples are equal. In this case we would use a paired two-sample t-test, because one person is responsible for each pair of scores. If we had a dozen people rating one type of athletic shoe and a completely different group of people rating the other brand of shoe, we would not use a paired test.

In the Data tab we select Data Analysis and then t-Test: Paired Two Sample for Means. We fill in the entries, as in Figure 17-13, dragging down the Variable 1 range and then the Variable 2 range.

t-Test: Paired Two Sample for Means

Input
Variable 1 Range: $C$4:$C$16
Variable 2 Range: $D$4:$D$16
Hypothesized Mean Difference:
Labels
Alpha: 0.05
Output options
Output Range:
New Worksheet Ply:
New Workbook
OK
Cancel
Help

Figure 17-13. Specifying the ranges for the t-test.

Clicking on OK yields a new worksheet with output produced by the t-Test: Paired Two Sample for Means tool, as shown in Figure 17-14. Examining this output, we see that the mean score for the Elite shoes is 1.9 whereas the mean for the well-known brand is 3.33.

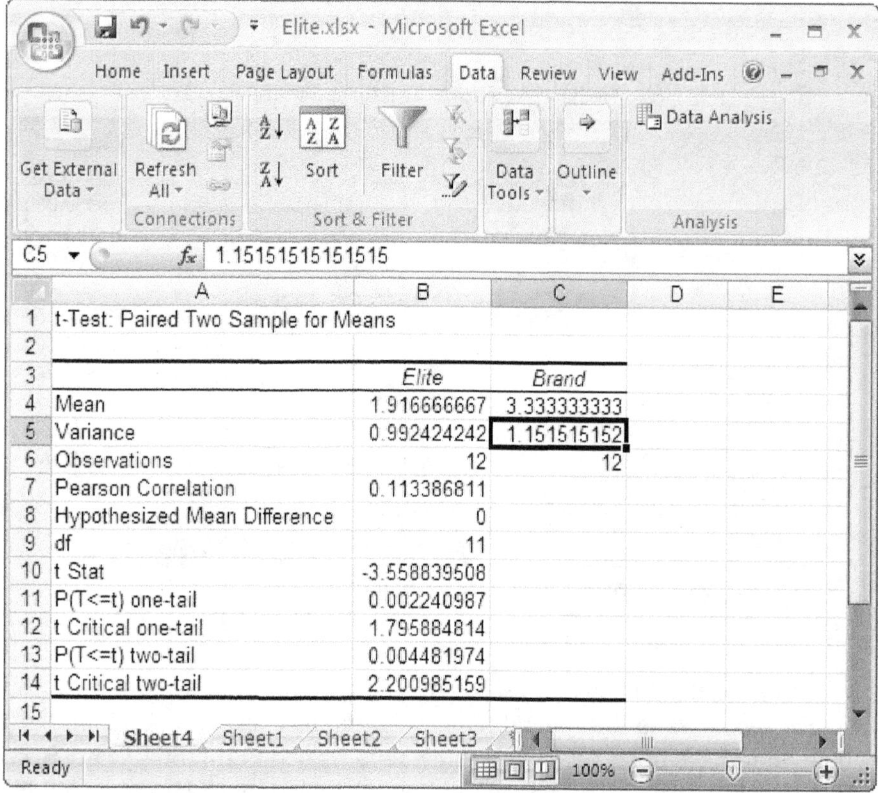

t-Test: Paired Two Sample for Means		
	Elite	*Brand*
Mean	1.916666667	3.333333333
Variance	0.992424242	1.151515152
Observations	12	12
Pearson Correlation	0.113386811	
Hypothesized Mean Difference	0	
df	11	
t Stat	-3.558839508	
P(T<=t) one-tail	0.002240987	
t Critical one-tail	1.795884814	
P(T<=t) two-tail	0.004481974	
t Critical two-tail	2.200985159	

Figure 17-14. The t-test result.

We asked only a dozen people. Is this difference in the mean statistically significant? Because we had no hypothesis before the study that one brand would score better than the other, it is appropriate to use a "two-tail" test.

We see in cell B14 of the worksheet in Figure 17-14 that the critical value of t for a two-tail test with this number of degrees of freedom is 2.20. The value of t calculated for these scores is 3.56, which is greater than 2.20. Thus, the difference between the two sets of scores is significant at the 5% level. If these scores were drawn randomly from populations having the same means, means as different as these would occur less than 5% of the time by chance. Looking at cell B13 we see that, indeed, if these scores were drawn randomly from populations having the same means, means as different as these would occur less than 0.45% of the time by chance or less than one out of 200 times. We reject the hypothesis that the Elite athletic shoes will score the same as the well-known brand. The students do not give equal scores to the two brands. This is bad news for the manufacturer of Elite.

USING THE REGRESSION TOOL

New Hires.xlsx - Microsoft Excel

Tracking New Hires at International Financial

	GPA	Sports	Summer	Interview	First Year Sales
1	2.7	3	$0	2	$100,000
2	3.6	0	$1,500	5	$30,000
3	2.4	5	$8,500	7	$9,800,000
4	3.6	1	$2,000	3	$200,000
5	2.6	7	$6,300	9	$7,450,000
6	3.2	0	$3,100	6	$1,300,000
7	3.7	0	$0	5	$65,000
8	2.9	0	$1,000	7	$300,000
9	3.0	1	$4,000	2	$2,604,000
10	3.3	0	$2,900	6	$80,000

Figure 17-15. Recent hires at International Financial.

International Financial hires recent college graduates to work on commission selling financial securities to the general public. Hiring has been a hit-and-miss affair. Some of the people hired have done very well; some have fizzled in the first year. Bringing new people on board is expensive. The VP of Sales and the Director of Hiring would like to get a handle on who succeeds and who does not. They would like to find out what factors, if any, they could use in predicting how well a person would do as a new hire. They brainstorm. They decide they like to hire athletes and students who are go-getters and report that they've made a lot of money during the previous summer. They come up with four measures that might predict how well a person would do in the sales position: grade point average (GPA) in college, the number of sports teams a person played on in college, the amount of money the person earned in the previous summer, and how well the person did in the job interview (a number between 1 and 10, where 10 is the best, given by the interviewer). Last year they hired ten new people. They decide to list each of these measures for each person as well as the person's total sales in the year. These data are given in the worksheet in Figure 17-15.

The **Regression tool** performs linear regression analysis. That is, it fits a line through a set of measures using the least squares method. Regression calculates an equation for predicting the sales performance of an employee based on the four measures given.

We call up the Regression tool by clicking on Data Analysis in the Data tab and then selecting Regression from the list of Tools available. In the Regression dialog box we fill in the location of the Sales data for the Input Y Range and the four measures for the Input X Range. (See Figure 17-16.) The ranges either can be typed in or you can click in the box for a range in the dialog box and then drag across the appropriate cells in the worksheet. The dialog box temporarily rolls up like a window shade to get out of the way and then unrolls when you are finished.

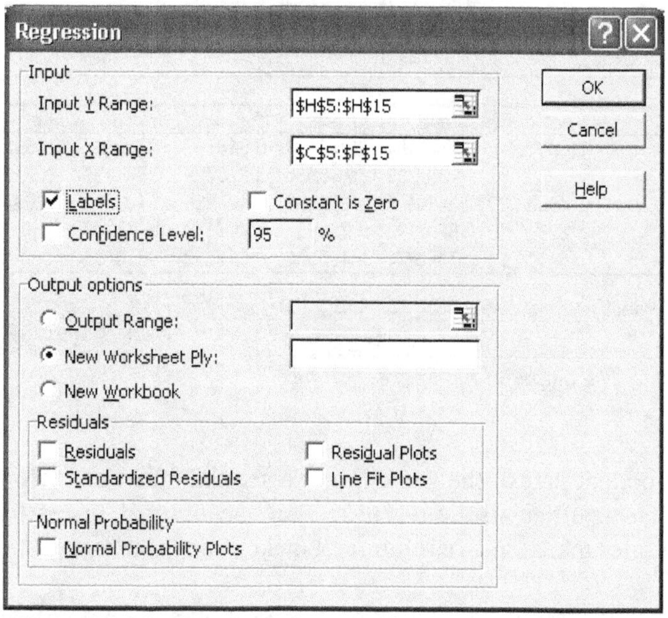

Figure 17-16. Specifying the variables for regression analysis.

Clicking on OK yields the output in Figure 17-17. There is a lot of information here. Starting at the top, in cell B4 we see that the multiple correlation coefficient R is 0.976, which is quite high. The value of R Square is 0.953 so the four factors account for more than 95% of the variance. The Y values are sales that are in the hundreds of thousands or millions, so the sums of squares in the analysis of variance table in C12:D14 are large numbers. Because the columns are narrow and the values are large, the numbers are displayed rounded off in **E format**. The "E" stands for "exponent" or power of 10. The number 2.67E+13 in D12 is 2.67 * 10^13 or 2.67 * 10000000000000. The exact value in D12 is 26716835260031.4, which is displayed in the formula bar in Figure 17-17.

New Hires.xlsx - Microsoft Excel

Home Insert Page Layout Formulas Data Review View Add-Ins

D12 fx 26716835260031.4

	A	B	C	D	E	F	G	H	I
1	SUMMARY OUTPUT								
2									
3	*Regression Statistics*								
4	Multiple R	0.976483							
5	R Square	0.953519							
6	Adjusted R Squ	0.916335							
7	Standard Error	1020725							
8	Observations	10							
9									
10	ANOVA								
11		*df*	*SS*	*MS*	*F*	*gnificance F*			
12	Regression	4	1.07E+14	2.67E+13	25.64293	0.001576			
13	Residual	5	5.21E+12	1.04E+12					
14	Total	9	1.12E+14						
15									
16		*Coefficient*	*standard Err*	*t Stat*	*P-value*	*Lower 95%*	*Upper 95%*	*ower 95.0%*	*pper 95.0%*
17	Intercept	168836.8	4077834	0.041404	0.968577	-1E+07	10651243	-1E+07	10651243
18	GPA	-522052	1188208	-0.43936	0.678739	-3576437	2532333	-3576437	2532333
19	Sports	460333.2	234609.1	1.962129	0.106996	-142749	1063415	-142749	1063415
20	Summer	825.7325	188.6696	4.376607	0.007177	340.7419	1310.723	340.7419	1310.723
21	Interview	84704.21	171686.4	0.493366	0.642658	-356630	526038.1	-356630	526038.1
22									

Sheet1 Data Sheet2 Sheet3

Ready 100%

Figure 17-17. The output of the Regression tool.

In the bottom part of the worksheet we see the effect of each of the four measures. We see from the coefficients in B17:B21 that the optimal linear formula for predicting the amount of sales that a first-year hire will make is approximately

= -522052*GPA + 460333*Sports + 825*Summer + 84704*Interview + 168836

Notice that the GPA has a negative coefficient. A recruit's Grade Point Average is associated negatively with sales. That is, the lower the GPA, the higher the sales! For each additional Sport that the person played, the formula predicts an additional $460,333 in First Year Sales. Each dollar the person made over the summer results in a predicted additional $825 in First Year Sales. Each point on the Interview is predicted to be worth an additional $84,704 in First Year Sales.

When we go back and plug the linear equation into column J, we can see what the predictions would be for the existing hires. (See Figure 17-18.) Even though according to our calculations we have done extremely well in predicting the first-year sales, there is plenty of error made in the predictions. Still, the formula comes close on the big winners among the salespeople, which probably is what we are most concerned about. We'd like more $8,000,000 sellers. According to the formula, some of the recent hires are predicted to have negative sales. No one actually can have negative sales, but these folks had very low actual first year sales and might do better in other jobs.

Once we have the equation, we use it in Figure 17-18 to predict the sales of new candidates. Candidate A has very low grades, played lots of sports, earned a lot of money last summer, and did very well on the interview. Candidate A is predicted to be a great salesperson. Candidate B was a straight-A student, played no sports, made no money last summer, and did not do very well in the interview. According to our regression model, all four factors are the kiss of death. Candidate C is a middling prospect.

New Hires.xlsx - Microsoft Excel

Home Insert Page Layout Formulas Data Review View Add-Ins

J11 f_x = -522052*C11 + 460333*D11 + 825*E11 + 84704*F11 + 168836

Tracking New Hires at International Financial

	GPA	Sports	Summer	Interview	First Year Sales	Predicted Sales
1	2.7	3	$0	2	$100,000	$309,703
2	3.6	0	$1,500	5	$30,000	($49,531)
3	2.4	5	$8,500	7	$9,800,000	$8,823,004
4	3.6	1	$2,000	3	$200,000	$653,894
5	2.6	7	$6,300	9	$7,450,000	$7,993,668
6	3.2	0	$3,100	6	$1,300,000	$1,563,994
7	3.7	0	$0	5	$65,000	($1,339,236)
8	2.9	0	$1,000	7	$300,000	$72,813
9	3.0	1	$4,000	2	$2,604,000	$2,532,421
10	3.3	0	$2,900	6	$80,000	$1,346,788
A	1.8	6	$11,200	9		$11,993,476
B	4.0	0	$0	3		($1,665,260)
C	3.1	2	$3,600	5		$2,864,661
null	0.0	0	$0	0		$168,836

Regression Data Sheet2 Sheet3

Ready 100%

Figure 17-18. Using the regression equation to predict the sales of three new candidates.

Also listed is "null". Notice from cell B17 in Figure 17-18 and from the prediction formula that the intercept is 168836. That is, if all of the four measures are 0, the candidate is predicted to have first-year sales of $168,836. If you wish, you can force the intercept to 0 by clicking on the Constant is 0 box in the Regression dialog box. Of course, this would result in different values for the four variable coefficients.

PAPER AND PENCIL EXERCISE

17-1. How might you go about investigating each of the following situations? For each situation you should: (1) describe your general approach, (2) describe the exact data collection method you would use, (3) design an Excel workbook for analyzing the data, (4) tell exactly which tool(s) or functions you would use in your workbook, and (5) specify exactly which results, which cells, you would look at and exactly how they would help you in your analysis of the situation.

(a) An automobile manufacturer would like to know which of five different shades of red paint customers would prefer on next year's model XLT convertible.

(b) A psychologist would like to know whether there is any difference in the mathematical ability of people who are left-handed versus people who are right-handed.

(c) A golf magazine would like to investigate the claim of a small manufacturer that its golf ball goes 25 yards farther than does a certain well-known golf ball.

(d) A producer of a popular TV series would like to know whether the viewers want a newly introduced character to be continued on the show or discontinued.

(e) A college admissions office would like to know whether it can predict a student's future success in its college given the information provided by each applicant.

(f) The Orange Growers' Association would like to know whether regularly drinking orange juice helps prevent people from getting colds.

(g) A finance company would like to automate the process of deciding which automobile loan applications it should approve. The finance company has access to all applications to the company for automobile loans over the past 10 years and the performance record of the loans it approved.

COMPUTER EXERCISES

17-2. A basketball coach has heard about visualization and decides it might be just what the team needs to improve its foul shooting. The idea is that in the moment before you take a foul shot you picture in your mind your successfully taking the shot and then the ball going through the hoop. Swish. Visualize success and it will be yours. To test out the idea he has the eleven members of his team shoot 20 foul shots each. Then he spends an hour describing visualization and having his team members try it. The next day at the beginning of practice he reminds them about the visualization technique and has each team member take 20 foul shots. Here are the results.

Player:	A	B	C	D	E	F	G	H	I	J	K
Day 1:	15	12	18	8	9	15	9	15	12	10	16
Day 2:	15	14	17	10	10	15	12	14	15	13	17

Summarize the data. Compare the performances without visualizing on day 1 and with visualizing on day 2. Was there an improvement? Was the improvement statistically significant? What do you conclude?

17-3. The Cranston Apperception Test was administered to 24 students majoring in Computers and 24 students majoring in English. The results were as follows:

Computer Majors
25 27 20 17 17 33 27 23 29 23 26 20 29 14 32 30 26 21 20 26 24 26 32 12

English Majors
21 29 16 7 26 23 21 18 28 18 17 29 31 25 20 32 14 32 26 24 27 23 23 17

(a) Generate descriptive statistics for both sets of data.

(b) Determine if there is any statistically significant difference in the means of the scores of the two groups at the 5% level.

17-4. A beverage company is considering a new fruit drink. To learn whether people like the drink they set up a booth at the mall. If you are willing to tell them your age and annual income, they will give you a free 8-ounce cup of the drink, which you are then asked to rate on a scale from 1 (awful) to 10 (nectar of the gods, best stuff I ever drank). You must be at least 18 years old to participate.

Here are the data they collect. The annual income is in thousands of dollars.

Person		A	B	C	D	E	F	G	H	I	J	K
Age	19	84	23	31	21	52	18	20	28	25	44	
Gender		M	M	F	M	F	M	F	F	M	M	F
Income		17	12	22	27	15	34	22	6	30	18	95
Rating		3	5	6	4	7	2	5	5	5	3	7

Person		L	M	N	O	P	Q	R	S	T	U	V
Age	33	20	73	18	25	19	22	24	32	36	68	
Gender		F	M	F	F	F	M	M	M	M	F	F
Income		57	19	31	15	32	13	23	26	30	55	28
Rating		9	6	5	6	6	4	5	3	4	8	5

Please enter the data into a worksheet (think about the best organization of the data). Apply the appropriate tools. What do you conclude about the new drink and to whom it appeals? Write up a professional report. Include appropriate worksheets and charts.

17-5. Consider again the real estate data in Figure 17-2. We are interested in constructing an equation to predict the price of a home based on the number of bedrooms, bathrooms, lot size, and age. Use the Regression tool to compute the coefficients of the equation. How good a fit is the equation? Enter the formula into the original worksheet and give the predicted prices for the existing homes. Now use the formula to set the prices of these homes that are about to come on the market:

15 Foxhall Road: 4 bedrooms, 2 baths, 0.6 acres, 15 years old
395 Washington Street: 3 bedrooms, 2 baths, 0.25 acres, 60 years old
24 Columbia Lane: 5 bedrooms, 3 baths, 2.1 acres, 2 years old

Write up a report. Be sure to include the formula, its predictions, and how good a job it does. Indicate how you might include the heating type in the prediction.

17-6. This problem is a little more open-ended. Many people are interested in being able to predict the price of a stock a month from now given data that are publicly available today. Examples of information that might be used include revenues, profits, price per earnings ratios, stock prices, stock volume, industry trends, market trends, and so on. For this assignment you are to come up with a formula that predicts the price of a given stock a month from now using your choice of any data available today. Try your formula by predicting historical results. Write up a report on your findings. If your formula is successful, please email your report, with your formula, to james.gips@bc.edu.

CHAPTER 18

SOLVER

OBJECTIVES

In this chapter you will learn how to:

- Use Solver tool to solve profit maximization problems
- Enter constraints into Solver
- Solve linear programming problems with Solver
- Solve transportation problems with Solver

SOLVER

In this final chapter we will be looking at some of the very powerful tools in **Solver** and how they can be used to help with many types of management problems. Solver is used for optimization and equation solving.

Solver is an add-in. As discussed at the beginning of Chapter 17 for the Analysis ToolPak, an add-in is a specialized feature of Excel that, because not everyone might want to use it and it takes up valuable space, is not automatically included when you run Excel on your computer. To see whether you have Solver ready to use, look in the Data tab and then at the right in the Analysis group. You should see Solver, perhaps below Data Analysis, as in Figure 18-1. If Solver is not present, select Excel Options at the bottom of the Office pull-down menu and then select Add-Ins and Go. Click on Solver Add-In and OK. For more information on installing Add-Ins, see the beginning of Chapter 17.

USING SOLVER TO MAXIMIZE PROFITS

As a first example, let's do a simple maximization problem. We decide to publish an "Uncensored Guide to Courses and Faculty" where students give their honest opinions about specific courses and faculty, including their recommendations (or warnings) to other students who are thinking about what courses to register for. We believe that if we gave the Guide away for free, we could give away 10,000 copies. For every $1.00 we charge for the Guide, we estimate that 1,000 fewer people will purchase it. So that if we charge $3.00 per copy, we figure we will sell 7,000 copies. If we charge $4.00 per copy, we figure we will sell 6,000 copies. We expect to have fixed expenses of $5,000 for manuscript preparation, delivery, promotion, and distribution. Each Guide will cost us $2.25 to print and bind. We would like to know the best price to charge for the Guide so we can make the most profit. We set up the worksheet in Figure 18-1 to help us.

Just for convenience, the formulas in the worksheet are included in text boxes to the right of the cells. We see that if we set the price at $4.00, we will sell 6,000 copies and end up with a profit of $5,500. Not bad. But we would like to find the price that will yield the maximum profits under these assumptions. We can't use Goal Seek because we don't have a particular profit we want to achieve. We just want to find the price that results in the highest profit. We could use trial and error, changing cell D4 until we maximize D17, but that would be tedious.

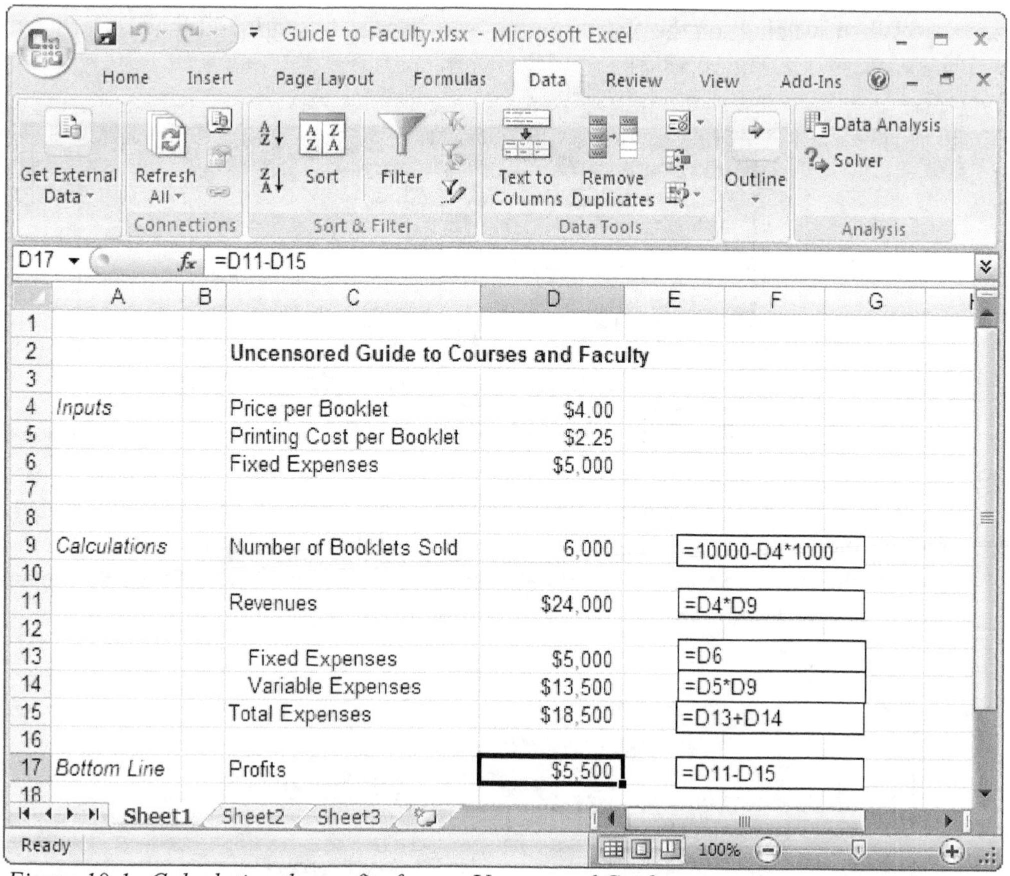

Guide to Faculty.xlsx - Microsoft Excel

D17 =D11-D15

	A	B	C	D	E	F
1						
2			**Uncensored Guide to Courses and Faculty**			
3						
4	*Inputs*		Price per Booklet	$4.00		
5			Printing Cost per Booklet	$2.25		
6			Fixed Expenses	$5,000		
7						
8						
9	*Calculations*		Number of Booklets Sold	6,000	=10000-D4*1000	
10						
11			Revenues	$24,000	=D4*D9	
12						
13			Fixed Expenses	$5,000	=D6	
14			Variable Expenses	$13,500	=D5*D9	
15			Total Expenses	$18,500	=D13+D14	
16						
17	*Bottom Line*		Profits	$5,500	=D11-D15	

Figure 18-1. Calculating the profits for our Uncensored Guide.

We click on Solver in the Analysis group of the Data tab. The Solver Parameters dialog box in Figure 18-2 is displayed. In the dialog box we specify that D17 is the Target cell and, on the next line, that we want to maximize the value in D17. We will allow Solver to change only D4.

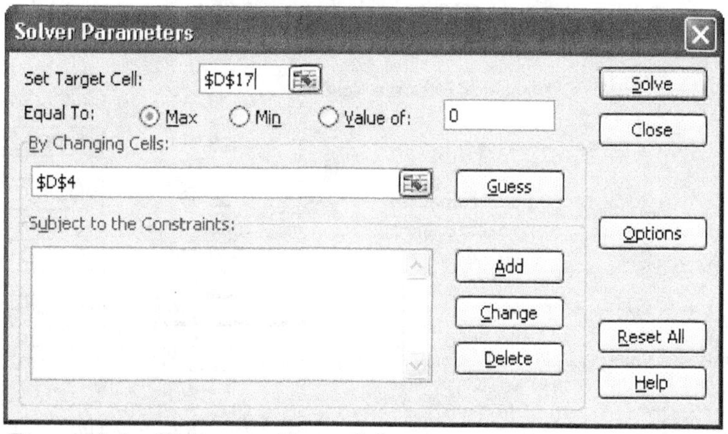

Solver Parameters
Set Target Cell: $D$17
Equal To: Max / Min / Value of: 0
By Changing Cells: $D$4
Subject to the Constraints:
Solve / Close / Guess / Options / Add / Change / Delete / Reset All / Help

Figure 18-2. Giving specifics to Solver.

When we click on the Solve button, Solver goes to work and in short order reports back its success (see Figure 18-3).

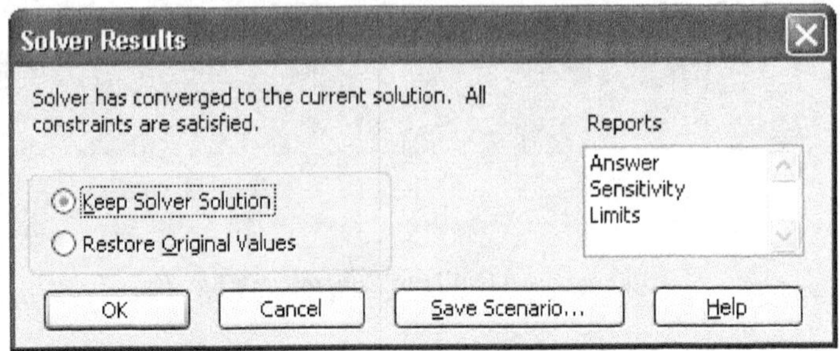

Figure 18-3. The results of using Solver.

Click on OK and we are returned to the original worksheet, but now cell D4 is changed so that the value in D17 is maximized. From Solver we learn that under these assumptions we should charge $6.12 per Guide and print up 3,875 copies. This will result in profits of $10,016. (See Figure 18-4.)

Guide to Faculty.xlsx - Microsoft Excel

D17 =D11-D15

	A	B	C	D	E	F
1						
2			**Uncensored Guide to Courses and Faculty**			
3						
4	*Inputs*		Price per Booklet	$6.12		
5			Printing Cost per Booklet	$2.25		
6			Fixed Expenses	$5,000		
7						
8						
9	*Calculations*		Number of Booklets Sold	3,875		=10000-D4*1000
10						
11			Revenues	$23,734		=D4*D9
12						
13			Fixed Expenses	$5,000		=D6
14			Variable Expenses	$8,719		=D5*D9
15			Total Expenses	$13,719		=D13+D14
16						
17	*Bottom Line*		Profits	$10,016		=D11-D15

Figure 18-4. Using Solver to adjust the Price per Booklet to maximize Profits.

USING SOLVER FOR A LINEAR PROGRAMMING PROBLEM

In our small manufacturing company we make grommits and widgets. Each grommit requires 4 hours of metal work and 2 hours of electrical work. Each widget requires 3 hours of metal work and 1 hour of electrical work. For each grommit we make we earn $70 of profit. For each widget we make we earn $50 of profit. Each week, given our employees and equipment, we have 240 hours of metal work available and 100 hours of electrical work. The question is, how many grommits and how many widgets should we make per week in order to maximize our profit?

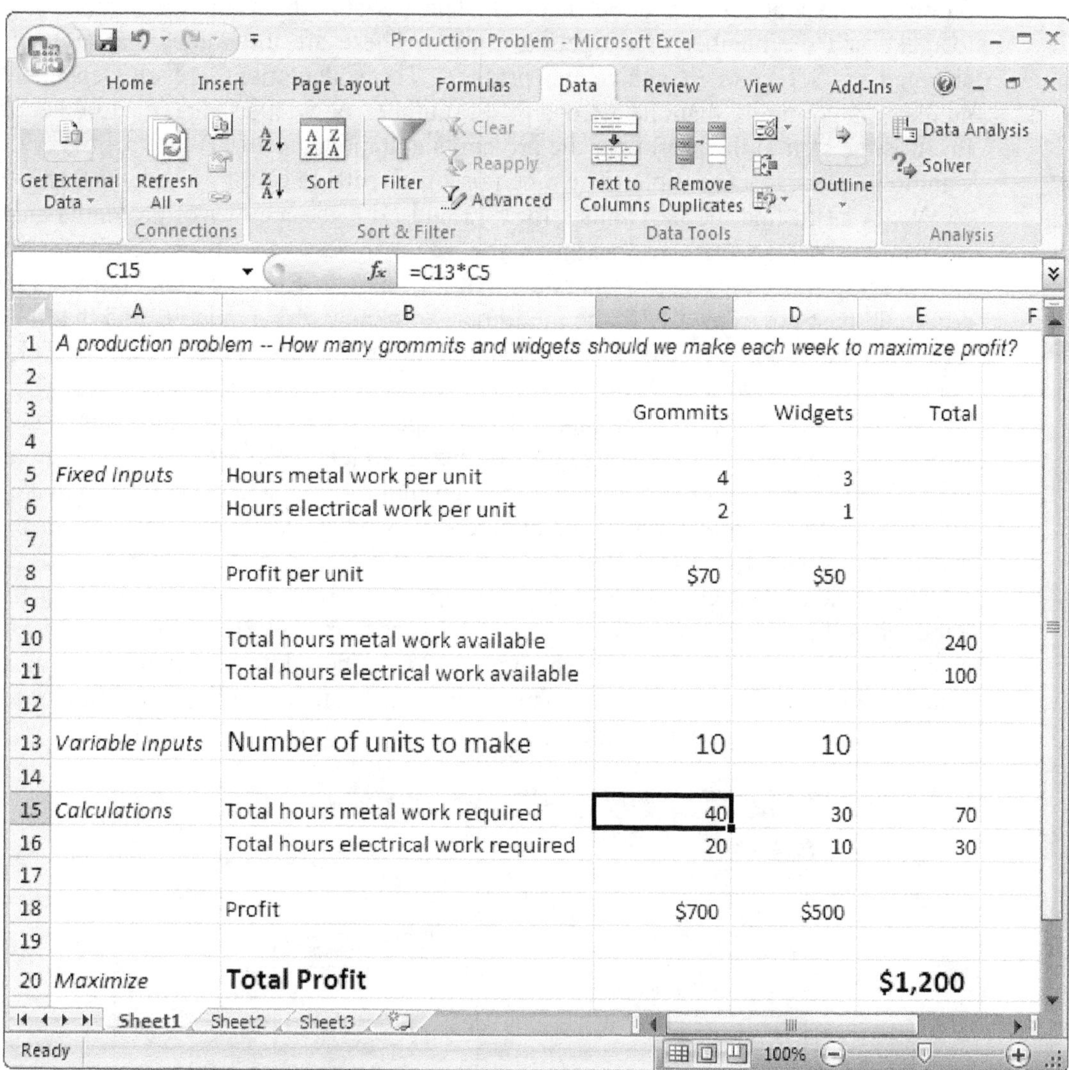

Figure 18-5. Setting up a production problem for Solver.

This problem is an example of a **linear programming** problem. We have a quantity we want to maximize, in this case profits. We have **constraints**, or restrictions, on the solution. In this case we have limits on the number of hours of metal work and electrical work available. We have a range of possible solutions to the problem. The objective and constraints can all be expressed in linear equations or inequalities.

Linear programming has been studied for over 50 years. Linear programming techniques are applicable in many different types of problems. Solver provides a powerful and easy-to-use tool for solving many linear programming problems.

To solve this production problem we set up the worksheet in Figure 8-5 that contains all of the inputs and calculations. The Fixed Inputs in the worksheet are the values given in the problem statement that cannot be changed. The Variable Inputs are the number of grommits to make and the number of widgets to make. These are the values that are going to be changed by Solver to maximize the profits. The Calculations are all dependent on the number of grommits manufactured and the number of widgets manufactured. The Total Profit is the sum of the profits for the grommits and the widgets. Total Profit is the value we want to be as large as possible. The nine non-blank cells in C15:E20 contain formulas.

We want to find the best values for C13 and D13, the number of grommits and widgets to manufacture, so that we maximize the value in E20, the Total Profit for the week. However, we have the added constraints that the value in E15, the total hours of metal work required, must not exceed E10, the total hours of metal work available, and that the value in E16, the total hours of electrical work required, must not exceed the number in E11, the total hours of electrical work available.

We currently show 10 grommits and 10 widgets being made, yielding a profit of $1,200. However, we have many available hours of metal work and electrical work that are not being utilized. We should increase the number of grommits and widgets we plan to make. But by how much? We could enter different numbers by hand and try to maximize the profit by trial and error. Instead, let's use Solver.

We click on Solver in the Analysis group of the Data tab. Excel displays the Solver Parameters dialog box, as before. We enter E20 (or point to E20) as the cell to maximize by changing cells C13 and D13. (See Figure 18-6.) The addresses of the cells that can be changed are separated by commas. There can be as many as 200 cells for Solver to be able to change! We have only two in this problem.

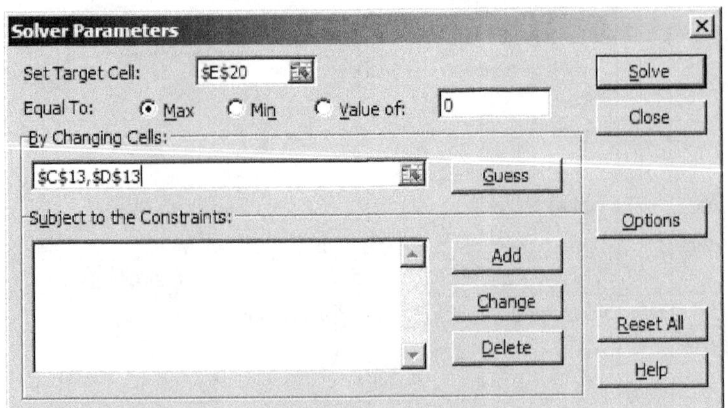

Figure 18-6. Beginning to fill in Solver parameters.

Now we have some constraints to add. We click on Add in the Constraints portion of the dialog box. We are confronted with the Add Constraint dialog box. We enter the constraint E15 <= E10, as shown in Figure 18-7. That is, the total number of hours of metal work required to manufacture the grommits and widgets each week must be less than the total number of hours of metal work available in the factory. Excel automatically adds $ signs so that all of the addresses are absolute references even if you type them in without $ signs.

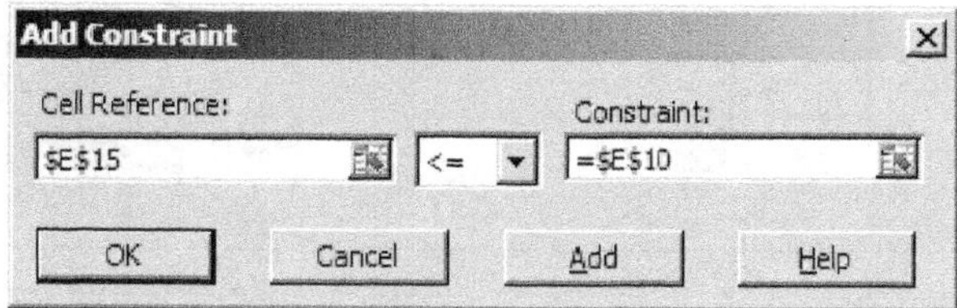

Figure 18-7. The dialog box for adding constraints.

We click on Add. The constraint automatically is entered into the Constraints field of the Solver Parameters dialog box. We fill in the constraint E16 <= E11 and click on Add, entering the second constraint.

It may not be obvious, but we have more constraints to add. The values in C13 and D13 must be greater than or equal to 0. That is, we cannot make a negative number of grommits or widgets even if it would help maximize profits. So we add the constraints C13 >= 0 and D13 >= 0. We might also want to require that C13 and D13 be integers, that is, that we do not make 3.25 grommits in a week. We could do this by clicking on C13 for the first field of the Add Constraint dialog box (or by typing C13) and then using the arrow in the operator pull-down menu in the middle of the dialog box to select int, as shown in Figure 18-8. We are allowed to specify up to 100 different constraints for Solver.

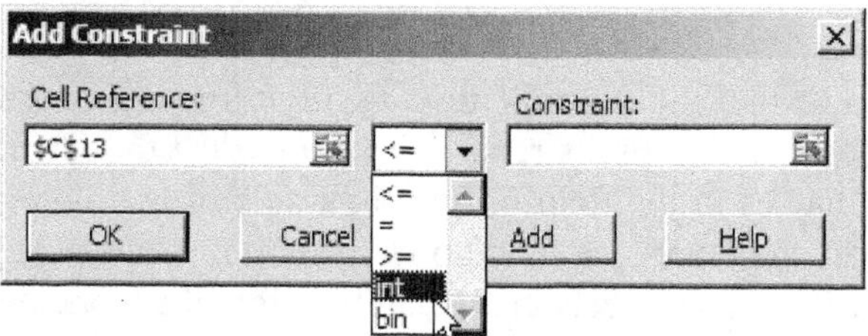

Figure 18-8. Specifying that cell C13must contain an integer.

After a constraint is specified in the Add Constraint dialog box, a click on Add will enter the constraint and keep you in the Add Constraint dialog box to enter another constraint. A click on OK will enter the constraint and bring you back to the Solver Parameter dialog box, as in Figure 18-9.

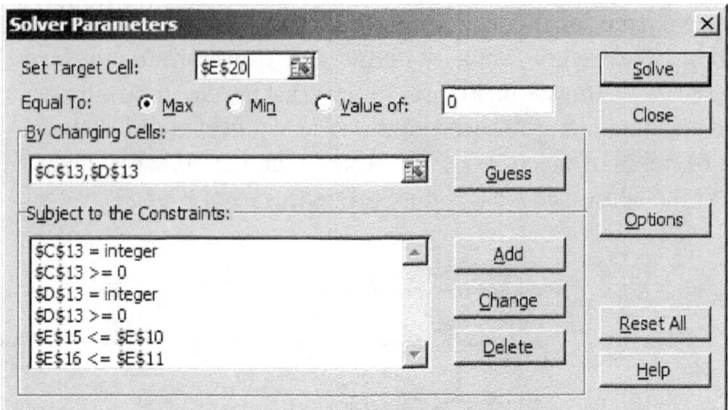

Figure 18-9. The final set of parameters for the production problem.

We click on Solve and Solver goes to work. In short order Solver reports back its success. (See Figure 18-10.)

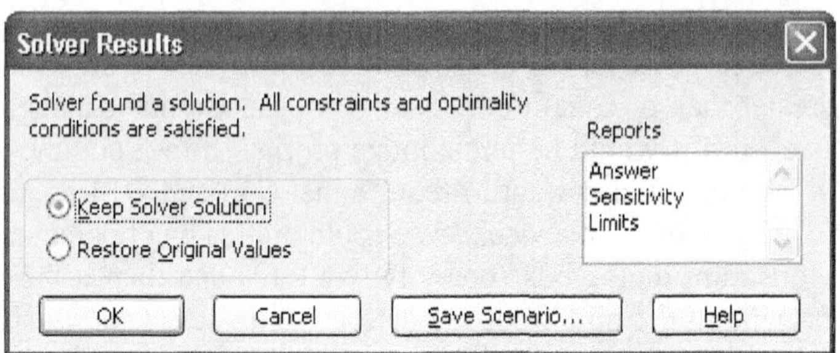

Figure 18-10. Solver has found an optimal solution.

If we would like, Solver will give us three reports on its work: an Answer report, a Sensitivity report, and a Limits report. We can select the reports we want to see by clicking on the report names in the field on the right side of the dialog box in Figure 18-11. If we want more than one report, we hold down the Ctrl or Control key while clicking. The reports will be inserted into new sheets immediately before the worksheet that contains the data. We select the Answer report and click on OK. The original worksheet is displayed with Solver's solutions entered into C13 and D13. (See Figure 18-11.)

Solver has found that if we make 30 Grommits and 40 Widgets this week, we will produce a maximal Total Profit of $4,100. With this solution, we utilize all of the metal work and electrical work capacity available, namely 240 hours of metal work and 100 hours of electrical work.

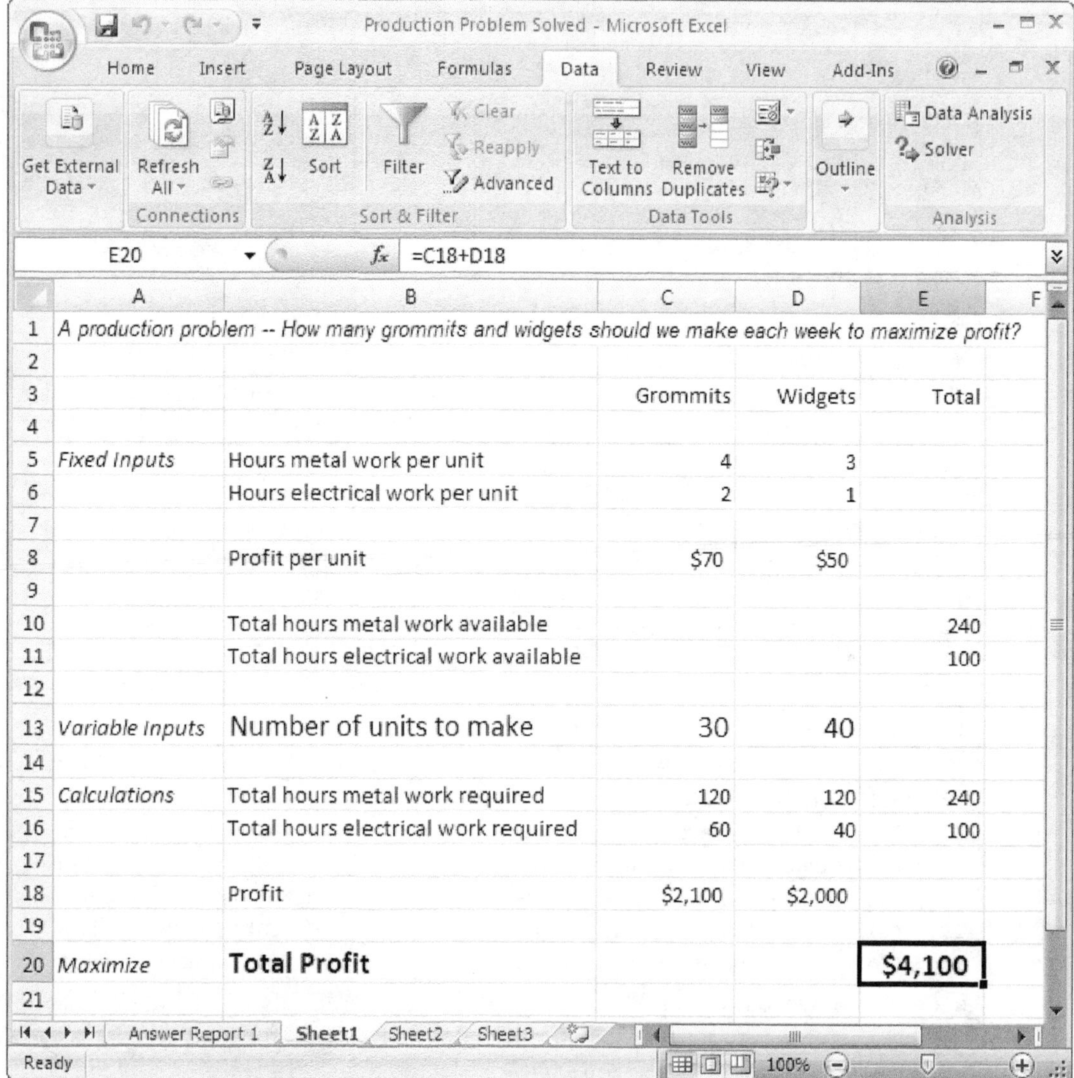

	A	B	C	D	E
1	*A production problem -- How many grommits and widgets should we make each week to maximize profit?*				
2					
3			Grommits	Widgets	Total
4					
5	*Fixed Inputs*	Hours metal work per unit	4	3	
6		Hours electrical work per unit	2	1	
7					
8		Profit per unit	$70	$50	
9					
10		Total hours metal work available			240
11		Total hours electrical work available			100
12					
13	*Variable Inputs*	Number of units to make	30	40	
14					
15	*Calculations*	Total hours metal work required	120	120	240
16		Total hours electrical work required	60	40	100
17					
18		Profit	$2,100	$2,000	
19					
20	*Maximize*	**Total Profit**			**$4,100**
21					

Figure 18-11. Solver's solution.

Clicking on the sheet tab for Answer Report 1 shows the worksheet in Figure 18-12. This worksheet summarizes the results of solving the linear programming problem.

If we want to change some of the data values in the original worksheet in Figure 18-5, we would need to run Solver again to produce a new optimal solution.

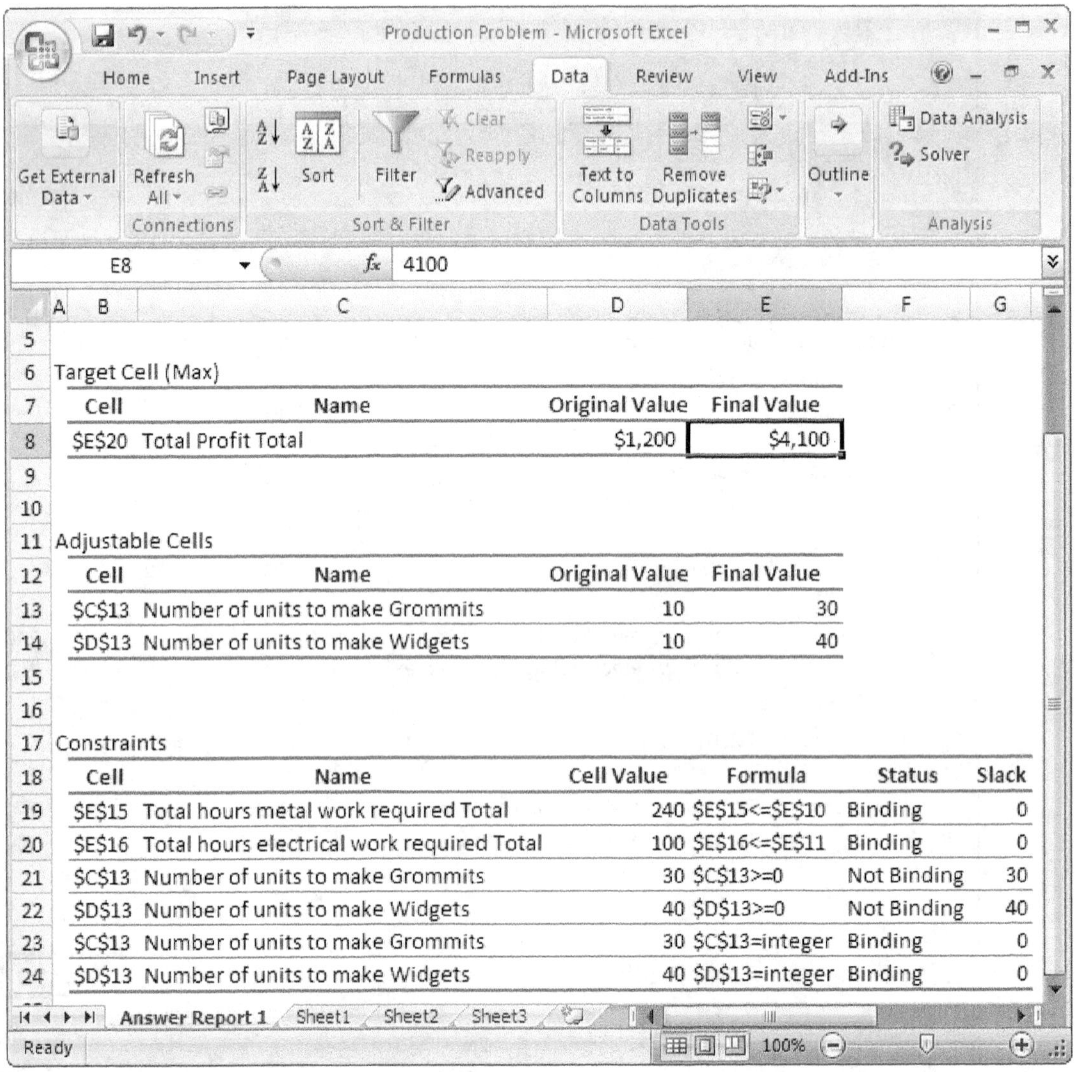

	A B	C	D	E	F	G
5						
6	Target Cell (Max)					
7	Cell	Name	Original Value	Final Value		
8	$E$20	Total Profit Total	$1,200	$4,100		
9						
10						
11	Adjustable Cells					
12	Cell	Name	Original Value	Final Value		
13	$C$13	Number of units to make Grommits	10	30		
14	$D$13	Number of units to make Widgets	10	40		
15						
16						
17	Constraints					
18	Cell	Name	Cell Value	Formula	Status	Slack
19	$E$15	Total hours metal work required Total	240	$E$15<=$E$10	Binding	0
20	$E$16	Total hours electrical work required Total	100	$E$16<=$E$11	Binding	0
21	$C$13	Number of units to make Grommits	30	$C$13>=0	Not Binding	30
22	$D$13	Number of units to make Widgets	40	$D$13>=0	Not Binding	40
23	$C$13	Number of units to make Grommits	30	$C$13=integer	Binding	0
24	$D$13	Number of units to make Widgets	40	$D$13=integer	Binding	0

Figure 18-12. The Answer Report from Solver.

USING SOLVER ON A TRANSPORTATION PROBLEM

We have three warehouses: in San Diego, Dubai, and Dublin. We have orders from customers in London, Delhi, Lagos, Seoul, and Auckland that need to be filled. Which customers should we ship to from which warehouse? The situation is summarized in the worksheet in Figure 18-13.

In the top half of the worksheet we see the cost of shipping from each warehouse to each customer. For example, it costs $50 per unit to ship from our warehouse in Dubai to the customer in Delhi.

In the bottom half of the worksheet we have quantity information. At the very bottom, in row 17, is the total number of units needed by each customer.

Transportation Problem.xlsx - Microsoft Excel

H17 f_x =SUM(B17:F17)

	A	B	C	D	E	F	G	H
1								
2		Cost of shipping one unit from warehouse to customer						
3		Customers						Total Cost
4	Warehouses	London	Delhi	Lagos	Seoul	Auckland		of Shipping
5	San Diego	$100	$80	$60	$60	$40		$840
6	Dubai	$60	$50	$40	$30	$60		
7	Dublin	$30	$40	$50	$50	$90		
8								
9		Number of units to ship from warehouse to customer						
10		Customers					Total to	Total in
11	Warehouses	London	Delhi	Lagos	Seoul	Auckland	Ship	Warehouse
12	San Diego	1	1	1	1	1	5	1550
13	Dubai	1	1	1	1	1	5	1300
14	Dublin	1	1	1	1	1	5	1400
15	Total to ship	3	3	3	3	3	15	4250
16								
17	Total ordered	900	400	1000	800	1100		4200
18								

Figure 18-13. A transportation problem. How many units should be shipped from each warehouse to each destination?

We can see that the customer in Delhi ordered 400 units. On the right, in H12:H14 we see the number of units in each warehouse. We currently have 1400 units in Dublin. The cells in B12:F14 currently contain 1's. These are the values we need to fill in, or rather that Solver will be filling in. These are the values that dictate how many units will be shipped from each warehouse to each customer.

The key cell is H5. This cell calculates the total cost of all the shipping, the value we want to minimize. The formula in H5 could be

= B12*B5 + C12*C5 + D12*D5 + E12*E5 + F12*F5 + B13*B6 + C13*C6 + D13 *D6 + E13*E6 + F13*F6 + B14*B7 + C14*C7 + D14*D7 + E14*E7 + F14*F7

Alternatively, the formula in H14 can use the **SUMPRODUCT** function

=SUMPRODUCT(B12:F14,B5:F7)

This formula calculates the sum of B12*B5 plus C12*C5 and so on, just as in the preceding formula.

There are 15 cells to be filled in (B12:F14) so that the value in H5 is minimized. Plus there are various constraints that must be satisfied. This is a problem for Solver.

The key in setting up any worksheet for Solver is to be sure all of the input values are included in separate cells and that all of the formulas needed are included, especially the formula for calculating the value that is to be minimized or maximized.

We click on Solver in the Analysis group of the Data tab. In the Solver Parameters dialog box, we indicate that the target cell is H5 and that we want the value in the cell to be minimized by changing the cells in B12:F14. Excel allows us to use ranges in both the By Changing Cells: entry and also in the constraints. The first constraint is

$B$12:$F$14 = Integer

All the values set from B12 through F14 must be integers. We can't ship fractions of units. The second constraint is

$B$12:$F$14 >= 0

We can only ship positive numbers of units. The third constraint is

$B$15:$F$15 = $B$17:$F17

This constraint specifies that B15 must equal B17, C15 must equal C17, and so on. That is, that the number of units shipped to each customer must be the same as the number ordered by the customer. The final constraint is

$G$12:$G$14 <= $H$12:$H$14

That is, from each warehouse we can ship at most the number of units in the warehouse. The final Solver Parameters dialog box is shown in Figure 18-14.

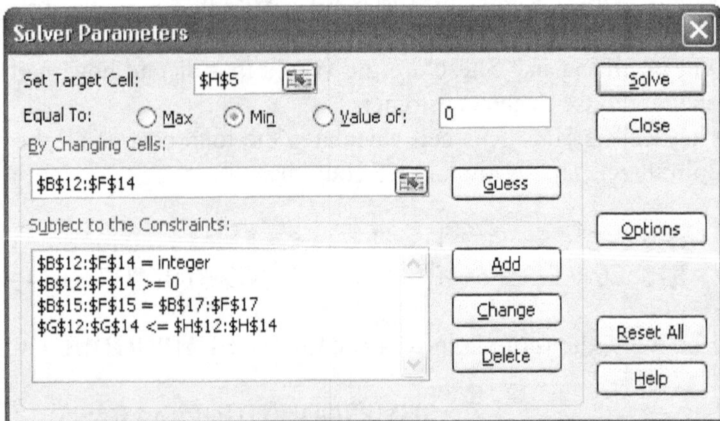

Figure 18-14. The Solver Parameters dialog box for the transportation problem.

We click on Solve and in a short time we obtain the solution shown in Figure 18-15.

Transportation Problem.xlsx - Microsoft Excel

H17 f_x =SUM(B17:F17)

	A	B	C	D	E	F	G	H
1								
2		Cost of shipping one unit from warehouse to customer						
3		Customers						Total Cost
4	Warehouses	London	Delhi	Lagos	Seoul	Auckland		of Shipping
5	San Diego	$100	$80	$60	$60	$40		$160,000
6	Dubai	$60	$50	$40	$30	$60		
7	Dublin	$30	$40	$50	$50	$90		
8								
9		Number of units to ship from warehouse to customer						
10		Customers					Total to	Total in
11	Warehouses	London	Delhi	Lagos	Seoul	Auckland	Ship	Warehouse
12	San Diego	0	0	400	0	1100	1500	1550
13	Dubai	0	0	500	800	0	1300	1300
14	Dublin	900	400	100	0	0	1400	1400
15	Total to ship	900	400	1000	800	1100	4200	4250
16								
17	Total ordered	900	400	1000	800	1100		4200
18								

Figure 18-15. The optimal solution found by Solver.

Note that Lagos is to receive units from all three warehouses.

Excel contains many powerful features. The key is to use them wisely.

COMPUTER EXERCISES

18-1. United Manufacturing is planning on spending up to $4,000,000 on new automated assembly machinery. They have decided to purchase two different models of equipment and are trying to decide how many of each model they should purchase. The F300 model costs $350,000 each. The S250 model costs $220,000 each. The F300 has some extra features so at least one third of the models purchased should be the F300. The annual maintenance budget for the new equipment is set at $120,000. The annual maintenance cost of each F300 is $12,000. The annual maintenance cost of each S250 is $7,500. Each F300 will produce 125 units per day. Each S250 will produce 81 units per day. Set up a worksheet and then use

Solver to determine how many of each model to purchase so that the daily production is maximized as long as the other constraints are met.

18-2. Seven new projects are being proposed for our division. Each would require investments over the next three years, but each ultimately would result in a positive return on our investment.

	Expenditures in $ Millions			Return
Project	Year 1	Year 2	Year 3	in $ Millions
A	5	1	8	20
B	4	7	9	36
C	3	8	4	28
D	3	9	2	20
E	7	4	1	18
F	3	2	3	12
G	6	8	9	40

The CEO has decided that we have a maximum of $25 million each year to invest. Just on the basis of the numbers, which combination of projects should we invest in so that the sum of the returns is maximized? Set up a worksheet and use Solver to come up with a solution. You should set up the worksheet so there is a cell for each project that contains either a 1 (meaning we invest in the project) or a 0 (meaning we do not invest in the project). Solver should find the combination of 1's and 0's that maximizes the sum of the returns subject to the constraints.

18-3. The Always Open Restaurant is, as the name implies, open 24 hours a day. It is always reasonably busy, but it is busier at some times than at others. Waiters work 8-hour shifts beginning at Midnight, 4 AM, 8 AM, Noon, 4 PM, or 8 PM. Management has decided that the minimal number of waiters required for each 4-hour period during the day is as follows:

Midnight to 4 AM	3
4 AM to 8 AM	10
8 AM to Noon	8
Noon to 4 PM	16
4 PM to 8 PM	14
8 PM to Midnight	8

Management would like to know how many waiters should begin their 8-hour shifts at each of the possible times, so that there is at least the minimum required waiters for each shift yet the fewest waiters possible hired.

18-4. The Greentree Financial Management Group manages funds for institutional clients. A pension fund has placed $100,000,000 with the Group. The Research Department at the Group identifies eight types of investments and rates them as follows.

	Expected Annual Yield	Risk Factor
Common stocks - aggressive	12%	2
Common stocks - growth	9%	1.5
Common stocks - conservative	7%	1
Corporate bonds	6%	0.5
Commodities	15%	3
Government bonds	4%	0
Real estate	15%	2.5
Venture capital	40%	5

The pension fund management would like the risk factor for the portfolio as a whole to be less than or equal to 1. Of course, given that constraint, they would like to maximize the yield for the entire portfolio.

Use Solver to find the best allocation of funds among the eight types of investments assuming the validity of the analyses supplied by Research. What is the expected annual yield of the entire portfolio?

18-5. We have three factories (A, B, C) and five distributors (P, Q, R, S, T) of our products. The products are shipped by truck from factory to distributor. At most 180 units of our product fit in a truck. The shipping cost is $1 per unit to load the truck and $1 per unit to unload the truck plus the mileage cost. The mileage cost is based on the mileage the truck must travel between the factory and the distributor. The mileage cost is independent of how many units are in the truck. The mileage cost is the same whether there are five units in the truck or 180 units, namely $15 per mile. The maximum monthly productions of the factories are: A 4000 units, B 2000 units, and C 1500 units. The monthly demands by the distributors are: P 1000 units, Q 1600 units, R 1500 units, S 2000 units, and T 1400 units. The mileage chart of the distances between factories and distributors is:

	Distributors				
Factories	P	Q	R	S	T
A	100	140	200	150	35
B	50	65	60	70	80
C	40	150	100	90	130

Use Solver to determine the number of units to send each month from each factory to each distributor so as to minimize the total shipping costs. Your worksheet also should show the number of trucks to send from each factory to each distributor and the total shipping cost.

18-6. Reformulate the Transportation problem worksheet in Figure 18-13 so it is divided into areas for Fixed Inputs, Variable Inputs, Calculations, and Outputs. Run Solver on your new worksheet. Do you obtain the same answers? Which worksheet is easier to understand?

INDEX

A

Absolute address, 102, 214, 288
Access, Microsoft, 6, 310
Accounting format, 41
Accounting Number Format button, 40
Active cell, 12, 14
Add-in program, 328, 348
Adobe Acrobat, 87
Aesthetics, 121
Align Left button, 37
Align Right button, 37
Alignment of cells, 36
Alphabetizing, 78, 314
Alt key, 86
Analysis ToolPak, 329
AND function, 186
Apple II, 5
Apple sales, 162, 170
Arguments of functions, 56
Arrow button, 41
Arrow keys, 14, 86
Arrow Shape, 130, 132
Attaching comments, 81
Audio International example, 139, 166
Auto dealership example, 312
Auto Fill, 67
AutoFilter, 316
Automobile expenses exercise, 154
Automobile loan example, 256
Automobile purchase exercise, 276
Automobile purchaser example, 312
AutoSum button, 59
AVERAGE function, 55, 59
Averosas exercise, 122

B

Backspace key, 16
Balloon payment, 257
Bar chart, 157, 160
BASIC, 4, 331
Beethoven, 94
Bin ranges, 335
Black hole exercise, 25
Blank cells, 8
Body Mass Index exercise, 28, 74
Bold, 35
Bollinger Bands exercise, 203
Boole, George, 186
Boolean function, 186
Borders button, 42
Break-Even Point exercise, 28
Bricklin, Dan, 5, 6

Budgeting exercise, 153
Built-in functions, 54
Business graphics, 3, 155

C

Caesar, Julius, 240
Calculations across worksheets, 142
Canarsie tribe, 106
Cancel button, 16
Case insensitive, 111, 218
Cash drawer exercise, 25
Caveat Emptor, 171
Cell, 8
Cell protection, 127
Center button, 37
Chart sheet, 166
Chart types, 156
Charting, 155
Check Box, 223
Checking account exercise, 153
Christmas, time until, exercise, 252
Chuck-A-Luck exercise, 304
Circular reference, 58, 364
Clip art, 132
Clipboard, 46, 82, 86
Close, 20
College admissions exercises, 197, 344
College costs exercise, 118
Colors, 43
Column chart, 157, 160, 171
Column index, 212, 220
Column width, 32
Columns, 2, 8, 14
Comma Style button, 40
Comments, 81
Comparison operators, 180
Compound interest, 104, 255
Compsys exercise, 120
Compound interest exercises, 26, 174, 275
Comma Separated Values (.csv) file, 177, 203, 237
Comma Style button, 40
Computer use exercise, 72
Conditional formatting, 125
Constraints, 336
Consulting billing exercise, 142
Conte Forum exercise, 280
Continents area exercise, 117
Continents, population example, 100, 157
Control buttons, 12
Control Panel, 242
Control-clicking, 34, 141, 160, 354
Conway, John, 197
Copy and Paste, 82
Copying worksheets, 140
Correcting errors, 16
Correlation, 164, 169, 336
Correlation tool, 336
COUNT function, 55, 59
COUNTIF function, 208, 294
Country GDP example, 208
Ctrl key, 34, 86, 141, 160, 354
Csv (Comma Separated Values) file, 177, 203, 257
Currency conversion exercise, 26
Currency format, 41
Custom format for numbers, 42
Custom Lists, 69
Customizing Quick Access toolbar, 49

D

Data Bars, 129
Data from web, 87, 90
Data management, 3, 311
Data Validation, 124
Database management, 312
Date formats, 245
DATE function, 245
Date systems, 240
Dates, 239
DAY function, 246
Days until July 1 example, 247
Decimal places, 40
Decrease Decimal button, 40
Delete key, 16
Deleting rows and columns, 77

Deleting worksheets, 140
Descriptive Statistics tool, 332
Design of workbooks, 150
Dice example, 294
Dice exercises, 306
Discount rate, 265
Displaying formulas, 47
Documentation, 152
Dollar signs in addresses, 103
Drag and drop, 76
Dragging, 33, 34
Drawing, 132

E

E format, 342
Eagles hockey example, 183
Economic Order Quantity exercise, 27
Electronic spreadsheet, 5, 9
Enter button, 15
Entering information, 15
Equal sign, 16
Erasing cells, 16, 77
Error message: #DIV/0, 102
Error message: #N/A, 213, 215, 218, 221
Error message: #NAME?, 182, 243, 285
Error message: #NUM!, 262, 264
Error message: #REF!, 78
Error message: #VALUE!, 230
Errors, 16
Esc key, 16
Evaluating formulas, 17
Exact matches in VLOOKUP, 214
Excel Options button, 12, 69, 223, 241, 331, 349
Executive decision maker exercise, 296
Exiting from excel, 12, 21
Exponentiation, 17

F

Factory wages exercise, 74
FALSE, 180
Family finances exercise, 301
Ferrari example, 256
Fibonacci series exercise, 120
Field, 312
Fill Color, 43, 132
Fill handle, 62, 142
Fill operation, 61
Filter, 314
Finance.google.com, 90, 177, 203
Fitting a straight line, 68, 164, 166
Flipping coins example, 285
Font Color button, 43, 87
Font menu, 35
Font Size, 35, 36
Fonts, 35
Football game exercise, 300
Forecasting, 166
Form Controls, 223
Format Painter button, 46
Formatting cells, 35
Formatting numbers, 39
Formula bar, 14
Formulas, 8, 15
Formulas, Display of, 47
Formulas, Printing, 47
Fortran, 4
Fortune Teller exercise, 297
Fortunes for the author exercise, 346
Frankston, Bob, 5
Freeze Panes, 114
Functions, 54
Functions, Nested, 60
Furniture discount exercise, 25
FV function, 260

G

Gasoline prices exercise, 72
Goal Seek, 65
Golden ratio exercise, 120
Google Finance, 90, 177, 203
Greenland ice core data, 177
Gregory XIII, 240

H

Harvard Business School, 5
Height conversion exercise, 25
Height distribution example, 162
Help, 39
Hill University tuition exercise, 193
Histogram tool, 335
Historical stock prices exercise, 236
HLOOKUP function, 214
Home purchase exercise, 279
Horizontal lookup table, 214
Horizontal scroll bar, 14
Horizontal Split Bar, 108
HOUR function, 250
HYPERLINK function, 94
Hyperlinks, 94

I

Ice core data, 177
Ice cream cone exercise, 28
IF function, 180, 208
IFERROR function, 215
Implementation of workbooks, 151
Income Statement example, 2
Income Statement exercise, 95
Income tax exercise, 232
Increase Decimal button, 40, 284
INDEX function, 219
Input validation, 124
Insert Clip Art, 132
Insert Function tool, 60, 258
Insert Hyperlink, 94
Insert Picture, 132
Inserting rows and columns, 78
Inserting New Worksheet button, 138
INT function, 202
Internet data, 87
Internet Shopping exercise, 119
Internet, Copying and pasting from, 87
IRR function, 263
Italics, 35

J

Jogger's calculator exercise, 27

K

Kapor, Mitch, 5
Keyboard accelerators, 86
Keyboard shortcuts, 86

L

Leap year, 240
Life, Game of, exercise, 197
Line chart, 162
Linear programming, 351
Linear regression, 69, 166, 340
Linear trendline, 166
Linking to a webpage, 94
Linking workbooks, 145
Lists, 312
Living expenses exercise, 174
Loan amortization table, 276
Logical functions, 179
Logical test, 180
Lottery example, 269
Lotus 1-2-3, 5, 86
Lotus Development, 5

M

Macintosh, 5, 241
Major League Baseball example, 164
Manhattan island example, 104
Mass. Pike speeding tickets exercise, 201
MATCH function, 219
MAX function, 55, 209
Maximizing profits example, 348
Merge and Center button, 38
Merge cells, 38
Microsoft, 2, 5
MIN function, 55

Minimize the Ribbon, 49
Minuit, Peter, 104
MINUTE function, 250
Mixed addressing, 113
Mobile Power exercise, 276
Molecular weight exercise, 26
Monte Carlo simulations, 284
MONTH function, 246
Mortgage payment example, 258
Mortgage payment exercise, 274
Moving cells, 76
Multiplan, 5
Multiple worksheets, 14, 138
Multiplication table example, 113
Music, playing, 94

N

Name box, 14, 111
Naming cells. 109
NASA Mission Control exercise, 253
Negative numbers, 42
Nested functions, 60
Nested IF functions, 182
Net present value, 265
New Ivy admissions exercise, 196
New Workbook, 12, 20
Noncontiguous range, 34
Noncontiguous ranges, Charting, 160
NOT function, 185
NOW function, 248
NPER function, 261
NPV function, 265
Number format 40

O

Oceans, Area of, 117
"Ode to Joy", 94
Office, Microsoft, 6
Office button, 12
Office menu, 13, 19
Option Button, 223
OR function, 185
Order of precedence, 17
Orientation button, 38

P

Page Layout button, 20
Page View buttons, 12
Paired t-Test tool, 338
Palindrome exercise, 195, 202
Palladia population exercise, 118
Panes, 114
Password protection, 128
Paste, 82
Paste Options, 84
Paste Special, 84
Paul and Maria exercise, 119
Payroll exercise, 73, 146
Percent operator, 17
Percent style button, 40
Peter Minuit example, 104
Phone directory example, 218
Pi, 304
PI function, 28
Picture, Inserting, 132
Pie chart, 157, 228
PivotTable Field List pane, 323
PivotTables, 321
PMT function, 256
Pointing, 57
Polynomial trendline, 170
Pope Gregory XIII, 240
Population by continents example, 100, 157
Population of world exercise, 175
Precedence of operators, 17
Price quote example, 8, 15, 33
Printing formulas, 47
Printing the worksheet, 20
Problem definition, 150
Protecting cells, 127
PV function, 260

Q

Queuing, 289
Quick Access toolbar, 12, 13, 16, 19, 49

R

R Square value in Regression tool, 340
R Square value in trendlines, 164, 169
RAND function, 284
RANDBETWEEN function, 293
Random integers, 293
Random numbers, 284
Random walk exercise, 302
Range, 34, 47, 56
RATE function, 262
Real estate listings example, 3, 129, 332
Real estate listings exercise, 326, 346
Real estate purchase exercise, 279
Recalculation, 10
Recalculation key, 200, 248, 253, 285
Record, 312
Redo, 16
Regional and Language Options, 242
Regression, linear, 69, 164, 167, 340
Regression tool, 340
Relative address, 102
Restore Window button, 144
Retirement exercise, 119, 194
Ribbon, 12, 49, 86
Ribbon Shape, 132
Rispoli, Fred, 306
Robot replication exercise, 121
Rock-Paper-Scissors exercise, 299
Roller coaster record example, 252
Roulette exercise, 303
Rows, 8
Rule of 72 exercise, 275

S

Salespeople commission exercise, 22
Salespeople hiring example, 340
Santa Claus example, 290
Save button, 12, 13, 19
Saving the workbook, 19
Scatter chart, 164
Sciore, Edward, 223
Scroll bars, 12, 14
Scrolling, 14, 76
SECOND function, 250
Selecting cells, 34
Serial numbers, 240
Shading, Three-Dimensional, 44
Shapes, 132
Shift-clicking, 141
Simulation, 284
Size of worksheet, 14
Skopi Project exercise, 277
Slot machine exercise, 297
SmartArt, 133
Smiley face, 132
Solver, 347
Sorting, 78, 314
Special numbers exercise, 197
Speeding ticket exercise, 194, 201
Spin Button, 228
Split bars, 108
Splitting the window, 108
Stack, 289
Standard deviation, 202, 334
Status bar, 12, 14
STDEV function, 202
Stock portfolio exercise, 29, 134, 147
Stock prices exercise, 236
Stock recommendations exercise, 191
Stock simulation exercise, 298, 308
Stock timing exercise, 203, 308
Straubing, Howard, 156
SUM function, 55
SUM function overuse, 59
SUMIF function, 209
SUMPRODUCT FUNCTION, 357
System clock, 244

T

Tables, 312
Temperature exercise, 25, 26, 51, 121
Testing IF functions, 189
Testing the engines example, 250
Testing worksheets, 147
Text alignment buttons, 37
Text Boxes, 130
Text cells, 8
Text Import Wizard, 237
Text to Columns tool, 89
Three-dimensional shading, 44
Tigers playoff exercise, 194
Time formats, 248
TIME function, 249
Time management exercise, 73, 147
Time value of money, 256
Title bar, 12
TODAY function, 244
Top 10 Filter, 319
Tortoise and hare exercise, 303
Total Row of a table, 319
Transportation problem, 356
Transportation problem exercise, 361
Trendlines, 166
Tropical Resort example, 185
TRUE, 180
t-Test tool, 338

U

Underline, 35
Undo button, 13
Unfreeze Panes, 114
Unmerging cells, 38
URL, 90, 94
U.S. government budget exercise, 176

V

Validating inputs, 124
Varying Pie chart, 228
Vending machine exercise, 299
Vertical lookup table, 211
Vertical scroll bar, 14
Vertical Split bar, 108
Viewing multiple worksheets, 144
VisiCalc, 5
Visualization exercise, 344
VLOOKUP function, 211, 287
Vostok ice core data, 227

W

Web-based data. 87
Weight conversion exercise, 24
"What if" analysis, 6, 110, 150, 265, 284, 289
Width of columns, 32
Wind chill factor exercise, 26, 121
Word, Microsoft, 6, 11
WordArt, 133
Workbook, 8, 19
Workbook names, 20
Worksheet, 8
Worksheet scrolling, 12, 14, 138
Worksheet tabs, 12, 138
Worksheets, Multiple, 139
World GDP example, 208
World population exercise, 175
Wrap Text button, 38

X

XIRR function, 268

Y

YEAR function, 246

Z

Zero coupon bond exercise, 274
Zoom slider, 12